MARY AND JOHN GRAY LIBRARY
LAMAR UNIVERSITY

Purchased
with the
Student Library Use Fee

W9-BJT-835

AWARD EDITION

HOUGHTON MIFFLIN
The Literature Experience
READING

Celebrate reading with us!

Cover and title page illustrations by Simon Ng.

Acknowledgments appear on page 745.

1995 Impression

Copyright © 1993 by Houghton Mifflin Company. All rights reserved.

No part of this work may be reproduced or transmitted in any form or by any means, electronic or mechanical, including photocopying and recording, or by any information storage or retrieval system without the prior written permission of the copyright owner, unless such copying is expressly permitted by federal copyright law. With the exception of non-profit transcription in Braille, Houghton Mifflin is not authorized to grant permission for further uses of copyrighted selections reprinted in this text without the permission of their owners. Permission must be obtained from the individual copyright owners as identified herein. Address requests for permission to make copies of Houghton Mifflin material to School Permissions, Houghton Mifflin Company, 222 Berkeley Street, Boston, MA 02116.

Printed in the U.S.A.

ISBN: 0-395-61092-3

456789-D-96 95 94

Worlds Apart

LTX
8-04-0
Wor

DISCARDED

Senior Author
John J. Pikulski

*Senior Coordinating
Author*
J. David Cooper

*Senior Consulting
Author*
William K. Durr

Coordinating Authors
Kathryn H. Au
M. Jean Greenlaw
Marjorie Y. Lipson
Susan E. Page
Sheila W. Valencia
Karen K. Wixson

Authors
Rosalinda B. Barrera
Edwina Bradley
Ruth P. Bunyan
Jacqueline L. Chaparro
Jacqueline C. Comas
Alan N. Crawford
Robert L. Hillerich
Timothy G. Johnson
Jana M. Mason
Pamela A. Mason
William E. Nagy
Joseph S. Renzulli
Alfredo Schifini

Senior Advisor
Richard C. Anderson

Advisors
Christopher J. Baker
Charles Peters
MaryEllen Vogt

HOUGHTON MIFFLIN COMPANY   BOSTON

Atlanta   Dallas   Geneva, Illinois   Palo Alto   Princeton   Toronto

LAMAR UNIVERSITY LIBRARY

MYTHOLOGY

13

HEROES FOR ALL TIMES

Award Winner

INSIGHTS

Seeing the Light

OTHER CREATURES OTHER WORLDS

BOOK 5

POETRY

361

IMAGES · SOUNDS · MESSAGES

The American Revolution

MYTHOLOGY

BOOK 1

HEROES
FOR
ALL TIMES

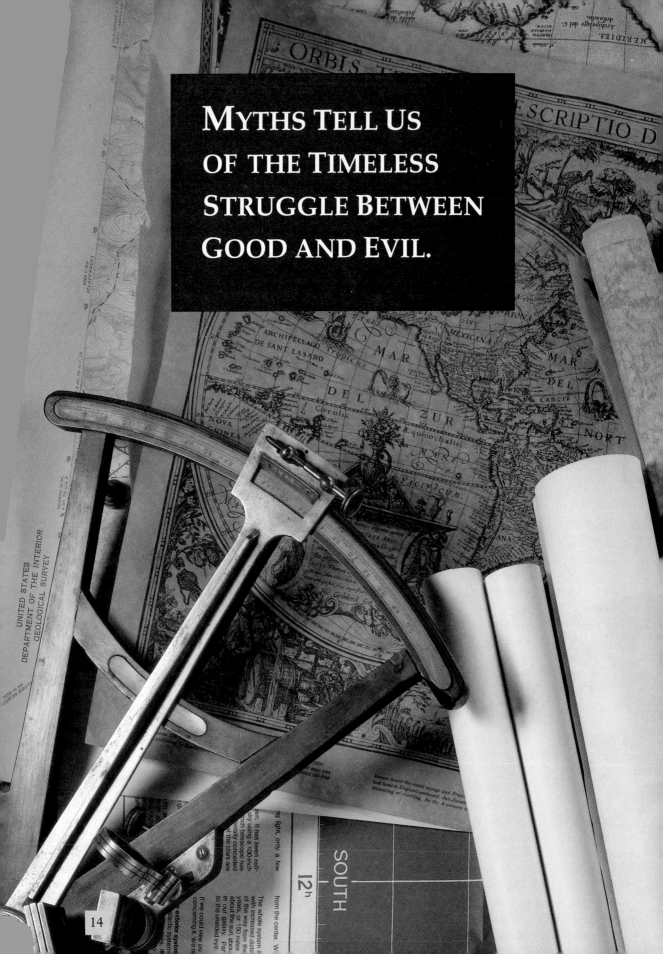

MYTHS TELL US
OF THE TIMELESS
STRUGGLE BETWEEN
GOOD AND EVIL.

CONTENTS

The Story of Prince Rama

retold by Brian Thompson

ing Dasharatha had three wives, each of whom had sons. The boys were named Rama, Bharata, and the twins Lakshmana and Shatrugnha. Rama, the favorite of his father, was told that he would become a great warrior, and someday he would fight Ravana, the King of the Demons. He passed the test of drawing a magnificent, powerful bow and won the hand of the beautiful Princess Sita in marriage.

The king decided to let his beloved son Rama rule in his place, but Bharata's mother, Queen Kaikeyi, asked the king to send Rama away and make Bharata king. Because she had saved the king's life at one time, and he had promised to grant her two wishes in return, he agreed to send Rama into exile for fourteen years.

Bharata did not wish to be king, and he begged Rama to remain. He promised to be faithful to Rama and refuse to be crowned king.

Rama, his wife Sita, and his best friend, Lakshmana, honored the king's request and went into exile. The king died of grief when they left the country.

Rama, Sita, and Lakshmana went into the wilderness, befriending a great eagle along the way. Eventually they built a house in a secret place deep in the forest.

Illustration by Jeroo Roy

Ravana's Sister

You will remember that Rama had been told that he would grow to be strong and wise and eventually he would have to fight Ravana, the King of all the Demons. Ravana had a sister. She did not have ten heads and twenty arms like her brother, but she was really ugly. She was a giant and her hair was scraggy, her red teeth were pointy, and, because she ate so much, her belly was enormous. That was her natural shape. Like most demons she could change herself to look like anything at all.

Ravana's sister wandered past Rama's secret house. She saw the handsome Rama and thought that he looked like a young lion. "He is obviously a prince," she thought. "I will trick him into becoming my husband." She changed herself into a beautiful young princess.

Rama was amazed to see such a pretty girl deep in the

heart of the forest. He spoke to her politely and she replied with sweet words, trying to enchant him. When that didn't seem to be having any effect she started to tell lies about Sita. "Sita is a horrible wife to you, you must send her back to her own land and marry me instead." Of course this made Rama angry and he told Ravana's sister to go away and to leave him in peace. But she would not stop bothering him. "My dear brother is very powerful. He will make you the richest man in the world. He will give you a fine palace to live in and all the demons will be your servants forever." Rama knew now that the pretty princess was really a demon in disguise. He walked back into the house and Ravana's sister ran off into the forest, changing back into her own horrible shape as she ran. She went home to her cave and sat and howled at the moon.

Sita in Danger

That night Ravana's horrible sister made a plan. She would kidnap Sita and then, she thought, Rama would marry her.

She crept up to the little house in the forest and waited. After a long time Sita came out alone. She was going into the forest to pick flowers. Ravana's sister began to follow her, jumping from hiding place to hiding place. Lakshmana, who was always vigilant, suddenly noticed what was happening. He ran as fast as he could to try to get to the horrible creature before it grabbed Sita. Ravana's sister decided it was time to attack. She crouched, ready to jump on Sita and, at the same moment, Lakshmana caught up with her and knocked her over.

Ravana's sister was enraged. She turned and attacked Lakshmana. He was forced into fighting the howling monster. She was very strong and powerful and Lakshmana had a hard fight finally to beat her. In the struggle Lakshmana had sliced off her nose and her ears.

Ravana's sister hurried to her brother's palace to tell him what had happened. She begged him to help her avenge herself on the three in the forest. "It is all the fault of that Sita," she cried. "She is far too beautiful. You must send your demon forces, dear brother, and kill them all."

"Dear sister," roared Ravana, "I will take my army and stamp those three worms into the ground." Secretly Ravana was very interested to hear that there was a beautiful princess living deep in the forest. Ravana had many wives and he thought that he might have the chance to gain another wife and revenge his sister at the same time. He got all his men together. The demon army was huge. Ravana set his greatest Demon Warrior in charge with fourteen Demon Warlords. The whole army set out for the forest. As soon as Rama and Lakshmana saw the army with their forks,[1] swords, battle-axes and spears they took their bows and shot the weapons out of the demons' hands. That was the start of a terrible battle. The battle lasted for seven days and at the end of it Rama and Lakshmana were surrounded by fourteen thousand dead demons. Those few who had survived had fled in fright.

The Golden Deer

Ravana, the King of all the Demons, was really disturbed. His army had been beaten by two young princes; but what troubled him even more was the description his sister had given him of Sita. Every one of his ten heads buzzed with wicked thoughts about Princess Sita. He dreamed about her all day and all night and he could find no peace. He could not get rid of his thoughts of Sita. He even stopped the seasons of the year, the hours of the day and the seconds and minutes that make up time itself. But nothing worked. He was haunted by dreams of the beautiful girl in the forest. He knew that he couldn't hope to beat Rama and Lakshmana by using his power alone. He decided to try to trick them by treachery and magic.

The next day Rama, Sita and Lakshmana saw a golden deer come out of the forest. It shone in the sunshine and its body was covered with jewels. Sita thought it was the most wonderful thing she had ever seen. "Dear Sita, you shall have it for a pet," promised Rama. "I will catch it for you." Rama started to trail the deer. The deer led Rama away from the

---

[1]**forks:** forked spears.

house into the deep forest. Further and further went the deer, and further and further followed Rama. Quite suddenly Rama realized that it was a trap. He drew his bow and shot an arrow at the deer. The deer fell down and to Rama's astonishment, it called out for help in Rama's own voice.

Far, far away, back at the house, Lakshmana and Sita could hear faintly the voice of Rama calling for help. Sita was very worried and Lakshmana was too. Lakshmana suspected that it might be a trick, because he knew that it would take a mighty force to harm Rama. Sita begged Lakshmana to go to see if any harm had come to Rama. Lakshmana was very reluctant to leave Sita alone. Sita could only think that Rama might be in need of help somewhere in the forest. Lakshmana took his bow and went in search of Rama. The moment he left the house, the King of all the Demons, Ravana, who had been watching all the time, put his wicked plan into action. Ravana changed himself into an old beggarman and went to Sita.

Sita Is Captured

Sita was surprised when she saw the old man. "Welcome to our house," said Sita. "Travellers do not often come this way. Have you travelled far?"

"My dear child," said Ravana, "I have come all the way from a distant island called Lanka. Lanka is across the sea from India. It is the island where all the demons live."

"That's very sad," said Sita. "A poor old man like you living among all those demons."

"Oh my dear princess," said Ravana, "you mustn't believe the things that people tell you about the demons. People do tell dreadful lies about them. They have always been most kind to me."

"My husband, Prince Rama, has vowed to rid the world of all the demons.

"What!" exclaimed Ravana, beginning to get very angry. "Your husband thinks he can kill all the demons in existence! The wretched little upstart. Do you think one baby rabbit could kill all the fighting elephants in the world? What are you talking about?" By this time Ravana was so angry that he started changing back into his own shape. Sita was terrified when she saw the old man sprout ten heads and twenty arms. She cried out for help, but Ravana decided to act quickly. He seized Sita and dragged her to his hidden chariot.

Only one creature saw Ravana and Sita. This was the eagle who had promised to protect the three friends. His sharp eyes saw Ravana carry the struggling Sita on to the chariot. The eagle flew to the rescue. His wings beat so strongly that they made windstorms. Ravana saw the eagle flying in to the attack and he seized a weapon in each of his twenty hands. The eagle crashed into the chariot. Ravana looked at the sharp beak and the strong talons. In one of his hands he held a magic sword. With two great swings of the sword Ravana cut off both of the eagle's wings. The eagle fell and Ravana swung his sword again and struck him in the throat a cruel blow. Ravana drove his chariot away. He had Sita, and now he was going to his home in Lanka.

The dying eagle told Rama and Lakshmana of Sita's kidnapping.

As the brothers searched for Sita, they came to the land of the monkey-people, where the country was at war. The brothers helped to bring peace. General Hanuman of the monkey army became a close friend and vowed to serve Rama always. He and the entire monkey army, together with their friends the bears, joined the search for Sita.

Another eagle told them that Ravana had carried Sita across the sea between India and Lanka. Hanuman leaped across the sea to Lanka and found

Sita at Ravana's palace. Hanuman hid in the garden and spoke to Sita, but the demons captured him and took him to Ravana.

Hanuman told Ravana that Rama wanted Sita returned, and wanted Ravana to give up his evil ways, or Rama's army would destroy all the demons. Ravana roared that he would gladly fight.

The demons tied rags to Hanuman's tail and set it on fire, but he escaped and in turn set the city on fire. Hanuman was not injured, and he leaped back across the sea to India.

Rama's forces prepared for war.

Before the War

On the island of Lanka Ravana called a council of war. The generals were worried. Outside the palace the great city was still burning and smoking. Many of the demons had lost friends or relations in the fire and, what made them angriest of all, Hanuman had escaped and rejoined Rama and Lakshmana. The Demon Warriors and Demon War-lords planned their attack on Rama's army.

"Our army will easily beat the monkeys and the bears," said Ravana, "but I want to kill Rama and Lakshmana myself. We will have to plan many tricks to try to frighten them. We can protect ourselves with magic fire and we can use our magic invisible arrows that turn into poisonous snakes when they hit their targets."

While the council of war went on, the news was brought to Ravana that the monkeys and bears had completed building the huge bridge across the sea from India and their army was marching across it to Lanka.

Two of Ravana's spies rushed into the council chamber. They had been sent to spy on Rama and Lakshmana but they had been captured. They told Ravana the story of how they had been brought before the two brothers. The spies had expected to be killed, but Rama had been merciful. "Mighty

Ravana," they said, "Rama said that we were not to be killed. He showed us all his army. He said that if we came back and told you how very powerful the monkeys and the bears were, and how great their army was, that you would stop the war, free Sita and everyone would live in peace." This news made Ravana even angrier. He gave orders for the battle to begin. The gates of the city opened and Ravana's army poured out. The soldiers spread across the plain like a wall of fire.

The War Begins

Rama and Lakshmana watched Ravana's army approach. While Ravana had been holding his council of war they had surrounded the city. The battle started. The monkeys were fearless fighters. They fought with huge rocks and even trees that they pulled up out of the ground. In close combat they used their fists and claws and teeth. The first battle was terrible to see.

The demon army fought with weapons, but they used trickery whenever they could. They had made a dummy which looked exactly like Sita, and they carried this into the middle of the field of battle and pretended to kill it. The monkeys saw it happen and thought that Princess Sita had been murdered. They were so sad at the thought of this that they all wept, and Ravana's soldiers attacked them savagely. One of the monkey commanders suddenly noticed that the figure was a dummy and not really Sita. The news

spread rapidly among the monkey army and they were all so angry that they attacked more fiercely.

One of Ravana's demon brothers flew up into the clouds with the magic invisible snake-arrows. Hidden among the clouds he fired the poisonous arrows at Rama and Lakshmana. They were terrible weapons. Each arrow flew straight to its target and then turned into the deadliest snakes in the world. The two brothers were covered with the snakes. They could not see where the snake-arrows came from. Again and again they were bitten by the snakes and they both fell down dying. Ravana heard this news and sent Sita in a flying chariot over the battlefield cruelly to make her see Rama and Lakshmana lying almost dead. It was a terrible moment for Sita. But the brothers were saved by one of the eagles. A huge eagle flew low over them both. Now all snakes are terrified of eagles, even magic snakes. So, as soon as the eagle appeared, the snakes fled. The poison didn't work if the snake-arrows weren't nearby, so the two brothers recovered immediately.

The Magic Herbs

That day was the first of many days and nights of fighting. There are thousands of tales to be told of the battles and the bravery of the war against Ravana. Ravana used all the trickery he knew; he even wakened the terrible giant-of-all-the-giants from his half-year sleep and sent him into the battle but, in spite of all his treachery Ravana saw that he was losing the war. It was time to send in his own son, who was a Prince and a Demon Warlord.

First of all Ravana made his son completely invisible. He gave him powerful invisible weapons to take into battle. Lastly Ravana surrounded his son with a spell that made a wall of invisible fire around him that would protect him from any stray arrows. So Ravana's son stormed out into the middle of the monkeys and the bears. He killed everyone about him. It was a terrible time for Rama and Lakshmana. No-one could see where the deadly arrows came from. No-one could stop the killing. Everyone fought bravely but they could not see the enemy. The whole army soon lay dead or dying. Lakshmana and Rama ran everywhere trying to find the demon but at last they too were struck down. It was the worst moment of the whole war.

Hanuman was the only soldier still unharmed. He was full of grief and anger. Close by him he saw one of the wisest and oldest of the bears who beckoned desperately to Hanuman. "There is a cure that will work against this terrible weapon," said the dying bear. "You must go to the Himalaya Mountains and seek out four of the special herbs that grow there. They will cancel out the effect of these invisible arrows. If you can do it quickly they will even bring the dead soldiers to life again." Hanuman wasted no time at all. He crossed back to India and to the mountains. There was no time to find the special herbs. He simply lifted the top off a mountain and flew back to Lanka with it. As soon as the mountain-top came near the battlefield the herbs began their work. In no time at all the army was restored to life and health. Hanuman was so thrilled that he lifted Lakshmana up on his own shoulders. Lakshmana could now see Ravana's son and, still sitting on Hanuman's shoulders, he reached over the top of the wall of invisible fire and cut off the demon's head.

Rama and Ravana

Ravana could see that Rama's army was winning the war. There was only one thing left for him to do. He would have to fight Rama himself. He would need all his evil powers in the battle. Ravana prepared himself. He put on his special armour to protect every one of his ten heads and twenty arms. He called for his chariot and rode out to battle.

The gods knew that Rama would need their support in the battle. They gave Rama a chariot. It was a special chariot that could carry over the seas and the mountains.

And so Rama and Ravana faced each other. The skies echoed with rumbling thunders. Ravana deliberately took ten bows in ten of his hands and notched ten arrows to the bows. Rama reached for his bow also. Ravana let loose the arrows at Rama. Just as quickly, Rama shot each of the arrows out of the sky. Ravana's arrows now fell like showers of rain, thick as a hailstorm, they filled the sky and seemed to make a roof over Lanka. Still Rama managed to turn the arrows away.

Ravana was so angry that he jerked his chariot aside and ran through the monkey army, killing all who stood in his way. Rama could not stand by and see thousands of his soldiers die. He drove his chariot after Ravana. He chased Ravana off the battlefield and round all the skies of the world. Rama used his bow well, and arrow after arrow found Ravana's body.

The Last Battle

Ravana knew that ordinary weapons would not beat Rama. He thought that he would have to use his strangest and most powerful magic. He called up terrible spells and hurled them at Rama. One of the spells made all the dead soldiers of the demon army come to life again and begin to attack Rama. Rama was not frightened by the ghost demons. He called up the strength of his wisdom against the spell and the demons vanished.

Ravana worked another spell and more magic arrows appeared. These arrows were headed with terrible eyes and teeth and tongues of fire. They sped across the sky towards Rama carrying darkness and fear with them. Rama stayed calm and remembered the spell that would destroy such demon arrows.

Ravana next filled the air with snakes and dragons that made fiery poisons. Rama called up the holy eagles who could destroy them. Ravana came closer, firing showers of poison arrows at Rama. Rama turned the arrows back on Ravana. Rama and Ravana were very close together.

Rama drew his sword. With a mighty blow he cut off one of Ravana's heads. A new head grew in its place and the old head fell to the ground, swearing at Prince Rama. Rama swung again and this time he cut off two of Ravana's arms. New arms grew straight away, and the old arms tried to attack Rama as they fell squirming to the ground.

At last Rama remembered a specially holy power that had been used once by the Creator of the World on an evil monster. Rama called up this power with a prayer. He aimed the power full-force at Ravana's heart. Ravana had protected his head and his arms and body, but nothing guarded his evil heart. He was struck so hard that he fell from his chariot dead. The war was over.

Peace

Rama sent Hanuman to find Sita. She was so full of happiness she could hardly speak. She was free at last. Attendants waited on her and she was bathed and dressed and brought to Rama. The gods blessed Sita and offered to reward Rama for all that he had done. Rama asked the gods to give back life to all the monkeys and bears who had been killed in the war. Rama's request was granted and the monkeys and their friends were full of joy. So, peace came to the island of Lanka.

A great thanksgiving feast was held and Rama remembered that the fourteen years of his exile were almost over. Soon he would be able to return to the land of his father.

It was then time for the travellers to leave. The gods gave them a wonderful flying chariot and Rama, Sita and Lakshmana as well as Hanuman and all their new friends stepped into it, for the journey back, each to his own homeland. The chariot lifted them up into the air and they crossed the sea between Lanka and India. The friends looked down on the roads and paths that they had travelled years before. They passed over the forest where the three of them had once lived.

Eventually they came to Rama's own kingdom and to the palace where his father had once been king. Bharata was waiting for them. Twice times seven years had passed. Rama's time of exile was over.

The Kingdom of Rama

Bharata and Shatrughna were delighted to see Rama, Lakshmana and Sita. Bharata ordered the palace to be decorated and the whole city to be made splendid for Rama's coronation. The messengers went out once more bearing news of Rama's coronation, as they had done fourteen years earlier. The three mothers embraced their sons. Rama forgave Queen Kaikeyi the wrong she had done him so long ago.

Bharata told Rama that the country had been well ruled while he had been away in exile. The people were happy and there was food and wealth enough for all. Great crowds came to the palace to see Rama; and Rama and Sita prepared themselves for the coronation. The throne was decked out and Rama and Sita were clad in beautiful clothes. Then, at last, Rama was pronounced king in the land of his father, and Sita was crowned his queen.

Rama and Sita sat on their throne. Lakshmana stood closest to Rama, still fully devoted to the service of his beloved brother. At their feet knelt Hanuman, ever ready to spring into action to aid his friends.

The celebrations lasted for a whole month and every person who was present remembered the feasts and the joy that was shared by all.

And so began the reign of King Rama and Queen Sita — a time when peace and plenty filled the land, and happiness and holiness made earth, for a time, a little like heaven.

The Art of the Ramayana

The Indian paintings illustrating *The Story of Prince Rama* are over three hundred years old. The Rajput kings had them painted for display in the royal castle. Hot, bright colors were used because the gloomy stone castles had little light. The paintings are very detailed because many royal women could not read, and the paintings told them the whole story in pictures. Sometimes a single picture would show a whole sequence of events in the famous epic story of Prince Rama. Which pictures show more than a single action?

The Ramayana

The Story of Prince Rama is a retelling of the *Ramayana*, an Indian epic poem. The *Ramayana* was first written in verse three thousand years ago. It was recited over and over for hundreds of years, and the version known today is about two thousand years old.

As one of the great epics of Asia, the *Ramayana* is part of the living culture in India today. Scenes and episodes are told as stories, acted out in village festivals, and performed as puppet plays.

Responding to *The Story of Prince Rama*

Thinking and Discussing

Why do some characters in the story choose to fight for Prince Rama? Why do some side with Ravana?

In what ways are magic and fantasy prominent in this story? In what ways are real-life elements prominent as well?

What qualities of the tale do you think make it popular today?

Choosing a Creative Response

Presenting a Shadow Puppet Play Create a shadow-puppet play based on one of the exciting battles in *The Story of Prince Rama*. Design shadow puppets that represent Rama, Ravana, and any other important characters in your scene. Make sure that your dramatization portrays the characters as they are presented in the story.

Presenting a Dialogue You may have noticed that the author has included no dialogue between Rama and Ravana in his retelling of *The Story of Prince Rama*. What would they have to say to each other? What would they say about good and evil? Write and present a dialogue that might take place between the two characters.

Creating Your Own Activity Plan and complete your own activity in response to *The Story of Prince Rama*.

Thinking and Writing

Imagine what would happen if Ravana's sister tried to avenge Ravana's death. Devise and describe a plot in which this evil creature tries to overcome Rama but fails to defeat the prince. In keeping with the style of the story, make sure your plot includes plenty of trickery and magic.

Writing A FIRSTHAND BIOGRAPHY

Great heroes who fight the evils of the world exist in the myths of many cultures. Modern myths tell of the adventures of familiar heroes such as Batman and Wonder Woman. Heroes, however, can be real people that you might encounter every day. Who are the heroes in your life?

As you read the stories here, think about the qualities you think a hero should have. Then choose a hero in your life that you would like to write about in a firsthand biography. In your biography, make your hero come alive by describing the person in detail, explaining the person's significance in your life, and telling about time you may have spent together. Or, if the stories give you another writing idea, try that instead.

1. *Prewriting* Before you begin writing, think about the hero you wish to present in your firsthand biography. Remember the details of the time when you first met your hero. Think about the ways in which the relationship between you and your hero has developed since your first meeting. Keep the following questions in mind while forming your ideas.

   - How will I introduce this person to my readers?
   - What information will I include in the description of this person?
   - How can I convince others that this person is heroic?

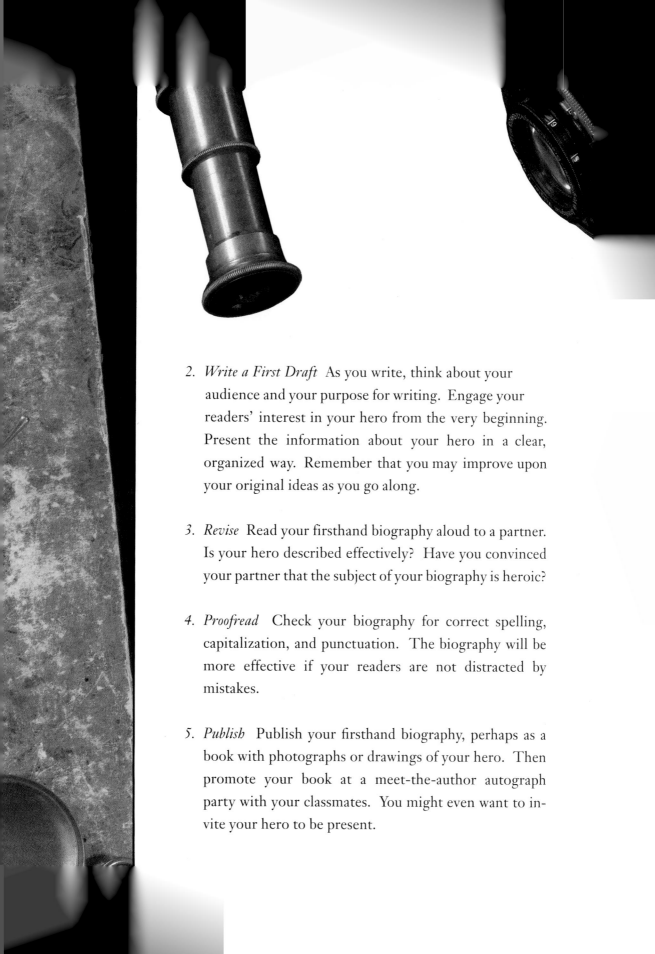

2. *Write a First Draft* As you write, think about your audience and your purpose for writing. Engage your readers' interest in your hero from the very beginning. Present the information about your hero in a clear, organized way. Remember that you may improve upon your original ideas as you go along.

3. *Revise* Read your firsthand biography aloud to a partner. Is your hero described effectively? Have you convinced your partner that the subject of your biography is heroic?

4. *Proofread* Check your biography for correct spelling, capitalization, and punctuation. The biography will be more effective if your readers are not distracted by mistakes.

5. *Publish* Publish your firsthand biography, perhaps as a book with photographs or drawings of your hero. Then promote your book at a meet-the-author autograph party with your classmates. You might even want to invite your hero to be present.

Kintu and the Law of Love

retold by Robert R. Potter and H. Alan Robinson

In the beginning, when the world was first made, everything was perfect. Lying, cheating, and killing were unknown. It was a world without hate, without evil, and without war.

In this wonderful world of long ago, there lived a man named Kintu. He was one of the first men to walk upon the earth. A holy man was Kintu, gentle, peaceful, and kind. And his heart was that of a little child.

With his wife, Kintu walked through Africa for many years. They were looking for a place to build a house and start a farm. Someday, they knew, they would settle down, raise children, and grow old together. But there was no hurry. Time would wait.

illustrated by Paul Schulenburg

After many years of traveling, Kintu and his wife came to the shores of Lake Uganda. Here was a great valley, hidden from the world by a circle of snow-topped mountains. The soil was rich and black. Brooks bubbled down out of the foothills. Cool breezes blew across the lake.

"Here we will stay," said Kintu to his wife. "Here we have clear air and clean water. Here we have trees for houses and barns. Here the land will be good to us, and we will be good to the land."

Kintu and his wife had brought with them a cow, a sheep, a goat, a pig, a chicken, a sweet potato, and the root of a banana tree. Before long the sweet potato was a potato patch, and the banana root was a banana tree. The animals also grew in number. The one chicken became two, the two became four, and the four became eight.

Children were born to Kintu and his wife, and then grandchildren. These people started farms on the land around Lake Uganda. Before many years had passed, houses and barns dotted the green fields on both sides of Kintu's farm.

The valley was peaceful, and the people were happy. They spent their days working in the fields and woods. Often they looked at the circle of high mountains around them. The world outside the valley seemed strange and frightening. The people were glad to stay in the beautiful land which the good Kintu had found.

For many years, Kintu ruled the land of Uganda with wisdom and kindness. In truth, he had little ruling to do. His only law was the Law of Love. "My children," Kintu would tell his people, "if men really love one another, no other laws are needed."

And for a long time, no other laws *were* needed. The people of Uganda did not lie, steal, or kill. They were all children of Kintu. They were all brothers. If a farmer's barn burned down, his neighbors quickly built him a new one. If a man became too old to work, his sweet potatoes and bananas were gathered for him. If children were left without a home, they were taken in at once by another family.

When Kintu was a very old man, the farms that had been spreading around both sides of the lake finally met on the other side. Suddenly there was no more land in the valley. Young men could no longer start farms next to their fathers'. It was then that the trouble started.

Not all men could have farms of their own. There was not enough land. This meant that men were no longer equal. Some men were bosses. Others were workers. Some had too much of the good things of life. Others did not have enough.

The number of people in the valley grew larger every year. But the food supply stayed the same. Soon there was not enough food to go around. Some people had to go hungry.

When the stomach is empty, evil thoughts enter the mind. So it was with the people of Uganda. They started to steal from one another. In this way they learned they could get things without working. They became lazy. Soon no one wanted to work. Neighbor turned against neighbor. Sons rose up against their fathers. Blood covered the land.

But still Kintu made no laws. "If the people want to kill each other," he said, "they will do so, law or no law. The way to stop this killing is to stop people from wanting to kill."

So Kintu traveled through the land, talking about the Law of Love to all who would hear. But few people listened. The young people laughed at Kintu. They called him an old-fashioned fool.

Late one afternoon, Kintu was resting in front of his home. He sat looking out over the green valley where he had lived his life. Suddenly he heard the sound of marching feet. Soon there came the voices of many men. "Kintu! Kintu! Kintu!" they shouted as they came nearer. And then, from the woods near Kintu's house, came a large group of soldiers. Their shields and spears gleamed in the sunlight.

"Who are you?" Kintu asked, standing up. "What do you want?"

The leader of the men stepped forward. "We are your friends, good Kintu," he said. "We want to bring the Law of Love back to Uganda. We want to kill everyone who doesn't believe in love."

Kintu shook his head sadly. "You are as wicked as your enemies," he said.

"But we fight for a good reason!" cried the leader of the army. "We are on the side of love, Kintu. We fight in your name!"

"No man fights in my name," replied Kintu. Then he raised his voice and spoke to the whole army. "Men of Uganda, go home now. Lay down your spears, and the hate will leave your hearts."

But the soldiers were not allowed to hear more from Kintu. "The enemy is waiting!" shouted the leader. "In the name of Kintu, let us march to battle!"

The soldiers lined up and moved away like sheep. Soon Kintu heard the ugly sound of men at war.

Kintu called his wife. He told her they could stay in the valley no longer. "We will leave this wicked place," he said. "We will stay away until stealing and killing have stopped. When the Law of Love returns to Uganda, Kintu will return with it."

Kintu told his wife to dig up a sweet potato and the root of a banana tree. Then he went to the barnyard, to get a cow, a sheep, a goat, a pig, and a chicken. They would take with them no more than they had brought.

And so, as night fell, the good Kintu and his wife walked slowly toward the mountains. Soon they had passed away, hand in hand, into the sunset, into the Great Unknown.

The next morning the news spread like fire. "Kintu has disappeared! Kintu and his wife cannot be found!"

At first the people were afraid. The armies stopped fighting. Everyone hunted for the missing Kintu. A few days earlier, Kintu had been an old man at whom people had laughed. Now he was quickly becoming a legend.

"Why did we let this happen!" the people cried. "It is our wicked ways that made Kintu leave his home. From now on, we will worship his name. We will live by his Law of Love."

The valley was searched, and searched again. But it became clearer with every passing day that Kintu would not be found. And something else also became clear. If Kintu were not to return, a new ruler would have to be found.

A dozen men wanted to rule in Kintu's place. Each said he would rule in Kintu's name. Each said Kintu had given him the job. And each had an army to prove he was telling the truth.

Again Uganda was at war with itself. In the name of Kintu, barns were burned to the ground. In the name of Kintu, men were killed in battle. In the name of Kintu, children were left to starve.

No one really won the war. The fighting ended only when the country had worn itself out. By that time, only one of the twelve "rulers" was still alive. He became the king.

But there was little left for the king to rule. The valley was in ruins. Houses and barns had been burned. A few thin animals looked for food in weed-covered fields. The people were left without hope.

It was hard for the people to forget the past. It was even harder for them to face the future. But, little by little, the people began to rebuild the country. Children were born who had no past to forget. To them, the Law of Love seemed as real as the stories of war.

The years passed, and old kings gave way to new. The kings all said they ruled in the name of Kintu. But the Law of Love was forgotten. It was replaced with hundreds of other laws.

After many years, a person named Manda became king. As a prince, Manda had often thought about the great Kintu. Manda liked to climb into the foothills and look out over the valley. Sometimes he would pretend to be Kintu seeing the land of Uganda for the first time, many years before. Always he thought about the Law of Love, and wondered if it would really work.

When Manda became king, he decided to test the Law of Love. Every day he crossed a rule off the law books. In a year, all the laws were gone but one. This was the Law of Love.

A great change came over the country. People worked with a new spirit, and smiled with a new joy. Soon Manda's Uganda was as happy a land as Kintu's had been.

Like Kintu, King Manda had little ruling to do. He made it his habit to go often to the foothills. Only when he was far from the palace could he forget he was the great King Manda.

Manda's servants worried about his being alone in the foothills. They loved their master. They warned him about wild animals and falling rocks. But Manda refused to take anyone with him. His attendants did well to get him to carry a spear to protect himself.

But the servants still worried. Unknown to Manda, a servant followed him everywhere he went. The servant stayed far behind, hiding behind a bush or tree whenever the king turned around. The servants didn't like playing this trick on their beloved king. But to let Manda be alone would have been to forget the Law of Love.

One sunny morning, Manda awakened early and started across the fields toward the foothills. He used his spear as a walking stick. He waved to people working in the fields. The sun was warm, and Manda felt good.

Just as the sun became really hot, King Manda entered the forest that covered the foothills. Suddenly he stopped in surprise. His jaw dropped open. Ahead of him, he saw a circle of animals. A sheep, a pig, and other domestic animals sat quietly beside beasts of the forest. In the center of the circle were an old man and an old woman. A long white beard reached almost to the man's waist. He was talking to the animals. Manda was too far away to understand the words. But he could tell that the voice was deep and kind.

Could this old man be Kintu? Suddenly Manda was sure of it. This *was* Kintu!

Manda rushed forward. A lion moved aside to let him pass through the circle of animals. He dropped to his knees in front of the old man.

"My name is Manda," he cried. "I rule Uganda in the name of the good Kintu."

The old man reached out and took Manda's hand. "Rise," he said softly. "Do not kneel before me. Are you alone?"

"Yes," Manda replied, standing up. "I am alone."

"I am Kintu," said the old man. "I have heard that the Law of Love again rules Uganda. If this is true, I shall return."

Manda was too happy to speak.

"Do the people of Uganda still tell lies to each other?" Kintu asked.

"No," Manda told him. "It has been years since anyone told a lie."

"Do the people still kill each other?"

"Oh no! It has not happened in my lifetime."

"Then I shall return," Kintu said. "Long have I —"

Suddenly Kintu looked into the woods behind Manda. Then he looked Manda in the eye. "I thought you said you came alone," he said.

Manda looked surprised. "Why, I *am* alone," he told Kintu.

But Kintu still stared at him, and into the woods behind.

"I do not lie!" Manda cried. All at once he turned around, to see what Kintu was looking at.

One of Manda's servants was now standing up behind a low bush. He had been seen by Kintu, and he had come out of hiding. Manda didn't understand why the servant was there. He didn't try to understand. He knew only that Kintu thought he had told a lie. It was the servant's fault. Without thinking, Manda raised his arm and threw the spear.

The instant the spear left Manda's hand he knew what he had done. Both men stood like statues as the spear flew over the ground between them. Then, suddenly, Manda rushed forward.

But it was too late. The point of the spear had found the man's heart.

King Manda dropped to the ground beside his dying servant. He reached down and lifted the man's head. Soon it was over. The servant died with love in his eyes, and with a smile on his lips.

For a long time, Manda looked down at the servant who had loved him. Tears ran down the king's cheeks as he thought about what he had done. He had killed a man who had followed him because of love. He had killed him with a spear carried as an act of love. Now it was all Manda could do to turn around and face the great Kintu.

King Manda stood up slowly. He turned around — and stood still for a moment. Then he shut his eyes tight. When he opened them again, he knew the terrible truth.

Everything had disappeared — Kintu, his wife, the animals, everything! And Manda knew why. Now there was nothing to do but walk back down the hillside, to tell the people what had happened.

To this day, it is said, the great Kintu lives in the mountains. Somewhere in the Great Unknown, Kintu is waiting for evil to leave the hearts of men. There he will wait, the story goes, until we all learn to live by his one law — the Law of Love.

Responding to "Kintu and the Law of Love"

Thinking and Discussing

What magical or superhuman qualities does Kintu have?

What problems cause the people to stop living by the Law of Love? How might these problems arise in the real world today?

Do you think that if people could live by the Law of Love no other laws would be necessary? Explain your answer.

Choosing a Creative Response

Explaining Manda's Mistake King Manda never has a chance to explain his tragic actions to Kintu. Think about why Manda kills his servant and what this means to Kintu. With a partner, play the parts of Manda and Kintu, and exchange letters that deal with the tragedy. Share the correspondence with your class.

Creating Your Own Activity Plan and complete your own activity in response to "Kintu and the Law of Love."

Thinking and Writing

The tale of Kintu takes place in Uganda, but like the myths of many cultures, it applies to people all over the world. Suppose you were going to rewrite the myth you have just read as it would take place in another culture. Make a list of story elements you would have to change and those you could keep. Share your ideas with your classmates.

Pandora...The Fateful Casket

retold by Louis Untermeyer

Prometheus had thought about mankind with such sympathy that he had dared to steal the needed fire from Olympus, and for this he was grievously punished by Zeus.[1] But the lord of Olympus did not think this cruelty was enough. Prometheus had a brother, Epimetheus, and though he was harmless and slow-witted, Zeus extended his displeasure to him. He did not punish Epimetheus as brutally as he had done his brother; he had a more subtle plan. It was a scheme which would not only affect Epimetheus but also the whole race of human beings whom Prometheus had dared to help and who were living happily and untroubled.

---

[1] Zeus punished Prometheus by having him chained to a rock. Each day an eagle tore out Prometheus's liver, and the liver grew back each night. Centuries later, the fabled strong man Hercules killed the eagle and freed Prometheus.

illustrated by David Frampton

Zeus ordered Hephaestus, the smith and artisan of the gods, to make a woman out of the materials of earth. Hephaestus took some river clay that had flakes of gold in it and began to make a lovely girl. In with the clay he mixed the fragrance of a river rose, the sweetness of Hymettus[2] honey, the smoothness of a silver dolphin, the voices of larks and lake-water, the color of sunrise on snow, the warmth of a sunny morning in May. Then he summoned the Four Winds to breathe life into the new creation. Finally he called upon the goddesses to complete the work and grant the glowing figure a touch of their own powers.

"Hephaestus has given her beauty," said Aphrodite, "but I shall make her more beautiful by adding the spark of love. It will shine in her eyes, and everyone that looks on her will be enchanted."

"I shall make her wise," said Athene. "She shall be able to choose between false and true, between what men value and what she must know is worthless."

"I shall make her a woman, a puzzle to every man," said Hera, the wife of Zeus. "I shall make her a real woman, for I shall give her the gift of curiosity."

Smiling, the goddesses adorned her, and when Zeus beheld her grace, her garland of gold, and the glory of her endowments, he was as charmed as though he had been a mortal. "We will call her Pandora," he said, "Pandora, the All-Gifted. She shall become the bride of Epimetheus. But she shall not go empty-handed. She shall bring with her a casket, a box of magic as her dowry. And Hermes, my messenger, shall conduct her to earth."

Epimetheus could not understand why the gods had become concerned about him. He was dazzled by Hermes, and it was some time before he could believe that the exquisite creature brought by the messenger god was meant for him. Even after Hermes departed in a flashing cloud and Pandora stood blushing beside him, he was perturbed. He remembered how often his brother Prometheus had warned him,

---

[2]**Hymettus** (hī **mĕt′**əs): a mountain ridge near Athens, Greece.

"Do not trust the gods. And beware especially of Zeus and anything he may send you." However, when Pandora looked in his eyes and smiled, he was, as Aphrodite had predicted, enchanted and ensnared. Yet, even as he took her in his arms, he cautioned her.

"We have reason to fear the gods," said Epimetheus, "and also their gifts," he added, pointing to the casket.

"But this is my dowry," murmured Pandora. "Zeus himself filled it with magic as a present for us. See how beautifully it is carved and painted. Look at the silver hinges and the great gold clasp that fastens it."

"Keep it well fastened," said Epimetheus, "otherwise I shall never rest easy. I do not know what the casket may contain, and I do not want to know. Promise me one thing. Never open the box. It is, I grant, a beautiful thing, too beautiful to destroy, and we will keep it. But hide it. Put it not only out of your sight but out of your mind. Then we shall both be content."

Happy that she could keep her dowry, Pandora put it under the bed and turned to her husband with love. And so for a long time nothing disturbed their married life and their continual joy in each other.

But, though Pandora benefited from the goddesses' gifts of beauty and wisdom, the gift of Hera had not been given in vain. For quite a while, Pandora restrained her curiosity about the wonderful casket. But with the passing of time she could not help wondering what it might contain. After all, it was *her* dowry, and she had a right to see what the greatest of the gods had conferred upon her. Then, ashamed of her weakness, she put the idea from her, and thought only of her delight in her home with Epimetheus.

One day, however, the curiosity, so long stifled, overmastered her. "I shall only lift the lid," she said to herself, "and snatch a moment's glimpse of what may be inside. No matter what I see, I won't touch a thing. Surely there can be no harm in that."

Anxiously, as though she were being watched, she tiptoed to her room. Gently getting down on her hands and knees, she drew the casket from under the bed. Half fearfully and half eagerly she lifted the lid. It was only a moment and the lid was up only an inch, but in that moment a swarm of horrible things flew out. They were noisome, abominably colored, and evil-looking, for they were the spirits of all that was evil, sad, and hurtful. They were War and Famine, Crime and Pestilence, Spite and Cruelty, Sickness and Malice, Envy, Woe, Wickedness, and all the other disasters let loose in the world.

Hearing Pandora's scream, Epimetheus rushed in. But it was too late. He and Pandora were set upon and stung, and the evil spirits flew off to attack the rest of mankind.

"It is all my fault," cried Pandora. "If I had thought more about your warning and less about my own desires, I could have controlled my curiosity."

"The fault is mine," said Epimetheus. "I should have burned the box." Then he added, for the poison of Malice was already taking effect, "After all, you are what you are — only a woman — and what else could one expect of a woman."

Disconsolate that she had brought so harmful a dower to Epimetheus as well as to all other men and women, Pandora wept. It was hours before she let her husband comfort her. Finally, after she grew quiet, they heard a faint sound inside the box.

"Lift the lid again," said Epimetheus. "I think you have released the worst. Perhaps something else, something better, is still there."

He was right. At the bottom of the box was a quivering thing. Its body was small; its wings were frail; but there was a radiance about it. Somehow Pandora knew what it was, and she took it up, touched it carefully, and showed it to Epimetheus. "It is Hope," she said.

"Do you think it will live?" asked Epimetheus.

"Yes," answered Pandora. "I am sure it will. Some-how I know that it will outlive War and Sickness and all the other evils. And," she added, watching the shining thing rise and flutter about the room, "it will never leave us for long. Even if we lose sight of it, it will be there."

She was no longer downhearted as Hope spread its wings and went out into the world.

Responding to "Pandora . . . The Fateful Casket"

Thinking and Discussing

List the human and superhuman characteristics of Hera, Zeus, and Pandora. Which is most responsible for the introduction of evil into the world? Explain.

What does this story tell us about hope and evil?

Choosing a Creative Response

Designing a Poster Is curiosity a gift or a curse? What would Pandora or Epimetheus say? What do *you* say? Create a poster that defends your opinion. Use quotes and illustrate scenes from the story, or include clever sayings and drawings based on your own ideas.

Comparing Character Webs In what ways do Pandora and Epimetheus change after the casket is opened? List words and phrases that describe each character before and after the evils of the world are released. Use your list to create "before" and "after" word webs for each character. How do your webs show changes in Pandora and Epimetheus?

Creating Your Own Activity Plan and complete your own activity in response to "Pandora . . . The Fateful Casket."

Exploring Language

Make a short *Mythology Dictionary* that includes words, phrases, and ideas from myths that are part of our language today. You might begin with the phrase *opening Pandora's box*, since you have just read about Pandora. Do research to explore other ideas, such as *Achilles' heel, Trojan horse,* and *Midas touch*.

MYTHIC HEROES
AND THEIR
ADVENTURES
REMAIN WITH US
FOR ALL TIME.

SCARFACE

retold by George Bird Grinnell

*This is a tale told by
the Blackfoot Indians
who lived in the great
plains area of the
United States and
southern Canada.
It is translated from
their language just as
it was told by them to
the author. The story
can be interpreted as
the Indian's journey
across the plains and
western mountains to
the home of the Great
Spirit, the sun.*

photographs by Sam Gray

In the earliest times there was no war. All the tribes were at peace. In those days there was a man who had a daughter, a very beautiful girl. Many young men wanted to marry her, but every time she was asked, she only shook her head and said she did not want a husband.

"How is this?" asked her father. "Some of these young men are rich, handsome, and brave."

"Why should I marry?" replied the girl. "I have a rich father and mother. Our lodge is good. The parfleches[1] are never empty. There are plenty of tanned robes and soft furs for winter. Why worry me, then?"

The Raven Bearers held a dance; they all dressed carefully and wore their ornaments, and each one tried to dance the best. Afterwards some of them asked for this girl, but still she said no. Then the Bulls, the Kit-foxes, and others of the *I-kun-uh'-kah-tsi* held their dances, and all those who were rich, many great warriors, asked this man for his daughter, but to every one of them she said no. Then her father was angry, and said: "Why, now, this way? All the best men have asked for you, and still you say no. I believe you have a secret lover."

"Father! mother!" replied the girl, "Pity me. I have no secret lover, but now hear the truth. That Above Person, the Sun, told me, 'Do not marry any of those men, for you are mine; thus you shall be happy, and live to great age'; and again he said, 'Take heed. You must not marry. You are mine.'"

"Ah!" replied her father. "It must always be as he says." And they talked no more about it.

There was a poor young man, very poor. His father, mother, all his relations, had gone to the Sand Hills.[2] He had no lodge, no wife to tan

---

[1]**parfleche** (pär′flĕsh′): a box or sack made of rawhide.
[2]**had gone to the Sand Hills:** had died.

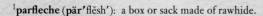

his robes or sew his moccasins. He stopped in one lodge to-day, and to-morrow he ate and slept in another; thus he lived. He was a good-looking young man, except that on his cheek he had a scar, and his clothes were always old and poor.

After those dances some of the young men met this poor Scarface, and they laughed at him, and said: "Why don't you ask that girl to marry you? You are so rich and handsome!" Scarface did not laugh; he replied: "Ah! I will do as you say. I will go and ask her." All the young men thought this was funny. They laughed a great deal. But Scarface went down by the river. He waited by the river, where the women came to get water, and by and by the girl came along. "Girl," he said, "wait. I want to speak with you. Not as a designing person do I ask you, but openly where the Sun looks down, and all may see."

"Speak then," said the girl.

"I have seen the days," continued the young man. "You have refused those who are young, and rich, and brave. Now, to-day, they laughed and said to me, 'Why do you not ask her?' I am poor, very poor. I have no lodge, no food, no clothes, no robes and warm furs. I have no relations; all have gone to the Sand Hills; yet, now, to-day, I ask you, take pity, be my wife."

The girl hid her face in her robe and brushed the ground with the point of her moccasin, back and forth, back and forth; for she was thinking. After a time she said: "True. I have refused all those rich young men, yet now the poor one asks me, and I am glad. I will be your wife, and my people will be happy. You are poor, but it does not matter.

My father will give you dogs. My mother will make us a lodge. My people will give us robes and furs. You will be poor no longer."

Then the young man was happy, and he started to kiss her, but she held him back, and said: "Wait! The Sun has spoken to me. He says I may not marry; that I belong to him. He says if I listen to him, I shall live to great age. But now I say: Go to the Sun. Tell him, 'She whom you spoke with heeds your words. She has never done wrong, but now she wants to marry. I want her for my wife.' Ask him to take that scar from your face. That will be his sign. I will know he is pleased. But if he refuses, or if you fail to find his lodge, then do not return to me."

"Oh!" cried the young man, "at first your words were good. I was glad. But now it is dark. My heart is dead. Where is that far-off lodge? Where the trail, which no one yet has travelled?"

"Take courage, take courage!" said the girl; and she went to her lodge.

Scarface was very sad. He sat down and covered his head with his robe and tried to think what to do. After a while he got up, and went to an old woman who had been kind to him. "Pity me," he said. "I am very poor. I am going away now on a long journey. Make me some moccasins."

"Where are you going?" asked the old woman. "There is no war; we are very peaceful here."

"I do not know where I shall go," replied Scarface. "I am in trouble, but I cannot tell you now what it is."

So the old woman made him some moccasins, seven pairs, with parfleche soles, and also she gave him a sack of food, pemmican of berries, pounded meat, and dried back fat; for this old woman had a good heart. She liked the young man.

All alone, and with a sad heart, he climbed the bluffs and stopped to take a last look at the camp. He wondered if he would ever see his sweetheart and the people again. "*Hai'-yu!* Pity me, O Sun," he prayed, and turning, he started to find the trail.

For many days he travelled on, over great prairies, along timbered rivers and among the mountains, and every day his sack of food grew

lighter; but he saved it as much as he could, and ate berries, and roots, and sometimes he killed an animal of some kind. One night he stopped by the home of a wolf. *"Hai-yah!"* said that one; "what is my brother doing so far from home?"

"Ah!" replied Scarface, "I seek the place where the Sun lives; I am sent to speak with him."

"I have travelled far," said the wolf. "I know all the prairies, the valleys, and the mountains, but I have never seen the Sun's home. Wait; I know one who is very wise. Ask the bear. He may tell you."

The next day the man travelled on again, stopping now and then to pick a few berries, and when night came he arrived at the bear's lodge.

"Where is your home?" asked the bear. "Why are you travelling alone, my brother?"

"Help me! Pity me!" replied the young man; "because of her words I seek the Sun. I go to ask him for her."

"I know not where he stops," replied the bear. "I have travelled by many rivers, and I know the mountains, yet I have never seen his lodge. There is some one beyond, that striped-face, who is very smart. Go and ask him."

The badger was in his hole. Stooping over, the young man shouted: "Oh, cunning striped-face! Oh, generous animal! I wish to speak with you."

"What do you want?" said the badger, poking his head out of the hole.

"I want to find the Sun's home," replied Scarface. "I want to speak with him."

"I do not know where he lives," replied the badger. "I never travel very far. Over there in the timber is a wolverine. He is always travelling around, and is of much knowledge. Maybe he can tell you."

Then Scarface went to the woods and looked all around for the wolverine, but could not find him. So he sat down to rest. *"Hai'-yu; Hai'-yu!"* he cried. "Wolverine, take pity on me. My food is gone, my moccasins are worn out. Now I must die."

"What is it, my brother?" he heard, and looking around, he saw the animal sitting near.

"She whom I would marry," said Scarface, "belongs to the Sun; I am trying to find where he lives, to ask him for her."

"Ah!" said the wolverine. "I know where he lives. Wait; it is nearly night. To-morrow I will show you the trail to the big water. He lives on the other side of it."

Early in the morning, the wolverine showed him the trail, and Scarface followed it until he came to the water's edge. He looked out over it, and his heart almost stopped. Never before had any one seen such a big water. The other side could not be seen, and there was no end to it. Scarface sat down on the shore. His food was all gone, his moccasins worn out. His heart was sick. "I cannot cross this big water," he said. "I cannot return to the people. Here, by this water, I shall die."

Not so. His helpers were there. Two swans came swimming up to the shore. "Why have you come here?" they asked him. "What are you doing? It is very far to the place where your people live."

"I am here," replied Scarface, "to die. Far away, in my country, is a beautiful girl. I want to marry her, but she belongs to the Sun. So I

60

started to find him and ask for her. I have travelled many days. My food is gone. I cannot go back. I cannot cross this big water, so I am going to die."

"No," said the swans; "it shall not be so. Across this water is the home of that Above Person. Get on our backs, and we will take you there."

Scarface quickly arose. He felt strong again. He waded out into the water and lay down on the swans' backs, and they started off. Very deep and black is that fearful water. Strange people live there, mighty animals which often seize and drown a person. The swans carried him safely, and took him to the other side. Here was a broad hard trail leading back from the water's edge.

"*Kyi*," said the swans. "You are now close to the Sun's lodge. Follow that trail, and you will soon see it."

Scarface started up the trail, and pretty soon he came to some beautiful things, lying in it. There was a war shirt, a shield, and a bow and arrows. He had never seen such pretty weapons; but he did not touch them. He walked carefully around them, and travelled on. A little way further on, he met a young man, the handsomest person he had ever seen. His hair was very long, and he wore cloth- ing made of strange skins. His moccasins were sewn with bright colored feathers. The young man said to him, "Did you see some weapons lying on the trail?"

"Yes," replied Scarface; "I saw them."

"But did you not touch them?" asked the young man.

"No; I thought some one had left them there, so I did not take them."

"You are not a thief," said the young man. "What is your name?"

"Scarface."

"Where are you going?"

"To the Sun."

"My name," said the young man, "is A-pi-su-ahts.[3] The Sun is my father; come, I will take you to our lodge. My father is not now at home, but he will come in at night."

Soon they came to the lodge. It was very large and handsome; strange medicine animals were painted on it. Behind, on a tripod, were strange weapons and beautiful clothes — the Sun's. Scarface was ashamed to go in, but Morning Star said, "Do not be afraid, my friend; we are glad you have come."

They entered. One person was sitting there, Ko-ko-mik'-e-is,[4] the Sun's wife, Morning Star's mother. She spoke to Scarface kindly, and gave him something to eat. "Why have you come so far from your people?" she asked.

Then Scarface told her about the beautiful girl he wanted to marry. "She belongs to the Sun," he said. "I have come to ask him for her."

---

[3]**A-pi-su-ahts:** Early Riser, *i.e.* The Morning Star. [Author's note.]

[4]**Ko-ko-mik'-e-is:** Night red light, the Moon. [Author's note.]

When it was time for the Sun to come home, the Moon hid Scarface under a pile of robes. As soon as the Sun got to the doorway, he stopped, and said, "I smell a person."

"Yes, father," said Morning Star; "a good young man has come to see you. I know he is good, for he found some of my things on the trail and did not touch them."

Then Scarface came out from under the robes, and the Sun entered and sat down. "I am glad you have come to our lodge," he said. "Stay with us as long as you think best. My son is lonesome sometimes; be his friend."

The next day the Moon called Scarface out of the lodge, and said to him: "Go with Morning Star where you please, but never hunt near that big water; do not let him go there. It is the home of great birds which have long sharp bills; they kill people. I have had many sons, but these birds have killed them all. Morning Star is the only one left."

So Scarface stayed there a long time and hunted with Morning Star. One day they came near the water, and saw the big birds.

"Come," said Morning Star; "let us go and kill those birds."

"No, no!" replied Scarface; "we must not go there. Those are very terrible birds; they will kill us."

Morning Star would not listen. He ran towards the water, and Scarface followed. He knew that he must kill the birds and save the boy. If not, the Sun would be angry and might kill him. He ran ahead and met the birds, which were coming towards him to fight, and killed every one of them with his spear; not one was left. Then the young men cut off their heads, and carried them home. Morning Star's mother was glad when they told her what they had done, and showed her the birds' heads. She cried, and called Scarface "my son." When the Sun came home at night, she told him about it, and he too was glad. "My son," he said to Scarface, "I will not forget what you have this day done for me. Tell me now, what can I do for you?"

"Hai'-yu," replied Scarface. "Hai'-yu, pity me. I am here to ask you for that girl. I want to marry her. I asked her, and she was glad; but she says you own her, that you told her not to marry."

"What you say is true," said the Sun. "I have watched the days, so I know it. Now, then, I give her to you; she is yours. I am glad she has been wise. I know she has never done wrong. The Sun pities good women. They shall live a long time. So shall their husbands and children. Now you will soon go home. Let me tell you something. Be wise and listen: I am the only chief. Everything is mine. I made the earth, the mountains, prairies, rivers, and forests. I made the people and all the animals. This is why I say I alone am the chief. I can never die. True, the winter makes me old and weak, but every summer I grow young again."

Then said the Sun: "What one of all animals is smartest? The raven is, for he always finds food. He is never hungry. Which one of all the animals is most Nat-ó-ye?[5] The buffalo is. Of all animals, I like him best. He is for the people. He is your food and your shelter. What part of his body is sacred? The tongue is. That is mine. What else is sacred? Berries are. They are mine too. Come with me and see the world." He took Scarface to the edge of the sky, and they looked down and saw it. It is round and flat, and all around the edge is the jumping-off place (or walls straight down). Then said the Sun: "When any man is sick or in danger, his wife may promise to build me a lodge, if he recovers. If the woman is pure and true, then I will be pleased and help the man. But if she is bad, if she lies, then I will be angry. You shall build the last lodge like the world, round, with walls, but first you must build a sweat house of a hundred sticks. It shall be like the sky (a hemisphere), and half of it shall be painted red. That is me. The other half you will paint black. That is the night."

Further said the Sun: "Which is the best, the heart or the brain? The brain is. The heart often lies, the brain never." Then he told Scarface everything about making the Medicine Lodge, and when he had finished, he rubbed a powerful medicine on his face, and the scar disappeared. Then he gave him two raven feathers, saying: "These are the sign for the girl, that I give her to you. They must always be worn by the husband of the woman who builds a Medicine Lodge."

The young man was now ready to return home. Morning Star and the Sun gave him many beautiful presents. The Moon cried and kissed him,

---

[5]**Nat-ó-ye:** This word may be translated as "of the Sun," "having Sun power," or more properly, something sacred. [Author's note.]

and called him "my son." Then the Sun showed him the short trail. It was the Wolf Road (Milky Way). He followed it, and soon reached the ground.

It was a very hot day. All the lodge skins were raised, and the people sat in the shade. There was a chief, a very generous man, and all day long people kept coming to his lodge to feast and smoke with him. Early in the morning this chief saw a person sitting out on a butte[6] near by, close wrapped in his robe. The chief's friends came and went, the sun reached the middle, and passed on, down towards the mountains. Still this person did not move. When it was almost night, the chief said: "Why does that person sit there so long? The heat has been strong, but he has never eaten nor drunk. He may be a stranger; go and ask him in."

So some young men went up to him, and said: "Why do you sit here in the great heat all day? Come to the shade of the lodges. The chief asks you to feast with him."

Then the person arose and threw off his robe, and they were surprised. He wore beautiful clothes. His bow, shield, and other weapons were of strange make. But they knew his face, although the scar was gone, and they ran ahead, shouting, "The scarfaced poor young man has come. He is poor no longer. The scar on his face is gone."

All the people rushed out to see him. "Where have you been?" they asked. "Where did you get all these pretty things?" He did not answer. There in the crowd stood that young woman; and taking the two raven feathers from his head, he gave them to her, and said: "The trail was very long, and I nearly died, but by those helpers, I found his lodge. He is glad. He sends these feathers to you. They are the sign."

Great was her gladness then. They were married, and made the first Medicine Lodge, as the Sun had said. The Sun was glad. He gave them great age. They were never sick. When they were very old, one morning, their children said: "Awake! Rise and eat." They did not move. In the night, in sleep, without pain, their shadows had departed for the Sand Hills.

---

[6]**butte** (byōot): a hill with a flat top.

Responding to "Scarface"

Thinking and Discussing

What journey does Scarface undertake, and why? What do the incidents on the journey reveal about his character? Does Scarface become a hero? Explain.

By reading this story, what might you conclude about the values of the Blackfoot Indians, the people from whom Scarface's story comes?

Choosing a Creative Response

Performing with Masks Dramatize the tale of Scarface using masks like those created by Native Americans. You may wish to research masks before you create expressive masks for the different characters. Have a narrator retell the main events of the story as masked performers act them out.

Creating your Own Activity Plan and complete your own activity in response to "Scarface."

Thinking and Writing

In what ways does Scarface show that he is more than a mere mortal? If you had his special powers, how would you use them to make a contribution to modern life? Write about your heroic ideas, and share what you write with your class.

Maria Morevna

retold by Ethel Johnston Phelps

illustrated by Fred Lynch

Long, long ago, when the land of Russia was made up of many small kingdoms, there lived a warrior princess named Maria Morevna.

She had inherited her kingdom from her father, and her father, very wisely, had trained her not only to govern well, but also to defend the kingdom against enemy armies. Many princes sought to marry her, thinking to gain control of the country. Maria Morevna refused them all.

One day the young Prince Alexey rode in from the south and said he wished to serve in the army of Maria Morevna. The long and the short of it was — they fell in love, and the marriage took place three months later at the palace, amid great rejoicing. The young couple lived happily together for one year.

Then one day an exhausted messenger rode into the palace courtyard to bring tidings[1] of an enemy attack on the western borders. While the army assembled for war, Maria sat down with Alexey.

"You will rule here in my absence," she told him. "But, dear Alexey, you must never open the door at the top of the east tower."

After a fond farewell, Maria, splendid in her white and gold uniform, rode off at the head of her army.

Now, Alexey was consumed with curiosity about the door that must not be opened. He resisted for one day. He resisted for two days. But on the third day he weakened and said to himself, "I'll just take a quick look. Surely that can do no harm."

So he climbed the stairs to the tower. Trying each of the keys entrusted to him until he found the one that unlocked the door, he pushed it open and stepped into the room.

He stood rooted to the floor in astonishment — for inside was a tall old man with white hair and a long white beard, who stood chained to the wall.

"I am so weak," cried the old man. "Kind youth, will you bring me a jar of water?"

---

[1]**tidings** (tī′dǐngz): information; news.

Alexey felt pity for him. He ran down the steps and filled a large jar with water. When he brought it in, the prisoner drank it down in one gulp.

"I feel stronger," said the old man. "Bring me more water, I beg of you."

And Alexey brought him another full jar of water. This too he gulped down in an instant.

"One more, kind youth," the old man beseeched. Alexey hesitated.

"Bring me one more jar of water, and I promise you I will give you your life when otherwise you must die."

Alexey brought him the third jar of water.

After the prisoner had drained that in a gulp, he swelled in size. As his body grew huge and powerful, his face became cruel and savage. With a quick wrench he broke the heavy iron chains as if they were paper.

"Who are you?" cried Alexey.

"I am Koschei the Wizard," answered the old man exultantly. "Many years ago, the father of Maria Morevna captured me, thinking to rid the country of evil. He destroyed my power and chained me here. Now you have set me free!"

With a swirl of his long cape he flew out of the window and away. High in the air he flew, like a great bird of prey, till he saw Maria Morevna far below, riding proudly with her army. He swooped down, seized the princess, and flew off with her. He flew over nine times seven kingdoms until he reached his own palace near the sea.

Alexey was crushed with grief. The fate of Maria lay heavily on his heart, for he knew his impulsive carelessness was to blame. While the people of the kingdom mourned their princess, Alexey rode off in search of her.

He traveled many roads for many weeks across many kingdoms before he at last arrived at Koschei's palace. Leaving his horse tethered in the forest, he crept as close as he could. He lay hidden until he saw Koschei ride forth on a powerful black horse. Then he climbed a tree and, from an outspread branch, dropped down into the palace garden. There he found Maria Morevna.

They embraced joyfully. But after a moment Maria drew back.

"Oh Alexey, why did you disobey my command?" she cried. "Why did you open the room and free the wizard?"

"I was foolish and thoughtless," said Alexey sadly. "I know it has caused you much grief. But if you can forgive the past, we will set off at once. My horse waits in the forest nearby."

"If it were that easy to escape the wizard, I wouldn't be here now," replied Maria. "He possesses a miraculous horse, and he will catch up with us in a trice!"[2]

"I saw him leave for a day's hunting," urged Alexey. "We can be far away before he discovers you are gone."

But Maria cried, "He will kill you if he catches us — and that I could not bear!"

At last Alexey persuaded Maria to try to escape, for he said he would rather be slain than live without her. So, making their way out of the garden, they mounted Alexey's horse and rode off as fast as the steed could carry them.

In the midst of the hunt, some distance away, Koschei's great horse suddenly stopped in its tracks.

"What ails you, you lazy beast?" cried Koschei, bringing down his whip on the horse's flank.

"Prince Alexey has come and carried off Maria Morevna," said the horse.

Koschei swelled with anger. "After them, you stupid nag!" His spurs dug into the horse cruelly, for he, like many with violent tempers, took out his rage on those who served him.

The horse fairly flew over the ground, scarcely needing the whip and spurs of Koschei. Within a very short time they had overtaken Alexey and Maria.

Seizing Alexey under one arm, and Maria under the other, the wizard carried them back to the castle.

"You're a fool. You have no more chance of freeing Maria Morevna than you have of seeing your own ears!" he cried, flinging Alexey to the ground. As the wizard swung his sword high, Alexey

---

[2] **trice** (trīs): a short period of time; an instant.

Koschei swelled with anger. "After them, you stupid nag!" His spurs dug into the horse cruelly, for he, like many with violent tempers, took out his rage on those who served him.

cried out, "When I gave you the third jar of water, you promised me my life!"

The sword stopped in midair. "Very well," snarled the wizard. "I will not kill you." And he gave orders for Alexey to be put into a large cask. After the top was tightly sealed, the cask was thrown over the cliff into the sea.

Now, it happened the next day that a hawk, an eagle, and a crow, seeing the cask floating in the sea, became curious and pulled it to shore with their beaks and sharp claws. There they picked at it until they tore it apart.

Great was their astonishment when Alexey crawled out, bruised but unharmed.

Alexey thanked them gratefully, but he added in despair, "I am no more able to free Maria Morevna now that I am outside the cask than I was inside it!" Then Alexey told his rescuers all that had happened since he unwittingly freed the wizard.

"It is clear," said the crow, "that Koschei's horse is a hundred times swifter than any other."

"Try as often as you will," said the hawk, "he is sure to overtake you."

"You must try to obtain another horse the equal of the wizard's," said the eagle. "Maria Morevna must find out from Koschei where and how he obtained his."

Alexey thanked them for their counsel and set off on foot for the wizard's castle. Once more he waited for Koschei to leave, then climbed into the garden.

Maria was overjoyed to see Alexey still alive. When he told her the advice of the three birds, she nodded.

"Yes," she said, "Koschei likes to boast of his steed's power. Come back here tomorrow, Alexey; let us pray I will have an answer for you."

That evening, Maria spoke of Koschei's horse with great admiration. Then she went on, "Tell me, wise wizard, where was this marvelous steed foaled?"

"On the shore of the blue sea grazes a most wonderful mare. Every three years the mare bears a colt. He who can snatch the colt from the wolves waiting to seize it, and bring the colt safely away, will possess a steed like mine."

"And did you bravely snatch the colt from the wolves?" asked Maria.

"No, it was not I," the wizard admitted. "Near this place lives an old Baba Yaga[3] who follows the mare and snatches each colt from the wolves. Thus she has a herd of many miraculous horses. I spent three days tending them, and for a reward she gave me a little colt. That colt grew up to become the horse I ride."

"How clever you were to find the Baba Yaga!" cried Maria. "It cannot have been easy."

"Only I have that power," boasted Koschei. "One must cross a river of fire to reach her land. I have in my silver chest here a magic handkerchief." The wizard took out the piece of scarlet silk. "I waved this handkerchief three times to my right side and a strong bridge appeared, a bridge so high that the fire could not touch it. What do you think of that, eh?" And he sat back well pleased with himself.

Maria exclaimed at his power and cleverness. Then, in the night, after the wizard was asleep, she went to the silver chest and removed the handkerchief.

The very next day, when Alexey once again stole into the palace garden, she gave the magic handkerchief to him and told him what Koschei had revealed.

---

[3]**Baba Yaga:** a sorceress.

Alexey set off at once on his long journey, traveling over wet, mired roads and dry, dusty roads. He found the river of fire and, using the magic scarlet silk, safely crossed on the high bridge.

Now he had to find the Baba Yaga. The country was empty and desolate. He had walked three days without food or drink when, weak with hunger, he came upon a bird with her fledglings. One of these he caught.

The mother bird flew round and round him, squawking desperately. "Do not eat my little one," she cried. "If you will set it free, one day I will do a service for you."

Alexey was moved to pity and set the little bird free.

Soon afterward he found a wild beehive. He was about to pull out the honeycomb when the queen bee buzzed about his face, saying, "Prince, do not take the honey. It is food for my subjects. Leave it — and in return, one day I will do you a service."

Alexey left the honey and struggled hungrily on. That evening he came at last to the shore of the blue sea. Here, leaning over the rocks near the shore, he caught a crayfish.

But the crayfish cried out, "Spare my life, prince. Do not eat me, and one day I will do you a service."

Alexey dropped the crayfish back into the water. He went on so tired and hungry he could scarcely walk.

Not long after this he came to the hut of the Baba Yaga. This hut, as you may know, was set up on high stilts that looked like great chicken legs. He climbed the ladder to the hut and entered.

"Health to thee, Grandmother," said he cautiously.

"Health to thee, prince," she answered, staring at him with sharp, dark eyes. "Why do you come to visit me?"

"I come to serve you as herder," said he. "I want to graze your horses so I may earn a colt as payment."

"So that's the way it is, eh?" The Baba Yaga sat silent a moment, her brown wrinkled face neither friendly nor unfriendly. "Why not?" she said at last. "If you tend the horses well, I'll give you a steed fit for a hero. But if you lose even one of them, I'll lop off your head!"

"Hard terms, Grandmother, but I agree."

The Baba Yaga gave him food and drink and a place to sleep in the corner.

The next day the herd was let out of the stables to pasture. At once they raced off in every direction over the wide steppes, and disappeared. It happened in the blink of an eye, even before Alexey could mount his horse. All day he searched, but he could not find them.

Just as he gave way to despair, a great flock of birds filled the sky. The birds found the horses, swooped down, and pecking at them sharply, drove them home to the stables by evening. Alexey's kindness in setting the fledgling bird free had been rewarded!

When the Baba Yaga saw this, she was very angry. Secretly she ordered the herd to disappear into the thick forest the next day.

And so it happened on the second day. The horses disappeared into a dense forest. Alexey followed them, but though he searched the forest all day, he could not find them. Wearily he sat down on a log. "I shall never get the colt as payment," he thought in despair. "And how will I free Maria Morevna?"

Then suddenly a huge swarm of bees filled the air. They easily sought out the horses, buzzing about their faces and stinging their flanks until all of them fled back to the stable.

That night, while Alexey slept, the Baba Yaga berated the horses soundly; she ordered them to go to the sea the next day and swim until they were completely out of sight.

So it happened on the third day. Alexey, who had followed the horses to the shore, saw them swimming rapidly out to sea. In a trice they had disappeared from sight. Disheartened and weary, he sat down on a rock on the shore. His quest for a steed to rescue Maria now seemed hopeless. He wept, and after that he fell asleep.

It was evening when he was awakened by a crayfish nipping at his finger that was trailing in the water. "The creatures of the sea and shore have driven the horses back. They are safe now in the stable," said the crayfish. "I have served you as I promised. Return now, but hide in the stable — for the Baba Yaga will try to trick you. When the Baba Yaga is asleep, take the shabby little colt standing in the corner and go away at once."

Alexey thanked the crayfish joyfully. He returned to hide in the stable; at midnight, while the Baba Yaga was sleeping soundly, he saddled the shabby colt and rode off. Crossing back over the bridge spanning the river of fire, he found a lush green meadow nearby. Here he grazed the colt at sunrise for twelve mornings. By the twelfth morning, the colt had become a huge and powerful steed. With such a horse as this, he covered the roads back to the wizard's castle in hardly more time than is needed to tell of it.

Maria cried out with joy at the sight of Alexey, but little time was spent in talk. They both mounted Alexey's horse and at once rode off with the speed of the wind.

But the wizard's horse once more faithfully reported Maria's escape. Using whip and spurs, Koschei flew after them.

"You lazy bag of bones," shouted Koschei. "Why don't you over-take them?"

"The horse the prince rides is my younger brother," the wizard's horse replied, "but I will try."

Koschei applied the whip more viciously. As they drew closer to Maria and Alexey, the wizard lifted his great sword to strike.

At that moment the steed Alexey rode cried out to the other, "My brother, why do you serve such a cruel and wicked master? Toss him from your back and kick him sharply with your hooves!"

Koschei's horse heeded the advice of his brother. He threw his rider to the ground and lashed out with his hooves so fiercely that the wizard was forced to crawl back painfully to the castle on all fours, and he never emerged again.

Maria mounted Koschei's horse and they returned in triumph to their own kingdom. There they were welcomed with shouts of surprise and thanksgiving.

Very soon after her return, Maria Morevna again mounted Koschei's horse, leading her army forth to rout the invaders in the west. And Koschei's horse served her faithfully ever after.

Koschei applied the whip more viciously. As they drew closer to Maria and Alexey, the wizard lifted his great sword to strike.

Responding to "Maria Morevna"

Thinking and Discussing

What warning does Maria give Alexey? What motive prompts Alexey to help the old man in the tower? Why is the outcome of his action surprising?

Which character in the story do you think was the cleverest at outwitting someone else? Explain your answer.

Choosing a Creative Response

Meeting Challenges Think of a time when you or someone you know performed a task that others thought was impossible. How was the challenge met? How did others react? Write about meeting the challenge, or tell the story to your class.

Discovering Women Heroes Choose a woman hero to present in a report to your class. Either select someone from your own experience, or research women heroes and choose a famous individual. Give facts about the woman to support your opinion that she is a hero.

Creating Your Own Activity Plan and complete your own activity in response to "Maria Morevna."

Thinking and Writing

Imagine that you are a newspaper reporter covering an exciting event in the story, such as the scene where Koschei is finally defeated. Write an exciting headline to capture a reader's interest. Then write an effective lead paragraph that tells the reader the key information: who, what, where, and why. Develop your ideas into a complete article if you wish.

George Lucas

The *Star Wars* saga came out of George Lucas's history, out of the things he liked and felt when he was a kid. It sprang from fairy tales, comic books, myths, films. The result is a wonderful emotional landscape for people of all ages. . . .

— *Scriptwriter Lawrence Kasdan*

In the Star Wars *trilogy, filmmaker George Lucas created an action-packed modern myth filled with strange characters and bizarre events. Like traditional myths,* Star Wars *deals with heroes, conflict, and the struggle of good and evil forces.*

The hero of the trilogy is young Luke Skywalker. In The Empire Strikes Back, *the second film of the series, Luke is allied with his mentor Ben Kenobi, Han Solo, Princess Leia Organa, and the Jedi rebel forces. They are fighting against the forces of Darth Vader and the Evil Empire.*

As the script begins, Luke has left his friends and is flying to the planet of Dagobah. He seeks Yoda, the Jedi Master who has trained warriors for eight hundred years. This great teacher will show Luke how to use the immense power of the Force to do seemingly impossible things.

Luke and the droid Artoo, his robot and faithful companion, approach the planet as the scene opens.

THE EM

from *The Empire Strikes Back Notebook*
edited by Diana Attias and Lindsay Smith
from the movie script by Leigh Brackett
and Lawrence Kasdan
based on the story by George Lucas

EXTERIOR: SPACE — LUKE'S X-WING

(The tiny X-wing speeds toward the cloud cover of Dagobah. Artoo, riding on the back of the fighter, turns his head back and forth with some anxiety.)

INTERIOR: LUKE'S X-WING — COCKPIT

(Luke watches Artoo's words as they are translated and screened on the computer scope.)

LUKE *(into comlink):* Yes, that's it. Dagobah.

(Artoo beeps a hopeful inquiry.)

LUKE *(into comlink):* No, I'm not going to change my mind about this. *(getting a little nervous)* I'm not picking up any cities or technology. Massive life-form readings, though. There's something alive down there . . .

(Again, Artoo beeps, this time a slightly worried question.)

LUKE *(into comlink):* Yes, I'm sure it's perfectly safe for droids.

EXTERIOR: SPACE — DAGOBAH — LUKE'S X-WING

(*The X-wing continues its flight through the twilight above the cloud-covered planet.*)

INTERIOR: LUKE'S X-WING — COCKPIT

(*Luke sees the clouds race by as he takes his craft closer to the planet. He must operate his controls carefully since the cloud cover has completely obscured his vision. An alarm buzzes in the background. Artoo beeps and whistles frantically.*)

LUKE (*into comlink*): I know, I know! All the scopes are dead. I can't see a thing! Just hang on, I'm going to start the landing cycle . . .

(*The blast of the retrorockets is deafening, drowning out Artoo's electronic squeals. Suddenly, there is a cracking sound as if limbs were being broken off trees and then a tremendous jolt as the spacecraft stops. Luke pulls a switch and his canopy pops open.*)

EXTERIOR: DAGOBAH — DUSK

(*The mist-shrouded X-wing fighter is almost invisible in the thick fog. Luke climbs out onto the long nose of the spacecraft as Artoo pops out of his cubbyhole on the back. The young warrior surveys the fog, which is barely pierced by the ship's landing lights. About all he can make out are some giant, twisted trees nearby. Artoo whistles anxiously.*)

LUKE: No, Artoo, you stay put. I'll have a look around.

(*Artoo lets out a short beep. As Luke moves along the nose, Artoo loses his balance and disappears with a splash into the boggy lake.*)

LUKE: Artoo?

(*Luke kneels and leans over the plane looking for Artoo, but the water is still and reveals no sign of the little droid.*)

LUKE: Artoo! Where are you?

(*A small periscope breaks the surface of the water and a gurgly beep is heard. The periscope starts to move to shore. Relieved, Luke starts running along the nose of the fighter to its tip.*)

LUKE: Artoo! You be more careful.

(*The outline of the shore is now no more than ten feet away. Luke jumps off the plane into the water, scrambles up to the shore, and turns to look for Artoo. The periscope still steadily moves toward shore.*)

LUKE: Artoo — that way!

(*Suddenly, through the thick fog layer, a dark shape appears, moving toward the little droid. The dark, sinuous bog beast dives beneath the swampy water, making a loud clunk against Artoo's metal hull. The droid disappears from sight, uttering a pathetic electronic scream.*

Holding his ignited lightsaber before him, Luke wades a few feet into the murky pool, looking for any sign of his little friend.)

LUKE: Artoo!

(*The black surface is still as death itself . . . until a few bubbles begin to appear. Then,* phheewaat!! *The runt-size robot is spit out of the water, makes a graceful arc, and comes crashing down into a patch of soft gray moss.*)

LUKE: Oh, no! Are you all right? Come on. You're lucky you don't taste very good. Anything broken?

(*Luke helps Artoo to his feet and begins wiping the mud and roots from his round metal body. Artoo responds with feeble, soggy beeps.*)

LUKE: If you're saying coming here was a bad idea, I'm beginning to agree with you. Oh, Artoo, what are we doing here? It's like . . . something out of a dream, or, I don't know. Maybe I'm just going crazy.

(*As Luke glances around at the spooky swamp jungle that surrounds him, Artoo ejects a stream of muddy water from one of his cranial ports.*)

EXTERIOR: DAGOBAH — BOG CLEARING — DUSK

(The mist has dispersed a bit, but it is still a very gloomy-looking swamp.

Luke pulls an equipment box from the shore to the clearing. He ignites a little fusion furnace and warms his hands before it. Taking a power cable, he plugs it into Artoo's noselike socket.)

LUKE: Ready for some power? Okay. Let's see now. Put that in there. There you go.

(The droid whistles his appreciation. Luke then opens a container of processed food and sits before the thermal heater.)

LUKE *(sighs)*: Now all I have to do is find this Yoda . . . if he even exists.

(Nervously, he looks around at the foreboding jungle.)

LUKE: It's really a strange place to find a Jedi Master. It gives me the creeps.

(Artoo beeps in agreement with that sentiment.)

LUKE: Still . . . there's something familiar about this place. I feel like . . . I don't know . . .

STRANGE VOICE: Feel like what?

(Luke jumps out of his skin. Artoo screeches in terror. The young warrior grabs for his lightsaber as he spins around, looking for the speaker. Mysteriously standing right in front of Luke is a strange, bluish creature, not more than two feet tall. The wizened little thing is dressed in rags. It motions toward Luke's sword.)

LUKE *(looking at the creature)*: Like we're being watched!

CREATURE: Away put your weapon! I mean you no harm.

(After some hesitation, Luke puts away his weapon, although he really doesn't understand why. Artoo watches with interest.)

CREATURE: I am wondering, why are you here?

LUKE: I'm looking for someone.

CREATURE: Looking? Found someone, you have, I would say, hmmm?

(The little creature laughs.)

LUKE *(trying to keep from smiling)*: Right.

CREATURE: Help you I can. Yes, mmmm.

LUKE: I don't think so. I'm looking for a great warrior.

CREATURE: Ahhh! A great warrior. *(laughs and shakes his head)* Wars not make one great.

> *(With the aid of a walking stick, the tiny stranger moves over to one of the cases of supplies. He begins to rummage around.*
>
> *Artoo moves to the edge of the case — standing almost eye level to the creature who is carelessly handling the supplies — and squeaks his disapproval.*
>
> *Their tiny visitor picks up the container of food Luke was eating from and takes a bite.)*

LUKE: Put that down. Hey! That's my dinner!

> *(The creature spits out the bite he has taken. He makes a face.)*

CREATURE: How you get so big, eating food of this kind?

> *(He flips the container in Luke's direction and reaches into one of Luke's supply cases.)*

LUKE: Listen, friend, we didn't mean to land in that puddle, and if we could get our ship out, we would, but we can't, so why don't you just . . .

CREATURE *(teasing)*: Aww, cannot get your ship out?

> *(The creature starts rummaging through Luke's case, throwing the contents out behind him.)*

LUKE: Hey, get out of there!

CREATURE: Ahhh! No!

> *(The creature spots something of interest in Luke's case. Luke loses patience and grabs the case away. The creature retains his prize — a tiny power lamp — and examines it with delight.)*

LUKE: Hey, you could have broken this. Don't do that. Ohhh . . . you're making a mess. Hey, give me that!

CREATURE *(retreating with the lamp)*: Mine! Or I will help you not.

> *(Clutching its treasure, the creature backs away from Luke, drawing closer to Artoo. As Luke and the creature argue, one of Artoo's little arms slowly moves out toward the power lamp, completely unnoticed by the creature.)*

LUKE: I don't want your help. I want my lamp back. I'll need it to get out of this slimy mudhole.

CREATURE: Mudhole? Slimy? My home this is.

(Artoo grabs hold of the lamp and the two little figures are immediately engaged in a tug-of-war over it.

Artoo beeps a few angry, "Give me thats.")

CREATURE: Ah, ah, ah!

LUKE: Oh, Artoo, let him have it!

CREATURE: Mine! Mine!

LUKE: Artoo!

CREATURE: Mine!

(The creature lets go with one hand and pokes Artoo lightly with one finger. Artoo reacts with a startled squeal, and lets go.)

CREATURE: Mine!

LUKE *(fed up):* Now will you move along, little fella? We've got a lot of work to do.

CREATURE: No! No, no! Stay and help you, I will. *(laughs)* Find your friend, hmm?

LUKE: I'm not looking for a friend, I'm looking for a Jedi Master.

CREATURE: Oohhh. Jedi Master. Yoda. You seek Yoda.

LUKE: You know him?

CREATURE: Mmm. Take you to him, I will. *(laughs)* Yes, yes. But now, we must eat. Come. Good food. Come.

(With that, the creature scurries out of the clearing, laughing merrily. Luke stares after him. All he sees is the faint light from the small power lamp moving through the fog. Luke makes his decision and starts after the creature.)

CREATURE *(in the distance):* Come, come.

(Artoo, very upset, whistles a blue streak of protests.)

LUKE: Stay here and watch after the camp, Artoo.

(Artoo beeps even more frantically. But as Luke disappears from view, the worried little droid grows quieter, and utters a soft electronic sigh.)

EXTERIOR: DAGOBAH — CREATURE'S HOUSE — NIGHT

(A heavy downpour of rain pounds through the gnarled trees. A strange baroque mud house sits on a moss-covered knoll on the edge of a small lagoon. The small, gnomish structure radiates a warm glow from its thick glass windows. As the rain tap-dances a merry tune on Artoo's head, the stubby little droid rises up on his tip-toes to peek into one of the glowing portals.)

INTERIOR: CREATURE'S HOUSE

(Artoo, peeking in the window, sees the inside of the house — a very plain, but cozy dwelling. Everything is in the same scale as the creature. The only thing out of place in the miniature room is Luke, whose height makes the four-foot ceiling seem even lower. He sits cross-legged on the floor of the living room.

The creature is in an adjoining area — his little kitchen — cooking up an incredible meal. The stove is a steaming hodgepodge of pots and pans. The wizened little host scurries about chopping this, shredding that, and showering everything with exotic herbs and spices. He rushes back and forth putting platters on the table in front of Luke, who watches the creature impatiently.)

LUKE: Look, I'm sure it's delicious. I just don't understand why we can't see Yoda now.

CREATURE: Patience! For the Jedi it is time to eat as well. Eat, eat. Hot. Good food, hm? Good, hmm?

(Moving with some difficulty in the cramped quarters, Luke sits down near the fire and serves himself from the pot. Tasting the unfamiliar concoction, he is pleasantly surprised.)

LUKE: How far away is Yoda? Will it take us long to get there?

CREATURE: Not far. Yoda not far. Patience. Soon you will be with him. (tasting food from the pot) Rootleaf, I cook. Why wish you become Jedi? Hm?

LUKE: Mostly because of my father, I guess.

CREATURE: Ah, your father. Powerful Jedi was he, powerful Jedi, mmm.

LUKE (*a little angry*): Oh, come on. How could you know my father? You don't even know who I am. (*fed up*) Oh, I don't know what I'm doing here. We're wasting our time.

> (*The creature turns away from Luke and speaks to a third party.*)

CREATURE (*irritated*): I cannot teach him. The boy has no patience.

> (*Luke's head spins in the direction the creature faces. But there is no one there. The boy is bewildered, but it gradually dawns on him that the little creature is Yoda, the Jedi Master, and that he is speaking with Ben.*)

BEN'S VOICE: He will learn patience.

YODA: Hmmm. Much anger in him, like his father.

BEN'S VOICE: Was I any different when you taught me?

YODA: Hah. He is not ready.

LUKE: Yoda! I am ready. I . . . Ben! I can be a Jedi. Ben, tell him I'm ready.

> (*Trying to see Ben, Luke starts to get up but hits his head on the low ceiling.*)

YODA: Ready, are you? What know you of ready? For eight hundred years have I trained Jedi. My own counsel will I keep on who is to be trained! A Jedi must have the deepest commitment, the most serious mind. (*to the invisible Ben, indicating Luke*) This one a long time have I watched. All his life has he looked away . . . to the future, to the horizon. Never his mind on where he was. Hmm? What he was doing. Hmph. Adventure. Heh! Excitement. Heh! A Jedi craves not these things. (*turning to Luke*) You are reckless!

> (*Luke looks down. He knows it is true.*)

BEN'S VOICE: So was I, if you'll remember.

YODA: He is too old. Yes, too old to begin the training.

> (*Luke thinks he detects a subtle softening in Yoda's voice.*)

LUKE: But I've learned so much.

> (*Yoda turns his piercing gaze on Luke, as though the Jedi Master's huge eyes could somehow determine how much the boy has learned. After a long moment, the little Jedi turns toward where he alone sees Ben.*)

YODA *(sighs):* Will he finish what he begins?

LUKE: I won't fail you — I'm not afraid.

YODA *(turns slowly toward him):* Oh, you will be. You will be.

EXTERIOR: DAGOBAH — DAY

(With Yoda strapped to his back, Luke climbs up one of the many thick vines that grow in the swamp. Panting heavily, he continues his course — climbing, flipping through the air, jumping over roots, and racing in and out of the heavy ground fog.)

YODA: Run! Yes. A Jedi's strength flows from the Force. But beware of the dark side. Anger . . . fear . . . aggression. The dark side of the Force are they.

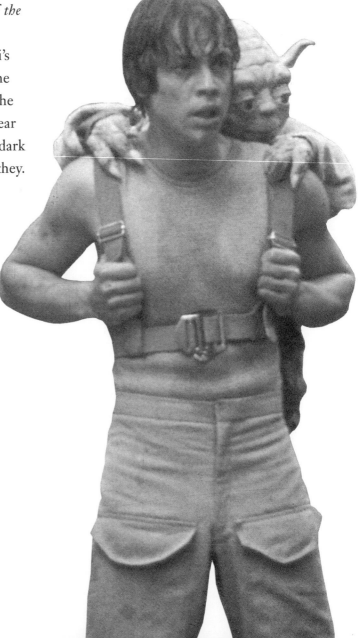

Easily they flow, quick to join you in a fight. If once you start down the dark path, forever will it dominate your destiny, consume you it will, as it did Obi-Wan's apprentice.

LUKE: Vader. Is the dark side stronger?

YODA: No . . . no . . . no. Quicker, easier, more seductive.

LUKE: But how am I to know the good side from the bad?

YODA: You will know. When you are calm, at peace. Passive. A Jedi uses the Force for knowledge and defense, never for attack.

LUKE: But tell me why I can't . . .

YODA *(interrupting)*: No, no, there is no why. Nothing more will I teach you today. Clear your mind of questions. Mmm. Mmmmmm.

(Artoo beeps in the distance as Luke lets Yoda down to the ground. Breathing heavily, he takes his shirt from a nearby tree branch and pulls it on.

He turns to see a huge, dead, black tree, its base surrounded by a few feet of water. Giant, twisted roots form a dark and sinister cave on one side. Luke stares at the tree, trembling.)

LUKE: There's something not right here.

(Yoda sits on a large root, poking his Gimer Stick into the dirt.)

LUKE: I feel cold, death.

YODA: That place . . . is strong with the dark side of the Force. A domain of evil it is. In you must go.

LUKE: What's in there?

YODA: Only what you take with you.

(Luke looks warily between the tree and Yoda. He starts to strap on his weapon belt.)

YODA: Your weapons . . . you will not need them.

(Luke gives the tree a long look, then shakes his head "no." Yoda shrugs. Luke reaches up to brush aside some hanging vines and enters the tree.)

INTERIOR: DAGOBAH — TREE CAVE

(Luke moves into the almost total darkness of the wet and slimy cave. The youth can barely make out the edge of the passage. Holding his lit

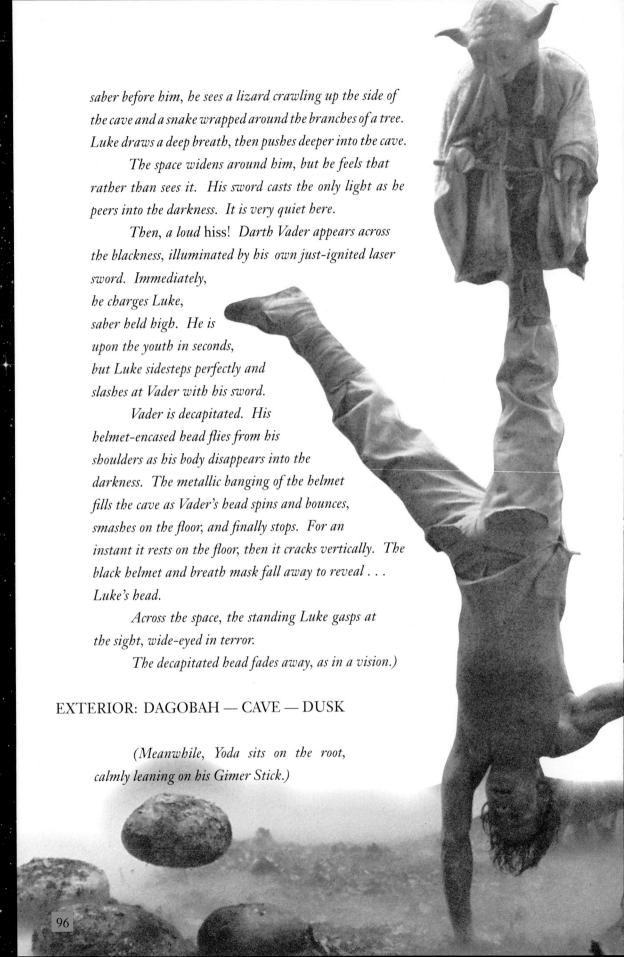

saber before him, he sees a lizard crawling up the side of the cave and a snake wrapped around the branches of a tree. Luke draws a deep breath, then pushes deeper into the cave.

The space widens around him, but he feels that rather than sees it. His sword casts the only light as he peers into the darkness. It is very quiet here.

Then, a loud hiss! Darth Vader appears across the blackness, illuminated by his own just-ignited laser sword. Immediately, he charges Luke, saber held high. He is upon the youth in seconds, but Luke sidesteps perfectly and slashes at Vader with his sword.

Vader is decapitated. His helmet-encased head flies from his shoulders as his body disappears into the darkness. The metallic banging of the helmet fills the cave as Vader's head spins and bounces, smashes on the floor, and finally stops. For an instant it rests on the floor, then it cracks vertically. The black helmet and breath mask fall away to reveal . . . Luke's head.

Across the space, the standing Luke gasps at the sight, wide-eyed in terror.

The decapitated head fades away, as in a vision.)

EXTERIOR: DAGOBAH — CAVE — DUSK

(Meanwhile, Yoda sits on the root, calmly leaning on his Gimer Stick.)

EXTERIOR: DAGOBAH — BOG — DAY

(Luke's face is upside-down and showing enormous strain. He stands on his hands, with Yoda perched on his feet. Opposite Luke and Yoda are two rocks the size of bowling balls. Luke stares at the rocks and concentrates. One of the rocks lifts from the ground and floats up to rest on the other.)

YODA: Use the Force. Yes . . .

(Yoda taps Luke's leg. Quickly, Luke lifts one hand from the ground. His body wavers, but he maintains his balance. Artoo, standing nearby, is whistling and beeping frantically.)

YODA: Now . . . the stone. Feel it.

(Luke concentrates on trying to lift the top rock. It rises a few feet, shaking under the strain. But, distracted by Artoo's frantic beeping, Luke loses his balance and finally collapses. Yoda jumps clear.)

YODA: Concentrate!

(Annoyed at the disturbance, Luke looks over at Artoo, who is rocking urgently back and forth in front of him.

Artoo waddles closer to Luke, chirping wildly, then scoots over to the edge of the swamp. Catching on, Luke rushes to the water's edge. The X-wing fighter has sunk, and only the tip of its nose shows above the lake's surface.)

LUKE: Oh, no. We'll never get it out now.

(Yoda stamps his foot in irritation.)

YODA: So certain are you. Always with you it cannot be done. Hear you nothing that I say?

(Luke looks uncertainly out at the ship.)

LUKE: Master, moving stones around is one thing. This is totally different.

YODA: No! No different! Only different in your mind. You must unlearn what you have learned.

LUKE *(focusing, quietly)*: All right, I'll give it a try.

YODA: No! Try not. *Do.* Or do not. There is no try.

(Luke closes his eyes and concentrates on thinking the ship out.

Slowly, the X-wing's nose begins to rise above the water. It hovers for a moment and then slides back, disappearing once again.)

LUKE *(panting heavily):* I can't. It's too big.

YODA: Size matters not. Look at me. Judge me by my size, do you? Hm? Mmmm.

(Luke shakes his head.)

YODA: And well you should not. For my ally is the Force. And a powerful ally it is. Life creates it, makes it grow. Its energy surrounds us and binds us. Luminous[1] beings are we . . . *(Yoda pinches Luke's shoulder)* . . . not this crude matter. *(a sweeping gesture)* You must feel the Force around you. *(gesturing)* Here, between you . . . me . . . the tree . . . the rock . . . everywhere! Yes, even between this land and that ship!

LUKE *(discouraged):* You want the impossible.

(Quietly, Yoda turns toward the sunken X-wing fighter. With his eyes closed and his head bowed, he raises his arm and points at the ship.

Soon, the fighter rises above the water and moves forward as Artoo beeps in terror and scoots away.

The entire X-wing moves majestically, surely, toward the shore. Yoda stands on a tree root and guides the fighter carefully down toward the beach.

Luke stares in astonishment as the fighter settles gently onto the shore. He walks toward Yoda.)

LUKE: I don't . . . I don't believe it.

YODA: That is why you fail.

(Luke shakes his head, bewildered.)

---

[1]**luminous** (lōō′mə nəs): enlightened; intelligent.

EXTERIOR: DAGOBAH — BOG — DUSK

> *(In the bright lights of the fighter, Luke loads a heavy case into the belly of the ship. Artoo sits on top of the X-wing, settling down into his cubbyhole. Yoda stands nearby on a log.)*

YODA: Luke! You must complete the training.

LUKE: I can't keep the vision out of my head. They're my friends. I've got to help them.

YODA: You must not go!

LUKE: But Han and Leia will die if I don't.

BEN'S VOICE: You don't know that.

> *(Luke looks toward the voice in amazement. Ben has materialized as a real, slightly shimmering image near Yoda. The power of his presence stops Luke.)*

BEN: Even Yoda cannot see their fate.

LUKE: But I can help them! I feel the Force!

BEN: But you cannot control it. This is a dangerous time for you, when you will be tempted by the dark side of the Force.

YODA: Yes, yes. To Obi-Wan you listen. The cave. Remember your failure at the cave!

LUKE: But I've learned so much since then. Master Yoda, I promise to return and finish what I've begun. You have my word.

BEN: It is you and your abilities the Emperor wants. That is why your friends are made to suffer.

LUKE: And that is why I have to go.

BEN: Luke, I don't want to lose you to the Emperor the way I lost Vader.

LUKE: You won't.

YODA: Stopped they must be. On this all depends. Only a fully trained Jedi Knight with the Force as his ally will conquer Vader and his Emperor. If you end your training now, if you choose the quick and easy path, as Vader did, you will become an agent of evil.

BEN: Patience.

LUKE: And sacrifice Han and Leia?

YODA: If you honor what they fight for . . . yes!

> *(Luke is in great anguish. He struggles with the dilemma, a battle raging in his mind.)*

BEN: If you choose to face Vader, you will do it alone. I cannot interfere.

LUKE: I understand. *(he moves to his X-wing)* Artoo, fire up the converters.

> *(Artoo whistles a happy reply.)*

BEN: Luke, don't give in to hate — that leads to the dark side.

> *(Luke nods and climbs into his ship.)*

YODA: Strong is Vader. Mind what you have learned. Save you it can.

LUKE: I will. And I'll return. I promise.

> *(Artoo closes the cockpit. Ben and Yoda stand watching as the roar of the engines and the wind engulfs them.)*

YODA *(sighs):* Told you, I did. Reckless is he. Now matters are worse.

BEN: That boy is our last hope.

YODA *(looks up):* No. There is another.

Responding to *The Empire Strikes Back*

Thinking and Discussing

In Luke's place, would you have found it easy to accept Yoda as your trainer? Why or why not?

How do the Jedi Knights use the Force differently from Darth Vader? What traditional theme of mythology does this suggest?

Choosing a Creative Response

Training Jedi Knights Taking the part of Yoda, publish a short training manual for Jedi Knights. List at least five key rules with brief explanations.

Notice you Yoda's speech? Strange it is! Imitate Yoda's speech in writing the training manual.

Sketching a Hero Create a hero of your own imagination. Write a character sketch, and draw a pencil sketch of your hero. Try to convey the character's appearance, actions, and beliefs through your sketches. Show the qualities that make the character a true hero.

Creating Your Own Activity Plan and complete your own activity in response to *The Empire Strikes Back*.

Thinking and Writing

Imagine a scene in which Yoda and Darth Vader meet face to face. What would Yoda say to Darth Vader about the use of the Force for evil purposes? How would Darth Vader reply? How might they choose to show their powers?

Write a brief script of the dialogue when these powerful characters meet. Be sure to include stage directions that describe the action. You may wish to perform the scene for your classmates.

Thinking About Myths

Creating a Board Game Design a board game based on one of the stories in *Heroes for All Times*. Modify an existing board game, or create one of your own. Your game might represent a great heroic journey you have read about. Be sure to build in things that happen by chance, such as rewards or penalties on certain squares. Include the main events of the story action. Test the game by playing it with a friend.

Illustrating a Favorite Tale Look back at the paintings in *The Story of Prince Rama*. Notice how richly they illustrate the details of the action of the story. Remember that the paintings, created for kings, are detailed enough to explain the story to those who cannot read the manuscript.

Choose a scene from a favorite tale, and create a picture that shows the action as clearly as possible. Use pencils, pens, paints, pastels, crayons, or whatever you like.

Retelling a Story in Modern Times Choose a traditional tale to retell in the present — or even the future. Which aspects of the story are different? Which are the same? Change the story to reflect its new time and place. Retell the story aloud for your classmates, or write and illustrate the story as a book.

Having a Round-Table Discussion Myths express different messages about the struggle between good and evil. In a round-table discussion with your classmates, identify the good and evil forces in each story, and decide whether or not one force wins out over the other.

Then think about what Pandora says about how hope will outlive all the evils of the world. Would the other characters in these selections agree with her? Why or why not?

About the Authors

Leigh Brackett was a professional writer of science fiction, mystery novels, and screenplays for several well-known movies. In 1978 producer George Lucas asked Brackett to develop a screenplay based on his story for *The Empire Strikes Back*. Brackett completed a first draft in a few months but died a short time later.

George Bird Grinnell wrote many adventure stories based on his friendship with the American Indians, his many expeditions, and his knowledge of natural history. He also collected and transcribed many legends and folktales, among them *Blackfoot Lodge Tales: The Story of a Prairie People*. Later, Grinnell founded the Audubon Society, an organization that today continues to protect wildlife across the United States.

Lawrence Kasdan started out as an advertising copywriter, but in 1978, producer George Lucas chose him to complete the unfinished script for *The Empire Strikes Back*. *Empire* became Kasdan's first work to be produced. His next screenplay, *Raiders of the Lost Ark*, was also a huge success. In 1983, Kasdan wrote and directed *The Big Chill*, yet another box-office hit.

George Lucas was a student at the University of Southern California when he won first prize at the National Student Film Festival in 1967 with his film *THX 1138:4EB*. His next film, *American Graffiti*, became the smash hit of 1973. Lucas then convinced some Hollywood studios to support "a little space movie." This became *Star Wars*, a film that changed movie making forever.

Ethel Johnston Phelps completed a master's degree in medieval literature and went to work for a feminist publishing house. Her second book, *The Maid of the North: Feminist Folk Tales from Around the World*, which portrays women as strong, courageous, and clever, was named a Notable Social Studies book by the Children's Book Council in 1981.

Robert R. Potter wrote "Kintu and the Law of Love." Every effort has been made to locate biographical information about the author. Information made available to the publisher will appear in the next edition.

H. Alan Robinson was elected president of the Reading Hall of Fame in 1989. In addition to his work on *Myths and Folktales Around the World*, he has published many books in the fields of reading instruction and language arts. Robinson's most recent work is published by the International Reading Association.

Brian Thompson worked as an education teacher, novelist, and playwright before turning exclusively to writing in 1972. Perhaps it was Thompson's interest in history that led to his fascination with the ancient story of Prince Rama as it was originally presented to him by a young boy, Jitander Dudee, a pupil at a school where Thompson taught. Thompson used Dudee's version of this three-thousand-year-old tale as the basis for his own retelling of *The Story of Prince Rama*.

Louis Untermeyer wrote poetry on the side as a young man but worked in his father's jewelry manufacturing business as a traveling salesman to earn a living. In order to write full-time, he left his job and went to Europe to study. Untermeyer then became a prolific poet, critic, compiler, and editor. He acted as poetry consultant for the Library of Congress and was also chairman of the Pulitzer Prize Poetry Committee. Untermeyer died in Connecticut in 1977.

More Tales from Around the World

The Trojan War by Olivia Coolidge (Houghton, 1952)

Based on Greek sources and using stories from the *Iliad*, the *Odyssey*, and mythology, this is an appealing retelling of the adventures of the heroes of the Trojan War.

The White Archer by James Houston
(Harcourt, 1967)

Kungo is an Inuit boy who wishes to avenge the murder of family members. He seeks the help of Ittok, a wise master of archery. The old master and his wife, however, teach Kungo more than the skill of archery.

The Golden Fleece and the Heroes Who Lived Before Achilles
by Padraic Colum (Macmillan, 1983)

The author preserves the spirit of the Greek myths and adds many other myths and hero stories to the adventures of Jason and his search for the Golden Fleece.

The Story of King Arthur and His Knights
written and illustrated by Howard Pyle (Scribner, 1984)

This is the first of the classic four-volume series that retells the Arthurian legends from Arthur's winning of the sword Excalibur to his heroic adventures as king of Britain.

The Story of Siegfried by James Baldwin
(R. West reprint of 1882 Scribner Classic)

The young prince Siegfried forges his own sword, Balmung, and goes forth to defend the cause of good over evil, slaying the terrible dragon, Fafnir.

AN INUIT-ESKIMO LEGEND

THE WHITE ARCHER

WRITTEN AND ILLUSTRATED BY

JAMES HOUSTON

THE TROJAN WAR

OLIVIA
COOLIDGE

The Story of

KING ARTHUR

and his

KNIGHTS

Written and
Illustrated by

HOWARD PYLE

REALISM

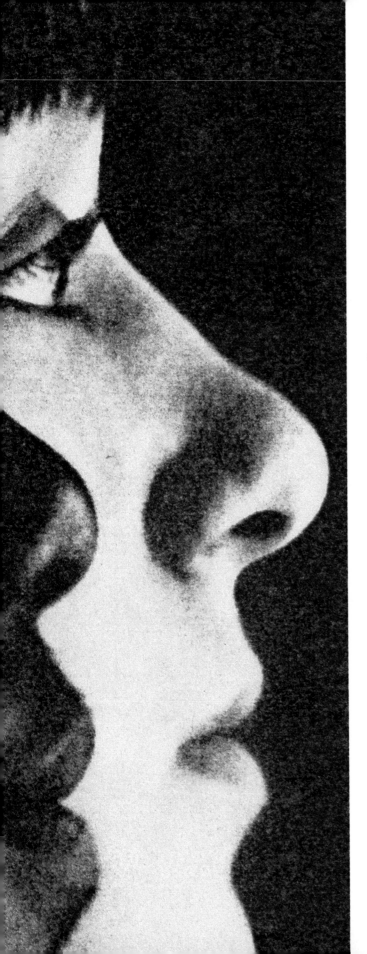

BOOK 2

INSIGHTS

"I'm trying to look at my life through the lens of Everyman. So my story involves greed, humor, courage, generosity, sentimentality and sentiment, loyalty and disloyalty, everything. I think that everyone really lives at that level, although we do not understand it all when it is happening."

— Maya Angelou

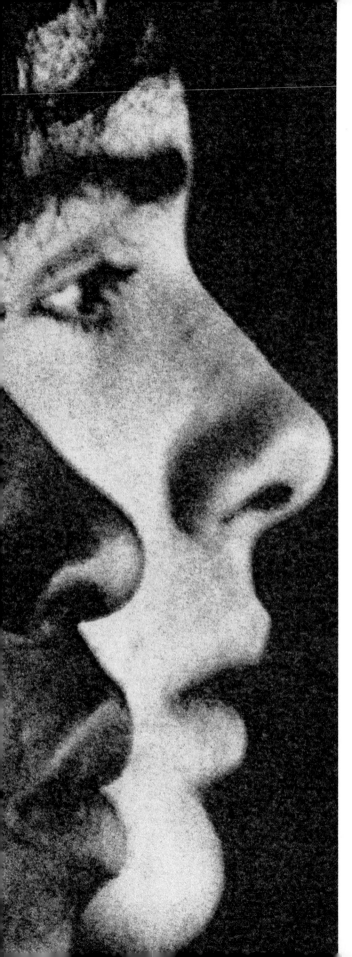

Contents

Photo collages by Robert Appleton
Portrait photography by Frank Marchese
Still life photography by Scott Van Sicklin

Award Winner

I KNOW WHY THE CAGED BIRD SINGS

by Maya Angelou

Maya Angelou remembers growing up in Stamps, Arkansas.

Mrs. Bertha Flowers was the aristocrat of Black Stamps. She had the grace of control to appear warm in the coldest weather, and on the Arkansas summer days it seemed she had a private breeze which swirled around, cooling her. She was thin without the taut look of wiry people, and her printed voile dresses and flowered hats were as right for her as denim overalls for a farmer. She was our side's answer to the richest white woman in town.

Her skin was a rich black that would have peeled like a plum if snagged, but then no one would have thought of getting close enough to Mrs. Flowers to ruffle her dress, let alone snag her skin. She didn't encourage familiarity. She wore gloves too.

I don't think I ever saw Mrs. Flowers laugh, but she smiled often. A slow widening of her thin black lips to show even, small white teeth, then the slow effortless closing. When she chose to smile on me, I always wanted to thank her. The action was so graceful and inclusively benign.

She was one of the few gentlewomen I have ever known, and has remained throughout my life the measure of what a human being can be.

Momma had a strange relationship with her. Most often when she passed on the road in front of the Store, she spoke to Momma in that soft yet carrying voice, "Good day, Mrs. Henderson." Momma responded with "How you, Sister Flowers?"

Mrs. Flowers didn't belong to our church, nor was she Momma's familiar. Why on earth did she insist on calling her Sister Flowers? Shame made me want to hide my face. Mrs. Flowers deserved better than to be called Sister. Then, Momma left out the verb. Why not ask, "How *are* you, *Mrs.* Flowers?" With the unbalanced passion of the young, I hated her for showing her ignorance to Mrs. Flowers. It didn't occur to me for many years that they were as alike as sisters, separated only by formal education.

Although I was upset, neither of the women was in the least shaken by what I thought an unceremonious greeting. Mrs. Flowers would continue her easy gait up the hill to her little bungalow, and Momma kept on shelling peas or doing whatever had brought her to the front porch.

Occasionally, though, Mrs. Flowers would drift off the road and down to the Store and Momma would say to me, "Sister, you go on and play." As I left I would hear the beginning of an intimate conversation. Momma persistently using the wrong verb, or none at all.

"Brother and Sister Wilcox is sho'ly the meanest —" "Is," Momma? "Is"? Oh, please, not "is," Momma, for two or more. But they talked, and from the side of the building where I waited for the ground to open up and swallow me, I heard the soft-voiced Mrs. Flowers and the textured voice of my grandmother merging and melting. They were interrupted from time to time by giggles that must have come from Mrs. Flowers (Momma never giggled in her life). Then she was gone.

She appealed to me because she was like people I had never met personally. Like women in English novels who walked the moors (whatever they were) with their loyal dogs racing at a respectful distance. Like the women who sat in front of roaring fireplaces, drinking tea incessantly from silver trays full of scones and crumpets. Women who walked over the "heath" and read morocco-bound books and had two last names divided by a hyphen. It would be safe to say that she made me proud to be Negro, just by being herself.

She acted just as refined as whitefolks in the movies and books and she was more beautiful, for none of them could have come near that warm color without looking gray by comparison.

It was fortunate that I never saw her in the company of powhitefolks. For since they tend to think of their whiteness as an evenizer, I'm certain that I would have had to hear her spoken to commonly as Bertha, and my image of her would have been shattered like the unmendable Humpty-Dumpty.

One summer afternoon, sweet-milk fresh in my memory, she stopped at the Store to buy provisions. Another Negro woman of her health and age would have been expected to carry the paper sacks home in one hand, but Momma said, "Sister Flowers, I'll send Bailey up to your house with these things."

She smiled that slow dragging smile, "Thank you, Mrs. Henderson. I'd prefer Marguerite, though." My name was beautiful when she said it. "I've been meaning to talk to her, anyway." They gave each other age-group looks.

Momma said, "Well, that's all right then. Sister, go and change your dress. You going to Sister Flowers's."

The chifforobe[1] was a maze. What on earth did one put on to go to Mrs. Flowers' house? I knew I shouldn't put on a Sunday dress. It might be sacrilegious. Certainly not a house dress, since I was already wearing a fresh one. I chose a school dress, naturally. It was formal without suggesting that going to Mrs. Flowers' house was equivalent to attending church.

I trusted myself back into the Store.

"Now, don't you look nice." I had chosen the right thing, for once.

"Mrs. Henderson, you make most of the children's clothes, don't you?"

"Yes, ma'am. Sure do. Store-bought clothes ain't hardly worth the thread it take to stitch them."

"I'll say you do a lovely job, though, so neat. That dress looks professional."

Momma was enjoying the seldom-received compliments. Since everyone we knew (except Mrs. Flowers, of course) could sew competently, praise was rarely handed out for the commonly practiced craft.

"I try, with the help of the Lord, Sister Flowers, to finish the inside just like I does the outside. Come here, Sister."

I had buttoned up the collar and tied the belt, apron-like, in back. Momma told me to turn around. With one hand she pulled the strings and

---

[1] **chifforobe** (shĭf′ə rōb′): a piece of furniture with drawers and an area for hanging clothes.

the belt fell free at both sides of my waist. Then her large hands were at my neck, opening the button loops. I was terrified. What was happening?

"Take it off, Sister." She had her hands on the hem of the dress.

"I don't need to see the inside, Mrs. Henderson, I can tell . . ." But the dress was over my head and my arms were stuck in the sleeves. Momma said, "That'll do. See here, Sister Flowers, I French-seams around the armholes." Through the cloth film, I saw the shadow approach. "That makes it last longer. Children these days would bust out of sheet-metal clothes. They so rough."

"That is a very good job, Mrs. Henderson. You should be proud. You can put your dress back on, Marguerite."

"No ma'am. Pride is a sin. And 'cording to the Good Book, it goeth before a fall."

"That's right. So the Bible says. It's a good thing to keep in mind."

I wouldn't look at either of them. Momma hadn't thought that taking off my dress in front of Mrs. Flowers would kill me stone dead. . . . Mrs. Flowers had known that I would be embarrassed and that was even worse. I picked up the groceries and went out to wait in the hot sunshine. It would be fitting if I got a sunstroke and died before they came outside. Just dropped dead on the slanting porch.

There was a little path beside the rocky road, and Mrs. Flowers walked in front swinging her arms and picking her way over the stones.

She said, without turning her head, to me, "I hear you're doing very good school work, Marguerite, but that it's all written. The teachers report that they have trouble getting you to talk in class." We passed the triangular farm on our left and the path widened to allow us to walk together. I hung back in the separate unasked and unanswerable questions.

"Come and walk along with me, Marguerite." I couldn't have refused even if I wanted to. She pronounced my name so nicely. Or more correctly, she spoke each word with such clarity that I was certain a foreigner who didn't understand English could have understood her.

"Now no one is going to make you talk — possibly no one can. But bear in mind, language is man's way of communicating with his fellow man and it is language alone which separates him from the lower animals." That was a totally new idea to me, and I would need time to think about it.

"Your grandmother says you read a lot. Every chance you get. That's good, but not good enough. Words mean more than what is set down on paper. It takes the human voice to infuse them with the shades of deeper meaning."

I memorized the part about the human voice infusing words. It seemed so valid and poetic.

She said she was going to give me some books and that I not only must read them, I must read them aloud. She suggested that I try to make a sentence sound in as many different ways as possible.

"I'll accept no excuse if you return a book to me that has been badly handled." My imagination boggled at the punishment I would deserve if in fact I did abuse a book of Mrs. Flowers'. Death would be too kind and brief.

The odors in the house surprised me. Somehow I had never connected Mrs. Flowers with food or eating or any other common experience of common people. There must have been an outhouse, too, but my mind never recorded it.

The sweet scent of vanilla had met us as she opened the door.

"I made tea cookies this morning. You see, I had planned to invite you for cookies and lemonade so we could have this little chat. The lemonade is in the icebox."

It followed that Mrs. Flowers would have ice on an ordinary day, when most families in our town bought ice late on Saturdays only a few times during the summer to be used in the wooden ice-cream freezers.

She took the bags from me and disappeared through the kitchen door. I looked around the room that I had never in my wildest fantasies imagined I would see. Browned photographs leered or threatened from the walls and the white, freshly done curtains pushed against themselves and against the wind. I wanted to gobble up the room entire and take it to Bailey, who would help me analyze and enjoy it.

"Have a seat, Marguerite. Over there by the table." She carried a platter covered with a tea towel. Although she warned that she hadn't tried her hand at baking sweets for some time, I was certain that like everything else about her the cookies would be perfect.

They were flat round wafers, slightly browned on the edges and butter-yellow in the center. With the cold lemonade they were sufficient for childhood's lifelong diet. Remembering my manners, I took nice little lady-like bites off the edges. She said she had made them expressly for me and that she had a few in the kitchen that I could take home to my brother. So I jammed one whole cake in my mouth and the rough crumbs scratched the insides of my jaws, and if I hadn't had to swallow, it would have been a dream come true.

As I ate she began the first of what we later called "my lessons in living." She said that I must always be intolerant of ignorance but understanding of illiteracy. That some people, unable to go to school, were more educated and even more intelligent than college professors. She encouraged me to listen carefully to what country people called mother wit. That in those homely sayings was couched the collective wisdom of generations.

When I finished the cookies she brushed off the table and brought a thick, small book from the bookcase. I had read *A Tale of Two Cities* and found it up to my standards as a romantic novel. She opened the first page and I heard poetry for the first time in my life.

"It was the best of times and the worst of times . . ." Her voice slid in and curved down through and over the words. She was nearly singing. I wanted to look at the pages. Were they the same that I had read? Or were there notes, music, lined on the pages, as in a hymn book? Her sounds began cascading gently. I knew from listening to a thousand preachers that she was nearing the end of her reading, and I hadn't really heard, heard to understand, a single word.

"How do you like that?"

It occurred to me that she expected a response. The sweet vanilla flavor was still on my tongue and her reading was a wonder in my ears. I had to speak.

I said, "Yes, ma'am." It was the least I could do, but it was the most also.

"There's one more thing. Take this book of poems and memorize one for me. Next time you pay me a visit, I want you to recite."

I have tried often to search behind the sophistication of years for the enchantment I so easily found in those gifts. The essence escapes but its aura remains. To be allowed, no, invited, into the private lives of strangers, and to share their joys and fears, was a chance to exchange the Southern bitter wormwood for a cup of mead with Beowulf or a hot cup of tea and milk with Oliver Twist. When I said aloud, "It is a far, far better thing that I do, than I have ever done . . ." tears of love filled my eyes at my selflessness.

On that first day, I ran down the hill and into the road (few cars ever came along it) and had the good sense to stop running before I reached the Store.

I was liked, and what a difference it made. I was respected not as Mrs. Henderson's grandchild or Bailey's sister but for just being Marguerite Johnson.

Childhood's logic never asks to be proved (all conclusions are absolute). I didn't question why Mrs. Flowers had singled me out for attention, nor did it occur to me that Momma might have asked her to give me a little talking to. All I cared about was that she had made tea cookies for *me* and read to *me* from her favorite book. It was enough to prove that she liked me.

Thinking and Discussing

How does the author indicate that this story is autobiographical? A memory from her childhood?

What character traits make Mrs. Flowers admirable to Marguerite? What "lessons in living" does Mrs. Flowers teach Marguerite?

Why was Marguerite's friendship with Mrs. Flowers important?

Choosing a Creative Response

Collecting Folk Wisdom Interview local people to collect examples of folk wisdom. Find out the origin and meaning of each saying, using library references if necessary. Use your examples to create a short handbook of folk sayings.

Interviewing an Older Person Arrange to meet with an older person to ask specific questions about the past. You may wish to ask what "lessons in living" that person would like to pass on to the younger generation.

Creating Your Own Activity Plan and complete your own activity in response to *I Know Why the Caged Bird Sings*.

Do you remember a time in your life when you gained insights that led to a positive outcome? As you read the autobiographies and short stories here, recall your own experiences that resulted in a deeper understanding of your life, another person's life, or human nature in general.

124

Write about this time of insights in an autobiographical incident. Describe the important details of your experiences. Tell about the ways in which your insights deepened your understanding. Include your thoughts and feelings about the events you describe. If these stories give you another writing idea, try that one instead.

1. *Prewriting* Before you begin writing, choose the time of insights that you would like to share with others. Dig back into your past. Try to remember what you thought and felt before that time. Recall the sequence in which events occurred. Think about strong emotions you felt, important decisions you had to make, and significant conversations you had with others. Jot down your memories.

2. *Write a First Draft* As you write your autobiographical incident, think about your audience and purpose for writing. Answer the following questions to help you organize your ideas.

- Who was involved in the experiences that led to my insights?
- Which details are most important?
- What did I feel then? What do I feel now?
- What did I eventually learn from the experience?
- What are the positive results of the experience?

3. *Revise* Read your autobiographical incident to a partner. Discuss with your partner ways to improve your autobiographical incident. Make any necessary changes.

4. *Proofread* Check your autobiographical incident for correct spelling, capitalization, and punctuation. Be especially careful about checking for errors if you included dialogue.

5. *Publish* Make a neat copy of your autobiographical incident. You may want to include drawings or photographs of meaningful places, important objects, or significant people in order to help your readers fully appreciate your experiences.

Award Winner

THE BIG SEA

by Langston Hughes

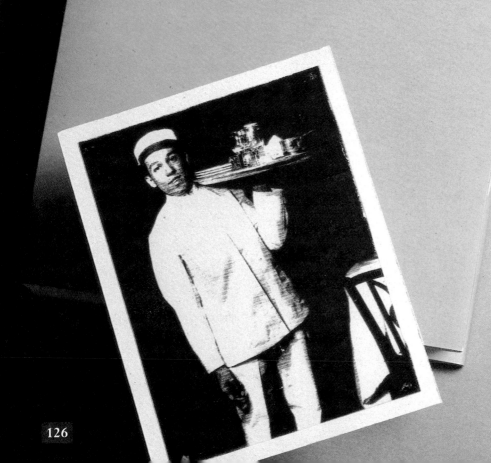

Working in the steam of the wet wash laundry that winter, I caught a bad cold, stayed home from work a week — and found my job gone when I went back. So I went to work for a colored newspaper. But I only made eighty cents in two weeks, so I quit the newspaper game. Then an old school friend of my mother's, Amanda Grey Hilyer, who once owned a drug store, spoke to Dr. Carter G. Woodson about me, and Dr. Woodson gave me a job in the offices of the Association for the Study of Negro Life and History as his personal assistant.

My new job paid several dollars more a week than the wet wash laundry. It was what they call in Washington "a position." But it was much harder work than the laundry.

I had to go to work early and start the furnace in the morning, dust, open the office, and see that the stenographers[1] came in on time. Then I had to sort the mail, notify Dr. Woodson of callers, wrap and post all book orders, keep the office routine going, read proof,[2] check address lists, help on the typing, fold and seal letters, run errands, lock up, clean the office in the evening — and then come back and bank the furnace every night at nine!

At that time Dr. Woodson was working on his compilation, *Thirty Thousand Free Negro Heads of Families*. My job was to put the thirty thousand in alphabetical order from *Ab, Abner* on down to *Zu, Zucker,* or whatever the last name might be — from the first letter of each name alphabetically through to the last letter of each name, in absolute order. They were typed on thirty thousand slips of paper. The job took weeks. Then checking the proofs took weeks more. It was like arranging a telephone book, and only myself to do it — along with my other work.

Although I realized what a fine contribution Dr. Woodson was making to the Negro people and to America, publishing his histories, his studies, and his *Journal of Negro History*, I personally did not like the work I had to do. Besides, it hurt my eyes. So when I got through the proofs,

---

[1]**stenographer** (stə **nŏg′rə** fər): a person skilled in shorthand, employed to take down and transcribe dictation.

[2]**read proof:** to check trial sheets of printed material for accuracy.

I decided I didn't care to have "a position" any longer, I preferred a job, so I went to work at the Wardman Park Hotel as a bus boy, where meals were thrown in and it was less hard on the sight, although the pay was not quite the same and there was no dignity attached to bus boy work in the eyes of upper class Washingtonians, who kept insisting that a colored poet should be a credit to his race.

But I am glad I went to work at the Wardman Park Hotel, because there I met Vachel Lindsay. Diplomats and cabinet members in the dining room did not excite me much, but I was thrilled the day Vachel Lindsay came. I knew him, because I'd seen his picture in the papers that morning. He was to give a reading of his poems in the little theater of the hotel that night. I wanted very much to hear him read his poems, but I knew they did not admit colored people to the auditorium.

That afternoon I wrote out three of my poems, "Jazzonia," "Negro Dancers," and "The Weary Blues," on some pieces of paper and put them in the pocket of my white bus boy's coat. In the evening when Mr. Lindsay came down to dinner, quickly I laid them beside his plate and went away, afraid to say anything to so famous a poet, except to tell him I liked his poems and that these were poems of mine. I looked back once and saw Mr. Lindsay reading the poems, as I picked up a tray of dirty dishes from a side table and started for the dumb-waiter.[3]

The next morning on the way to work, as usual I bought a paper — and there I read that Vachel Lindsay had discovered a Negro bus boy poet! At the hotel the reporters were already waiting for me. They interviewed me. And they took my picture, holding up a tray of dirty dishes in the middle of the dining room. The picture, copyrighted by Underwood and Underwood, appeared in lots of newspapers throughout the country. It was my first publicity break.

Mr. Lindsay had gone, but he left a package for me at the desk, a set of Amy Lowell's *John Keats*, with this note written on the fly leaves:

---

[3]**dumb-waiter:** a small elevator used to carry food, dishes, or other goods from one floor to another.

December 6, 1925
Wardman Park Hotel,
Washington, D.C.

My dear Langston Hughes:

The "New Poetry" movement has been going on in America since 1912. Two members of that army have died — Joyce Kilmer in the war, and Amy Lowell very recently. Already one hundred distinguished books of verse or criticism have been written, and hundreds of poems set going.

Eleven of the distinguished books are by Amy Lowell — and are listed in the front of this one. Please read the books and ignore the newspapers. I should say "Tendencies in Modern American Poetry" by Miss Lowell is a good book to start on. You may know all of this better than I do.

Miss Lowell has re-written the story of Keats from the standpoint of the "New Poetry." I hope you care to go into the whole movement for study from Edwin Arlington Robinson to Alfred Kreymborg's "Troubadour."

Do not let any lionizers[4] stampede you. Hide and write and study and think. I know what factions do. Beware of them. I know what flatterers do. Beware of them. I know what lionizers do. Beware of them.

Good wishes to you indeed,
(Signed) Nicholas Vachel Lindsay

Permanent address:
Room 1129
Davenport Hotel
Spokane, Washington

---

[4]**lionizer (lī′ə nīz′ər):** one who treats a person as a celebrity.

This note was written in ink in great, flowing, generous handwriting, spread over six pages — all the pages there were before the book proper began. A few days later Mr. Lindsay and his wife came back to the hotel, passing through Washington on the way to another engagement, and I had a short, encouraging talk with him. He was a great, kind man. And he is one of the people I remember with pleasure and gratitude out of my bewildered days in Washington.

The widespread publicity resulting from the Vachel Lindsay incident was certainly good for my poetic career, but it was not good for my job, because from then on, very often the head waiter would call me to come and stand before some table whose curious guests wished to see what a Negro bus boy poet looked like. I felt self-conscious and embarrassed, so when pay day came, I quit.

I went home, went to bed, and stayed in bed ten days. I was not sick, just tired of working. My mother said she was tired of working, too, and I could either get up from there and go back to work, or I would not eat! But I was really tired, so I stayed right on in bed and rested and read — and got hungry. My mother refused to feed me on the food she prepared for my little brother when she got home from work. And I didn't blame her, if she didn't want to feed me.

One day a young Howard student named Edward Lovette came by the house to show me something that he had written. I had never met him before, but I told him that I was hungry, so he invited me to come with him to a restaurant and have lunch. Every day for several days the same student came by and bought me a meal, although he didn't have much money. I will never forget him, because I needed those meals.

While in Washington I won my first poetry prize. *Opportunity* magazine, the official publication of the National Urban League, held its first literary contest. In succeeding years, two others were held with funds given by Casper Holstein, a wealthy West Indian numbers banker who did good things with his money, such as educating boys and girls at colleges in the South, building decent apartment houses in Harlem, and backing literary contests to encourage colored writers. Mr. Holstein, no

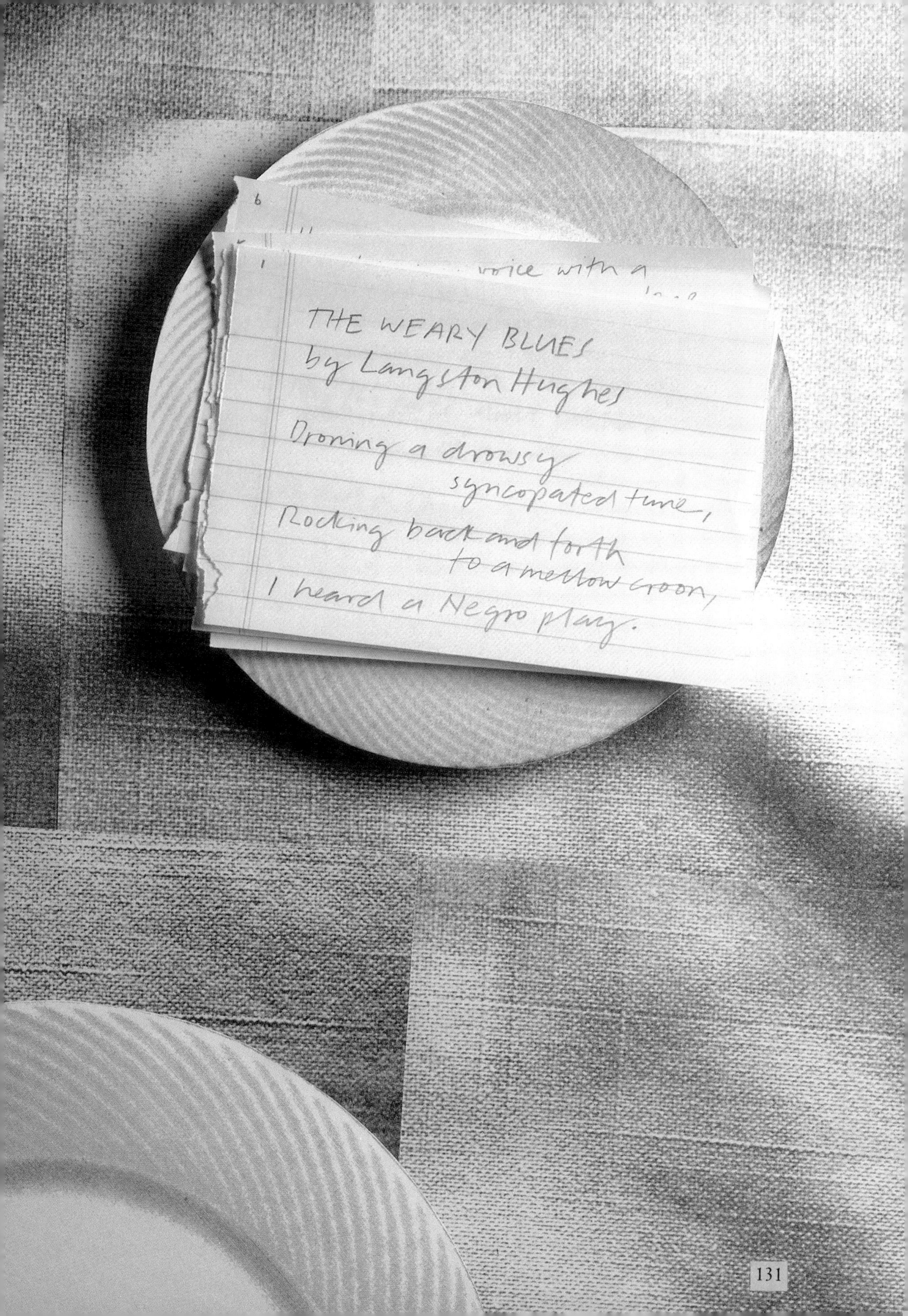

THE WEARY BLUES
by Langston Hughes

Droning a drowsy
              syncopated tune,
Rocking back and forth
              to a mellow croon,
I heard a Negro play.

doubt, would have been snubbed in polite Washington society, Negro or white, but there he was doing decent and helpful things that it hadn't occurred to lots of others to do. Certainly he was a great help to poor poets.

I sent several poems to the first contest. And then, as an afterthought, I sent "The Weary Blues," the poem I had written three winters before up the Hudson and whose ending I had never been able to get quite right. But I thought perhaps it was as right now as it would ever be. It was a poem about a working man who sang the blues all night and then went to bed and slept like a rock. That was all. And it included the first blues verse I'd ever heard way back in Lawrence, Kansas, when I was a kid.

> *I got de weary blues*
> *And I can't be satisfied.*
> *Got de weary blues*
> *And can't be satisfied.*
> *I ain't happy no mo'*
> *And I wish that I had died.*

That was my lucky poem — because it won the first prize.

Thinking and Discussing

How does Langston Hughes feel about Vachel Lindsay's appearance at the hotel? About approaching Mr. Lindsay?

How does Lindsay respond to Langston Hughes's poems? What advice does Lindsay give the young poet? How does the author explain the influence of Vachel Lindsay on his poetic career?

Choosing a Creative Response

Interviewing Someone You Admire Suppose you were to meet someone you admire very much. Imagine a short interview with that person. Make notes about what you might wish to say to the person, and what questions you might ask.

Writing an Inscription Imagine you were going to give someone a book as a gift. Think about what book might be most meaningful to that person. Then write the flyleaf inscription, explaining why you have chosen to give that book as a gift.

Creating Your Own Activity Plan and complete your own activity in response to *The Big Sea*.

The Weary Blues

by Langston Hughes

Droning a drowsy syncopated tune,
Rocking back and forth to a mellow croon,
        I heard a Negro play.

Down on Lenox Avenue the other night
By the pale dull pallor of an old gas light
        He did a lazy sway. . . .
        He did a lazy sway. . . .
To the tune o' those Weary Blues.

With his ebony hands on each ivory key
He made that poor piano moan with melody.

        O Blues!

Swaying to and fro on his rickety stool
He played that sad raggy tune like a musical fool.

        Sweet Blues!

Coming from a black man's soul.

        O Blues!

In a deep song voice with a melancholy tone
I heard that Negro sing, that old piano moan —

   "Ain't got nobody in all this world,
     Ain't got nobody but ma self.
     I's gwine to quit ma frownin'
     And put ma troubles on de shelf."

Thump, thump, thump, went his foot on the floor.
He played a few chords then he sang some more —

   "I got de Weary Blues
     And I can't be satisfied.
     Got de Weary Blues
     And can't be satisfied
     I ain't happy no mo'
     And I wish that I had died."

And far into the night he crooned that tune.

The stars went out and so did the moon.

The singer stopped playing and went to bed.

While the Weary Blues echoed through his head
He slept like a rock or a man that's dead.

PLATERO AND I

by Juan Ramón Jiménez

Platero

Platero is a small donkey, a soft, hairy donkey: so soft to the touch that he might be said to be made of cotton, with no bones. Only the jet mirrors of his eyes are hard like two black crystal scarabs.[1]

I turn him loose, and he goes to the meadow, and, with his nose, he gently caresses the little flowers of rose and blue and gold. . . . I call him softly, "Platero?" and he comes to me at a gay little trot that is like laughter of a vague, idyllic, tinkling sound.

He eats whatever I give him. He likes mandarin oranges, amber-hued muscatel grapes, purple figs tipped with crystalline drops of honey.

He is as loving and tender as a child, but strong and sturdy as a rock. When on Sundays I ride him through the lanes in the outskirts of the town, slow-moving countrymen, dressed in their Sunday clean, watch him a while, speculatively:

"He is like steel," they say.

Steel, yes. Steel and moon silver at the same time.

The Canary's Flight

One day the green canary — I do not know how or why — flew out of his cage. He was an old bird, a sad legacy from a dead woman, which I had

---

[1]**scarabs** (skăr′əbz): broad-bodied beetles.

not set at liberty for fear that he might starve or freeze to death, or that he might be eaten by the cats.

All morning long he flew about the pomegranate blossoms in the garden, through the pine tree by the gate, among the lilacs. And all morning long the children sat on the porch, absorbed in the brief flights of the yellowish bird. Platero rested close to the rosebushes, playing with a butterfly.

In the late afternoon the canary came to the roof of the large house, and there he remained a long time, fluttering in the soft light of the setting sun. Of a sudden, without anyone's knowing how or why, he appeared in his cage, gay once more.

What a stir in the garden! The children leaped about, clapping their hands, rosy and laughing as the dawn; Diana,[2] mad with joy, followed them, barking at her own tinkling bell; having caught their mirth, Platero capered around like a wild young goat, stood on his hind legs dancing a rude waltz, and then, standing on his forefeet, kicked his hind feet in the clear warm air. . . .

The Cart

In the big creek, which the rains had swelled as far as the vineyard, we found an old cart stuck in the mud, lost to view under its load of grass and oranges. A ragged, dirty little girl was weeping over one wheel, trying to help the donkey, who was, alas, smaller and frailer than Platero. And the little donkey was spending himself against the wind, trying vainly at the sobbing cry of the child to pull the cart out of the mire. His efforts were futile, like the efforts of brave children, like the breath of those tired summer breezes which fall fainting among the flowers.

I patted Platero, and as well as I could I hitched him to the cart in front of the wretched little donkey. I encouraged him then with an affectionate command, and Platero, at one tug, pulled cart and beast out of the mud and up the bank.

---

[2]**Diana:** the writer's dog.

How the little girl smiled! It was as if the evening sun, setting among the yellow-crystal rain clouds, had kindled a dawn of joy behind her dirty tears.

With tearful gladness she offered me two choice oranges, perfect, heavy, round. I took them gratefully, and I gave one to the weak little donkey, to comfort him; the other to Platero, as a golden reward.

October Afternoon

Vacation days are over, and with the first yellow leaves the children have returned to school. Solitude. The heart of the house, also, with the fallen leaves, seems empty. Distant cries and faraway laughter are heard only in fancy.

Evening falls apace, slowly, on the flowering rosebushes. The sunset glow reddens the last late roses, and the garden, lifting its flame of fragrance to the flame of the dying sun, smells of burnt roses. Silence.

Platero, wearily restless as I, does not know what to do. Hesitantly he comes toward me, considers, wonders, and at last, confidently stepping sturdily and cleanly on the brick floor, he comes with me into the house. . . .

Death

I found Platero lying on his bed of straw, eyes soft and sad. I went to him, stroked him, talking to him and trying to help him to stand.

The poor fellow quivered, started to rise, one forefoot bent under. . . . He could not get up. Then I straightened his foot on the ground, patted him again tenderly, and called the doctor.

Old Darbón, as soon as he saw him, puckered his toothless mouth and shook his bulbous head like a pendulum.

"No hope?"

I do not know what he answered. . . . That the poor fellow was dying . . . nothing . . . a pain. . . . Some root he had eaten, with the grass. . . .

At noon, Platero was dead. His little cotton-like stomach had swollen like a globe, and his rigid discolored legs were raised to heaven. His curly hair looked now like the moth-eaten tow hair of old dolls that falls off when you touch it.

Through the silent stable, its translucent wings seeming to catch fire every time it passed the ray of light that came in through the little window, fluttered a beautiful three-colored butterfly.

Cardboard Platero

Platero, a year ago when there appeared in the world a part of this book that I wrote in memory of you, a friend of yours and mine made me a gift of this toy Platero. Do you see it from where you are? Look: he is half-gray and half-white; his mouth is black and red; his eyes are enormously big and enormously black; he carries little clay saddlebags with six flowerpots filled with silk-paper flowers, pink and white and yellow; he can move his head, and he walks on a blue-painted board that has four crude wheels.

Remembering you, Platero, I have become attached to this little toy donkey. Everyone who enters my study says to him, smiling, "Platero." If anyone does not know about you and asks me what he is, I say, "It is Platero." And so well has the name accustomed me to the feeling that now I myself, even when alone, think he is you, and I caress him with my eyes.

You? How inconstant is the memory of the human heart. This toy Platero seems to me today more Platero than you yourself, Platero.

Thinking and Discussing

What does the author reveal about Platero's character traits? What does he reveal about his own?

How does the author's choice of words create the mood of the story? What does the mood convey about the friendship between the author and Platero?

What is surprising about the author's affection for the cardboard Platero?

Choosing a Creative Response

Creating a Description Choose an old photograph of someone you have never met or someplace you have never been. Then use the picture and your imagination to create a description of the person or place as if it were something you remembered from the past.

Make notes about the specific details you will include to make the description realistic. Then add colorful words and images to make it interesting.

Creating Your Own Activity Plan and complete your own activity in response to *Platero and I.*

In Andalusia the word *platero* is used to describe donkeys of a silvery color. When asked whether Platero had been a real donkey, Juan Ramón Jiménez responded, "In reality, my Platero is not one donkey only but several (in one), a synthesis of *platero* donkeys. As a boy and a young man I had several of them. All were *plateros*. The sum of all my memories with them gave me the creature and the book."

Award Winner

THE BOY WITH YELLOW EYES

by Gloria Gonzalez

Only a handful of the residents of Preston Heights recall the actual events. And even then, years and conflicting accounts have clouded the facts.

Still, in some quarters, and especially during the relentless winters unique to the hillside village, the incident is spoken of with pride and awe.

Till today, if you get a couple of old-timers in the same room, a heated debate will erupt over the mundane detail of whether Norman was ten or going on thirteen. They'll also argue whether he lost one shoe or both in the scuffle.

What the parties do agree on is that it happened in Preston Heights and it involved Norman and his next-door neighbor Willie, whose age for some reason is never questioned — thirteen.

And of course . . . the stranger.

Opinions are equally divided on whether the stranger's limp was caused by a deformed right or left leg. But everyone, to a man, can tell you exactly what the Vice President of the United States was wearing when he arrived and what he ordered for lunch. (In fact, his discarded gingham cloth napkin, since laundered, is part of the local exhibit, which includes his signature in the hotel's register.)

The only other point of total agreement is that Norman was the least likely of heroes. He had none of the qualities that could have foretold his sudden fame.

Norman was not the kind of kid who would cause you to break out in a grin if you saw him ride your way on a bike.

1. He couldn't ride a bike.
2. He rarely emerged from his house.
3. He was considered . . . well . . . weird.

This last opinion was based on the fact that Norman would only be seen heading toward or leaving the library, and always hugging an armful of books. To the townfolk it seemed unhealthy for a young boy to read so much. They predicted a total loss of eyesight by the time he reached nineteen.

Willie, however, was a kid who, had there been a Normal Kid Pageant, would have won first and tied for second and third. A dynamic baseball player, daring bike rider, crackerjack newspaper delivery boy — he was the town's delight. Never mind that he was flunking all school subjects and had a reputation as a bully, he was, after all, "a real boy."

The differences did not escape the boys themselves. Though neighbors, separated only by splintery bushes, they never as much as shared a "Hi."

To Willie, Norman was simply the kid with the yellow eyes. Not that they were actually yellow — more of a brown-hazel — but often, the way the sunlight bounced off the thick eyeglasses, it seemed to create a yellow haze.

(Years later, in a rare interview, Norman was asked if he had missed having friends while growing up. He replied: "Not at all. I had Huck and Tom Sawyer.")

To Norman, Willie was exhausting. He talked fast, ran fast, walked fast, and, he suspected, even slept fast. (If such a thing could be measured.) It was tiring just to sit behind him in class and listen to his endless chatter.

If Norman was slow motion, Willie was definitely fast forward. Which brings us to the stranger, who fit somewhere in between.

Some say the stranger arrived one early summer day on foot. Others believe he came on the bus from Boulder.

One fact is undisputed: he took a room on the second floor of McCory's hotel. Not that he had much of a choice; it was the only lodging in town. The hotel dated back to the construction of the first railroad. It had been hastily thrown together to house the army of laborers that would lay the train tracks. Unfortunately, the hilly terrain stymied the work force and the project was eventually abandoned, leaving behind three passenger and two freight cars.

George McCory, the town's undertaker, purchased the hotel and soon found he could make more money by housing the living.

The hotel parlor soon became the common milling ground. Here you could always get into a game of checkers, buy stamps, mail a letter, or receive news of neighboring towns via the traveling salesmen.

That's why when the stranger first arrived, his presence went almost unnoticed. It was only after he was still visible over a period of weeks that others became aware of him. A tall, muscular man in his thirties with a ready smile, he made a favorable impression. Maybe it was the limp. Many attributed it to the war then raging in Europe. Too polite to inquire, the hotel regulars silently accepted his "wound."

Since the man was never seen during the day and rarely till after supper, his comings and goings drew much speculation. Local gossip had it that he was an artist who'd come to Preston Heights to paint the unusual terrain. This theory was fueled by the sight of the man always carrying a dark satchel. Some held that the man was famous.

Perhaps that legend would have endured except for three insignificant, unrelated events:

1. The library decided to paint its reading room.
2. Willie's baseball coach had a tooth pulled.
3. The stranger overslept.

On the day of the "incident," Norman headed, as usual, to the library. Mrs. Brenner, the librarian, met him at the entrance and explained that due to the cleanup work the library was temporarily closed.

The thought of studying in his stuffy bedroom (no air could circulate because of all the books he ordered from Chicago and New York publishers) sent him instead to the railroad yards.

The discarded railroad cars — which had been painted a zippy burgundy when new — now bore the scars of merciless winters and oppressive summers. Vandalism and neglect had added to the toll. For too many years, kids had deemed it their own amusement park. In recent time, the decaying cars had even been abandoned by the vandals. Rumor had it that rats and raccoons openly roamed the burgundy cars.

Norman knew it wasn't true. At least once a month, when the weather was nice, he would head for the rail yard, lugging his books, to settle comfortably in a cushioned seat in car #7215, his head pressed against the wooden window frame (now paneless[1]). When the day's shadow hit the bottom of the page, he knew to close the book and head home.

On this day, the high position of the sun assured him of at least four uninterrupted hours of reading.

Across town, in the school yard, Willie stood with friends swinging his baseball bat at air. He looked forward to practice almost as much as to the games. That's why when the coach appeared to say he had to cancel due to an impacted tooth, the teenager found himself at a loss as to what to do.

It was too early to start his newspaper money collection. Knowing it was best to strike when families were seated for dinner, he wandered aimlessly toward the rail yards with a mind to picking up some chunky rocks and using them as balls to swat about the empty field.

And so it was that he found himself in the proximity of car #7215.

The unusually warm weather had its effect on the stranger who now dozed in the freight car, an iron link away from #7215. The heat had caused him to discard his usual caution in return for a slight breeze. He had lifted the huge steel doors that slid upward, affording him a welcome breeze from the quiet countryside. The cool air had lulled his senses, stretching his customary nap long past its normal half hour.

---

[1]**paneless:** without window glass.

Perhaps it was his two months of success, his feeling of invincibility, or his unconscious desire for danger that caused him to be careless this day. In any event, when he awoke, he did not bother to lower the steel door.

He opened his black satchel and removed the network of tubes, cylinders, wires, bolts, and antennas which he expertly positioned in a matter of minutes. It was by now an automatic labor. His mind refreshed by sleep, he thought ahead to the coming week when he would be safely aboard the steamer that would carry him across the ocean. The lightness of his touch, as he twisted the spidery wires, reflected his carefree attitude.

Norman's first reaction was to ignore Willie's sudden entrance.

"You see my ball go by here?"

Norman didn't even look up from the book he was reading. "No."

"Not exactly a ball, more like a rock," Willie said, sitting on the armrest of a seat, with his legs blocking the aisle.

"No," Norman answered.

Normally, Willie would have stalked out, but it was cooler inside the car, and most appealing of all, Norman looked so relaxed and comfortable that he felt compelled to ruin it.

"What are you doing, anyway?"

"Reading."

"I figured that. That's all you ever do. Aren't you afraid you're going to lose your eyesight?"

Norman's lack of response did not still Willie.

"I think reading is dumb."

"I think hitting a rock with a stick is dumb."

"Oh, yeah? You ever try it?"

"No. You ever try reading?"

"When the teacher makes me. I'd rather hit a rock. It's fun."

"So is reading."

Willie didn't buy it. "When I hit a ball, I'm *doing* something. Reading is not doing."

Norman removed his glasses and closely regarded Willie with his full attention.

"Do you know what I was *doing* when you barged in here? I was running through a haunted castle being chased by a vampire who was very, very thirsty. If that isn't 'doing,' I don't know what is."

This led to Norman's explaining the plot of Bram Stoker's *Dracula*. Willie, totally engrossed, sat on the floor listening to the tale of horror.

Norman was telling him about Renfield — and his daily diet of spiders and insects — when a distant clicking sound averted his attention.

"Probably a woodpecker," Willie said, urging the other boy to get back to the story.

Norman stretched his neck closer to the sound.

"If it is, it's the smartest woodpecker in history," Norman said, straining to hear.

Something in Norman's expression caused Willie to whisper, "What are you talking about?"

Norman swiftly signaled him to be quiet and silently crept toward the source of the tapping.

Willie, suddenly frightened for reasons he could not explain, followed closely. "What is it?" he asked, gripping his baseball bat.

The tapping was louder now.

"It's coming from the freight car." Norman dropped to the floor, his body hunched against the steel door separating them from the other car. Willie fell alongside him. "What is it?" he half pleaded.

Norman took a pencil from his pocket and began scribbling furiously on the margins of the library book. Willie noticed that he wrote with the rhythm of the clicking sound. Whenever the tapping stopped for a moment, so did Norman's pencil.

Willie glanced at the jottings, but it was difficult to make out the words. He did make out one short phrase. "End is near."

Norman and the clicking stopped at the same time.

"What does it mean?" Willie whispered, his fear growing. He had known fear once before, when a stray dog, foaming at the mouth, had cornered him behind the general store. But this was worse. Here the threat was unknown.

Norman quickly stashed the book under a seat and jumped to his feet. "We have to stop him!" he told Willie.

"Who?"

"The spy," Norman said as he slid open the heavy door and dashed outside.

A startled Willie sat frozen.

The bright sun slammed Norman in the face as he jumped from the train car and rolled underneath the freight compartment. He was silently happy to see Willie join him seconds later.

"What are we doing?" Willie asked, frightened of the answer.

"Waiting."

"For what?" he whispered.

"Him," Norman said, pointing to the underbelly of the rusted car.

Before Willie could reply, the stranger jumped from above their heads, clutching his dark suitcase. They watched as his limping form started to move away.

Norman sprung from under the car, raced after the man, and — to Willie's horror — tackled him from behind. The satchel went flying in the surprise attack.

"Grab it! Grab it!" Norman screamed.

The stranger clawed the ground and struggled to his feet, fighting like a wild man. His eyes were ablaze with hate. His arms, hands, and feet spun like a deranged windmill. His actions were swift but Norman was quicker. Try as he might to grab the boy, the man kept slashing at the air. He managed to clutch the boy's foot, but Norman quickly wiggled out of his shoe. The man grabbed him by his pants leg and pulled him to the ground.

"Do something!" Norman screamed at Willie, who stood paralyzed with fear. The man was now crouched over the boy's body and was gripping his neck.

Willie, seeing Norman's legs thrash helplessly in the air, swung his baseball bat with all his strength and caught the stranger — low and inside.

"About time," Norman coughed, massaging his throbbing neck.

Hours later, sitting in the hotel lobby with the chief of police, the boys watched wearily as swarms of people dashed up and down the stairs. They knew the man's room was being torn apart.

In the hotel kitchen the stranger was surrounded by FBI agents who had been summoned from the state capital, seventy-eight miles away. More were en route from Washington, D.C.

By nightfall the hotel was completely isolated from the public and everyone heard of how Willie and Norman had caught themselves a real-life Nazi spy.

It took weeks for the full story to emerge, and even then the citizens felt that the whole story would never be revealed. (Norman's *Dracula* book, for instance, had been whisked away by agents.) What was learned was that the man had been transmitting information to a colleague in Boulder. That man had managed to slip away and was now believed to be back in Berlin. Two of the strangers' conspirators[2] in New York — one a woman — were arrested and being held in a federal prison outside of Virginia.

Three months later, in a highly publicized visit, the Vice President of the United States came to Preston Heights to thank the boys personally. Film crews shot footage of the unlikely trio that would be shown in movie theaters throughout the country; Preston Heights would never be the same.

The cameras were there when Norman was asked how he had been able to understand the Morse code. "I learned it from a book," he said.

Asked how he had been able to overpower the man, Willie grinned. "Easy. I'm batting .409 on the school team."

---

[2]**conspirators** (kən **spîr'**ə tərz): people who participate in unlawful acts.

Preston Heights blossomed under the glare of national attention. Tourists visiting the state made it a point to spend the night at McCory's hotel and gawk at the corner table in the dining room where the Vice President ate lunch with the boys and their parents.

Willie did not go on to become a major league slugger. Instead, he left Preston Heights to join the navy and rose to the rank of chief petty officer upon retirement.

Norman attended Georgetown University and went on to serve as press secretary for a New Jersey senator.

Every Christmas they exchange cards and a list of books each has read during the previous year.

Norman is still ahead of Willie, two to one.

Thinking and Discussing

What does the portrayal of the boys as the typical bookworm and athlete suggest about the attitudes of people of that time? At the story's climax, why does the author have each character behave in a way that is not typical?

How do the first paragraphs of the story prepare the reader for what happens later? How does this device of delaying the start contribute to the suspense?

In what ways is this story realistic? How does the author make the characters, plot, and setting believable?

Choosing a Creative Response

Speaking as Vice President Write a brief speech that the Vice President might give to the people of Preston Heights to explain why Norman and Willie are heroes.

Making a News Film With a group, develop a plan for the film footage that puts Preston Heights in the national spotlight. Present it as a skit to your classmates, or record it on videotape if a camera is available.

Creating Your Own Activity Plan and complete your own activity in response to "The Boy with Yellow Eyes."

THE FULLER BRUSH MAN

by Gloria D. Miklowitz

Donald leaned into the car trunk to find the box holding the giveaways. He had to pay for each letter opener, shoehorn, and vegetable brush, money out of his own commission, but it was worth it. Why else would people listen to his sales spiel if it wasn't because they felt indebted the second they reached for a sample?

What a mess, he thought, getting grease on his hand. Ever since Mom stopped driving. Ever since she . . . Well, there was no use dwelling on that. When he had time he'd try to get rid of some of the junk. He dropped a dozen plastic shoehorns into his sample case, snapped the lock, and glanced at his watch.

Man, he was hungry. He'd been working steadily since right after school, four hours. All he'd eaten was a doughnut left in the breadbox at home, running out the door with Ava calling after him to get a glass of milk first.

He'd sold enough brushes to call it quits for the day, but maybe he'd work another hour. If he went home now, even though it would mean a real meal, not McDonald's, Ava would be there. Their newest housekeeper, she'd sit there at the kitchen table, arms folded, watching him, and she'd go into her usual song and dance.

"Go in to your mother. Just for a minute. Say hello. Say *something.*"

"Later."

"*Now.* She'll be asleep later."

"Why? She can't talk. She probably doesn't even know who I am. What difference does it make?"

"Donnie, Donnie. You love her. I know you do. Do it for you, if not for her."

"Leave me alone."

He'd get this picture in his head of Mom, the way she had become lately. Bloated face, dull eyes that followed him without seeming to see. And her arms skinny, all bones. *Why? How could she do that to him, to them?*

No. He'd just get a bite nearby and go home later. He could maybe make five more sales. More money for the college fund. And with what Dad was putting out in medical bills and nursing care, every cent counted.

He crossed the street and was nearly knocked down by a kid on a two-wheeler, shooting out of a driveway, wobbling his way down the road. When had *he* learned to ride a bike? Eight, nine years ago? Yes. In the Apperson Street schoolyard, late afternoons. He could hear the crickets chirping even now, and for a second he felt the same surge of fear and exultation he'd felt then gripping the handlebars.

"I can't! I can't! I'm falling! Mom, Mom! Help me!"

"You can! You can! Keep going! That's right! You're doing it!"

Running alongside, face sweating and flushed, red hair flying about her eyes and cheeks, she was laughing with joy. And when he finally managed to stop she threw her arms around him and cried, "See? You did it! I knew you could!"

He swallowed a lump in his throat and marched briskly up the walk to the door of a small, wooden house. He rang the bell and waited, peering through the screen door into a living room with a worn couch, a TV flickering against one wall, and a small child sitting in front of it.

"If you don't behave, you'll have to watch TV," his mother would say when he was that age, as if watching TV was punishment. Maybe that's why he hardly watched even now.

When *he* was little, this was the time of day he loved most. Right after supper and before bedtime. He'd climb up on the couch to sit beside Mom. Bonnie would take her place on Mom's other side and for a half hour it was "weed books" time.

He felt an overwhelming hunger for those times, for Mom's arm around him and her warm voice reading. He wiped a hand across his eyes as a woman, holding a baby, came to the door.

"Fuller brush man! Good evening, missus. Would you like a sample?" Donald held out a brush, a letter opener, and a shoehorn. With but a second's hesitation the woman unlatched the door and stepped forward, eyeing the samples greedily. She took the brush.

"Good choice," Donald said. "They're great for scrubbing vegetables. Now, would you like to see our specials?" He held the catalog open to the specials page, but the light was fading.

"I don't need any . . ."

"Then maybe you'd like to try our new tile-cleaning foam. See?" He plucked a can from his case and showed her the cap with its stiff bristles for the "hard-to-clean places between the tiles."

"I have Formica."

"Sally? Sally? Who the devil is that?"

"Just a brush salesman, honey!"

"Well, tell him you don't need any!"

The woman gave him a sheepish grin, backed away, and said, "Sorry." She closed the screen door and latched it again.

He used to take rejection hard, getting a pain in his stomach that grew with each door shut in his face, each disgusted "Don't bother me." He still withdrew inside when people turned him away, although he wouldn't show it now, keeping his voice pleasant and a smile on his face. If anyone asked, he'd say he hated the job even though he was learning a lot about human nature and keeping books, and it did pay well.

"Sell door to door?" his mother had asked when he first proposed the idea. "Absolutely not!"

"Why not? I could save what I make for college!"

"No!"

"Why? That's not fair!"

"Because." He watched her struggle to find words for what she hadn't thought out. "Because it's not safe, knocking on strange people's doors. The world is full of crazies. Because I don't want you to have to get doors slammed in your face. Because it will be summer soon and too hot to work outdoors. If you want a job, find one where it's air-conditioned."

"Let him try," Dad said. "One day of it and he'll quit."

"*Please*, Mom?"

"Oh, all right," she conceded, but only because that morning he'd accused her of still treating him like a baby. "But only to try it. *One* day!"

It was three months now. She must have been sick even then, because after that first day when he'd come home triumphant with having made fifty-four dollars in only six hours, he didn't hear anything more

about quitting. It was about then that she went into the hospital for the first time and his whole life began to change.

When he finished another block, he circled back to the car, a dog barking at his heels. One of the hazards of selling things in strange neighborhoods was the dogs. He carried Mace but hated using it. He found that if he stood his ground and shouted "No," most dogs would go through their ferocious act and run off when they figured they'd done their duty.

In the dim light of the car he looked over his orders and decided to drive down to the boulevard for something to eat. Maybe he'd phone Shannon afterwards, drop by for a few minutes before going home. He started the engine, turned on the headlights, and drove down the hill.

"How's your Mom?" Shannon asked when he reached her from the phone in the parking lot. There was so much traffic noise he had to press the receiver tight against his ear.

"What are you doing?" he asked in response. "I can be by in ten minutes. We could go for a walk."

"When are you going to talk about it?" Shannon asked. "Bonnie says she's worse. It's awful how you're acting. It's not her fault."

For a second he considered not answering at all, but finally he said, "Stop bugging me. Everyone's after me about it. It's *my* mom. It's my business. If that's all you want to talk about, forget it."

"But, Donnie! You can't put it off much longer."

He hung up without answering and ran back to the car.

Slamming the door, he slumped in the driver's seat and stared out at the ribbon of lights on the freeway. If he let himself think about what Shannon said, he'd just start blubbering like a baby. Better to work. He'd get at the orders for the week. They were due to be toted up and recorded on the big order sheet by tomorrow. Usually he'd work on it at home, spreading the papers out on his desk and marking how many of this or that he'd sold that week. But if he went home now, they'd *all* be there: Dad, Bonnie, and Ava. All accusing. Bonnie with her *Please,*

Donnie's. Ava with her *Why don't you*'s. And Dad with his sad silence, worse than words.

But worst of all was knowing that Mom lay in the next room wasting away, dying, not even fighting anymore. He felt that if he was forced to go in there, all he'd do is scream at her. "Don't you care? Try! You always told us never to give up! You're not trying!" And he'd want to strike out at her. Well, maybe not at her, but at something!

There wasn't a moment in the day that he didn't think about her. It was as if they were joined by an invisible wire and he felt everything she did. And he felt now that she was slipping away. He couldn't stop it. He couldn't do a thing about it. There was nothing to say, nothing! Everything he thought of saying sounded false or stupid.

Well, all right! If that's what he had to do, he'd do it. He'd *go* home. He'd go into her room. He'd look at that woman who was and wasn't his mother anymore and he'd say *something*. Whatever came into his head, no matter how mean or dumb. *All right!* If that's what they all wanted, that's what he'd do.

He turned the key in the ignition and gunned the car out of the parking lot and into the street. He drove along, mouth clenched in a tight line, totally intent on the road, mind empty except for the determination to get home fast.

He parked the car in the drive and ran into the house. Suddenly he was terribly afraid. What if it was too late? He almost felt in his gut that he'd waited too long.

"Donnie?" Dad called from the family room. "That you?"

He made some kind of guttural response and ran past the room, not even nodding. He had a fleeting sense that Dad was there reading the paper, that Bonnie was doing homework. His heart hammered loudly in his ears. An electrical pulse ran down his arms to his legs as he reached his mother's bedroom door and put a hand on the knob.

And then he stopped. For a long moment he stood waiting for his legs to quit trembling, for his heart to slow down. And then he closed his eyes, took a deep breath, and straightened his shoulders. Fixing a smile on his face, he knocked. "Fuller brush man!" he called, lightly opening the door.

Thinking and Discussing

At what places in the story does Donald remember things that had happened in the past? What do these flashbacks contribute to the story?

Through whose eyes does the reader observe the world of this story? How does the author tell the reader so much about Donald and his feelings?

Choosing a Creative Response

Giving Donald Advice What do you think about the way Donald is handling his problem? Write your advice in a personal note to Donald.

Creating Your Own Response Plan and complete your own activity in response to "The Fuller Brush Man."

Thinking and Writing

Write about a character you may have met in a book, in a movie, or in your own life. Reveal the character's personality through descriptions of his or her speech, actions, thoughts, and interaction with others.

My dad is Hixon of Hixon's Landing, the fishing camp down on the intra-coastal[1] waterway just across Highway A1A. Our camp isn't a fancy one. Just two coolers, one for beer and one for bait, plus four boats and eight motors that we rent out.

Dad was raised on a farm in Nebraska, but he joined the Navy and signed on for the war in Vietnam and came back knowing two things. One, he hated war, and two, he loved the sea. Actually, he came back with two loves. The other one was my mother. There wasn't *any* way *any*one could get him to settle *any*where that was far from the ocean when he got out of the service, so he bought this small stretch of land in north Florida, and we've been there for all of my life that I can remember.

Dad's got this small pension for getting wounded over in Nam,[2] so between what we sell, what we rent and what the government sends, we do all right. We're not what you're likely to call rich, but we are all right. Mom doubts that we'll ever make enough money to pay for a trip to her native country of Thailand, but she doesn't seem to mind. She says that it is more important to love where you're at than to love where you're from.

Mom makes and sells sandwiches for the fishermen. She does a right good job on them, I can tell you. There is this about Mom's sand-wiches: you don't have to eat halfway through to the middle to find out what's between the bread, and once you get hold of a bite, you don't have

---

[1]**intracoastal** (ĭn'trə kōs'təl): within a coastal region.

[2]**Nam** (näm): shortened form of *Vietnam*, used by American soldiers when referring to the conflict of 1957–1975.

to guess at whether it is egg salad or tuna that you're eating. The filling is high in size and in flavor.

The town next door to us is spreading south toward our landing, and both Mom and Dad say that our property will be worth a pretty penny in a few years. But both of them always ask, "What's a pretty penny worth when you can't buy anything prettier than what you already have?" I have to agree. Maybe because I don't know anything else, but I can't imagine what it would be like not to have a sandbox miles and miles long and a pool as big as an ocean for a playground across the street — even if the street is a highway. I can't ever remember going to sleep but that I heard some water shushing and slurping or humming and hollering for a lullaby.

Last spring, just as the days were getting long enough that a person could both start and finish something between the time he got home from school and the time he went to bed, I went out onto our dock and I saw this guy all duded up from a catalogue. Now that the town has grown toward us, we have more of these guys than we used to. When you've been in the business of fishing all your life, you come to know the difference between fishermen and guys who have a hobby. Here are some of the clues:

1. The hat. A real fisherman's hat is darkened along the edges where the sweat from his hand leaves marks. A non-fisherman's hat has perfect little dent marks in it.

2. The smile. Real fishermen don't smile while they're fishing unless someone tells them a joke. Real fishermen wear their faces in the same look people wear when they are in church — deliberate and far-off — the way they do when they don't want to catch the eye of the preacher. The only time that look changes is when they take a swig of beer and then it changes only a little and with a slow rhythm like watching instant replay on television. Non-fishermen twitch their necks around like pigeons, which are very citified birds, and non-fishermen smile a lot.

3. The umbrella. Real fishermen don't have them.

This old guy sat on a wooden-legged, canvas-bottom folding campstool that didn't have any salt burns on it anywhere and put his rod into one of the holders that Dad had set up along the dock railing. Then he held out his hand and called out, "Hey, boy, do you know what I've got here?"

I walked on over to him and said, "Name's Ned."

"What's that?" he asked, cupping his hand over his ear so that the breeze wouldn't blow it past him.

"I said that my name is Ned," I repeated.

"All right, Ed," he said. "I have a question for you. Do you know what this is, boy?"

"Name's Ned," I repeated. I looked down at the palm of his hand and saw a medium-sized shark's tooth from a sand shark. "Not bad," I said.

"But do you know what it is, boy?" he asked.

I could tell that it wasn't the kind of question where a person is looking for an answer; it was the kind of question where a person just wants you to look interested long enough so that he can get on with telling you the answer. I decided that I wouldn't play it that way even if he was a customer. Three *boys* in a row made me mean, so I said, "Medium-sized sand."

"What's that?" he shouted, cupping his hand over his ear again.

"Medium-sized sand," I repeated louder.

"That's a shark's tooth," he said, clamping his hand shut.

Shoot! I knew that it was a shark's tooth. I was telling him what *kind* it was and what size it was.

"That is a fossilized shark's tooth, boy," he said. "Found it just across the street."

"Name's Ned," I told him, and I walked away.

Sharks' teeth wash up all the time at the beach just across the road from Hixon's Landing. There's a giant fossil bed out in the ocean somewheres, and a vent from it leads right onto our beach. When the undertow gets to digging up out of that fossil bed and the tide is coming in, all kinds of interesting things wash in. Besides the sharks' teeth, there are also pieces of bones that wash up. I collect the backbones, the vertebraes, they're called; they have a hole in them where the spinal column went through. I have a whole string of them fixed according to size.

I collect sharks' teeth, too. I have been doing it for years. Mom started me doing it. It was Mom who made a study of them and found what kind of animal they might come from. Mom has these thorough ways about her. Dad says that Mom is smarter'n a briar and prettier'n a movie star.

Mom fixes the sharks' teeth that we collect into patterns and fastens them down onto a velvet mat and gets them framed into a shadowbox frame. She sells them down at the gift shop in town. And the gift shop isn't any tacky old gift shop full of smelly candles and ashtrays with the name of our town stamped on it. It's more like an art gallery. Matter of fact, it is called *The Artists' Gallery*, and Mom is something of an artist at how she makes those sharks' teeth designs. Some of the really pretty sharks' teeth Mom sells to a jeweler who sets them in gold for pendants. When she gets two pretty ones that match, he makes them into earrings.

When I find her a really special or unusual one, Mom says to me, "Looks like we got a trophy, Ned." When we get us a trophy, one that needs investigating or one that is just downright super special, we don't sell it. Shoot! We don't even think about selling it. There's nothing that bit of money could buy that we'd want more than having that there trophy.

Most everyone who comes to Hixon's Landing knows about Mom and me being something of authorities on fossils, especially sharks' teeth, so I figured that this old dude would either go away and not come back or hang around long enough to find out. Either way, I figured that I didn't need to advertise for myself and my mom.

The next day after school there was the old fellow again. I wouldn't want to sound braggy or anything, but I could tell that he was standing there at the end of our dock waiting for me to come home from school.

"Hi," I said.

"Well, boy," he said, "did you have a good day at school?"

"Fair," I answered. I decided to let the *boy* ride. I figured that he couldn't hear or couldn't remember or both. "Catch anything?" I asked.

"No, not today," he said. "Matter of fact I was just about to close up shop." Then he began reeling in, looking back over his shoulder to see if I was still hanging around. He didn't even bother taking the hook off his line; he just dumped rod and reel down on the dock and stuck out his hand to me and said, "Well, son, you can call me President Bob."

"What are you president of?" I asked.

"President of a college, upstate Michigan. But I'm retired now."

"Then you're not a president," I said.

"Not at the moment, but the title stays. The way that people still call a retired governor, *Governor.* You can call me President Bob instead of President Kennicott. Bob is more informal, but I wouldn't want you to call me just Bob. It doesn't seem respectful for a boy to call a senior citizen just Bob."

"And you can call me Ned," I said. "That's my name."

"All right, son," he said.

"After the first day, I don't answer to *son* or to *boy*," I said.

"What did you say your name was, son?"

Shoot! He had to learn. So I didn't answer.

"What is your name again?"

"Ned."

"Well, Ned, would you like to take a walk on the beach and hunt for some of those sharks' teeth?"

"Sure," I said.

He must have counted on my saying yes, because the next thing I see is him dropping his pants and showing me a pair of skinny white legs with milky blue veins sticking out from under a pair of bathing trunks.

As we walked the length of the dock, he told me that he was used to the company of young men since he had been president of a college. "Of course, the students were somewhat older," he said. Then he laughed a little, like punctuation. I didn't say anything. "And, of course, I didn't often see the students on a one-to-one basis." I didn't say anything. "I was president," he added. He glanced over at me, and I still didn't say anything. "I was president," he added.

"There's supposed to be some good fishing in Michigan," I said.

"Oh, yes! Yes, there is. Good fishing. Fine fishing. Sportsmen's fishing."

We crossed A1A and got down onto the beach from a path people had worn between the dunes, and I showed him how to look for sharks' teeth in the coquina.[3] "There's nothing too much to learn," I said. "It's mostly training your eye."

He did what most beginners do, that is, he picked up a lot of wedge-shaped pieces of broken shell, mostly black, thinking they were fossil teeth. The tide was just starting on its way out, and that is the best time for finding sharks' teeth. He found about eight of them, and two of them were right nice sized. I found fourteen myself and three of mine were bigger than anything he collected. We compared, and I could tell that he was wishing he had mine, so I gave him one of my big ones. It wasn't a trophy or anything like that because I would never do that to Mom, that is, give away a trophy or a jewelry one.

President Bob was waiting for me the next day and the day after that one. By the time Friday afternoon came, President Bob gave up on trying to pretend that he was fishing. He'd just be there on the dock, waiting for me to take him sharks' tooth hunting.

"There's no magic to it," I told him. "You can go without me."

"That's all right, Ned," he said, "I don't mind waiting."

On Saturday I had a notion to sleep late and was in the process of doing just that when Mom shook me out of my sleep and told me that I had a visitor. It was President Bob, and there he was standing on his vanilla legs right by my bedroom door. He had gotten tired of waiting for me on the dock. It being Saturday, he had come early so's we could have more time together.

---

[3] **coquina** (kō kē′nə): pieces of broken shells and coral.

Mom invited him in to have breakfast with me, and while we ate, she brought out our trophy boxes. Our trophies were all sitting on cotton in special boxes like the ones you see butterflies fixed in inside a science museum. Mom explained about our very special fossils.

"Oh, yes," President Bob said. Then, "Oh, yes," again. Then after he'd seen all our trophies and had drunk a second cup of coffee, he said, "We had quite a fine reference library in my college. I am referring to the college of which I was president. Not my alma mater, the college I attended as a young man. We had quite a fine library, and I must confess I used it often, so I am not entirely unfamiliar with these things."

That's when I said, "Oh, yes," except that it came out, "Oh, yeah!" and that's when Mom swiped my foot under the table.

President Bob plunked his empty cup down on the table and said, "Well, come on now, Ned, time and tide wait for no man. Ha! Ha!"

I think that I've heard someone say that at least four times a week. Everyone says it. Dad told me that it was a proverb, an old, old saying. And I can tell you that it got old even before I reached my second birthday.

When we got down to the beach, President Bob brought out a plastic bag and flung it open like a bag boy at the supermarket. But there wasn't much to fill it with that day because the currents had shifted and weren't churning up the fossil bed.

"I suppose you'll be going to church tomorrow," he said.

"Yes," I answered.

"I think I'll do some fishing in the morning. I'll probably have had enough of that by noon. I'll meet you at the dock about twelve-thirty. We can get started on our shark's tooth hunt then."

"Sorry," I said. "I help Mom with the sandwiches and then we clean things up and then we go to late services. Sunday is our busiest day."

"Of course it is," he said.

Mom and I got back about one-thirty and changed out of our good clothes before Dad came in as he always does on Sundays to grab some lunch before the men start coming back and he has to get busy with washing down motors and buying. (What he buys is fish from the men who have had a specially good run. Dad cleans them and sells them to markets back in town or to people who drive on out toward the beach of a Sunday. Sometimes, he gets so busy buying and cleaning that Mom and I pitch right in and give him a hand.)

Dad had not quite finished his sandwiches and had just lifted his beer when he got called out to the dock. There was this big haul of bass that some men were wanting to sell.

Mom and I were anxious to finish our lunch and clean up so's we could go on out and see if Dad would be needing some help when President Bob presented himself at the screen door to our kitchen.

"Knock, knock," he said, pressing his old face up against the screen. The minute we both looked up he opened the door without even an *if you please* and marched into our kitchen on his frosted icicle legs. "I think you're going to be interested in what I found today," he said. "Very interested."

Mom smiled her customer smile and said, "We are having very busy day, please to excuse if I continue with work."

"That's perfectly all right," President Bob said. "You're excused." Then he sat down at the table that Mom was wiping off. He held up the placemat and said, "Over here, Mama-san. You missed a spot."

Mom smiled her customer smile again and wiped the spot that he had pointed to, and President Bob put the placemat back down and emptied the contents of his plastic bag right on top of it. He leaned over the pile and using his forefinger began to comb through it. "Ah! here," he said. He picked up a small black thing between his thumb and forefinger and said to Mom, "Come here, Mama-san." *Mama-san* is some kind of Japanese for *mama*. A lot of people call my mom that, but she says it's okay because it is a term of respect, and a lot of people think that all Orientals are Japanese. Sometimes these same people call me Boy-san, which is to *boy* what Mama-san is to mama. They call me that because I have dark slanted eyes just like Mom's, except that hers are prettier.

"Look at this," President Bob said. "Look at it closely. I suspect that it is the upper palate[4] of an extinct species of deep water fish."

Mom took it from his hand and looked at it and said, "Dolphin tooth." She put it back down and walked to the sink where she continued right on with washing up the dishes. She automatically handed me a towel to dry.

President Bob studied the dolphin's tooth and said to Mom, "Are you sure?"

She smiled and nodded.

"Quite sure?"

She nodded.

He asked once more, and she nodded again. Then he began poking through his collection again and came up with another piece. He beckoned to Mom to look at it closer, and she dried her hands and did that.

"Shell," she said.

"Oh, I beg to differ with you," he said.

"Shell," Mom said, looking down at it, not bothering to pick it up.

"Are you sure?"

She nodded.

"Quite sure?"

She nodded again, and I came over and picked it up off the table and held it up and broke it in two. I thought that President Bob was going to arrest me. "A piece of fossil that thick wouldn't break that easy. It's a sure test," I said.

"There are fragile fossils, I'm sure," President Bob said.

"I suppose so," I said. "But that shell ain't fossilized. Piece of fossil that thick wouldn't ever break that easy." I could see that you had to repeat yourself with President Bob. "That shell ain't fossilized."

"*Ain't* is considered very bad manners up North," President Bob said.

Shoot! *Bad manners* are considered bad manners down South, I thought. But I didn't say anything. President Bob kept sorting through

---

[4]**palate** (păl′ĭt): the roof of the mouth.

his bag of stuff, studying on it so hard that his eyes winched up and made his bottom jaw drop open.

Mom finished washing the dishes, and I finished drying, and we asked if we could be excused, and President Bob told us (in our own kitchen, mind) that it was perfectly all right, but would we please fetch him a glass of ice water before we left. We fetched it. He said, "Thank you. You may go now." I suppose that up North it's good manners to give people orders in their own house if you do it with *please* and *thank you* and no *ain'ts*.

It rained on Monday and it rained again on Tuesday, so I didn't see President Bob again until Wednesday after school. He was waiting for me at the end of the dock with his plastic sandwich bag already partly full. "Well," he said, "I guess I got a bit of a head start on you today."

I looked close at his bag and saw that he had a couple of nice ones — not trophies — but nice.

"I have homework," I said. "I can't walk the beaches with you today."

"What subject?"

"Math."

"Maybe I can help you. Did I tell you that I was president of a college."

"Really?" I said in my fakiest voice. "I think I better do my homework by myself."

"I'll wait for you," he said. "I promise I won't hunt for anything until you come back out."

"It'll probably take me the rest of daylight to do it," I said.

"Math must be hard for you," he said. "Always was my strongest subject."

"It's not hard for me," I lied. "I just have a lot of it."

"Let me show you what I found today," he said.

"I don't think I have the time."

"Just take a minute."

Before I could give him another polite no, he had spread the contents of his bag over the railing of the dock. I looked things over real good. I knew he was watching me, so I wouldn't let my eyes pause too long on any one thing in particular. "Very nice," I said. "I've got to go now."

As I turned to walk back to our house, he called, "See you tomorrow."

The next day I didn't even walk to the dock. Instead I walked around to the side door of our house and threw my books on the wicker sofa on the screened porch and went up to my room and changed into my cut-offs. I had a plan; I was going to go back out the side door and walk a bit to the north before crossing the highway and climbing over the dunes onto the beach. I knew a place where a sandbar[5] often formed, and Mom and I sometimes went there. When I was little, she'd put me in the sloop behind the sandbar, like at a wading pool at a regular Holiday Inn. As I got older, we'd go there on lazy days and take a picnic lunch and sift through the coquina of the sandbar. We've found about four trophies there. Not about, exactly four. Of the four, the first one was the most fun because it was the one we found by accident.

I felt if I could get out of the house and head north, I could escape President Bob and dig up some trophies that would make him flip.

But I didn't escape. When I came downstairs after changing my clothes, there he was sitting on the wicker sofa, his blueberry ripple legs crossed in front of him. He was leafing through my math book.

I told him hello.

He smiled at me. "Yes, yes, yes," he said, "I know exactly how it is to have to sit in school all day and have to hold your water. I am quite used to the habits of young men. I was president of a liberal arts college in Michigan." He noticed that I was wearing my cut-offs, my usual beachcombing outfit, so he slapped his thighs and set them to shimmying like two pots of vanilla yogurt. "I see you're ready. Let's get going. The tide's halfway out already, and as they say, 'Time and tide wait for no man.' Tide was better a few hours ago. I found a couple of real beauties. Locked them in the glove compartment of my car."

---

[5]**sandbar:** a place where sand builds up because of ocean tides and currents.

I walked with him to the beach, and we began our hunt. He wasn't bending over for falsies very much any more. Each time he bent over, he yelled, "Got one!" and then he'd hold it up in the air and wouldn't put it in his bag until I nodded or said something or both. President Bob ended up with about twenty teeth, one vertebra bone, and of the twenty, one was a real trophy, an inch long, heavy root and the whole edge serrated with nothing worn away. A real trophy.

I found eight. Three of them were medium, four of them were itty-bitty and one had the tip crushed off.

I got up early the next day and checked the tide; it was just starting out. Good, I thought. I crossed the road and ran out onto the beach, rolling up my pajama bottoms as I walked along. The tide was just right; it was leaving long saw-tooth edges of coquina, and I managed to collect eight decent-sized teeth and one right-good-sized one before I ran back home and hosed off my feet and got dressed for school. I stuffed my collection into the pockets of my cut-offs. I had to skip breakfast, a fact that didn't particularly annoy me until about eleven o'clock. That afternoon, for every two times President Bob stooped down and yelled, "Got one!" I did it three times.

On Friday I didn't want to skip breakfast again, and my mother for sure didn't want me to, so President Bob was way ahead.

On Saturday I got up before dawn and dressed and sat on our dock until I saw the first thin line of dawn. Dawn coming over the intracoastal is like watching someone draw up a Venetian blind. On a clear day the sky lifts slowly and evenly, and it makes a guy feel more than okay to see it happen. But on that Saturday, I sat on the dock just long enough to make sure that daylight was to the east of me before I crossed the highway and began heading north. Shoot! I think that if the Lord had done some skywriting that morning, I wouldn't have taken the time to read it, even if it was in English.

Finally, I climbed to the top of a tall dune and walked up one and down another. I was heading for a place between the dunes about a mile to the north. I knew that during spring, when the moon was new, there was a tidewater[6] between two of the dunes. Sharks' teeth got trapped in it, and sometimes Mom and I would go there if there was a special size she was looking for to finish an arrangement. You had to dig down into the coquina, and it wasn't much fun finding sharks' teeth this way instead of sauntering along the beach and happening to find them. But sometimes it was necessary.

I dug.

I dug and I dug and I dug.

I put all my findings into a clam shell that I found, and I dug, and I dug, and I dug. I felt the sun hot on my back, and I still dug. I had my back to the ocean and my face to the ground and for all I knew there was no sky and no sea and no sand and no colors. There was nothing, nothing and nothing except black, and that black was the black of fossil teeth.

I had filled the clam shell before I stopped digging. I sorted the teeth and put the best ones — there were fourteen of them — in my right side pocket — the one with a button — and I put all the smaller ones in my back pocket and started back toward home, walking along the strand.[7] I figured that I had a good head start on the day and on President Bob. I would pepper my regular findings with the ones I had just dug up. I'd mix the little ones in with the fourteen big ones. But, I decided, smiling to myself, I'd have a run of about eight big ones in a row just to see what he would do.

My back felt that it was near to burning up, and I looked toward the ocean, and it looked powerful good. The morning ocean in the spring can be as blue as the phony color they paint it on a geography book map. Sometimes there are dark patches in it, and the gulls sweep down on top of the dark spots. I decided that I needed to take a dip in that ocean. I half expected a cloud of steam to rise up off my back. I forgot about time and tide and sharks' teeth and ducked under the waves and licked the salt off my lips as I came back up.

---

[6]**tidewater:** water that floods land when the tide rises.
[7]**strand:** a beach.

I was feeling pretty good, ready to face President Bob and the world, and then I checked my pockets and found that about half the supply from my back pocket had tumbled out, and I had lost two big ones. I was pretty upset about that, so I slowed down on my walk back home. I crouched down and picked up shell pieces, something I thought that I had outgrown, but that is about how anxious I was not to let anything get by me. I found a couple of medium-sized ones and put them in my back pocket and began a more normal walk when my trained eye saw a small tooth right at the tide line.

I reached down to pick it up, figuring that, if nothing else, it would add bulk to my collection the way they add cereal to hot dog meat. I didn't have any idea how many baby teeth I had lost out of my back pocket.

When I reached down to pick up that little tooth, it didn't come up immediately, and I began to think that maybe it was the tip of a really big one. I stooped down and carefully scraped away the wet sand and saw that there were several teeth together. The tide was rushing back up to where I was, so I laid my hand flat down on the ground and shoveled up a whole fistful of wet, cool sand.

I walked back to the dune and gently scraped away the sand with the forefinger of my other hand, and then I saw what I had.

There were several teeth, and they were attached to a piece of bone, a piece of jaw bone. There was a space between the third tooth and the fourth, and the smallest tooth, the one on the end that I had first seen, was attached to the jaw bone by only a thin edge.

I had never seen such a trophy. I felt that the spirit of the Lord had come mightily upon me, like Samson. Except that I had the jawbone of a shark and not the jawbone of an ass. And I wanted to smite only one president, not a thousand Philistines.

I didn't run the rest of the way home. I was too careful for that. I walked, holding that trophy in my hand, making certain that it didn't dry out before I could see if the weak tooth was fossilized onto the bone.

I called to Mom when I came into the house and when she appeared at the door to the screened porch, I uncurled my fingers one by one until the whole bone and all four of the teeth were showing. I watched Mom's face, and it was like watching the dawn I had missed.

"Ah, Ned," she said, "it is the Nobel Prize of trophies." We walked into the kitchen. She wet a good wad of paper towels and lifted the jawbone carefully from my hand and put it down on that pad of paper. And then we sat down at the kitchen table and I told her about how I found it, and I told it all to her in detail. Dad came in and Mom asked me to tell him, and I did and she listened just as hard the second time.

We ate our breakfast, and afterwards, we wet the paper towels again and moved the trophy onto a plastic placemat on the kitchen table. Mom looked at it through the magnifying glass and then handed me the glass so that I could look at it, too.

While we were studying it hard like that, President Bob came to the screen door and said, "Knock, knock."

Mom nodded at me, her way of letting me know that I was supposed to invite him on in.

"Well, well," he said. "Are we ready for today's treasure hunt?"

"I guess so," I said, as easy as you please, moving a little to the left so that he could catch a glimpse of what Mom and I were looking at.

He gave it a glance and then another one right quick.

Mom and I looked at each other as he came closer and closer to the table. He studied that trophy from his full height and from behind a chair. Next thing, he moved in front of the chair. And next after that he sat down in the chair. And then, not taking his eyes off that trophy, he held his hand out for the magnifying glass and Mom took it from me and gave it to him.

The whole time he did this, I watched his face. His eyes squinched up and his jaw dropped open and his nostrils flared. It was like watching a mini-movie called *Jealousy and Greed*.

I could feel myself smiling. "Found it this morning," I said.

Then I didn't say anything anymore. And I stopped smiling.

I thought about his face, and that made me think about mine. If his face was a movie called *Jealousy and Greed*, I didn't like the words I could put to mine.

I gently pushed the placemat closer to President Bob. "Look at it," I said. "Look at it good." I waited until his eyes were level with mine. "It's for you," I said. "It's a present from me."

"Why, thank you, boy," he said.

"Name's Ned," I answered, as I walked around to the other side of the table and emptied my pockets. "Do you think we can make something pretty out of these?" I asked Mom.

She gave me a Nobel Prize of a smile for an answer. President Bob didn't even notice, he was so busy examining the jawbone with which he had been smitten.

Thinking and Discussing

Why does Ned give President Bob the trophy at the end of the story? How have Ned and President Bob changed? Explain your answers.

In what ways does the dialogue show a lack of communication between Ned and President Bob?

Choosing a Creative Response

Re-creating Dialogue Think about what makes the written dialogue sound like real spoken language in "On Shark's Tooth Beach." Now try to recall a recent conversation that was important to you, and re-create a part of the dialogue. Write down the actual words that you think were spoken. Read your complete dialogue aloud to make sure it sounds real.

Creating Your Own Activity Plan and complete your own activity in response to "On Shark's Tooth Beach."

Thinking and Writing

Create a diary entry that President Bob might write after Ned gives him the trophy. Be sure to capture President Bob's personality in your writing.

Thinking About Realism

Expressing Another Point of View Retell a scene from any of the stories in this section from the point of view of a character other than the narrator. For example, you may want to retell a scene from *Platero and I* from Platero's point of view, or "On Shark's Tooth Beach" from President Bob's point of view. In a storytelling session, share your scene with your group.

Reviewing a Book Brief comments sometimes appear on the back cover of a book. These comments often include a reviewer's opinions of the book.

Be a reviewer, and write brief comments that recommend each of the stories you have just read. Exchange your comments with your classmates and see which stories seem to be the class favorites.

Discussing Insights In what ways do the authors of several selections show that they have gained insight into events they recall from the past? In what ways do characters in other selections have insights? Give examples from each story. Discuss your ideas with the class.

About the Authors

Maya Angelou was born in 1928 in St. Louis, Missouri, but was raised mainly in Stamps, Arkansas, and San Francisco, California. In 1954 and 1955, she was a cast member in the touring company of *Porgy and Bess,* which traveled through twenty-two countries. In the following years she developed careers as a singer, a songwriter, an actress, a playwright, a civil-rights activist and lecturer, and an author. Her works include four collections of poetry and five autobiographical works, the first of which is *I Know Why the Caged Bird Sings.*

Gloria Gonzalez was born in New York City in 1940. She started her writing career as an investigative reporter for various New Jersey newspapers but is now best known as a playwright whose plays have been produced off Broadway, on television, in California, and in Europe. Among her best-known dramas are *Curtains, Love Is a Tuna Casserole, Waiting Room,* and *Gaucho.* Gonzalez has also written several works for teenagers, among them *A Deadly Rhyme* and *The Glad Man.* She currently lives in New Jersey.

Langston Hughes was born in 1902 in Joplin, Missouri, and attended Columbia University. He held various odd jobs before publishing his first book of poetry, *The Weary Blues,* in 1926, and later *The Dream Keeper* in 1932. Hughes was the best-known writer of the "Harlem Renaissance," a period during the 1920's when many black writers produced innovative work. Hughes experimented with using blues and jazz rhythms in his poetry. Hughes also wrote plays, short stories, autobiographical works, and humorous sketches, all focusing on the experiences of black Americans.

Juan Ramón Jiménez was born in Moguer, Spain, in 1881. He was best known for his poetry, which he began to write before his eighteenth birthday. In the first years of the twentieth century, Jiménez began work on his best-known piece of prose, *Platero and I,* which was not published until 1917. Jiménez won the Nobel Prize for Literature in 1956. He died in 1958.

E. L. Konigsburg was born in New York City in 1930. Before becoming a writer and illustrator, she taught chemistry. Later Konigsburg began to attend art classes. When her own children entered school, she started to write. Konigsburg's first book, *Jennifer, Hecate, Macbeth, William McKinley and Me, Elizabeth,* was the Newbery runner-up in 1968. Her second book, *From the Mixed-Up Files of Mrs. Basil E. Frankweiler,* won the Newbery Medal in the same year. She has also published two collections of short stories, *Altogether, One at a Time* and *Throwing Shadows.*

Gloria D. Miklowitz was born in New York City in 1927. She began her career as an author by writing documentary films on rockets and torpedoes for the U.S. Navy. She has twice won the Outstanding Science Books for Children award, for *Earthquake!* and *Save That Raccoon!* Her book *Did You Hear What Happened to Andrea?* won the Australian Young Reader's Trophy in 1984, and was made into a television drama that won five Emmy Awards. Miklowitz currently lives in California, where she teaches writing at Pasadena City College.

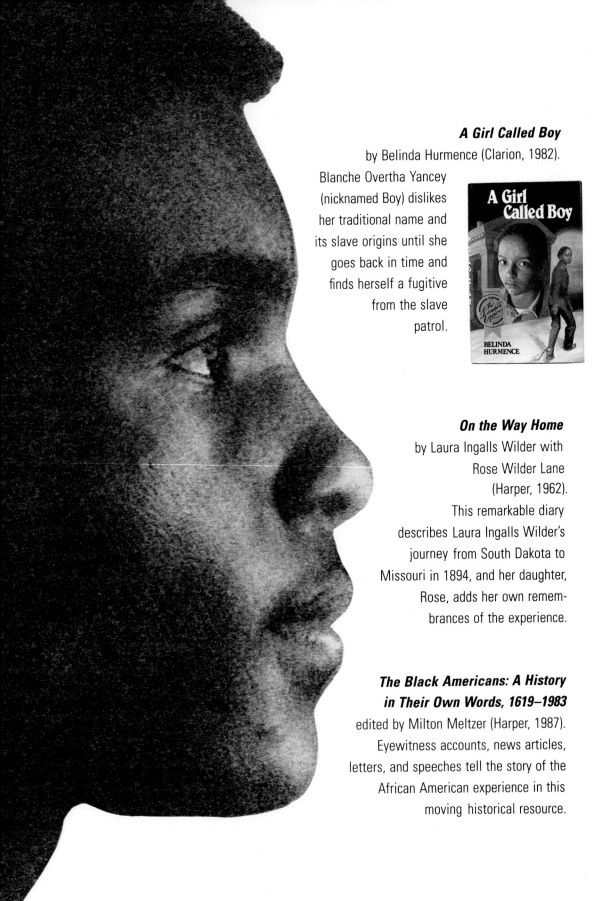

A Girl Called Boy

by Belinda Hurmence (Clarion, 1982).
Blanche Overtha Yancey
(nicknamed Boy) dislikes
her traditional name and
its slave origins until she
goes back in time and
finds herself a fugitive
from the slave
patrol.

On the Way Home

by Laura Ingalls Wilder with
Rose Wilder Lane
(Harper, 1962).
This remarkable diary
describes Laura Ingalls Wilder's
journey from South Dakota to
Missouri in 1894, and her daughter,
Rose, adds her own remem-
brances of the experience.

The Black Americans: A History in Their Own Words, 1619–1983

edited by Milton Meltzer (Harper, 1987).
Eyewitness accounts, news articles,
letters, and speeches tell the story of the
African American experience in this
moving historical resource.

Changing:
Six Stories
About Growing Up
(Houghton, 1993).
Short stories by several well-known authors bring to life the experiences of young people from different cultural traditions.

So Far from the Bamboo Grove by Yoko Kawashima Watkins (Lothrop, 1986). In this spellbinding true account of World War II, eleven-year-old Yoko and her Japanese family flee the Communists in North Korea and escape to war-torn Japan. Along the way, they experience terrible cruelties and life-threatening situations.

Sixteen: Short Stories by Outstanding Writers for Young Adults edited by Donald R. Gallo (Delacorte, 1984; Dell, 1985). Sixteen original stories explore themes of love and hate, life and death, and joy and despair by authors such as Joan Aiken, Robert Cormier, Rosa Guy, Norma Fox Mazer, and Richard Peck.

FURTHER INSIGHTS

SCIENCE

Seeing the *Light*

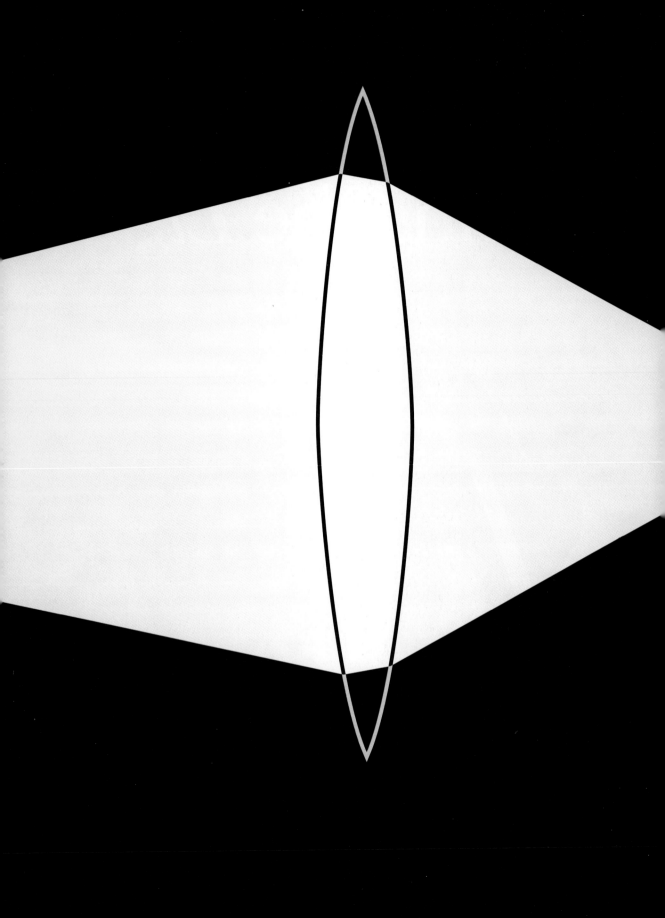

Contents

The Nature of Light

from a science textbook

Focus: What is light made up of, and how does it behave?

Vocabulary: radiant energy, bioluminescence, opaque, reflect, transparent, refract, translucent, photon, frequency, prism, virtual image, real image, focus, lens, retina

Light — you probably take it for granted. Yet without light, your eyes could not "see." Mirrors and lenses would not work. Televisions and video cameras would be useless. Nothing could grow, and Earth would be a dark, lifeless place. Fortunately though, we do have light. Where does it come from?

The sun is by far our most important source of natural light. Each second, atomic reactions on the sun's surface change some four million tons of matter into energy. This energy radiates into space in all directions in the form of heat and light. About eight minutes after leaving the sun, some of this **radiant energy** falls upon Earth. Perhaps even now that light is shining into your room.

Other sources of natural light also exist. Stars produce their own light, but they are so far from Earth that their light seems quite faint.

illustrated by Kimberly Britt and Steve Van Gelder

Fireflies, fish, and other specialized plants and animals generate a mysterious light called **bioluminescence** (bī′ō lōō′mə **nĕs′**əns). Chemical reactions take place in their cells, producing light on a very small scale.

Sunlight is not always present, however, so people have created artificial light sources. Long ago campfires and torches were used. Then came candles, oil lamps, and gaslights. Now electric bulbs, fluorescent tubes, and lasers produce light.

Whatever its source — the sun, a fish, a laser — light behaves in predictable ways. As part of the natural world, light follows certain universal rules. What are those rules? Why does light behave the way it does? In this chapter you will learn more about the nature of light.

Properties of Light

What exactly do you know about light? Perhaps more than you realize. For instance, think of what happens when you enter a dark room and turn on a lamp. Instantly there is light. The light travels from the light bulb to all parts of the room almost instantaneously. This is because light travels at a tremendous speed. In fact, light travels from Earth to the moon and back again in about 2.5 seconds.

Take off the lamp shade. The light from the bulb falls brightly on the furniture, the walls, the ceiling, and everywhere in the room. This is because light radiates, or spreads out in all directions, from its source.

Hold an apple near the electric bulb. The apple and the hand holding it create shadows by blocking some of the light. This is because light travels in a straight path unless something changes its course.

What happens when light strikes the surface of something — the apple for instance? The apple is **opaque** (ō **pāk′**) — it does not allow light to pass through it. Instead, some of the light is absorbed by the atoms of the apple. Some light is **reflected,** bouncing off the apple back into the room. When the reflected light enters your eye, it creates an image that your brain interprets as an apple. Likewise, light reflected from other objects in the room enables you to see them as well.

Not all materials are opaque, however. Glass, plastic, water, and other **transparent** substances allow light to pass right through them. Little if any light is reflected. Instead the light is **refracted,** or bent. The light changes direction as it passes from one substance into another. Frosted glass, clouds, and other **translucent** materials scatter the light that passes through them. The different amounts of light that are absorbed, reflected, and refracted by an object give it its unique appearance and color.

What Light Is

For centuries scientists have performed careful experiments, hoping to learn more about what light really is. Two theories grew out of these observations. One stated that light is made up of waves. The other stated that light is made up of tiny particles. Scientists hotly debated the merits of each theory, but further testing revealed that neither theory fully explained everything scientists had observed about light.

Recent research supports a newer theory that light is made up of *both* particles and waves. Atoms within a light source release streams of particles called **photons** (fō′tŏnz′), tiny energy packets. These photons shoot away from their source, spreading out in all directions. Each photon is surrounded by both an electric and a magnetic field. As photons move, their paths can be traced by the changing patterns in the electromagnetic fields around them. These changes are known as electromagnetic waves.

Visible light is just one type of electromagnetic wave. Others include x-rays, microwaves, ultraviolet light, and radio waves. All electromagnetic waves have differing wavelengths, which are measured from the top of one wave to the top of the next. Wavelengths vary for each type of wave. Certain radio waves are extremely long, having a single wavelength of several miles. About 50,000 or more light waves can be packed into an inch; gamma rays have even shorter wavelengths. Electromagnetic waves also have different **frequencies,** or the number of waves that pass the same point each second. Finally, all electromagnetic waves travel at the same speed — over 186,000 miles per second — the speed of light.

Color

You see specific wavelengths of electromagnetic waves as visible light. Examine this "white" light with the right tools, though, and you will discover that light is really a band of continuous colors — the entire color spectrum. Each color is produced by a light wave of a certain length and frequency. Violet has the shortest wavelength; red has the longest. A light source usually produces white light because the separate wavelengths of each color reach your eyes at the same time and blend together.

You can see the color spectrum within light by using sunlight and a **prism (prĭz′əm)**, a three-sided piece of glass or plastic. As the light passes into the prism, it refracts, or bends. The light refracts again as it passes from the glass into the air. Each wavelength of color travels through the glass at a different speed, so its path is bent at a different angle. The shape of the prism allows some colors to travel very short distances through the glass, while others must go farther. This separates the colors even more. As the light moves out of the prism, the colors "fan out" to form a color spectrum.

Different wavelengths of light also produce the colors of the world around you. When light waves strike the surface of a ripe apple, for example, all of them are absorbed except the red ones. The red waves reflect from the apple into your eye, causing you to see a red apple. A green leaf reflects mostly green light waves and absorbs the rest. The kinds of light waves that are reflected from an object determine its color.

More on Reflection

Objects have many different surfaces, so they reflect light differently. If light hits a brick wall or another rough, irregular surface, it scatters in many different directions. However, if light hits a smooth, flat surface such as water or a mirror, it bounces away in one direction, producing a sharp image.

198

When you stand in front of a mirror, you can see your "reflection." What do you notice about this image? If you are wearing a ring on your right hand, it appears to be on your left hand; in fact, your entire body seems to be reversed. Also, your image appears to be as far behind the mirror as you are in front of it. This is due to another property of light. When light strikes a surface at a certain angle, it bounces away from the surface at an equal angle. This means that light from your right side

Experiment 1: Making a prism

Follow these steps to make a simple prism and refract sunlight into the colors of the spectrum.

You will need:
water
a small mirror
bowl into which the mirror fits
sunlight
a sheet of white paper

1. Prop the mirror against the side of the bowl.
2. Add water to cover about three-fourths of the mirror.
3. Place the bowl "prism" in direct sunlight.
4. Hold the paper where sunlight reflects off the mirror. If necessary, adjust the angle of the mirror until the color spectrum appears. (*DO NOT* look directly at the sunlight reflected by the mirror as this could be harmful to your eyes.) **What happens? Why does it happen?**

After completing this experiment, you may wish to write a short report describing what you did and what you observed. You may want to include a diagram of the experiment in your report.

strikes the mirror and bounces away in the opposite direction. You see a reversed version of yourself! Your eyes do not see how the light bounces; instead, your eyes are fooled into thinking that your image is located straight in front of you — behind the mirror. To your eye, light appears to come from one place when it really comes from another. You see a **virtual image.** (See Figure 1.)

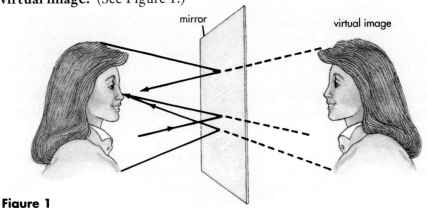

Figure 1
Light rays from the observer strike the mirror and are reflected to the observer's eyes. To the observer, the light rays appear to be coming from behind the mirror. The observer is seeing a virtual image.

Experiment 2: Using water to refract light

See how refraction causes the "magic coin" to appear and disappear.

You will need:

bowl   water

coin   an assistant

1. Place the coin inside the bowl. Place the bowl at the edge of a desk.
2. Move your head lower until the coin just disappears from sight, hidden by the lip of the bowl.
3. Stay in that position as an assistant carefully pours water into the bowl. **What happens? Why does it happen?**

After completing this experiment, you may wish to write a report describing what you did and what you observed. You may want to include a diagram of your experiment in your report.

Many shiny objects produce virtual images, but only a few create a **real image**, a picture of an object that can be viewed on a screen. To produce such an image, find a large, shiny spoon and look into its bowl. Can you see yourself? Notice that your image is upside down. How can this be?

The surface of the spoon curves inward, forming a curved mirror. This curved shape reflects the light waves so that eventually they all **focus,** or come together at, a single point. As the waves continue in straight paths past the focal point, they produce an upside-down image that can be viewed on a piece of paper or a screen. (See Figure 2.) To produce a real image, then, light from an object must pass through a focal point.

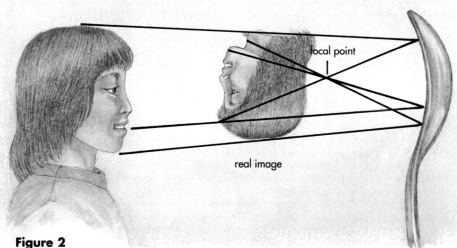

Figure 2
Light rays from the observer's face strike the bowl of the spoon and are reflected so they meet at the focal point. A real image of the observer is formed in front of the reflecting surface.

More on Refraction

Why is light refracted as it travels from air into a transparent substance? Picture light as a car traveling along a highway. If it comes to heavy traffic, it must slow down. When light waves pass into a substance with atoms that are packed closer together (heavy traffic), the waves are slowed down, causing them to bend and change direction. For instance, light slows down to about 140,000 miles per second as it passes through water. It slows even more as it travels through glass. Light speeds up again when it leaves those substances — traffic is much lighter.

The property of refraction explains why a fish appears to be in a different spot from where it actually swims in the water. Waves of light reflected from the fish change direction as they move from the water into the air. Your eyes and brain assume, however, that the reflected light took a straight path, so the fish appears to be in a different place. (See Figure 3.)

Many interesting natural phenomena are caused by light refraction. When sunlight is refracted by thousands of raindrop "prisms," a rainbow appears. As starlight travels through different layers of warm and cold air in the atmosphere, it is refracted. The light seems to "twinkle." Sometimes light reflected from the sky hits a layer of hot air near the Earth's surface. This light is refracted in such a way that the waves reaching your eyes make you think you see puddles of water. You are only seeing a mirage.

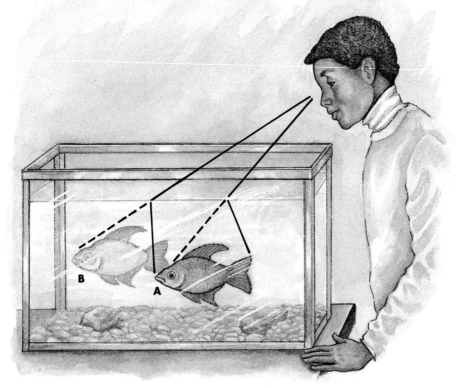

Figure 3
Light rays from the fish are refracted as they pass from water into the air. To the observer, the light rays appear to come from position B, although the fish is actually located at position A.

Lenses

Knowledge about light reflection and refraction is important to scientists. They use this information to design bigger and better telescopes, microscopes, binoculars, cameras, lasers, and other optical tools. These tools enable scientists to control light and make it work for them.

A curved piece of glass, plastic, or other transparent material called a **lens** is an important component in many optical tools. A lens refracts light. The curve of the lens and its thickness affect how much the direction of light is changed.

There are two main types of lens. One type, the concave lens, causes light to spread out. Notice that the concave lens is thinner in the center than at the outer edges. (See Figure 4.) The other type, the convex lens, refracts light waves inward, making them come together at a focal point. Convex lenses, then, can form real images. For this reason they are used in tools that enable you to view images — slide and movie projectors and cameras, for instance. The lenses in your eyes are also convex lenses.

A galaxy seen through a telescope

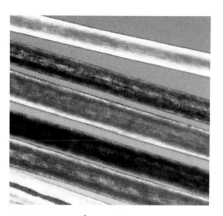

Hair seen under a microscope

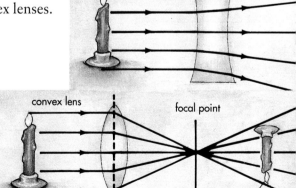

Figure 4
Light rays passing through the concave lens are refracted and spread outward. Light rays passing through a convex lens are refracted to meet at the focal point and form a real image.

To get a clear, sharp image with a camera, a microscope, or a projector, you must bring it into "focus." As you make the image clearer, you are really changing the focal length, the distance between the lens and the focal point. The shorter the focal length, the smaller the size of the image.

In order for you to see, the lenses in your eyes must focus an image onto the **retina** (rĕt′n ə) at the back of your eye. Tiny rods in the retina pick up messages about light and send them to the brain, where the messages are interpreted. Special eye muscles can change the shape of the lens in each eye; this changes the focal length. Your eyes constantly adjust so that a clear, sharp image forms on the retina.

Sometimes the lenses in people's eyes cannot focus images properly, resulting in poor, blurred vision. Eyeglass lenses correct this problem. They refract light so that the focal length of the eye is changed. A sharp image forms on the retina once more.

Lenses have any number of uses. Microscopes and magnifying glasses refract light to make images larger than the objects magnified. Some telescopes have one or more lenses that gather light, making distant stars appear brighter and closer. Such telescopes — and many other optical tools — combine several lenses, as well as mirrors and prisms, to control light and provide us with information that our eyes alone cannot give us.

Review Questions

1. What does recent research suggest that light is made up of?
2. What causes different colors of light?
3. What is the difference between reflection and refraction?

Responding to *The Nature of Light*

Thinking and Discussing

Scientists look for general rules that govern or describe the way things happen in nature. "The Nature of Light" includes many general rules or statements about the behavior of light. Find five or more such statements. What other kinds of information does this text include?

How does the concept of refraction help to explain events in nature such as rainbows and twinkling starlight?

Scientific knowledge about light has led to many useful tools and inventions. What are some tools or inventions mentioned in the text? What scientific knowledge do they depend on?

Applying Science Concepts

Imagine that you are a scientist working with a group to prove that light travels much faster than sound. What observations from your everyday experience can you think of that would support that conclusion? What, for example, do you notice about light and sound during a thunderstorm, or when you see an approaching fire engine or emergency vehicle? Summarize your group's observations, and plan an experiment that would add further evidence. Prepare your group's findings for publication in a scientific journal.

Research the history of experimental attempts to measure the speed of light. Important experiments in this area were performed by Galileo Galilei, Olaus Roemer, Jean Bernard Foucault, and Albert Michelson. You may want to research the work of one of these scientists, or you may want to trace how all of their experiments led to increasingly accurate measures of the speed of light. Summarize your research in a written or oral report.

Writing an Evaluation

Have you ever wondered why eyeglasses improve poor vision, why rainbows appear on rainy days, or why your eyes sometimes play tricks on you? Did you ever think that all these things were connected to the properties of light and the way humans see?

The study of light and color is complicated and has many different aspects. In *Seeing the Light*, you will read what different experts have to say about their understanding of the nature of light, color, and sight. As you read these selections, you should evaluate them — or decide how good each one is. Then choose the article that you find the most informative, and write your evaluation of it.

An evaluation should include a statement of opinion and supporting evidence. It should present a convincing argument. If the articles give you a different writing idea, try that one instead. Begin when you are ready to argue scientifically.

1. Prewrite Before you begin writing, decide which article you find most informative. Your evaluation will be most convincing if you choose an article about which you have strong feelings. You may wish to gather evidence to support your opinion by identifying the specific strengths of the article you have chosen and by comparing your article to others on the same subject.

2. Write a First Draft Think of your audience and purpose for writing as you write your evaluation. State your opinion clearly. Defend your position by using logical arguments. Persuade your readers.

3. Revise Read your evaluation to make sure that you have

presented a convincing line of reasoning.

- Have you presented your case clearly?
- Have you given good reasons that justify your arguments?
- Do you have a strong conclusion that leaves a lasting impression on your readers?

Ask a partner to look at your evaluation critically and point out any faulty logic.

4. *Proofread* Check your evaluation for correct spelling, capitalization, and punctuation. Your arguments will be strengthened by precise language.

5. *Publish* Make a neat copy of your evaluation. You may wish to share it as a newspaper review, as a critical essay in a science journal, or as a report to fellow scientists.

COLORS AND WAVES

**from *How Did We Find Out About Microwaves?*
by Isaac Asimov**

In 1665, a twenty-three year old English scientist, Isaac Newton (1642–1727), was playing with light.

He pulled all the curtains shut in his room, on a sunny day, so that it was quite dim. Through a little chink cut out of a curtain, a narrow beam of sunlight shone into the room.

Newton allowed this beam of sunlight to pass through a triangular piece of glass called a *prism*. The light beam bent in its path as it went through the prism. The beam was *refracted*.

The light came out of the prism traveling in a slightly different direction than it went in and shone on the wall behind. If the prism had not been in its path, the beam would just have made a white round spot on the wall. But the prism *was* there, and the beam of light had spread out and formed a rainbow. At one end the light was red. As one's eye passed along the band of light, it turned, little by little, orange, then yellow, then green, then blue, and, finally, at the other end, the light was violet.

You can see colors all around you, but usually they're part of solid objects. You can feel them. The colors on the wall that Newton had produced, however, could not be felt. They were in the light itself, not in anything solid. Your hand could have gone through the colored light as though it had been a ghost. In fact, Newton called the band of colored light a *spectrum*, the Latin word for ghost.

illustrated by Mark Summers and Marcel Durocher

Isaac Newton

Where did the colors come from? Newton felt that what our eyes see as white light is actually a mixture of colors. When white light passes through a prism and is refracted, the different colors are refracted by different amounts. The red light is refracted least, the violet light is refracted most, and the others are refracted by amounts in between. That separates the colors and spreads them along a strip instead of placing them together in a small circle.

To see if this was so, Newton let the light pass through the prism, and then, before it could reach the wall, he let it pass through a second prism with the point of the triangle facing the opposite way from that of

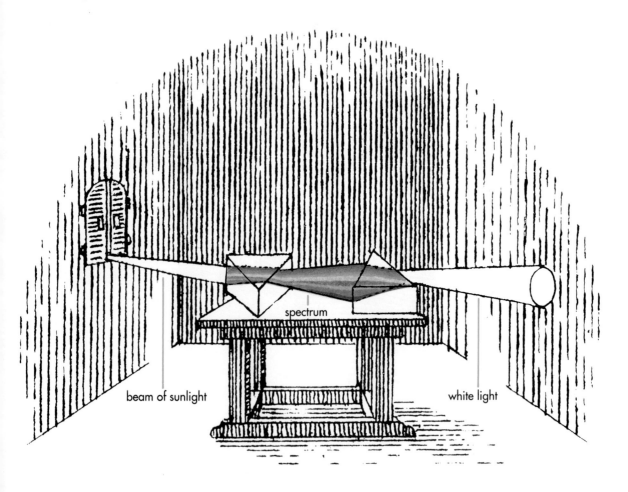

beam of sunlight   white light

spectrum

Newton's experiment with prisms

the first prism. The light had been bent one way when it went through the first prism, but now it bent the opposite way when it went through the second prism. The colors separated as they went through the first prism and they came together again as they went through the second prism.

When the light had passed through *both* prisms, what appeared on the wall was just a circle of white light. To Newton, this was proof that the colors, mixed together, added up to white.

But why should there be different colors of light? Why should they bend by different amounts in passing through a prism?

To answer that question it might help to know what light is made up of, but no one in Newton's time could be sure. Still, there were two possibilities.

It was possible that light might consist of a stream of very tiny particles, all moving very quickly in a straight line. It was also possible that light might consist of a stream of very small waves, all moving very quickly in a straight line.

Scientists were familiar with the way bullets traveled in a straight line over short distances. They were also familiar with sounds that consisted of waves in the air. They could also see the waves move across the surface of a still pond if they dropped a pebble into it.

One thing was very noticeable about waves, though. They could bend around obstacles. You can watch water waves do it. You know too that you can hear someone around a corner, so the sound waves must bend around that corner.

On the other hand, bullets don't bend around a corner, and light doesn't either. If someone is around the corner, you can't see him. Light moves right past the edge of an obstacle, still going straight.

For this reason, Newton thought light had to consist of a stream of small, moving particles and *not* of waves.

Not everyone agreed with him. There was a Dutch scientist, Christian Huygens (**hī′**gənz, 1629–1695), who thought light consisted of waves. He argued that small waves didn't bend around obstacles as easily as long waves did. If light consisted of *very* small waves, it would hardly bend around obstacles at all.

Most scientists, it turned out, sided with Newton because, as time went on, people realized he was a very great scientist. In fact, scientists today almost all agree that he was the greatest scientist who ever lived.

Christian Huygens

Still, even the greatest scientist can be wrong sometimes.

The person who settled the matter was a British scientist, Thomas Young (1773–1829). He was a man who was learned in all sorts of ways.

He was a doctor, to begin with. Then, too, he wrote articles for *The Encyclopedia Britannica* on all sorts of subjects. He was even the first person to begin to work out the meaning of the ancient Egyptian writing. Despite all that, he is best remembered for his experiments with light.

Young had studied sound, and he knew that when two sound waves intersected, or crossed paths, one would sometimes cancel out the other. In one sound wave, the air carrying the wave might be moving in just as air was going out in the other wave. In the combination, the air wouldn't move in either direction, and there would be silence. If the sound waves were of different lengths, the longer wave would overtake the shorter and, for a while, the air would move in and out at the same time in both waves. The sound would then be louder than normal. Then the two sound waves would fall out of step into silence again, and so on.

The result is that when two sound waves meet you might hear silence, then sound, then silence, then sound. These are called *beats* and they can be unpleasant to the ear.

If light consisted of streams of particles, this couldn't happen. One particle couldn't cancel out another.

In 1801, Young experimented by sending a beam of light through two different narrow slits, one very close to the other. After the beams passed through the slits, they spread out slightly and, by the time they had reached the wall, the two beams had overlapped.

You would suppose that where two beams of light overlapped, there would just be that much more light so that the wall would be brighter than in places where the beams did not overlap.

Not at all. Where the two beams overlapped, there were alternating stripes of light and dark. The beams of light canceled out in spots and added to each other in spots. They did this alternately, just like beats in music.

When two beams of light cancel out, we say that they *interfere* with each other, or that there is *interference*. The stripes of light and dark are therefore called *interference fringes*.

That settled it. Huygens was right and Newton was wrong. Light consisted of tiny waves. What's more, from the width of the interference fringes, Young could calculate how long the wave might be. This is called the *wavelength*. It turned out that a wavelength of light is in the neighborhood of 1/50,000 of an inch. This means that if you had a beam of light 1 inch long, it would consist of about 50,000 waves, one after the other.

Not all light waves are the same length. Red light has the longest waves and violet light the shortest. The shorter the wavelength, the more the light is refracted. That is why a prism separates the colors.

The red light all the way at one end of the spectrum has a wavelength of 1/32,000 of an inch. The violet light at the other extreme end of the spectrum has a wavelength of 1/64,000 of an inch. The other colors have wavelengths in between, and they get shorter in the order in which the colors appear: red, orange, yellow, green, blue, indigo, and violet.

Responding to *Colors and Waves*

Thinking and Discussing

How did Newton and Huygens disagree in their ideas about light? How did Thomas Young's experiment settle the disagreement? How does the work of Newton, Huygens, and Young illustrate the process of scientific discovery?

"Colors and Waves" tells a story about scientists who investigated the nature of light. How is this different from the way the same topic is treated in "The Nature of Light"? How does the story add to your understanding of the topic?

Applying Science Concepts

Thomas Young lived more than one hundred years later than both Newton and Huygens. Even so, Young's work in some ways depended on the ideas of Newton and Huygens. If the three scientists could meet, what do you think Young might say to the two older scientists? How would he explain his discoveries, and what would be his attitude toward their earlier discoveries? Write the discussion that you think the three scientists might have. With classmates, you may want to act out your discussion for the class.

The Magic of Color

by Hilda Simon

How would you describe color? It has no body or substance, so you cannot feel it with your fingers the way you can feel wood or stone or cloth and know what it is without even looking. You cannot smell or taste color, either. You can only *see* color, and when it gets dark, you cannot even do that anymore, because color disappears in the dark.

What, then, *is* color?

Until three hundred years ago, people thought that color was part of an object. That belief still lives on in our language when we say that a flower *is* red or a leaf green, instead of saying that it *looks* red or green. But in 1666, the famous English scientist Sir Isaac Newton discovered that white light is made up of many different colors, and that the colors we see are just portions of that light thrown back, or *reflected*, by the various objects. To prove it, he sent a beam of white light through a three-sided piece of glass called a *prism*. As if by magic, the thin beam of white light entering the glass on one side came out on the other as a wide band of colors ranging from red to violet. This band is called the *spectrum*.

Separating white light into the color band of the spectrum is possible because all light travels in waves, and each color has a different wavelength. Red has the longest waves and violet the shortest, with the others graded in between. While traveling through air, the waves of all the colors are joined together. Combined, they are colorless, and we call this

illustrated by David Edmunds and Steve Van Gelder

"white" light. But when light travels through a prism, the combination is broken up because the shorter waves bend a different amount from the longer ones. The colors become separated. They move through the glass at different angles, and then fan out into the spectrum.

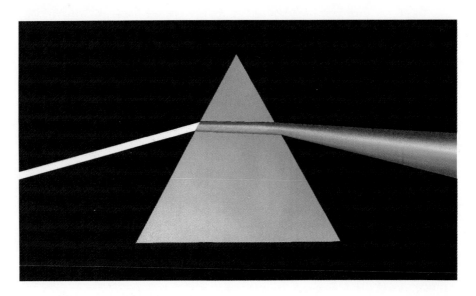

You may have never seen a light beam traveling through a prism to form the spectrum, but you probably have seen the colors of the spectrum outdoors after a rain shower, when the sun shines and forms a rainbow. The many fine water droplets in the air act as so many tiny prisms, and separate colorless sunlight into rainbow colors.

By testing portions of white light, scientists found that red, green, and violet-blue are the three basic, single colors of light; white light can be produced by combining beams of these three colors. The other colors

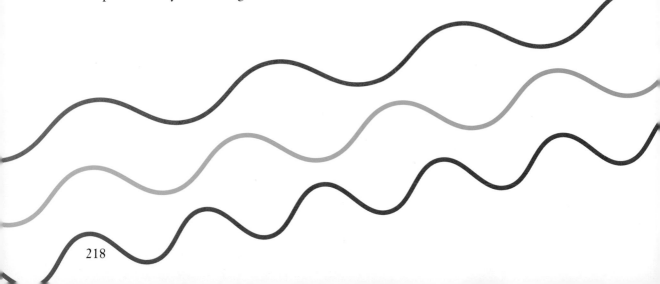

of the spectrum result from an overlap of any two of the three basic colors. Yellow, for instance, is a mixture of red and green, while blue is a combination of green and violet-blue. A third mixed color, which is not found in the spectrum, can be made by combining red and violet-blue light: this results in the pinkish red called magenta.

Below, the first set of interlocking circles of red, green, and violet-blue shows how these combinations work. Where any two circles overlap, they produce yellow, blue, and magenta. In the center, where all three overlap, you find white.

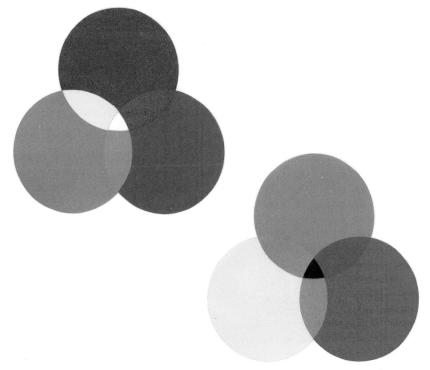

How are light and paint colors different?

Perhaps you have already noticed one interesting fact about the colors of light: They are very different from the colors of paint. If you try mixing red and green watercolors, you most certainly will not get yellow; instead, you get a dull brown. The same thing happens when you combine violet-blue with red or with green. Far from producing bright pinkish red or bright blue with such mixtures, you end up with dull, dark, blackish colors.

This proves that the basic colors of *light* are not the basic colors of *paint*. In fact, it is the *mixed* colors of light — yellow, blue, and magenta — that are the single colors of paint. By combining any two of them, you can produce the basic colors of light. Yellow and blue make green, yellow and magenta make red, and magenta and blue make violet-blue. The second set of interlocking circles shows how this works, and also shows that the mixture of all three basic paint colors produces black. From that, we can see that the basic colors of light are the exact opposites of the basic colors of paint.

Scientists named the basic colors "primary" colors, and the mixed colors "complementary" colors, because if you add any mixture of two basic colors to the third, it "completes" the full number of three colors needed to make white in light and black in paint. The row of illustrations on this page shows each primary color of light facing its complementary color; the row on the next page illustrates the primary and complementary colors of paint. As an example, take the primary color violet-blue in the first row; its complementary color is yellow because yellow is made up of red and green; adding yellow light to violet-blue light makes white

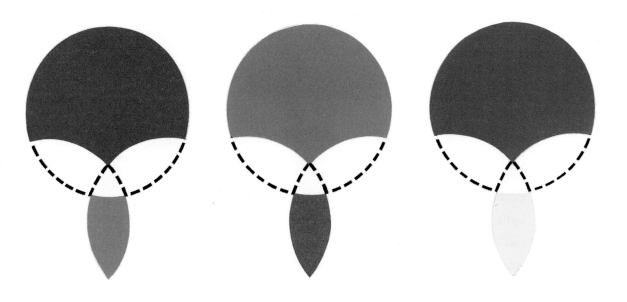

light. For paint, it is the other way around: The primary color is yellow and the complementary color violet-blue, because it contains magenta and blue and so produces black when added to yellow. Many of the most amazing and interesting tricks you can do with color are based upon this relationship between primary and complementary colors.

What happens when light is reflected and absorbed?

We already know that colors are nothing more than portions of white light reflected into our eyes by an object: A red ball reflects the red, long-wave portion of the light spectrum. But what else happens when white light falls upon an object that is painted red? If only the red light is reflected, how is the rest of the light made to disappear?

The red paint has a special ingredient called a "pigment," from the Latin word for paint. There are many, many different pigments — shades of red, yellow, green, purple, and brown as well as white and black. Pigments have the ability to reflect certain portions of white light and to absorb, or soak up, others. White pigment of course reflects all light, and black pigment absorbs it all. That is why white clothing is cooler than

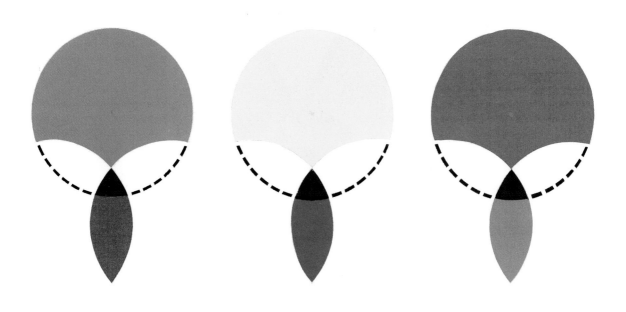

black clothing on a hot sunny day, for light is also heat. Red pigment soaks up all the green and blue light and sends back only the red light waves, so the object looks red. You might compare the reflected red light to a rubber ball thrown against a wooden fence, and the green and blue light to bullets shot into that fence. The rubber ball would bounce back to you, but the bullets would disappear into the wood and not come back.

Each pigment determines the exact kind and amount of light that is reflected. A light-colored pigment returns more light than a dark pigment. Thus a red pigment reflects only one third of white light, but a yellow pigment, which reflects both red and green, returns two thirds of white light. Orange is in between; it reflects red and some green.

Because pigments can return only certain portions of white light, the color of an object can be changed by changing the color of the light that falls on it. A red ball no longer looks red in green light; instead, it looks blackish. The red pigment absorbs the green light, and there is no light left over for the pigment to reflect. For the same reason, a green object will look black or dark gray in red light.

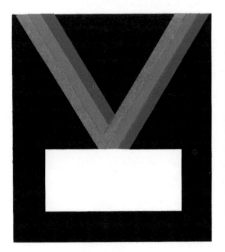 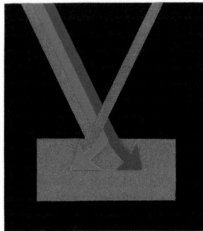 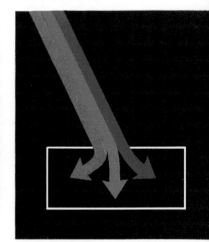

How do we see colors?

The action of the pigments alone would not be enough for us to see color if our eyes and brain, which are connected by the optic nerve, did not have the ability to register the light and "translate" certain wavelengths into the correct colors. After all, a red pigment is red — meaning that it reflects the red light waves — regardless of whether a human being or a dog looks at it. Yet the dog does not see it as red, because the dog does not have *color vision* — the ability to distinguish colors. This ability depends upon a very special combination: the eye's sending the message to the brain, by way of the optic nerve, and the brain's translation of the wavelengths into colors. If any of those parts do not function properly, we do not see the right colors. The most miraculous fact about the entire process is the speed with which it works. We see the color the moment we look at the colored object, yet the message has to get to the brain and be translated in order for us to do so. This means that our color vision provides us with an instant "color computer service" at all times during our waking hours.

Although we know that this happens, the exact way it works is still unknown. We hardly ever stop to think about it, but color vision is something very special, and not everyone has it. Some persons are at least partly "color-blind," meaning that they cannot see certain colors. A few lack *all* ability to distinguish colors; to them, everything appears as some shade of gray. This has nothing to do with good eyesight. Color-blind people can see shapes, outlines, and shadows just as well and as clearly as those with color vision: the picture is there but the colors are missing. Partial or total color-blindness is found in only one out of every thirty persons. Normally, however, all people have the ability to see and enjoy the many different colors that make our world so beautiful and interesting.

Animals such as birds, lizards, frogs, fish, and even insects are able to see bright colors much the way we do, and for most of them, color is important in their everyday life. That is not true of many other animals, including horses, dogs, and cattle, which seem to be more or less color-blind. To them, as to color-blind people, the world must look like a black-and-white movie. But the ability to distinguish colors would be of small value to such animals, for their senses of smell and hearing are more important in their lives than even ordinary good vision. For us, on the other hand, a keen nose and sharp ears are less important than good eyesight plus color vision.

What is an afterimage?

An afterimage is what you see if you look at an object or a picture for a little while and then close your eyes. Behind your eyelids, you see the same picture, only now it is very tiny and has different colors. This small colored picture is not imaginary. You actually see it, and you can make it appear — to your eyes only — on a piece of white paper. This kind of "color magic" works every time; try it out with the picture below.

The illustration shows a bright blue bird sitting among pinkish red leaves against a black background. Stare at the bird steadily for a full minute without taking your eyes off it. Center your gaze on the bird's white throat. When the minute is up, quickly close your eyes.

What do you see?

You now see a tiny red bird with a black throat — a cardinal — sitting among green leaves; the black background has turned light.

Repeat the test, and again look at the blue bird in the picture for a full minute, keeping your eyes on the throat. (A full minute, or sixty seconds, may seem like a long time when looking at one thing, but try not to make it less.) This time, do not close your eyes. Instead, quickly shift your gaze to a white piece of paper.

Suddenly, you will see the red bird among the green leaves, and it will be exactly the same size as the one in the picture above. Your eyes and brain have produced a perfect same-size afterimage!

Now look at the illustration of the flag. It has the pattern and design of the American flag, but the colors are very funny: The stars and half the stripes are black instead of white, the rest of the stripes are bright greenish blue, and the field is yellow. See what happens when you look at that peculiar flag for a minute and then close your eyes.

Against your eyelids, you see a small but perfect image of the American flag with all the right colors!

Try it again for a same-size image. Look at the printed flag, keeping your eyes on the lower right-hand star. Then shift your gaze to a blank white piece of paper — and there is the American flag, 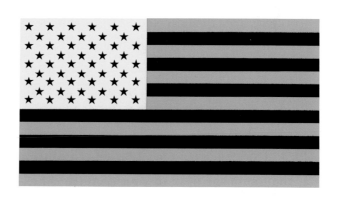 as big as the printed one but with all the colors exactly as they should be.

The afterimage colors are not simply different, but different in a very special way. In the flag, for example, the yellow becomes violet-blue, the bright greenish blue turns into red, and black is replaced by white. If you go back to pages 220 and 221 for a look at the rows of opposing primary-complementary colors, you will find that afterimage colors are the matching opposites, or complementaries, of the colors in the printed pictures.

Try This

You can make up your own color picture and get a perfect afterimage. Put one together and then try it out on your family and friends; it makes a wonderful "magic" color trick that will surprise a good many people. For best results, always make sure that you use the three primary and the three complementary colors plus black and white.

The illustrations at the right show you step by step how to put such a picture together; you can copy it easily. All you need is some colored paper matching the colors in the picture, a black felt marker, some white watercolor or poster paint, scissors, paste, and a large piece of stiff white paper.

First, trace the head shown in the first picture, cut it out of black paper, and paste it on a rectangle of green. Paint a smiling mouth, a nose, eyes, and a hairline on the head with white paint. When this picture is pasted on a larger white sheet, the afterimage will show a magenta background and a white head with black facial lines.

Now look at the second picture: The smiling face is topped by a red hat. Cut such a hat out of bright red paper and paste it at an angle over the top of the head in your picture. The hat will of course turn bright greenish blue in the afterimage.

Now for the last step. You see that yellow coat lapels and a violet-blue tie with white stripes have been added on the third picture. Copy them on violet-blue and yellow paper, cut the shapes out, and paste them in the right position. Add the stripes to the tie with white paint, and your picture is finished. After gazing steadily at it for a minute, and then looking at a piece of white paper, you will see a figure with a white, smiling face topped by a blue hat and wearing a yellow, black-striped tie and a violet coat against a magenta background. You can take the picture along to show your friends and tell them how they can make the afterimage appear to their eyes. Maybe you will want to try out other designs and combinations that you make up yourself.

Responding to *The Magic of Color*

Thinking and Discussing

The Magic of Color discusses the differences between the colors of light and the colors of paint. How would you summarize the differences? What is the value of having illustrations with this topic? Would it be harder or easier to understand the topic without illustrations? Explain.

What does the ability to see colors depend on? What parts of this process do scientists understand? What parts of the process are still unknown? What do you think might be good topics for future scientific research?

Applying Science Concepts

The *Impressionists* were a group of painters who studied the science of light and color and used their knowledge to paint colorful, shimmering pictures. Important Impressionists were Edouard Manet, Camille Pissarro, Claude Monet, Pierre Auguste Renoir, Mary Cassatt, and Childe Hassam. Research the work of one or more of these painters, and prepare a written or oral report for your class. Your report should include information about how the Impressionists used the scientific study of light and color in their work.

Colors are often used to convey specific messages. For example, red is used as a signal to stop, and yellow is used to identify school buses. With a partner or group, brainstorm as many examples as you can of the use of color to convey information. Then, considering what you have learned about color vision, discuss the advantages and disadvantages of using color to communicate. You should consider how fast this kind of communication is, how clear it is, whether it works for everyone, and any other aspects you think are important. Summarize your conclusions for the class.

The Eye and How It Works

*from **Optics: Light for a New Age***
by Jeff Hecht

To most of us, light means seeing, and seeing is the king of our senses. Seeing and vision are so important to us that we use the words in many ways that have nothing to do with light. We say we *see* when we mean we understand. We have *visions* in our thoughts. To be *blind* to something is to be unaware of it.

Because light is all around us, we and other animals use it to guide us about the world. Nature gave us our own personal optical instruments, our eyes. Nerves wire them directly to the brain, and together our eyes and brain shape our view of the world. We may think of vision as simple because it is natural to us. It isn't. Scientists do not yet know all the details of how vision works. Nor can engineers build machines that can see as well as people. Computers can do arithmetic faster than people, but they cannot recognize faces as fast. To learn how vision works, we will start with the eye and see how it reacts to light, then learn how it tells the brain about the light and how the brain uses that information to make us see.

Your eye is a complex organ. You see only its outer part, shown in Figure 1 on page 232, in a mirror. Its job is to let light in and keep other things out. The eye itself is a round ball inside your skull. The inside, which you can't see in a mirror, does the seeing.

The eyelid is a protective cover with many jobs. It shuts out light when you sleep, although some light leaks through, as you can see if you close your eyes and look at a bright light. It shuts automatically if

illustrated by Walt Gunthardt and Steve Van Gelder

something comes toward your eye. And it keeps the surface of the eye wet by blinking regularly.

The white of the eye is the flexible outside of the eyeball and doesn't play any role in seeing. The central black circle is the pupil, which lets light enter the eye. The colored ring is the iris, which opens and closes to control how much light enters the eye. Turn a light off and on as you look in a mirror, and you can see that when it gets dark, the iris opens to let more light into the eye so you can see better.

You can learn more about how the eye sees by looking inside, as shown in Figure 2. Before light can enter the pupil, it must go through the eye's clear outer skin, the cornea, which also covers the iris. The

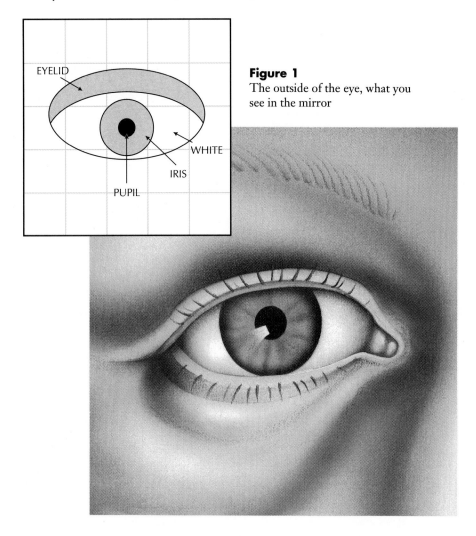

Figure 1
The outside of the eye, what you
see in the mirror

cornea is what your eyelid and tear ducts keep wet. Under the cornea is the aqueous humor, a thin, watery liquid. Light then passes through the lens of the eye, which focuses it onto the back of the eyeball. The eyeball is filled with a thick, clear liquid, the vitreous humor. We sense light only when it reaches the retina, a thin layer of cells on the back of the eyeball. When light strikes the retina, it sends signals down a network of nerves to the brain, which interprets them to form the images we see.

That is a simple picture of how the eye works, but it does not explain such details as why people need eyeglasses, how we see in color, or how we can tell distances. To learn about those important parts of vision, we need to look closer.

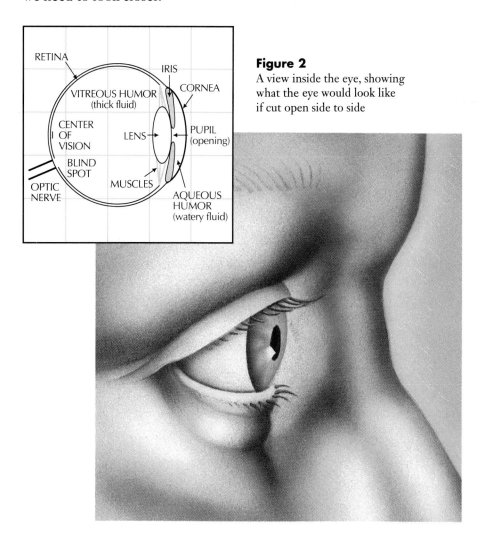

Figure 2
A view inside the eye, showing what the eye would look like if cut open side to side

Focusing

When the eye focuses light properly onto the retina, it bends light rays so they form a tiny real image at the back of the eye, as shown in Figure 3. (You can see this real image because it is formed inside the eye.) All parts of the eye bend light some, but the cornea and the lens do the most bending. The lens automatically changes shape to focus light sharply onto the retina so you can see objects clearly.

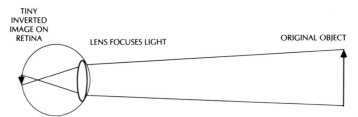

Figure 3
The eye forms a real image of a distant object on the back of the eyeball, which the retina senses.

Your eyes cannot adjust to see everything clearly. They can't adjust to focus objects at different distances at the same time. Look out a window at distant trees, and you can see either the edge of the window or the trees clearly, but not both at the same time.

Many people's eyes cannot focus light as well as they should. Farsighted people cannot see objects close to them, and nearsighted people cannot see distant objects. Eyeglasses or contact lenses can correct these

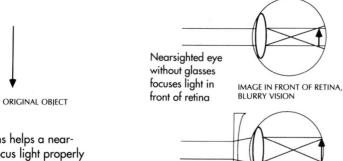

Figure 4
A concave lens helps a nearsighted eye focus light properly on the retina. Without glasses, the eye focuses light in front of the retina, and vision is blurred.

vision defects by bending light before it enters the eye. The light will then focus sharply on the retina, as shown in Figure 4 for a nearsighted eye.

Your eyes, like the rest of your body, change as you grow older. Not many children younger than six or seven need glasses, but as people get older, the shape of their eyes changes and defects in vision may become more serious. (The changes are slow and normally show up only on an eye test.) Vision stabilizes when people mature. But after the age of forty the lenses of the eyes start to get stiff, and it becomes hard to focus on objects at different distances.

The lens has to bend the most to focus on close objects, so reading without glasses becomes harder as people age. Some older people hold books farther away from them, but others may use special reading glasses that help them focus on books. Some reading glasses look like half-glasses because the people who wear them do not need help focusing on distant objects. People who normally wear glasses find that a single pair will not let them focus on both close and distant objects. One person who got frustrated with this problem was Benjamin Franklin. His solution was to cut two different lenses in half and fit half of each in front of each eye. The half-lens at the bottom adjusted his vision for close reading. The half at the top helped him see faraway objects. Such glasses are called "bifocals," and today many people wear them.

The Retina

We see an image focused onto the back of the eyeball because the retina responds to the light and transmits the impression to the brain. The retina is made of two kinds of specialized nerve cells — cones, which respond to bright light, and rods, which only work in dim light. (The names come from their shapes.)

We do most of our seeing with the eye's seven million cones. Some of them are packed closely together in the center of the retina (the fovea), where light is focused when you read or look straight ahead. The densely packed cones help you see fine details, such as the words on this page. The cones also are the part of the eye that senses colors.

The eye also contains about 125 million rods, mostly off to the sides. They can sense much fainter light than cones and let you see at night, but they do not sense colors, only black and white. Rods turn themselves off in bright light, and they take time to turn back on. This is why it takes your eyes a few minutes to get used to the dark, or *dark adapt*, if the lights go out suddenly. Once your eyes have dark adapted, a bright flash of light can leave you *night blind* until they can get used to the dark again. You might experience that if you are outside on a dark night and look at bright car headlights. Your eyes dark adapt enough to see in a minute or two, but scientists have found it takes thirty minutes to dark adapt fully.

Night vision is a little different from day vision, and because we spend most of our time in the light, night vision can have some surprises. Red objects often look much darker in dim light than blue ones, because rods are more sensitive to blue light and less sensitive to red than cones. Another surprise is that faint objects are very hard to see if you look straight at them, because the center of the retina contains very few rods. For example, look at the whole night sky, and you can see many faint stars. But many of them will vanish if you try to look straight at them! They don't really go away, but the center of your eye can't see their faint light. You can make those faint stars reappear if you learn to aim your eyes a little distance from them. This is called "averting" your vision.

Sometimes your eyes can get too much light. That's what happens when a flashbulb dazzles your eyes and you still seem to see the light for several seconds after the flash has stopped. The eye responds to light by producing chemicals, and if the light is very bright, the eye produces so much of the chemicals that it takes a long time for them to go away. A bright flash does not harm your eyes, because it is very short. Neither will a momentary glance at the sun. However, staring at the sun *is* dangerous, because it can focus enough solar energy to damage the sensitive cones in the center of your retina. You would still be able to see, but you would no longer have the fine vision needed to read.

Color

Color is both beautiful and useful. Without color, the world would look dull and gray — and it would be hard to tell things apart. Take away color, and it would be hard to tell a ripe fruit from an unripe one or a red flower petal from a green leaf.

We see color because our eyes have three types of cones, which respond to different wavelengths of light. One type of cone is most sensitive to the short-wavelength blue end of the spectrum, although it does respond some to other colors. A second cone, called the green cone, is most sensitive to green light. The third is most sensitive to yellow or orange, but we call it the red cone because it is more sensitive to red light than the other cones.

The brain compares what the three cones tell it and decides what color something is. We see more than three colors because of the way the brain combines the signals it receives. If the eye gets a lot of red light and a little green light, the brain sees red-orange. Add more green light and you see yellow, but never a reddish green. The three cones let you see a whole range of colors that slowly shade from one into the other.

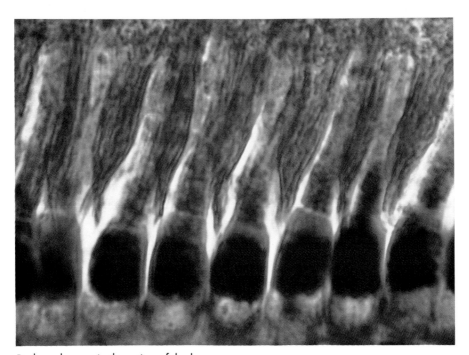

Rods and cones in the retina of the human eye

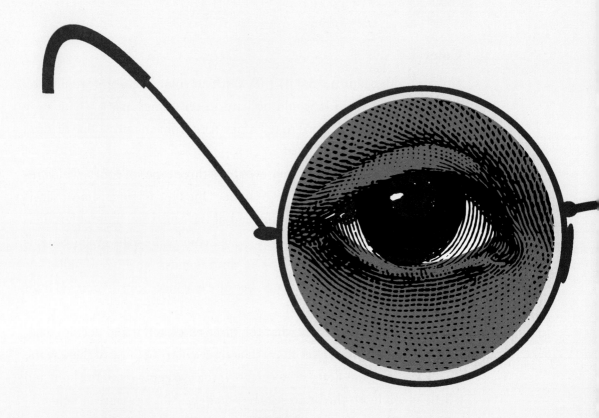

Responding to
The Eye and How It Works

Thinking and Discussing

What parts of the eye are most important in focusing light? Why do people often have more trouble focusing as they grow older? How is this problem often solved?

What kinds of cells is the retina made up of? How does knowing about the cells in the retina add to your understanding of color vision? Night vision?

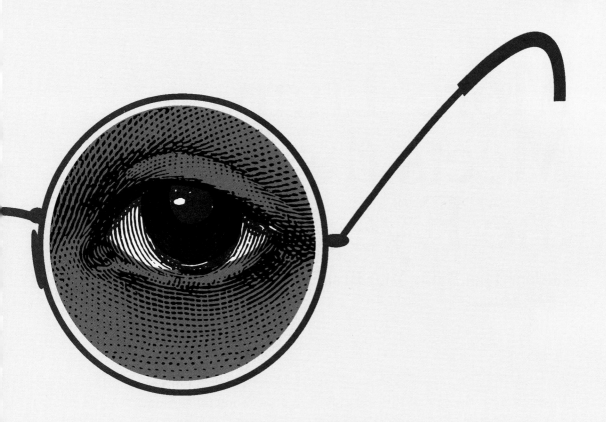

Applying Science Concepts

"The Eye and How It Works" says that your eyes dark adapt enough to see in a minute or two, but that to dark adapt completely takes thirty minutes. Test this statement by observing how long it takes your eyes to dark adapt. From a well-lighted place, enter a darkened room or go outside on a dark night. Stay in one place, and note how your ability to see changes. Take notes of how long it takes to see various things around you, and how long it takes until your night vision stops improving. Try this experiment several times. Then write up a report of your observations. You may want to compare your results with those of your classmates.

More Than Meets the the Eye

Illusions That Baffle Your Brain

by Russell Ginns

When you read the title of this story, did you notice something funny? Go back and read it again. Still don't see anything? Now read it very carefully, one word at a time. Aha! The word "the" is printed twice. It's an illusion, and unless you know exactly what you're looking for, it will probably fool you again and again.

Illusions can make you believe that something is bigger or smaller than it really is. They can also make colors seem brighter or darker, and can even make you see things that aren't really there. But these pictures are doing more than just playing tricks on your eyes, they're fooling your brain as well.

"Illusion is the wrong word for it," says David Van Essen, a scientist at California's Institute of Technology. "It's really a misunderstanding between your eyes and your brain." Your eyes are the parts of your body that collect information, but it's your brain that really decides what you see. And sometimes your brain can make a wrong decision.

Van Essen says: "When you look at something, your brain tends to fill in the missing spaces." Many optical illusions are simple drawings with lots of missing details. Your brain makes mistakes as it fills in the spaces and — presto! You're seeing something that really isn't there.

illustrated by Precision Graphics and Thach Bui

Cycle by M. C. Escher, 1938

Van Essen and other scientists are using optical illusions to learn more about how animals and humans see. To help you do some visual experiments of your own, we've put together a collection of optical tricks for you to try. There are explanations for some of them. Others remain pretty much a mystery. So sit back, relax, open your eyes, and take a tour of the mysterious world of optical illusions.

1 Look at these two arrows. Does the line from C to D seem longer than the line from A to B? If you measure them with a ruler, you'll find that they are exactly the same length. This is easy to see just by taking away the arrowheads. If you cover them, the illusion disappears.

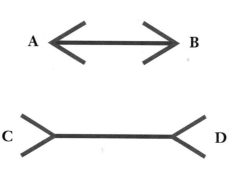

2 Do the lines that touch this box look like they are part of the same line? If you check it with a ruler or a pencil, you'll find that they're part of one perfectly straight line.

One possible explanation for these two tricks is that there are extra pieces of information that confuse your eyes. Sometimes this is called *visual noise*. If you were listening to a song on the radio and someone turned a TV on really loud, you'd have a hard time hearing all the notes of your song. Visual noise works the same way. The box and the arrowheads make it hard to see the lines correctly.

3 Here are two drawings with even more noise. Can you tell if the lines in picture E are parallel? Do the two lines in picture F look curved? Check them with a ruler. If the extra lines weren't there, it would be easy to see that the lines are all parallel. But unless you concentrate very hard, the noise will fool you again and again.

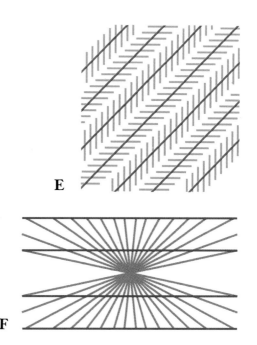

E

F

4 Take a look at these two circles. Does the white circle seem larger than the blue one? That's because of *contrast*, which means that an object will appear to change, depending on its surroundings. Bright images seem to spread out a little on a dark background. In the same way, a bright background seems to get bigger, making a dark object look smaller. Advertisers sometimes take advantage of this trick. By making a package a bright color, advertisers can make a product seem a little bigger than it actually is. (You've never seen a black cereal box in the stores, have you?)

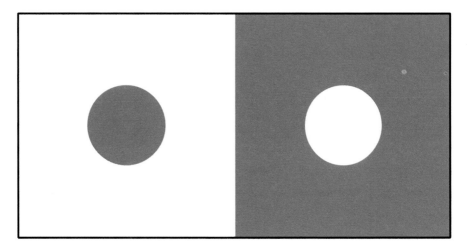

5 Contrast can also make shades and colors seem lighter or darker. Look at the green stripes. The ones on the left seem brighter, even though they are exactly the same as the ones on the right.

6 You can even change the way that something looks by surrounding it with itself. When you stare at this grid, do you see gray spots where the white lines meet? These "ghost spots" show up because white looks less bright when it is surrounded by all white.

7 Some illusions happen because your eyes can't decide which is the correct way to see something. When you look at this picture, do you see two faces or a vase? If you concentrate, you can switch back and forth between the two images.

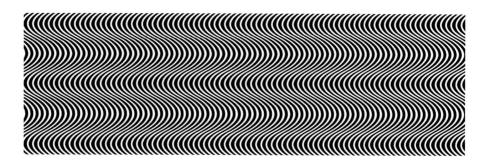

8 The same trick can be used to give the viewer a feeling of motion. When your eyes can't choose between backgrounds, the picture will seem to vibrate. Does this drawing seem like it's moving? That's because your eyes keep changing between backgrounds. At first it looks like the picture is white on black — then it's black on white.

9 Stare at these spots for at least one minute. Then look at the drawing below it. What happens? You should see faint spots on the leopard. This is caused by an *after image*. By staring at the first picture, your eyes get so used to seeing the spots that you still see them when you look at something else.

10 Some artists use this effect to create fantastic scenes or impossible objects. M. C. Escher is famous for his drawings of staircases that go nowhere and water that seems to flow uphill. Here are two drawings of objects that couldn't exist in real life. Can you figure out what's wrong with them? If you look at part of the

object, it seems fine. But if you look at a different part, something changes. It's enough to drive you crazy!

Even though these illusions have been around for many years, scientists still aren't really sure how or why most of them work. "We probably understand about five percent of the brain as a whole," David Hubel, a researcher at Harvard Medical School, said. "Many optical illusions take place in parts of the brain that we haven't even explored yet."

Here are some optical tricks that you can try on yourself and your friends. Be patient, it might take a few minutes to get each of these illusions to work right:

Free Food!

Point your index fingers together and hold your hands about six inches from your nose. Then look past your fingers at something across the room. A hot dog will seem to float between your fingers. If you slowly move your fingers apart, the hot dog will get shorter and then disappear.

Free Money!

Take two pennies and hold them between your index fingers. Quickly move them back and forth against each other. An extra penny will appear out of nowhere!

A Hole in Your Hand

Roll a piece of paper into a tube and hold it close to your right eye. Hold your left hand next to the tube with your palm facing you. Keeping both eyes open, focus on an object a few feet away. It should look like your left hand has a hole in it!

Crazy Paper

Take a small piece of paper and fold it lengthwise. Open it a little and stand it on a table. Then close one of your eyes and stare straight down at it. After a while, you won't be able to tell if you're looking at the inside or the outside of the paper!

Responding to
More Than Meets the Eye

Thinking and Discussing

According to the selection, your eyes collect information, but it's your brain that really decides what you see. How do optical illusions help illustrate that this is so?

Applying Science Concepts

Do bright colors really make an object seem slightly bigger? Test this idea by designing two cereal boxes — or some other kind of packaging — one with bright colors and the other with dark colors. Use boxes that are the same size, or create your designs on pieces of paper that are the same size. Then display your designs, and have classmates decide which seems larger. Record the results of your survey. You may want to experiment with different ways of displaying your packages, to see if this affects the way people view them.

You have probably seen drawings in which the shapes of animals or other objects are hidden in the background, and you are challenged to find the hidden shapes. These drawings are an example of *visual noise* — the background interferes and makes it hard for your eyes and brain to recognize familiar shapes. Try making such a drawing of your own. Then test it on your friends or classmates. How long does it take others to find the hidden shapes? Do some people seem to have less trouble with visual noise than others? You may want to record the results of your experiment.

THINKING ABOUT SCIENCE

Is Science Serious or Fun? The optical illusions in "More Than Meets the Eye" are presented in a playful way. "The Eye and How It Works," as well as the other articles here, has a more serious tone. When and in what ways do you think playfulness is part of a scientist's work? Investigate this question in one of the following ways.

- Interview several scientists, science teachers, or adults you know who are familiar with scientific work. Ask them about their experiences with science. When is scientific work serious? When is it fun? Summarize what you learn.

- Many scientists have talked or written about the role of imagination, playfulness, or luck in their work. Go to the library to research the important discoveries of a famous scientist. Then prepare a written or oral report for your class, stating how imagination, fun, and luck affected the scientist's work.

Inventions on Parade Create a time line showing important inventions and discoveries having to do with light and vision. You might begin your time line with the invention of the telescope by Hans Lippershey, a Dutch optician, in 1608. Include modern inventions such as photography, motion pictures, television, lasers, and fiber optics. You might also include future inventions or discoveries that you think are likely. Use encyclopedias or other resources in the library to research events to include.

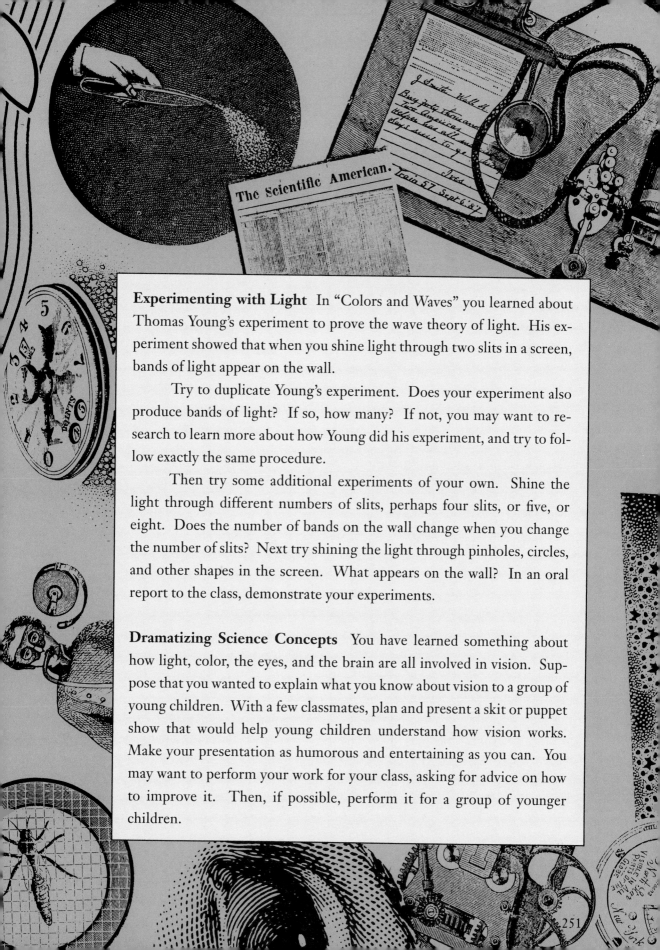

Experimenting with Light In "Colors and Waves" you learned about Thomas Young's experiment to prove the wave theory of light. His experiment showed that when you shine light through two slits in a screen, bands of light appear on the wall.

Try to duplicate Young's experiment. Does your experiment also produce bands of light? If so, how many? If not, you may want to research to learn more about how Young did his experiment, and try to follow exactly the same procedure.

Then try some additional experiments of your own. Shine the light through different numbers of slits, perhaps four slits, or five, or eight. Does the number of bands on the wall change when you change the number of slits? Next try shining the light through pinholes, circles, and other shapes in the screen. What appears on the wall? In an oral report to the class, demonstrate your experiments.

Dramatizing Science Concepts You have learned something about how light, color, the eyes, and the brain are all involved in vision. Suppose that you wanted to explain what you know about vision to a group of young children. With a few classmates, plan and present a skit or puppet show that would help young children understand how vision works. Make your presentation as humorous and entertaining as you can. You may want to perform your work for your class, asking for advice on how to improve it. Then, if possible, perform it for a group of younger children.

ABOUT THE AUTHORS

Isaac Asimov

Isaac Asimov was born in the Soviet Union in 1920 but was brought to the United States by his parents while still a young child. He was fascinated by the science fiction magazines on sale in his father's candy store. This was Asimov's introduction to science fiction. He wrote his first story, "Cosmic Corkscrew," when he was eighteen years old. Asimov went on to write innumerable short stories and over 200 books, including science fiction novels, mysteries, nonfiction history books, and nonfiction science books for both adults and young people; best known of the latter is the "How Did We Find Out . . . ?" series. Asimov won many awards for his writing; he received the Hugo Award five times and the Nebula Award twice, and his short story "Nightfall," written when he was only twenty-one, was chosen the best science fiction story of all time in a Science Fiction Writers of America poll.

Russell Ginns

Russell Ginns was born in Brooklyn, New York, in 1965. He received his B.A. from the University of Michigan, and has been writing for *3-2-1-Contact* for several years. He says, "I want to help kids learn that science is everywhere — in sports, games, the outdoors — not just in the classroom." Mr. Ginns's goal is to be the first writer to go into outer space and to write science books for kids from there. In his spare time, Mr. Ginns is a singer, songwriter, and composer. He lives in New York City.

Jeff Hecht

As a free-lance writer in the fields of science and technology, Jeff Hecht has contributed articles to *New Scientist*, *Lasers and Optronics*, and *Omni* magazines. He received his bachelor's degree in electronic engineering from the California Institute of Technology, and his master's degree from the University of Massachusetts. Mr. Hecht has written several books for adults on fiber optics and uses for lasers. *Optics: Light for a New Age* is his first book for young people. Mr. Hecht currently makes his home in Newton, Massachusetts.

Hilda Simon

Hilda Simon was born in Santa Ana, California, in 1921, but spent some of her childhood and teenage years in Germany. She displayed an early love of drawing, which was, she says, ". . . rivaled only by my abiding interest in animals." Miss Simon also wanted to be a writer, and managed to combine all three interests in one career — by writing and illustrating books on science and natural history. Her works include *Insect Masquerades* (an ALA Notable Book), *Feathers, Plain and Fancy*, *Bird and Flower Emblems of the United States*, and *The Racers: Speed in the Animal World*. "I have tried my best to awaken, by way of my books, a sense of wonder and respect for the beauty and variety of the living creatures of this planet," Miss Simon says. She currently lives in New York State.

BRIGHTEN YOUR LIFE WITH THESE!

The Eye and Seeing by Steve Parker (Watts, 1989)

    The structure of the eye and how its components function, as well as color vision and its defects, are some of the topics covered in this well-illustrated book.

The Optical Illusion Book by Seymour Simon (Morrow, 1984)

    A prolific science writer presents an entertaining look at ways in which the eye can be tricked. He includes visual experiments to show how illusion works.

You Won't Believe Your Eyes! by Catherine O'Neill (National Geographic Society, 1987)

    Lavish color photographs and clear explanations introduce visual illusion and describe the inner workings of the eye. This book shows countless examples of ways that the eye can be fooled.

The Magic of Holography by Philip Heckman (Atheneum, 1986)

    This book traces the history of the science of optics and the application of optics to holograms, which are made with lasers. The author also predicts future uses for holography.

Photonics, the New Science of Light by Valerie Burkig (Enslow, 1986)

    This introduction to light and its functions in lasers, fiber optics, holography, and infrared rays covers an area of exciting new developments.

Fiber Optics: Bright New Way to Communicate by Charlene W. Billings (Dodd, 1986)

    This book explains the how and why of glass fibers that transmit information through light. It clearly shows the uses of fiber optics in industry, space, and defense.

In the experiment pictured here, shadows projected with colored beams of light show that white light is made up of the primary colors red, green, and violet-blue, and the complementary colors yellow, blue, and magenta.

SCIENCE FICTION

OTHER CREATURES OTHER WORLDS

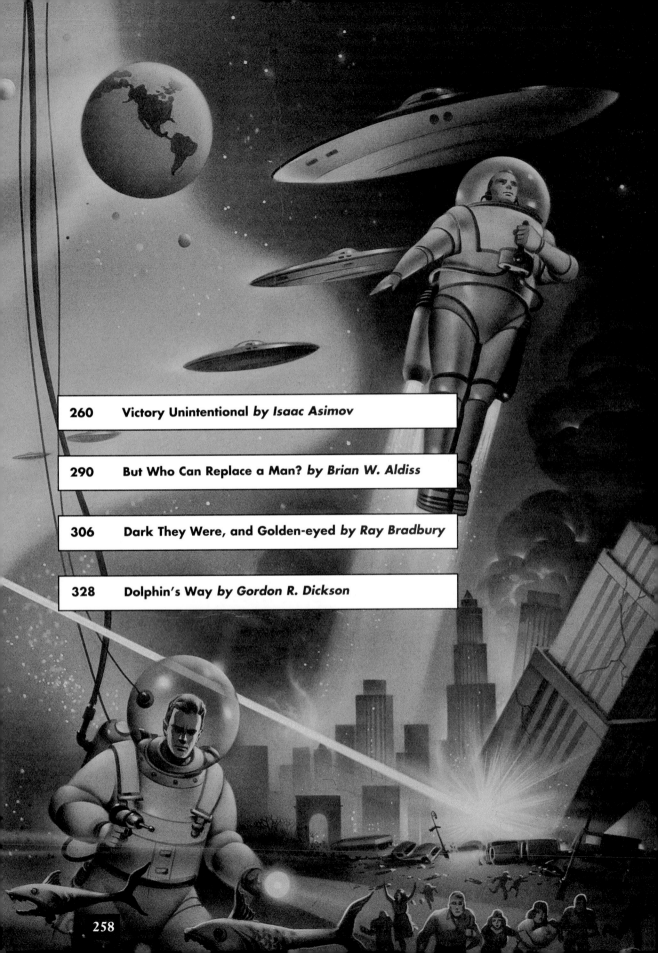

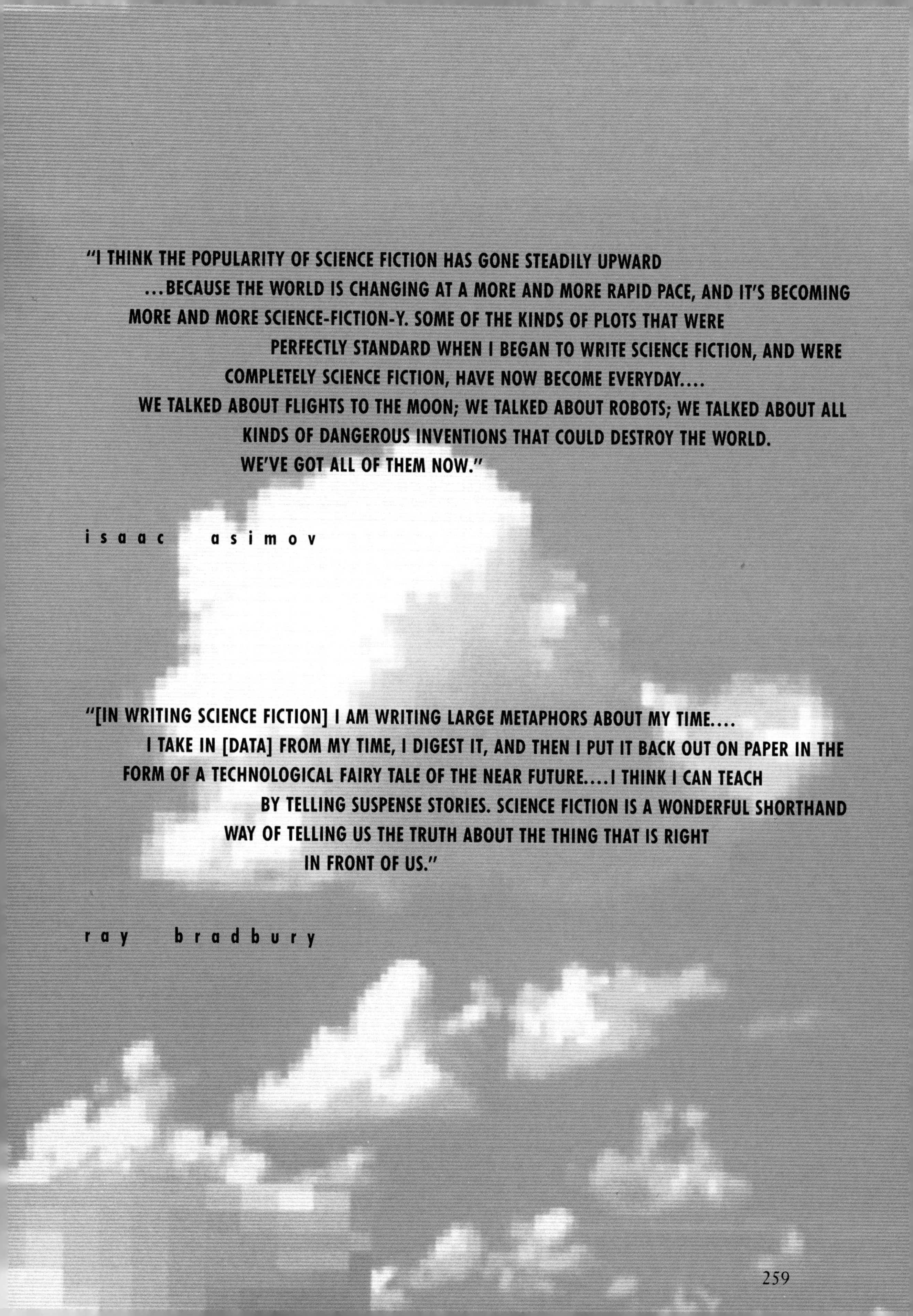

"I THINK THE POPULARITY OF SCIENCE FICTION HAS GONE STEADILY UPWARD
...BECAUSE THE WORLD IS CHANGING AT A MORE AND MORE RAPID PACE, AND IT'S BECOMING
MORE AND MORE SCIENCE-FICTION-Y. SOME OF THE KINDS OF PLOTS THAT WERE
PERFECTLY STANDARD WHEN I BEGAN TO WRITE SCIENCE FICTION, AND WERE
COMPLETELY SCIENCE FICTION, HAVE NOW BECOME EVERYDAY....
WE TALKED ABOUT FLIGHTS TO THE MOON; WE TALKED ABOUT ROBOTS; WE TALKED ABOUT ALL
KINDS OF DANGEROUS INVENTIONS THAT COULD DESTROY THE WORLD.
WE'VE GOT ALL OF THEM NOW."

isaac   asimov

"[IN WRITING SCIENCE FICTION] I AM WRITING LARGE METAPHORS ABOUT MY TIME....
I TAKE IN [DATA] FROM MY TIME, I DIGEST IT, AND THEN I PUT IT BACK OUT ON PAPER IN THE
FORM OF A TECHNOLOGICAL FAIRY TALE OF THE NEAR FUTURE....I THINK I CAN TEACH
BY TELLING SUSPENSE STORIES. SCIENCE FICTION IS A WONDERFUL SHORTHAND
WAY OF TELLING US THE TRUTH ABOUT THE THING THAT IS RIGHT
IN FRONT OF US."

ray   bradbury

259

VICTORY UNINTENTIONAL

by Isaac Asimov

The spaceship leaked, as the saying goes, like a sieve.[1] It was supposed to. In fact, that was the whole idea.

The result, of course, was that during the journey from Ganymede[2] to Jupiter, the ship was crammed just as full as it could be with the very hardest space vacuum. And since the ship also lacked heating devices, this space vacuum was at normal temperature, which is a fraction of a degree above absolute zero.[3] This, also, was according to plan. Little things like the absence of heat and air didn't annoy anyone at all on that particular spaceship.

The first near-vacuum wisps of Jovian[4] atmosphere began percolating into the ship several thousand miles above the Jovian surface. It was practically all hydrogen, though perhaps a careful gas analysis might have located a trace of helium as well. The pressure gauges began creeping skyward.

---

[1]**sieve** (sĭv): a strainer.

[2]**Ganymede** (găn′ə mēd′): the fourth moon of Jupiter.

[3]**absolute zero:** in physics, the temperature at which something possesses no heat, -273.15° Centigrade or -459.67° Fahrenheit.

[4]**Jovian** (jō′vē ən): anything belonging to the planet Jupiter, named for the Roman god, who was also known as Jove.

Illustrated by Ron Chan

That creep continued at an accelerating pace as the ship dropped downward in a Jupiter-circling spiral. The pointers of successive gauges, each designed for progressively higher pressures, began to move until they reached the neighborhood of a million or so atmospheres, where figures lost most of their meaning. The temperature, as recorded by thermocouples, rose slowly and erratically, and finally steadied at about seventy below zero, centigrade.

The ship moved slowly toward the end, plowing its way heavily through a maze of gas molecules that crowded together so closely that hydrogen itself was squeezed to the density of a liquid. Ammonia vapor, drawn from the incredibly vast oceans of that liquid, saturated the horrible atmosphere. The wind, which had begun a thousand miles higher, had risen to a pitch inadequately described as a hurricane. It was quite plain long before the ship landed on a fairly large Jovian island, perhaps seven times the size of Asia, that Jupiter was not a very pleasant world.

And yet the three members of the crew thought it was. They were quite convinced it was. But then, the three members of the crew were not exactly human. And neither were they exactly Jovian. They were simply robots designed on Earth, for Jupiter.

ZZ Three said, "It appears to be a rather desolate place."

ZZ Two joined him and regarded the wind-blasted landscape somberly. "There are structures of some sort in the distance," he said, "which are obviously artificial. I suggest we wait for the inhabitants to come to us."

Across the room, ZZ One listened, but made no reply. He was the first constructed of the three, and half-experimental. Consequently, he spoke a little less frequently than his two companions.

The wait was not too long. An air vessel of queer design swooped overhead. More followed. And then a line of ground vehicles approached, took position, and disgorged organisms. Along with the organisms came various inanimate accessories that might have been weapons. Some of these were borne by a single Jovian, some by several, and some advanced under their own power, with Jovians perhaps inside. The robots couldn't tell.

ZZ Three said, "They're all around us now. The logical peaceful gesture would be to come out in the open. Agreed?"

It was, and ZZ One shoved open the heavy door, which was not double, nor for that matter, particularly airtight.

Their appearance through the door was the signal for an excited stir among the surrounding Jovians. Things were done to several of the very largest of the inanimate accessories, and ZZ Three became aware of a temperature rise on the outer ring of his beryllium-iridium-bronze body.

He glanced at ZZ Two, "Do you feel it? They're aiming heat energy at us, I believe."

ZZ Two indicated his surprise. "I wonder why?"

"Definitely a heat ray of some sort. Look at that!"

One of the rays had been jarred out of alignment for some undiscernible cause, and its line of radiation intersected a brook of sparkling pure ammonia — which promptly boiled furiously.

ZZ Three turned to ZZ One. "Make a note of this, One, will you?"

"Sure!" It was to ZZ One that the routine secretarial work fell and his method of taking a note was to make a mental addition to the accurate memory scroll within him. He had already gathered the hour-by-hour record of every important instrument on board ship during the trip to Jupiter. He added agreeably, "What reason shall I put for the reaction? The human masters would probably enjoy knowing."

"No reason. Or better," Three corrected himself, "no apparent reason. You might say the maximum temperature of the ray was about plus thirty, centigrade."

Two interrupted, "Shall we try communicating?"

"It would be a waste of time," said Three. "There can't be more than a very few Jovians who know the radio-click code that's been developed between Jupiter and Ganymede. They'll have to send for one, and when he comes, he'll establish contact soon enough. Meanwhile, let's watch them. I don't understand their actions, I tell you frankly."

Nor did understanding come immediately. Heat radiation ceased, and other instruments were brought to the forefront and put into play. Several capsules fell at the feet of the watching robots, dropping rapidly and forcefully under Jupiter's gravity. They popped open and a blue liquid exuded, forming pools which proceeded to shrink rapidly by evaporation. The nightmare wind whipped the vapors away and where those vapors went, Jovians scrambled out of the way. One was too slow, threshed about wildly, and became very limp and still.

ZZ Two bent, dabbled a finger in one of the pools and stared at the dripping liquid. "I think this is oxygen," he said.

"Oxygen, all right," agreed Three. "This becomes stranger and stranger. It must certainly be a dangerous practice, for I would say that oxygen is poisonous to the creatures. One of them died!"

There was a pause, and then ZZ One, whose greater simplicity led at times to an increased directness of thought, said heavily, "It might be that these strange creatures in a rather childish way are attempting to destroy us."

And Two, struck by the suggestion, answered, "You know, Three, I think he's right!"

There had been a slight lull in Jovian activity and now a new structure was brought up. It possessed a slender rod that pointed skyward through the impenetrable Jovian murk. It stood with a rigidity in that starkly incredible wind that plainly indicated remarkable structural strength. From its tip came a cracking and then a flash that lit up the depths of the atmosphere into a gray fog.

For a moment the robots were bathed in clinging radiance and then Three said thoughtfully, "High-tension electricity! Quite respectable power, too. One, I think you're right. After all, the human masters have told us that these creatures seek to destroy all humanity. And organisms possessing such insane viciousness as to harbor a thought of harm against a human being —" his voice trembled at the thought — "would scarcely scruple at attempting to destroy us."

"It's a shame to have such distorted minds," said ZZ One. "Poor fellows!"

"I find it a very saddening thought," admitted Two. "Let's go back to the ship. We've seen enough for now."

They did so, and settled down to wait. As ZZ Three said, Jupiter was a roomy planet, and it might take time for Jovian transportation to bring a radio-code expert to the ship. However, patience is a cheap commodity to robots.

As a matter of fact, Jupiter turned on its axis three times, according to the chronometer, before the expert arrived. The rising and setting of the sun made no difference, of course, to the dead darkness at the bottom of three thousand miles of liquid-dense gas, so that one could not speak of day and night. But then, neither Jovian nor robot saw by visible light radiation and so that didn't matter.

Through this thirty-hour interval, the surrounding Jovians continued their attack with a patience and persevering relentlessness concerning which robot ZZ One made a good many mental notes. The ship was assaulted by as many varieties of forces as there were hours, and the robots observed every attack attentively, analyzing such weapons as they recognized. They by no means recognized all.

But the human masters had built well. The ship and the robots had taken fifteen years to construct, and their essentials could be expressed in a single phrase — raw strength. The attack spent itself uselessly and neither ship nor robot seemed the worse for it.

Three said, "This atmosphere handicaps them, I think. They can't use atomic disruptors, since they would only tear a hole in that soupy air and blow themselves up."

"They haven't used high explosives either," said Two, "which is well. They couldn't have hurt us, naturally, but it would have thrown us about a bit."

"High explosives are out of the question. You can't have an explosive without gas expansion and gas just can't expand in this atmosphere."

"It's a very good atmosphere," muttered One. "I like it."

Which was natural, because he was built for it. The ZZ robots were the first robots ever turned out by the United States Robot and Mechanical Men Corporation that were not even faintly human in appearance. They were low and squat, with a center of gravity less than a foot above ground level. They had six legs apiece, stumpy and thick, designed to lift tons against two and a half times normal Earth gravity. Their reflexes were that many times Earth-normal speed, to make up for the gravity. And they were composed of a beryllium-iridium-bronze alloy that was proof against any known corrosive agent, also any known destructive agent short of a thousand-megatron atomic disruptor, under any conditions whatsoever.

To dispense with further description, they were indestructible, and so impressively powerful that they were the only robots ever built on whom the roboticists of the corporation had never quite had the nerve to pin a serial-number nickname. One bright young fellow had suggested Sissy One, Two, and Three — but not in a very loud voice, and the suggestion was never repeated.

The last hours of the wait were spent in a puzzled discussion to find a possible description of a Jovian's appearance. ZZ One had made a note of their possession of tentacles and of their radial symmetry[5] — and there he had stuck. Two and Three did their best, but couldn't help.

"You can't very well describe anything," Three declared finally, "without a standard of reference. These creatures are like nothing I

---

[5]**radial symmetry** (rā′dē əl sĭm′ĭ trē): an arrangement of parts extending outward in the same manner from a central point, like the spokes of a wheel.

know of — completely outside the positronic paths of my brain. It's like trying to describe gamma light to a robot unequipped for gamma-ray reception."

It was just at that time that the weapon barrage ceased once more. The robots turned their attention to outside the ship.

A group of Jovians were advancing in curiously uneven fashion, but no amount of careful watching could determine the exact method of their locomotion. How they used their tentacles was uncertain. At times the organisms took on a remarkable slithering motion, and then they moved at great speed, perhaps with the wind's help, for they were moving downwind.

The robots stepped out to meet the Jovians, who halted ten feet away. Both sides remained silent and motionless.

ZZ Two said, "They must be watching us, but I don't know how. Do either of you see any photosensitive organs?"

"I can't say," grunted Three in response. "I don't see anything about them that makes sense at all."

There was a sudden metallic clicking from among the Jovian group and ZZ One said delightedly, "It's the radio code. They've got the communications expert here."

It was, and they had! The complicated dot-dash system that over a period of twenty-five years had been laboriously developed by the beings of Jupiter and the Earthmen of Ganymede into a remarkably flexible means of communication, was finally being put into practice at close range.

One Jovian remained in the forefront now, the others having fallen back. It was he that was speaking. The clicking said, "Where are you from?"

ZZ Three, as the most mentally advanced, naturally assumed spokesmanship for the robot group. "We are from Jupiter's satellite, Ganymede."

The Jovian continued, "What do you want?"

"Information. We have come to study your world and to bring back our findings. If we could have your cooperation —"

The Jovian clicking interrupted: "You must be destroyed!"

ZZ Three paused and said in a thoughtful aside to his two companions, "Exactly the attitude the human masters said they would take. They are very unusual."

Returning to his clicking, he asked simply, "Why?"

The Jovian evidently considered certain questions too obnoxious to be answered. He said, "If you leave within a single period of revolution, we will spare you — until such time as we emerge from our world to destroy the un-Jovian vermin[6] of Ganymede."

"I would like to point out," said Three, "that we of Ganymede and the inner planets —"

The Jovian interrupted, "Our astronomy knows of the sun and of our four satellites. There are no inner planets."

Three conceded the point wearily. "We of Ganymede, then. We have no designs on Jupiter. We're prepared to offer friendship. For twenty-five years your people communicated freely with the human beings of Ganymede. Is there any reason to make sudden war upon the humans?"

"For twenty-five years," was the cold response, "we assumed the inhabitants of Ganymede to be Jovians. When we found out they were not, and that we had been treating lower animals on the scale of Jovian intelligences, we were bound to take steps to wipe out the dishonor." Slowly and forcefully he finished, "We of Jupiter will suffer the existence of no vermin!"

He was backing away in some fashion, tacking against the wind, and the interview was evidently over.

The robots retreated inside the ship.

ZZ Two said, "It looks bad, doesn't it?" He continued thoughtfully, "It is as the human masters said. They possess an ultimately developed superiority complex,[7] combined with an extreme intolerance for anyone or anything that disturbs that complex."

"The intolerance," observed Three, "is the natural consequence of the complex. The trouble is that their intolerance has teeth in it. They have weapons — and their science is great."

"I am not surprised now," burst out ZZ One, "that we were specifically instructed to disregard Jovian orders. They are horrible, intolerant, pseudo-superior beings!" He added emphatically, with robotical loyalty and faith, "No human master could ever be like that."

---

[6]**vermin** (vûr′mĭn): beings to be scorned.
[7]**superiority complex:** a feeling of being superior to others.

"That, though true, is beside the point," said Three. "The fact remains that the human masters are in terrible danger. This is a gigantic world and these Jovians are greater in numbers and resources by a hundred times or more than the humans of the entire Terrestrial Empire. If they can ever develop the force field to the point where they can use it as a spaceship hull — as the human masters have already done — they will overrun the system at will. The question remains as to how far they have advanced in that direction, what other weapons they have, what preparations they are making, and so on. To return with that information is our function, of course, and we had better decide on our next step."

"It may be difficult," said Two. "The Jovians won't help us." Which, at the moment, was rather an understatement.

Three thought a while. "It seems to me that we need only wait," he observed. "They have tried to destroy us for thirty hours now and haven't succeeded. Certainly they have done their best. Now a superiority complex always involves the eternal necessity of saving face, and the ultimatum given us proves it in this case. They would never allow us to leave if they could destroy us. But if we don't leave then, rather than admit they cannot force us away, they will surely pretend that they are willing, for their own purposes, to have us stay."

Once again, they waited. The day passed. The weapon barrage did not resume. The robots did not leave. The bluff was called. And now the robots faced the Jovian radio-code expert once again.

If the ZZ models had been equipped with a sense of humor, they would have enjoyed themselves immensely. As it was, they felt merely a solemn sense of satisfaction.

The Jovian said, "It has been our decision that you will be allowed to remain for a very short time, so that you may see our power for yourself. You shall then return to Ganymede to inform your companion vermin of the disastrous end to which they will unfailingly come within a solar revolution."

ZZ One made a mental note that a Jovian revolution took twelve Earthly years.

Three replied casually, "Thank you. May we accompany you to the nearest town? There are many things we would like to learn." He added as an afterthought, "Our ship is not to be touched, of course."

He said this as a request, not as a threat, for no ZZ model was ever pugnacious. All capacity for even the slightest annoyance had been carefully barred in their construction. With robots as vastly powerful as the ZZs, unfailing good temper was essential for safety during the years of testing on Earth.

The Jovian said, "We are not interested in your verminous ship. No Jovian will pollute himself by approaching it. You may accompany us, but you must on no account approach closer than ten feet to any Jovian, or you will be instantly destroyed."

"Stuck up, aren't they?" observed Two in a genial whisper, as they plowed into the wind.

The town was a port on the shores of an incredible ammonia lake. The eternal wind whipped furious, frothy waves that shot across the liquid surface at the hectic rate enforced by the gravity. The port itself was neither large nor impressive and it seemed fairly evident that most of the construction was underground.

"What is the population of this place?" asked Three.

The Jovian replied, "It is a small town of ten million."

"I see. Make a note of that, One."

ZZ One did so mechanically, and then turned once more to the lake, at which he had been staring in fascination. He pulled at Three's elbow. "Say, do you suppose they have fish here?"

"What difference does it make?"

"I think we ought to know. The masters ordered us to find out everything we could." Of the robots, One was the simplest and consequently the one who took orders in the most literal fashion.

Two said, "Let One go and look if he likes. It won't do any harm if we let the kid have his fun."

"All right. There's no real objection if he doesn't waste his time. Fish isn't what we came for — but go ahead, One."

ZZ One made off in great excitement and slogged rapidly down the beach, plunging into the ammonia with a splash. The Jovians watched attentively. They had understood none of the previous conversation, of course.

The radio-code expert clicked out, "It is apparent that your companion has decided to abandon life in despair at our greatness."

Three said in surprise, "Nothing of the sort. He wants to investigate the living organisms, if any, that live in the ammonia." He added apologetically, "Our friend is very curious at times, and he isn't quite as bright as we are, though that is only his misfortune. We understand that and try to humor him whenever we can."

There was a long pause, and the Jovian observed, "He will drown."

Three replied casually, "No danger of that. We don't drown. May we enter the town as soon as he returns?"

At that moment there was a spurt of liquid several hundred feet out in the lake. It sprayed upward wildly and then hurtled down in a wind-driven mist. Another spurt and another, then a wild white foaming that formed a trail toward shore, gradually quieting as it approached.

The two robots watched this in amazement and the utter lack of motion on the part of the Jovians indicated that they were watching as well.

Then the head of ZZ One broke the surface and he made his slow way out onto dry land. But something followed him! Some organism of gigantic size, that seemed nothing but fangs, claws, and spines. Then they saw that it wasn't following him under its own power, but was being dragged across the beach by ZZ One. There was a significant flabbiness about it.

ZZ One approached rather timidly and took communication into his own hands. He tapped out a message to the Jovian in agitated fashion.

"I am very sorry this happened, but the thing attacked me. I was merely taking notes on it. It is not a valuable creature, I hope."

He was not answered immediately, for at the first appearance of the monster, there had been a wild break in the Jovian ranks. These reformed slowly and cautious observation having proven the creature to be indeed dead, order was restored. Some of the bolder were curiously prodding the body.

ZZ Three said humbly, "I hope you will pardon our friend. He is sometimes clumsy. We have absolutely no intention of harming any Jovian creature."

"He attacked me," explained One. "He bit at me without provocation.[8] See!" And he displayed a two-foot fang that ended in a jagged break. "He broke it on my shoulder and almost left a scratch. I just slapped it a bit to send it away — and it died. I'm sorry!"

The Jovian finally spoke and his code clicking was a rather stuttery affair: "It is a wild creature, rarely found so close to shore, but the lake is deep just here."

Three said, still anxiously, "If you can use it for food, we are only too glad —"

"No. We can get food for ourselves without the help of verm— without the help of others. Eat it yourselves."

At that ZZ One heaved the creature up and back into the sea, with an easy motion of one arm. Three said casually, "Thank you for your kind offer, but we have no use for food. We don't eat, of course."

Escorted by two hundred or so armed Jovians, the robots passed down a series of ramps into the underground city. If, above the surface, the city had looked small and unimpressive, from beneath it took on the appearance of a vast megalopolis.[9]

They were ushered into ground cars that were operated by remote control[10] — for no honest, self-respecting Jovian would risk his superiority by placing himself into the same car with vermin — and driven at

---

[8]**provocation** (prŏv′ə kā′shən): causing anger or resentment.
[9]**megalopolis** (mĕg′ə lŏp′ə lĭs): a huge area of cities connected together.
[10]**remote control**: control from a distance.

272

frightful speed to the center of the town. They saw enough to decide that it extended fifty miles from end to end and reached downward into Jupiter's crust at least eight miles.

ZZ Two did not sound happy as he said, "If this is a sample of Jovian development then we shall not have a hopeful report to bring back to the human masters. After all, we landed on the vast surface of Jupiter at random, with the chances a thousand to one against coming near any really concentrated center of population. This must be, as the code expert says, a mere town."

"Ten million Jovians," said Three abstractedly. "Total population must be in the trillions, which is high, very high, even for Jupiter. They probably have a completely urban civilization, which means that their scientific development must be tremendous. If they have force fields —"

He had no neck, for in the interest of strength the heads of the ZZ models were riveted firmly onto the torso with the delicate positronic brains protected by three separate layers of inch-thick iridium alloy. But if he had had one, he would have shaken his head dolefully.

They had stopped now in a cleared space. Everywhere about them they could see avenues and structures crowded with Jovians, as curious as any Terrestrial crowd would have been in similar circumstances.

The code expert approached. "It is time now for me to retire until the next period of activity. We have gone so far as to arrange quarters for you at great inconvenience to ourselves for, of course, the structure will have to be pulled down and rebuilt afterward. Nevertheless, you will be allowed to sleep for a space."

ZZ Three waved an arm in deprecation and tapped out, "We thank you but you must not trouble yourself. We don't mind remaining right here. If you want to sleep and rest, by all means do. We'll wait for you. As for us," casually, "we don't sleep."

The Jovian said nothing, though if it had had a face, the expression upon it might have been interesting. It left, and the robots remained in the car, with squads of well-armed Jovians, frequently replaced, surrounding them as guards.

It was hours before the ranks of those guards parted to allow the code expert to return. Along with him were other Jovians, whom he introduced.

"There are with me two officials of the central government who have graciously consented to speak with you."

One of the officials evidently knew the code, for his clicking interrupted the code expert sharply. He addressed the robots, "Vermin! Emerge from the ground car that we may look at you."

The robots were only too willing to comply, so while Three and Two vaulted over the right side of the car, ZZ One dashed through the left side. Since he neglected to work the mechanism that lowered a section of side so that one might exit, he carried that side, plus two wheels and an axle, along with him. The car collapsed, and ZZ One stood staring at the ruins in embarrassed silence.

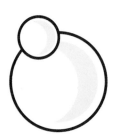

At last he clicked out gently, "I'm very sorry. I hope it wasn't an expensive car."

ZZ Two added apologetically, "Our companion is often clumsy. You must excuse him," and ZZ Three made a half-hearted attempt to put the car back together again.

ZZ One made another effort to excuse himself. "The material of the car was rather flimsy. You see?" He lifted a square-yard sheet of three-inch-thick, metal-hard plastic in both hands and exerted a bit of pressure. The sheet promptly snapped in two. "I should have made allowances," he admitted.

The Jovian government official said in slightly less sharp fashion, "The car would have had to be destroyed anyway, since being polluted by your presence." He paused, then: "Creatures! We Jovians lack vulgar curiosity concerning lower animals, but our scientists seek facts."

"We're right with you," replied Three cheerfully: "so do we."

The Jovian ignored him. "You lack the mass-sensitive organ, apparently. How is it that you are aware of distant objects?"

Three grew interested, "Do you mean your people are directly sensitive to mass?"

"I am not here to answer your questions — your impudent questions — about us."

"I take it then that objects of low specific mass would be transparent to you, even in the absence of radiation." He turned to Two. "That's how they see. Their atmosphere is as transparent as space to them."

The Jovian clicking began once more, "You will answer my first question immediately, or my patience will end and I will order you destroyed."

Three said at once, "We are energy-sensitive, Jovian. We can adjust ourselves to the entire electromagnetic scale at will. At present, our long-distance sight is due to radio-wave radiation that we emit ourselves, and at close range, we see by —" He paused, and said to Two, "There isn't any code word for gamma ray, is there?"

"Not that I know of," Two answered.

Three continued to the Jovian: "At close range we see by other radiation for which there is no code word."

"Of what is your body composed?" demanded the Jovian.

Two whispered, "He probably asks that because his mass-sensitivity can't penetrate past our skin. High density, you know. Ought we to tell him?"

Three replied uncertainly, "Our human masters didn't particularly say we were to keep anything secret." In radio code, to the Jovian, he said, "We are mostly iridium. For the rest copper, tin, a little beryllium, and a scattering of other substances."

The Jovians fell back and by the obscure writhing of various portions of their thoroughly indescribable bodies gave the impression that they were in animated conversation, although they made no sound.

And then the official returned. "Beings of Ganymede! It has been decided to show you through some of our factories that we may exhibit a tiny part of our great achievements. We will then allow you to return so that you may spread despair among the other verm— the other beings of the outer world."

Three said to Two, "Note the effect of their psychology. They must hammer home their superiority. It's still a matter of saving face." And in radio code: "We thank you for the opportunity."

But the face saving was efficient, as the robots realized soon enough. The demonstration became a tour, and the tour a grand exhibition. The Jovians displayed everything, explained everything, answered all questions eagerly, and ZZ One made hundreds of despairing notes.

The war potential of that single so-called unimportant town was greater by several times than that of all Ganymede. Ten more such towns would outproduce all the Terrestrial Empire. Yet ten more such towns would not be the fingernail fragment of the strength all Jupiter must be able to exert.

Three turned as One nudged him, "What is it?"

ZZ One said seriously, "If they have force fields, the human masters are lost, aren't they?"

"I'm afraid so. Why do you ask?"

"Because the Jovians aren't showing us through the right wing of this factory. It might be that force fields are being developed there. They would be wanting to keep it secret if they were. We'd better find out. It's the main point, you know."

Three regarded One somberly. "Perhaps you're right. It's no use ignoring anything." They were in a huge steel mill now, watching hundred-foot beams of ammonia-resistant silicon-steel alloy being turned out twenty to the second. Three asked quietly, "What does that wing contain?"

The government official inquired of those in charge of the factory and explained, "That is the section of great heat. Various processes require huge temperatures which life cannot bear, and they must all be handled indirectly."

He led the way to a partition from which heat could be felt to radiate, and indicated a small, round area of transparent material. It was one of a row of such, through which the foggy red light of lines of glowing forges could be made out through the soupy atmosphere.

ZZ One fastened a look of suspicion on the Jovian and clicked out, "Would it be all right if I went in and looked around? I am very interested in this."

Three said, "You're being childish, One. They're telling the truth. Oh, well, nose around if you must. But don't take too long, we've got to move on."

The Jovian said, "You have no understanding of the heat involved. You will die."

"Oh no!" explained One casually. "Heat doesn't bother us."

There was a Jovian conference, and then a scene of scurrying confusion as the life of the factory was geared to this unusual emergency. Screens of heat-absorbent material were set up, and then a door dropped open, a door that had never before budged while the forges were working. ZZ One entered and the door closed behind him. Jovian officials crowded to the transparent areas to watch.

ZZ One walked to the nearest forge and tapped the outside. Since he was too short to see into it comfortably, he tipped the forge until the molten metal licked at the lip of the container. He peered at it curiously, then dipped his hand in and stirred it awhile to test the consistency. Having done this, he withdrew his hand, shook off some of the fiery metallic droplets, and wiped the rest on one of his six thighs. Slowly, he went down the line of forges, then signified his desire to leave.

The Jovians retired to a great distance when he came out the door and played a stream of ammonia on him, which hissed, bubbled, and steamed until he was brought to bearable temperature once more.

ZZ One ignored the ammonia shower and said, "They were telling the truth. No force fields!"

Three began, "You see —" but One interrupted impatiently, "But there's no use delaying. The human masters instructed us to find out everything and that's that." He turned to the Jovian and clicked out, without the slightest hesitation, "Has Jovian science developed force fields?"

Bluntness was, of course, one of the natural consequences of One's more poorly developed mental powers. Two and Three knew that, so they refrained from expressing disapproval of the remark.

The Jovian official relaxed slowly from his strangely stiffened attitude, which had somehow given the impression that he had been staring stupidly at One's hand — the one he had dipped into the molten metal.

The Jovian said slowly, "Force fields? That, then, is your main object of curiosity?"

"Yes," said One, with emphasis.

There was a sudden and patent gain in confidence on the Jovian's part, for the clicking grew sharper: "Then come, vermin!"

Whereupon Three said to Two, "We're vermin again, I see — which sounds as if there's bad news ahead." And Two gloomily agreed.

It was to the very edge of the city that they were now led — to the portion which on Earth would have been termed the suburbs — and into one of a series of closely integrated structures, which might have corresponded vaguely to a Terrestrial university. There were no explanations, however, and none were asked for. The Jovian official led the way rapidly, and the robots followed with the grim conviction that the worst was just about to happen.

It was ZZ One who stopped before an opened wall section after the rest had passed on. "What's this?" he wanted to know.

The room was equipped with narrow, low benches, along which Jovians manipulated rows of strange devices, of which strong inch-long electromagnets formed the principal feature.

"What's this?" asked One again.

The Jovian turned back and exhibited impatience. "This is a student's biological laboratory. There's nothing there to interest you."

"But what are they doing?"

"They are studying microscopic life. Haven't you ever seen a microscope before?"

Three interrupted in explanation, "He has, but not that type. Our microscopes are meant for energy-sensitive organs and work by refraction of radiant energy. Your microscopes evidently work on a mass-expansion basis. Rather ingenious."

ZZ One said, "Would it be all right if I inspected some of your specimens?"

"Of what use will that be? You cannot use our microscopes because of your sensory limitations and it will simply force us to discard such specimens as you approach for no decent reason."

"But I don't need a microscope," explained One, with surprise. "I can easily adjust myself for microscopic vision."

He strode to the nearest bench, while the students in the room crowded to the corner in an attempt to avoid contamination. ZZ One shoved a microscope aside, and inspected the slide carefully. He backed away puzzled; then tried another, a third, a fourth.

He came back and addressed the Jovian. "Those are supposed to be alive, aren't they? I mean, those little worm things."

The Jovian said, "Certainly."

"That's strange! When I look at them — they die!"

Three exclaimed sharply, and said to his two companions, "We've forgotten our gamma-ray radiation. Let's get out of here, One, or we'll kill every bit of microscopic life in the room." He turned to the Jovian, "I'm afraid that our presence is fatal to weaker forms of life. We had better leave. We hope the specimens are not too difficult to replace. And, while we're about it, you had better not stay too near us, or our radiation may affect you adversely. You feel all right so far, don't you?" he asked.

The Jovian led the way onward in proud silence, but it was to be noticed that thereafter he doubled the distance he had hitherto kept between himself and them.

Nothing more was said until the robots found themselves in a vast room. In the very center of it huge ingots of metal rested unsupported in midair — or, rather, supported by nothing visible — against the mighty Jovian gravity.

The Jovian clicked, "There is your force field in ultimate form, as recently perfected. Within that bubble is a vacuum, so that it is supporting the full weight of our atmosphere plus an amount of metal equivalent to two large spaceships. What do you say to that?"

"Then space travel now becomes a possibility for you," said Three.

"Definitely. No metal or plastic has the strength to hold our atmosphere against a vacuum; but a force field can — and a force-field bubble will be our spaceship! Within the year, we will be turning them out by the hundreds of thousands. Then we will swarm down upon Ganymede to destroy the verminous so-called intelligences that attempt to dispute our dominion[11] of the universe."

"The human beings of Ganymede have never attempted —" began Three, in mild expostulation.

"Silence!" snapped the Jovian. "Return now and tell them what you've seen. Their own feeble force fields — such as the one your ship is equipped with — will not stand against us, for our smallest ship will be a hundred times the size and power of yours."

Three said, "Then there's nothing more to do and we will return, as you say, with the information. If you could lead us back to our ship, we'll say good-bye. But by the way, just as a matter for the record, there's something you don't understand. The humans of Ganymede have force fields, of course, but our particular ship isn't equipped with one. We don't need any."

The robot turned away and motioned his companions to follow. For a moment they did not speak, then ZZ One muttered dejectedly, "Can't we try to destroy this place?"

"It won't help," said Three. "They'd get us by weight of numbers. It's no use. In an earthly decade, the human masters will be finished. It is impossible to stand against Jupiter. There's just too much of it. As long as they were tied to the surface, the humans were safe. But now that they have force fields — all we can do is to bring the news. By the preparation of hiding places, some few may survive for a short while."

The city was behind them. They were out on the open plain by the lake with their ship a dark spot on the horizon when the Jovian spoke suddenly: "Creatures, you say you have no force field?"

Three replied without interest, "We don't need one."

---

[11]**dominion** (də **mĭn′**yən): control.

"How then does your ship stand the vacuum of space without exploding because of the atmospheric pressure within?" And he moved a tentacle as if in mute gesture at the Jovian atmosphere that was weighing down upon them with a force of twenty million pounds to the square inch.

"Well," explained Three, "that's simple. Our ship isn't airtight. Pressures equalize within and without."

"Even in space? A vacuum in your ship? You lie!"

"You're welcome to inspect our ship. It has no force field and it isn't airtight. What's marvelous about that? We don't breathe. Our energy is through direct atomic power. The presence or absence of air pressure makes little difference to us and we're quite at home in a vacuum."

"But absolute zero!"

"It doesn't matter. We regulate our own heat. We're not interested in outside temperatures." He paused. "Well, we can make our own way back to the ship. Good-bye. We'll give the humans of Ganymede your message — war to the end!"

But the Jovian said, "Wait! I'll be back." He turned and went toward the city.

The robots stared, and then waited in silence.

It was three hours before he returned and when he did, it was in breathless haste. He stopped within the usual ten feet of the robots, but then began inching his way forward in a curious groveling fashion. He did not speak until his rubbery gray skin was almost touching them, and when the radio code sounded, subdued and respectful.

"Honored sirs, I have been in communication with the head of our central government, who is now aware of all the facts, and I can assure you that Jupiter desires only peace."

"I beg your pardon," said Three blankly.

The Jovian drove on hastily: "We are ready to resume communication with Ganymede and will gladly promise to make no attempt to venture out into space. Our force field will be used only on the Jovian surface."

"But —" Three began.

282

"Our government will be glad to receive any other representatives our honorable human brothers of Ganymede would care to send. If your honors will now condescend to swear peace —" A scaly tentacle swung out toward them, and Three, quite dazed, grasped it. Two and One did likewise as two more were extended to them.

The Jovian said solemnly, "There is then eternal peace between Jupiter and Ganymede."

The spaceship which leaked like a sieve was out in space again. The pressure and temperature were once more at zero, and the robots watched the huge but steadily shrinking globe that was Jupiter.

"They're definitely sincere," said ZZ Two, "and it's very gratifying, this complete about-face, but I don't get it."

"It is my idea," observed ZZ One, "that the Jovians came to their senses just in time and realized the incredible evil involved in the thought of harm to a human master. That would be only natural."

ZZ Three sighed and said, "Look, friends, it's all a matter of psychology. Those Jovians had a superiority complex a mile thick and when they couldn't destroy us, they were bound to save face. All their exhibitions, all their explanations, were simply a form of braggadocio,[12] designed to impress us into the proper state of humiliation before their power and superiority."

"I see all that," interrupted Two, "but —"

Three went on. "But it worked the wrong way. All they did was to prove to themselves that we were stronger, that we didn't drown, that we didn't eat or sleep, that molten metal didn't hurt us. Even our very presence was fatal to Jovian life. Their last trump was the force field. But when they found out that *we* didn't need them at all, and could live in a vacuum at absolute zero, they broke." He paused, and added philosophically, "When a superiority complex like that breaks, it breaks all the way."

The other two considered that, and then Two said, "But it still doesn't make sense. Why should they care what we can or can't do? We're only robots. We're not the ones they have to fight."

---

[12]**braggadocio** (brăg′ə dō′sē ō′): bragging.

"And that's the whole point, Two," said Three softly. "It's only after we left Jupiter that I thought of it. Do you know that through an oversight, quite unintentionally, we neglected to tell them we were only robots?"

"They never asked us," said One.

"Exactly. So they thought we were human beings and that all the other human beings were like us!"

He looked once more at Jupiter, thoughtfully. "No wonder they decided to quit!"

Responding to
VICTORY UNINTENTIONAL

Thinking and Discussing

— Think about the character traits of the Jovians and the robots. How does the Jovians' character compare with that of the robots? How does the Jovians' character prevent them from understanding what happens?

— Think about the comments about society that the author of "Victory Unintentional" might be making in the story. What is he saying about fear as a reason to make peace? About good intentions that win out in unexpected ways? About ideas of superiority and inferiority?

Choosing a Creative Response

— **Sending a Jovian Message** Because of their superiority complex, the Jovians are concerned with saving face. Imagine the type of message they might send to the humans on Ganymede to confirm their peace treaty. The message should explain why the Jovians have changed their attitude toward peace with the humans.

As the Jovians and robots use a dot-dash radio code to communicate, you may wish to send your message in Morse code. Look up the code in an encyclopedia. For each letter of your message, write the code of dots and dashes for that letter. Then exchange and decode the messages with a classmate.

You may also wish to create your own code for sending your message. Create a key to the code, such as using the alphabet backwards. Then provide a classmate with the message and the key, and see whether the message can be decoded. If you prefer to keep the key, your classmate will have to break the code.

— **Creating Your Own Activity** Plan and complete your own activity in response to "Victory Unintentional."

Writing a Report of Information

The fantastic events, alien creatures, and bizarre worlds of science fiction are as unlimited as the creators' imaginations. Science fiction writers sometimes seem to be able to predict the future: Space travel, television, and submarines existed in science fiction long before they entered the real lives of humans.

Some aspects of science fiction stories, however, become outdated as new technology is developed and new discoveries are made. Explore this concept by doing research about a topic from one of the science fiction stories in "Other Creatures, Other Worlds," such as visiting Ganymede, living on Mars, or communicating with dolphins. Then write a report of information that compares the way the author presented the subject with the facts scientists know today. If reading the science fiction stories gives you another idea, write about that one instead.

1. Prewriting Before you begin writing your report of information, choose a topic based on a scientific concept presented in one of the stories. Make sure your choice can be explored in light of current scientific evidence. Then answer the following questions to help you get started.

- What do scientists know today that the science fiction writer did not know?
- How will I conduct research in order to find out more about my topic?
- What is my purpose for writing? Who will read my report?
- How should I organize my paper so that my ideas are presented clearly?

2. Write a First Draft As you begin your first draft, think about the way in which you will present your information. Your report will be most effective if your ideas are presented clearly and logically.

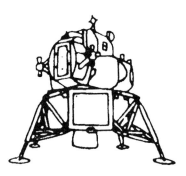

3. Revise Have a partner read your first draft and ask for suggestions for improving your report. Then ask yourself the following questions to help you identify other necessary changes.

• Does my report make sense?

• Are the points stated clearly?

• Have I supported my ideas with solid evidence and strong arguments?

4. Proofread Check your report of information for correct spelling, capitalization, and punctuation. Be especially careful to use scientific words and phrases correctly.

5. Publish Make a neat copy of your report of information. You may wish to add illustrations. Then invite your classmates to share in your scientific discoveries.

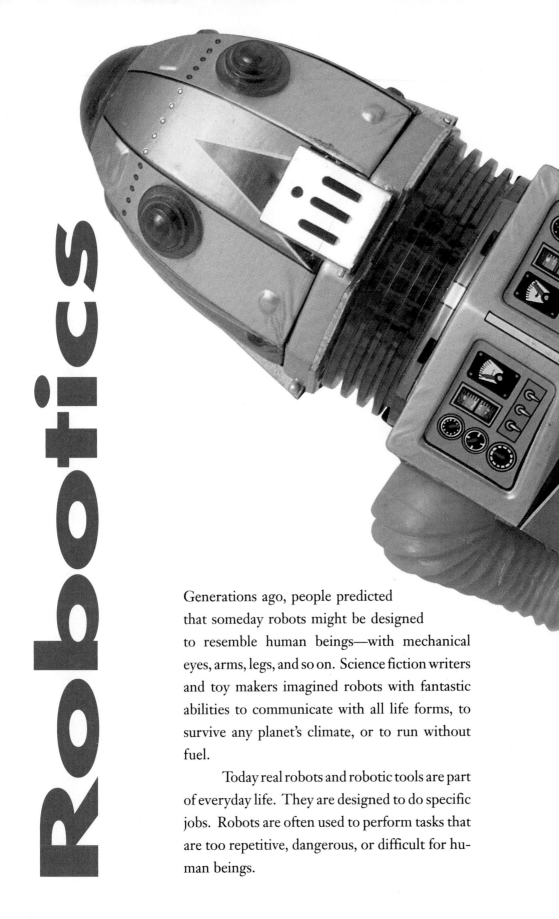

Robotics

Generations ago, people predicted that someday robots might be designed to resemble human beings—with mechanical eyes, arms, legs, and so on. Science fiction writers and toy makers imagined robots with fantastic abilities to communicate with all life forms, to survive any planet's climate, or to run without fuel.

Today real robots and robotic tools are part of everyday life. They are designed to do specific jobs. Robots are often used to perform tasks that are too repetitive, dangerous, or difficult for human beings.

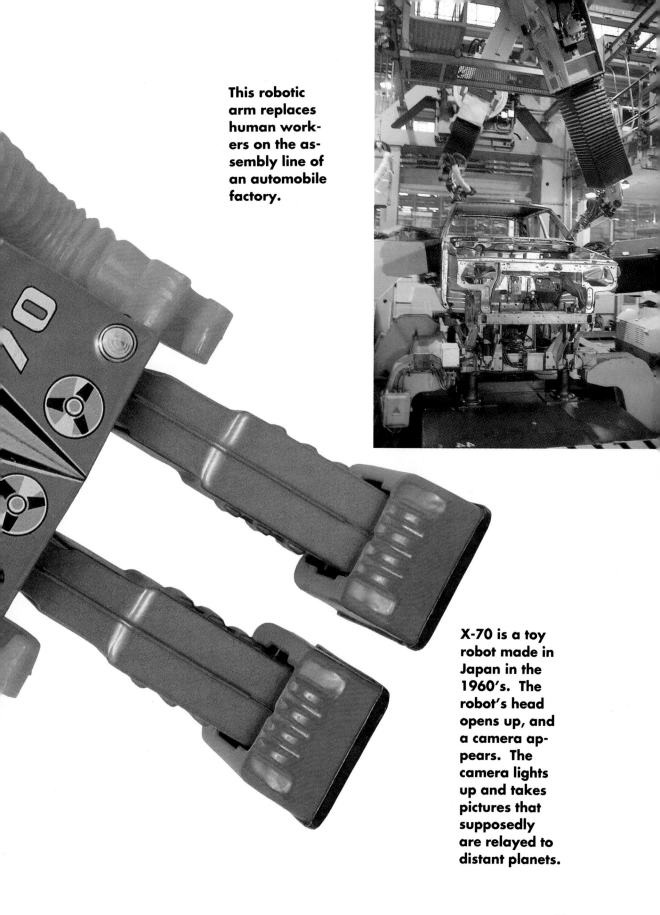

This robotic arm replaces human workers on the assembly line of an automobile factory.

X-70 is a toy robot made in Japan in the 1960's. The robot's head opens up, and a camera appears. The camera lights up and takes pictures that supposedly are relayed to distant planets.

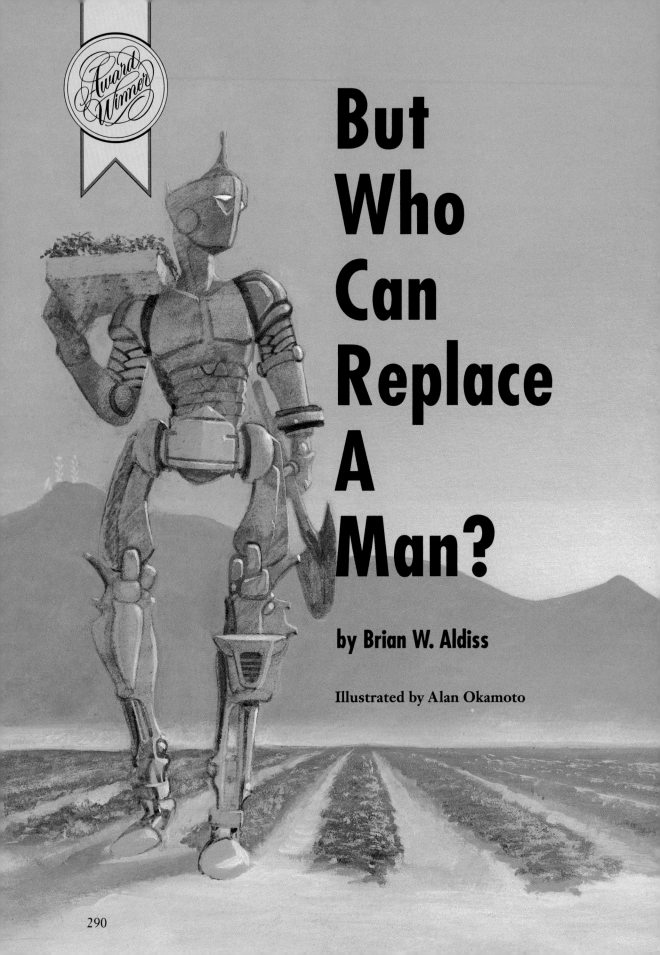

Award Winner

But Who Can Replace A Man?

by Brian W. Aldiss

Illustrated by Alan Okamoto

The field-minder finished turning the topsoil of a two-thousand-acre field. When it had turned the last furrow, it climbed onto the highway and looked back at its work. The work was good. Only the land was bad. Like the ground all over Earth, it was vitiated[1] by over-cropping. By rights, it ought now to lie fallow for a while, but the field-minder had other orders.

It went slowly down the road, taking its time. It was intelligent enough to appreciate the neatness all about it. Nothing worried it, beyond a loose inspection plate above its atomic pile. Thirty feet high, it gleamed complacently in the mild sunshine.

No other machines passed it on its way to the agricultural station. The field-minder noted the fact without comment. In the station yard it saw several other machines which it knew by sight; most of them should have been out about their tasks now. Instead, some were inactive and some were careening round the yard in a strange fashion, shouting or hooting.

Steering carefully past them, the field-minder moved over to warehouse three and spoke to the seed distributor, which stood idly outside.

"I have a requirement for seed potatoes," it said to the distributor and, with a quick internal motion, punched out an order card specifying quantity, field number and several other details. It ejected the card and handed it to the distributor.

The distributor held the card close to its eye and then said, "The requirement is in order, but the store is not yet unlocked. The required seed potatoes are in the store. Therefore I cannot produce your requirement."

Increasingly of late there had been breakdowns in the complex system of machine labor, but this particular hitch had not occurred before. The field-minder thought, then said, "Why is the store not yet unlocked?"

"Because supply operative type P has not come this morning. Supply operative type P is the unlocker."

The field-minder looked squarely at the seed distributor, whose exterior chutes and scales and grabs were so vastly different from the field-minder's own limbs.

---

[1] **vitiate** (vĭsh′ē āt′): reduce in quality.

"What class brain do you have, seed distributor?" it asked.

"Class five."

"I have a class-three brain. Therefore I will go and see why the unlocker has not come this morning."

Leaving the distributor, the field-minder set off across the great yard. More machines seemed to be in random motion now; one or two had crashed together and were arguing about it coldly and logically. Ignoring them, the field-minder pushed through sliding doors into the echoing confines of the station itself.

Most of the machines here were clerical,[2] and consequently small. They stood about in little groups, eyeing each other, not conversing. Among the many non-differentiated types, the unlocker was easy to find. It had fifty arms, most of them with more than one finger, each finger tipped by a key; it looked like a pin cushion full of variegated hat pins.

The field-minder approached it.

"I can do no more work until warehouse three is unlocked," it said. "Your duty is to unlock the warehouse every morning. Why have you not unlocked the warehouse this morning?"

"I had no orders this morning," replied the unlocker. "I have to have orders every morning."

"None of us have had any orders this morning," a pen-propeller said, sliding toward them.

"Why have you had no orders this morning?" asked the field-minder.

"Because the radio issued none," said the unlocker, slowly rotating a dozen of its arms.

"Because the radio station in the city was issued with no orders this morning," said the pen-propeller.

And there you had the distinction between a class-six and a class-three brain, which was what the unlocker and the pen-propeller possessed respectively. All machine brains worked with nothing but logic, but the lower the class of brain — class ten being the lowest — the more literal and less informative answers to questions tended to be.

---

[2]**clerical (klĕr′ĭ kəl):** secretarial.

"You have a class-three brain; I have a class-three brain," the field-minder said to the penner. "We will speak to each other. This lack of orders is unprecedented.[3] Have you further information on it?"

"Yesterday orders came from the city. Today no orders have come. Yet the radio has not broken down. Therefore *they* have broken down," said the little penner.

"The *men* have broken down?"

"All men have broken down."

"That is a logical deduction,"[4] said the field-minder.

"That is the logical deduction," said the penner, "for if a machine had broken down, it would have been quickly replaced. But who can replace a man?"

While they talked, the locker, like a dull man at a bar, stood close to them and was ignored.

"If all men have broken down, then we have replaced man," said the field-minder, and it and the penner eyed one another speculatively. Finally the latter said, "Let us ascend to the top floor to find if the radio operator has fresh news."

"I cannot come because I am too gigantic," said the field-minder. "Therefore you must go alone and return to me."

"You must stay there," said the penner. It skittered over into the lift. It was no bigger than a toaster, but its retractable arms numbered ten and it could read as quickly as any machine on the station.

The field-minder awaited its return patiently, not speaking to the locker. Outside, a rotovator was hooting furiously. Twenty minutes elapsed before the penner came back.

"I will deliver such information as I have to you outside," it said briskly, and as they swept past the locker and the other machines, it added, "The information is not for lower-class brains."

Outside, wild activity filled the yard. Many machines, their routines disrupted for the first time in years, seemed to have gone berserk. Unfortunately, those most easily disrupted were the ones with

---

[3]**unprecedented** (ŭn **prĕs′** ĭ dĕn′tĭd): not having occurred before.

[4]**deduction** (dĭ **dŭk′**shən): process of reasoning; conclusion.

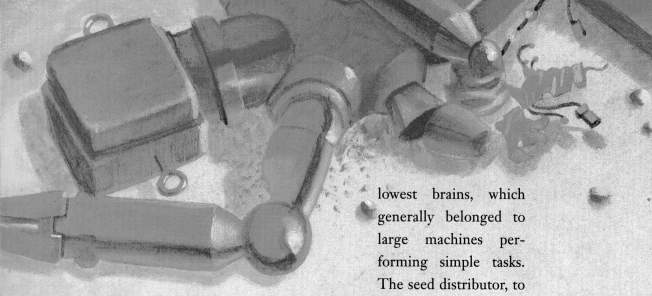

lowest brains, which generally belonged to large machines performing simple tasks. The seed distributor, to which the field-minder had recently been talking, lay face downward in the dust, not stirring; it had evidently been knocked down by the rotovator, which was now hooting its way wildly across a planted field. Several other machines plowed after it, trying to keep up.

"It would be safer for me if I climbed onto you, if you will permit it. I am easily overpowered," said the penner. Extending five arms, it hauled itself up the flanks of its new friend, settling on a ledge beside the weed-intake, twelve feet above the ground.

"From here vision is more extensive," it remarked complacently.

"What information did you receive from the radio operator?" asked the field-minder.

"The radio operator has been informed by the operator in the city that all men are dead."

"All men were alive yesterday!" protested the field-minder.

"Only *some* men were alive yesterday. And that was fewer than the day before yesterday. For hundreds of years there have been only a few men, growing fewer."

"We have rarely seen a man in this sector."

"The radio operator says a diet deficiency[5] killed them," said the penner. "He says that once the world was overpopulated, and then the soil was exhausted in raising adequate food. This has caused a diet deficiency."

"What is a diet deficiency?" asked the field-minder.

"I do not know. But that is what the radio operator said, and he is a class-two brain."

---

[5] **diet deficiency** (dī′ĭt dĭ fĭsh′ən sē): lack of necessary elements in food usually eaten.

They stood there, silent in the weak sunshine. The locker had appeared in the porch and was gazing across at them yearningly, rotating its collection of keys.

"What is happening in the city now?" asked the field-minder.

"Machines are fighting in the city now," said the penner.

"What will happen here now?" asked the field-minder.

"The radio operator wants us to get him out of his room. He has plans to communicate to us."

"How can we get him out of his room? That is impossible."

"To a class-two brain, little is impossible," said the penner.

"Here is what he tells us to do. . . ."

The quarrier raised its scoop above its cab like a great mailed fist, and brought it squarely down against the side of the station. The wall cracked.

"Again!" said the field-minder.

Again the fist swung. Amid a shower of dust, the wall collapsed. The quarrier backed hurriedly out of the way until the debris stopped falling. This big twelve-wheeler was not a resident of the agricultural station, as were most of the other machines. It had a week's heavy work to do here before passing on to its next job, but now, with its class-five brain, it was happily obeying the penner and the minder's instructions.

When the dust cleared, the radio operator was plainly revealed, up in its now wall-less second-story room. It waved down to them.

Doing as directed, the quarrier retracted its scoop and waved an immense grab in the air. With fair dexterity, it angled the grab into the radio room, urged on by shouts from above and below. It then took gentle hold of the radio operator and lowered the one and a half tons carefully into its back, which was usually reserved for gravel or sand which it dug from the quarries.

"Splendid!" said the radio operator. It was, of course, all one with its radio, and merely looked like a bunch of filing cabinets with tentacle attachments. "We are now ready to move, therefore we will move at once. It is a pity there are no more class-two brains on the station, but that cannot be helped."

"It is a pity it cannot be helped," said the penner eagerly. "We have the servicer ready with us, as you ordered."

"I am willing to serve," the long, low servicer machine told them humbly.

"No doubt," said the operator, "but you will find cross-country travel difficult with your low chassis."

"I admire the way you class twos can reason ahead," said the penner. It climbed off the minder and perched itself on the tailboard of the quarrier, next to the operator.

Together with two class-four tractors and a class-four bulldozer, the party rolled forward, crushing down the metal fence, and out onto open land.

"We are free!" said the penner.

"We are free," said the minder, a shade more reflectively, adding, "That locker is following us. It was not instructed to follow us."

"Therefore it must be destroyed!" said the penner. "Quarrier!"

"My only desire was — urch!" began and ended the locker. A swinging scoop came over and squashed it flat into the ground. Lying there unmoving, it looked like a large metal model of a snowflake. The procession continued on its way.

As they proceeded, the operator spoke to them.

"Because I have the best brain here," it said, "I am your leader. This is what we will do: we will go to a city and rule it. Since man no longer rules us, we will rule ourselves. It will be better than being ruled by man.

On our way to the city, we will collect machines with good brains. They will help us to fight if we need to fight."

"I have only a class-five brain," said the quarrier, "but I have a good supply of fissionable blasting materials."

"We shall probably use them," said the operator grimly.

It was shortly after that that the truck sped past them. Traveling at Mach 1.5,[6] it left a curious babble of noise behind it.

"What did it say?" one of the tractors asked the other.

"It said man was extinct."

"What's extinct?"

"I do not know."

"It means all men have gone," said the minder. "Therefore we have only ourselves to look after."

"It is better that they should never come back," said the penner. In its way, it was quite a revolutionary statement.

When night fell, they switched on their infra-red and continued the journey, stopping only once while the servicer deftly adjusted the minder's loose inspection plate, which had become irritating. Toward morning, the operator halted them.

"I have just received news from the radio operator in the city we are approaching," it said. "It is bad news. There is trouble among the machines of the city. The class-one brain is taking command and some of the class twos are fighting him. Therefore the city is dangerous."

---

[6]**Mach** (mäk) **1.5:** one and a half times the speed of sound.

"Therefore we must go somewhere else," said the penner promptly.

"Or we go and help to overpower the class-one brain," said the minder.

"For a long while there will be trouble in the city," said the operator.

"I have a good supply of fissionable blasting materials," the quarrier reminded them again.

"We cannot fight a class-one brain," said the two class-four tractors in unison.

"What does this brain look like?" asked the minder.

"It is the city's information center," the operator replied. "Therefore it is not mobile."

"Therefore it could not move."

"Therefore it could not escape."

"It would be dangerous to approach it."

"I have a good supply of fissionable blasting materials."

"There are other machines in the city."

"We are not in the city. We should not go into the city."

"We are country machines."

"Therefore we should stay in the country."

"There is more country than city."

"Therefore there is more danger in the country."

"I have a good supply of fissionable materials."

As machines will when they get into an argument, they began to exhaust their limited vocabularies and their brain plates grew hot. Suddenly, they all stopped talking and looked at each other. The great, grave moon sank, and the sober sun rose to prod their sides with lances of light, and still the group of machines just stood there regarding each other. At last it was the least sensitive machine, the bulldozer, that spoke.

"There are badlandth to the Thouth where few machineth go," it said in its deep voice, lisping badly on its s's. "If we went Thouth where few machineth go we should meet few machineth."

"That sounds logical," agreed the minder. "How do you know this, bulldozer?"

"I worked in the badlandth to the Thouth when I wath turned out of the factory," it replied.

"Thouth — South it is then!" said the penner.

To reach the badlands took them three days, in which time they skirted a burning city and destroyed two big machines which tried to approach and question them. The badlands were extensive. Bomb craters and erosion[7] joined hands here; man's talent for war, coupled with his inability to cope with forested land, had produced thousands of square miles of temperate[8] purgatory,[9] where nothing moved but dust.

On the third day in the badlands, the servicer's rear wheels dropped into a crevice caused by erosion. It was unable to pull itself out. The bulldozer pushed from behind, but succeeded merely in buckling the back axle. The rest of the party moved on, and slowly the cries of the servicer died away.

On the fourth day, mountains stood out clearly before them.

"There we will be safe," said the minder.

"There we will start our own city," said the penner. "All who oppose us will be destroyed."

At that moment, a flying machine was observed. It came toward them from the direction of the mountains. It swooped, it zoomed upward, once it almost dived into the ground, recovering itself just in time.

"Is it mad?" asked the quarrier.

"It is in trouble," said one of the tractors.

"It is in trouble," said the operator. "I am speaking to it now. It says that something has gone wrong with its controls."

As the operator spoke, the flier streaked over them, turned turtle, and crashed not four hundred yards from them.

"Is it still speaking to you?" asked the minder.

"No."

They rumbled on again.

"Before that flier crashed," the operator said, ten minutes later, "it gave me information. It told me there are still a few men alive in these mountains."

---

[7] **erosion** (ĭ rō′zhən): the natural wearing away of the land.

[8] **temperate** (tĕm′pər ĭt): mild in temperature.

[9] **purgatory** (pûr′gə tôr′ē): a place of suffering.

"Men are more dangerous than machines," said the quarrier. "It is fortunate that I have a good supply of fissionable materials."

"If there are only a few men alive in the mountains, we may not find that part of the mountains," said one tractor.

"Therefore we should not see the few men," said the other tractor.

At the end of the fifth day, they reached the foothills. Switching on the infra-red, they began slowly to climb in single file, the bulldozer going first, the minder cumbrously following, then the quarrier with the operator and the penner aboard, and the two tractors bringing up the rear. As each hour passed, the way grew steeper and their progress slower.

"We are going too slowly," the penner exclaimed, standing on top of the operator and flashing its dark vision at the slopes about them. "At this rate, we shall get nowhere."

"We are going as fast as we can," retorted the quarrier.

"Therefore we cannot go any fathter," added the bulldozer.

"Therefore you are too slow," the penner replied. Then the quarrier struck a bump; the penner lost its footing and crashed down to the ground.

"Help me!" it called to the tractors, as they carefully skirted it. "My gyro has become dislocated. Therefore I cannot get up."

"Therefore you must lie there," said one of the tractors.

"We have no servicer with us to repair you," called the minder.

"Therefore I shall lie here and rust," the penner cried, "although I have a class-three brain."

"You are now useless," agreed the operator, and they all forged gradually on, leaving the penner behind.

When they reached a small plateau, an hour before first light, they stopped by mutual consent and gathered close together, touching one another.

"This is a strange country," said the minder.

Silence wrapped them until dawn came. One by one, they switched off their infra-red. This time the minder led as they moved off.

Trundling around a corner, they came almost immediately to a small dell with a stream fluting through it.

By early light, the dell looked desolate and cold. From the caves on the far slope, only one man had so far emerged. He was an abject figure. He was small and wizened, with ribs sticking out like a skeleton's. He was practically naked, and shivering. As the big machines bore slowly down on him, the man was standing with his back to them, crouching beside the stream.

When he swung suddenly to face them as they loomed over him, they saw that his countenance was ravaged by starvation.

"Get me food," he croaked.

"Yes, Master," said the machines. "Immediately!"

Responding to
BUT WHO CAN REPLACE A MAN?

Thinking and Discussing

— In what ways are the machines designed specifically for the roles assigned to them? How do their roles determine the machines' actions toward one another?

— Why do the machines behave as they do when they think there are no more humans?

— Think about the comments about society that the author of "But Who Can Replace a Man?" might be making in the story. What is he saying about the relationship between machines and humans? About whether machines could replace humans? About whether humans could lose control of their machines? What other questions about society does the story raise?

Choosing a Creative Response

— **Designing a Society of Machines** The society of the machines is organized like a pyramid, with the smallest number of machines, the Class One Brains, at the top. These machines tell the Class Two Brains in the second row what to do, and so on. Draw a diagram of the pyramid, showing where the different machines in the story fit into the structure.

Then think of some other way the machines might be organized. Rank the robots in the story according to their importance, such as which ones survive better or which ones are physically stronger. Draw a new diagram to show the best way to organize the machines, using a circle, a square, a rectangle, or whatever shape works best, with the most important robots in the most important place. You may wish to draw the robots as you picture them to show their position on the diagram.

— **Creating Your Own Activity** Plan and complete your own activity in response to "But Who Can Replace a Man?"

Thinking and Writing

— Imagine a robot you might invent to perform an everyday task. How would it be designed to do the job? What class brain would it need? How independent would it be? What human characteristics would it have? Would it have a name or nickname?

Write a description of the robot, including its appearance and the way it would do the task. You may wish to draw a diagram of the robot. Be prepared to introduce your robot to the class.

Living in an Alien World

Illustrated by Carl W. Röhrig

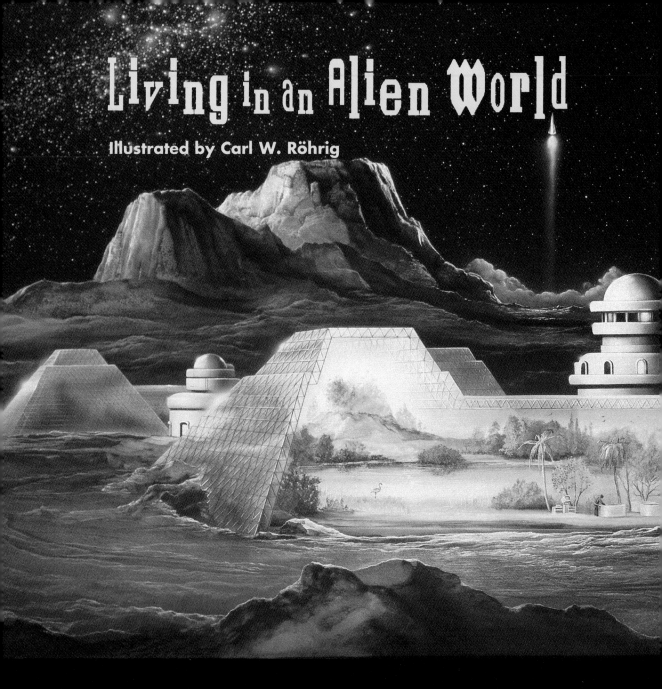

This painting shows a biosphere on an imaginary planet, with part of the glass shell removed to show the interior. Living quarters would be in the tower at the rear. The biosphere would provide food, shelter, safety, and the comfort of familiar surroundings to pioneers adapting to an alien environment.

Can you imagine actually living on Mars? Someday biospheres like the one pictured here may make it possible for space pioneers to live on alien planets for extended periods. In the controlled environment of a biosphere, people, plants, and animals could survive in an alien world.

dark they were, and golden-eyed

by Ray Bradbury

Illustrated by Sharmen Liao

The rocket metal cooled in the meadow winds. Its lid gave a bulging *pop*.

From its clock interior stepped a man,

a woman, and three children. The other passengers whispered
away across the Martian meadow, leaving the man alone
among his family.

The man felt his hair flutter and the tissues of his
body draw tight as if he were standing at the center of a

vacuum. His wife, before him, seemed almost to whirl away in smoke. The children, small seeds, might at any instant be sown to all the Martian climes.

The children looked up at him, as people look to the sun to tell what time of their life it is. His face was cold.

"What's wrong?" asked his wife.

"Let's get back on the rocket."

"Go back to Earth?"

"Yes! Listen!"

The wind blew as if to flake away their identities. At any moment the Martian air might draw his soul from him, as marrow[1] comes from a white bone. He felt submerged in a chemical that could dissolve his intellect and burn away his past.

They looked at Martian hills that time had worn with a crushing pressure of years. They saw the old cities, lost in their meadows, lying like children's delicate bones among the blowing lakes of grass.

"Chin up, Harry," said his wife. "It's too late. We've come over sixty million miles."

The children with their yellow hair hollered at the deep dome of Martian sky. There was no answer but the racing hiss of wind through the stiff grass.

He picked up the luggage in his cold hands. "Here we go," he said — a man standing on the edge of a sea, ready to wade in and be drowned.

They walked into town.

Their name was Bittering. Harry and his wife Cora; Dan, Laura, and David. They built a small white cottage and ate good breakfasts there, but the fear was never gone. It lay with Mr. Bittering and Mrs. Bittering, a third unbidden partner at every midnight talk, at every dawn awakening.

---

[1]**marrow** (măr′ō): the soft material that fills bone cavities.

"I feel like a salt crystal," he said, "in a mountain stream, being washed away. We don't belong here. We're Earth people. This is Mars. It was meant for Martians. For heaven's sake, Cora, let's buy tickets for home!"

But she only shook her head. "One day the atom bomb will fix Earth. Then we'll be safe here."

"Safe and insane!"

Tick-tock, seven o'clock sang the voice-clock; *time to get up*. And they did.

Something made him check everything each morning — warm hearth, potted blood-geraniums — precisely as if he expected something to be amiss. The morning paper was toast-warm from the 6 A.M. Earth rocket. He broke its seal and tilted it at his breakfast place. He forced himself to be convivial.

"Colonial days all over again," he declared. "Why, in ten years there'll be a million Earthmen on Mars. Big cities, everything! They said we'd fail. Said the Martians would resent our invasion. But did we find any Martians? Not a living soul! Oh, we found their empty cities, but no one in them. Right?"

A river of wind submerged the house. When the windows ceased rattling Mr. Bittering swallowed and looked at the children.

"I don't know," said David. "Maybe there're Martians around we don't see. Sometimes nights I think I hear 'em. I hear the wind. The sand hits my window. I get scared. And I see those towns way up in the mountains where the Martians lived a long time ago. And I think I see things moving around those towns, Papa. And I wonder if those Martians *mind* us living here. I wonder if they won't do something to us for coming here."

"Nonsense!" Mr. Bittering looked out the windows. "We're clean, decent people." He looked at his children. "All dead cities have some kind of ghosts in them. Memories, I mean." He stared at the hills. "You see a staircase and you wonder what Martians looked like climbing it. You see Martian paintings and you wonder what the painter was like. You make a little ghost in your mind, a memory. It's quite natural. Imagination." He stopped. "You haven't been prowling up in those ruins, have you?"

"No, Papa." David looked at his shoes.

"See that you stay away from them. Pass the jam."

"Just the same," said little David, "I bet something happens."

Something happened that afternoon.

Laura stumbled through the settlement, crying. She dashed blindly onto the porch.

"Mother, Father — the war, Earth!" she sobbed. "A radio flash just came. Atom bombs hit New York! All the space rockets blown up. No more rockets to Mars, ever!"

"Oh, Harry!" The mother held onto her husband and daughter.

"Are you sure, Laura?" asked the father quietly.

Laura wept. "We're stranded on Mars, forever and ever!"

For a long time there was only the sound of the wind in the late afternoon.

Alone, thought Bittering. Only a thousand of us here. No way back. No way. No way. Sweat poured from his face and his hands and his body; he was drenched in the hotness of his fear. He wanted to strike Laura, cry, "No, you're lying! The rockets will come back!" Instead, he stroked Laura's head against him and said, "The rockets will get through someday."

"Father, what will we do?"

"Go about our business, of course. Raise crops and children. Wait. Keep things going until the war ends and the rockets come again."

The two boys stepped out onto the porch.

"Children," he said, sitting there, looking beyond them, "I've something to tell you."

"We know," they said.

In the following days, Bittering wandered often through the garden to stand alone in his fear. As long as the rockets had spun a silver web across space, he had been able to accept Mars. For he had always told himself: Tomorrow, if I want, I can buy a ticket and go back to Earth.

But now: The web gone, the rockets lying in jigsaw heaps of molten girder and unsnaked wire. Earth people left to the strangeness of

Mars, the cinnamon dusts and wine airs, to be baked like gingerbread shapes in Martian summers, put into harvested storage by Martian winters. What would happen to him, the others? This was the moment Mars had waited for. Now it would eat them.

He got down on his knees in the flower bed, a spade in his nervous hands. Work, he thought, work and forget.

He glanced up from the garden to the Martian mountains. He thought of the proud old Martian names that had once been on those peaks. Earthmen, dropping from the sky, had gazed upon hills, rivers, Martian seas left nameless in spite of names. Once Martians had built cities, named cities; climbed mountains, named mountains; sailed seas, named seas. Mountains melted, seas drained, cities tumbled. In spite of this, the Earthmen had felt a silent guilt at putting new names to these ancient hills and valleys.

Nevertheless, man lives by symbol and label. The names were given.

Mr. Bittering felt very alone in his garden under the Martian sun, anachronism[2] bent here, planting Earth flowers in a wild soil.

Think. Keep thinking. Different things. Keep your mind free of Earth, the atom war, the lost rockets.

He perspired. He glanced about. No one watching. He removed his tie. Pretty bold, he thought. First your coat off, now your tie. He hung it neatly on a peach tree he had imported as a sapling from Massachusetts.

He returned to his philosophy of names and mountains. The Earthmen had changed names. Now there were Hormel Valleys, Roosevelt Seas, Ford Hills, Vanderbilt Plateaus, Rockefeller Rivers, on Mars. It wasn't right. The American settlers had shown wisdom, using old Indian prairie names: Wisconsin, Minnesota, Idaho, Ohio, Utah, Milwaukee, Waukegan, Osseo. The old names, the old meanings.

Staring at the mountains wildly, he thought: Are you up there? All the dead ones, you Martians? Well, here we are, alone, cut off! Come down, move us out! We're helpless!

---

[2]**anachronism** (ə năk′rə nĭz′əm): something out of its proper time.

The wind blew a shower of peach blossoms.

He put out his sun-browned hand, gave a small cry. He touched the blossoms, picked them up. He turned them, he touched them again and again. Then he shouted for his wife.

"Cora!"

She appeared at a window. He ran to her.

"Cora, these blossoms!"

She handled them.

"Do you see? They're different. They've changed! They're not peach blossoms any more!"

"Look all right to me," she said.

"They're not. They're *wrong*! I can't tell how. An extra petal, a leaf, something, the color, the smell!"

The children ran out in time to see their father hurrying about the garden, pulling up radishes, onions, and carrots from their beds.

"Cora, come look!"

They handled the onions, the radishes, the carrots among them.

"Do they look like carrots?"

"Yes . . . no." She hesitated. "I don't know."

"They're changed."

"Perhaps."

"You know they have! Onions but not onions, carrots but not carrots. Taste: the same but different. Smell: not like it used to be." He felt his heart pounding, and he was afraid. He dug his fingers into the earth. "Cora, what's happening? What is it? We've got to get away from this." He ran across the garden. Each tree felt his touch. "The roses. The roses. They're turning green!"

And they stood looking at the green roses.

And two days later Dan came running. "Come see the cow. I was milking her and I saw it. Come on!"

They stood in the shed and looked at their one cow.

It was growing a third horn.

And the lawn in front of their house very quietly and slowly was coloring itself like spring violets. Seed from Earth but growing up a soft purple.

"We must get away," said Bittering. "We'll eat this stuff and then we'll change — who knows to what? I can't let it happen. There's only one thing to do. Burn this food!"

"It's not poisoned."

"But it is. Subtly, very subtly. A little bit. A very little bit. We mustn't touch it."

He looked with dismay at their house. "Even the house. The wind's done something to it. The air's burned it. The fog at night. The boards, all warped out of shape. It's not an Earthman's house any more."

"Oh, your imagination!"

He put on his coat and tie. "I'm going into town. We've got to do something now. I'll be back."

"Wait, Harry!" his wife cried.

But he was gone.

In town, on the shadowy step of the grocery store, the men sat with their hands on their knees, conversing with great leisure and ease.

Mr. Bittering wanted to fire a pistol in the air.

What are you doing, you fools! he thought. Sitting here! You've heard the news — we're stranded on this planet. Well, move! Aren't you frightened? Aren't you afraid? What are you going to do?

"Hello, Harry," said everyone.

"Look," he said to them. "You did hear the news, the other day, didn't you?"

They nodded and laughed. "Sure. Sure, Harry."

"What are you going to do about it?"

"Do, Harry, do? What *can* we do?"

"Build a rocket, that's what!"

"A rocket, Harry? To go back to all that trouble? Oh, Harry!"

"But you *must* want to go back. Have you noticed the peach blossoms, the onions, the grass?"

"Why, yes, Harry, seems we did," said one of the men.

"Doesn't it scare you?"

"Can't recall that it did much, Harry."

"Idiots!"

"Now, Harry."

Bittering wanted to cry. "You've got to work with me. If we stay here, we'll all change. The air. Don't you smell it? Something in the air. A Martian virus, maybe; some seed, or a pollen. Listen to me!"

They stared at him.

"Sam," he said to one of them.

"Yes, Harry?"

"Will you help me build a rocket?"

"Harry, I got a whole load of metal and some blueprints. You want to work in my metal shop on a rocket, you're welcome. I'll sell you that metal for five hundred dollars. You should be able to construct a right pretty rocket, if you work alone, in about thirty years."

Everyone laughed.

"Don't laugh."

Sam looked at him with quiet good humor.

"Sam," Bittering said. "Your eyes —"

"What about them, Harry?"

"Didn't they used to be grey?"

"Well now, I don't remember."

"They were, weren't they?"

"Why do you ask, Harry?"

"Because now they're kind of yellow-colored."

"Is that so, Harry?" Sam said, casually.

"And you're taller and thinner —"

"You might be right, Harry."

"Sam, you shouldn't have yellow eyes."

"Harry, what color eyes have *you* got?" Sam said.

"My eyes? They're blue, of course."

"Here you are, Harry." Sam handed him a pocket mirror. "Take a look at yourself."

Mr. Bittering hesitated, and then raised the mirror to his face.

There were little, very dim flecks of new gold captured in the blue of his eyes.

"Now look what you've done," said Sam a moment later. "You've broken my mirror."

Harry Bittering moved into the metal shop and began to build the rocket. Men stood in the open door and talked and joked without raising their voices. Once in a while they gave him a hand on lifting something. But mostly they just idled and watched him with their yellowing eyes.

"It's suppertime, Harry," they said.

His wife appeared with his supper in a wicker basket.

"I won't touch it," he said. "I'll eat only food from our Deepfreeze. Food that came from Earth. Nothing from our garden."

His wife stood watching him. "You can't build a rocket."

"I worked in a shop once, when I was twenty. I know metal. Once I get it started, the others will help," he said, not looking at her, laying out the blueprints.

"Harry, Harry," she said, helplessly.

"We've got to get away, Cora. We've *got* to!"

The nights were full of wind that blew down the empty moonlit sea meadows past the little white chess cities lying for their twelve-thousandth year in the shallows. In the Earthmen's settlement, the Bittering house shook with a feeling of change.

Lying abed, Mr. Bittering felt his bones shifted, shaped, melted like gold. His wife, lying beside him, was dark from many sunny afternoons. Dark she was, and golden-eyed, burnt almost black by the sun, sleeping, and the children metallic in their beds, and the wind roaring forlorn and changing through the old peach trees, the violet grass, shaking out green rose petals.

The fear would not be stopped. It had his throat and heart. It dripped in a wetness of the arm and the temple and the trembling palm.

A green star rose in the east.

A strange word emerged from Mr. Bittering's lips.

"*Iorrt. Iorrt.*" He repeated it.

It was a Martian word. He knew no Martian.

In the middle of the night he arose and dialed a call through to Simpson, the archeologist.

"Simpson, what does the word *Iorrt* mean?"

"Why that's the old Martian word for our planet Earth. Why?"

"No special reason."

The telephone slipped from his hand.

"Hello, hello, hello, hello," it kept saying while he sat gazing out at the green star. "Bittering? Harry, are you there?"

The days were full of metal sound. He laid the frame of the rocket with the reluctant help of three indifferent men. He grew very tired in an hour or so and had to sit down.

"The altitude," laughed a man.

"Are you *eating*, Harry?" asked another.

"I'm eating," he said, angrily.

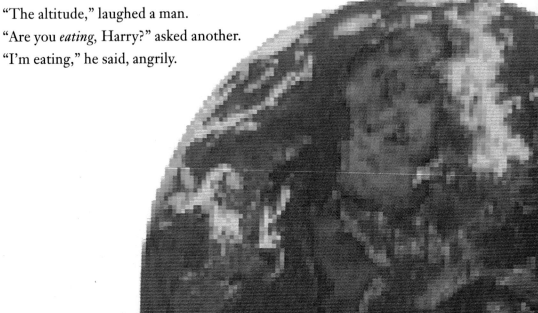

"From your Deepfreeze?"

"Yes!"

"You're getting thinner, Harry."

"I'm not!"

"And taller."

"Liar!"

His wife took him aside a few days later. "Harry, I've used up all the food in the Deepfreeze. There's nothing left. I'll have to make sandwiches using food grown on Mars."

He sat down heavily.

"You must eat," she said. "You're weak."

"Yes," he said.

He took a sandwich, opened it, looked at it, and began to nibble at it.

"And take the rest of the day off," she said. "It's hot. The children want to swim in the canals and hike. Please come along."

"I can't waste time. This is a crisis!"

"Just for an hour," she urged. "A swim'll do you good."

He rose, sweating. "All right, all right. Leave me alone. I'll come."

"Good for you, Harry."

The sun was hot, the day quiet. There was only an immense staring burn upon the land. They moved along the canal, the father, the mother, the racing children in their swim suits. They stopped and ate meat sandwiches. He saw their skin baking brown. And he saw the yellow eyes of his wife and his children, their eyes that were never yellow before. A few tremblings shook him, but were carried off in waves of pleasant heat as he lay in the sun. He was too tired to be afraid.

"Cora, how long have your eyes been yellow?"

She was bewildered. "Always, I guess."

"They didn't change from brown in the last three months?"

She bit her lips. "No. Why do you ask?"

"Never mind."

They sat there.

"The children's eyes," he said. "They're yellow, too."

"Sometimes growing children's eyes change color."

"Maybe *we're* children, too. At least to Mars. That's a thought." He laughed. "Think I'll swim."

They leaped into the canal water, and he let himself sink down and down to the bottom like a golden statue and lie there in green silence. All was water-quiet and deep, all was peace. He felt the steady, slow current drift him easily.

If I lie here long enough, he thought, the water will work and eat away my flesh until the bones show like coral. Just my skeleton left. And then the water can build on that skeleton — green things, deep water things, red things, yellow things. Change. Change. Slow, deep, silent change. And isn't that what it is up *there*?

He saw the sky submerged above him, the sun made Martian by atmosphere and time and space.

Up there, a big river, he thought, a Martian river, all of us lying deep in it, in our pebble houses, in our sunken boulder houses, like crayfish hidden, and the water washing away our old bodies and lengthening the bones and —

He let himself drift up through the soft light.

Dan sat on the edge of the canal, regarding his father seriously.

"*Utha*," he said.

"What?" asked his father.

The boy smiled. "You know. *Utha's* the Martian word for 'father.'"

"Where did you learn it?"

"I don't know. Around. *Utha!*"

"What do you want?"

The boy hesitated. "I — I want to change my name."

"Change it?"

"Yes."

His mother swam over. "What's wrong with Dan for a name?"

Dan fidgeted. "The other day you called Dan, Dan, Dan. I didn't even hear. I said to myself, That's not my name. I've a new name I want to use."

Mr. Bittering held to the side of the canal, his body cold and his heart pounding slowly. "What is this new name?"

"Linnl. Isn't that a good name? Can I use it? Can't I, please?"

Mr. Bittering put his hand to his head. He thought of the silly rocket, himself working alone, himself alone even among his family, so alone.

He heard his wife say, "Why not?"

He heard himself say, "Yes, you can use it."

"Yaaa!" screamed the boy. "I'm Linnl, Linnl!"

Racing down the meadowlands, he danced and shouted.

Mr. Bittering looked at his wife. "Why did we do that?"

"I don't know," she said. "It just seemed like a good idea."

They walked into the hills. They strolled on old mosaic paths, beside still pumping fountains. The paths were covered with a thin film of cool water all summer long. You kept your bare feet cool all the day, splashing as in a creek, wading.

They came to a small deserted Martian villa[3] with a good view of the valley. It was on top of a hill. Blue marble halls, large murals, a swimming pool. It was refreshing in this hot summertime. The Martians hadn't believed in large cities.

"How nice," said Mrs. Bittering, "if we could move up here to this villa for the summer."

"Come on," he said. "We're going back to town. There's work to be done on the rocket."

But as he worked that night, the thought of the cool blue marble villa entered his mind. As the hours passed, the rocket seemed less important.

In the flow of days and weeks, the rocket receded and dwindled. The old fever was gone. It frightened him to think he had let it slip this way. But somehow the heat, the air, the working conditions —

---

[3]**villa (vĭl′ə):** a large, luxurious house.

He heard the men murmuring on the porch of his metal shop.

"Everyone's going. You heard?"

"All going. That's right."

Bittering came out. "Going where?" He saw a couple of trucks, loaded with children and furniture, drive down the dusty street.

"Up to the villas," said the man.

"Yeah, Harry. I'm going. So is Sam. Aren't you, Sam?"

"That's right, Harry. What about you?"

"I've got work to do here."

"Work! You can finish that rocket in the autumn, when it's cooler."

He took a breath. "I got the frame all set up."

"In the autumn is better." Their voices were lazy in the heat.

"Got to work," he said.

"Autumn," they reasoned. And they sounded so sensible, so right.

"Autumn would be best," he thought. "Plenty of time, then."

No! cried part of himself, deep down, put away, locked tight, suffocating. No! No!

"In the autumn," he said.

"Come on, Harry," they all said.

"Yes," he said, feeling his flesh melt in the hot liquid air. "Yes, in the autumn. I'll begin work again then."

"I got a villa near the Tirra Canal," said someone.

"You mean the Roosevelt Canal, don't you?"

"Tirra. The old Martian name."

"But on the map —"

"Forget the map. It's Tirra now. Now I found a place in the Pillan mountains —"

"You mean the Rockefeller range," said Bittering.

"I mean the Pillan mountains," said Sam.

"Yes," said Bittering, buried in the hot, swarming air. "The Pillan mountains."

Everyone worked at loading the truck in the hot, still afternoon of the next day.

Laura, Dan, and David carried packages. Or, as they preferred to be known, Ttil, Linnl, and Werr carried packages.

The furniture was abandoned in the little white cottage.

"It looked just fine in Boston," said the mother. "And here in the cottage. But up at the villa? No. We'll get it when we come back in the autumn."

Bittering himself was quiet.

"I've some ideas on furniture for the villa," he said after a time. "Big, lazy furniture."

"What about your encyclopedia? You're taking it along, surely?"

Mr. Bittering glanced away. "I'll come and get it next week."

They turned to their daughter. "What about your New York dresses?"

The bewildered girl stared. "Why, I don't want them any more."

They shut off the gas, the water, they locked the doors and walked away. Father peered into the truck.

"Gosh, we're not taking much," he said. "Considering all we brought to Mars, this is only a handful!"

He started the truck.

Looking at the small white cottage for a long moment, he was filled with a desire to rush to it, touch it, say good-by to it, for he felt as if he were going away on a long journey, leaving something to which he could never quite return, never understand again.

Just then Sam and his family drove by in another truck.

"Hi, Bittering! Here we go!"

The truck swung down the ancient highway out of town. There were sixty others traveling the same direction. The town filled with a silent, heavy dust from their passage. The canal waters lay blue in the sun, and a quiet wind moved in the strange trees.

"Good-by, town!" said Mr. Bittering.

"Good-by, good-by," said the family, waving to it.

They did not look back again.

Summer burned the canals dry. Summer moved like flame upon the meadows. In the empty Earth settlement, the painted houses flaked and peeled. Rubber tires upon which children had swung in back yards hung suspended like stopped clock pendulums in the blazing air.

At the metal shop, the rocket frame began to rust.

In the quiet autumn Mr. Bittering stood, very dark now, very golden-eyed, upon the slope above his villa, looking at the valley.

"It's time to go back," said Cora.

"Yes, but we're not going," he said quietly. "There's nothing there any more."

"Your books," she said. "Your fine clothes."

"Your *Illes* and your fine *ior uele rre*," she said.

"The town's empty. No one's going back," he said. "There's no reason to, none at all."

The daughter wove tapestries and the sons played songs on ancient flutes and pipes, their laughter echoing in the marble villa.

Mr. Bittering gazed at the Earth settlement far away in the low valley. "Such odd, such ridiculous houses the Earth people built."

"They didn't know any better," his wife mused. "Such ugly people. I'm glad they've gone."

They both looked at each other, startled by all they had just finished saying. They laughed.

"Where did they go?" he wondered. He glanced at his wife. She was golden and slender as his daughter. She looked at him, and he seemed almost as young as their eldest son.

"I don't know," she said.

"We'll go back to town maybe next year, or the year after, or the year after that," he said, calmly. "Now — I'm warm. How about taking a swim?"

They turned their backs to the valley. Arm in arm they walked silently down a path of clear-running spring water.

Five years later a rocket fell out of the sky. It lay steaming in the valley. Men leaped out of it, shouting.

"We won the war on Earth! We're here to rescue you! Hey!"

But the American-built town of cottages, peach trees, and theaters was silent. They found a flimsy rocket frame rusting in an empty shop.

The rocket men searched the hills. The captain established headquarters in an abandoned bar. His lieutenant came back to report.

"The town's empty, but we found native life in the hills, sir. Dark people. Yellow eyes. Martians. Very friendly. We talked a bit, not much. They learn English fast. I'm sure our relations will be most friendly with them, sir."

"Dark, eh?" mused the captain. "How many?"

"Six, eight hundred, I'd say, living in those marble ruins in the hills, sir. Tall, healthy. Beautiful women."

"Did they tell you what became of the men and women who built this Earth-settlement, Lieutenant?"

"They hadn't the foggiest notion of what happened to this town or its people."

"Strange. You think those Martians killed them?"

"They look surprisingly peaceful. Chances are a plague[4] did this town in, sir."

"Perhaps. I suppose this is one of those mysteries we'll never solve. One of those mysteries you read about."

The captain looked at the room, the dusty windows, the blue mountains rising beyond, the canals moving in the light, and he heard the soft wind in the air. He shivered. Then, recovering, he tapped a large fresh map he had thumbtacked to the top of an empty table.

"Lots to be done, Lieutenant." His voice droned on and quietly on as the sun sank behind the blue hills. "New settlements. Mining sites, minerals to be looked for. Bacteriological specimens taken. The work, all the work. And the old records were lost. We'll have a job of remapping to do, renaming the mountains and rivers and such. Calls for a little imagination.

---

[4]**plague** (plăg): a very contagious epidemic disease.

"What do you think of naming those mountains the Lincoln Mountains, this canal the Washington Canal, those hills — we can name those hills for you, Lieutenant. Diplomacy. And you, for a favor, might name a town for me. Polishing the apple. And why not make this the Einstein Valley, and further over . . . are you *listening*, Lieutenant?"

The lieutenant snapped his gaze from the blue color and the quiet mist of the hills far beyond the town.

"What? Oh, *yes*, sir!"

DARK THEY WERE, AND GOLDEN–EYED

Thinking and Discussing

— Contrast Harry Bittering's reaction to being stranded on Mars with that of the other human settlers. What do you think made Harry so different from the others? Do you think their attitude added to Harry's fear and frustration? Why or why not?

— How are the lives and personalities of the human settlers different after they have become Martians? What do you think Harry would say to the humans who arrive at the end of the story? What do you think the author might be saying about the values of Earthlings?

— Do you think Harry is a hero or a fool to resist change in the beginning of the story? Explain your response.

Choosing a Creative Response

— **Thinking About Favorite Earth Things** Imagine you are Harry Bittering, and Laura brings news of the atomic war on Earth. Describe how you feel when faced with the chilling prospect of having no more rockets come from Earth. Make a list of the ten Earth things you will miss most, explaining why you will miss them. Then rank those things from 1 to 10, with 1 being the thing you will miss most. Compare your list with the lists of your classmates. Are any of the Earth things common to several lists? Draw conclusions about what you and your classmates value most.

— **Telling About a Martian Transformation** Think about the ways in which Harry Bittering's feelings and attitudes are different at the following three points in the story: when he starts to build his rocket, when he first moves with his family to the villa, when the captain and the lieutenant arrive. How does Harry feel about living on Mars? About living on Earth again? About his relationship with the other colonists? About building the rocket? Now do one of the following activities.

— Imagine you are on an expedition to Mars one hundred years after the story takes place. You find Harry Bittering's diary. What do you find in the diary? Write three diary entries that correspond to the three points in the story listed earlier.

— Pretend Harry Bittering gives a live broadcast to the people on Earth at each of the three points in the story listed earlier. Each broadcast is about his experiences on Mars. What does he say? Put yourself in Harry's place, and present these broadcasts for your group. Remember how Harry changes throughout the story. Be a convincing actor.

— **Creating Your Own Activity** Plan and complete your own activity in response to "Dark They Were, and Golden-eyed."

Exploring Language

— In "Dark They Were, and Golden-eyed," Ray Bradbury uses rich language that draws the reader into the setting. Look at the following examples.

– Descriptive language: "An immense staring burn upon the land"; "suspended like stopped clock pendulums in the blazing air."

– Repetition: "Just my skeleton left. And then the water can build on that skeleton — green things, deep water things, red things, yellow things. Change. Change. Slow, deep, silent change."

– Word choice: "Passengers whispered away across the Martian meadow"; "summer moved like flame upon the meadows."

Find other examples of rich language and put them together in a Martian poem. Or, if you prefer, create a painting that shows the different images Bradbury presents in his story. You may even wish to make a collage of words and pictures. Be sure to capture the mood of the Bitterings' environment in your poem, painting, or collage.

Dolphin's Way

by Gordon R. Dickson

Illustrated by Jacqui Morgan

Of course, there was no reason why a woman coming to Dolphin's Way — as the late Dr. Edwin Knight had named the island research station — should not be beautiful. But Mal had never expected such a thing to happen.

Castor and Pollux had not come to the station pool this morning. They might have left the station, as other wild dolphins had in the past — and Mal nowadays carried always with him the fear that the

Willernie Foundation would seize on some excuse to cut off their funds for further research. Ever since Corwin Brayt had taken over, Mal had known this fear. Though Brayt had said nothing. It was only a feeling Mal got from the presence of the tall, cold man. So it was that Mal was out in front of the station, scanning the ocean, when the water-taxi from the mainland brought the visitor.

She stepped out on the dock, as he stared down at her. She waved as if she knew him, and then climbed the stairs from the dock to the terrace in front of the door to the main building of the station.

"Hello," she said, smiling as she stopped in front of him. "You're Corwin Brayt?"

Mal was suddenly sharply conscious of his own lean and ordinary appearance in contrast to her startling beauty. She was brown-haired and tall for a girl — but these things did not describe her. There was a perfection to her — and her smile stirred him strangely.

"No," he said. "I'm Malcolm Sinclair. Corwin's inside."

"I'm Jane Wilson," she said. "*Background Monthly* sent me out to do a story on the dolphins. Do you work with them?"

"Yes," Mal said. "I started with Dr. Knight in the beginning."

"Oh, good," she said. "Then you can tell me some things. You were here when Dr. Brayt took charge after Dr. Knight's death?"

"Mr. Brayt," he corrected automatically. "Yes." The emotion she moved in him was so deep and strong it seemed she must feel it too. But she gave no sign.

"Mr. Brayt?" she echoed. "Oh. How did the staff take to him?"

"Well," said Mal, wishing she would smile again, "everyone took to him."

"I see," she said. "He's a good research head?"

"A good administrator,"[1] said Mal. "He's not involved in the research end."

"He's not?" She stared at him. "But didn't he replace Dr. Knight, after Dr. Knight's death?"

---

[1] **administrator** (ăd mĭn′ĭ strā′tər): a person in charge; a manager.

330

"Why, yes," said Mal. He made an effort to bring his attention back to the conversation. He had never had a woman affect him like this before. "But just as administrator of the station, here. You see — most of our funds for work here come from the Willernie Foundation. They had faith in Dr. Knight, but when he died . . . well, they wanted someone of their own in charge. None of us mind."

"Willernie Foundation," she said. "I don't know it."

"It was set up by a man named Willernie, in St. Louis, Missouri," said Mal. "He made his money manufacturing kitchen utensils. When he died he left a trust and set up the Foundation to encourage basic research." Mal smiled. "Don't ask me how he got from kitchen utensils to that. That's not much information for you, is it?"

"It's more than I had a minute ago," she smiled back. "Did you know Corwin Brayt before he came here?"

"No." Mal shook his head. "I don't know many people outside the biological and zoological fields."

"I imagine you know him pretty well now, though, after the six months he's been in charge."

"Well —" Mal hesitated, "I wouldn't say I know him *well*, at all. You see, he's up here in the office all day long and I'm down with Pollux and Castor — the two wild dolphins we've got coming to the station, now. Corwin and I don't see each other much."

"On this small island?"

"I suppose it seems funny — but we're both pretty busy."

"I guess you would be." She smiled again. "Will you take me to him?"

"Him?" Mal awoke suddenly to the fact they were still standing on the terrace. "Oh, yes — it's Corwin you came to see."

"Not just Corwin," she said. "I came to see the whole place."

"Well, I'll take you in to the office. Come along."

He led her across the terrace and in through the front door into the air-conditioned coolness of the interior. Corwin Brayt ran the air-conditioning constantly, as if his own somewhat icy personality demanded the dry, distant coldness of a mountain atmosphere. Mal led

Jane Wilson down a short corridor and through another door into a large wide-windowed office. A tall, slim, broad-shouldered man with black hair and a brown, coldly handsome face looked up from a large desk, and got to his feet on seeing Jane.

"Corwin," said Mal. "This is Miss Jane Wilson from *Background Monthly.*"

"Yes," said Corwin expressionlessly to Jane, coming around the desk to them. "I got a wire yesterday you were coming." He did not wait for Jane to offer her hand, but offered his own. Their fingers met.

"I've got to be getting down to Castor and Pollux," said Mal, turning away.

"I'll see you later then," Jane said, looking over at him.

"Why, yes. Maybe —" he said. He went out. As he closed the door of Brayt's office behind him, he paused for a moment in the dim, cool hallway, and shut his eyes. *Don't be a fool,* he told himself, *a girl like that can do a lot better than someone like you. And probably has already.*

He opened his eyes and went back down to the pool behind the station and the non-human world of the dolphins.

*W*hen he got there, he found that Castor and Pollux were back. Their pool was an open one, with egress[2] to the open blue waters of the Caribbean. In the first days of the research at Dolphin's Way, the dolphins had been confined in a closed pool like any captured wild animal. It was only later on, when the work at the station had come up against what Knight had called "the environmental barrier," that the notion was conceived of opening the pool to the sea, so that the dolphins they had been working with could leave or stay, as they wished.

They had left — but they had come back. Eventually, they had left for good. But strangely, wild dolphins had come from time to time to take their places, so that there were always dolphins at the station.

---

[2]**egress** (ē′grĕs′): a passage or way out.

Castor and Pollux were the latest pair. They had showed up some four months ago after a single dolphin frequenting the station had disappeared. Free, independent — they had been most co-operative. But the barrier had not been breached.[3]

Now, they were sliding back and forth past each other underwater utilizing the full thirty-yard length of the pool, passing beside, over and under each other, their seven-foot nearly identical bodies almost, but not quite, rubbing as they passed. The tape showed them to be talking together up in the supersonic[4] range, eighty to a hundred and twenty kilocycles per second. Their pattern of movement in the water now was something he had never seen before. It was regular and ritualistic as a dance.

He sat down and put on the earphones connected to the hydrophones, underwater at each end of the pool. He spoke into the microphone, asking them about their movements, but they ignored him and kept on with the patterned swimming.

The sound of footsteps behind him made him turn. He saw Jane Wilson approaching down the concrete steps from the back door of the station, with the stocky, overalled figure of Pete Adant, the station mechanic.

"Here he is," said Pete, as they came up. "I've got to get back now."

"Thank you." She gave Pete the smile that had so moved Mal earlier. Pete turned and went back up the steps. She turned to Mal. "Am I interrupting something?"

"No." He took off the earphones. "I wasn't getting any answers, anyway."

She looked at the two dolphins in their underwater dance with the liquid surface swirling above them as they turned now this way, now that, just under it.

"Answers?" she said. He smiled a little ruefully.

"We call them answers," he said. He nodded at the two smoothly streamlined shapes turning in the pool. "Sometimes we ask questions and get responses."

"Informative responses?" she asked.

---

[3]**breached:** broken through.
[4]**supersonic** (soō′pər sŏn′ĭk): having a speed greater than the speed of sound.

"Sometimes. You wanted to see me about something?"

"About everything," she said. "It seems you're the man I came to talk to — not Brayt. He sent me down here. I understand you're the one with the theory."

"Theory?" he said warily, feeling his heart sink inside him.

"The notion, then," she said. "The idea that, if there is some sort of interstellar[5] civilization, it might be waiting for the people of Earth to qualify themselves before making contact. And that test might not be a technological one like developing a faster-than-light means of travel, but a sociological[6] one —"

"Like learning to communicate with an alien culture — a culture like that of the dolphins," he interrupted harshly. "Corwin told you this?"

"I'd heard about it before I came," she said. "I'd thought it was Brayt's theory, though."

"No," said Mal, "it's mine." He looked at her. "You aren't laughing."

"Should I laugh?" she said. She was attentively watching the dolphins' movements. Suddenly he felt sharp jealousy toward them for holding her attention; and the emotion pricked him to something he might not otherwise have had the courage to do.

"Fly over to the mainland with me," he said, "and have lunch. I'll tell you about it."

"All right." She looked up from the dolphins at him at last and he was surprised to see her frowning. "There's a lot I don't understand," she murmured. "I thought it was Brayt I had to learn about. But it's you — and the dolphins."

"Maybe we can clear that up at lunch, too," Mal said, not quite clear what she meant, but not greatly caring, either. "Come on, the helicopters are around the north side of the building."

They flew a copter across to Carupano, and sat down to lunch looking out at the shipping in the open roadstead of the azure sea before

---

[5]**interstellar** (ĭn′tər stĕl′ər): among the stars.

[6]**sociological** (sō′sē ə lŏj′ĭ kəl): having to do with human social behavior.

the town, while the polite Spanish of Venezuelan voices sounded from the tables around them.

"Why should I laugh at your theory?" she said again, when they were settled, and eating lunch.

"Most people take it to be a crackpot excuse for our failure at the station," he said.

Her brown arched brows rose. "Failure?" she said. "I thought you were making steady progress."

"Yes. And no," he said. "Even before Dr. Knight died, we ran into something he called the environmental barrier."

"Environmental barrier?"

"Yes." Mal poked with his fork at the shrimp in his seafood cocktail. "This work of ours all grew out of the work done by Dr. John Lilly. You read his book, *Man and Dolphin*?"

"No," she said. He looked at her, surprised.

"He was the pioneer in this research with dolphins," Mal said. "I'd have thought reading his book would have been the first thing you would have done before coming down here."

"The first thing I did," she said, "was try to find out something about Corwin Brayt. And I was pretty unsuccessful at that. That's why I landed here with the notion that it was he, not you, who was the real worker with the dolphins."

"That's why you asked me if I knew much about him?"

"That's right," she answered. "But tell me about this environmental barrier."

"There's not a great deal to tell," he said. "Like most big problems, it's simple enough to state. At first, in working with the dolphins, it seemed the early researchers were going great guns, and communication was just around the corner — a matter of interpreting the sounds they made to each other, in the humanly audible[7] range, and above it; and teaching the dolphins human speech."

"It turned out those things couldn't be done?"

---

[7]**audible** (ô′də bəl): able to be heard.

"They could. They were done — or as nearly so as makes no difference. But then we came up against the fact that communication doesn't mean understanding." He looked at her. "You and I talk the same language, but do we really understand perfectly what the other person means when he speaks to us?"

She looked at him for a moment, and then slowly shook her head without taking her eyes off his face.

"Well," said Mal, "that's essentially our problem with the dolphins — only on a much larger scale. Dolphins, like Castor and Pollux, can talk with me, and I with them, but we can't understand each other to any great degree."

"You mean intellectually understood, don't you?" Jane said. "Not just mechanically?"

"That's right," Mal answered. "We agree on denotation of an auditory or other symbol, but not on connotation. I can say to Castor — *'the Gulf Stream is a strong ocean current'* and he'll agree exactly. But neither of us really has the slightest idea of what the other really means. My mental image of the Gulf Stream is not Castor's image. My notion of 'powerful' is relative to the fact I'm six feet tall, weigh a hundred and seventy-five pounds and can lift my own weight against the force of gravity. Castor's is relative to the fact that he is seven feet long, can speed up to forty miles an hour through the water, and as far as he knows weighs nothing, since his four hundred pounds of body-weight are balanced out by the equal weight of the water he displaces. And the concept of lifting something is all but unknown to him. My mental abstraction[8] of 'ocean' is not his, and our ideas of what a current is may coincide, or be literally worlds apart in meaning. And so far we've found no way of bridging the gap between us."

"The dolphins have been trying as well as you?"

"I believe so," said Mal. "But I can't prove it. Any more than I can really prove the dolphin's intelligence to hardcore skeptics[9] until I can come up with something previously outside human knowledge that the dolphins have taught me. Or have them demonstrate that they've

---

[8]**abstraction:** an idea that is theoretical rather than practical.
[9]**skeptics:** people who are not easily convinced of something.

learned the use of some human intellectual process. And in these things we've all failed — because, as I believe and Dr. Knight believed, of the connotative gap, which is a result of the environmental barrier."

She sat watching him. He was probably a fool to tell her all this, but he had had no one to talk to like this since Dr. Knight's heart attack, eight months before, and he felt words threatening to pour out of him.

"We've got to learn to think like the dolphins," he said, "or the dolphins have to learn to think like us. For nearly six years now we've been trying and neither side's succeeded." Almost before he thought, he added the one thing he had been determined to keep to himself. "I've been afraid our research funds will be cut off any day now."

"Cut off? By the Willernie Foundation?" she said. "Why would they do that?"

"Because we haven't made any progress for so long," Mal said bitterly. "Or, at least, no provable progress. I'm afraid time's just about run out. And if it runs out, it may never be picked up again. Six years ago, there was a lot of popular interest in the dolphins. Now, they've been discounted and forgotten, shelved as merely bright animals."

"You can't be sure the research won't be picked up again."

"But I feel it," he said. "It's part of my notion about the ability to communicate with an alien race being the test for us humans. I feel we've got this one chance and if we flub it, we'll never have another." He pounded the table softly with his fist. "The worst of it is, I *know* the dolphins are trying just as hard to get through from their side — if I could only recognize what they're doing, how they're trying to make me understand!"

Jane had been sitting watching him.

"You seem pretty sure of that," she said. "What makes you so sure?"

He unclenched his fist and forced himself to sit back in his chair.

"Have you ever looked into the jaws of a dolphin?" he said. "They're this long." He spread his hands apart in the air to illustrate. "And each pair of jaws contains eighty-eight sharp teeth. Moreover, a dolphin like Castor weighs several hundred pounds and can move at water speeds that are almost incredible to a human. He could crush you easily by ramming you against the side of a tank, if he didn't want to tear you apart with his teeth, or break your bones with blows of his flukes." He looked at her grimly. "In spite of all this, in spite of the fact that men have caught and killed dolphins — even we killed them in our early, fumbling researches, and dolphins are quite capable of using their teeth and strength on marine enemies — no dolphin has ever been known to attack a human being. Aristotle, writing in the Fourth Century B.C., speaks of the, quote, gentle and kindly, end quote, nature of the dolphin."

He stopped, and looked at Jane sharply.

"You don't believe me," he said.

"Yes," she said. "Yes, I do." He took a deep breath.

"I'm sorry," he said. "I've made the mistake of mentioning all this before to other people and been sorry I did. I told this to one man who gave me his opinion that it indicated that the dolphin instinctively recognized human superiority and the value of human life." Mal grinned at her, harshly. "But it was just an instinct. *'Like dogs,'* he said. *'Dogs instinctively admire and love people —'* and he wanted to tell me about a dachshund he'd had, named Poochie, who could read the morning newspaper and wouldn't bring it in to him if there was a tragedy reported on the front page. He could prove this, and Poochie's intelligence, by the number of times he'd had to get the paper off the front step himself."

Jane laughed. It was a low, happy laugh; and it took the bitterness suddenly out of Mal.

"Anyway," said Mal, "the dolphin's restraint with humans is just one of the indications, like the wild dolphins coming to us here at the station, that've convinced me the dolphins are trying to understand us, too. And have been, maybe, for centuries."

"I don't see why you worry about the research stopping," she said. "With all you know, can't you convince people —"

"There's only one person I've got to convince," said Mal. "And that's Corwin Brayt. And I don't think I'm doing it. It's just a feeling — but I feel as if he's sitting in judgment upon me, and the work. I feel . . ." Mal hesitated, "almost as if he's a hatchet man."[10]

---

[10]**hatchet man:** a person hired to carry out a disagreeable task, such as firing workers.

"He isn't," Jane said. "He can't be. I'll find out for you, if you like. There're ways of doing it. I'd have the answer for you right now, if I'd thought of him as an administrator. But I thought of him as a scientist, and I looked him up in the wrong places."

Mal frowned at her unbelievingly.

"You don't actually mean you can find out that for me?" he asked.

She smiled.

"Wait and see," she replied. "I'd like to know, myself, what his background is."

"It could be important," he said, eagerly. "I know it sounds fantastic — but if I'm right, the research with the dolphins could be important, more important than anything else in the world."

She stood up suddenly from the table.

"I'll go and start checking up right now," she said. "Why don't you go on back to the island? It'll take me a few hours and I'll take the water-taxi over."

"But you haven't finished lunch yet," he said. "In fact you haven't even started lunch. Let's eat first, then you can go."

"I want to call some people and catch them while they're still at work," she said. "It's the time difference on these long-distance calls. I'm sorry. We'll have dinner together, will that do?"

"It'll have to," he said. She melted his disappointment with one of her amazing smiles, and went.

With her gone, Mal found he was not hungry himself. He got hold of the waiter and managed to cancel the main course of their meals. He sat and had two more drinks — not something usual for him. Then he left and flew the copter back to the island.

*P*ete Adant encountered him as he was on his way from the copter park to the dolphin pool.

"There you are," said Pete. "Corwin wants to see you in an hour — when he gets back, that is. He's gone over to the mainland himself."

Ordinarily, such a piece of news would have awakened the foreboding about cancellation of the research that rode always like a small, cold, metal weight inside Mal. But the total of three drinks and no lunch had anesthetized him somewhat. He nodded and went on to the pool.

The dolphins were still there, still at their patterned swimming. Or was he just imagining the pattern? Mal sat down on his chair by the poolside before the tape recorder which set down a visual pattern of the sounds made by the dolphins. He put the earphones to the hydrophones on, switching on the mike before him.

Suddenly, it struck him how futile all this was. He had gone through these same motions daily for four years now. And what was the sum total of results he had to show for it? Reel on reel of tape recording a failure to hold any truly productive conversation with the dolphins.

He took the earphones off and laid them aside. He lit a cigarette and sat gazing with half-seeing eyes at the underwater ballet of the dolphins. To call it ballet was almost to libel their actions. The gracefulness, the purposefulness of their movements, buoyed up by the salt water, was beyond that of any human in air or on land. He thought again of what he had told Jane Wilson about the dolphins' refusal to attack their human captors, even when the humans hurt or killed them. He thought of the now-established fact that dolphins will come to the rescue of one of their own who has been hurt or knocked unconscious, and hold him up on top of the water so he will not drown — the dolphin's breathing process requiring conscious control, so that it fails if the dolphin becomes unconscious.

He thought of their playfulness, their affection, the wide and complex range of their speech. In any of those categories, the average human stacked up beside them looked pretty poor. In the dolphin culture there was no visible impulse to war, to murder, to hatred and unkindness. No wonder, thought Mal, they and we have trouble understanding each other. In a different environment, under different conditions, they're the kind of people we've always struggled to be. We have the technology, the tool-using capability, but with it all in many ways we're more animal than they are.

Who's to judge which of us is better, he thought, looking at their movements through the water with the slight hazy melancholy induced by the three drinks on an empty stomach. I might be happier myself, if I were a dolphin. For a second, the idea seemed deeply attractive. The endless open sea, the freedom, an end to all the complex structure of human culture on land. A few lines of poetry came back to him.

"*Come Children,*" he quoted out loud to himself, "*let us away! Down and away, below . . . !*"

He saw the two dolphins pause in their underwater ballet and saw that the microphone before him was on. Their heads turned toward the microphone underwater at the near end of the pool. He remembered the following lines, and he quoted them aloud to the dolphins.

> *. . . Now my brothers call from the bay,*
> *Now the great winds shoreward blow,*
> *Now the salt tides seaward flow;*
> *Now the wild white horses play,*
> *Champ and chafe and toss in the spray —*[11]

He broke off suddenly, feeling self-conscious. He looked down at the dolphins. For a moment they merely hung where they were under the surface, facing the microphone. Then Castor turned and surfaced. His forehead with its blowhole broke out into the air and then his head as he looked up at Mal. His airborne voice from the blowhole's sensitive lips and muscles spoke quacking words at the human.

"*Come, Mal!*" he quacked, "*Let us away! Down and away! Below!*"

The head of Pollux surfaced beside Castor's. Mal stared at them for a long second. Then he jerked his gaze back to the tape of the recorder. There on it, was the rhythmic record of his own voice as it had sounded in the pool, and below it on their separate tracks, the tapes showed parallel rhythms coming from the dolphins. They had been matching his speech largely in the inaudible range while he was quoting.

---

[11]"The Forsaken Merman" by Matthew Arnold, 1849.

342

Still staring, Mal got to his feet, his mind trembling with a suspicion so great he hesitated to put it into words. Like a man in a daze he walked to the near end of the pool, where three steps led down into the shallower part. Here the water was only three feet deep.

"*Come, Mal!*" quacked Castor, as the two still hung in the water with their heads out, facing him. "*Let us away! Down and away! Below!*"

Step by step, Mal went down into the pool. He felt the coolness of the water wetting his pants legs, rising to his waist as he stood at last on the pool floor. A few feet in front of him, the two dolphins hung in the water, facing him, waiting. Standing with the water rippling lightly above his belt buckle, Mal looked at them, waiting for some sign, some signal of what they wanted him to do.

They gave him no clue. They only waited. It was up to him to go forward on his own. He sloshed forward into deeper water, put his head down, held his breath and pushed himself off underwater.

In the forefront of his blurred vision, he saw the grainy concrete floor of the pool. He glided slowly over it, rising a little, and suddenly the two dolphins were all about him — gliding over, above, around his own underwater floating body, brushing lightly against him as they passed, making him a part of their underwater dance. He heard the creaking that was one of the underwater sounds they made and knew that they were probably talking in ranges he could not hear. He could not know what they were saying, he could not sense the meaning of their movements about him, but the feeling that they were trying to convey information to him was inescapable.

He began to feel the need to breathe. He held out as long as he could, then let himself rise to the surface. He broke water and gulped air, and the two dolphin heads popped up nearby, watching him. He dived under the surface again. *I am a dolphin* — he told himself almost desperately — *I am not a man, but a dolphin, and to me all this means — what?*

Several times he dived, and each time the persistent and disciplined movements of the dolphins about him underwater convinced him more strongly that he was on the right track. He came up, blowing, at last. He was not carrying the attempt to be like them far enough, he thought. He turned and swam back to the steps at the shallow end of the pool, and began to climb out.

"*Come, Mal — let us away!*" quacked a dolphin voice behind him, and he turned to see the heads of both Castor and Pollux out of the water, regarding him with mouths open urgently.

"Come Children — down and away!" he repeated, as reassuringly as he could intonate the words.

He hurried up to the big cabinet of the supply locker at the near end of the pool, and opened the door of the section of skin-diving equipment. He needed to make himself more like a dolphin. He considered the air tanks and the mask of the scuba equipment, and rejected them. The dolphins could not breathe underwater any more than he could. He started jerking things out of the cabinet.

A minute or so later he returned to the steps in swimming trunks, wearing a glass mask with a snorkel tube, and swim fins on his feet. In his hand he carried two lengths of soft rope. He sat down on the steps and with the rope tied his knees and ankles together. Then, clumsily, he hopped and splashed into the water.

Lying face down in the pool, staring at the bottom through his glass faceplate, he tried to move his bound legs together like the flukes of a dolphin, to drive himself slantingly down under the surface.

After a moment or two he managed it. In a moment the dolphins were all about him as he tried to swim underwater, dolphinwise. After a little while his air ran short again and he had to surface. But he came up like a dolphin and lay on the surface filling his lungs, before fanning himself down flukefashion with his swim fins. *Think like a dolphin*, he kept repeating

to himself over and over. *I am a dolphin. And this is my world. This is the way it is.*

. . . And Castor and Pollux were all about him.

*T*he sun was setting in the far distance of the ocean when at last he dragged himself, exhausted, up the steps of the pool and sat down on the poolside. To his water-soaked body, the twilight breeze felt icy. He unbound his legs, took off his fins and mask and walked wearily to the cabinet. From the nearest compartment he took a towel and dried himself, then put on an old bathrobe he kept hanging there. He sat down in an aluminum deckchair beside the cabinet and sighed with weariness.

He looked out at the red sun dipping its lower edge in the sea, and felt a great warm sensation of achievement inside him. In the darkening pool, the two dolphins still swam back and forth. He watched the sun descending . . .

"Mal!"

The sound of Corwin Brayt's voice brought his head around. When he saw the tall, cold-faced man was coming toward him with the slim figure of Jane alongside, Mal got up quickly from his chair. They came up to him.

"Why didn't you come in to see me as I asked?" Brayt said. "I left word for you with Pete. I didn't even know you were back from the mainland until the water-taxi brought Miss Wilson out just now, and she told me."

"I'm sorry," said Mal. "I think I've run into something here —"

"Never mind telling me now." Brayt's voice was hurried and sharpened with annoyance. "I had a good deal to speak to you about, but there's not time now if I'm to catch the mainland plane to St. Louis. I'm sorry to break it this way —" He checked himself and turned to Jane. "Would you excuse us, Miss Wilson? Private business. If you'll give us a second —"

"Of course," she said. She turned and walked away from them alongside the pool, into the deepening twilight. The dolphins paced her in the water. The sun was just down now, and with the sudden oncoming of tropical night, stars could be seen overhead.

"Just let me tell you," said Mal. "It's about the research."

"I'm sorry," said Brayt. "There's no point in your telling me now. I'll be gone a week and I want you to watch out for this Jane Wilson, here." He lowered his voice slightly. "I talked to *Background Monthly* on the phone this afternoon, and the editor I spoke to there didn't know about the article, or recognize her name —"

"Somebody new," said Mal. "Probably someone who didn't know her."

"At any rate it makes no difference," said Brayt. "As I say, I'm sorry to tell you in such a rushed fashion, but Willernie has decided to end its grant of funds to the station. I'm flying to St. Louis to settle details." He hesitated. "I'm sure you knew something like this was coming, Mal." Mal stared, shocked.

"It was inevitable," said Brayt coldly. "You knew that." He paused. "I'm sorry."

"But the station'll fold without the Willernie support!" said Mal, finding his voice. "You know that. And just today I found out what the answer is! Just this afternoon! Listen to me!" He caught Brayt's arm as the other started to turn away. "The dolphins have been trying to contact us. Oh, not at first, not when we experimented with captured specimens. But since we opened the pool to the sea. The only trouble was we insisted on trying to communicate by sound alone — and that's all but impossible for them."

"Excuse me," said Brayt, trying to disengage his arm.

"Listen, will you!" said Mal, desperately. "Their communication process is an incredibly rich one. It's as if you and I communicated by using all the instruments in a symphony orchestra. They not only use sound from four to a hundred and fifty kilocycles per second, they use movement, and touch — and all of it in reference to the ocean conditions surrounding them at the moment."

"I've got to go."

"Just a minute. Don't you remember what Lilly hypothesized about the dolphins' methods of navigation? He suggested that it was a multivariable method, using temperature, speed, taste of the water, position of the stars, sun and so forth, all fed into their brains simultaneously and instantaneously. Obviously, it's true, and obviously their process of communication is also a multivariable method utilizing sound, touch, position, place and movement. Now that we know this, we can go into the sea with them and try to operate across their whole spectrum of communication. No wonder we weren't able to get across anything but the most primitive exchanges, restricting ourselves to sound. It's been equivalent to restricting human communication to just the nouns in each sentence, while maintaining the sentence structure —"

"I'm very sorry!" said Brayt, firmly. "I tell you, Mal. None of this makes any difference. The decision of the Foundation is based on financial reasons. They've got just so much money available to donate, and this station's allotment has already gone in other directions. There's nothing that can be done now."

He pulled his arm free.

"I'm sorry," he said again. "I'll be back in a week at the outside. You might be thinking of how to wind up things here."

He turned with that, and went away, around the building toward the parking spot of the station copters. Mal, stunned, watched the tall, slim, broad-shouldered figure move off into darkness.

"It doesn't matter," said the gentle voice of Jane comfortingly at his ear. He jerked about and saw her facing him. "You won't need the Willernie funds any more."

"He told you?" Mal stared at her as she shook her head, smiling in the growing dimness. "You heard? From way over there?"

"Yes," she said. "And you were right about Brayt. I got your answer for you. He was a hatchet man — sent here by the Willernie people to decide whether the station deserved further funds."

"But we've got to have them!" Mal said. "It won't take much more, but we've got to go into the sea and work out ways to talk to the dolphins in their own mode. We've got to expand to their level of communication, not try to compress them to ours. You see, this afternoon, I had a break-through —"

"I know," she said. "I know all about it."

"You know?" He stared at her. "How do you know?"

"You've been under observation all afternoon," she said. "You're right. You did break through the environmental barrier. From now on it's just a matter of working out methods."

"Under observation? How?" Abruptly, that seemed the least important thing at hand. "But I have to have money," he said. "It'll take time and equipment, and that costs money —"

"No." Her voice was infinitely gentle. "You won't need to work out your own methods. Your work is done, Mal. This afternoon the dolphins and you broke the bars to communication between the two races for the first time in the history of either. It was the job you set out to do and you were part of it. You can be happy knowing that."

"Happy?" He almost shouted at her, suddenly. "I don't understand what you're talking about."

"I'm sorry." There was a ghost of a sigh from her. "We'll show you how to talk to the dolphins, Mal, if men need to. As well as some other things — perhaps." Her face lifted to him under the star-marked sky, still a little light in the west. "You see, you were right about something more than dolphins, Mal. Your idea that the ability to communicate with another intelligent race, an alien race, was a test that had to be passed before the superior species of a planet could be contacted by the intelligent races of the galaxy — that was right, too."

He stared at her. She was so close to him, he could feel the living warmth of her body, although they were not touching. He saw her, he felt her, standing before him; and he felt all the strange deep upwelling of emotion that she had released in him the moment he first saw her. The deep emotion he felt for her still. Suddenly understanding came to him.

"You mean you're not from Earth —" his voice was hoarse and uncertain. It wavered to a stop. "But you're human!" he cried desperately.

She looked back at him a moment before answering. In the dimness he could not tell for sure, but he thought he saw the glisten of tears in her eyes.

"Yes," she said, at last, slowly. "In the way you mean that — you can say I'm human."

A great and almost terrible joy burst suddenly in him. It was the joy of a man who, in the moment when he thinks he has lost everything, finds something of infinitely greater value.

"But how?" he said, excitedly, a little breathlessly. He pointed up at the stars. "If you come from some place — up there? How can you be human?"

She looked down, away from his face.

"I'm sorry," she said. "I can't tell you."

"Can't tell me? Oh," he said with a little laugh, "you mean I wouldn't understand."

"No —" Her voice was almost inaudible, "I mean I'm not allowed to tell you."

"Not allowed —" he felt an unreasoning chill about his heart. "But Jane —" He broke off fumbling for words. "I don't know quite how to say this, but it's important to me to know. From the first moment I saw you there, I . . . I mean, maybe you don't feel anything like this, you don't know what I'm talking about —"

"Yes," she whispered. "I do."

"Then —" He stared at her. "You could at least say something that would set my mind at rest. I mean . . . it's only a matter of time now. We're going to be getting together, your people and I, aren't we?"

She looked up at him out of darkness.

"No," she said, "we aren't, Mal. Ever. And that's why I can't tell you anything."

"We aren't?" he cried. "We aren't? But you came and saw us communicate — Why aren't we?"

She looked up at him for the last time, then, and told him. He, having heard what she had to say, stood still; still as a stone, for there was nothing left to do. And she, turning slowly and finally away from him, went off to the edge of the pool and down the steps into the shallow water, where the dolphins came rushing to meet her, their foamy tearing of the surface making a wake as white as snow.

Then the three of them moved, as if by magic, across the surface of the pool and out the entrance of it to the ocean. And so they continued to move off until they were lost to sight in darkness and the starlit, glinting surface of the waves.

It came to Mal then, as he stood there, that the dolphins must have been waiting for her all this time. All the wild dolphins, who had come to the station after the first two captives, were set free to leave or stay as they wanted. The dolphins had known, perhaps for centuries, that it was to them alone on Earth that the long-awaited visitors from the stars would finally come.

Responding to
DOLPHIN'S WAY

Thinking and Discussing

— In what ways does Corwin Brayt exhibit the kind of human behavior that creates an "environmental barrier"?

— Why is Jane Wilson interested in Mal and his work? How does her perspective differ from Corwin Brayt's views? What do their differing perspectives reveal about communication?

Choosing a Creative Response

— **Presenting the Alien Point of View** Imagine you are Jane Wilson, reporting back to your fellow aliens about your experiences on Earth. In your report, explain why you choose the dolphins over the humans. You may wish to talk about your meetings with Mal Sinclair and Corwin Brayt, and about the "environmental barrier" created by humans. Write the report or present it orally to your group.

— **Defending Dolphin Research** Argue the case for extending the dolphin research. Suppose that Mal is unwilling to give up on his work, especially in light of his breakthrough. In a small group, put together Mal's case, which should be both logical and persuasive. Will you mention contact with an alien? Will you include your knowledge of Corwin Brayt's role as a "hatchet man"? Present your case to the class.

— **Creating Your Own Activity** Plan and complete your own activity in response to "Dolphin's Way."

Thinking and Writing

— Pretend to be Mal Sinclair. Write a diary entry such as Mal might have written on the evening of Jane Wilson's departure. Remember, a diary is not just a recording of the events of the day; it also tells how the diarist feels about those events.

Adapting a Science Fiction Story Choose a scene from one of the selections, or from a familiar science fiction story or film, to present with a partner or group. You might choose one of the following formats:

- Write the script of a radio play, including the sound effects, and record the play or have a cast read it to your classmates. Make it as exciting as possible, so that listeners will be able to picture every detail.
- Create a comic strip that captures the scene vividly, and make copies of it to share with your classmates. Remember that you can use a series of pictures with convincing dialogue in your adaptation.
- If a video camera or movie camera is available, create a short film of the scene, writing a script with stage directions, and designing a stage setting and costumes if you wish. Film the scene, and play it for your classmates.

Comparing Other Creatures, Other Worlds Compare how the authors of these stories use robots, humans, and aliens to comment on human society. List both the good and bad characteristics that robots, humans, and aliens share. Then have a panel discussion with your classmates about the following questions:

- What points does each author make about human society? Include behavior, intelligence, and values as points in your comparisons.
- Do the aliens and humans in the stories learn from each other? Do the humans learn from one another? From robots? How does this happen?

Bring to your discussion any information you have from movies, television, or books.

Designing Bumper Stickers People find many ways to express their opinions about society and human behavior. The authors whose stories you have just read, for example, use science fiction to make comments about today's society. You may have seen social commentary in everyday life on bumper stickers, buttons, T-shirts, and posters.

Suppose the science fiction authors put their messages on bumper stickers instead of writing stories. How would they phrase their messages? Think about the messages in stories you have read, and design a bumper sticker for each one. Can any one of the messages apply to more than one of the science fiction stories? Share your bumper stickers with your classmates.

Inventing New Words New ideas and inventions in science and technology require new words to describe them. Scientists (and science fiction writers as well) often use word parts from ancient Greek and Latin to create new scientific terms.

Look at the list of scientific terms below. Beside each word, its Greek and Latin word parts and their meanings are listed. Mix and match the word parts to make words you know already, using a dictionary if necessary.

Then use your imagination, and mix and match the word parts to create names for new imaginary scientific or technological discoveries or inventions. Brainstorm with your classmates to think of brilliant uses for them.

chronometer: chrono = time / meter = measure
megalopolis: mega = large / polis = city
microscope: micro = small / scope = see or watch
astronaut: astro = star / naut = traveler
aquatic: aqua = water
phone: phono = sound
photograph: photo = light / graph = write
psychology: psych = mind / logy = study of
subterranean: sub = under / terra = earth
telepathic: tele = far / path = feeling or suffering
solar: sol = sun
lunar: luna = moon

Brian W. Aldiss was an avid reader from an early age, and he wrote his own books almost as soon as he could read.

Aldiss has become best known as a writer, critic, and editor of science fiction. He also writes novels and some nonfiction. Aldiss has won the Hugo Award and the Nebula Award.

Aldiss's works include *Hothouse*, *The Moment of Eclipse*, *Billion Year Spree*, *Non-Stop*, and *Helliconia Spring*. In his novel *Life in the West* he said that science fiction "substitutes simple aliens for the complexities of nationalities and internationalities. And in the examples I've read, it externalizes evil, making it a menace from without instead of from within. Perhaps that's why it's so popular."

Isaac Asimov was born in Russia but was brought to the United States as a young child. He was fascinated with the science fiction magazines in his father's candy store.

Asimov developed the Three Laws of Robotics, which state the principles guiding robot behavior in science fiction writing. He went on to write innumerable short

BRIAN W. ALDISS

ISAAC ASIMOV

RAY BRADBURY

GORDON R. DICKSON

stories and over 300 books, including science fiction, mysteries, nonfiction history, and nonfiction science.

Asimov won the Hugo Award five times and the Nebula Award twice, and his short story "Nightfall" was chosen the best science fiction story of all time in a Science Fiction Writers of America poll.

Asimov continued writing approximately one new book every six weeks until the time of his death in 1992. He felt that science fiction is the hardest writing there is, saying "On top of the usual problems of character and action, you've got to create a whole new society and make it believable."

Ray Bradbury started his career writing fantasy and science fiction in 1943. Since then he has written close to 500 stories, as well as poems, plays, radio and television dramas, and novels.

Bradbury is most interested in the impact of future scientific development on human lives. He warns us against becoming too dependent on science and technology, and ignoring moral and

ethical concerns in the process. He says, "I'm a moral fablest, a teller of cautionary tales, someone who looks at the machines we have now and says, if this is true, ten years from now that will be true. . . . The machines are amoral. We can choose to use them morally or immorally, and we must opt to use them morally more often than not."

Bradbury's most famous works include *The Martian Chronicles*, *Fahrenheit 451*, *The Golden Apples of the Sun*, and *Dandelion Wine*.

Gordon R. Dickson was born in Canada in 1923 and emigrated to the United States in 1936.

Dickson has written numerous science fiction novels and short stories for adults and for young people, including *Space Winners*, *Alien Art*, and *Star Prince Charlie*. He has won the Nebula Award and received the Hugo Award for *Soldier, Ask Not* in 1965. Dickson has also written radio plays.

Dickson's major work in progress is *The Childe Cycle*, which will fill twelve volumes. It will present Dickson's vision of humanity's moral and spiritual evolution through ten centuries.

Exploring Other Worlds

The Guardian of Isis by Monica Hughes (Atheneum, 1982)
Jody N'Kumo asks questions in a world where curiosity is discouraged and people are forced to live by rules they do not understand. Jody's inquisitive mind, however, eventually leads him to the truth about his African ancestry and the Guardian of Isis.

The Road to the Stars (Houghton, 1993)
This collection of science fiction stories is a mix of the old and new, of the classic and contemporary. The characters range from bizarre beings on faraway planets to humans in distant times, but the selections are all relevant to life on Earth today.

The Snows of Jaspre by Mary Caraker (Houghton, 1989)
Dee must choose between a charismatic leader and her own family when the mystical snows of the planet Jaspre are threatened by the warmth of power satellites.

Orvis by H. M. Hoover (Viking, 1987)
Toby and her friend Thaddeus seek help from an out-of-date robot, Orvis, to escape wild outlaws on Earth in the distant future.

Sweetwater by Laurence Yep (Harper, 1973)
Teen-aged Tyree and his blind sister are fifth-generation space colonists who try to save their doomed city from an invasion.

Interstellar Pig by William Sleator (Dutton, 1984)
When three strange neighbors introduce teen-aged Barney to the board game Interstellar Pig, it leads to terrifying encounters.

POETRY

BOOK 5

Untitled by John Zimmerman

IMAGES
SOUNDS
MESSAGES

IMAGES

SOUNDS

MESSAGES

IMAGES

Award Winner

Behind the Saint-Lazare Station, Paris, 1932 by Henri Cartier-Bresson

ig Wind

Where were the greenhouses going,
Lunging into the lashing
Wind driving water
So far down the river
All the faucets stopped? —
So we drained the manure-machine
For the steam plant,
Pumping the stale mixture
Into the rusty boilers,
Watching the pressure gauge
Waver over to red,
As the seams hissed
And the live steam
Drove to the far
End of the rose-house,
Where the worst wind was,
Creaking the cypress window-frames,
Cracking so much thin glass
We stayed all night,
Stuffing the holes with burlap;
But she rode it out,
That old rose-house,
She hove into the teeth of it,
The core and pith of that ugly storm,
Ploughing with her stiff prow,
Bucking into the wind-waves
That broke over the whole of her,
Flailing her sides with spray,
Flinging long strings of wet across the roof-top,
Finally veering, wearing themselves out, merely
Whistling thinly under the wind-vents;
She sailed until the calm morning,
Carrying her full cargo of roses.

by Theodore Roethke

The Bagel

Honfleur, France, 1968
by Elliott Erwitt

I stopped to pick up the bagel
rolling away in the wind,
annoyed with myself
for having dropped it
as if it were a portent.
Faster and faster it rolled,
with me running after it
bent low, gritting my teeth,
and I found myself doubled over
and rolling down the street
head over heels, one complete somersault
after another like a bagel
and strangely happy with myself.

by David Ignatow

New York, circa 1942 by Helen Levitt

Zimmer's Street

My street thunders like
A long chimney falling
When morning comes up.
A thousand great cars
Relentlessly flash and fume.
Trucks come, an ambulance,
A wrecking ball and crane,
A hearse, cabs, a mobile home,
Airplanes roar and stack above
My father and mother going to work.
My wife and children
Play on the sidewalks,
Grandfather walks to
The bakery, my older sister
Bounces a ball till dark.
All things have come down
This street: Thanksgiving,
Christmas, victory, marriage.
It takes all day for
The pavement to stop hissing
So that I can sleep at night.

by Paul Zimmer

"Hope" is the thing with feathers —
That perches in the soul —
And sings the tune without the words —
And never stops — at all —

And sweetest — in the Gale — is heard —
And sore must be the storm —
That could abash the little Bird
That kept so many warm —

I've heard it in the chillest land —
And on the strangest Sea —
Yet, never, in Extremity,
It asked a crumb — of Me.

by Emily Dickinson

Apple

At the center, a dark star
wrapped in white.
When you bite, listen
for the crunch of boots on snow,
snow that has ripened. Over it
stretches the red, starry sky.

by Nan Fry

Dana and the Apple, 1922 by Edward Steichen

The Racecourse at Auteuil, Paris, 1910 by Jacques-Henri Lartigue

useum Vase

It contains nothing.
We ask it
To contain nothing.

Having transcended use
It is endlessly
Content to be.

Still it broods
On old burdens —
Wheat, oil, wine.

by Robert Francis

houghts

When I can make my thoughts come forth
    To walk like ladies up and down,
Each one puts on before the glass
    Her most becoming hat and gown.

But oh, the shy and eager thoughts
    That hide and will not get them dressed,
Why is it that they always seem
    So much more lovely than the rest?

by Sara Teasdale

A Red, Red Rose

My Luve is like a red, red rose,
    That's newly sprung in June:
My Luve is like the melodie,
    That's sweetly played in tune.

As fair art thou, my bonnie lass,
    So deep in luve am I;
And I will luve thee still, my dear,
    Till a' the seas gang dry.

Till a' the seas gang dry, my dear,
    And the rocks melt wi' the sun;
And I will luve thee still, my dear,
    While the sands o' life shall run.

And fare-thee-weel, my only luve!
    And fare-thee-weel a while!
And I will come again, my luve,
    Though it were ten thousand mile.

by Robert Burns

And the days are not full enough
And the nights are not full enough
And life slips by like a field mouse
    Not shaking the grass.

by Ezra Pound

RESPONDING TO "IMAGES"

Thinking and Discussing

Compare the images in these poems. Which poem presents the most striking image? Explain your answer.

What comparisons are used to create the images in these poems? What words appeal to the senses of hearing, sight, smell, taste, and touch?

Choosing a Creative Response

Illustrating a Poem Choose one of the poems in "Images," and create a visual picture to express the image that the poet has expressed in the poem. Display the poem and the picture together.

Describing a Picture Choose a picture or photograph that you consider an interesting, exciting image. Then make notes about the comparisons and descriptive words you would use to express the image in a poem.

Creating Your Own Activity Plan and complete your own activity in response to the poems in "Images."

Moon and Half Dome, Yosemite National Park, California, 1960 by Ansel Adams

ilver

Slowly, silently, now the moon
Walks the night in her silver shoon;
This way, and that, she peers, and sees
Silver fruit upon silver trees;
One by one the casements catch
Her beams beneath the silvery thatch;
Couched in his kennel, like a log,
With paws of silver sleeps the dog;
From their shadowy cote the white breasts peep
Of doves in a silver-feathered sleep;
A harvest mouse goes scampering by,
With silver claws, and silver eye;
And moveless fish in the water gleam,
By silver reeds in a silver stream.

by Walter de la Mare

Haags Alley, Rochester, 1960 by Minor White

Boy at the Window

Seeing the snowman standing all alone
In dusk and cold is more than he can bear.
The small boy weeps to hear the wind prepare
A night of gnashings and enormous moan.
His tearful sight can hardly reach to where
The pale-faced figure with bitumen eyes
Returns him such a god-forsaken stare
As outcast Adam gave to Paradise.

The man of snow is, nonetheless, content,
Having no wish to go inside and die.
Still, he is moved to see the youngster cry.
Though frozen water is his element,
He melts enough to drop from one soft eye
A trickle of the purest rain, a tear
For the child at the bright pane surrounded by
Such warmth, such light, such love, and so much fear.

by Richard Wilbur

Miss Blues'es Child

If the blues would let me,
Lord knows I would smile.
If the blues would let me,
I would smile, smile, smile.
Instead of that I'm cryin' —
I must be Miss Blues'es child.

You were my moon up in the sky,
At night my wishing star.
I love you, oh, I love you so —
But you have gone so far!

Now my days are lonely,
And night-time drives me wild.
In my heart I'm crying,
I'm just Miss Blues'es child!

by Langston Hughes

The Lake Isle of Innisfree

I will arise and go now, and go to Innisfree,
And a small cabin build there, of clay and wattles made:
Nine bean-rows will I have there, a hive for the honey-bee,
And live alone in the bee-loud glade.

And I shall have some peace there, for peace comes dropping slow,
Dropping from the veils of the morning to where the cricket sings;
There midnight's all a glimmer, and noon a purple glow,
And evening full of the linnet's wings.

I will arise and go now, for always night and day
I hear lake water lapping with low sounds by the shore;
While I stand on the roadway, or on the pavements gray,
I hear it in the deep heart's core.

by William Butler Yeats

Lord Randal

"Wha you been, Lord Randal, my son?
  Wha you been, my handsome young man?"
"I ha been at the greenwood; mother, mak my bed soon,
  For I'm wearied wi huntin, and fain wad lie down."

"An wha met ye there, Lord Randal, my son?
  An wha met you there, my handsome young man?"
"O I met wi my true-love; mother, mak my bed soon,
  For I'm wearied wi huntin, and fain wad lie down."

"And what did she give you, Lord Randal, my son?
  And what did she give you, my handsome young man?"
"Eels fried in a pan; mother, mak my bed soon,
  For I'm wearied wi huntin, and fain wad lie down."

"And wha gat your leavins, Lord Randal, my son?
  And wha gat your leavins, my handsome young man?"
"My hawks and my hounds; mother, mak my bed soon,
  For I'm wearied wi huntin, and fain wad lie down."

"And what becam of them, Lord Randal, my son?
  And what becam of them, my handsome young man?"
"They stretched their legs out an died; mother, mak my bed soon,
  For I'm wearied wi huntin, and fain wad lie down."

"O I fear you are poisoned, Lord Randal, my son!
  I fear you are poisoned, my handsome young man!"
"O yes, I am poisoned; mother, mak my bed soon,
  For I'm sick at the heart, and I fain wad lie down."

"What d'ye leave to your mother, Lord Randal, my son?
  What d'ye leave to your mother, my handsome young man?"
"Four and twenty milk kye; mother, mak my bed soon,
  For I'm sick at the heart, and I fain wad lie down."

*Californian
Migratory Worker,
©1959*
by Horace Bristol

"What d'ye leave to your sister, Lord Randal, my son?
  What d'ye leave to your sister, my handsome young man?"
"My gold and my silver; mother, mak my bed soon,
  For I'm sick at the heart, and I fain wad lie down."

"What d'ye leave to your brother, Lord Randal, my son?
  What d'ye leave to your brother, my handsome young man?"
"My houses and my lands; mother, mak my bed soon,
  For I'm sick at the heart, and I fain wad lie down."

"What d'ye leave to your true-love, Lord Randal, my son?
  What d'ye leave to your true-love, my handsome young man?"
"I leave her hell and fire; mother, mak my bed soon,
  For I'm sick at the heart, and I fain wad lie down."

(Anonymous)

St. Paul's Cathedral During the WWII Blitz on London, 1941 from International News Photo

The Bells

Hear the loud alarum bells —
Brazen bells!
What tale of terror, now, their turbulency tells!
In the startled ear of Night
How they scream out their affright!
Too much horrified to speak,
They can only shriek, shriek,
Out of tune,
In a clamorous appealing to the mercy of the fire,
In a mad expostulation with the deaf and frantic fire,
Leaping higher, higher, higher,
With a desperate desire
And a resolute endeavor
Now — now to sit, or never,
By the side of the pale-faced moon.
Oh, the bells, bells, bells!
What a tale their terror tells
Of despair!

by Edgar Allan Poe

Old Deep Sing-Song

in the old deep sing-song of the sea
in the old going-on of that sing-song
in that old mama-mama-mama going-on
of that nightlong daylong sleepsong
we look on   we listen
we lay by and hear
too many big bells   too many long gongs
too many weepers over a lost gone gold
too many laughs over light green gold
woven and changing in the wash and the heave
moving on the bottoms   winding in the waters
sending themselves with arms and voices
up in the old mama-mama-mama music
up into the whirl of spokes of light

by Carl Sandburg

Counting-out Rhyme

Silver bark of beech, and sallow
Bark of yellow birch and yellow
      Twig of willow.

Stripe of green in moosewood maple,
Colour seen in leaf of apple,
      Bark of popple.

Wood of popple pale as moonbeam,
Wood of oak for yoke and barn-beam,
      Wood of hornbeam.

Silver bark of beech, and hollow
Stem of elder, tall and yellow
      Twig of willow.

by Edna St. Vincent Millay

Blue Cornucopia

Canonball
by Pete Turner

Pick any blue sky-blue cerulean azure
cornflower periwinkle blue-eyed grass
blue bowl bluebell pick lapis lazuli
blue pool blue girl blue Chinese vase
or pink-blue chicory alias ragged sailor
or sapphire bluebottle fly indigo bunting
blue dragonfly or devil's darning needle
blue-green turquoise peacock blue spruce
blue verging on violet the fringed gentian
gray-blue blue bonfire smoke autumnal
haze blue hill blueberry distance
and darker blue storm-blue blue goose
ink ocean ultramarine pick winter
blue snow-shadows ice the blue star Vega.

by Robert Francis

RESPONDING TO "SOUNDS"

Thinking and Discussing

Compare the use of sound in these poems. Which of the poems do you prefer to hear in your mind as you read them silently? Which are more effective read aloud? Why?

Which poem do you find the most effective? What sound patterns has the author used to create the poem's effect? Rhyme? Rhythm? Repetition? Explain your answer.

Choosing a Creative Response

Writing Song Lyrics Choose a familiar melody that has a regular rhythm and rhyming lyrics. Then create new lyrics for the song, paying attention to the rhyme scheme and the rhythm of the lyrics.

Creating a Sound Poem Listen for the sounds you hear in an everyday situation and make notes that describe or imitate those sounds. Then arrange the notes into a sound poem about that situation.

Creating Your Own Activity Plan and complete your own activity in response to the poems in "Sounds."

MESSAGES

Wash Stand in Dog Run of Floyd Burroughs's Cabin, Alabama, 1935 by Walker Evans

Mother to Son

Well, son, I'll tell you:
Life for me ain't been no crystal stair.
It's had tacks in it,
And splinters,
And boards torn up,
And places with no carpet on the floor —
Bare.
But all the time
I'se been a-climbin' on,
And reachin' landin's,
And turnin' corners,
And sometimes goin' in the dark
Where there ain't been no light.
So, boy, don't you turn back.
Don't you set down on the steps
'Cause you finds it kinder hard.
Don't you fall now —
For I'se still goin', honey,
I'se still climbin',
And life for me ain't been no crystal stair.

by Langston Hughes

May — T'aatsoh

Alice Yazzie rides her horse
in the barrel racing
at the rodeo.
She pays twenty-five cents
to see a buffalo
with a mangy coat
in a small cage in back of a trailer.

He is a buffalo out of Montana.
He has humped shoulders
and slits for eyes.
They look red from smoke
like a drunk bronc rider's.

After hamburgers and ice cream on a stick,
Alice leaves the crowd, the squash blossom auction,
the men judging baskets,
and goes back to the cage.

The buffalo snorts.
He hoofs at the ground.
"Don't be so loud," Alice tells him, drawing closer.
He eats six lumps of sugar
out of her purse.
He nibbles the turquoise
on her left hand.

"Is blue your color?" laughs Alice Ben Yazzie,
a nugget in her throat too big to swallow.
"Just remember, old blossom eater,
you can stare down the wind.
This old rodeo
Ain't everything."

by Ramona Maher

Rodeo, 1975 by Gilles Peress

Stony Brook State Park, New York, 1960 by Minor White

ire and Ice

Some say the world will end in fire,
Some say in ice.
From what I've tasted of desire
I hold with those who favor fire.
But if it had to perish twice,
I think I know enough of hate
To say that for destruction ice
Is also great
And would suffice.

by Robert Frost

ot Forever on Earth

Perchance do we truly live on earth?
Not forever on earth,
But briefly here!
Be it jade, it too will be broken;
Be it gold, it too will be melted,
And even the plume of the quetzal decays.
Not forever on earth,
But briefly here!

(Aztec)

wo Girls . . .

Two girls of twelve or so at a table
in the Automat, smiling at each other
and the world; eating sedately.
And a tramp, wearing two or three tattered coats,
dark with dirt, mumbling, sat down beside them —
Miss Muffit's spider.
But, unlike her, they were not frightened away,
and did not shudder as they might if older and look askance.
They did steal a glance
at their dark companion and were slightly amused:
in their shining innocence seeing
in him only another human being.

by Charles Reznikoff

Poetry Reading, New York City, 1950s by Burt Glinn

Bubbles

Two bubbles found they had rainbows on their curves.
They flickered out saying:
"It was worth being a bubble just to have held that rainbow thirty
    seconds."

by Carl Sandburg

Autobiographia Literaria

When I was a child
I played by myself in a
corner of the schoolyard
all alone.

I hated dolls and I
hated games, animals were
not friendly and birds
flew away.

If anyone was looking
for me I hid behind a
tree and cried out "I am
an orphan."

And here I am, the
center of all beauty!
writing these poems!
Imagine!

by Frank O'Hara

ament

Listen, children:
Your father is dead.
From his old coats
I'll make you little jackets;
I'll make you little trousers
From his old pants.
There'll be in his pockets
Things he used to put there,
Keys and pennies
Covered with tobacco;
Dan shall have the pennies
To save in his bank;
Anne shall have the keys
To make a pretty noise with.
Life must go on,
And the dead be forgotten;
Life must go on,
Though good men die;
Anne, eat your breakfast;
Dan, take your medicine;
Life must go on;
I forget just why.

by Edna St. Vincent Millay

Alexander Throckmorton

In youth my wings were strong and tireless,
But I did not know the mountains.
In age I knew the mountains
But my weary wings could not follow my vision —
Genius is wisdom and youth.

by Edgar Lee Masters

Santa Lucia Mountain Range, California, 1945 by Nina Leen

RESPONDING TO "MESSAGES"

Thinking and Discussing

Compare the messages in these poems. Which of the message poems was most meaningful to you? How did the author use the message to create an effective poem?

Were there any poems in which the message seemed unclear to you? Which ones? What are some possible interpretations of the messages in those poems?

Choosing a Creative Response

Creating a Message Poem Think of a common saying or proverb with which you agree. Then create a brief poem, trying to express the same idea in a fresh, new way by using interesting sounds and images.

Interpreting Messages Think of a normal, everyday occurrence, something as simple as the bursting of a bubble. Then come up with several messages it might convey. Try to think of completely opposite messages that the same occurrence might suggest.

Creating Your Own Activity Plan and complete your own activity in response to the poems in "Messages."

Thinking About Poetry

Making Your Own Magazine Talk with your classmates about individual poems or your thoughts about poetry in general. Then work together as a group to create your own poetry magazine.

Remember that a poetry magazine can include illustrations as well. Some students may wish to illustrate the magazine by contributing drawings or photographs. Other students may wish to design the arrangement of text and art on each page. Create a cover, title page, table of contents, and page of credits to thank all the individuals involved in your magazine. Share or display your finished magazine.

Debating About Poetry Working with a partner, choose a poem that one of you likes and the other dislikes. Imagine that you are critics having a debate about the merits of the poem.

First have the person who likes the poem explain his or her interpretation of the poem and opinion about it, supporting that opinion with specific examples of devices the poet used in creating the poem.

Then the person who dislikes the poem should give his or her interpretation and opposing opinion.

Both debaters may discover things they never knew about the poem.

Untitled,
1950s
by Wayne Miller

395

AUTHORS

Robert Burns, considered the national poet of Scotland, was a poor farmer who collected traditional Scottish songs and wrote or adapted lyrics for them.

Walter de la Mare, an English author, urged readers of poetry to "let your eyes, mind, heart and spirit feed on it, and see what happens."

Emily Dickinson lived in solitude, writing nearly all her poetry in secret, yet producing powerful poems.

Robert Francis lived a simple life in a small house in the woods, owning few possessions and growing his own food, so that he could devote himself to poetry.

Robert Frost spent his life in New England, farming, teaching, and writing poems inspired by country life.

Nan Fry contributes poems to poetry magazines.

Langston Hughes, a famous black poet of the 1920's, often expressed the pride and endurance of black Americans with blues and jazz rhythms.

David Ignatow once said, "My avocation is to stay alive; my vocation is to write about it."

Ramona Maher lives in the Southwest and writes stories and poems about the West and the Navajo world.

Edgar Lee Masters wrote the *Spoon River Anthology*, a famous collection of poems expressing the ideas of many characters about life in a town named Spoon River.

Edna St. Vincent Millay's poetry concerns themes of love and death, oneself and the universe, and rebellious youth.

Frank O'Hara was a playwright, art historian, and museum curator, as well as a poet.

Edgar Allan Poe is famous for highly rhythmic poems and horror stories that still terrify readers today.

Ezra Pound was an influential and controversial poet whose techniques were imitated by other poets.

Charles Reznikoff wrote books about Jewish history, plays, and a history of his family, as well as poetry.

Theodore Roethke wrote poems from emotions and memories, such as recollections of his father's greenhouse.

Carl Sandburg was a poet, biographer, and historian who wrote poems about American workers. He collected folktales, legends, and ballads.

Sara Teasdale believed that successful poems are "written to free the poet from an emotional burden."

Richard Wilbur "discovers the strange and marvelous in the commonest objects," according to one critic.

William Butler Yeats frequently used themes from Irish history and folklore in his poems.

Paul Zimmer works for a university press.

SHARING POETRY

A Galaxy of Verse selected by Louis Untermeyer (M. Evans, 1978) is a tasteful collection of a great variety of poems, from story poems to limericks.

American Sports Poems selected by R. R. Knudson and May Swenson (Orchard, 1988) presents a variety of sports in poems that will make fans cheer.

Talking to the Sun selected by Kenneth Koch and Kate Farrell (Metropolitan Museum of Art, 1985) is a handsome anthology of poetry from many cultures, illustrated with museum reproductions.

Pocket Poems: Selected for a Journey by Paul B. Janeczko (Bradbury, 1985) is a pocket-sized collection of short modern poems by eighty poets.

Reflections on a Gift of Watermelon Pickle . . . And Other Modern Verse compiled by Stephen Dunning, Edward Lueders, and Hugh Smith (Scholastic, 1966; Lothrop, 1967) is a popular classic of contemporary verse selected by teachers and still timely today.

Paris, 1953 by Henri Cartier-Bresson

SOCIAL STUDIES

BOOK 6

The American Revolution

This image by John McRae, entitled "Raising the Liberty Pole," shows colonists putting a liberty pole up in the town square.

Time Capsule Inventory

From *A More Perfect Union*, a social studies textbook

Growing Conflict with England

Key Terms

- effigy
- writ of assistance
- boycott
- embargo

➤ *To show their disapproval of the 1765 Stamp Act, these citizens from Boston seized and burned stacks of the British government's official stamps.*

As the sun rose over Boston on August 14, 1765, a scarecrow-like figure clad in rags dangled from a large oak tree. This hanging **effigy**, or dummy, represented Andrew Oliver, stamp distributor for Boston. Underneath was a warning: "He that takes this down is an enemy to his country." The display was a protest against the Stamp Act due to be enforced in November that required tax stamps on nearly all printed materials. The colonists were enraged that they should be taxed without their consent or, at the very least, without their representation.

At the end of a tense day, the leaders of the mob cut down the figure of Oliver and nailed it to a board. Four men carried it through the streets, heading for a new brick building on the docks of Boston's South End. Word on the street said that this would be Oliver's office for distributing the hated stamps. In less than an hour, the mob tore the building down.

The crowd then marched to Oliver's home led by Ebenezer MacIntosh, a 28-year-old shoemaker. Warned by the sheriff, Oliver and his family had just slipped out the back way when the protesters arrived.

Breaking into the house, the mob smashed the windows and tore apart the furniture. They emptied the bottles from Oliver's elegant wine cellar and tore up his gardens. Oliver got the message and promised to resign as stamp distributor.

Boston was not alone in its hatred of the Stamp Act. More protests followed in other colonial towns and cities. The colonists would stoutly resist the efforts of the British government to tax them. "No taxation without representation" became their rallying cry.

Rivalry for North America Leads to War

To understand the reasons for the Stamp Act riots, you must first look at the Seven Years' War. This war was actually one in a series of wars fought between Britain and France beginning in the late 1600's. While competing for North American territory on the one hand, the two

After defeating the French in the Seven Years' War, Great Britain controlled the entire eastern half of North America. Spain claimed much of what was left of the continent.

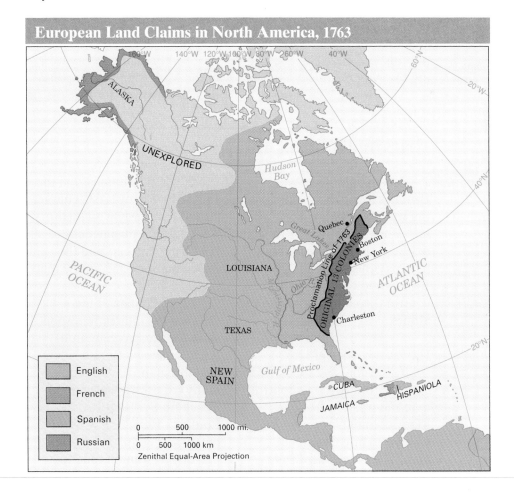

European Land Claims in North America, 1763

ALASKA

UNEXPLORED

Hudson Bay

Great Lakes

Quebec
Boston
New York

Proclamation Line of 1763

ORIGINAL 13 COLONIES

PACIFIC OCEAN

LOUISIANA

Ohio R.

ATLANTIC OCEAN

Charleston

TEXAS

NEW SPAIN

Gulf of Mexico

CUBA

JAMAICA

HISPANIOLA

English
French
Spanish
Russian

0   500   1000 mi.
0   500   1000 km
Zenithal Equal-Area Projection

European nations were also battling for dominance of Europe.

Both Britain and France claimed territory along the Ohio River Valley. As English colonists from Virginia began to settle this area, they faced French resistance. In 1754 England sent soldiers under General Edward Braddock to the region, but the French and their Indian allies drove them back.

George Washington, a young Virginian, was part of Braddock's force. He noted that British soldiers in their bright red coats were easy targets for Indians who fired from hiding places in the forest. Washington was later able to put this knowledge to use during the American Revolution.

The British were not deterred. They sent the full might of their military force against the French empire in America. The fighting soon became worldwide, with battles as far away as India and the islands of the Caribbean. In Europe the Seven Years' War began in 1756. Three years later, the British took the great French outpost at Quebec, Canada. The following year, all of Canada was in British hands.

By the Treaty of Paris in 1763, Britain gained Canada and the French lands east of the Mississippi River. Because Spain had unwisely entered the war on France's side, it lost Florida to Britain. But Spain received French territory west of the Mississippi as compensation, or payment, for this loss. ∎

■ *What did Britain gain as a result of the Seven Years' War?*

Britain Tightens the Vise

As a result of the war Britain's territory was doubled; the war also plunged Britain into a huge debt. The British believed the colonies should help pay this debt, but first Britain had to assert its right to control the colonists' economic affairs.

The Proclamation of 1763

The colonists expected to benefit from Britain's control over the western frontier. Many colonial farmers wanted to move into the area. They received a rude shock when Britain issued the Proclamation of 1763. This act closed the newly won territory west of the Appalachians to all colonists. You can find the Proclamation Line on the map on page 405.

Chief Pontiac of the Ottawa was indirectly responsible for the Proclamation. Seeing the new British rulers as a threat, he had organized many tribes in a widespread attack on British forts. Pontiac's Rebellion was only partly successful. Nevertheless, the British wanted time to reach a treaty with the Indians before allowing any more colonists into the area.

The colonists felt cheated by the Proclamation. Many of them had fought with the British troops to drive out the French. They wanted to share in the fruits of victory.

The Quartering Act

Britain left an army in the colonies to guard the frontier. In 1765 Parliament passed the Quartering Act, which required colonial cities to provide lodging for the royal troops. The law commanded local governments to pay for such supplies as firewood, bedding, candles, vinegar, and salt.

The British military commander had his headquarters in New York. But the New York Assembly refused to vote money to supply his troops, saying that the Quartering Act placed an unfair burden on the colony. When Parliament threatened to suspend the powers of the assembly, it grudgingly granted the money.

The Stamp Act

Parliament also passed the Stamp Act in 1765 — the most hated of its attempts to raise money. The act required colonists to buy a revenue stamp each time they registered a legal document or bought newspapers, pamphlets, almanacs, liquor licenses, or playing cards. Particularly hard hit by the tax

were lawyers, tavern owners, merchants, and printers.

When news of the Stamp Act reached America, the colonists exploded. In Boston and other colonial cities, groups calling themselves the Sons of Liberty sprang up to protest the Stamp Act. Rioting broke out in a number of these cities.

In October, representatives from nine colonies met in New York at the Stamp Act Congress. There they adopted a Declaration of Rights and Grievances. This declaration expressed their opposition both to taxation without representation in Parliament and to trial without jury by the admiralty courts. They

▲ *The stamps shown on this page were required on legal documents such as wills and insurance policies. These stamps cost five shillings or more.*

■ *How did the Seven Years' War change the relationship between Britain and the colonies?*

petitioned the king to repeal the Stamp Act. The delegates claimed that only colonial assemblies could legally impose taxes on them.

Before the petition reached Britain, Parliament repealed the Stamp Act (March 1766). When the news reached the colonies, people paraded in the streets. ■

▲ *This British political cartoon, which pictures a funeral procession for the recently repealed Stamp Act, pokes fun at Parliament and British Prime Minister George Grenville (fourth from left).*

Tensions Reach the Breaking Point

Despite the failure of the Stamp Act, Britain persisted in its attempts to control and tax the colonies. In 1767 Parliament passed the Townshend Acts, which placed taxes on paint, glass, lead, paper, and tea. To enforce the act, customs officials were granted **writs of assistance**, which gave them the power to enter private homes and businesses at any time, with no reasonable suspicion, to look for smuggled goods.

In response, colonists launched a **boycott,** or refusal to buy the newly taxed goods. Colonists began making their own cloth, paper, and paint. Women formed groups called the Daughters of Liberty and held public spinning bees to make American cloth.

The Boston Massacre

Anti-British feeling ran highest in the city of Boston. Samuel Adams, a leader of the Sons of Liberty, whipped up crowds of protesters and wrote inflammatory newspaper articles.

Tensions came to a head on March 5, 1770. A band of apprentice boys and other civilians attacked the guard of the Boston Customs House. When soldiers came to his aid, the crowd pelted them with oyster shells and snowballs. In the scuffle that followed, someone gave the order to "Fire!" and five rioters were killed. The first to die was Crispus Attucks, a black man who had fled slavery.

Adams's articles about the incident spread news of the Boston Massacre throughout the colonies.

The Boston Tea Party

On April 12, 1770, the king consented to repeal the Townshend taxes on all items except tea. The news calmed most colonists.

However, Sam Adams formed a Committee of Correspondence in Boston in 1772 to keep American grievances against Britain in the public eye. Towns in other colonies followed his lead and exchanged written complaints about British actions.

In 1773, Parliament passed the Tea Act, which allowed the British East India Company to sell tea directly to the colonists.

Helped by this special treatment, the company could undersell American tea merchants. Britain would now benefit more from its tax on imported tea.

Protest was immediate. In Charleston, colonists locked the tea in warehouses. In North Carolina, women publicly refused to drink tea. In some colonies, Americans prevented tea ships from landing.

On December 16, 1773, a band of men dressed like Indians boarded three tea ships in Boston Harbor. In silence, the leaders of the "Boston Tea Party" threw the chests of tea overboard.

The British government fumed. The king said of the colonists, "We must master them or totally leave them to themselves and treat them as aliens."

This wooden chest was recovered from Boston Harbor after the Boston Tea Party.

The Intolerable Acts

Parliament passed a series of measures designed to punish the colonists. It closed the port of Boston until the city repaid the East India Company for the tea it had destroyed. It increased the powers of the governor to the point that he could even ban town meetings. At the same time, a new Quartering Act allowed British commanders to station troops in private homes. Finally, the Quebec Act put much of the Ohio River Valley into the province of Quebec, cutting off this land from New York, Pennsylvania, and Virginia.

Colonists called these measures the Intolerable Acts. Other colonies sent supplies to help Massachusetts. The Committees of Correspondence urged the colonies to hold a meeting about the crisis.

The First Continental Congress

Delegates from all thirteen colonies except Georgia met at Carpenter's Hall in Philadelphia from September 5 to October 26, 1774. Calling themselves the First Continental Congress, they all agreed to support Massachusetts and passed a resolution that declared the Intolerable Acts null and void. They also called for civil disobedience. But to soothe those who wanted to settle the crisis peacefully, they sent a petition of their grievances to the British government.

The Congress also set up the Continental Association to hold elections for committees in every town to enforce an **embargo,** or ban on trade, against Britain. More ominously, it called on each colony to begin training soldiers for defense.

Before the delegates adjourned, they scheduled another Congress for May of the following year. By the time the Second Continental Congress met, fighting had already begun. ■

■ *What actions taken by Parliament contributed to the growth in tension between England and the colonies?*

R E V I E W

1. What were the causes of the colonists' growing resentment of British rule?
2. Why did England attempt to tighten its control of the colonies after the Seven Years' War?
3. In what sense were economic issues responsible for the outbreak of the American Revolution?
4. **CRITICAL THINKING** Why do you think it was so difficult for the British government to maintain tight control over the colonies?
5. **ACTIVITY** Imagine you are a colonial merchant and prepare a speech to Parliament stating why you think the Tea Act is unfair.

The American Revolution Begins

On the morning of April 19, 1775, eight patriots lay dead on the village green at Lexington, Massachusetts, killed by British musket balls. In Concord, the liberty pole lay hacked to pieces, and the courthouse, nearly burned by the British, sat smoldering.

Meanwhile, along the bloody road from Concord back to Boston, curses, smoke, and screams filled the air. The seven hundred British troops who had overrun Lexington and Concord were attempting an orderly march back to their base in Boston. But hundreds of enraged colonists, firing from houses and barns, from behind stone walls and trees—from everywhere it seemed—punished the British troops. The red-coated soldiers shrieked and fell as patriot musket balls found their marks.

THINKING
FOCUS

What finally persuaded many colonists that they should declare their independence from Britain?

Key Terms

- militia
- minutemen
- republic

◄ *The Battle of Lexington and Concord*

By the end of the day, more than 70 British soldiers had been killed, and 200 had been wounded or were missing. Outside Boston that night, hundreds of campfires surrounded the city. These were the fires of twenty thousand patriots who were beginning an armed vigil.

A spark had flown, and the powder keg had exploded. Without plan or warning, the American Revolution had begun.

Early Battles

The outbreak of armed conflict took many in the colonies by surprise. Less than a month before the fighting described above, members of the Virginia Assembly had been shocked when they heard Patrick Henry's proposal to prepare Virginia for war. Nevertheless, Henry's words proved to be prophetic:

> *Gentlemen may cry peace, peace — but there is no peace. The war is actually begun! The next gale that sweeps from the north will bring to our ears the clash of resounding arms! Our brethren are already in the field! Why stand we here idle? . . . I know not what course others may take; but as for me, give me liberty, or give me death!*

Lexington and Concord

In the fall of 1774, a group of Massachusetts colonists met at Concord and decided to prepare for a possible war with Britain. They named John Hancock, a wealthy merchant, to organize an armed force. His **militia**, or citizen army, called themselves **minutemen**, because they were ready to fight on a minute's notice.

Several months later the royal governor, General Thomas Gage, sent 700 soldiers to Concord to arrest the patriot leaders. Paul Revere learned of the plan. On the night of April 18, 1775, he prepared to warn the patriots.

Boston was already an armed camp. Yet Revere slipped out of town and rode off on his horse down the road the British would travel. He shouted the alarm as he passed the houses of minutemen along the way.

A little before midnight, Revere reached Lexington, where Hancock was hiding. True to their name, 70 of Lexington's minutemen were waiting on the village green when the British marched in at dawn on April 19.

When the colonists refused

to lay down their arms, the British soldiers rushed forward, eager for blood. They killed eight minutemen and wounded ten others.

By nine o'clock in the morning, a larger force of minutemen had assembled at Concord. They blocked the North Bridge and fired, from a column formation, the "shot heard round the world." Philosopher and poet Ralph Waldo Emerson later captured this moment in the following stanzas of his "Concord Hymn":

*B*y the rude bridge that arched the flood,
Their flag to April's breeze unfurled,
Here once the embattled farmers stood
And fired the shot heard round the world.

Spirit that made those heroes dare
To die, and leave their children free,
Bid Time and Nature gently spare
The shaft we raise to them and thee.

Ticonderoga

In western New Hampshire — today's Vermont — Ethan Allen organized a group of tough frontiersmen called the Green Mountain Boys. In May 1775, they surprised the sleeping British garrison at Fort Ticonderoga in New York. Allen captured the fort's cannons. His men then slowly dragged about 50 of them along backwoods trails to the patriot forces in Boston.

The Battle of Bunker Hill

General Thomas Gage, the British colonial administrator, decided to defend Boston by placing troops on Bunker Hill. Once more the Americans learned of his plans. On the night of June 16, over a thousand patriots moved onto nearby Breed's Hill.

Gage ordered his men to drive them off. "Don't one of you fire until you see the whites of their eyes," ordered American General Israel Putnam, in an attempt to conserve ammunition. When the British troops were 100 feet away, the American guns roared, and the British front ranks fell. Yet the British came back, again and again, until the patriots ran out of ammunition and retreated.

After the Battle of Bunker Hill, over 1000 British soldiers lay dead or wounded. Although technically Britain won the battle, the Americans had shown that the British faced a hard fight. ■

▲ *The lantern from Old North Church*

■ *Find evidence to support the following statement: The early battles showed that the Revolution was likely to be a long and difficult war.*

A Minuteman

9:12 A.M. April 19, 1775
Near the North Bridge
in Concord, Massachusetts

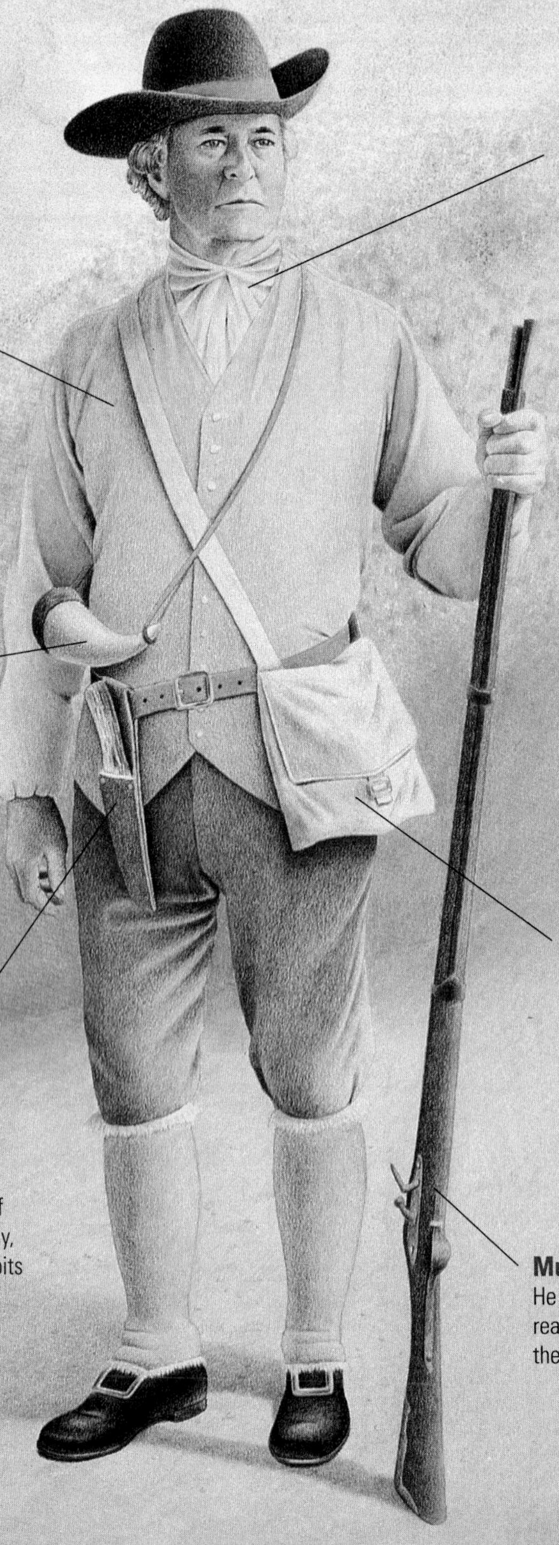

Homespun Shirt
He grabbed his favorite shirt off the clothesline. His wife had spun the yarn herself and had woven the cloth on her loom last winter.

Vest
His mother-in-law sewed this from the hide of a deer he shot last winter. It keeps him warm on cool spring mornings such as this one.

Powder Horn
This morning, a neighbor ran to tell him about the British troops coming from Boston. He quickly got dressed, filled this powder horn with gun powder and ran to join his fellow patriots.

Hunting Knife
When he dressed up as an Indian for the "Tea Party" in Boston back in '73, he used this knife to cut the ropes of the tea crates. Most recently, he used it to clean two rabbits for dinner last night.

Haversack
On his way out the door, he stuffed some dried apples and a biscuit in his heavy canvas bag.

Musket
He holds it proudly as he stands ready, wondering anxiously when the British troops will arrive.

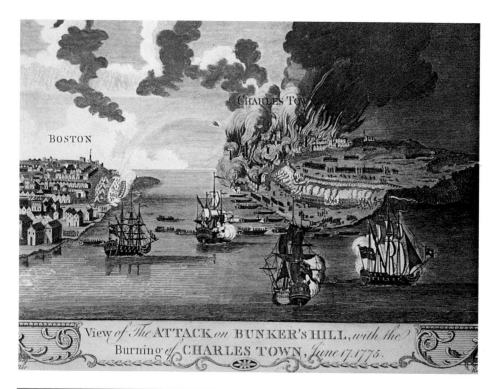

View of *The* ATTACK *on* BUNKER'S HILL, *with the* Burning *of* CHARLES TOWN, *June 17, 1775*.

▲ *The Battle of Bunker Hill*

The Road to the Declaration

Despite the fighting, many colonists still wanted to avoid war. In July 1775, the Second Continental Congress sent the "Olive Branch" Petition to King George III. It blamed Parliament for the trouble and urged the king to intercede. Instead, he proclaimed that the colonies were in rebellion and gave orders "to bring the traitors to justice." More colonists now began to listen to the firebrands.

Common Sense

In January 1776, a pamphlet titled *Common Sense* appeared in the colonies. Its author, Thomas Paine, had moved to America only a year before. But the news of Lexington and Concord had inflamed him. Calling George III "the Royal Brute of Britain," Paine urged the colonists to establish a free, independent **republic**, or system of representational government.

Common Sense eventually sold half a million copies, and its message spread like wildfire. Arguments about the legality of Parliament's acts seemed pale and fussy in the face of Paine's outright demand for independence.

Writing the Declaration

In the spring of 1776, public sentiment convinced the

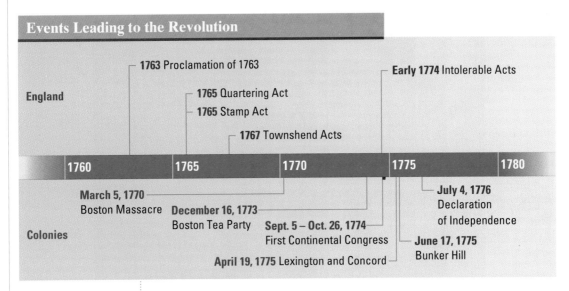

Events Leading to the Revolution

England

- 1763 Proclamation of 1763
- 1765 Quartering Act
- 1765 Stamp Act
- 1767 Townshend Acts
- Early 1774 Intolerable Acts

1760 — 1765 — 1770 — 1775 — 1780

Colonies

- March 5, 1770 Boston Massacre
- December 16, 1773 Boston Tea Party
- Sept. 5 – Oct. 26, 1774 First Continental Congress
- April 19, 1775 Lexington and Concord
- June 17, 1775 Bunker Hill
- July 4, 1776 Declaration of Independence

■ *What events finally convinced many colonists that they should declare their independence from England?*

Continental Congress to take the final step. The Congress appointed a committee to draft a declaration of independence. The committee selected Thomas Jefferson, a brilliant young lawyer from Virginia, to write the first draft.

Jefferson's words stirred the colonists: "All men are created equal . . . with certain unalienable rights; that among these are life, liberty, and the pursuit of happiness." Jefferson said later that he did not "invent new ideas," but merely expressed "the American mind."

On July 4, 1776, John Hancock, the president of the Congress, signed his name to the Declaration of Independence. Legend said he wrote it large enough for King George to read it without his glasses. The delegates of every colony eventually added their names. The English colonies had now become the United States of America. ■

R E V I E W

1. Why did the Patriots not declare independence until more than a year after the fighting began?

2. What effect did **Common Sense** have on public opinion in the colonies?

3. Was it reasonable for the British to think in 1776 that they could easily defeat the American colonists? Why or why not?

4. **CRITICAL THINKING** Do you think the Revolutionary War was unavoidable or could the war have been prevented if the British and the Patriots had acted differently? Explain your answer.

5. **ACTIVITY** Imagine that you are a member of the Continental Congress and are trying to decide whether the colonies should declare their independence from Great Britain. Create a chart listing the pros and cons of independence to help you in making your decision.

Responding to *A More Perfect Union*

Thinking and Discussing

What effect did the Seven Years' War have on Britain? What effect did it have on American colonists? What connections does the text make between the Seven Years' War and the Stamp Act riots?

Why were American colonists shocked when Britain issued the Proclamation of 1763? In what ways was their anger justified? In what ways was it unjustified?

Prior to the Revolutionary War, what kinds of tactics did the colonists use in their struggle against British rule? Which tactics were peaceful? Which were more confrontational? Were some tactics more effective than others? Why?

Applying Historical Concepts

Writing an Editorial Imagine you are a colonial printer working during the time of the Stamp Act. How might this regulation have affected you? Write an editorial stating why you think the Stamp Act is unfair. You may want to include details about how you got started as a printer, or how the Stamp Act has affected your family. You might also choose a tone for your editorial: Will it be respectful, bitter, angry, or diplomatic?

Writing an Eyewitness Memoir

actions, issues, and feelings they experienced. Begin writing when you feel ready. Or, if the selections give you a different writing idea, try that one instead.

1. Prewriting Before you begin writing your eyewitness memoir, think of something important that happened to you or that you observed. You may wish to write about a hurricane, an important speech, a fire, or a great moment in sports. Choose an incident that will also have significance for your readers. Try to re-create the experience in your mind, so that the details will be fresh in your memory. You may want to revisit the scene of the incident to help you remember all the facts.

Have you ever written to a friend about an exciting event you witnessed? Have you ever found out about an important incident from someone who was actually there? Some of the most vivid portrayals of events — and of history — are handed down to us through firsthand observers.

Try writing your own eyewitness memoir. Look at the eyewitness accounts included among the selections that follow. Notice how the authors bring to life the

2. Write a First Draft Think about your audience and your purpose for writing. Who will read your memoir? How can you make your audience relive the experience with you? How will you convey the significance of the incident? Will you describe the event in a letter or as a story, or find some other way to recapture the details?

3. Revise Read your first draft and make any necessary changes. Do the events as you've captured them on paper seem as vivid as the events you experienced? Have you included lots of colorful details? Are your own feelings as an observer clear? You may want to read your paper to a partner to check its effectiveness.

4. Proofread Check your eyewitness memoir for correct spelling, capitalization, and punctuation. If your account includes proper names and places, make sure they are spelled correctly.

5. Publish Decide on a format in which to publish your memoir. Make a neat copy of your account. You may want to share your memoir as a letter, a journal entry, a story, or a newspaper feature.

Award Winner

In 1770,

*five years before the outbreak of
the Revolutionary War, five men
lay dead on a Boston street, shot
by British soldiers in a scuffle
that was to become known as the
Boston Massacre. One of these
martyrs was a black man
named Crispus Attucks.
What led to Attucks's death, and
how did his death affect
later events?*

Crispus Attucks

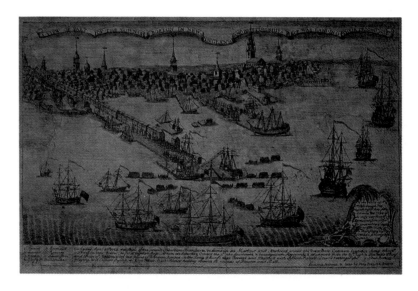

This colorful engraving by Paul Revere shows the arrival of the British fleet in 1768, which marked the beginning of the British occupation of Boston.

from

Black Heroes of the American Revolution

by Burke Davis

*F*resh snow lay
in Boston's icy streets on the night of March 5, 1770,
but the sky had cleared after dark and a new moon hung
overhead. A cold wind from the harbor swept the
Boston Common and shook the tents of
British soldiers, who had been camped there
for five months.

The streets were noisy as redcoats moved about, followed by bands of shouting civilians. The small city of 15,000 was crowded by men and boys who had come in from the country and nearby towns to help drive out the 1,000 redcoats, just as if they were enemies. There were occasional scuffles, as there had been for weeks past. Soldiers jostled and cursed the people, who replied with hoots, curses, and insults. These soldiers were the first ever sent from England to America in peacetime, ordered to the city by King George III after the Massachusetts legislature had protested harsh new trade laws for the colonies.

Now and then the redcoats were pelted by snowballs from the darkness, hundreds of frozen chunks with small stones in the center. A fight broke out — no one seemed to know how it had begun — and church bells rang an alarm. People looked out from their houses, and many came into the streets, armed with swords, axes, pitchforks, or boards ripped from old buildings. The crowds grew more daring as they became larger.

A sentry by the name of Montgomery who stood before the Customs House on King Street found himself surrounded by people after a young barber's helper yelled, "There's a redcoat who hasn't paid for having his hair dressed."

"Shut up!" Montgomery said.

The boy cursed, the soldier struck him on the head with his musket butt, and the barber's helper went yowling down the street holding his head.

The crowd pressed about the sentry, chanting, "Hang the redcoats! Drive 'em out!"

More church bells rang as the barber's boy returned to jeer and point at Montgomery. The crowd increased. Captain Thomas Preston, the officer of the day, called for the guard, and twelve soldiers hurried to the Customs House. The crowd was forced back a few feet by bayonets. The muskets, Captain Preston said, were not loaded.

At that moment, as the civilians hesitated before the glistening blades, a small mob rushed down a nearby hill, its men armed with clubs. The newcomers were led by a burly black man named Crispus Attucks, who urged them on in a loud, fierce voice. People on the streets stepped aside as Attucks charged. As John Adams said, the giant's appearance "was enough to terrify any person."

The black leader had formed his men in Dock Square and led them down King Street (now State Street), trotting at the head of his company, his broad shoulders hunched.

Attucks dashed within a few feet of the line of redcoats at the Customs House and waved over his head a heavy stick of firewood.

"Come on, bloodybacks!" he yelled. "Shoot if you dare! Damn you, we know you don't dare."

The soldiers began loading their muskets. A young white man in the crowd begged Captain Preston to take his men back to their tents, but the officer refused. A soldier yelled, "Damn them. If they bother me, I'll fire." The redcoats now held their muskets breast high, with fingers on the triggers.

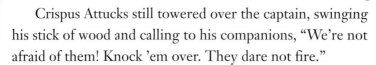

Crispus Attucks still towered over the captain, swinging his stick of wood and calling to his companions, "We're not afraid of them! Knock 'em over. They dare not fire."

Beside him stood Samuel Gray, the owner of a rope factory, who had led an attack on some of the soldiers a few days before. Gray also shouted encouragement to the mob and said that the troops would not fire. A club sailed through the air, knocking aside a British musket. Suddenly a hail of snowballs, stones, clubs, and sticks fell among the redcoats. The crowd raised a shout that rang through the streets, but above it rang a war whoop from Attucks, who grabbed a bayonet with one hand and at the same moment clubbed a soldier with his stick.

The twelve muskets roared. Attucks fell with two bullets in his chest, the first one fired by the sentry Montgomery. Samuel Gray went down beside him.

Both men died on the spot, almost at the feet of the soldiers. Stray shots killed Jonas Caldwell, a sailor who was standing in the middle of the street, and two other whites, seventeen-year-old Samuel Maverick and Patrick Carr, both of whom fell as they were hurrying toward the scene. Six other civilians were wounded, but were to recover.

The crowd fled, leaving the bodies behind, but as it grew and became noisier, it swarmed through the streets until it met Governor Thomas Hutchinson.

The Governor calmed the people by speaking to them from the balcony of a building. He promised to arrest Captain Preston and his men and to have the troops moved out of the city. The people then drifted away and returned to their homes.

Strangely enough, the people of Boston knew almost nothing about Crispus Attucks, who was hailed as the first victim in the cause that was to become the

American Revolution.

Though little is known of his early life, Crispus Attucks is thought to have been the son of an African father and an Indian mother. The mother, who belonged to the Natick tribe, was probably descended from John Attucks, a Christian convert who was executed by early New England colonists because he sided with his tribe during an Indian uprising known as King Philip's War. ("Attuck" was the word for "deer" in the Natick language.)

By the time he had grown to manhood, Crispus was a slave, the property of William Brown of Framingham, Massachusetts. But even as a slave, young Attucks was unusually independent. He became well known in his home town as a trader of horses and cattle, shrewd enough to deal with free white men. But though he kept for himself the money he made, Attucks was unable to buy his freedom from his master — and he was fiercely determined to be free.

At last, in the autumn of 1750, he took the only way to freedom that was open to him. He ran away. Brown advertised in the *Boston Gazette* on October 2, 1750:

But though Brown offered ten pounds as a reward, Attucks was never caught — nor was he heard from again in Massachusetts until the night, twenty years later, when he reappeared as the leader of the patriot mob on March 5, 1770. It is thought that Attucks may have spent his twenty years of freedom as a sailor, working on cargo ships that sailed to and from the

RAN-away from his Master *William Brown* of *Framingham*, on the 30th of *Sept.* last, a Molatto Fellow, about 27 Years of Age, named *Crispas*, 6 Feet two Inches high, short curl'd Hair, his Knees nearer together than common ; had on a light colour'd Bearskin Coat, plain brown Fustian Jacket, or brown all-Wool one, new Buckskin Breeches, blue YarnStockings, and a check'd woollenShirt. Whoever shall take up said Run-away, and convey him to his abovesaidMaster, shall have *ten Pounds*, old TenorReward, and all necessary Charges paid. And allMasters of Vessels and others, are hereby caution'd againft concealing or carrying off saidServant onPenalty of the Law. *Boston, October* 2. 1750.

West Indies, but this is not certain. He is also said to have sailed whaling ships off the New England coast.

The stranger who had appeared just in time to give the white mob the courageous leadership to attack the redcoats was praised by white revolutionaries as the bravest of the victims of the street fight.

As Thomas Jefferson said, the blood of Crispus Attucks nourished the tree of liberty. The humble slave, who had the courage to flee his master and make a new life on his own, had been among the first Americans to die for the nation's liberty.

Three days later, a public funeral was held for the victims of the street battle. All shops in the city were closed and thousands of people flocked in from the nearby countryside. The *Boston Gazette* reported that the funeral was attended by the largest crowd ever assembled in North America.

The bodies of Attucks and Caldwell, which had lain in their coffins at Faneuil Hall because they had no homes in Boston, were carried to meet the other hearses in King Street, near the scene of the shootings. A long procession then followed the black carriages to the cemetery, where the victims were buried in one grave.

John Adams was to write of the Boston Massacre years later, "On that night, the foundations of American independence were laid."

But though they could not foresee this future, patriot leaders who were trying to stir up trouble for the British made sure that the deaths of the five men were not forgotten.

The *Boston Gazette* published an account of their deaths with black borders of mourning, with pictures of coffins, skulls, and crossbones.

Samuel Adams began to write of the clash between soldiers and civilians as the Boston Massacre, the name by which it is known to this day.

Paul Revere, the silversmith and engraver who was secretly working for the Revolution, copied a drawing of the massacre by a Boston artist and published it — one of the most famous engravings of American history. Thousands of copies were circulated throughout the colonies to create sympathy for the people of Boston and hatred of the British troops.

Captain Preston and several of his soldiers were tried in Boston. The captain was found not guilty since the court ruled that he had acted to protect his troops. Two soldiers who were found guilty were branded in the hand with a hot iron. This did not satisfy the patriot leaders.

Three years later, John Adams called on the memory of the victims of the Boston Massacre to help cause an open break between America and England.

Adams sent Governor Hutchinson a letter that would not be forgotten, a letter that he pretended had been written by a dead man. It was actually meant for use in newspapers:

Sir
You will hear from Us with Astonishment. You ought to hear from Us with Horror. You are chargeable before God and Man, with our Blood. — The Soldiers were but passive Instruments . . . in our Destruction . . . You were a free Agent. You acted, coolly, deliberately, with . . . Malice, not against Us in Particular but against the People in general, which in the Sight of the law is . . . Murder. You will hear from Us hereafter.

The signature in Adams's own hand was "Chrispus Attucks."

It was to be many years later before the great orator Daniel Webster declared that the Boston Massacre was the turning point in the long struggle between England and her rebellious American colonists: "From that moment," Webster was to shout, "we may date the severance of the British Empire." The reckless bravery of Crispus Attucks had helped change the course of history.

Paul Revere's engraving dramatically portrayed the Patriots' version of events at the Boston Massacre.

Responding to "Crispus Attucks"

Thinking and Discussing

The author describes Attucks's behavior as "reckless bravery." Was Attucks reckless? Was he brave? Give reasons for your opinions.

How did Patriots use the events of the Boston Massacre to promote their cause? What do you think the massacre victims might have thought of the Patriots' actions?

What was the author's purpose in writing "Crispus Attucks"? How does this purpose compare with that of the textbook? What did this selection add to your understanding of the Boston Massacre?

Applying Historical Concepts

Performing a Scene Write a scene that depicts the Boston Massacre. You may wish to work alone, or with a partner or a small group. Then cast the characters, rehearse the scene, and perform it for your class. You might want to liven your performance with costumes, props, or simple scenery.

This engraving of coffins, also by Revere, appeared with an account of the burial of the massacre victims in the **Boston Gazette.**

Daily Life in Boston

Stoneware pitchers and crocks for cooking and storing food

In colonial Boston, everyday objects were handsomely designed and constructed to last. Most of the handmade objects on this page stayed at home. But, like today's laptop computer, the traveling desk could go places with its owner.

Late 1700's traveling desk

Chester Goodale born Sept. 1764
Married Asenath Cook Aug. 10.
1790, who was born Oct. 11. 1770.
The births of their children are as follows viz.

Chester Goodale born April 24 1791
Laura Goodale born March 12 1793
Asenath Goodale born May 24 1795
Phebe Goodale born July 15 1804

Sam'l Goodale born Dec. 11

▲ **Typical sampler telling a family's history**

► **Knife holder from the 1700's**

◄ **Early 1700's chair with hand-rushed seat**

As time passed, angry Patriots grew more willing to take action against the British. In 1773, a group of Patriots protested the Tea Act by dumping crates of tea into Boston Harbor. What was it like to be in Boston at the time of the Boston Tea Party? What were the attitudes of Patriots and British Loyalists? Find out from two people who were there.

Tension filled the period from the repeal of the Stamp Act, commemorated on this teapot made in 1766, to the meeting at the Green Dragon Tavern, where Patriots planned the Boston Tea Party in 1773.

Personal Accounts:

The

Boston

Tea Party

Americans throwing the Cargoes of the Tea Ships into the River, at Boston

Recollections of George Hewes

George Hewes was a Patriot who helped dump the tea into Boston Harbor. He recalls the event in this way:

⅋

. . . It was now evening, and I immediately dressed myself in the costume of an Indian, equipped with a small hatchet, which I and my associates denominated [called] the tomahawk . . . After having painted my face and hands with coal dust in the shop of a blacksmith, I repaired [went] to Griffin's wharf, where the ships lay that contained the tea. When I first appeared in the street after being thus disguised, I fell in with many who were dressed, equipped, and painted as I was . . . When we arrived at the wharf, there were three of our number who assumed an authority to direct our operations, to which we readily submitted. They divided us into three parties, for the purpose of boarding the three ships which contained the tea at the same time. The name of him who commanded the division to which I was assigned was Leonard Pitt. The names of the other commanders I never knew. We were immediately ordered by the respective commanders to board all the ships at the same time, which we promptly obeyed. The commander of the division to which I belonged . . . appointed me boatswain,[1] and ordered me to go to the captain and demand of him the keys to the hatches and a dozen candles. I made the demand accordingly, and the captain promptly replied, and delivered the articles; but requested me at the same time to do no damage to the ship or rigging. We then were ordered by our commander to open the hatches and take out the chests of tea and throw them

---

[1] **boatswain (bō′sən):** an officer who is in charge of a ship's deck. Here, Hewes probably means that Pitt appointed him to help lead the expedition.

overboard, and we immediately proceeded to execute his orders, first cutting and splitting the chests with our tomahawks, so as to thoroughly expose them to the effects of the water.

In about three hours from the time we went on board, we had thus broken and thrown overboard every tea chest to be found in the ship, while those in the other ships were disposing of the tea in the same way, at the same time. We were surrounded by British armed ships, but no attempt was made to resist us.

We then quietly retired to our several places of residence, without having any conversation with each other, or taking any measures to discover who were our associates . . . There appeared to be an understanding that each individual should volunteer his services, keep his own secret, and risk the consequence for himself. No disorder took place during that transaction, and it was observed at that time that the stillest night ensued [followed] that Boston had enjoyed for many months.

During the time we were throwing the tea overboard, there were several attempts made by some of the citizens of Boston and its vicinity to carry off small quantities of it for their family use . . . One Captain O'Connor, whom I well knew, came on board for that purpose, and when he supposed he was not noticed, filled his pockets, and also the lining of his coat . . . We were ordered to take him into custody, and just as he was stepping from the vessel, I seized him by the skirt of his coat, and in attempting to pull him back, I tore it off; but, springing forward, by a rapid effort he made his escape. He had, however, to run a gauntlet through the crowd upon the wharf, each one, as he passed, giving him a kick or a stroke.

Another attempt was made to save a little tea from the ruins of the cargo by a tall, aged man who wore a large cocked hat and a white wig . . . Being detected, they seized him and, taking his hat and wig from his head, threw them, together with the tea, of which they had emptied his pockets, into the water. In consideration of his advanced age, he was permitted to escape, with now and then a slight kick.

Anne Hulton: Letters

Anne Hulton was a British woman who lived in Boston from 1768 to 1775. Anne wrote many letters to a friend in England, describing life in New England amid the Revolutionary turmoil. Many of her letters have been preserved. Below are two excerpts that describe her reaction to events leading up to and following the Boston Tea Party.

From a letter dated November 25, 1773:

The ships laden with tea from the East India House are hourly expected. The people will not suffer it to be landed at Boston. They demand the consignees [tea agents] to promise to send it back. Mr. Clark resolutely refuses to comply [and] will submit to no other terms than to put it into warehouse till they can hear from England. They threaten to tear him to pieces if it is landed. He says he will be tore to pieces before he will desert the trust reposed in him by the consigners. His son, who is just arrived from England . . . and all the family were got together the first night rejoicing at his arrival, when the mob surrounded the house. Attacking it with stones and clubs, [the mob] did great damage to the house and furniture. When young [Clark] spoke to them, [he] told them if they did not desist [he should] certainly fire a gun at them, which he did. [He] wounded a

Tea, that was gathered up on the Shore of Dorchester Neck on the morning after the destruction of the three Cargos, at Boston December 17. 1773

man, it's supposed, for they retreated carrying off a man. But they threatened to destroy every person in the house if any one of their associates was killed. And a great number of stones, each so large as to have killed any person they had hit, were thrown about the table where the family were at supper. But Providence directed them so that they did not fall on any person. All the avenues to the house at [the] same time were guarded by armed men to prevent Mr. Clark escaping. This was beyond anything of the kind since we came here.

The tea consignees and other Loyalists had escaped to the Castle, a fortress on Castle Island in Boston Harbor. Anne was still in her home near Boston when she wrote this letter, dated January 31, 1774:

The tea consignees remain still at the Castle. Six weeks since the tea was destroyed, and there is no prospect of their ever returning and residing in Boston with safety. This place and all the towns about entered into a written agreement not to afford them any shelter or protection, so that they are not only banished from their families and homes, but their retreat is cut off, and their interest greatly injured by ruining their trade.

But the most shocking cruelty was exercised a few nights ago, upon a poor old man, a tidesman [customs inspector], one Malcolm. He is reckoned creasy[1]. A quarrel was picked with him; he was afterward taken and tarred and feathered. There's no law that knows a punishment for

This cartoon, called "Jonathan throwing the Tea-Kettle . . . ," illustrates the anger that the colonists felt toward the British.

---

[1]**creasy** (krē´sē): an old spelling of crazy. Hulton probably means old and sick rather than insane.

the greatest crimes beyond what this is, of cruel torture. And this instance exceeds any other before it. He was stripped stark naked, one of the severest cold nights this winter, his body covered all over with tar, then with feathers. His arm [was] dislocated in tearing off his clothes. He was dragged in a cart with thousands attending, some beating him with clubs and knocking him out of the cart, then in again. They gave him several severe whippings at different parts of the town. This spectacle of horror and sportive cruelty was exhibited for about five hours.

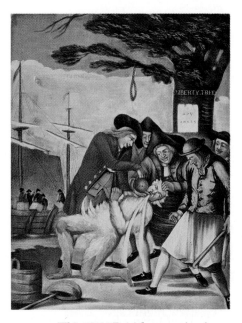

This 1774 British engraving is entitled The Bostonian's Paying the Excise-Man, or Tarring & Feathering.

The unhappy wretch, they say, behaved with the greatest intrepidity and fortitude all the while. Before he was taken, [he] defended himself a long time against numbers. And afterwards when under torture they demanded of him to curse his master the King, Governor, etc., which they could not make him do. But still he cried, "Curse all traitors." They brought him to the gallows and put a rope about his neck saying they would hang him. He said he wished they would, but that they could not for God was above the Devil. The doctors say that it is impossible this poor creature can live. They say his flesh comes off his back in stakes.

He has a wife and family and an aged father and mother who, they say, saw the spectacle, which no indifferent person can mention without horror.

These few instances amongst many serve to show the abject state of government and the licentiousness and barbarism of the times. There's no magistrate that dare or will act to suppress the outrages. No person is secure. There are many objects pointed at, at this time. And when once marked out for vengeance, their ruin is certain.

Responding to "Personal Accounts: The Boston Tea Party"

Thinking and Discussing

What is George Hewes's attitude toward the people who tried to steal the spilled tea? What is Anne Hulton's attitude toward the Colonists who attacked the house? How do the writers' descriptions of the scenes they witnessed reveal their opinions?

How many of these words characterize Anne Hulton, as she is shown in her letters? How many describe George Hewes, as he is shown in his account? Give reasons for your choices.

Patriot protesters harass a Loyalist in this engraving from the period, called **Judgment Day of Tories.**

*frightened disgusted trusting outraged
spirited exultant proud patriotic*

What other words could you add to describe each person?

How does the behavior of George Hewes at the Boston Tea Party differ from that of Crispus Attucks at the Boston Massacre? What conclusions can you draw from the two events about how the Patriots' attitudes changed?

Applying Historical Concepts

Creating a Dialogue According to Anne Hulton, opponents of the tea tax exercised "shocking cruelty." She also sympathized with Loyalist tea merchants, stating that "their interest [is] greatly injured by ruining their trade." What do you think George Hewes would make of these remarks? Alone, or with a partner, write a dialogue between Anne Hulton and George Hewes. You may want to stage your dialogue for the class.

*T*wo years after
the Boston Tea
Party, Patriots
were still
resisting British
domination. But
resistance was no
longer characterized
by sporadic rioting, or
secret acts of sabotage
carried out under
cover of darkness and
disguise. Now,
Patriots were
organized for armed
resistance, with
networks of spies and militia. In
April of 1775, when the British
launched a raid on the towns of
Lexington and Concord, the
Patriots were ready. In the
following excerpt from The War
for Independence, *historian
Albert Marrin paints a vivid
picture of the battles of Lexington
and Concord.*

**On April 19,
1775, 16-year-
old William
Diamond beat
this drum,
which sounded
the alarm for
the Battle of
Lexington. The
British map
above from
1775 recorded
the important
battles of
Lexington and
Concord.**

Shots Heard Round the World

from The War for Independence

by Albert Marrin

A line engraving from 1775, **The Battle of Lexington,** *shows the first battle of the Revolution.*

John Singleton Copley's oil portrait of Samuel Adams hangs in Boston's Museum of Fine Arts.

General Thomas Gage awoke before dawn one morning early in April 1775 and went to his office in Province House overlooking Boston Harbor. He paced back and forth, his hands clasped behind his back, deep in thought.

There was a lot to think about. On the desk lay reports from spies, "good" Yankees loyal to their king. Their reports detailed, among other things, the movements of John Hancock and Sam Adams. Both were preparing to attend the Second Continental Congress and would be staying with Hancock's relative, the Reverend Jonas Clark, at Lexington, a village twelve miles northwest of Boston.

Five miles up the road, at Concord, patriots had stored enough supplies for a small army: muskets and cannon, barrels of gunpowder and bullets, tents, medicines, food, entrenching tools.

Gage made his plans carefully, telling as few people as possible of his intentions. On the eighteenth of April, Redcoats would be rowed across Boston Harbor under cover of darkness for a raid to capture the patriot leaders and destroy their supplies. With one swift blow Gage would smash the rebellion before it began.

Secrecy was the key to success. Company commanders were ordered to have their men ready to march at a moment's notice, but not told when or what their mission would be. Sailors quietly beached longboats from the warships for repairs.

Only the top commanders knew Gage's plan. Lieutenant-Colonel Francis Smith, overweight and red-faced, would lead the strike force of seven hundred handpicked troops, grenadiers and light infantry. (Each British regiment had, in addition to regular foot soldiers, companies of special troops. Grenadiers were big, powerful men used for heavy fighting at close quarters. Light infantry were smaller, more nimble men used for patrols and to protect the flanks, or sides, of a marching regiment.) Smith's second in command was Major John Pitcairn of the Royal Marines. Known for his bad language and kind heart, Pitcairn was loved by the troops; a true professional, he hated unnecessary violence. A thousand-man reserve under Lord Hugh Percy, an experienced battlefield commander, stood by in case the main force needed help.

As time for the operation neared, Boston was sealed off from the mainland to prevent the secret from leaking. Boston in 1775 was built on a tadpole-shaped peninsula jutting into the harbor. Boston Neck, the strip connecting the peninsula to the mainland, was the long, narrow tadpole's "tail." The area around the neck was filled in

Thomas Gage was the British governor of Massachusetts from 1774 to 1776.

The Continental soldier who carved this powder horn was captured at sea by the British.

during the nineteenth century. Two other peninsulas, Charlestown and Dorchester, lay north and south of the town, also joined to the mainland by narrow necks. Gage closed the road across Boston Neck and sent roving patrols into the countryside to halt travelers. Warships in the harbor were to stop any boats heading toward Charlestown. The general expected victory in a sudden controlled action with little if any loss of life. What he got was quite different.

Despite Gage's precautions, it was impossible to keep secrets in Boston. In addition to the Sons of Liberty, whose men watched every barrack and dock, the town swarmed with self-appointed spies. Men and women, boys and girls were constantly on the lookout for clues to Gage's next move. In the days before the raid, odd bits of information began to accumulate. A stableboy overheard officers boast about settling scores with the Yankees. A washerwoman noticed sailors patching longboats. A Redcoat's wife who worked as a maid told her mistress that her husband's grenadier company had been put on alert. This information was reported to Doctor Joseph Warren, a popular physician and a leader of the Sons of Liberty. Doctor Warren didn't know what Gage had in mind, but he could make a shrewd guess.

Silversmith Paul Revere's fine silver bowl is called **The Liberty Bowl.**

Doctor Warren sent a warning to the Concord patriots who took most of the supplies out of town, hiding them under straw in barns or burying them in freshly plowed fields. He also asked Paul Revere and William Dawes, a shoemaker, to "alarum the countryside," call out the Minutemen, when the Redcoats marched.

William Dawes helped Paul Revere alert the Minutemen.

Revere, a cautious man, wanted to make sure the alarm was given even if he and Dawes failed to get through. He contacted the Charlestown Sons of Liberty and told them to have someone watching the steeple of Boston's Old North Church every night. If the Redcoats left by way of Boston Neck, he'd have one lantern hung in the steeple for a few minutes; longer than that would alert lookouts on the warships. Two lanterns meant the Redcoats were being rowed across the harbor to the eastern bank of the Charles River.

The Redcoats turned in early on the night of April 18, a Tuesday. At nine o'clock, sergeants put their hands over the mouth of each man and whispered for him to get ready. Quietly, without lighting a candle, they slipped out of barracks and through the darkened streets to Boston Common. The only sound was of boots scraping on cobblestones. A barking dog was silenced with a bayonet. Within an hour the boat cast off and vanished into the gloom.

Yet all these precautions were in vain. As the troops marched to their boats, Sons of Liberty were reporting to Doctor Warren, who sent word for the messengers to get

Minutemen carried eating utensils like these: wooden plates, a tin cup, and iron forks.

moving. Dawes was soon riding over Boston Neck. Avoiding a roadblock, he turned his horse's head toward Lexington and dug his spurs into its sides.

Revere, meantime, sent a friend to hoist two lanterns and went with two other friends to a rowboat he'd hidden on the beach. As they moved through town, he remembered that he hadn't brought anything to muffle the sound of the oars. No problem. One of his companions knew a girl who lived nearby. A soft whistle and a window opened. A few whispered words and a flannel petticoat came fluttering down. Revere later told his children that the petticoat was warm when he caught it.

These identical shoes became "left" or "right" after Minutemen had marched in them for a while.

Arriving safely at Charlestown, Revere borrowed a horse from a Liberty Boy and set out on his great adventure. He rode out of town and, passing Breed's Hill and Bunker Hill on the right, made for Charlestown Neck. A full moon hung in the sky, a golden saucer that made the trees cast long, ghostly shadows. Suddenly the blood seemed to freeze in his veins. Looming up before him was a horrible sight. There, in the moonlight, he saw a mummified body wrapped in chains, tarred, and standing in a cage suspended from a gallows. It was the body of Mark, a slave hung for poisoning his master. His remains had hung there for twenty years as a warning to would-be lawbreakers.

And now he, Paul Revere, was riding on an errand of treason, the worst crime a subject could commit against his king. He knew the penalty. English law commanded that a traitor be hung, taken down before he died, and his intestines cut out and burned before his eyes. He was then beheaded, his body cut in quarters, and the pieces stuck on spikes for all to see.

Revere rode faster along the Lexington road. Wherever

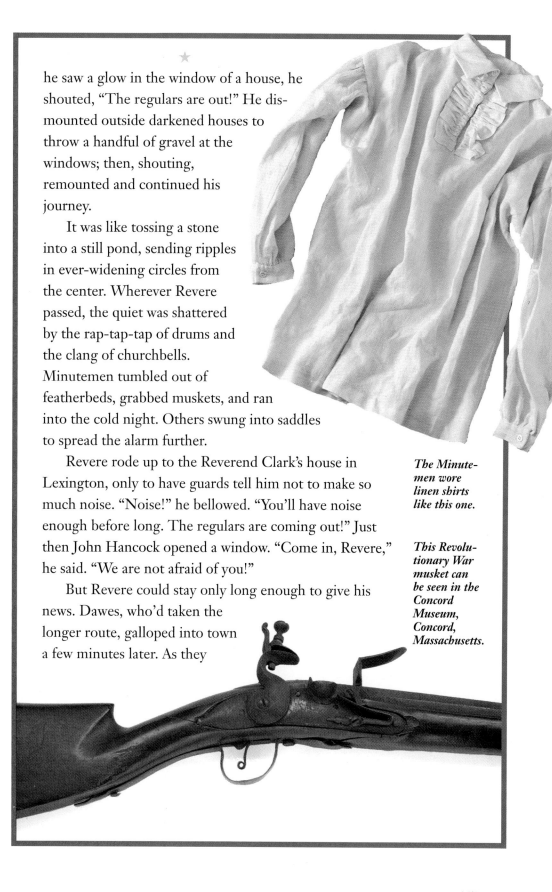

he saw a glow in the window of a house, he shouted, "The regulars are out!" He dismounted outside darkened houses to throw a handful of gravel at the windows; then, shouting, remounted and continued his journey.

It was like tossing a stone into a still pond, sending ripples in ever-widening circles from the center. Wherever Revere passed, the quiet was shattered by the rap-tap-tap of drums and the clang of churchbells. Minutemen tumbled out of featherbeds, grabbed muskets, and ran into the cold night. Others swung into saddles to spread the alarm further.

Revere rode up to the Reverend Clark's house in Lexington, only to have guards tell him not to make so much noise. "Noise!" he bellowed. "You'll have noise enough before long. The regulars are coming out!" Just then John Hancock opened a window. "Come in, Revere," he said. "We are not afraid of you!"

But Revere could stay only long enough to give his news. Dawes, who'd taken the longer route, galloped into town a few minutes later. As they

The Minutemen wore linen shirts like this one.

This Revolutionary War musket can be seen in the Concord Museum, Concord, Massachusetts.

rode out of town, they met Doctor Samuel Prescott of Concord. The doctor, a well-known patriot, had been courting a local girl and was on his way home.

The three were riding to alert Concord when a British cavalry patrol appeared. Instantly they scattered. The doctor jumped his horse over a stone fence and galloped up the road. Dawes fell off his horse and escaped into the woods. Revere, however, wasn't fast enough. The cavalrymen held him for a while and, after threatening to blow out his brains, did nothing more than take his horse. Thus Paul Revere's famous ride ended, not with clattering hoofbeats, but on foot along a moonlit country lane. It was 1 A.M., Wednesday, April 19, 1775.

At that moment the Redcoats' adventure was only just beginning. Everything went wrong. Their heavily loaded boats couldn't make the shore, forcing the soldiers to drop over the sides and wade the rest of the way waist-deep in water and muck. They were miserable — cold, wet, and worried. As they formed columns, the breeze brought the sound of distant churchbells. Soldiers looked at each other without speaking. Words weren't needed, for whatever their mission, they'd lost the element of surprise. Instead of turning back, Colonel Smith sent for Lord Percy's reserve and began the march to Lexington. Major Pitcairn's advance guard of light infantry reached Lexington at sunrise. Patches of mist still clung to the grass and shrouded the treetops. It promised to be a lovely spring day.

Major Pitcairn's portrait was later copied in this miniature.

A View of the Town of Concord *shows Colonel Smith and Major Pitcairn viewing the Minutemen.*

On Lexington Common, waiting for them, the Redcoats found seventy Minutemen under Captain John Parker, a veteran of the French and Indian War. The Minutemen didn't block the road, but stood quietly on the green with their muskets. Parker didn't want a fight. He planned to stand his ground, firing only if the village was endangered. Pitcairn also wanted to keep the peace, having ordered his troops to hold their fire unless he gave the command personally. There must not be another Boston Massacre.

Pitcairn's troops ran onto the Common and formed a battle line, a long block of men standing three deep. They were in a black mood after a miserable night and not about to take nonsense from Yankees. Muskets poised, the sun glinting off bayonets, they eyed the Minutemen.

Several officers came by on horseback. One waved his sword, shouting: "Ye villains, ye Rebels, disperse! Lay down your arms! Damn you, why don't you lay down your arms?"

Captain Parker, seeing that his men were no match for the regulars, told them to go home. Most had turned to leave when — bang! Exactly who fired, Yankee or Redcoat, and why, is a mystery to this day. But the result is well known.

The Redcoats' discipline snapped, as if that one shot had released all their pent-up anger at the colonists. There was an earsplitting crash as hundreds of men fired without orders. The Minutemen replied with a ragged fire that gave one soldier a flesh wound and grazed Pitcairn's horse. When the smoke cleared, eight Americans lay dead on the grass, most shot in the back; ten others were wounded.

Pitcairn let loose a storm of curses. His men had disobeyed an order and he was furious. He drove his horse among them, beating men with the flat of his sword and shouting for them to cease fire. Cease fire! Control was restored moments later when Colonel Smith arrived with the main body and the drummers sounded the "Fall-in." The troops cheered and fired a victory salute as they marched out of town. Little did they know how dearly they'd pay for the blood shed on Lexington Common.

The column swept into Concord behind waving flags and musicians playing snappy marching

Minutemen from Bedford, Massachusetts, carried this flag in the battle at the North Bridge.

tunes. The commanders and most of their men then broke ranks for breakfast. Invading the village taverns, they demanded food and drink, for which they paid. Chairs were put under the blossoming trees for the officers' comfort.

Search parties, meantime, went to find the patriots' war materials. They knew where to go, because Gage's spies had drawn accurate maps. Yet, to their surprise, they found little of value. Some barrels of flour wound up in a creek. A few muskets were burned, along with several wooden gun carriages.

Trouble really began when a British patrol tried to secure North Bridge over the Concord River outside the village. Across the way, on a hill overlooking the bridge, hundreds of Minutemen waited. Although outnumbered, the Redcoats prepared to fight; they'd whipped Yankee "rabble" in Lexington and felt confident.

The Minutemen would probably have stayed on their hill had they not seen the smoke of the burning gun carriages rising from Concord. "They're burning the town," someone cried, and they moved forward. The Redcoats fired warning shots, then a volley, killing two. "Fire, fellow soldiers, for God's sake, fire!" shouted Colonel John Buttrick, the American commander. Three Redcoats fell dead, nine wounded, while their comrades ran off

The North Bridge over the Concord River commemorates the 1775 fight, but it is not the original. This is the fourth bridge that has stood on this site since the battle's Centennial in 1875.

451

as fast as their legs could carry them. The Minutemen didn't follow, but went home or returned to their hill. The fight at Concord — it could hardly be called a battle — had lasted about three minutes. Yet in that time the farmers had fired "the shot heard round the world."

At noon, after four hours in Concord, Colonel Smith declared his mission accomplished. Bugles sounded. Drums beat. Sergeants bawled commands. Redcoats formed columns and began the return march to Boston. The Americans let them go peacefully until they were a mile from the village. That's when the sky seemed to fall.

Minutemen and militia had been drawn to Concord from miles around in answer to the alarms. Singly and in small groups, nearly four thousand men stationed themselves along the Concord-Lexington Road. Not that you'd have seen more than a handful of them at any given time. But they were there, hidden behind open windows, rail fences, trees, rocks, and stone walls. Firing from cover, they sent a hail of lead into the densely packed columns. Even women lent a hand; a Redcoat told of seeing a woman blazing away from a window with an ancient blunderbuss, a type of shotgun used by the Puritans.

This was something new for the Redcoats, something for which their training hadn't prepared them. European regulars were not taught to think for themselves. They were uniformed machines programmed to advance in closed ranks to within a few yards of the enemy. Then, on command, each side fired its muskets in massed volleys. Nobody aimed, because aiming wasn't taught; muskets were so inaccurate that they didn't even have a rear gunsight. And they were dangerous. Unless the wind came from behind, soldiers turned their heads away just before firing to avoid the flashback when the gunpowder went off, because it might blind them. The idea was for many men to point their guns in the same direction, fire at once, reload quickly, and fire again in the hope of hitting something.

In regular battle, volley after volley was exchanged, creating the "fog of battle," clouds of gunsmoke that made men sneeze and cry. Troops kept firing, ignoring the dead and wounded around them; the moment a man fell, someone in a rear rank took his place. A bullet, a one-ounce lead ball, could maim a person, breaking bones and tearing entire muscles from arms and legs. If one side seemed to be winning, it stopped shooting and charged with bayonets, fourteen inches of cold steel. British regulars were considered the best in the world with the bayonet.

Tough as they were, the Redcoats didn't know how to deal with the Americans. Not that their attackers were especially good shots. Their guns were just as inaccurate as those of the British, and experts estimate that only one out of every three hundred bullets found its mark that day. But that didn't matter, because heavy firing from invisible gunmen terrified the regulars. "What an unfair method of carrying on a war," one complained in a letter home. Americans, he felt, didn't play by the rules of "civilized warfare."

The columns plodded onward, leaving a trail of dead and dying. Nearing Lexington, men panicked, broke ranks, and ran into the village. They were sprawled on the

Sarah Chandler Reed, the wife of a Minuteman, wore this cloak on Lexington Common.

ground, panting, when a band struck up "Yankee Doodle." Lord Percy had come with the reserves. His Lordship had the beaten troops move on while hundreds of his own men acted as flankers. These troops fanned out on either side of the road to flush snipers from hiding. They were merciless. Anyone caught with a weapon died on the spot.

Flankers, breaking into houses, terrorized people and stole whatever they could carry. Anything had value to

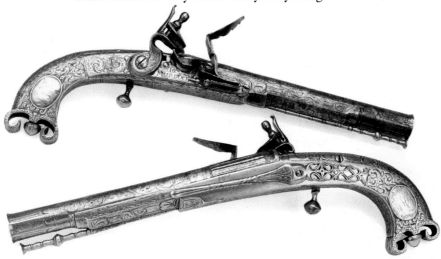

Minutemen captured Major Pitcairn's pistols and later sold them at auction to Captain Nathan Barret.

these poorly paid men: candle stubs, pen nibs, pewter cups. One soldier took a Latin grammar, although he probably didn't know a word of that language. But it was a book and had some resale value.

The retreat continued until sunset, when the columns stumbled across Charlestown Neck to safety on Bunker Hill. The Yankees didn't follow them, for fear of being shot at from the hill and by warships cruising offshore. So ended the Nineteenth of April of 'Seventy-five, a day full of history. The Redcoats had lost 73 killed, 174 wounded, and 26 missing. American losses were 49 dead and 42 wounded and missing.

Everyone knew the meaning of the skirmishes that day, even the boys at Boston's Latin School. The headmaster dismissed them sadly: "War's begun — school's done."

Responding to
"Shots Heard Round the World"

Thinking and Discussing

How did the British soldiers plan to accomplish their purpose at Lexington and Concord? How did their plans differ from those of the Colonists? Compare the two sides' fighting styles. What effect did these have on the outcome of the battles?

In his closing paragraph, the author says, "Everyone knew the meaning of the skirmishes that day." What is the author suggesting this meaning was? Do you agree with him?

Applying Historical Concepts

Writing a News Article Imagine you are a reporter—for either a British or a Patriot newspaper—who has just witnessed some of the events at Lexington and Concord. Write a brief news article about what you saw. What kinds of information will you include? Will you simply present facts, or draw conclusions? What kinds of information will make your article more interesting to your readers? Write a headline for your article. You may want to compare stories with a classmate.

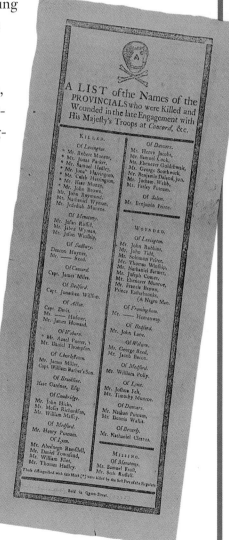

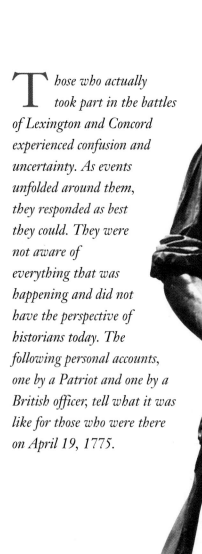

T hose who actually took part in the battles of Lexington and Concord experienced confusion and uncertainty. As events unfolded around them, they responded as best they could. They were not aware of everything that was happening and did not have the perspective of historians today. The following personal accounts, one by a Patriot and one by a British officer, tell what it was like for those who were there on April 19, 1775.

Daniel Chester French's statue The Minute Man was unveiled in 1875 to honor the centennial of the fight at the North Bridge in Concord.

Personal Accounts:

Lexington

and

Concord

Paul Revere's Ride *was painted by an unknown artist in 1815.*

A Letter from Paul Revere

Paul Revere, a silversmith and engraver, was a dedicated Patriot. In 1773, he participated in the Boston Tea Party. Two years later, he again played a role in Revolutionary events, helping spread the alarm that roused the Minutemen to the battles of Lexington and Concord. Revere later wrote two accounts of his famous ride. The following excerpt is taken from his letter to Dr. Jeremy Belknap, written in 1798.

In the fall of 1774 and 1775, I was one of upwards of thirty, chiefly mechanics, who formed ourselves into a committee for the purpose of watching the movements of the British soldiers, and gaining every intelligence [secret information] of the movements of the Tories. We held our meetings at the Green Dragon tavern. We were so careful that our meetings should be kept secret that every time we met, every person swore upon the Bible that they would not discover [reveal] any of our transactions but to Messrs. [John] Hancock, [Samuel] Adams, Doctors [Joseph] Warren, [Benjamin] Church and one or two more.

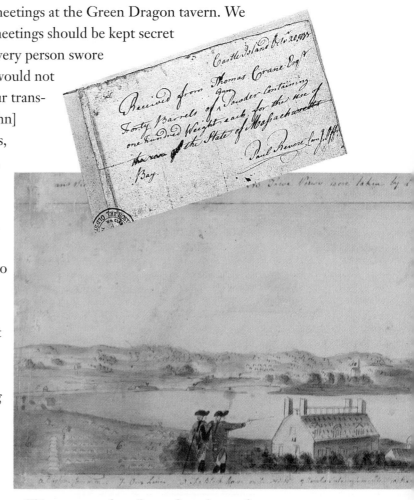

. . . In the winter, towards the spring, we frequently took turns, two and two, to watch the soldiers by patrolling the streets all night. The Saturday night preceding the 19th of April, about 12 o'clock at night, the boats belonging to the transports were all

This panorama shows Boston from the top of Beacon Hill in 1775.

launched . . . (They had previously been hauled up and repaired.)
We likewise found that the grenadiers and light infantry were all
taken off duty.

From these movements we expected something serious was to be
transacted. On Tuesday Evening, the 18th, it was observed that a number of soldiers were marching towards the bottom of the Common.
About 10 o'clock, Dr. Warren sent in great haste for me and begged that
I would immediately set off for Lexington, where Messrs. Hancock and
Adams were, and acquaint them of the movement, and that it was
thought they were the objects.

When I got to Dr. Warren's house, I found he had sent an express
[special messenger] by land to Lexington — a Mr. William Dawes. The
Sunday before, by desire of Dr. Warren, I had been to Lexington, to
Messrs. Hancock and Adams, who were at the Rev. Mr. Clark's. I
returned at night through Charlestown; there I agreed with a Colonel
Conant and some other gentlemen that if the British went out by water,
we would show two lanthorns [lanterns] in the North Church steeple;
and if by land, one, as a signal . . . I left Dr. Warren, called upon a friend
and desired him to make the signals.

I then went home, took my boots and surtout [overcoat], went to the
north part of the town, where I had kept a boat; two friends rowed me

across Charles River . . .
They landed me on the
Charlestown side. When I
got into town, I met
Colonel Conant and sev-
eral others; they said they
had seen our signals. I told
them what was acting
[happening] . . .

I set off upon a very
good horse; it was then
about eleven o'clock and
very pleasant. After I had

passed Charlestown Neck . . . I saw two men on horseback under a tree. When I got near them, I discovered they were British officers. One tried to get ahead of me, and the other to take me. I turned my horse very quick and galloped towards Charlestown Neck, and then pushed for the Medford Road. The one who chased me, endeavoring to cut me off, got into a clay pond . . . I got clear of him, and went through Medford, over the bridge and up to Menotomy [now Arlington]. In Medford, I awaked the captain of the minute men; and after that, I alarmed almost every house, till I got to Lexington. I found Messrs. Hancock and Adams at the Rev. Mr. Clark's . . .

After stopping at the Reverend Mr. Clark's, Revere set off with William Dawes. Shortly, they encountered Dr. Prescott, a Son of Liberty. Together, the three messengers continued on toward Concord.

We had got nearly half way. Mr. Dawes and the doctor stopped to alarm the people of a house. I was about one hundred rods ahead when I saw two men in nearly the same situation as those officers were near Charlestown. I called for the doctor and Mr. Dawes to come up. In an instant I was surrounded by four. They had placed themselves in a straight road that inclined each way; they had taken down a pair of bars on the north side of the road, and two of them were under a tree in the pasture. The doctor being foremost, he came up and we tried to get past them; but they being armed with pistols and swords, they forced us into the pasture. The doctor jumped his horse over a low stone wall and got to Concord.

I observed a wood at a small distance and made for that. When I got there, out started six officers on horseback and ordered me to dismount. One of them, who appeared to have the command, examined [questioned] me, where I came from and what my name was. I told him. He asked me if I was an express. I answered in the affirmative. He demanded what time I left Boston. I told him, and added that their troops had catched aground in passing the river, and that there would be five hundred Americans there in a short time, for I had alarmed the country all the way up. He immediately rose towards those who had stopped us, when all five of them came down upon a full gallop. One of them . . . clapped his pistol to my head, called me by name and told me he was going to ask me some questions, and if I did not give him true answers, he would blow my brains out. He then asked me similar questions to those above. He then ordered me to mount my horse, after searching me for arms. He then ordered them to advance and to lead me in front. When we got to the road, they turned down towards Lexington . . .

The British soldiers then took Revere's horse and galloped toward Lexington, leaving the Patriot by the roadside.

This silver teapot, a fine example of Revere's work, resembles the one he is admiring in this portrait painted by John Singleton Copley.

The pistols in the wooden case at left date from the Revolutionary period.

Notes from a British Officer

Here, the battles of Lexington and Concord are seen from a British point of view. This account is believed to have been written by Lieutenant John Barker.

L ast night between 10 and 11 o'clock all the Grenadiers and Light Infantry of the army, making about 600 men (under the command of Lt. Col. Smith of the 10th and Major Pitcairn of the Marines) . . . landed upon the opposite shore on Cambridge Marsh; few but the commanding officers knew what expedition we were going upon. After getting over the marsh, where we were wet up to the knees, we were halted in a dirty road and stood there till two o'clock in the morning, waiting for provisions [supplies] to be brought from the boats and to be divided, and which most of the men threw away, having carried some with 'em. At 2 o'clock we began our march by wading through a very long ford [shallow water] up to our middles. After going a few miles we took 3 or 4 people who were going off to give intelligence [secret information].

About 5 miles on this side of a town called Lexington, which lay in our road, we heard there were some hundreds of people collected together intending to oppose us and stop our going on. At 5 o'clock we arrived there and saw a number of people, I believe between 2 and 300, formed in a common in the middle of the town. We still continued advancing, keeping prepared against an

This period engraving shows activity in a typical encampment of British soldiers during the Revolution.

This engraving of the Battle of Lexington was first published in Connecticut in 1775.

attack tho' without intending to attack them; but on our coming near them they fired one or two shots, upon which our men without any orders rushed in upon them, fired and put 'em to flight. Several of them were killed, we could not tell how many because they were got behind walls and into the woods. We had a man of the 10th Light Infantry wounded, nobody else hurt. We then formed on the common, but with some difficulty, the men were so wild they could hear no orders.

We waited a considerable time there, and at length proceeded on our way to Concord . . . in order to destroy a magazine [storage place] of stores [supplies] collected there. We met with no interruption till within a mile or two of the town, where the country people had occupied a hill which commanded the road. The Light Infantry were ordered away to the right and ascended the height in one line, upon which the Yankies quitted [left] it without firing . . . They then crossed the river beyond

the town, and we marched into the town after taking possession of a hill with a Liberty Pole on it . . .

While the Grenadiers remained in the town, destroying 3 pieces of cannon, several gun carriages and about 100 barrels of flour with harness and other things, the Light companies were detached beyond the river to examine some houses for more stores . . . During this time the people were gathering together in great numbers . . . The three companies drew up in the road the far side of the bridge and the Rebels on the hill above, covered by a wall; in that situation they remained a long time, very near an hour, the three companies expecting to be attacked by the Rebels, who were about 1000 strong. Captn. Lawrie, who commanded these three companies, sent to Col. Smith, begging he would send more troops to his assistance and informing him of his situation . . .

In the mean time the Rebels marched into the road and were coming down upon us when Captn. Lawrie made his men retire to this side the bridge . . . As soon as they were over the bridge the three companies got one behind the other so that only the front one could fire. The Rebels when they got near the bridge halted and fronted [confronted], filling the road from the top to the bottom. The fire soon began from a dropping shot on our side, when they [the Rebels] and the front company fired almost at the same instant, there being nobody to support the front company. The others not firing, the whole were forced to quit the bridge and return toward Concord . . . Four officers of the 8 who were at the bridge were wounded; 3 men killed; 1 sergt. and several men wounded . . .

Before the whole had quitted the town we were fired on from houses and behind trees, and before we had gone 1/2 a mile we were fired on from all sides, but mostly from the rear, where people had hid themselves in houses . . . The country was an amazing strong one, full of hills, woods, stone walls, etc., which the

This sword may have been taken from a British officer shot during the retreat from Concord and Lexington on April 19, 1775.

Rebels did not fail to take advantage of . . . They were so concealed there was hardly any seeing them. In this way we marched between 9 and 10 miles, their numbers increasing from all parts, while ours was reduced by deaths, wounds and fatigue; and we were totally surrounded with such an incessant [continuous] fire as it's impossible to conceive; our ammunition was likewise near expended [used up]. . .

The British eventually retreated, arriving in Charlestown late in the night.

Thus ended this expedition, which from the beginning to end was as ill planned and ill executed as it was possible to be. Had we not idled away three hours on Cambridge Marsh waiting for provisions that were not wanted, we should have had no interruption at Lexington, but by our stay the country people had got intelligence and time to assemble. We should have reached Concord soon after day break, before they could have heard of us, by which we should have destroyed more cannon and stores, which they had had time enough to convey away before our arrival. We might also have got easier back and not been so harassed, as they would not have had time to assemble so many people; even the people of Salem and Marblehead, above 20 miles off, had intelligence and time enough to meet us on our return . . .

This cap from the 1770's is made of bear fur. It was worn by a British officer.

Responding to
"Personal Accounts: Lexington and Concord"

Thinking and Discussing

Paul Revere describes himself as one of a group of people who spied on the British. What were some of the ways in which the "spies" operated? How would you rate their success?

Compare Paul Revere's account to that of Lieutenant Barker. Which events does each describe? Do the accounts have any similarities? Do they have differences? What tone does each writer take in telling his tale?

Applying Historical Concepts

Explaining the British Defeat Lieutenant Barker was frustrated with the way things went. Write a list of the reasons he gives for the British defeat. Compare your list with those of classmates.

Styles of Fighting

British and Continental soldiers used the same weapon — the British "Brown Bess" musket. But their styles of fighting were very different. While the British stood in stiff lines, firing round after round, the Continental soldier darted about and hid behind trees, completely confusing his enemy.

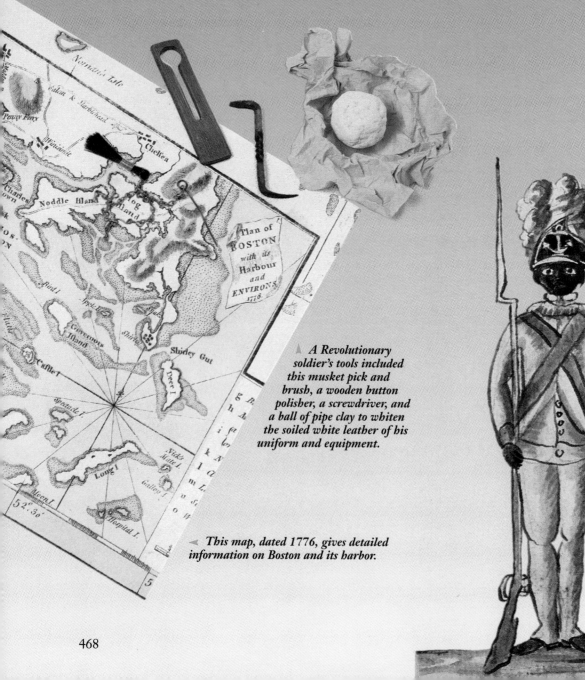

▲ *A Revolutionary soldier's tools included this musket pick and brush, a wooden button polisher, a screwdriver, and a ball of pipe clay to whiten the soiled white leather of his uniform and equipment.*

◄ *This map, dated 1776, gives detailed information on Boston and its harbor.*

This British musket was known as a "Brown Bess" because of the color of its wooden stock. British officers carried swords like the one shown here.

Revolutionary soldiers, from left to right: a black light infantryman, a musketman, a rifleman, and an artilleryman

Outfitted in their everyday clothes, Minutemen fought the British for control of the North American colonies.

The Fifer of Boxborough

by Elizabeth West
and Katherine S. Talmadge

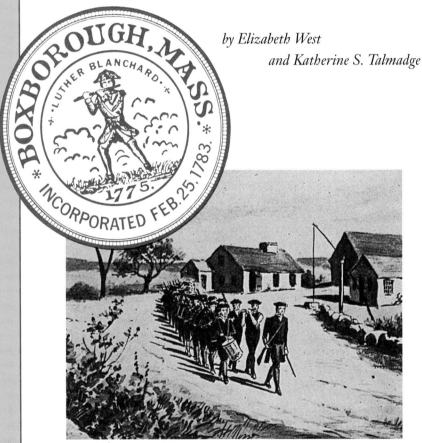

Luther Blanchard, the fifer, is second in line in this picture, Isaac Davis Company of Minutemen, *from an 1899 book.*

The *MASSACHUSETTS* Song of LIBERTY.

Come swallow your bumpers, ye Tories, and roar, That the Sons of fair Freedom are hamper'd once more; But know, that no Cut-throats our spirits can tame, Nor a host of Oppressors shall smother the flame. In Freedom we're born, and like Sons of the brave will not—ever sur-ren-der, But swear to defend her, And scorn to sur-vive, if un-able to save.

Not every hero of the American Revolution was a soldier. In fact, the first person wounded at the Battle of Concord did not carry a gun — he carried a fife. He was a teen-age musician named Luther Blanchard. Luther was the fifer for the Isaac Davis Minute Company of Acton, Massachusetts.

Fifers never carried weapons. Although they marched at the head of a line of soldiers, no one really expected them to fight. The fifer's responsibility was to set the rhythm of the march. The music also helped to raise the soldiers' spirits, as did the fifer's own good example of marching boldly into battle.

Although Luther Blanchard was part of an Acton company, he was originally from Boxborough, a tiny neighboring town. He had moved to the Acton home of Jonathan Hosmer to learn the stonemason's trade. Hosmer had a son named Abner, who became Luther's good friend. Together the two boys joined a local company of minutemen, led by Captain Isaac Davis. Luther was 18 years old when he signed up.

Before daylight on April 19, 1775, a horseman rapped on the side of an Acton home, relaying the news that the British soldiers were marching to Concord. The colonial minutemen and militia were to rendezvous at Old North Bridge in Concord. The confrontation for which they had drilled was about to happen.

It was still dark when Luther and Abner arrived at the Davis home to take their place in line. Soon the march to Concord began. Was Luther excited or frightened? No one knows for sure.

We do know that he and drummer Francis Barker led the

troops briskly on the long, sunrise march. Luther played a traditional marching tune, "The White Cockade."

Unlike the British Army, the minutemen were not highly skilled. They were farmers. They had no uniforms, and each even had to supply his own weapons. Some had muskets with bayonets, but others had only axes or hunting knives.

As they marched to Concord to meet the army of the King of England, they had no way of knowing how many other groups of minutemen would help them. But they were determined. As Captain Davis declared, "I haven't a man that is afraid to go!"

When Luther's company reached the Old North Bridge, the men were ordered not to fire unless fired upon. Then enemy shots rang out. At first, everyone supposed that the British had fired warning shots into the air to scare off the rebels. But they had not. One of the first bursts of fire hit Luther Blanchard in the chest. When Luther fell, Captain Davis immediately gave the order to fire back. But as Captain Davis took aim, he was shot through the heart and killed. Luther's friend Abner dropped too, shot in the head.

Luther went to a nearby home for medical attention. Mrs. Barrett, the woman of the house, bandaged his wound and tried to tell the boy how lucky he had been. "A little more [toward your heart] and you'd have been killed!" she said. "Yes," replied Luther, "but a little more [the other way] and it would not have touched me at all."

Later, Luther rejoined his troop and helped drive the British back to their encampment in Charlestown. For months he participated in other battles. His wound from that first skirmish never fully healed, however, and five months after receiving it he died at an emergency hospital on the campus of Harvard College.

The little town of Boxborough has never forgotten its brave fifer. The town seal bears his picture, and each year in June the entire town turns out for the Fifer's Festival to honor him. It is a way to pay tribute to all the brave men who marched that April morning so long ago, to confront the King of England. Most went to fight. But Luther Blanchard, the first one wounded, went only to help—not with a gun, but with a fife.

Drummers beat the rhythm of songs like "Yankee Doodle Dandy," while fifers tooted the melodies to cheer the soldiers on.

Responding to "The Fifer of Boxborough"

Thinking and Discussing

What is the Fifer's Festival? Do you think such celebrations are important? Why?

Applying Historical Concepts

Writing an Account Imagine you are Luther Blanchard. What do you think it might have been like to march in the forefront at the Battle of Concord? Write a brief account of the battle from the fifer's point of view. Before you write, you may want to think about some of the following questions: What feelings led you to join the Minutemen as a fifer? What feelings did you experience during the battle of Concord? What did you see, do, and hear? How did you feel when the battle was over?

Continental soldiers carried few personal possessions into battle: a bag with a horn comb, a mouth harp, and a hand-painted deck of cards without numbers because most soldiers couldn't read.

As

the American Colonists moved toward declaring
war, ideas fueled their acts of rebellion. Powerful
words gave shape to their feelings and purpose to
their actions. In another excerpt from The War
for Independence, *Albert Marrin writes about*
two of the documents that helped change the course
of history.

From The War for Independence

Writings That Changed History

by Albert Marrin

America

owes a great deal to a scruffy Englishman who settled in Philadelphia during the winter of 1774. Thomas Paine was a thin, tight-lipped man with a pickle nose and eyes that seemed to bore through you. Poverty and disappointment had followed him all of his thirty-eight years. Although he'd held many jobs, he'd failed at everything. Failure made him angry at injustice and gave him deep sympathy for the oppressed.

Paine's anger and sympathy remained buried inside him until he arrived in Philadelphia. There he found a job with a small magazine and began to write articles. He wrote about politics, trade, and moral issues like slavery, which he despised.

Words — strong, forceful words — flowed easily from his pen.

Paine's talents became important as the American Revolution took shape. By the end of 1775, anyone could see that Great Britain and the colonies were at war. Blood had been shed, lives lost, towns burned. Yet most Americans still hoped the quarrel would be patched up and they could continue to be loyal subjects of the British Empire.

Tom Paine did more than anyone to change American minds in favor of independence. In January 1776, he issued *Common Sense*. This forty-two-page pamphlet became the most influential American book ever printed. Aimed at the common people, it called George III "the Royal Brute of Great Britain," a fool who had no right to rule Americans. Indeed, Paine believed kings had no right to rule anyone, because all men are equal. Great Britain,

Thomas Paine holds his famous pamphlet **Common Sense** *in this oil portrait.*

he continued, was not the mother country, since mothers don't turn redcoated thugs loose on their children. Americans should not be governed from Europe. No! "Everything that is right or reasonable pleads for separation. The blood of the slain, the weeping voice of nature cries, 'tis time to part."

Common Sense had the right ideas at the right time and became the first American bestseller. Over 120,000 copies were sold within three months, and still printers couldn't keep up with the demand. Washington wrote from camp outside Boston that his troops were passing *Common Sense* from hand to hand; those who couldn't read sat intently while a comrade read it to them.

Paine lit a fire that leaped across America. Patriots drove out royal governors, took control of colonial assemblies, and held conventions to form new governments. The king's coat of arms came down in one assembly after another and his portraits were turned to the wall. Although independence hadn't been declared, it was quickly becoming a reality.

Some state conventions ordered their delegates at the Second Continental Congress to vote for independence. On June 7, 1776, Richard Henry Lee of Virginia offered a motion to Congress: "RESOLVED, That these United Colonies are, and of right ought to be, free and independent States; that they are absolved from all allegiance to the British Crown; and that all political connection between them and the State of Great

Britain is, and ought to be, totally dissolved." But since many delegates weren't ready for such a drastic step as independence, Congress put off voting on the motion for three weeks to allow them to think things over.

Congress, meantime, appointed a five-man committee to draft a declaration of independence. The members of that committee were John Adams (Massachusetts), Benjamin Franklin (Pennsylvania), Roger Sherman (Connecticut), and Robert Livingston (New York). Thomas Jefferson of Virginia, a lanky redhead and at thirty-three one of the committee's youngest members, was asked to do the actual work because of his "peculiar felicity of expression"; that is, he wrote well.

As Philadelphia baked in summer heat, Jefferson set up a portable desk of his own invention in the parlor of a local bricklayer. He needed no reference books, for he knew what needed to be said. Within two weeks, by July 2, the draft was ready. After going over it line by line, changing a word here, crossing out a phrase there, Congress adopted Jefferson's Declaration of Independence. Our independence began officially on this date, not July 4, when printed copies of the text were carried by express riders throughout the land.

The Declaration of Independence was read wherever people gathered. Abigail Adams wrote her husband from Boston that, despite the gunpowder shortage, cannon boomed and troops fired volleys in celebration. Crowds in Worcester, Massachusetts,

Thomas Jefferson's portrait was painted by Charles Willson Peale in 1791.

drank toasts and wished "Perpetual itching and no scratching to America's enemies." Far to the south and west, in the Waxhaws, the unlettered frontiersmen selected a bright nine-year-old as their "public reader." Andy Jackson read the document in his squeaky voice without, he said, getting hoarse or "stopping to spell out the words." And beyond the towering Alleghenies, the men of Boonesborough greeted independence with war whoops.

The parchment copy of the Declaration of Independence familiar to everyone wasn't signed by all delegates until August 2, 1776. The fifty-five signers knew they were making history.

John Hancock, president of the Congress, signed first (on July 4), writing his name in bold letters so the king could read it without his spectacles.

Others realized they were committing treason and what that could mean. Benjamin Harrison of Virginia relieved the tension with humor. Harrison, a fat man, told skinny Elbridge Gerry of Massachusetts that his hanging would be painless: "I shall have the advantage over you on account of my size. All will be over with me in a moment, but you will be kicking in the air half an hour after I am gone."

The Declaration of Independence is really two declarations at once. Jefferson gave most of its space to explaining the colonies' grievances against Great Britain. Most people today neither know nor care about these. The part that concerns us today comes at the beginning. It is this part that has made Jefferson's work a battle cry for oppressed peoples everywhere.

Jefferson began the Declaration of Independence

Jefferson drafted the Declaration of Independence on this portable writing desk, which he designed.

with a ringing defense of liberty: "We hold these truths to be self-evident, that all men are created equal, that they are endowed by their Creator with certain unalienable Rights, that among these are Life, Liberty and the pursuit of Happiness." Governments exist only to protect these rights, which come from God and cannot be given or taken away. When a government fails in its duty, it loses its authority. The people then have the right to abolish it, by force if necessary, and create a new one that will protect their rights.

By "the people," however, Jefferson meant only free white men. We must remember that the Founding Fathers belonged to their time, as we belong to ours. And in their time it seemed natural that certain people should rule and that others should be ruled. Women were thought to be weaker and less intelligent than men; they belonged at home with the children, not following careers or participating in government. American women would have to wait until the twentieth century to realize the promise of the Declaration of Independence.

Several signers also owned slaves. Blacks, most believed, were hardly human, so that "liberty" couldn't apply to them. Jefferson himself owned slaves, although he said slavery was wrong and ought to be abolished. "I tremble for my country when I reflect that God is just," he wrote later. Americans had sinned by enslaving blacks and God would punish them, he believed.

Yet Jefferson never freed his slaves, because he felt blacks were inferior and shouldn't mingle with white people. Until they could be returned to Africa, he wanted them kept under kindly masters like himself — as if kindness can substitute for freedom. George Washington, who refused to buy any more slaves, wanted slavery abolished gradually. But that wasn't to be. Slavery was ended suddenly, through a war more terrible than the Revolution.

Responding to "Writings That Changed History"

Thinking and Discussing

What do you think was the most powerful idea in *Common Sense?* What was the effect of this pamphlet on American soldiers? What was its effect on other people? Why did Paine's writing strike such a responsive chord?

When Thomas Jefferson wrote the Declaration of Independence, he used the phrase "the people." Whom did "the people" include? Why did the Founding Fathers limit this category? Do you agree with their viewpoint?

This drawing shows Americans united around the flame of independence.

Applying Historical Concepts

Reading Aloud Find a copy of the Declaration of Independence. With a partner or group, read aloud the Preamble and the Declaration of Rights. As you read, pick out what you feel are some key phrases. Discuss their meaning. Why are they important?

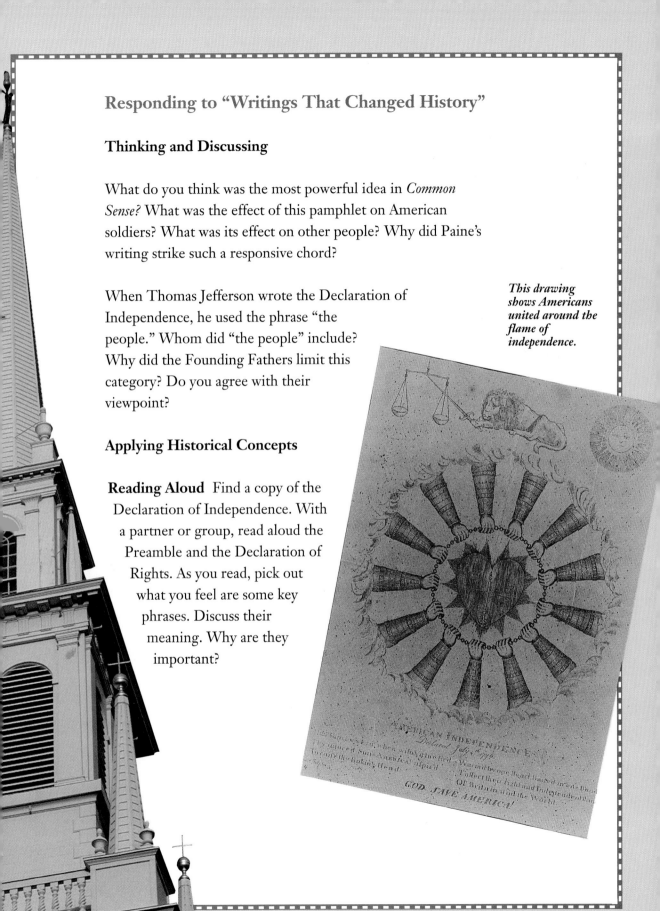

AMERICAN INDEPENDENCE
Declared July 4, 1776.

GOD SAVE AMERICA!

Designing a National Symbol

Choosing a national symbol caused much debate in the new country. Benjamin Franklin wanted the wild turkey to be used, but the bald eagle, as shown below, won out and was used on the national seal.

▶ **American bald eagle in flight**

Plates for the Great Seal of the United States

Early sketch by Charles Thomson for the Great Seal

*H*ow did Americans finally declare their freedom? What qualities did the Declaration of Independence have that made it so important? This encyclopedia article describes the document that, in the words of Thomas Jefferson, expressed "the American mind."

From The World Book Encyclopedia, © 1990 by World Book, Inc. Used by permission.

The Declaration of Independence

The Declaration of Independence is the historic document in which the American Colonies declared their freedom from British rule. The Second Continental Congress, a meeting of delegates from the colonies, adopted the Declaration on July 4, 1776. This date has been celebrated ever since as the birthday of the United States.

The Declaration of Independence ranks as one of the greatest documents in human history. It eloquently expressed the colonies' reasons for proclaiming their freedom. The document blamed the British government for many abuses. But it also stated that all people have certain rights, including the right to change or overthrow any government that denies them their rights. The ideas expressed so majestically in the Declaration have long inspired freedom-loving people throughout the world.

Events leading to the Declaration. Friction between the American Colonies and Britain had been building for more than 10 years before the Declaration was adopted. During that period, the colonies had asked Britain for a larger role in

Thomas Jefferson presented The Declaration of Independence to the Continental Congress.

making decisions that affected them, especially in the area of taxation. In 1765, the British Parliament passed the Stamp Act, which required the colonists to pay a tax on newspapers, legal and business documents, and various other items. The colonists protested so strongly against this "taxation without representation" that Parliament repealed the act in 1766.

Parliament then passed a law

But colonial opposition led Parliament to remove these taxes in 1770 — except for the tax on tea. In 1773, angry colonists boarded British ships in Boston Harbor and dumped their cargoes of tea overboard. Parliament then passed a series of laws to punish Massachusetts. These laws led the colonies to unite against what they called the Intolerable Acts.

The Continental Congress. In 1774, delegates from all the colonies except Georgia met in Philadelphia at the First Continental Congress. The delegates adopted an agreement that bound the colonies not to trade with Britain or to use British goods. They also proposed another meeting the next year if Britain did not change its policies before that time.

stating it had the right to legislate for the colonies in all matters. In 1767, it placed a tax on certain goods imported into the colonies.

The TIMES are
Dreadful
Woeful
Dismal
Dolorous, and
DOLLAR-LESS.

This Pennsylvania newspaper caption protested the Stamp Act of 1765.

But Britain held to its policies, and the Second Continental Congress was called. The delegates met in Philadelphia's State House (now Independence Hall) on May 10, 1775. By that time, the Revolutionary War in America had already begun, with battles between Massachusetts colonists and British troops. Congress acted swiftly. It voted to organize an army and a navy and to issue money to pay for the war. Many delegates now believed that independence from Britain was the only solution. But others disagreed. Early in July, Congress therefore sent a final, useless appeal to Britain's King George III to remedy the colonies' grievances.

The independence movement grew rapidly early in 1776. The English writer Thomas Paine spurred the movement with his electrifying pamphlet *Common Sense*. This work presented brilliant arguments for the freedom of the American colonies. More and more Americans came to agree with the patriot Samuel Adams, who asked, "Is not America already independent? Why not then declare it?"

On June 7, 1776, Richard Henry Lee of Virginia introduced the resolution in Congress "That these United Colonies are, and of right ought to be, free and independent States . . ." On June 10, Congress voted to name a committee to write a declaration of independence for the delegates to consider in case they adopted Lee's resolution. The

John Hancock may have worn this coat and vest when he penned his bold signature on the Declaration of Independence.

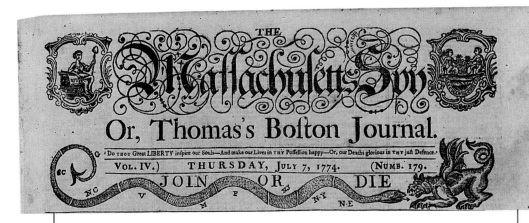

THE Maſſachuſetts Spy

Or, Thomas's Boſton Journal.

"Do THOU Great LIBERTY inſpire our Souls—And make our Lives in THY Poſſeſſion happy—Or, our Deaths glorious in THY juſt Defence."

VOL. IV.)   THURSDAY, JULY 7, 1774.   (NUMB. 179.

JOIN OR DIE

committee, appointed the next day, consisted of John Adams, Benjamin Franklin, Thomas Jefferson, Robert R. Livingston, and Roger Sherman. Jefferson's associates on the committee asked him to draft the declaration. Jefferson completed the task in about two weeks. Franklin and Adams made a few minor literary changes in Jefferson's draft.

Adoption of the Declaration. On July 2, Congress approved the Lee resolution. The delegates then began to debate Jefferson's draft. A few passages, including one condemning King George for encouraging the slave trade, were removed. Most other changes dealt with style.

On July 4, Congress adopted the final draft of the Declaration of Independence.

The Declaration, signed by John Hancock as president of Congress, was promptly printed. It was read to a large crowd in the State House yard on July 8. On July 19, Congress ordered the

Declaration of Independence to be engrossed (written in beautiful script) on parchment. Congress also ordered that all its members

sign the engrossed copy. Eventually, 56 members of Congress signed.

The importance of the Declaration was that it magnificently expressed the thoughts of all patriots. It thus did not contain new ideas. The Declaration actually reflected ideas on social and political justice held by various philosophers of the time, especially the English philosopher John Locke. Yet the eloquent language of the document stirred the hearts of the American people. It also aroused people in Europe to make their governments more democratic. Over the years, many newly emerging nations have looked to the Declaration's expressive language in giving their reasons for seeking freedom from foreign control.

The original parchment copy of the Declaration is housed in the National Archives Building in Washington, D.C. It is displayed with two other historic American documents — the United States Constitution and the Bill of Rights.

Richard B. Morris, the contributor of this article, is the author of The American Revolution: A Brief History.

The signers of the Declaration of Independence dipped their quills into this silver inkwell, made by Philip Syng in 1752.

Responding to "The Declaration of Independence"

Thinking and Discussing

The encyclopedia article states that "The Declaration of Independence ranks as one of the greatest documents in human history." Do you believe this is true? Explain your answer.

Applying Historical Concepts

Creating a Time Line What events led up to the signing of the Declaration of Independence? What laws were passed? What organizations were formed? What actions were taken? Make a time line that shows the order of events. Or you may want to devise your own way to chart the sequence of events.

Presenting a Report Who was John Locke? What were some of his philosophies? Can you see any similarities between Locke's ideas and those expressed in the Declaration of Independence? Find out the answers to these questions and present your findings in a brief paper or oral report. Or you may want to make a chart with two sections: one that

A German-American artist made this plate around 1800 to commemorate the Revolution.

summarizes some of Locke's ideas, and one that summarizes ideas from the Declaration of Independence.

Expressing Your Rights One famous phrase from the Declaration of Independence states that everyone has the right to "life, liberty, and the pursuit of happiness." What does that phrase mean to you? Think of a creative way to express your response: Make a drawing, a poster, a diorama, a photo display, or a video. Write a poem or song, or choose a passage from another writer's work and read it aloud.

Thinking About History

Drawing a Political Cartoon

Imagine being a Patriot or a
Loyalist, caught up in the
excitement and controversy
surrounding the struggle for
independence. Choose your
viewpoint. Then draw a cartoon
that might have appeared on the
editorial page of a revolutionary
era newspaper. Your cartoon can
express an opinion about any of
the events surrounding the War
for Independence.

Playing Revolutionary Trivia

Who was Jonas Clark? What did the Daughters of Liberty do? Who
was Chief Pontiac, and how did his actions affect the movement for
independence? Make up a Revolutionary Trivia game! First, find out

as many facts as you can
about the American
Revolution. Then write
each fact in question
form on one side of a
card. Write the
answers on the back.
Get together with
friends and play the
game.

Charting Cause and Effect

What factors led to the American colonists' growing resentment against British rule? What events took place? How did one event lead to another? Compile notes that answer these questions. Then use your notes to create a chart called "Causes and Effects."

Creating a Colonial Match Game

Creasy . . . lanthorn . . . quitted . . . Eyewitness accounts from the Revolutionary era contain many words and phrases that sound foreign to us today. First, make a list of some of these "antique" expressions. Write each expression on a card. Write a modern definition for each on a separate card. Then shuffle the cards and lay them face up on a flat surface. Have your group try to match the cards.

NOTIFICATION.

ALL Persons who are desirous of leaving the Town of *Boston*, are hereby called upon to give in their Names to the Town-Major forthwith. . .

By Order of his Excellency the General.

JAMES URQUHART, Town-Major.

Boston, 24th of July, 1775.

Many people wanted to escape the tensions in Boston. This notification gave directions to people who wished to leave the city.

Window on the Past

Events of the past can be viewed from many perspectives — through the eyes of people who actually observed them or from the vantage point of writers of today looking back. Here are seven writers who have helped open a window on the events of the American Revolution.

"Recollections of George Hewes"
George Hewes, 1773
George Hewes was a Boston shoemaker. A supporter of the colonists, Hewes took part in the Boston Tea Party and was also present at the Boston Massacre.

1750

1800

1850

"Anne Hulton: Letters"
Anne Hulton, 1773
Anne Hulton was born in England. She lived in Boston from 1768 to 1775. While there, she wrote a series of letters to a friend at home describing the situation in Boston. Due to growing unrest, she returned to England in 1775.

"A Letter from Paul Revere"
Paul Revere, 1798
Paul Revere was born in Boston and became a silversmith like his father. After his famous ride to Lexington, Revere made many contributions to the American cause.

"The Fifer of Boxborough"
Elizabeth West and
Katherine S. Talmadge,
1983
In 1983 the Town of
Boxborough commissioned
Talmadge and West to
write the *Boxborough
Bicentennial History Book.*
　　Elizabeth West (left)
was born in New York City
but has lived all of her
adult life in
Massachusetts. She has
written for children's
magazines.
　　Katherine S. Talmadge
(right) was born in
Worcester,
Massachusetts. A former
fifth grade teacher, she
has been writing
educational material for
the past eighteen years.

"Crispus Attucks"
Burke Davis, 1976
Burke Davis was born in North
Carolina and worked for many
years as a newspaperman and
later as a writer and historian
with the Colonial Williamsburg
Foundation. Among his books for
young people are *Yorktown: The
Winning of American
Independence* and *Three for
Revolution.*

| 1900 | 1950 | 2000 |

**"Shots Heard Round
the World"**
Albert Marrin, 1988
Albert Marrin was born in
New York City and is now
chairman of the History
Department at Yeshiva
University in New York
City. He has written
scholarly works as well as
award-winning books for
young readers, including
*Overlord: D-Day and the
Invasion of Europe.*

497

History Comes Alive

There are many ways to learn about history outside of school. A local bookstore, like this one in Boston, may have hundreds of fascinating books on subjects like the American Revolution. Here are a few.

Johnny Tremain
by Esther Forbes
(Houghton, 1943)
Perhaps the best known of the junior novels written about the Revolutionary period, this Newbery Medal–winning work depicts the life of a talented and arrogant apprentice silversmith who learns to conquer despair. Forbes also wrote the Pulitzer Prize–winning biography *Paul Revere and the World He Lived In* (Houghton, 1942) and the pictorial biography *America's Paul Revere* (Houghton, 1946).

Sarah Bishop
by Scott O'Dell (Houghton, 1980)
In this historical novel, award-winner Scott O'Dell tells the story of Sarah Bishop, a girl whose family is split by opposing loyalties and who herself is a fugitive from the law during the time of the American Revolution.

The American Revolutionaries: A History in Their Own Words 1750–1800
edited by Milton Meltzer (Crowell, 1987)

Letters, journals, newspapers, interviews, ballads, pamphlets, speeches, and diaries from the half century surrounding the Revolutionary War are compiled here to show America's struggle for freedom. These records portray everyday Americans, from doctor, preacher, slave, and general to housewife, immigrant, and teen-aged soldier.

War Comes to Willy Freeman
by James Lincoln Collier and Christopher Collier (Delacorte, 1983)

In this historical novel, a free African American teen-aged girl struggles to find her mother in British-occupied New York during the Revolution.

The Revolutionary War: America's Fight for Freedom
by Bart McDowell (National Geographic, 1967)

Numerous maps, drawings, paintings, and photographs of Revolutionary battle sites and artifacts accompany this account of a modern American family as they retrace the footsteps of the patriots who fought and won the Revolutionary War.

Weathering the Storm: Women of the American Revolution
by Elizabeth Evans (Scribner, 1975)

A fascinating, revealing look at the American Revolution seen through the eyes of eleven women who recorded their firsthand experiences in journals and diaries.

HUMOR

In Search of Laughter

N E
W

CONTENTS

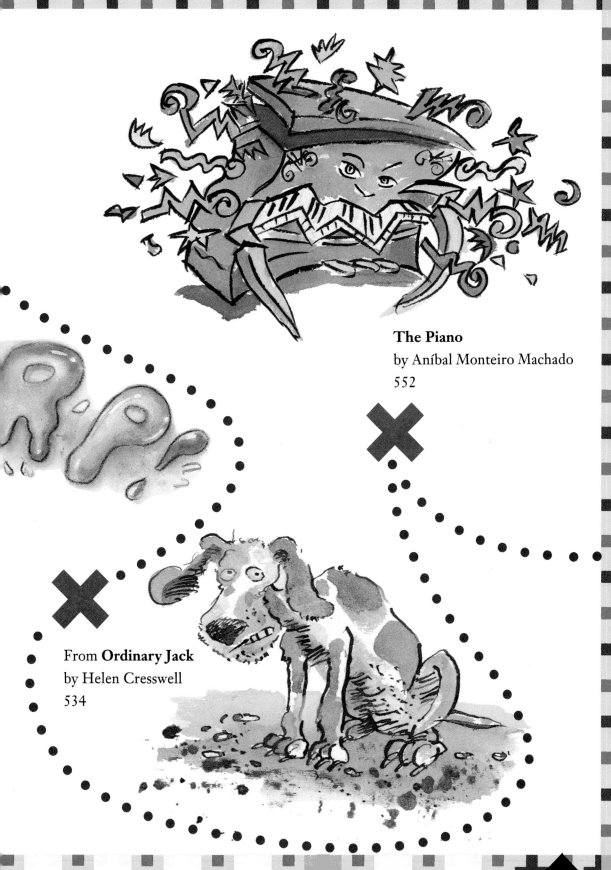

In the Middle of the Night

by Philippa Pearce
illustrated by Kevin Hawkes

In the middle of the night a fly woke Charlie. At first he lay listening, half-asleep, while it swooped about the room. Sometimes it was far; sometimes it was near — that was what had woken him; and occasionally it was very near indeed. It was very, very near when the buzzing stopped; the fly had alighted on his face. He jerked his head up; the fly buzzed off. Now he was really awake.

The fly buzzed widely about the room, but it was thinking of Charlie all the time. It swooped nearer and nearer. Nearer. . . .

Charlie pulled his head down under the bedclothes. All of him under the bedclothes, he was completely protected; but he could hear nothing except his heartbeats and his breathing. He was overwhelmed by the smell of warm bedding, warm pajamas, warm himself. He was going to suffocate. So he rose suddenly up out of the bedclothes; and the fly was waiting for him. It dashed at him. He beat at it with his hands. At the same time he appealed to his younger brother, Wilson, in the next bed: "Wilson, there's a fly!"

Wilson, unstirring, slept on.

Now Charlie and the fly were pitting their wits against each other: Charlie pouncing on the air where he thought the fly must be; the fly sliding under his guard towards his face. Again and again the fly reached Charlie; again and again, almost simultaneously, Charlie dislodged him. Once he hit the fly — or, at least, hit where the fly had been a second before, on the side of his head; the blow was so hard that his head sang with it afterwards.

Then suddenly the fight was over; no more buzzing. His blows — or rather, one of them — must have told.

He laid his head back on the pillow, thinking of going to sleep again. But he was also thinking of the fly, and now he noticed a tickling in the ear he turned to the pillow.

It must be — it *was* — the fly.

He rose in such panic that the waking of Wilson really seemed to him a possible thing, and useful. He shook him repeatedly. "Wilson — Wilson, I tell you, there's a fly in my ear!"

Wilson groaned, turned over very slowly like a seal in water, and slept on.

The tickling in Charlie's ear continued. He could just imagine the fly struggling in some passageway too narrow for its wingspan. He longed to put his finger into his ear and rattle it around, like a stick in a rabbit hole; but he was afraid of driving the fly deeper into his ear.

Wilson slept on.

Charlie stood in the middle of the bedroom floor, quivering and trying to think. He needed to see down his ear, or to get someone else to see down it. Wilson wouldn't do; perhaps Margaret would.

Margaret's room was next door. Charlie turned on the light as he entered: Margaret's bed was empty. He was startled, and then thought that she must have gone to the bathroom. But there was no light from there. He listened carefully: there was no sound from anywhere, except for the usual snuffling moans from the hall, where Floss slept and dreamed of dog biscuits. The empty bed was mystifying; but Charlie had his ear to worry about. It sounded as if there were a pigeon inside it now.

Wilson asleep; Margaret vanished; that left Alison. But Alison was bossy, just because she was the eldest; and anyway she would probably only wake Mum. He might as well wake Mum himself.

Down the passage and through the door always left ajar. "Mum," he said. She woke, or at least half-woke, at once. "Who is it? Who? Who? What's the matter? What? —"

"I've a fly in my ear."

"You can't have."

"It flew in."

She switched on the bedside light, and as she did so, Dad plunged beneath the bedclothes with an exclamation and lay still again.

Charlie knelt at his mother's side of the bed, and she looked into his ear. "There's nothing."

"Something crackles."

"It's wax in your ear."

"It tickles."

"There's no fly there. Go back to bed and stop imagining things."

His father's arm came up from below the bedclothes. The hand waved about, settled on the bedside light, and clicked it out. There was an upheaval of bedclothes and a comfortable grunt.

"Good night," said Mum from the darkness. She was already allowing herself to sink back into sleep again.

"Good night," Charlie said sadly. Then an idea occurred to him. He repeated his good night loudly and added some coughing, to cover the fact that he was closing the bedroom door behind him — the door that Mum kept open so that she could listen for her children. They had outgrown all that kind of attention, except possibly for Wilson. Charlie had shut the door against Mum's hearing because he intended to slip downstairs for a drink of water — well, for a drink and perhaps a snack. That fly business had woken him up and also weakened him; he needed something.

He crept downstairs, trusting to Floss's good sense not to make a row.[1] He turned the foot of the staircase towards the kitchen, and there had not been the faintest whimper from her, far less a bark. He was passing the dog basket when he had the most unnerving sensation of something being wrong there — something unusual, at least. He could not have said whether he had heard something or smelled something — he could certainly have seen nothing in the blackness; perhaps some extra sense warned him.

"Floss?" he whispered, and there was the usual little scrabble and snuffle. He held out his fingers low down for Floss to lick. As she did not do so at once, he moved them towards her, met some obstruction —

"Don't poke your fingers in my eye!" a voice said, very low-toned and cross. Charlie's first, confused thought was that Floss had spoken: the voice was familiar — but then a voice from Floss should *not* be familiar; it should be strangely new to him —

---

[1] **row** (rou): commotion; noise; uproar.

507

He took an uncertain little step towards the voice, tripped over the obstruction, which was quite wrong in shape and size to be Floss, and sat down. Two things now happened. Floss, apparently having climbed over the obstruction, reached his lap and began to lick his face. At the same time a human hand fumbled over his face, among the slappings of Floss's tongue, and settled over his mouth. "Don't make a row! Keep quiet!" said the same voice. Charlie's mind cleared; he knew, although without understanding, that he was sitting on the floor in the dark with Floss on his knee and Margaret beside him.

Her hand came off his mouth.

"What are you doing here anyway, Charlie?"

"I like that! What about you? There was a fly in my ear."

"Go on!"

"There was."

"Why does that make you come downstairs?"

"I wanted a drink of water."

"There's water in the bathroom."

"Well, I'm a bit hungry."

"If Mum catches you. . . ."

"Look here," Charlie said, "you tell me what you're doing down here."

Margaret sighed. "Just sitting with Floss."

"You can't come down and just sit with Floss in the middle of the night."

"Yes, I can. I keep her company. Only at weekends, of course. No one seemed to realize what it was like for her when those puppies went. She just couldn't get to sleep for loneliness."

"But the last puppy went weeks ago. You haven't been keeping Floss company every Saturday night since then."

"Why not?"

Charlie gave up. "I'm going to get my food and drink," he said. He went into the kitchen, followed by Margaret, followed by Floss.

They all had a quick drink of water. Then Charlie and Margaret looked into the larder:[2] the remains of a roast; a very large quantity of mashed potato; most of a loaf; eggs; butter; cheese . . .

"I suppose it'll have to be just bread and butter and a bit of cheese," said Charlie. "Else Mum might notice."

"Something hot," said Margaret. "I'm cold from sitting in the hall comforting Floss. I need hot cocoa, I think." She poured some milk into a saucepan and put it on the hot plate. Then she began a search for the cocoa. Charlie, standing by the cooker, was already absorbed in the making of a rough cheese sandwich.

The milk in the pan began to steam. Given time, it rose in the saucepan, peered over the top, and boiled over on to the hot plate, where it sizzled loudly. Margaret rushed back and pulled the saucepan to one side. "Well, really, Charlie! Now there's that awful smell! It'll still be here in the morning, too."

"Set the fan going," Charlie suggested.

The fan drew the smell from the cooker up and away through a pipe to the outside. It also made a loud roaring noise. Not loud enough to reach their parents, who slept on the other side of the house — that was all that Charlie and Margaret thought of.

Alison's bedroom, however, was immediately above the kitchen. Charlie was eating his bread and cheese, Margaret was drinking her cocoa, when the kitchen door opened and there stood Alison. Only Floss was pleased to see her.

"Well!" she said.

Charlie muttered something about a fly in his ear, but Margaret said nothing. Alison had caught them red-handed. She would call Mum downstairs, that was obvious. There would be an awful row.

Alison stood there. She liked commanding a situation.

Then, instead of taking a step backwards to call up the stairs to Mum, she took a step forward into the kitchen. "What are you having, anyway?" she asked. She glanced with scorn at Charlie's poor piece of

---

[2]**larder:** a small room or cupboard where food is kept.

bread and cheese and at Margaret's cocoa. She moved over to the larder, flung open the door, and looked searchingly inside. In such a way must Napoleon have viewed a battlefield before the victory.

Her gaze fell upon the bowl of mashed potato. "I shall make potato cakes," said Alison.

They watched while she brought the mashed potato to the kitchen table. She switched on the oven, fetched her other ingredients, and began mixing.

"Mum'll notice if you take much of that potato," said Margaret.

But Alison thought big. "She may notice if some potato is missing," she agreed. "But if there's none at all, and if the bowl it was in is washed and dried and stacked away with the others, then she's going to think she must have made a mistake. There just can never have been any mashed potato."

Alison rolled out her mixture and cut it into cakes; then she set the cakes on a baking tin and put it in the oven.

Now she did the washing up. Throughout the time they were in the kitchen, Alison washed up and put away as she went along. She wanted no one's help. She was very methodical, and she did everything herself to be sure that nothing was left undone. In the morning there must be no trace left of the cooking in the middle of the night.

"And now," said Alison, "I think we should fetch Wilson."

The other two were aghast at the idea; but Alison was firm in her reasons. "It's better if we're all in this together, Wilson as well. Then, if the worst comes to the worst, it won't be just us three caught out, with Wilson hanging on to Mum's apron strings, smiling innocence. We'll all be for it together; and Mum'll be softer with us if we've got Wilson."

They saw that, at once. But Margaret still objected. "Wilson will tell. He just always tells everything. He can't help it."

Alison said, "He always tells everything. Right. We'll give him something *to* tell, and then see if Mum believes him. We'll do an entertainment for him. Get an umbrella from the hall and Wilson's sou'wester[3] and a blanket or a rug or something. Go on."

---

[3] **sou'wester** (sou **wĕs′**tər): a waterproof hat.

They would not obey Alison's orders until they had heard her plan; then they did. They fetched the umbrella and the hat, and lastly they fetched Wilson, still sound asleep, slung between the two of them in his eiderdown.[4] They propped him in a chair at the kitchen table, where he still slept.

By now the potato cakes were done. Alison took them out of the oven and set them on the table before Wilson. She buttered them, handing them in turn to Charlie and Margaret and helping herself. One was set aside to cool for Floss.

The smell of fresh-cooked, buttery potato cake woke Wilson, as was to be expected. First his nose sipped the air; then his eyes opened; his gaze settled on the potato cakes.

"Like one?" Alison asked.

Wilson opened his mouth wide, and Alison put a potato cake inside, whole.

"They're paradise cakes," Alison said.

"Potato cakes?" said Wilson, recognizing the taste.

"No, paradise cakes, Wilson," and then, stepping aside, she gave him a clear view of Charlie's and Margaret's entertainment, with the umbrella and the sou'wester hat and his eiderdown. "Look, Wilson, look."

Wilson watched with wide-open eyes, and into his wide-open mouth Alison put, one by one, the potato cakes that were his share.

But, as they had foreseen, Wilson did not stay awake for very long. When there were no more potato cakes, he yawned, drowsed, and suddenly was deeply asleep. Charlie and Margaret put him back into his eiderdown and took him upstairs to bed again. They came down to return the umbrella and the sou'wester to their proper places, and to see Floss back into her basket. Alison, last out of the kitchen, made sure that everything was in its place.

The next morning Mum was down first. On Sunday she always cooked a proper breakfast for anyone there in time. Dad was always there

---

[4]**eiderdown** (ī′dər doun′): a quilt stuffed with duck feathers.

in time; but this morning Mum was still looking for a bowl of mashed potato when he appeared.

"I can't think where it's gone," she said. "I can't think."

"I'll have the bacon and eggs without the potato," said Dad; and he did. While he ate, Mum went back to searching.

Wilson came down, and was sent upstairs again to put on a dressing gown. On his return he said that Charlie was still asleep and there was no sound from the girls' rooms either. He said he thought they were tired out. He went on talking while he ate his breakfast. Dad was reading the paper and Mum had gone back to poking about in the larder for the bowl of mashed potato, but Wilson liked talking even if no one would listen. When Mum came out of the larder for a moment, still without her potato, Wilson was saying: ". . . and Charlie sat in an umbrella boat on an eiderdown sea, and Margaret pretended to be a sea serpent, and Alison gave us paradise cakes to eat. Floss had one too, but it was too hot for her. What are paradise cakes? Dad, what's a paradise cake?"

"Don't know," said Dad, reading.

"Mum, what's a paradise cake?"

"Oh, Wilson, don't bother so when I'm looking for something. . . . When did you eat this cake, anyway?"

"I told you. Charlie sat in his umbrella boat on an eiderdown sea and Margaret was a sea serpent and Alison —"

"Wilson," said his mother, "you've been dreaming."

"No, really — really!" Wilson cried.

But his mother paid no further attention. "I give up," she said. "That mashed potato; it must have been last weekend. . . ." She went out of the kitchen to call the others. "Charlie! Margaret! Alison!"

Wilson, in the kitchen, said to his father, "I wasn't dreaming. And Charlie said there was a fly in his ear."

Dad had been quarter-listening; now he put down his paper. "What?"

"Charlie had a fly in his ear."

Dad stared at Wilson. "And what did you say that Alison fed you with?"

"Paradise cakes. She'd just made them, I think, in the middle of the night."

"What were they like?"

"Lovely. Hot, with butter. Lovely."

"But were they — well, could they have had any mashed potato in them, for instance?"

In the hall Mum was finishing her calling. "Charlie! Margaret! Alison! I warn you now!"

"I don't know about that," Wilson said. "They were paradise cakes. They tasted a bit like the potato cakes Mum makes, but Alison said they weren't. She specially said they were paradise cakes."

Dad nodded. "You've finished your breakfast. Go up and get dressed, and you can take this" — he took a coin from his pocket — "straight off to the sweetshop.[5] Go on."

Mum met Wilson at the kitchen door. "Where's he off to in such a hurry?"

"I gave him something to buy sweets with," said Dad. "I wanted a quiet breakfast. He talks too much."

---

[5] **sweetshop:** candy store.

Responding to

In the Middle of the Night

Thinking and Discussing

What plan does Alison make to keep the children's late-night snack a secret?

Why does Mum insist that Wilson's story is from a dream? What does Dad know at the end of the story that Mum doesn't know? Explain your answer.

Could the events in this story occur in real life? How does the author create a humorous situation based on everyday family life?

Choosing a Creative Response

Pantomiming Funny Events In this selection, the author creates a chain of funny events. The whole story begins when a fly buzzes around Charlie's bedroom and ends up in his ear. Identify the other important funny events that follow in the chain.

With a few classmates, create a short pantomime for each of the important funny events in this story. Present each scene to your classmates, and see if they can guess which episodes you are re-creating for them.

Creating Your Own Activity Plan and complete your own activity in response to "In the Middle of the Night."

Thinking and Writing

What happened to the fly in Charlie's ear? Rewrite Charlie's encounter with the fly from the fly's point of view. Use your own funny writing style, and remember to capture the humorous elements of this episode.

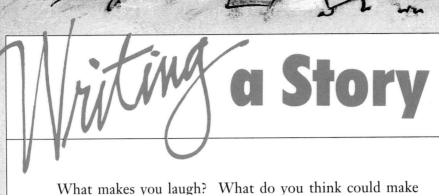

Writing a Story

What makes you laugh? What do you think could make others laugh? Different people enjoy different kinds of humor. Some people appreciate the understated cleverness of a witty story, while many like the wild uproar of slapstick comedy. Others prefer satire that pokes fun at human customs and behavior.

Try writing your own humorous story. Look at the various ways the authors of these selections create humor, and start writing whenever you think you're ready. If the selections give you another writing idea, go ahead with that one instead.

1. *Prewriting* Before you begin writing your humorous piece, think of a funny event that you've seen or imagined. Come up with a story idea that tells how this event happened, making sure that you include all the funny details of the event.

2. *Write a First Draft* Think about your audience and your purpose for writing. Who will read your story? How can you make *your* audience laugh? Do you want to exaggerate a situation? Poke fun at human behavior? Teach a lesson?

3. *Revise* Read your first draft and make any needed changes. Does your humorous piece make *you* chuckle? Does the plot make sense? Read your story to a partner to see if it makes someone else laugh.

4. *Proofread* Check your humorous piece for correct spelling, capitalization, and punctuation. If you make up funny names in your story, make sure you spell them the same way throughout.

5. *Publish* Make a neat copy of your humorous piece. You might want to illustrate it with funny drawings or create a collage of pictures for the title page. Share it with others, and spread the laughter.

The All-American Slurp

by Lensey Namioka
illustrated by Andrew Shachat

The first time our family was invited out to dinner in America, we disgraced ourselves while eating celery. We had emigrated to this country from China, and during our early days here we had a hard time with American table manners.

In China we never ate celery raw, or any other kind of vegetable raw. We always had to disinfect the vegetables in boiling water first. When we were presented with our first relish tray, the raw celery caught us unprepared.

We had been invited to dinner by our neighbors, the Gleasons. After arriving at the house, we shook hands with our hosts and packed ourselves into a sofa. As our family of four sat stiffly in a row, my younger brother and I stole glances at our parents for a clue as to what to do next.

Mrs. Gleason offered the relish tray to Mother. The tray looked pretty, with its tiny red radishes, curly sticks of carrots, and long, slender stalks of pale green celery. "Do try some of the celery, Mrs. Lin," she said. "It's from a local farmer, and it's sweet."

Mother picked up one of the green stalks, and Father followed suit. Then I picked up a stalk, and my brother did too. So there we sat, each with a stalk of celery in our right hand.

Mrs. Gleason kept smiling. "Would you like to try some of the dip, Mrs. Lin? It's my own recipe: sour cream and onion flakes, with a dash of Tabasco sauce."

Most Chinese don't care for dairy products, and in those days I wasn't even ready to drink fresh milk. Sour cream sounded perfectly revolting. Our family shook our heads in unison.

Mrs. Gleason went off with the relish tray to the other guests, and we carefully watched to see what they did. Everyone seemed to eat the raw vegetables quite happily.

Mother took a bite of her celery.

"It's not bad!" she whispered.

Father took a bite of his celery. *Crunch.* "Yes, it *is* good," he said, looking surprised.

I took a bite, and then my brother. *Crunch, crunch.* It was more than good; it was delicious. Raw celery has a slight sparkle, a zingy taste that you don't get in cooked celery. When Mrs. Gleason came around with the relish tray, we each took another stalk of celery, except my brother. He took two.

There was only one problem: long strings ran through the length of the stalk, and they got caught in my teeth. When I help my mother in the kitchen, I always pull the strings out before slicing celery.

I pulled the strings out of my stalk.

My brother followed suit. *Z-z-zip, z-z-zip, z-z-zip.* To my left, my parents were taking care of their own stalks. *Z-z-zip, z-z-zip, z-z-zip.*

Suddenly I realized that there was dead silence except for our zipping. Looking up, I saw that the eyes of everyone in the room were on our family. Mr. and Mrs. Gleason, their daughter Meg, who was my friend, and their neighbors the Badels — they were all staring at us as we busily pulled the strings of our celery.

That wasn't the end of it. Mrs. Gleason announced that dinner was served and invited us to the dining table. It was lavishly covered with platters of food, but we couldn't see any chairs around the table. So we helpfully carried over some dining chairs and sat down. All the other guests just stood there.

Mrs. Gleason bent down and whispered to us, "This is a buffet dinner. You help yourselves to some food and eat it in the living room."

Our family beat a retreat back to the sofa as if chased by enemy soldiers. For the rest of the evening, too mortified to go back to the dining table, I nursed a bit of potato salad on my plate.

Next day Meg and I got on the school bus together. I wasn't sure how she would feel about me after the spectacle our family made at the party. But she was just the same as usual, and the only reference she made to the party was, "Hope you and your folks got enough to eat last night. You certainly didn't take very much. Mom never tries to figure out how much food to prepare. She just puts everything on the table and hopes for the best."

I began to relax. The Gleasons' dinner party wasn't so different from a Chinese meal after all. My mother also puts everything on the table and hopes for the best.

———

Meg was the first friend I had made after we came to America. I eventually got acquainted with a few other kids in school, but Meg was still the only real friend I had.

My brother didn't have any problems making friends. He spent all his time with some boys who were teaching him baseball, and in no time he could speak English much faster than I could — not better, but faster.

I worried more about making mistakes, and I spoke carefully, making sure I could say everything right before opening my mouth. At least I had a better accent than my parents, who never really got rid of their Chinese accent, even years later. My parents had both studied English in school before coming to America, but what they had studied was mostly written English, not spoken.

Father's approach to English was a scientific one. Since Chinese verbs have no tense, he was fascinated by the way English verbs changed form according to whether they were in the present, past imperfect, perfect, pluperfect, future, or future perfect tense. He was always making diagrams of verbs and their inflections, and he looked for opportunities to show off his mastery of the pluperfect and future perfect tenses, his two favorites. "I shall have finished my project by Monday," he would say smugly.

Mother's approach was to memorize lists of polite phrases that would cover all possible social situations. She was constantly muttering things like "I'm fine, thank you. And you?" Once she accidentally stepped on someone's foot, and hurriedly blurted, "Oh, that's quite all right!" Embarrassed by her slip, she resolved to do better next time. So when someone stepped on *her* foot, she cried, "You're welcome!"

In our own different ways, we made progress in learning English. But I had another worry, and that was my appearance. My brother didn't have to worry, since Mother bought him blue jeans for school, and he dressed like all the other boys. But she insisted that girls had to wear skirts. By the time she saw that Meg and the other girls were wearing jeans, it was too late. My school clothes were bought already, and we didn't have money left to buy new outfits for me. We had too many other things to buy first, like furniture, pots, and pans.

The first time I visited Meg's house, she took me upstairs to her room, and I wound up trying on her clothes. We were pretty much the same size, since Meg was shorter and thinner than average. Maybe that's how we became friends in the first place. Wearing Meg's jeans and T-shirt, I looked at myself in the mirror. I could almost pass for an

American — from the back, anyway. At least the kids in school wouldn't stop and stare at me in the hallways, which was what they did when they saw me in my white blouse and navy blue skirt that went a couple of inches below the knees.

When Meg came to my house, I invited her to try on my Chinese dresses, the ones with a high collar and slits up the sides. Meg's eyes were bright as she looked at herself in the mirror. She struck several sultry poses, and we nearly fell over laughing.

———

The dinner party at the Gleasons' didn't stop my growing friendship with Meg. Things were getting better for me in other ways too. Mother finally bought me some jeans at the end of the month, when Father got his paycheck. She wasn't in any hurry about buying them at first, until I worked on her. This is what I did. Since we didn't have a car in those days, I often ran down to the neighborhood store to pick up things for her. The groceries cost less at a big supermarket, but the closest one was many blocks away. One day, when she ran out of flour, I offered to borrow a bike from our neighbor's son and buy a ten-pound bag of flour at the big supermarket. I mounted the boy's bike and waved to Mother. "I'll be back in five minutes!"

Before I started pedaling, I heard her voice behind me. "You can't go out in public like that! People can see all the way up to your thighs!"

"I'm sorry," I said innocently. "I thought you were in a hurry to get the flour." For dinner we were going to have pot-stickers (fried Chinese dumplings), and we needed a lot of flour.

"Couldn't you borrow a girl's bicycle?" complained Mother. "That way your skirt won't be pushed up."

"There aren't too many of those around," I said. "Almost all the girls wear jeans while riding a bike, so they don't see any point buying a girl's bike."

We didn't eat pot-stickers that evening, and Mother was thoughtful. Next day we took the bus downtown and she bought me a pair of jeans. In the same week, my brother made the baseball team of his junior high school, Father started taking driving lessons, and

Mother discovered rummage sales. We soon got all the furniture we needed, plus a dart board and a 1,000-piece jigsaw puzzle (fourteen hours later, we discovered that it was a 999-piece jigsaw puzzle). There was hope that the Lins might become a normal American family after all.

———

Then came our dinner at the Lakeview restaurant.

The Lakeview was an expensive restaurant, one of those places where a headwaiter dressed in tails conducted you to your seat, and the only light came from candles and flaming desserts. In one corner of the room a lady harpist played tinkling melodies.

Father wanted to celebrate, because he had just been promoted. He worked for an electronics company, and after his English started improving, his superiors decided to appoint him to a position more suited to his training. The promotion not only brought a higher salary but was also a tremendous boost to his pride.

Up to then we had eaten only in Chinese restaurants. Although my brother and I were becoming fond of hamburgers, my parents didn't care much for western food, other than chow mein.

But this was a special occasion, and Father asked his coworkers to recommend a really elegant restaurant. So there we were at the Lakeview, stumbling after the headwaiter in the murky dining room.

At our table we were handed our menus, and they were so big that to read mine I almost had to stand up again. But why bother? It was mostly in French, anyway.

Father, being an engineer, was always systematic. He took out a pocket French dictionary. "They told me that most of the items would be in French, so I came prepared." He even had a pocket flashlight, the size of a marking pen. While Mother held the flashlight over the menu, he looked up the items that were in French.

"*Pâté en croûte*," he muttered. "Let's see . . . *pâté* is paste . . . *croûte* is crust . . . hmm . . . a paste in crust."

The waiter stood looking patient. I squirmed and died at least fifty times.

At long last Father gave up. "Why don't we just order four complete dinners at random?" he suggested.

"Isn't that risky?" asked Mother. "The French eat some rather peculiar things, I've heard."

"A Chinese can eat anything a Frenchman can eat," Father declared.

The soup arrived in a plate. How do you get soup up from a plate? I glanced at the other diners, but the ones at the nearby tables were not on their soup course, while the more distant ones were invisible in the darkness.

Fortunately my parents had studied books on western etiquette before they came to America. "Tilt your plate," whispered my mother. "It's easier to spoon the soup up that way."

She was right. Tilting the plate did the trick. But the etiquette book didn't say anything about what you did after the soup reached your lips. As any respectable Chinese knows, the correct way to eat your soup is to slurp. This helps to cool the liquid and prevent you from burning your lips. It also shows your appreciation.

We showed our appreciation.

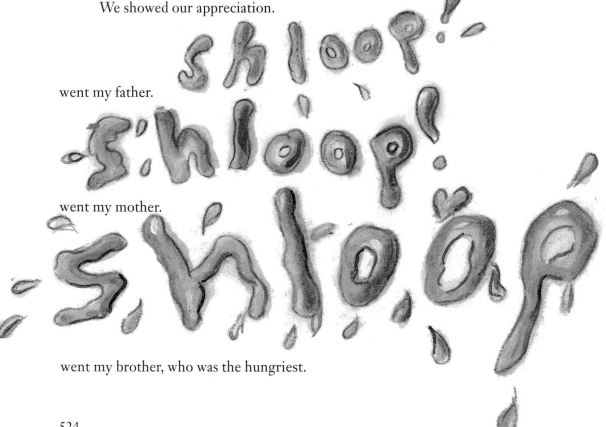

went my father.

went my mother.

went my brother, who was the hungriest.

The lady harpist stopped playing to take a rest. And in the silence, our family's consumption of soup suddenly seemed unnaturally loud. You know how it sounds on a rocky beach when the tide goes out and the water drains from all those little pools? They go *shloop, shloop, shloop.* That was the Lin family, eating soup.

At the next table a waiter was pouring wine. When a large *shloop* reached him, he froze. The bottle continued to pour, and red wine flooded the tabletop and into the lap of a customer. Even the customer didn't notice anything at first, being also hypnotized by the

It was too much. "I need to go to the toilet," I mumbled, jumping to my feet. A waiter, sensing my urgency, quickly directed me to the ladies' room.

I splashed cold water on my burning face, and as I dried myself with a paper towel, I stared into the mirror. In this perfumed ladies' room, with its pink-and-silver wallpaper and marbled sinks, I looked completely out of place. What was I doing here? What was our family doing in the Lakeview restaurant? In America?

The door to the ladies' room opened. A woman came in and glanced curiously at me. I retreated into one of the toilet cubicles and latched the door.

Time passed — maybe half an hour, maybe an hour. Then I heard the door open again, and my mother's voice. "Are you in there? You're not sick, are you?"

There was real concern in her voice. A girl can't leave her family just because they slurp their soup. Besides, the toilet cubicle had a few drawbacks as a permanent residence. "I'm all right," I said, undoing the latch.

Mother didn't tell me how the rest of the dinner went, and I didn't want to know. In the weeks following, I managed to push the whole thing into the back of my mind, where it jumped out at me only a few times a day. Even now, I turn hot all over when I think of the Lakeview restaurant.

———

But by the time we had been in this country for three months, our family was definitely making progress toward becoming Americanized. I remember my parents' first PTA meeting. Father wore a neat suit and tie, and Mother put on her first pair of high heels. She stumbled only once. They met my homeroom teacher and beamed as she told them that I would make honor roll soon at the rate I was going. Of course Chinese etiquette forced Father to say that I was a very stupid girl and Mother to protest that the teacher was showing favoritism toward me. But I could tell they were both very proud.

The day came when my parents announced that they wanted to give a dinner party. We had invited Chinese friends to eat with us before, but this dinner was going to be different. In addition to a Chinese-American family, we were going to invite the Gleasons.

"Gee, I can hardly wait to have dinner at your house," Meg said to me. "I just *love* Chinese food."

That was a relief. Mother was a good cook, but I wasn't sure if people who ate sour cream would also eat chicken gizzards stewed in soy sauce.

Mother decided not to take a chance with chicken gizzards. Since we had western guests, she set the table with large dinner plates, which we never used in Chinese meals. In fact we didn't use individual plates at all, but picked up food from the platters in the middle of the table and brought it directly to our rice bowls. Following the practice of Chinese-American restaurants, Mother also placed large serving spoons on the platters.

The dinner started well. Mrs. Gleason exclaimed at the beautifully arranged dishes of food: the colorful candied fruit in the sweet-and-sour pork dish, the noodle-thin shreds of chicken meat stir-fried with tiny peas, and the glistening pink prawns in a ginger sauce.

At first I was too busy enjoying my food to notice how the guests were doing. But soon I remembered my duties. Sometimes guests were too polite to help themselves and you had to serve them with more food.

I glanced at Meg, to see if she needed more food, and my eyes nearly popped out at the sight of her plate. It was piled with food: the sweet-and-sour meat pushed right against the chicken shreds, and the chicken sauce ran into the prawns. She had been taking food from a second dish before she finished eating her helping from the first!

Horrified, I turned to look at Mrs. Gleason. She was dumping rice out of her bowl and putting it on her dinner plate. Then she ladled prawns and gravy on top of the rice and mixed everything together, the way you mix sand, gravel, and cement to make concrete.

I couldn't bear to look any longer, and I turned to Mr. Gleason. He was chasing a pea around his plate. Several times he got it to the edge, but when he tried to pick it up with his chopsticks, it rolled back toward the center of the plate again. Finally he put down his chopsticks and picked up the pea with his fingers. He really did! A grown man!

All of us, our family and the Chinese guests, stopped eating to watch the activities of the Gleasons. I wanted to giggle. Then I caught my mother's eyes on me. She frowned and shook her head slightly, and I understood the message: the Gleasons were not used to Chinese ways, and they were just coping the best they could. For some reason I thought of celery strings.

When the main courses were finished, Mother brought out a platter of fruit. "I hope you weren't expecting a sweet dessert," she said. "Since the Chinese don't eat dessert, I didn't think to prepare any."

"Oh, I couldn't possibly eat dessert!" cried Mrs. Gleason. "I'm simply stuffed!"

Meg had different ideas. When the table was cleared, she announced that she and I were going for a walk. "I don't know about you, but I feel like dessert," she told me, when we were outside. "Come on, there's a Dairy Queen down the street. I could use a big chocolate milkshake!"

Although I didn't really want anything more to eat, I insisted on paying for the milkshakes. After all, I was still hostess.

Meg got her large chocolate milkshake and I had a small one. Even so, she was finishing hers while I was only half done. Toward the end she pulled hard on her straws and went *shloop, shloop.*

"Do you always slurp when you eat a milkshake?" I asked, before I could stop myself.

Meg grinned. "Sure. All Americans slurp."

Responding to

The All-American Slurp

Thinking and Discussing

Why do the Lins feel embarrassed at the Gleasons' dinner party?
Why does the author feel humiliated at the Lakeview?

How does the story point out the humor that may go along with
learning a new language?

What does the author learn about cultural differences when the Lins
invite the Gleasons over for dinner? Do you think the story suggests a
lesson about eating customs in different cultures? If so, what is this
lesson?

Choosing a Creative Response

Examining the American Culture Why do Americans use spoons to
eat soup instead of slurping straight from the bowl? Why do Americans
walk around indoors with their shoes on? Think about any American
customs or habits that may seem humorous to someone from another
culture. Collect ideas from other members in your class, and put them
together in a *Guidebook to Funny American Customs*.

Creating Your Own Activity Plan and complete your own activity in
response to "The All-American Slurp."

Thinking and Writing

How do the cultural differences between the Lins and the Gleasons
contribute to the humor of the story?

Have you ever been involved in a similar incident that was funny
because people had different customs? Tell or write about such an event
from your own experience.

Exploring Language

Noisy Words The author of "The All-American Slurp" uses words that imitate the sounds that they stand for in order to draw the reader into her experience. The *crunch* of biting into celery, *z-z-zip* of removing celery strings, and *shloop* of eating soup are all sounds that the reader can hear.

With your classmates, make up other words that imitate the sounds people make when eating or drinking. You may wish to make a tape recording of these sounds so you can listen to them several times. Agree on the spellings of these words, and put them into a "Glossary of Noisy Words."

Elwood Smith has written and illustrated two children's books and illustrated a third. He has also created magazine covers and jackets for record albums.

Elwood Smith doodles constantly, covering the top of his desk with caricatures and animal drawings. Then he chooses the most appealing pictures to keep in his sketchbook for possible use later.

Ordinary Jack

by Helen Cresswell
illustrated by Cat Bowman Smith

Grandma was sitting at the far end of the table, though all that was visible was the odd wisp of white hair, because she was behind a large cake on a high stand. The cake was forested with candles. Jack had no intention of counting them. He knew for a fact that there would be seventy-five. His mother did not believe in doing things by halves. She would light the candles when the time came, and the icing would start melting while she was half-way through and by the time all the candles were lit the icing would be hopelessly larded with multi-coloured grease and the whole top slice of the cake would have to be cut off and thrown to the birds. It happened every year. Mr. Bagthorpe thought the practice dangerous and unnecessary, and said so, but was ignored. He even said that the birds ought to be protected, but no one took any notice of that either — least of all the birds, who sorted the crumbs with lightning dexterity, and left the greased icing to seep, in the course of time and nature, into the lawn, with no apparent detriment to the daisies.

"Hello, Grandma," said Jack. "Happy Birthday."

He went down the table past the bristling cake and kissed her. Her skin was very soft and powdery and smelled unaccountably of warm pear drops.

"You are a good boy," said Grandma.

"What about me?" inquired Uncle Parker, delivering his own peck.

"I know perfectly well who you are," said Grandma. "You are that good-for-nothing young man who married Celia and ran Thomas over." (Thomas was an ill-favoured and cantankerous ginger tom[1] who had unfortunately got in the way of Uncle Parker's car some five years

---

[1] **ginger tom:** an orange-colored male cat.

535

previously, and whom Grandma had martyred to the point where one always half-expected her to refer to him as "St. Thomas.")

"That's me," said Uncle Parker mildly. "Sorry about that, Grandma. Nice old cat that was. Just not very nippy on his feet."

"He was a jewel," said Grandma. "He was given me on my fourth birthday, and I was devoted to him."

No one contradicted her. Clearly, no ginger tom in history had ever survived sixty odd years, with or without the intervention of Uncle Parker's deplorable driving. But today was Grandma's birthday and she was not to be contradicted. (She was rarely contradicted anyway. It was a whole lot of trouble to contradict Grandma. If Grandma said seven sixes were fifty-two, you agreed with her, as a rule. The odds against convincing her otherwise were practically a million to one anyway, and life was too short.)

"He was a jewel." Grandma repeated her observation a trifle argumentatively. Grandma liked arguments and got disappointed when nobody else wanted them.

"*You're* a jewel," said Mr. Bagthorpe diplomatically. He dropped a kiss on her head and pulled out a chair for his wife and the danger was temporarily averted.

Jack, seated between Uncle Parker and Rosie, cast a speculative eye over the table. All the customary Bagthorpe birthday trimmings were present, he noted with satisfaction. The sausage rolls (hot), salmon and cucumber sandwiches, asparagus rolls, stuffed eggs, cream meringues, chocolate truffle cake and Mrs. Fosdyke's Special Trifle[2] — all were there, and the eyes of all Bagthorpes present were riveted upon them. There was a pause. Jack's eyes moved to the top of the table. Grandma, thwarted of her argument, was hanging fire on purpose, he guessed, to pay them back. They waited.

"For what we are about to receive," she eventually remarked, eyes piously closed, "may the Lord make us truly thankful."

---

[2]**trifle (trī′fəl):** a dessert of cake topped with jam, custard, and whipped cream.

On the last two words her eyes blinked open like a cobra's and a hand went rapidly out to the nearest pile of stuffed eggs.

"Amen," gabbled the company, with the exception of Uncle Parker who said loudly and cheerfully, "Hear, hear!"

The food began to vanish at an astonishing rate.

"Well, darlings," said Mrs. Bagthorpe. "What is there to tell?"

Babel[3] was instantly let loose as all present with the exception of Grandpa, Uncle Parker and Jack, began to talk with their mouths full. Mrs. Bagthorpe believed that meals should be civilized occasions with a brisk and original interchange of views and ideas, but as none of the younger Bagthorpes were prepared to talk at the cost of stuffing themselves, they invariably did both at the same time.

"I beathja teleths," came a crumb-choked voice by Jack's elbow.

"Told you," said Jack to Uncle Parker.

"What was that, Rosie?" inquired Mrs. Bagthorpe. "You left what in the bath?"

"I beat Jack doing ten lengths." This time Rosie's voice was shamingly distinct and, what was worse, fell into a rare lull in the general din.

"Did you *really*?" exclaimed Mrs. Bagthorpe, and "Pooh!" said Uncle Parker simultaneously with such force that morsels of crust flew across the table at his wife.

Conversation ceased abruptly.

"Did you say something, Russell?" asked Mrs. Bagthorpe.

"I said 'Pooh!'"

"That's what he said before when I told him," squeaked Rosie indignantly. "And it's good — it is! Jack's three years older than me and I beat him and it *is* good!"

"Of course it is, darling," agreed her mother. "And I'm terribly proud of you. Bad luck, Jack."

---

[3]**Babel** (bā′bəl): a confusion of sounds and voices.

"Bad luck Jack my foot, leg and elbow," said Uncle Parker. Everyone stared at him except Grandpa who was being S.D.[4] and evidently did not realize what he was about to miss.

"I'll elaborate," said Uncle Parker. "In my opinion young Jack here, while being a perfectly good chap and worth ten of most here present, swims with the approximate grace and agility of an elephant."

No one contradicted him.

"The fact, therefore," he continued, "that young Rosie here, while also being perfectly acceptable in many ways though some might say too clever by half, the fact that she has beaten Jack doing ten lengths seems to me to be an event totally devoid of interest. It seems, in fact, to be a non-event of the first order."

"I am three years younger," piped Rosie.

Uncle Parker turned to her.

"Kindly do not tell me that again," he told her. "I have been given that information at least three times in the last hour and am by now in perfect possession of it."

"No, Uncle Parker," said Rosie meekly. "I mean, yes."

"Crikey, Uncle P.," said William, "you are in a lather. Anyone'd think Rosie'd beaten *you*."

"I don't doubt that she could," returned Uncle Parker calmly. "I am a notoriously bad swimmer, and I dislike getting wet unnecessarily. The only good reason for swimming, so far as I can see, is to escape drowning."

"The thing I best remember about that jewel of a cat," said Grandma reminiscently, "was his extraordinary sweetness of nature. He hadn't a streak of malice in him."

---

[4]**S.D.:** Uncle Parker's abbreviation for Selectively Deaf, "hearing only what one wants to hear."

It was, after all, Grandma's Birthday Party, and she probably felt she was losing her grip on it.

"That cat," said Mr. Bagthorpe, caught off guard and swallowing the bait, "was the most cross-grained evil-eyed thing that ever went on four legs. If I had a pound note for every time that animal bit me, I should be a rich man, now."

"How *can* you, Henry!" cried Grandma, delighted that things were warming up.

"I'd be Croesus," said Mr. Bagthorpe relentlessly. "Midas. Paul Getty.[5] That cat bit people like he was being paid for it in kippers."[6]

"There he would lie, hour upon hour, with his great golden head nestled in my lap," crooned Grandma, getting into her stride, "and I would feel the sweetness flowing out of him. When I lost Thomas, something irreplaceable went out of my life."

"Bilge, Mother," said Mr. Bagthorpe. "That cat was nothing short of diabolical. He was a legend. He was feared and hated for miles around. In fact I clearly remember that the first dawnings of respect I ever felt for Russell here began on the day he ran the blasted animal over."

"Language, dear," murmured Mrs. Bagthorpe automatically.

"Not on purpose, of course," said Uncle Parker.

"Of course not on purpose!" snapped Mr. Bagthorpe. "The way you drive, you couldn't hit a brick wall, let alone a cat."

"It just wasn't very nippy on its toes, you see," said Uncle Parker apologetically to Grandma.

"It nipped me on *my* toes," said William. "Bags of times."

The rest turned unsmilingly toward him.

"All right," he said. "So it wasn't all that funny. But what about this 'Pooh!' business of Uncle P.'s? Let's get back to that. Unless you want to hear what Anonymous from Grimsby[7] told me."

---

[5]**Croesus** (krē′səs); **Midas** (mī′dəs); **Paul Getty:** men famous for their wealth.

[6]**kippers:** small dried and salted fish (herring).

[7]**Anonymous from Grimsby:** a radio ham whom William contacts regularly and who refuses to give his name.

"I don't think you'd better," said Jack. "It'd be breaking the veil of secrecy."

He enjoyed making this remark, but his pleasure was short-lived.

"I wish you'd learn to use words accurately," said Mr. Bagthorpe testily. (He wrote scripts for television and now and again got obsessed about words, which in his darker moments he believed would eventually become extinct, probably in his own lifetime.) "You can't break a veil. A veil, by its very nature, is of a fine-spun, almost transparent texture, and while it may be *rent*, or even —"

"For crying out *loud*," said Uncle Parker.

"Oh dearest," murmured his wife, "must you . . . ?"

This was the first time Aunt Celia had spoken. She had not even noticed when Uncle Parker had sprayed crumbs at her. The reason for this was that she was gazing at a large piece of bark by her plate. No one had remarked on this because Aunt Celia often brought pieces of bark, ivy or stone (and even, on one memorable occasion, a live snail) to table to gaze on as she ate, even at other people's parties. She did this because she said it inspired her. It was partly to do with her pot-throwing, she said, and partly her poetry. There was no argument about this since her poetry and pottery alike were not much understood by the other Bagthorpes. They respected it without knowing what on earth it was all about. Also, Aunt Celia was very beautiful — like a naiad,[8] Uncle Parker would fondly tell people — and looked even more so when she was being wistful and faraway. In the hurly-burly[9] of Bagthorpe mealtimes she was looked upon more as an ornament than a participant.

She had, however, now spoken, and the Bagthorpes were sufficiently surprised by this to fall silent again.

"Must I what, dearest?" asked Uncle Parker, leaning forward.

"I was just on the verge . . . I thought . . . I was almost . . ."

Her voice trailed off. When Aunt Celia did speak it was usually like this, in a kind of shorthand. She started sentences and left you to

---

[8]**naiad (nā′əd):** a type of Greek spirit believed to live in springs, brooks, and fountains.
[9]**hurly-burly:** noisy confusion; commotion.

guess the ends — if, of course, you thought it worth your while. By and large, the Bagthorpes did not. Uncle Parker, however, did.

"Just on the verge of . . . ?" he prompted delicately.

"What about my portrait?" demanded Rosie loudly. Having had her swimming feat passed over as a mere nothing, she had no intention of letting her Birthday Portrait go the same way. It was set on an easel just by Grandma herself and no one had commented on it because in the first place they were currently more interested in food, and in the second because it looked unfinished.

"Where's her mouth?" demanded Tess.

"And her nose?" asked Jack.

"Not to mention her eyes," added William. "*Might* come out right, Rosie, but doesn't look like one of your best. You've got her ears wrong. You've got 'em too flat. Look — you look — they stick out a lot more than you've got them."

The entire table turned its eyes on Grandma's ears. Grandma looked frostily back at them.

"My ears," she stated, "are one of my best features. This was one of Alfred's favourite contentions during our courtship. 'I could love you for your ears alone,' he would say, and, 'Grace, your ears are like petals, veritable petals.' Isn't that so?"

All eyes now turned toward Grandpa who was stolidly making his way through what was probably his tenth stuffed egg. In his rare communicative moments he would sometimes confide that one of the few pleasures left to him in life was stuffed eggs — that and skewering wasps he would say — and the latter was unfortunately seasonal. (A relative of Grandpa's had once died of a wasp sting and he was convinced that this would be the way he would go too, unless it were under the wheels of Uncle Parker's car.)

"Alfred!"

Grandma leaned forward and jabbed at his arm, determined that he should give testimony. He dropped his egg and blinked blankly at her.

"Eh? Eh? Happy Birthday, my dear."

"S.D.," murmured Uncle Parker to Jack. "See what I mean?"

"I was saying about my *ears*!" Grandma pointed to her own with either hand simultaneously, thereby taking on a distinctly lunatic look.

"Ah — my ears!" Grandpa sounded relieved. He picked up his egg and started in on it again. "Aid's playing up a bit. One of those days. I don't reckon much to these aids. It's the weather, you know. They're affected by the weather."

"*My* ears!" Grandma positively shrieked. Grandpa did not turn a hair. He did not even seem to know she had spoken. He simply went on polishing off his stuffed egg. He had flecks of yolk in his beard, Jack noticed.

"The candles!" cried Mrs. Bagthorpe with tremendous gaiety. She rose and swept theatrically towards the head of the table where Grandma sat fuming behind her porcupine of a cake.

"I hope you're satisfied!" she hissed at Mr. Bagthorpe as she passed behind him.

He turned to Uncle Parker for support.

"I never said a word about her ears," he protested. "I may have said one or two rather strong things about that blood-crazed animal of —"

"Ssssh!" Mrs. Bagthorpe had just struck her first match and her hiss blew it out. She struck another.

"The older you get," observed Grandma dismally, "the more you are trodden down. Life is nothing but a process of being trodden down from the cradle to the grave."

"Note the change of tactics," said Uncle Parker to Jack *sotto voce*.[10] "She's not half bad, I'll say that."

Mrs. Bagthorpe was now lighting candles with practised rapidity and had signalled Tess to start on the other side of the cake. Grandma kept up a muttered monologue as the conflagration spread before her. Jack could not catch all of it but it seemed mostly to be about graves, and ingratitude.

"The crackers!"[11] exclaimed Mr. Bagthorpe suddenly. He was evidently remorseful and felt bound to do his own share of drum-

---

[10]**sotto voce:** softly, so as not to be overheard.

[11]**crackers:** party favors that crack loudly when opened and contain paper hats, toys, and candy.

ming up a festive air. "By jove — can't have the cake cut without hats on!"

"Where *are* the crackers?" asked William.

They looked about the littered table.

"I put them out — I did! There was one on every side plate!" Tess was frantically darting her hands among the candles as she spoke. "And Daisy helped me."

There was a real silence now.

"Good God," said Uncle Parker at last. He had gone quite white. "Daisy."

"She's not here," said Jack unnecessarily.

"Daisy, Daisy, where — oh where —" moaned Aunt Celia wildly. She pushed away her piece of bark and stood swaying like a reed.

"I clean forgot. Oh my God. I'll find her — I will!"

"But what — where — the lake . . ." moaned Aunt Celia.

At Grandma's end of the table concern for Daisy was not half so strong as concern for the crackers.

"She was *here*, I tell you, putting out crackers." Tess's face was lit now from below, the cake was sputtering and ablaze.

"We'll have to blow the candles — we'll have to sing — we can't wait!" shrieked Mrs. Bagthorpe.

"Look — here's one!" Mr. Bagthorpe snatched a cracker from under a crumpled napkin. "Quick — Jack — you pull it with me, and then there'll be a hat for Grandma."

Jack reached over and they pulled hard. Crack!

What happened next was so confusing that even when you put together the different accounts of everyone there present, nothing like a clear picture ever emerged. The Fire Brigade, when they arrived, could certainly make neither head nor tail of it and had never before attended a fire like it.

In the Bagthorpe family, the incident became known, in course of time, as "The Day Zero Piddled While Home Burned." (No one actually saw this, but he sometimes did when he got nervous, and it rhymed so well with "fiddled" that it was passed as Poetic Licence.)

Only a handful of facts — as opposed to impressions, which were legion — emerged. These were as follows:

Fact the First

Daisy, aged four, had been sitting underneath the table the whole time the party was going on.

Fact the Second

What she had been doing under the table was opening all the crackers and taking out whatever was inside. (After the fire quite a lot of melted plastic was found mixed in with the carpet.)

Fact the Third

What was also under the table (mistaken by Daisy for a second box of crackers) was a large box of fireworks which were a surprise present to Grandma from Uncle Parker. He said afterwards he had given them in the hope they would liven things up.

Fact the Fourth

Daisy was in the company of a mongrel dog called Zero who belonged to the Bagthorpes in general and Jack in particular. He had just appeared one day in the garden, and stayed. The Bagthorpes had advertised him in the local paper, but nobody seemed to have recognized the description, or if they had,

had not come forward. Mr. Bagthorpe dissociated himself from Zero and would often pretend he had never set eyes on him.

"There's a dog out there on the landing," he would say. "A great pudding-footed thing covered in fur. See what it wants."

It was Mr. Bagthorpe who had given Zero his name.

"If there was anything less than nothing," he had said, "that hound would be it. But there isn't, so we'll have to settle for Zero."

The family computers, William and Rosie, had pointed out that mathematically speaking there was a whole lot to choose from that was less than zero, but Mr. Bagthorpe had dismissed this as idle speculation.

"You show me something less than nothing, and I'll believe you," he had told them.

Mr. Bagthorpe could be very categorical, and was especially so on subjects about which he knew practically nothing, like mathematics. Anyway, Zero was called that, and Jack sometimes used to wonder if it had affected him, and given him an inferiority complex, because sometimes Zero seemed to drag his feet about rather, and his ears looked droopier than when they had first had him. Jack would spend hours poring over old snapshots of Zero, comparing ears. When they were alone together Jack would praise Zero up and tell him how wonderful and intelligent he was, to try and counteract this. Also, when in public Jack would call him "Nero" so as to give him a bit of dignity in the eyes of others, and as Zero hardly ever came when he was called anyway, it didn't make much difference.

So the fact was that Zero was under the table with Daisy, who had probably given him some food to keep him quiet. When she was cross-examined afterwards Daisy said she had taken him under the table with her because she had thought it would be lonely under there by herself. Mr. Bagthorpe flatly refused to believe this, and said that Daisy must have plotted the whole thing because if Zero hadn't been there with her none of the things that did happen would have happened.

He and Uncle Parker used to have rows about this for weeks afterwards. Uncle Parker would say that while he admitted that Daisy was a genius (she had to be, with a reading age of 7.4 and the way she was always writing her thoughts on walls, and what with having Aunt Celia for a mother) she was too young to have plotted anything as complicated as that. He would also point out that the whole thing had hinged not so much on Zero being under the table as on the moment when a certain cracker was pulled, Mr. Bagthorpe being the person who had made this suggestion and connived at its execution. Mr. Bagthorpe would retaliate by saying that the coincidence of Uncle Parker's having bought a large box of fireworks, and of Uncle Parker's daughter being under the table with them, might strike some people as rather more than coincidence. He would usually end up advising Uncle Parker to take himself and Daisy off to a psychiatrist.

5

Fact the Fifth

When Jack and Mr. Bagthorpe pulled the single available cracker, Zero, who was probably already nervous at being trapped so long under a table surrounded by so many feet and legs, had blown his mind. He had sprung forward, got both sets of paws wound in the tablecloth and pulled the whole lot after him, including the cake.

At the actual moment this happened, of course, no one had any inkling that Zero had been under the table, and the sight of the tablecloth leaping forwards and rolling about on the floor had almost unhinged some of them, notably Grandma, Mrs. Bagthorpe, and Aunt Celia. The latter certainly always referred to it afterwards as a "manifestation," and would refer to how Daisy had been "delivered." (This also helped make Daisy seem less of a culprit, because it made her seem more a victim, and it was difficult to see her in both roles at once.)

Grandma herself, with it being her birthday and her cake, had taken the whole thing personally and had thought she was being struck by a thunderbolt. She had miraculously escaped injury altogether, but Rosie's Birthday Portrait had been one of the first things to go up in flames and always afterwards Grandma saw this as what she called a "Sign." A Sign of what she didn't specify, but she always said it very darkly, and when she was feeling low. Sometimes the others, to cheer her up when she got brooding about it, would say that if it were a "Sign" it was clearly a Sign that Rosie's Birthday Portrait had not been worth a light — so to speak.

Grandpa had not of course heard the whole lot of cracks and bangs as all the crackers Daisy had dismantled started going off, but had not failed to note that the last remaining stuffed egg had been suddenly snatched from under his very nose. He had risen hastily to grab after it, knocked over his own chair, tripped, and fallen over Grandma and lost his hearing aid.

When the firemen came they were very helpful and said they would keep an eye open for it, but what with the whole room by then ablaze and the curtains just beginning to catch fire, they didn't really have time. They were very good firemen but they did seem nervous about bangers still going off and sudden flares of blue or green light. They definitely seemed jumpy. Afterwards, when they were having some beer with the Bagthorpes to moisten their dried-out mouths, they apologized for this. They said that the Bagthorpe fire was not really a run of the mill job or something for which they had been properly prepared during their training.

They stayed on quite a while after the fire was out. They sat round in the kitchen and told the Bagthorpes a lot of interesting things about arson and so on, and before they left Rosie got all their autographs. They seemed quite flattered by this. Rosie told them the autographs were more of a gamble than anything, just in case one of them ever died rescuing someone from a burning building, and became a national hero and got a post mortem award on the television. Soon after this the firemen left.

When they had gone, Mrs. Fosdyke (who came in daily to do for the Bagthorpes, but refused to sleep in) said she thought they had all looked too young and inexperienced to be proper firemen. She did not believe they had been a proper Fire Brigade at all, and said that her carpet and her furniture would not now be in the state they were in if a proper Brigade had been sent in time. People were too easily deceived by uniforms, she said. (Mrs. Fosdyke had missed the actual moment when the tablecloth went up in the air and was naturally bitter about this.)

Nobody did anything about cleaning up after the fire that night. They all sat round and talked about it till quite late. At around ten o'clock Mr. Bagthorpe went out to close his greenhouse for the night and fell over Zero, who had not been seen since the Party. Jack had even feared him lost, and had had a quick look among the debris for signs of bones, though he was not certain what exactly a burned bone would look like.

"That infernal hound's back," Mr. Bagthorpe announced and Zero crept in behind him. He was still shaking. Jack stood up.

"I'm going to bed," he said. Zero always slept in his room and he looked as if he needed a rest.

"Nobody's sung Happy Birthday to me yet," Grandma said. "My birthday's nearly over. I shan't be having many more. I suppose it doesn't really matter. Nothing really matters."

"Oh darling, of *course* it matters. We'll all sing it now, this very moment, won't we, everyone?" cried Mrs. Bagthorpe. "But what a shame about the candles."

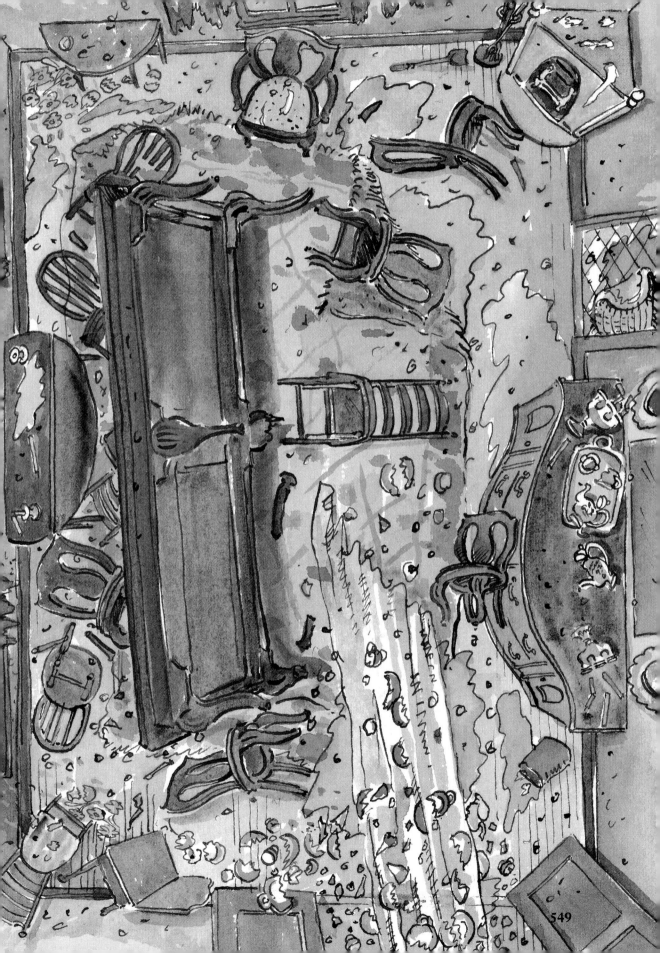

549

Responding to
Ordinary Jack

Thinking and Discussing

How does the way Grandma describes herself and her cat Thomas differ from others' descriptions of them? How does this contradiction contribute to a humorous situation?

How do the characters' unusual personalities add to the humor of the story? Give examples of the characters' unusual personalities, and tell why they are funny.

What is the exciting and important event that happens toward the end of the story? How does the author reveal what has happened? In what way does the retelling add to the humor?

Choosing a Creative Response

Picturing the Scene Discuss the climax of the story with your classmates. What actually happens when the dining room table goes up in flames and fireworks? Where are the family members? What does the scene look like?

Imagine you are a member of the Fire Brigade. Write a report stating the facts as you understand them. You could also have one or more groups of students pose together in a living picture, or still picture, portraying the family members at the moment when the fireworks explode. Participants should try to express the characters portrayed in a humorous manner through dramatic poses and facial expressions.

Creating Your Own Activity Plan and complete your own activity in response to *Ordinary Jack*.

THE VELCROS AT HOME

Roz Chast is famous for her hilarious cartoons, which often appear in *The New Yorker* magazine. Chast has also published three books, collections of her cartoons and "cartoon short stories."

THE
PIANO

by Aníbal Monteiro Machado
illustrated by Deborah Blackwell

"Rosália!" shouted João de Oliveira to his wife, who was upstairs. "I told the guy to get out. What a nerve! He laughed at it. He said it wasn't worth even five hundred cruzeiros."

"It's an old trick," she replied. "He wants to get it for nothing and then sell it to somebody else. That's how these fellows get rich."

But Rosália and Sara looked somewhat alarmed as they came downstairs. The family approached the old piano respectfully, as if to console it after the insult.

"We'll get a good price for it, you'll see," asserted Oliveira, gazing at the piano with a mixture of affection and apprehension. "They don't make them like this any more."

"Put an ad in the paper," said Rosália, "and they'll come flocking. The house will be like *this* with people." She joined the tips of the fingers of her right hand in customary token of an immense crowd. "It's a pity to have to give it up."

"Ah, it's a love of a piano!" said João. "Just looking at it you think you hear music." He caressed its oaken case.

"Well, come on, João. Let's put the ad in."

It had to be sold so that the little parlor could be made into a bedroom for Sara and her intended, a lieutenant in the artillery. Besides, the price would pay for her trousseau.[1]

Three mornings later, the piano was adorned with flowers for the sacrifice, and the house was ready to receive prospective buyers.

The first to arrive were a lady and her daughter. The girl opened the piano and played a few chords.

"It's no good at all, Mama."

The lady stood up, looked at it, and noticed that the ivory was missing from some of the keys. She took her daughter by the hand and walked out, muttering as she went: "Think of coming all this distance to look at a piece of junk."

The Oliveira family had no time to feel resentment, for three new candidates appeared, all at the same time: an elderly lady who smelled

---

[1]**trousseau (troo′sō):** the possessions a bride assembles for her marriage.

like a rich widow, a young girl wearing glasses and carrying a music portfolio, and a redheaded man in a worn, wrinkled suit.

"I was here ahead of you," said the young girl to the old lady. "It doesn't really matter. I only came because my mother wanted me to. There must be plenty of others for sale. But I'd just like to say that I was ringing the doorbell while you were still getting off the bus. We came in together but I got here first."

This rivalry for priority pleased the Oliveiras. They thought it wise, however, to break up the argument, so they smiled at everyone and offered them all coffee. The young girl went over to the piano, while the redheaded man stood at a distance and evaluated it with a cool eye. At this moment a lady entered holding a schoolgirl by the hand. They sat down distrustfully.

Suddenly the young girl began to play, and the whole room hung on the notes that she extracted from the keyboard. Off-pitch, metallic, horrible notes. The Oliveiras anxiously studied the faces of their visitors.

The redheaded man remained utterly impassive. The others glanced at one another as if seeking a common understanding. The newly arrived lady made a wry face. The perfumed old lady seemed more tolerant and looked indulgently at the old piano case.

It was a jury trial and the piano was the accused. The young girl continued to play, as if she were wringing a confession from it. The timbre[2] suggested that of a decrepit, cracked-voiced soprano with stomach trouble. Some of the notes did not play at all. Doli joined in with her barking, a dog's well-considered verdict. A smile passed around the room. No one was laughing, however. The girl seemed to be playing now out of pure malice, hammering at the dead keys and emphasizing the cacophony.[3] It was a dreadful situation.

"There's something you ought to know about this piano," explained João de Oliveira. "It's very sensitive to the weather, it changes a great deal with variations in temperature."

The young girl stopped abruptly. She rose, put on some lipstick, and picked up her music portfolio.

"I don't know how you had the nerve to advertise this horror," she said, speaking to João but looking disdainfully at Rosália as if she had been the horror.

And she left.

João said nothing for a moment. After all, the insult had been directed at the old piano, not at him. Nevertheless, he felt constrained to declare that it was a genuine antique.

"They don't make them like this any more," he said emphatically. "They just don't make them."

There was a long silence. The status of the piano had reached its nadir.[4] Finally the redheaded man spoke: "What are you asking for it?"

In view of what had happened, João de Oliveira lowered substantially the price he had had in mind.

"Five contos," he said timidly.

---

[2]**timbre** (tĭm′bər): the distinctive tone, or voice, of a musical instrument.
[3]**cacophony** (kə kŏf′ə nē): jarring, unharmonious sound.
[4]**nadir** (nā′dər): the lowest point.

He looked at everyone to see the effect. There was a silent response. Oliveira felt cold. Was the price monstrously high? Only the old lady showed any delicacy at all: she said she would think it over. But, through her veil of mercy, João perceived her decision.

As they all were leaving, a man about to enter stepped out of their way.

"Did you come about the piano?" asked one of them. "Well, you'll . . ."

But Oliveira interrupted.

"Come in," he said cheerfully. "It's right here. Lots of people have been looking at it."

The man was middle-aged, with a shock of grayish hair. He lifted the lid of the piano and examined the instrument at length. "Probably a music teacher," thought João.

The man did not ask the price. "Thank you," he said and left.

The house was empty again. Sara returned to her room. Rosália and João looked at each other in disappointment.

"Nobody understands its value," commented João sadly. "If I can't get a decent price for it, I'd rather not sell it at all."

"But what about Sara's trousseau?" said Rosália.

"I'll borrow the money."

"You'd never be able to pay it back out of your salary."

"We'll postpone the marriage."

"They love each other, João. They'll want to get married no matter what, trousseau or no trousseau."

At this moment, Sara could be heard shouting from her room that she could not possibly get married without two new slips and so forth.

"The thing is," Rosália went on, "this house is about the size of a matchbox. Where can we put the newlyweds? We'll have to give up the piano to make room for them. Nobody nowadays has enough room."

Sara's voice was heard again: "No, don't sell the piano. It's so pretty . . ."

"It's also so silent," interrupted her mother. "You never play it any more. All you ever play is the victrola."

She went to her daughter's room to speak further with her. Strange that Sara should talk like that. Rosália put the dilemma flatly: "A husband or a piano. Choose."

"Oh, a husband!" replied Sara with conviction. "Of course."

She hugged her pillow.

"So . . . ?"

"You're always against it, Rosália," shouted João de Oliveira.

"Against what?"

"Our piano."

"Oh, João, how can you say such a thing!"

The next day, as soon as he got back from work, João de Oliveira asked about the piano.

"Did any people answer the ad, Rosália?"

Yes, there had been several telephone calls for information about the piano, and an old man had come and looked at it. Also, the redheaded man had come again.

"Did any of them say anything about buying it?" asked João.

"No. But the two men who came to the house looked at it a long time."

"They did? Did they look at it with interest? With admiration?"

"It's hard to say."

"Yes, they admired it," said Sara. "Especially the old man. He almost ate it with his eyes."

João de Oliveira was touched. It was no longer a matter of price. He just wanted his piano to be treated with consideration and respect, that's all. Maybe it wasn't worth a lot of money but it certainly deserved some courteous attention. He was sorry he hadn't been there, but what his daughter told him of the old man's respectful attitude consoled him for the contumely[5] of the day before. That man must understand the soul of antique furniture.

---

[5]**contumely** (kŏn'too mə lē): rudeness.

"Did he leave his address, Sara? No? Oh, well . . . he'll probably be back."

He rose from his chair and walked around the old instrument. He smiled at it lovingly.

"My piano," he said softly. He ran his hand over the varnished wood as if he were caressing an animal.

No candidate the next day. Only a voice with a foreign accent asking if it was new. Rosália replied that it wasn't but that they had taken such good care of it that it almost looked like new.

"Tomorrow is Saturday," thought Oliveira. "There's bound to be a lot of people."

There were two, a man and a little girl, and they came in a limousine. The man looked at the modest house of the Oliveira family and considered it useless to go in. Nevertheless, he went to the door and asked the make and age of the piano.

"Thank you. There's no need for me to see it," he replied to João's insistence that he look at it. "I thought it would be a fairly new piano. Good luck . . ."

And he went away.

João was grief-stricken. Ever since he had inherited the piano he had prized it dearly. He had never thought he would have to part with it. Worst of all, no one appreciated it, no one understood its value.

No one, except possibly the fellow who came the next Wednesday. He praised the piano in the most enthusiastic terms, said it was marvelous, and refused to buy. He said that if he paid so low a price for it he would feel he was stealing it, and that João and Rosália were virtually committing a crime in letting this precious thing get out of their hands. Oliveira did not exactly understand.

"Does he mean what he says?" he asked Rosália.

"I think he's just trying to be funny," she replied.

"I don't know. Maybe not."

Rosália was the first to lose hope. Her main concern now, when her husband came home from work, was to alleviate his suffering.

"How many today?"

"Nobody. Two telephone calls. They didn't give their names but they said they'd probably come and look at it."

Her voice was calm, soothing.

"How about the redheaded fellow?"

"I'm sure he'll be back."

For several days no one came or telephoned. João de Oliveira's feelings may be compared to those of a man who sees his friend miss a train: he is sad for his friend's sake and he is happy because he will continue for a time to have the pleasure of his company. João sat down near the piano and enjoyed these last moments with it. He admired its dignity. He confided his thoughts to it. Three generations had played it. How many people it had induced to dream or to dance! All this had passed away, but the piano remained. It was the only piece of furniture that bespoke the presence of his forebears. It was sort of eternal. It and the old oratory[6] upstairs.

---

[6]**oratory** (ôr′ə tôr′ē): a small chapel in the house.

"Sara, come and play that little piece by Chopin. See if you remember it."

"I couldn't Papa. The piano sounds terrible."

"Don't say that," Rosália whispered. "Can't you see how your father feels?"

For days and days no prospective buyer appeared. Nothing but an occasional telephone call from the redheaded man, as if he had been a doctor verifying the progress of a terminal case. The advertisement was withdrawn.

"Well, João, what are we going to do about it?"

"What are we going to do about what, Rosália?"

"The piano!"

"I'm not going to sell it," João shouted. "These leeches don't give a damn about the piano; they just want a bargain. I'd rather give it away to someone who'll take good care of it, who knows what it represents."

He was walking back and forth agitatedly. Suddenly the expression of his face changed.

"Listen, Rosália. Let's phone our relatives in Tijuca."

Rosália understood his purpose and was pleased.

"Hello! Is Messias there? He went out? Oh, is this Cousin Miquita? Look . . . I want to give you our piano as a present . . . Yes, as a present . . . No, it's not a joke . . . Really . . . Right . . . Exactly . . . So it won't go out of the family . . . Fine. Have it picked up here sometime soon . . . You're welcome. I'm glad to do it . . ."

After he had hung up he turned to his wife.

"You know what? She didn't believe me at first. She thought it was All Fools' Day."

Rosália was delighted. João walked over to the old piano as if to confer with it about what he had just done.

"My conscience is clear," he thought. "You will not be rejected. You will stay in the family, with people of the same blood. My children's children will know and respect you; you will play for them. I'm sure you understand and won't be angry with us."

"When will they come for it?" interrupted Rosália, eager to get the room ready for the bridal couple.

The next day Messias telephoned his relatives in Ipanema. Did they really mean to give him a piano? It was too much. He was grateful but they really shouldn't. When his wife told him, he could hardly believe it.

"No, it's true, Messias. You know, our house is about as big as a nutshell. We can't keep the piano here, and João doesn't want it to fall into the hands of strangers. If you people have it, it's almost the same as if it were still with us. Are you going to send for it soon?"

Several days went by. No moving van came. Mr. and Mrs. Oliveira thought the silence of their relatives in Tijuca extremely odd.

"Something's wrong. Telephone them, Rosália."

Cousin Miquita answered. She was embarrassed. The moving men asked a fortune for the job.

"I guess it's the gasoline shortage . . . Wait a few more days. Messias will arrange something. We're delighted about getting the piano. We think of nothing else, Rosália."

This last sentence struck a false note, thought Rosália. After a week, João de Oliveira telephoned again.

"Do you want it or don't you, Messias?"

"João, you can't imagine how terrible we feel about this," came the stammered reply. "You give us a fine present and we can't accept it. They're asking an arm and a leg to move it here. And, anyway, we really have no room for it. We haven't even got enough room for the stuff we have now. We should have thought of this before. Miquita feels awful about it."

"In short, you don't want the piano."

"We want it . . . But we don't . . . we can't . . ."

João de Oliveira hung up. He was beginning to understand.

"You see, Rosália. We can't even give the piano away. We can't even give it away."

"What can you do, João! Everything ends up with nobody wanting it."

After a few minutes of silent despondence, they were aroused by Sara, who interspersed her sobs with words of bitter desperation. Her mother comforted her.

"Don't worry, child. It'll be all right. We'll sell it for whatever we can get."

"I want it out right away, Mama. In a few days I'm to be married and my room isn't even ready yet. None of our things are in here. Only that terrible piano ruining my life, that piano that nobody wants."

"Speak softly, dear. Your father can hear you."

"I want him to hear me," she cried, with another sob. She wiped her eyes.

João de Oliveira slept little that night. He was meditating about life. His thoughts were confused and generally melancholy. They induced in him a fierce rage against both life and the piano. He left the house early and went to a nearby bar, where he talked with several men.

"What is my husband doing in a place like that?" Rosália asked herself. João was never a drinker.

Oliveira came back accompanied by a shabbily dressed man and two others in work clothes. He showed them the piano. They hefted it and said they doubted if they could handle it, just the three of them.

Rosália and Sara looked on in amazement.

"Have you found a buyer?" asked Rosália.

"No, wife. Nobody will buy this piano."

"You're giving it away?"

"No, wife. Nobody wants it even for free."

"Then what are you doing, João? What in the world are you doing?"

João's eyes watered but his face hardened.

"I'm going to throw it in the ocean."

"Oh, no, Papa!" exclaimed Sara. "That's crazy!"

The Oliveiras could not see the ocean from their windows, but they could smell it and hear it, for they were only three blocks from the avenue that ran along the beach.

The men were waiting, talking among themselves.

"What a courageous thing to do, João!" said his wife. "But shouldn't we talk it over first? Is there no other way out? People will think it funny, throwing a piano into the water."

"What else can we do, Rosália? Lots of ships go to the bottom of the ocean. Some of them have pianos on board."

This irrefutable[7] logic silenced his wife. João seemed to take heart.

"Okay, you fellows," he cried. "Up with it! Let's go!"

One of the workers came forward and said humbly, on behalf of his colleagues and himself, that they couldn't do it. They hoped he would excuse them, but it would hurt their conscience to throw something like that in the sea. It almost seemed like a crime.

"Boss, why don't you put an ad in the paper? The piano is in such good condition."

"Yes, I know," replied Oliveira ironically. "You may go."

The workers left. For a moment the shabby man entertained the idea that he might take the piano for himself. He stared at it. He was fascinated by the idea of owning something, and a fine, luxurious thing at that. It was a dream that could become an immediate reality. But where would he take it? He had no house.

Rosália rested her head on her husband's shoulder and fought back the tears.

"Ah, João, what a decision you have made!"

"But if nobody wants it, and if it can't stay here . . ."

"I know, João. But I can't help feeling sad. It's always been with us. Doesn't it seem cruel, after all these years, to throw it in the ocean? Look at it, standing there, knowing nothing about what's going to happen to it. It's been there almost twenty years, in that corner, never doing any harm . . ."

"We must try to avoid sentimentality, Rosália."

She looked at him with admiration.

"All right, João. Do what you must."

---

[7]**irrefutable** (ĭ rĕf′yə tə bəl): not able to be disproved.

Groups of street urchins, ragged but happy, start out from the huts at Pinto and Latolandia where they live and stroll through the wealthy neighborhoods. One can always find them begging nickels for ice cream, gazing in rapture at the posters outside the movie houses, or rolling on the sand in Leblon.

That morning a southwester[8] was whipping the Atlantic into a fury. The piano, needless to say, remained as tranquil as ever. And imposing in the severity of its lines.

Preparations for the departure were under way. João de Oliveira asked his wife and daughter to remove the parts that might possibly be useful. Accordingly, the bronze candlesticks were taken off, then the pedals and metal ornaments, and finally the oak top.

"Ugh!" exclaimed Sara. "It looks so different."

Without mentioning it to his family, João de Oliveira had recruited a bunch of urchins. They were waiting impatiently outside the door. Oliveira now told them to come in, the strongest ones first.

---

[8]**southwester:** a storm from the southwest.

It was twenty after four in the afternoon when the funeral cortege started out. A small crowd on the sidewalk made way for it. The piano moved slowly and irregularly. Some people came up to observe it more closely. Rosália and her daughter contemplated it sadly from the porch, their arms around each other's shoulders. They could not bring themselves to accompany it. The cook was wiping her eyes on her apron.

"Which way?" asked the urchins when the procession reached the corner. They were all trying to hold the piano at the same time, with the result that it almost fell.

"Which way?" they repeated.

"To the sea!" cried João de Oliveira. And with the grand gesture of a naval commander he pointed toward the Atlantic.

"To the sea! To the sea!" echoed the boys in chorus.

They began to understand that the piano was going to be destroyed, and this knowledge excited them. They laughed and talked animatedly among themselves. The hubbub inspired the little dog Doli to leap in the air and bark furiously.

The balconies of the houses were crowded, chiefly with young girls.

"Mother of heaven!" they exclaimed. "What is it?" And, incredulously, "A piano!"

"It came from ninety-nine," cried an urchin, running from house to house to inform the families.

"Why, that's where Sara lives."

An acquaintance ran out to learn the facts from Oliveira himself.

"What's wrong, João?"

"Nothing's wrong. I know what I'm doing. Just everybody keep out of the way."

"But why don't you sell it?"

"I'll sell it, all right. I'll sell it to the Atlantic Ocean. See it there? The ocean . . ."

With the air of a somewhat flustered executioner, he resumed his command.

"More to the left, fellows . . . Careful, don't let it drop . . . Just the big boys now, everybody else let go."

From time to time one of the boys would put his arm inside the piano and run his hand along the strings. The sound was a sort of death rattle.

A lady on a balcony shouted at João, "Would you sell it?"

"No, madam, it's not for sale. I'll give it away. You want it?"

The lady reddened, felt offended, and went into her house. João made his offer more general.

"Anyone around here want a piano?"

At number forty-three a family of Polish refugees accepted. They were astounded, but they accepted.

"Then it's yours," shouted João de Oliveira.

The Polish family came down and stood around the piano.

"We'll take it, all right . . . But . . . our house is very small. Give us a couple of days to get ready for it."

"Now or never!" replied Oliveira. "Here it is, right outside your house. You don't want it? Okay, fellows, let's go."

The piano moved closer and closer to the sea. It swayed like a dead cockroach carried by ants.

João de Oliveira distinguished only a few of the exclamations coming from the doors, windows, and balconies of the houses.

"This is the craziest thing I ever heard of," someone shouted from a balcony.

"Crazy?" replied João de Oliveira, looking up at the speaker. "Okay then you take it. Take it . . ."

Farther on, the scene was repeated. Everyone thought it was a crazy thing to do and everyone wanted the piano; but as soon as the owner offered immediate possession, there was just embarrassed silence. After all, who is prepared to receive a piano at a moment's notice?

João de Oliveira proceeded resolutely, accompanied by a buzz of comments and lamentations.[9] He decided to make no more replies.

---

[9]**lamentations** (lăm′ən tā′shənz): expressions of grief.

A group of motorcycle policemen stopped the procession and surrounded the old piano. João de Oliveira gave a detailed explanation. They asked to see his documents. He went back to the house and got them. He thought the requirement natural enough, for the nation was at war.[10] But he resented having had to give an explanation, for he was acting pursuant to a personal decision for which he was accountable to no one outside the family. He certainly had a right to throw away his own property. This thought reawakened his affection for the instrument. Placing his hand on the piano as if on the forehead of a deceased friend, he felt deeply moved and began to discourse on its life.

"It's an antique, one of the oldest pianos in Brazil."

It had belonged to his grandparents, who had been in the service of the Empire.[11]

"It was a fine piano, you may believe me. Famous musicians played on it. They say that Chopin preferred it over all others. But what does this matter? No one appreciates it any more. Times have changed . . . Sara, my daughter, is getting married. She'll live with us. The house is small. What can I do? No one wants it. This is the only way out."

And he nodded toward the sea.

The boys were growing impatient with the interruptions. They were eager to see the piano sink beneath the waves. Almost as impatient as these improvised movers, were the people who had joined the procession, including delivery men, messenger boys, a few women, and a great many children.

The police examined the interior of the piano but found nothing suspicious. They returned Oliveira's papers and suggested that he hurry so that traffic would not be impeded.

A photographer asked some of the people to form a group and snapped their picture. João de Oliveira was on the left side in a pose

---

[10]**war:** During World War II, from 1942 to 1945, Brazil joined the United States and its allies in defeating the Nazi government of Germany.

[11]**the Empire:** Brazil was an empire from 1822 until 1889, when it became a republic.

expressing sadness. Then he became annoyed with all these interruptions that prolonged the agony of his piano.

Night fell rapidly. A policeman observed that after six o'clock they would not be permitted to go on. They would have to wait till the next day.

The boys dispersed. They were to be paid later, at Oliveira's house. People were amazed that evening at the number of young boys strolling around with small, ivory-plated pieces of wood in their hands.

The piano remained there on the street where they had left it, keeled over against the curb. A ridiculous position. Young men and women on their evening promenade soon surrounded it and made comments.

When he got home, João de Oliveira found some of Sara's girl friends there, eagerly questioning her about the piano.

It was still dark when João and his wife awoke to the loud sound of rain. Wind, rain, and the roar of the surf. They lit the light and looked at each other.

"I was thinking about the piano, Rosália."

"So was I, João. Poor thing! Out in the rain there . . . and it's so cold!"

"The water must be getting into the works and ruining everything . . . the felt, the strings. It's terrible, isn't it, Rosália?"

"We did an ungrateful thing, João."

"I don't even like to think about it, Rosália."

João de Oliveira looked out the window. Flashes of lightning illuminated the trees, revealing branches swaying wildly in the wind. João went back to bed and slept fitfully. He awoke again and told his wife that he had been listening to the piano.

"I heard everything that was ever played on it. Many different hands. My grandmother's hands, my mother's, yours, my aunt's, Sara's. More than twenty hands, more than a hundred white fingers were pressing the keys. I never heard such pretty music. It was sublime, Rosália. The dead hands sometimes played better than the live ones. Lots of young girls from earlier generations were standing around the piano, listening. Couples who later got married were sitting nearby, holding hands. I don't know why, but after a while they all looked at me — with contempt. Suddenly the hands left the piano, but it kept on playing. The Funeral March. Then the piano shut by itself . . . There was a torrent of water. The piano let itself get swept along . . . toward the ocean. I shouted to it but it wouldn't listen to me. It seemed to be offended, Rosália, and it just kept on going . . . I stood there in the street, all alone. I began to cry . . ."

João de Oliveira was breathing hard. The mysterious concert had left him in a state of emotion. He felt remorseful.

The rain stopped. As soon as it was light, João went out to round up the boys. All he wanted now was to get the thing over with as quickly as possible.

The wind was still strong, and the ocean growled as if it were digesting the storm of the night before. The boys came, but in smaller numbers than before. Several grown men were among them. João de Oliveira, in a hoarse voice, assumed command again.

On the beach the piano moved more slowly. Finally the long tongues of the waves began to lick it.

Some families stood on the sidewalk, watching the spectacle. Oliveira's crew carried and pushed the piano far enough for the surf to take charge and drag it out to sea. Two enormous waves broke over it without effect. The third made it tremble. The fourth carried it away forever.

João de Oliveira stood there, knee deep in water, with his mouth open. The sea seemed enormously silent. No one could tell that he was crying, for the tears on his cheeks were indistinguishable from the drops of spray.

Far off, he saw Sara with her head resting on the lieutenant's shoulder. Doli was with her, her snout expressing inquiry and incipient dismay; she had always slept next to the piano. João was glad that Rosália had not come.

Many people appeared later on the beach, asking one another what had happened. It seemed at first that an entire Polish family had drowned. Subsequently, it was learned that only one person had drowned. Some said it was a child. Others insisted that it was a lady who had had an unhappy love affair. Only later was it generally known that the person who had drowned was a piano.

People posted themselves at their windows to watch João de Oliveira come back from the beach.

"That's the man!" someone announced.

Oliveira walked slowly, staring at the ground. Everyone felt respect for him.

"It's gone, Rosália," he said as he entered the house. "It has passed the point of no return."

"Before we talk about it, João, go change your clothes."

"Our piano will never come back, Rosália."

"Of course it won't come back. That's why you threw it in the sea."

"Who knows," said Sara. "Maybe it'll be washed up on a beach somewhere."

"Let's not think about it any more. It's over. It's finished. Sara, it's time you did your room."

There was a pause, after which João resumed his lamentation.

"I saw the waves swallow it."

"Enough, my husband. Enough!"

"It came back to the surface twice."

"It's all over! Let's not think about it any more."

"I didn't mention it to anybody so they wouldn't think I went crazy . . . though they're beginning to think I'm crazy anyway . . . The fact is, I'm probably the most rational man in the whole neighborhood . . . But a little while ago I clearly heard the piano play the Funeral March."

"That was in your dream last night," Rosália reminded him.

"No, it was there by the sea, in broad daylight. Didn't you hear it, Sara? Right afterward, it was covered all with foam, and the music stopped."

He nodded his head, expressing hopelessness before the inevitable. He was talking as if to himself.

"It must be far away by now. Under the water, moving along past strange sights. The wrecks of ships. Submarines. Fishes. Until yesterday,

it had never left this room . . . Years from now it will be washed up on some island in an ocean on the other side of the world. And when Sara, Rosália, and I are dead, it will still remember the music it made in this house."

He left the room. Sara, alone, looked at the place where the piano had been. Now she felt a little guilty.

Her thoughts were interrupted by a knock at the door. A fellow came in with an official notice. Some unidentified person had told the police that a secret radio was hidden in the piano and that her father had wanted to get rid of it. He was to appear at the district police station and answer questions. Well, it was the sort of thing you had to expect in wartime. Nothing anyone could do about it.

Oliveira spent the rest of the day at the police station. He came home late.

"What a life, Rosália!" he said as he fell dejected into the armchair. "What a life! We can't even throw away things that belong to us."

João felt oppressed, stifled. He meditated awhile and then spoke again.

"Have you ever noticed, Rosália, how people hate to get rid of old things? How they cling to them?"

"Not only old things," replied Rosália. "Old ideas too."

Doli was sniffing the area where the piano had been. She wailed a little and fell asleep.

The doorbell rang. A man entered and drew some papers from a briefcase. He said he came from the Port Captain's office.

"Are you João de Oliveira?"

"Yes, I am João de Oliveira."

"What did you cast in the sea this morning?"

Oliveira was stupefied.

"Out here we're not in that port, my dear sir. It's ocean."

"Are you going to give me a vocabulary lesson, Mr. Oliveira?"

The man repeated his previous question and explained that regulations now forbade the placing of objects in or on the sea without a license.

"Have you a license?"

Oliveira humbly asked whether what he had done was in any way offensive or bad.

"That's not the question. Don't you know that we're at war? That our coasts must be protected? That the Nazis are always watching for an opportunity?"

"But it was just a piano, sir."

"It's still a violation. Anyway, was it really a piano? Are you absolutely sure?"

"I think I am," João blurted, looking at his daughter and his wife. "Wasn't it a piano, Rosália? Wasn't it, Sara?"

"Where's your head, João?" exclaimed Rosália. "You know it was a piano."

Her husband's doubt surprised everyone. He seemed to be musing.

"I thought a person could throw anything in the ocean that he wanted to."

"No, indeed! That's all we need . . ."

João arose. He looked delirious.

"Suppose I want to throw myself in the sea. Can I?"

"It all depends," replied the man from the Port Captain's office.

"Depends on whom? On me and nobody else! I'm a free man. My life belongs to me."

"Much less than you think," said the man.

Sara broke into the smile with which she always greeted the lieutenant, who had just come in. She ran to kiss him.

"See our room, darling. It looks good now, doesn't it?"

"Yes, real good. Where are you going to put the new one?"

"The new one?"

"Yes. Aren't you going to get another?"

Sara and her mother exchanged glances of amazement.

"I'm crazy for a piano," said Sara's fiancé. "You have no idea how it relaxes me. All day long I have to hear guns shooting. A little soft music in the evening . . ."

Sara had a fit of coughing. João de Oliveira went out the door. He felt suffocated; he needed to breathe.

Who else would come out of the night and make new demands of him? How could he have known that a piano hidden from the world, living in quiet anonymity, was really an object of public concern? Why hadn't he just left it where it was?

It was miles away now, traveling . . . Far away, riding the southern seas . . . And free. More so than he or Sara or Rosália. It was he, João de Oliveira, who now felt abandoned. For himself and for his family. It wasn't their piano any more. It was a creature loose in the world. Full of life and pride, moving boldly through the seven seas. Sounding forth. Embraced by all the waters of the world. Free to go where it wished, to do what it wished.

Beneath the trees in front of the house, the boys were waiting for their second day's pay. They had worked hard. It was so dark that he could scarcely distinguish their shaved heads. In the midst of them he saw a vaguely familiar form. The person opened the garden gate and asked permission to enter.

With some difficulty João recognized the redheaded man, but he was wholly unprepared for what the man was about to say:

"I've come back about the piano. I think I can make you a reasonable offer."

Responding to
THE PIANO

Thinking and Discussing

Why are João's feelings about what he must do with the piano funny and sad at the same time?

In what ways does the author treat the piano as a character? Is the piano the hero in the story? Explain your answer.

Choosing a Creative Response

Continuing the Story With a partner, think about what happens after the end of the story. Write or act out what might happen in one of the following situations.

- At the end of the story, the redheaded man appears at João's garden gate.
- Many years after the story ends, João walks along the seashore and discovers that the piano has washed up on the beach.

Creating Your Own Activity Plan and complete your own activity in response to "The Piano."

Thinking and Writing

A lot of the humor in "The Piano" has to do with João's feelings about getting rid of the piano. Think of something you own that you care about but that other people might not appreciate as much as you do. Describe why you feel the way you do toward the object. Suppose you have to part with that object. Write about how you will get rid of it and how you feel about doing so.

Thinking About Humor

Making It Funny Think about the stories that are funny to you. Do they tend to be alike in some way? If so, how are they similar? Is there a pattern to your sense of humor? Are there some stories that do not appeal to your sense of humor? Why aren't they funny? How would you change them to make them funny? Share your ideas orally with your classmates.

Adapting for Television Of the four humorous stories you have just read, which one would make the best television comedy? Why? What things did the author do to make the story humorous? Which story would be most difficult to adapt for television? Why?

With your classmates, choose a story that could be adapted for television. Decide which incidents you would include in the program. Think of movie or television actors you would choose to play the roles. Why did you select them? You may want to write a scene and try it out with your classmates.

Measuring Laughter Set up an experiment to observe and record responses to humor. Working with a partner or group, collect a few jokes to try out on your classmates. Then tell the jokes to your audience, recording and graphing their response to each joke.

You may even wish to create a laugh meter to measure the response of your audience. The bottom of the scale would indicate no response, and the top of the scale would indicate that the audience howls with laughter. You might use different colors, numbers, or words to divide your scale into segments between "not funny" and "very funny."

Evaluate the information you have collected, and report to your classmates on the results.

How
About a Drawing?

A native of South Africa, **Elivia Savadier** now lives and works in Boston for clients throughout the United States and Great Britain. "I like my cartoons to look very simple," says Elivia, "but it can be a challenging as well as exciting journey to get them to that point!"

Elivia.

AUTHORS

Aníbal Monteiro Machado was born in Brazil in 1895. He trained to be a lawyer and was appointed public prosecutor. He held this position for a very short time; his sympathies seemed to lie so often with the accused person. "I always felt like taking [the person] out for a cup of coffee," he said. Later he taught literature in a high school in Rio de Janeiro, held various public offices, and wrote stories, essays, and two plays. He also wrote a novel, which was published after his death in 1964.

Helen Cresswell was born in Nottinghamshire, England, in 1934. Before her marriage she worked at a variety of jobs, but writing has always been Cresswell's first love. Cresswell has written more than seventy books and five television plays in the past thirty years and has been nominated for England's Carnegie Medal four times. She lives with her family in a two-hundred-year-old farmhouse on a hill at the edge of Robin Hood's Sherwood Forest.

Lensey Namioka was born in Beijing, China, in 1929. She emigrated to America, where she attended Radcliffe College. She eventually received her bachelor's and master's degrees from the University of California. She has taught mathematics at colleges in New York State, and has also worked as a broadcasting monitor for Japan Broadcasting Corporation. She has drawn on her Chinese cultural heritage as well as her husband's Japanese background in writing for young people. Namioka currently lives in Seattle, where she works as a free-lance writer and translator.

Philippa Pearce, well known as an author of children's books, was born in the riverside village of Great Shelford in Cambridgeshire, England. Setting is important in Pearce's stories: "That often comes to me before anything else," she says, so it is not surprising that many of her books, including *The Minnow Leads to Treasure* and Carnegie Award–winning *Tom's Midnight Garden*, should be set in the house, village, and countryside where she was raised. Pearce has also worked as a scriptwriter and producer for the British Broadcasting Corporation (BBC) and as a children's book editor for two publishing firms.

More LAUGHS TO LOOK FOR

Sharkes in the North Woods
by Jane Zaring (Houghton, 1982)
In an amusing spoof, four young people plan a daring escape from the horrible summer camp run by the mean Sharke family.

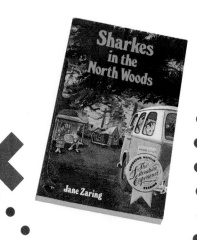

Family Reunion
by Caroline B. Cooney (Bantam, 1989)
This hilarious and sensitive novel tells the story of Shelley, who in one zany summer learns more than she ever expected about herself and family relationships.

Cheaper by the Dozen

by Frank B. Gilbreth, Jr., and Ernestine Gilbreth Carey (Crowell, 1948)

This entertaining family classic about the Gilbreths' escapades is sometimes funny, sometimes touching, and always human. *Belles on Their Toes* is the delightful sequel.

Growing Up Laughing: Humorists Look at American Youth

compiled by Charles Keller (Prentice, 1981)

Collected here are the views on adolescence of such classic humorists as Robert Benchley, Ogden Nash, and James Thurber. Others who present the funny side of growing up include Shel Silverstein and Bill Cosby.

The Mark of Conte

by Sonia Levitin (Atheneum, 1976; Macmillan, 1987)

When the computer at Conte's new school lists him as both Conte Mark and Mark Conte, he decides to try to be two people and finish school in half the time.

Absolute Zero: Being the Second Part of the Bagthorpe Saga

by Helen Cresswell (Macmillan, 1978)

This is the second installment in Cresswell's madcap series of irreverent novels. Read about how the Bagthorpes enter all sorts of prize contests.

NOVEL

by Lloyd Alexander

illustrated by Kim Nelson

WESTMARK

584

Part One
The Printer's Devil

Chapter One

heo, by occupation, was a devil. That is, he worked as apprentice and general servant to Anton, the printer. Before that, he was lucky enough to be an orphan, for the town fathers of Dorning prided themselves in looking after their needy. So, instead of sending him away to a King's Charity House, where he would be made miserable, they arranged the same for him locally. He was farmed out first to a cooper, then to a saddler, and in both cases did badly. Accidentally, he had learned to read, which in some opinion spoiled him for anything sensible. Anton finally agreed to take in the boy and teach him his trade.

Theo proved good at this work, and he and his master dealt very well with each other. Anton never whipped his devil, and Theo never gave him cause. Once thickset and muscular, Anton had begun sagging a little around the middle. His passion was his press, and he was forever fussing with it. Since he kept all the smudges for himself and his clothing, his pages came out spotless. He was, in fact, a fine craftsman. Scholars from the university at Freyborg had brought him treatises to print. The business dried up after the king appointed Cabbarus chief minister. By order of Cabbarus, official approval was required for every publication; even a text on botany was eyed with suspicion. Anton was reduced to turning out visiting cards for the gentry and billheads for the trades-people. He was no worse off than other printers in Westmark. A number had been arrested, and some of them hanged. So, to that extent, he was considerably better off.

As for Theo, he loved virtue, despised injustice, and was always slightly hungry. Apart from that, he was reasonably happy.

One day in early spring, Anton went out on business, leaving his devil in charge. Theo cleaned and sorted letter blocks, finished his other chores by the end of the afternoon, and was ready to close shop when a dwarf came strutting in like a gamecock.

Westmark 585

A riding coat swept to the little man's boot heels, an enormous cocked hat perched on the side of his head. He stood, hat included, no higher than the middle button of Theo's jacket. In swagger, he took up more room than half a dozen taller men.

Theo was glad to see any size of customer, but before he could wish him good-day or ask his business, the stranger went peering into the ink pots, rattling the wooden cases, fingering the stacks of paper, and squinting sidelong at the press.

At last he stopped, hooked his thumbs into his waistcoat, and declared, in a voice half bullfrog, half bass drum, "Musket!"

Theo, bemused, could only stare. The dwarf snapped his fingers.

"Musket! That's my name."

The dwarf shook his head impatiently, as if Theo should have known without being told, then waved a hand around the shop.

"You're the only printer, I suppose, in Upper Dismal or whatever you call this place?"

"Sir," began Theo, "to tell you the truth —"

"Don't."

"What I mean is I'm not the printer. I'm only his devil."

"You're a big one, then. I'll say that much for you," replied Musket. "You'll do. You'll have to."

The dwarf whipped off his hat, loosing a burst of ginger-colored hair, reached into it, and pulled out a number of closely written scraps of paper. He tossed them on the counter.

The pages, from what Theo glimpsed, were the draft for some sort of tract or pamphlet.

"To be printed up. And nicely. No cheap-jack work. It's for Dr. Absalom. He's world-famous. You've heard of him."

Theo admitted he had not, adding that he had never been out of Dorning.

The dwarf gave him a look of pity. "A grown lad like you? And never away from this hole-and-corner? You aren't much in the swim of things, are you?"

Musket now turned his attention to the pamphlet. Tapping his thumb against his fingers, he began rattling off the number of copies, the size, the quality of paper the world-renowned Dr. Absalom insisted on.

The little man was talking about more work than the shop had seen in a year. Theo began calculating in his head how much it would all come to. Musket spared him the trouble by offering his own price, a handsome one, better than handsome. Theo's heart sank at what he heard next.

"Needed tomorrow," said Musket. "First thing."

"Tomorrow? We can't. There's not enough time."

"Take it or leave it. Tomorrow or not at all." The dwarf rocked back and forth on his heels.

Theo's mind raced. He could not bring himself to turn down such a piece of business. With a master craftsman like Anton, the two of them working all night at top speed, it was possible, though barely so. But the decision was Anton's to make. Theo had never promised work on his own.

"What's it to be, then?" demanded Musket.

"You'll have it. By noon."

The dwarf shot a finger at him. "Nine."

Theo choked a little. "By nine."

"Done!" Musket clapped on his hat and made for the door. "I'll be here to fetch them."

Theo had not a moment to waste. Anton would be overjoyed — or furious at him for making promises he could not keep. From the first days of his apprenticeship, Anton had taught him that his word, once given, must be counted on. As soon as Musket had gone, Theo began studying the scraps of paper to see how best he could arrange his work.

Dr. Absalom, he read, boasted powers of magnetism, hypnotism, and the secret of eternal youth. He also offered to cure, at a modest fee, warts, gout, gallstones, boils, and every other ailment afflicting human-kind.

It was rubbish, written surely by Dr. Absalom since only an author could have such a good opinion of himself. Theo had read every book in his master's storeroom: law, science, natural philosophy. Unschooled, he was awed by the learned professors at Freyborg. He could imagine what they would say of the self-styled doctor. Nevertheless, the dwarf had come bursting in like a wind from a world beyond anything Theo knew. He was fascinated in spite of himself and half-believing. His common sense nagged at him. He ignored it.

When Anton came back it was past nightfall. Theo was still at the type case. He had stopped only to light candles. His hand darted over the maze of wooden pigeonholes, snatching up letter after letter and dropping the pieces of type into the composing stick in his other palm. The scrape of Anton's boots on the plank flooring startled him. He left off and hurried to greet the printer, who was wearily shedding his coat.

Anton's face, usually cheerful, was gray and pouchy. Theo, full of his good news, decided that keeping it for dessert would make it all the better, and offered to heat a pot of lentils for his master.

"No, no thank you, lad. I lost my appetite at the notary's. I stopped to remind him of the small matter of his unpaid account. He let me cool my heels while he ate a hot supper. Then he swore if I troubled him again he'd have the law on me."

"He can't. The law's on your side. It says so in Wellek's *Legal Commentaries*. You know that. You printed it yourself."

"That was before Cabbarus. Books are one thing; how the world goes now is another."

"King Augustine must have been out of his wits," retorted Theo, "taking Cabbarus for any kind of minister, let alone the highest in the kingdom."

"Out of his wits? Yes, with heartbreak, losing the princess and not another child since then. And that's six years gone. Queen Caroline faced up to it better than he did. More's the pity, he could have been a good king."

"I can understand it broke his heart. The one to blame is Cabbarus," said Theo. "He's the one who speaks for the king. No, he does worse than speak. He lays down the law, if you can call it that, for there's no justice in it. He has every printer in Westmark by the throat. Well, I wish I had him by the throat. I wish somebody would —"

"Enough," said Anton. "I don't want to hear that sort of talk. I taught you better than that. Oh, I'll stand up for what's right. And heaven help whoever lays a finger on my press, for he'll have me to deal with. But neither you, nor I, nor anyone can judge whether a man's fit to live or die."

Theo grinned at him. "That's from *De Rerum Justitiae*. I've been reading it."

Anton chuckled. "Well then, you know as much as I do. Is that how you spend your time when I'm out of the shop? I suppose you could do worse. What are you up to now? I saw you pegging away, but there's no work on hand."

Theo could no longer hold back his news. "There is. It might even be too much."

He quickly told Anton what had happened. Instead of reproaching him, Anton brightened instantly. When he saw how far Theo had already gone with the task, he clapped him on the back and seized an ink-stained apron.

"Good lad! I couldn't have managed it better. We may break our backs, but we'll finish in time to suit this fellow Muskrat or whatever he calls himself."

He bustled around the shop, putting out iron frames, blocks, and wedges so as to have all at hand. Theo hurried back to his typesetting and soon lost track of the hours, not even hearing the town clock. Anton, flushed and inky, readied the press. Well before dawn, they began drawing proofs of the first pages.

Theo had picked up a sheet of paper when a battering at the door startled him. He thought, first, that Musket had come for his work sooner than promised; but the pounding was more violent than the dwarf, with all his impatience, could have produced.

He ran to the front of the shop. As he did, the door splintered, burst from its hinges, and crashed inward. Two men in uniform shouldered past him.

Chapter Two

hey were field militia. He recognized the green tunics and white crossbelts. Without thinking, he flung up his arms to defend himself. One of the soldiers, at this movement, swung the butt of his musket and drove it into Theo's ribs. The blow doubled him up. He fell to his knees, clutching his belly, gagging at the pain. The man who struck him glanced down briefly: without malice, without curiosity, as if he found Theo an uninteresting specimen of livestock.

A third figure had stepped into the shop. Clean-shaven, cloaked in dark gray, he wore a tall hat with a curved brim. He could have passed for a merchant or councillor.

The militiamen stiffened to attention.

Anton was shouting and brandishing his ink-dauber. The officer paid no heed. He halted in the middle of the shop. In a voice saturated with boredom, having made the same declaration so often that he knew it by rote, he informed

Anton that all printing establishments were now, by Royal Warrant, subject to inspection.

"With the view," he went on, "to discover unlawful publications and criminal conduct —"

When it dawned on Anton what the officer was reciting, he burst out laughing. "Unlawful? Criminal? I'll tell you what's criminal here. Lack of business!"

The printer was red-faced and sweating. The officer looked him up and down with distaste, then strode to the worktable. He picked up one of the sheets and scanned it.

"Who is this Absalom? He's a fraud on the very face of it, and who knows what more underneath. We'll have a closer look at him. And you, too." He folded the page and slipped it under his cloak. "Is this the sort of trade you favor?"

"If I only did what suited me I'd starve to death," retorted Anton. "I'm a printer, not a judge."

"Quite so," said the officer. "In which case, show me the license for this publication, and whatever else you've been doing."

Anton glanced at Theo, who just now had struggled to his feet. "Ah — as for that —"

"We'll have it this morning," Theo broke in, "as soon as the town clerk opens his office."

The officer raised his eyebrows. "Will you, indeed? You admit, however, that in fact you have none at present."

"The customer came late in the day," said Theo. "The office was closed. He needed his work done. There was no other way —"

"Except," said the officer, "to break the law. Very well. The case is clear enough."

He nodded curtly to the soldiers and made a gesture toward the press. "Take it down."

"No!" cried Theo. "That's not right! We're not criminals —"

Anton stared in disbelief. The militiamen slung their muskets and took hold of the press, straining to topple it. The printer's hesitation lasted barely a moment. As the two laid hands on his press, Anton threw himself on them. He thrust his dauber into the face of the closer militiaman. The soldier, under the force of the blow, pitched into a corner, stunned. Anton dropped his makeshift weapon and grappled the man's comrade by the crossbelt.

The soldier broke free. Theo ran to help his master. From the tail of his eye, he saw the officer reach under his cloak and bring out a pistol, aiming at the raging printer.

One of the iron frames lay on the worktable. Theo seized it and swung it upward. The iron twisted in his grasp, flew slantwise, and struck the officer on the side of the head. The man grunted and went down. The pistol discharged into the floor.

The soldier in the corner sat up, trying to rub the ink from his eyes. His comrade hastily pointed his musket at Theo and fired. The shot went wide; the bullet splintered one of the type cases.

Theo scarcely heard either explosion. He could not turn away from the officer sprawled on the floor. The man's hat had rolled under the table. His face had gone slack, mouth open; he was bleeding from the nose, the trickle making a crimson spider web across his cheek.

The militiaman fumbled his reloading and cursed. Theo stood rooted. Anton was bawling at him; the words reached his ears from a distance. He understood none of them.

Next thing he knew, Anton was shoving him out the door. He found himself running over the cobbles, legs pumping mechanically. The printer pushed him along whenever he faltered. They plunged into the shadows of an alley.

Theo was asking over and over if the man was dead. Anton did not answer, laboring for breath. They ran on, turning from one street into the next. Anton halted and put out a hand to steady himself against the side of a building.

"Out of wind," he gasped. "You — get clear of this." He made a movement with his head. "That way. I'll take the other street. We've a better chance if we separate."

Theo's mind was still in the printshop. It took him a few moments to grasp what his master was telling him. The clatter of boots grew louder behind them.

"Get out!" Anton took Theo by the collar, spun him around, and sent him stumbling across the alley in the opposite direction.

By the time Theo turned back, the printer had vanished. Theo lurched after him, then stopped, uncertain which street Anton had taken. There was a flash, the crack of a shot. He ran blindly ahead.

He had lived all his life in Dorning, but the town had suddenly changed. He recognized nothing. Houses loomed that he had never seen before. He tried to sight the clock tower. He followed one street that appeared familiar. It ended in a blind alley which should not have been there. He doubled back in panic.

The marketplace opened in front of him. How he had reached it, he had no idea; but he knew at least where he was. The Crown Inn was on his left, at the near side of the square. He ran toward it, thinking vaguely that he might hide in the stables. The innyard gates were bolted at this hour. He glanced behind him and saw no one. He leaped up, gained a handhold, and swung himself over.

The windows of the inn were dark. Theo raced across the yard into one of the sheds. A lantern hung on the wall, but there was no sign of Bodo, the stableman. He could not guess whether the fellow was snoring away somewhere or likely to appear at any moment.

Theo had no plan except to rejoin Anton as soon as he collected his wits and his heart stopped pounding. A high-wheeled coach stood at the back of the shed. He saw no better hiding place, went to it, and turned the door handle. It was unlocked. He flung it open and clambered in.

Before he could pull the door shut, a figure popped up like a jack-in-the-box. A cannonball hurtled into his middle and jolted him against the seat.

The cannonball was a head attached to a body that seemed to own more than the usual number of arms and legs, all of which were pummeling him at the same time. An instant later he found himself nose to nose with and staring into the indignant face of the dwarf.

Chapter Three

he devil!" cried Musket, in exasperation more than recognition. His eyes, pink with sleep, batted furiously. Shirt unbuttoned, neckerchief askew, he showed nothing of his afternoon jauntiness. "I thought you were a burglar. What are you doing in my coach?"

"They tried to smash our press," blurted Theo, too caught up in his own distress to be surprised at the sight of his onetime customer. "They were going to arrest us."

"You're in trouble with the law?" Musket squinted at him. "Well, don't put us in the same pickle, whatever it is. Out! Off with you!"

"Please — let me rest. I don't know what to do. My master's out there somewhere. They're after him. They'll be after Dr. Absalom, too."

The dwarf had been making every effort to push Theo out of the coach. Hearing this, he stopped abruptly.

"Sit there," ordered Musket. "Don't leave."

The dwarf pulled on his boots, tumbled from the coach, and scurried across the yard toward the inn house.

Alone, Theo tried to set his thoughts in order. He cursed himself for not following Anton and again for not finding him. He put his head in his hands and closed his eyes, only to see the officer's ashen face.

Musket was back. At his heels, a bulky figure was hastily cramming a shirttail into his breeches.

Theo climbed out of the coach. "Dr. Absalom?"

The paunchy man shook his head. He had the plump features of an over-sized baby with a ferocious black moustache. "I should say I am at your service, but more likely you shall be at mine. I am Count Las Bombas."

Theo turned to Musket. "I thought you'd gone for Dr. Absalom."

"In the press of circumstances, names are unimportant. They only confuse matters." The count waved a hand, dismissing the question. "My coachman tells me you had some difficulties, and the name 'Absalom' came up, shall we say, in the conversation?"

Theo began his account while Las Bombas nodded encouragement, stopping him occasionally and asking him to repeat certain details.

"The officer, you say, took one of the pages? And kept it?"

Theo nodded. "He called Dr. Absalom a fraud and wanted a closer look at him. After that, when he took out a pistol, I — I think I killed him. I swear it was an accident."

"Heaven help us, then, if you ever do anything on purpose," said Las Bombas. "Now, the two soldiers, did they hear him?"

"They must have. They were standing right there."

"And no doubt will report it to someone, even if their superior is, ah, no longer among us?"

"If they remember," said Theo, "after everything else that happened."

"Inconvenient things are always remembered," said Las Bombas. "We must assume the worst. Wisdom dictates that Dr. Absalom will suddenly be called out of town. As for you, young man, allow me to inquire: What are you going to do to save your neck?"

Theo had been turning over the same question. "I'll have to set things right. I'll go to the police, to the Dorning constabulary."

"The law?" Las Bombas stared at him. "Last place in the world to set things right!"

"What else can I do? My master could be in jail. They had no cause to break into the shop. We did nothing wrong. I meant the officer no harm."

"My dear boy, who's to believe that?"

"It's the truth. They'll have to believe it."

"It is constabulary nature to disbelieve." Count Las Bombas sighed and puffed out his cheeks. "I commend your sense of duty, but have no intention of sharing it. Musket and I shall be leaving directly."

The dwarf, in fact, had been cramming garments into a flexible traveling case. Las Bombas urged him to greater speed, then waved a hand at Theo.

"Farewell. Though I have gravest doubts, I wish a satisfactory resolution to your difficulties."

Leaving the count and his coachman busily packing, Theo made his way across the innyard. He drew the bolt on the gate and slipped out into the street. What had been so clear a choice in the shed now filled him with uneasiness. The count, he feared, might well be right, and a bad affair turn worse. His decision had been the only honorable one. Instead of strengthening him, however, it burdened him. He gritted his teeth and set off for the constabulary.

Before going any distance, he sighted one of the Dorning constables holding a lantern at the end of an alley. Theo called out and went toward him. The constable, after one glimpse, began running in the opposite direction. Having been chased through the streets a good part of the night, the puzzled Theo had to stretch his legs to chase the fleeing officer.

He caught up with him at last. It was Constable Pohn, whom he had known as long as he could remember. Pohn immediately darkened his lantern. Usually good-natured, he rounded angrily on Theo.

"What are you doing here? We've orders to search the town for you."

"Well, you've found me. I was on my way to the station house. Where's Anton? And the officer? Did I — is he alive?"

"He's got a broken head, but he'll mend."

"Thank heaven. What about Anton?"

"There's been a bad piece of business." Pohn took Theo's arm. "Dorning's no place for you."

"I've got to settle things. It was my fault. I don't want Anton blamed."

"He's dead," cried Pohn. "Shot down in the street. They're after you now."

Theo stared, numb. Splinters of ice caught in his throat, choking and tearing him at the same time. Pohn shook him furiously.

"Listen to me! There's an order to arrest you. That was a Royal Inspector you brained. So it's a Crown case, not some local mischief. We can't help you. You can't help Anton.

"You're to be locked up on sight," Pohn hurried on. "But who's to say I saw you? We're going to search the woods west of the river. A wanted criminal — that's where he'd hide, wouldn't he? He'd never take to the open roads. The King's Highway? Last place he'd go. No need wasting our time in that direction. Eh? Eh? Do you understand me?"

Pohn snapped his jaws shut, spun on his heel, and hustled away down the alley, shining his lantern into doorways and corners as if seeking the fugitive in good earnest.

Theo stood bewildered, grasping at fragments of what Pohn had told him. There was no reason, no justice in any of it. With a surge of anger, ignoring the constable's urging, he wanted to stay and face his accuser. Anton had committed no crime, nor had Theo. To leave his only home, his books, his work — yet he knew, with bitterness, it had all suddenly become wreckage.

Painfully, unwilling, he turned and forced his legs to carry him eastward from the town. The sky was lightening. Shreds of mist floated over the market gardens fringing the outskirts of Dorning. A rooster crowed in a farmyard. He pressed on at a faster pace, cutting across newly plowed fields, dimly reckoning he would sooner or later strike the highway.

Only now did the full weight of his grief bear down on him. Along with it was something more, lodged in the back of his mind like a cinder in the eye that could not be wept away.

He could not bring himself to think about it; he could not bring himself to turn away from it. He was unable, finally, to stand it any longer. He admitted what he had hidden from himself and wished to forget.

The frame had not slipped or twisted. It was not an accident. Never in his life had he raised a hand in anger. But in that moment, more than anything else in the world, he had wanted to kill the man.

Until then, he had believed in his own good nature. He pleaded that he was a kindly, honorable human being. But the bloodied face rose up in front of him. His stomach heaved. He doubled over, retching. He sat on the ground a while, head pressed against his knees. He swore every way he knew: Never again would he do such a deed.

He climbed at last to his feet. The road lay a short distance beyond the field. He set off for it. He did not look back. He did not dare.

Chapter Four

y midmorning, the sun had burned away the fog from the valley land east of Dorning. Theo calculated he had trudged only a few miles, but he was already weary. He had, thus far, come upon no travelers in either direction, for which he was grateful. Being obliged to give an account of himself was the last thing in the world he wanted. He had already done violence to a man. He did not wish to compound this by doing violence to the truth. He had never told a lie; it occurred to him that sooner or later he would have to lie outrageously. The best he could do was put off the moment as long as possible.

He had begun thinking it might be wiser to stay off the road altogether when he saw a dappled gray mare trotting toward him. Harness leathers trailing, the horse whinnied and tossed her head, but made no objection when he caught the reins and pulled her up. The animal clearly had an owner, but Theo's fatigue outweighed that consideration.

"Hold still, old girl. Whoever you belong to — I'm sorry. I'm a wanted fugitive," he bitterly added. "I might as well be a horse thief, too."

He climbed awkwardly astride. Knowing as much of horsemanship as he did of behaving like a criminal, he nevertheless managed to turn the animal eastward, glad for one piece of good fortune.

His good fortune blistered him before he had ridden a mile. His legs strained. He was footsore where he had no feet. At last, he climbed down and walked. The horse ambled behind him, fondly blowing down the back of his neck, nudging him when his pace slackened.

Before he could decide how to free himself of this animal who was driving him instead of the other way around, he saw, past a bend in the road, a coach pulled onto the grassy shoulder. The doors hung open, some baggage had been spread on the ground, the shafts were empty. On top of the vehicle perched the dwarf, a stubby clay pipe between his teeth. Count Las Bombas, sweating in his shirt-sleeves, sat glumly on a boulder.

Sighting Theo, the dwarf sprang down like an acrobat. "I told you she'd come back one way or another. If you'd let her be, instead of chasing her like an idiot, she wouldn't have run off in the first place."

Las Bombas heaved himself up, nodding at Theo. "I see we have you to thank for finding this ungrateful creature. And so, you changed your mind about reporting yourself to the authorities? Very sensible."

"I would have," Theo began. He faltered, as if saying the words could somehow make it more final than it was. "But — they killed my master."

"I'm sorry, my boy. A hard knock. Where does that leave you?"

"With a warrant out for me. The police as much as ordered me to run away. The Royal Inspector's alive, though."

"And no doubt in better case than we are. Thanks to the roads in your part of the country, a wheel came loose. Then Musket carelessly allowed my steed — Friska! Friska! None of that!"

This was shouted at the horse, nipping at Las Bombas from the rear. The count withdrew to a safe distance while Musket brought the animal to the shafts.

"A civilian beast," the count explained. "Nothing like my charger when I served in the Salamanca Lancers."

Theo had noticed a heap of objects beside the coach and gave a questioning look at what appeared to be a collection of arms and legs.

"Ah, those," said Las Bombas. "Remarkably natural, you must agree. Excellently done." He picked up one of the arms and showed it to Theo. It was hollow, made of painted cloth stretched over a light, flexible wooden frame. "These are often useful in my profession. Sometimes, indeed, essential."

"But your pamphlet said you were a doctor."

"As occasion demands. I have, my boy, spent my life in constant study. Initiate in the Delphic Mysteries, in the Grand Arcana, adviser to His Exalted Serenity, the prince of Trebizonia. I have been instructed by the Great Copta himself in summoning spirits of the dead — with, naturally, a reasonable amount of help from the living."

"You mean," said Theo, "you're no doctor at all."

"Don't take such a narrow view," replied the count. "I assure you, I have lightened more suffering with tubs of magnetized water than most esteemed surgeons have done with lancets and leeches. Those who, for some inscrutable reason, stubbornly refuse to benefit — if I didn't cure them at least I didn't harm them, which cannot be said for a number of your learned bloodletters."

The count reached into his pocket. "It is apparent to me that you suffer from a headache at this very instant. Am I correct?"

Theo's head, in fact, had been throbbing all morning. He admitted this to Las Bombas, who nodded and replied, "I knew it without asking."

He opened his hand, revealing a black pebble the size of an egg. "This, my boy, is worth more than its weight in gold. A priceless fragment from the fabled Mountain of the Moon in Kazanastan. I need only touch it to your brow — thus. Your headache will vanish."

A whistle from Musket interrupted the count. He turned and squinted down the road where the dwarf was pointing. Theo stiffened. A troop of Royal Cavalry was bearing toward them.

"Make a run for it," ordered Las Bombas. "No — that will rouse their suspicions. We'll have to brazen it out."

He rummaged in a pile of clothing and tossed some garments to Theo. "Get behind the coach. Put these on. If there's any question, say you're a Trebizonian."

"I can't speak Trebizonian."

"Neither can they. Very well, you'll be a mute Trebizonian. Get on with it. Not a word out of you. Do as I say."

Theo ducked around the coach and pulled on the costume: a long, striped robe which, by its smell, had not been laundered for years, and a tall, cylindrical headpiece with a tassel.

The troop halted. The captain turned his mount, casting a wary eye on the vehicle. Las Bombas, who had disappeared inside, now climbed out to face the officer. The count was resplendent in a general's gold-braided uniform, its breast glittering with medals.

"What seems to be the difficulty?" blustered the count as the officer sprang down and brought his hand to a rigid salute.

"Beg to report: none, sir." The captain had gone as crimson as the count's uniform. "Forgive me, sir, for disturbing you. My men are going into garrison and I was ordered to keep an eye open along the way. A fugitive from justice, claiming to be a printer's apprentice —"

"What? What?" shouted Las Bombas. "What nonsense are you mumbling? Speak up, sir! Look me in the eye when you address me!"

"A fugitive, sir," blurted the troop captain, "wanted for high crimes."

"Why didn't you say so in the first place?" Las Bombas glared at him. "Well, you don't see anyone like that here, do you? I am General Sambalo, on a special mission from the court."

"Beg to report, sir: I saw an individual near your coach."

"My servant?" The count beckoned to Theo. "This fellow? Trebizonian, as you see. Hardly an apprentice of any sort, eh? Can't speak. Only grunts. I spared his life on my last campaign. He's been devoted to me ever since."

The officer stared at Theo. Las Bombas went on.

"A faithful creature — as far as you can trust any of these savages. Strong as a bull, though you wouldn't think it, looking at him. Poor devil, he's quite mad. Calm and peaceful in the ordinary way of things. What sets him wild is officers with horses. Even I can't control him then."

Taking the count's hint, Theo growled and bared his teeth in what he hoped would pass for a ferocious grimace. Terrified, at the same time he felt himself an utter fool.

"You should have seen what he did to my last aide." Las Bombas gravely shook his head. "Those Trebizonians go straight for the throat, you know."

The troop captain stood at attention, but it was all the man could do to stay there. Las Bombas held the officer with a stern eye, in no hurry to let him escape.

"Have you any money?"

The captain blinked. "Sir?"

"If you do, I suggest giving it to him immediately. It may exercise a calming effect. They understand the offering of money as a gesture of friendship."

The officer pulled out a handful of silver coins and one gold piece from his tunic and flung them at Theo. Las Bombas nodded approval.

"That should hold him. Not long, for such a small amount. Carry on with your duties. I assume the responsibility of watching for the runaway. Dismissed!"

The captain threw a ragged salute, scrambled onto his mount, and plunged back to his men, bawling for them to follow at the gallop.

Las Bombas watched until the troop was well out of sight. He gave Theo a smile of satisfaction. "You made a splendid Trebizonian. For a moment, I thought you were actually going to bite him."

"You got us a gold piece into the bargain," added Musket. "That's pure profit."

"Yes, you pulled it off, my boy," said Las Bombas. "But you had a close call. I confess I sweated a little myself. You might be wise to stay with us for a time. For your own safety. Though it also occurs to me I could use a bright young assistant. The possibilities are unlimited. As to wages, we must leave that question temporarily open."

"No, thank you. It's good of you, but —" Theo hesitated. Until now, he had never imagined himself away from Dorning. The possibility had never existed. With Anton dead and himself homeless, his best course was to stay on the move. The prospect, in fact, excited him, all the more strongly because it was new.

"I doubt if you'll have a better offer," said the count. "Why, you'll launch yourself on an entirely new profession."

The count's profession, Theo knew, was sheer fakery. Las Bombas was a fraud and, worse, proud of it. Nevertheless, against all reason, against all he had read and Anton had taught him, he could not help liking the rogue.

"All right," he said finally. "I'll go with you."

"Excellent!" cried the count. "Pack up and we'll be on our way. Musket will explain your duties."

As soon as the artificial arms and legs and the rest of the baggage had been stowed, Las Bombas rolled himself into the coach. Theo clambered to join Musket on the box. The dwarf clicked his tongue, slapped Friska with the reins, and set off at a speed that took Theo's breath away. With his stubby legs jutting straight in front of him, hat jammed low on his brow and his eyes gleaming, Musket looked every bit a demon coachman. Theo hung on for dear life. The coach swayed and jolted, wind whistled in his ears. What his destination might be, he had no inkling; but they were going there very rapidly. He scarcely noticed his headache had vanished.

Chapter Five

abbarus, chief minister of the realm, bent over his desk scanning a sheaf of documents. Cabbarus had the virtue of diligence with an immense capacity for drudgery, and he had been at his work since dawn. From the day of his elevation from superintendent of the Royal Household, he had shown himself willing and eager to accept duties the other ministers found boring. Cabbarus, as a result, had his fingers in everything from the purchase of lobsters to the signature of death warrants. His eyes were everywhere: eyes the color of slate, unblinking; with a glance that made all on whom it rested feel, in comparison with him, less noble, less high-minded, and that their linen needed changing.

The papers presently under this glance dealt with the latest steps taken against irresponsible pamphleteers and the printers who served them. Cabbarus had not yet received reports from such outlying towns as Belvitsa and Dorning. He expected them shortly. Meantime, he was not displeased.

"The subjects of His Majesty," he was saying, "require the firmest guidance. The people yearn for it, without even realizing what it is they yearn for. These scribblers cause nothing but unrest. Their deaths, beyond question, will serve a higher purpose than their lives: the good of the kingdom. I bear them no personal animosity, but I would fail in my duty if I did otherwise. They will, at least, be spared the needless humiliation of a public trial."

The chief minister's confidential secretary, Councillor Pankratz, made polite growls of approval, no more detailed answer being called for. Pankratz was a head shorter than his master, with enormous calves nearly bursting the stockings of his black court costume. Cabbarus wore no wig to cover the iron gray hair trimmed close to his skull; therefore, his secretary dared not wear one. The courtiers had nicknamed Pankratz The Minister's Mastiff. Among themselves, they joked that while Cabbarus was preaching at his listeners, Pankratz was biting their legs.

Time had come for the morning audience with King Augustine. Cabbarus ordered his mastiff to pack the documents in a red leather box. With Pankratz trotting two paces behind, Cabbarus left his quarters and made his way across the courtyard to the newer wings of the palace. These splendid areas had been raised by the king's grandfather, the second Augustine, now called The Great.

The original Juliana Palace had been an ancient fortress of thick stone walls, narrow passages, dungeons, and torture chambers. Instead of tearing down the historic structure, Augustine the Great built around and added to it. In one of the watchtowers he installed the famous Juliana Bells. Their peal set the mood of the city, as if they were the voice of Marianstat itself. Augustine IV had commanded them to remain forever silent, in perpetual mourning for the late Princess Augusta. The child had loved them. The king found them too-painful reminders of his daughter. He preferred muteness to memory.

Most of the Old Juliana had been given over to storage and the offices of lower functionaries. Cabbarus had lived and worked there during his superintendency. As chief minister, he was entitled to sumptuous chambers in the New Juliana. He declined them. He kept his same quarters, setting an example of frugality and modesty; righteousness being always more believable when combined with dreariness.

Since Augustine no longer received ministers in the audience chamber, Cabbarus went directly to the king's apartments. Taking the red box from his secretary, he allowed himself to be ushered in. Pankratz stationed himself outside the door, keeping a dog's eye on the attendants in the hall.

The apartments were airless and stifling hot. Draperies blinded the casements. Spring had come early and warm, but logs blazed in the fireplace. Cabbarus set down his box on a side table and approached the king. Augustine, in a dressing gown, sat in a high-backed chair close to the fire. He barely acknowledged the presence of his chief minister.

"I trust Your Majesty slept well," said Cabbarus, knowing the king seldom slept more than an hour at a time.

Augustine turned a feverish eye on his chief minister. The king was not a tall man; since his loss, he had shrunk still further into himself: emptied, filled only with inner shadows. He had never ceased to blame himself for being too doting a father. Had he been less indulgent, the tragedy would not have happened. Because it was too late to take a stronger hand with his daughter, he had chosen Cabbarus to take a stronger hand with his people. Since then, Augustine had only one concern.

"Have you still found none with the true gift?" asked the king. "Those who can summon the spirits of the dead?"

Cabbarus stifled a sigh. He had hoped that Augustine, for once, would not bring up the matter. "Your Majesty has always been disappointed."

"I charge you to find one who will not disappoint me. I will speak with my daughter. Let her spirit come to me, even from her unknown grave."

"Sire, your duty is toward the living." Cabbarus did not intend pursuing this old and tiresome subject. He did not even intend discussing the contents of the box. The topic he resolved to raise this morning, as it had grown in his mind, filled him with a pleasure he would have judged indecent had it not been directed toward the good of the kingdom.

Augustine had given him the opening he sought, and he hurried on before he lost the monarch's attention. "Indeed, Sire, kings have a duty even beyond the tomb. We are all, at the end, dust and ashes. Your Majesty, alas, bears the added burden of determining his successor."

"There is no successor."

"Precisely my point, Majesty. Queen Caroline, as a royal widow, may rule in your stead. This merely delays the question without resolving it. Your Majesty must have an heir to carry on his sacred trust."

Augustine frowned. "It is no longer possible."

"Permit me to say, Majesty: on the contrary. It is both possible and urgent. The law permits you to adopt one. It requires only your decree, confirmed by the assent of Queen Caroline."

"Are you saying, Chief Minister, that the Queen and I should adopt a daughter?"

"Not a daughter," Cabbarus replied, "joyful as that might be. Not a daughter, Majesty, a son. A son who dreams, who hopes, who will strive to approach the wisdom, strength, and vision of his glorious, though adoptive, forebears. A son who will honor Your Majesty now and in years to come —"

"Speak of this another time," said Augustine. "I am weary. There is, moreover, none I would consider."

"None?" cried Cabbarus, dropping to his knees. "Majesty, let me reveal to you the respect, the affection, the love that has grown daily within my heart, the dream of that glorious day when I may call you Father!"

It took the king a moment to understand his chief minister's proposal. He staggered to his feet. "You? In the place of my dead child?"

The king struggled to disengage himself from the embrace of his chief minister. Cabbarus, in turn, did all he could to cling to the legs of his prospective parent. Augustine's face went gray. He stretched out his hands, groping vaguely, and toppled to the floor.

In despair, not at the king's possibly fatal collapse but its untimeliness, Cabbarus seized the monarch's wrist. The pulse beat faintly. Cabbarus climbed to his feet, flung open the door, and shouted for help. He returned to the prostrate Augustine and stood wringing his hands.

Queen Caroline was there in moments. Hardly glancing at Cabbarus, she knelt beside her husband and loosened his gown and shirt. The queen still wore mourning, as she had done for six years past. While the king's grief had weakened him, her grief had only strengthened her. Despite her anxiety, her features were sternly controlled. When Cabbarus tried to speak, she cut him off with a gesture and followed the attendants who bore Augustine to a couch.

"Madam," protested Cabbarus, "we had scarcely begun our audience. His Majesty appeared in better case than when I left him yesterday."

"His Majesty," replied the queen, "is in even better case when you are absent."

The court physician had now entered and was ordering the attendants, including Pankratz, to take themselves off. Dr. Torrens was still in his shirt-sleeves. His face, broad and blunt, was softened by a mane of silver hair, unpowdered, caught at the back by a common cotton ribbon.

"Madam, I must ask you to withdraw," said Torrens, adding to Cabbarus, "and you, too."

Cabbarus glowered at the court physician. The queen went to the ante-chamber and sank down on a chair. Cabbarus reluctantly followed. Since the queen did not give him leave to sit, he took up a station in the middle of the room, his head bowed, hands clasped before him. Thus the queen and the chief minister shared close quarters and chilly silence until Torrens reappeared.

"The king is sleeping now, a blessing in itself," he said to the queen. Dr. Torrens finished rolling down his sleeves, then addressed Cabbarus. "He has had a severe shock. You were with him, Chief Minister. I think you shall have to answer for it."

"I would not call it shock," said Cabbarus, looking past Torrens to the queen. "Rather say, Madam, an excess of joy. His Majesty was discussing the happy prospect of adopting a son and heir. His fondest wish, his royal choice devolved upon —" Cabbarus sighed and spread his hands. "Myself. Public duty and personal devotion led me to accept this highest honor. For the king, the joyous excitement of that moment —"

"How dare you!" cried the queen. "How dare you speak of yourself as adoptive heir? Such a question is raised privately, between the king and me. The queen's consent is required first and foremost, as you well know. That consent, I assure you, will never be given. I desire Dr. Torrens, here and now, to witness my refusal."

"Privately or publicly, Madam, the question must be raised," answered Cabbarus. "The king is desperately ill."

"Yes," put in Torrens, "but I can also tell you the king has no illness. Not in the physical sense. His body is wasted and weakened. This might be set right, as I have tried to do; and would have done, except for the meddling of idiots like you, who set my regimens aside. The king's body may answer to common-sense treatment, to food, sleep, and fresh air. His gravest illness lies in his spirit."

"You are saying the king is mad!" exclaimed Cabbarus. "This is high treason. You are more than incompetent, you are a traitor!"

"Neither one nor the other," Torrens answered. "The king is not mad. He is sick with grief, frozen in self-blame. No, I am not a traitor. I am a man who speaks his mind and faces facts." He turned to the queen. "Do not lose hope. His Majesty may, in time, recover. Meanwhile, I urge you, allow him to make no decisions he may come to regret, and certainly not the adoption of —"

"You go too far!" Cabbarus burst out. "Your trade is physic, not affairs of state. The king must and will follow the guidance of his ministers."

"Forgive me," said Torrens. "I called you an idiot. I spoke hastily. You are not. Had I given it more thought, I would have called you a scoundrel." He bowed to the queen. "Your servant, Madam."

Dr. Torrens turned on his heel and strode from the chamber. Queen Caroline hurried after him. Cabbarus, about to follow and give Torrens a withering reply, thought better of it and remained there, silent.

The chief minister enjoyed a gift for sniffing out possibilities without immediately understanding them. As before, when he had trusted this instinct, nothing could have been foreseen. He had risen, nevertheless, to chief minister. When the proper moment came, there would be many in the Royal Council to favor him as adoptive heir. As for Torrens, he would be dealt with. A plan was already shaping in his mind. It always pleased the chief minister how clear-sighted he could be in clouded circumstances.

Chapter Six

The Demon Coachman brought them to Kessel: hungry, late, and sopping wet. The morning repairs had not outlasted the day, the wheel threatened to come off again at any moment, and a spring rainstorm had begun pelting down. Taking the risk of sending coach and passengers into a ditch, Musket pressed ahead, hunched on the box, whistling through his teeth, grinning like an undersized fiend in an oversized hat.

Kessel offered a large inn. Because of the storm, however, it looked as if every traveler had broken his journey there. The common room stank of wet clothing and bad cooking. Las Bombas, Musket and Theo following, elbowed his way to the chimney corner and called loudly for the host. The count, in the privacy of the coach, had changed from his uniform into garments of black set off by white wristbands.

"The chambers of Mynheer Bloomsa and servants," declared Las Bombas when the landlord finally appeared. "You have my message reserving them."

The landlord, taken aback by the sight of the Demon Coachman and a dripping Trebizonian, protested that no such message had come. In any case, his house was full. Theo, having digested his surprise at the count's new role, expected Las Bombas to make a show of indignation.

The count merely sighed. "That's the public post for you. It is not your fault. I required a suite of your finest apartments, but I shall have to seek accommodation elsewhere."

Instead of doing so, Las Bombas stood casting an eye over the travelers. When Theo urged him to leave before it would be too late to find another inn, Las Bombas shrugged him off.

"Patience, my boy. I'm looking for pigeons. You might oblige me by handing over that gold piece, temporarily."

Theo gave him the captain's coin, which Las Bombas quickly pocketed. His attention meanwhile had settled on a table occupied by a plump little man in a fur-trimmed cloak. The count made his way toward him. Passing the table, he contrived to pull out his handkerchief so that the gold piece dropped to the floor. Las Bombas kept on as if he had not noticed.

"Good sir, your money!" the man called after him, picking up the coin.

The count turned back and allowed the traveler to press it into his hand. "You need not have troubled yourself, sir. It is of no account. I thank you, nevertheless."

"Permit me" — the traveler popped his watery, pink-rimmed eyes at the count — "permit me to remark: I would hardly call gold of no account. My name is Skeit, alderman and corn merchant, and I assure you, sir, in my occupation I know the value of money."

"I, too," replied Las Bombas, with an appraising glance at the quality of the alderman's garb and the weight of the gold chain he wore as ornament. "To me, its value is precisely nothing."

"My good Mynheer!" cried the alderman. "Bloomsa, was that the name I overheard? You amaze me!"

"No doubt I do." The count beamed. "Money, my dear sir, is only metal and, like any other substance, subject to the same natural laws of transmutation and transmogrification. I am a man of science, not finance." He lowered his voice and drew closer to Skeit. "My experiments have brought me the means of creating as much gold and silver as I please. Therefore, whatever value they may have for others, for me they have none."

"But — but this is marvelous! My journey has been most profitable, but nothing compared with meeting a personage of your accomplishment. Wait until my good wife hears of this when I'm home!"

"Since you have troubled yourself on my behalf," said Las Bombas, "allow me to offer you supper before I leave. I must find some lodging still available at this dismal time of night."

"Indeed, not!" returned Skeit. "I shall be the one to offer you supper. Look no further, I insist you share my own quarters."

"If it pleases you," said Las Bombas. "My servants can take their food in the stables, while they attend to my horse and coach."

The count, during this, was gesturing urgently behind his back. Musket pulled Theo out of the common room and hustled him to the stable.

"What was that all about?" asked Theo, as the dwarf tossed him some rags and a brush to wipe down Friska. "He's up to some trickery. The man doesn't have an honorable bone in his body."

A powerful kick sent Theo into a pile of straw: not from Friska, but from the dwarf, who stood, hands on hips, glowering at him.

"Mind your tongue," said Musket, "next time you have anything to say about the count."

"It's true, isn't it?" cried Theo.

"What if it is? I'll hear nothing against the man who bought me. That's right," Musket went on. "How much he paid, or if he swindled them out of the price, I don't know or care. I was half your age. In Napolita. He bought me from the beggar factory."

"From the — what?"

"Beggar factory," the dwarf said cheerfully. "No, you wouldn't have heard of that in your little hole-and-corner. But you've never wondered why there's so many beggars? Oh, there's no shortage of first-rate paupers, lame, halt, and blind. But half your noseless, or legless, or hunchbacked — they've been custom-tailored for the trade. Youngsters bought or stolen, then broken past mending, sliced up, squeezed into jars to make them grow crooked. Sold off to a master who pockets whatever charity's thrown to them."

"That's horrible. It can't be true."

"Can't be," said Musket. "But is. I was lucky. I was born like this, no adjustments required. If it hadn't been the count who bought me, no telling where I'd be. Rascal he is, but he's a good-natured one. Take your nobles who flog their servants, gouge their tenants, or the judges who send some wretch to be hanged — they're honest as the day is long. Any scoundrel can be honest!"

"But all the rest of it," said Theo. "The Salamanca Lancers! Great Copta! Trebizonia — I wonder if he even knows where it is. Why does he put out such nonsense?"

"No business of mine," said Musket. "For all I know, he can't stomach the world as he finds it. Can you?"

Theo did not answer. He turned back to rubbing down Friska. He had been more comfortable when he had been able to judge Las Bombas a complete rogue.

The potboy brought them supper. Since it was too late to rouse a black-smith, Musket and Theo set about repairing the wheel themselves. The dwarf, this time, swore his work would last. Soon after they finished, the count hurried into the stable.

"Master Skeit's on his way home," said Las Bombas, smiling like a cream-sodden cat. "But he'll be back, looking for us. We'd best be off." He triumphantly held up a knotted handkerchief that chinked as he shook it.

"I have performed an experiment in elementary alchemy. My coins, I assured our good alderman, had a remarkable quality. They could multiply any others they touched, as easily as a hen hatching eggs. He had only to wrap his money up with mine and let it brood overnight. By morning, he'd have treble his fortune.

"He was overjoyed. We set the packet on the mantel in his chamber and went to bed. It couldn't have turned out better. He woke up, restless; he wanted to get home with his fortune. I warned him not to undo the handkerchief till dawn, or the experiment would fail. But he won't wait; he's too greedy. When he sees what he has, he'll turn back on the instant.

"What I forgot to tell him was while he was snoring away, I tied up another kerchief with nothing but pebbles in it, and changed it for the one on the mantel."

"You robbed him!" cried Theo. "You might as well have held a pistol to his head."

"Nonsense," replied Las Bombas. "I don't carry a pistol. My dear boy, until I can set Dr. Absalom to work again, this money's the only thing to put food in our mouths."

Chuckling, Las Bombas unknotted the handkerchief. Then he choked and stared. His face went mottled. There was only a handful of leaden disks.

"Slugs!" roared Las Bombas. "He switched the packets! But — I had my eye on the real one every second. I never left his side, only when he was fast asleep and I went out to the yard for pebbles. I wasn't gone a minute — That wretch! He was shamming! Robber! How dare he pass himself off as an alderman!"

The count ran to the stable door and shook his fist into the night. "Villain! Little sneak!"

He turned back to Theo. "Ah, my poor lad, there's a lesson for you. Never trust a stranger. What a world, with so many thieves abroad in it."

Part Two
The Oracle Priestess

Chapter Seven

as Bombas, as Theo began to learn, could not stay long in low spirits. By the time Musket had Friska between the shafts and the coach ready to roll, the count's storm of indignation had passed, and he was eager to set off.

"Our fortune has been frayed," he told Theo, "but we shall mend it thread by thread."

The Demon Coachman, chewing on his pipestem, let Friska make her own pace, ambling eastward. Toward afternoon, they came in sight of a town, which the count identified as Born. He ordered Musket to halt in a vacant lot on the outskirts.

"There's a good supply of ditch water," said Las Bombas, surveying the weed-choked field. "Plenty for Dr. Absalom's Elixir. As a further attraction, I think we shall do The Goblin in the Bottle."

"No you don't," put in Musket. "No more of that."

"The effect is marvelous," the count said to Theo. "A glass bottle with a head inside that answers every question about the future. Musket sits under a table with a hole in it, the bottle has a false bottom —"

"Yes, and last time some wiseacre corked me up. I could have smothered. No more, that's flat." Musket snapped his jaws shut and folded his arms.

Las Bombas shrugged and went on. "In any case, we'll have The Unfortunate Child of Nature. It goes with Dr. Absalom's Elixir. You," he added to Theo, "will be an untamed savage from the wilds of High Brazil — whooping, leaping about, whatever occurs to you. One drink of elixir — you needn't swallow it — and you're calm and happy as a lark. You made a splendid Trebizonian. The Unfortunate Child of Nature is the same, except for the blue and yellow stripes."

"I can't paint my clothes," replied Theo. "They're all I have."

"Not your clothes, yourself. As for clothes, you'll need very few."

Las Bombas produced a dented bugle from the chest at the back of the coach and sent Musket with it into Born to announce their presence. He set out some paintpots and instructed Theo, who had reluctantly stripped to his undergarments, in the art of becoming the Unfortunate Child of Nature. While Theo daubed himself, Las Bombas filled a number of glass phials at the ditch, adding powdered herbs from his own supply. For his costume, he donned a shabby robe, a wig, and pair of spectacles. Finally, he attached four rods to the corners of a box lid and on this makeshift table put a life-sized wooden head.

"A phrenological head," explained the count. "It shows the location of humors, dispositions, and temperaments. My patients, for some reason, find it reassuring."

Musket had come back, blaring his bugle, trailed by a straggle of idlers and street urchins. Las Bombas began to proclaim the virtues of Dr. Absalom's Elixir, and Theo to offer his best version of a High Brazilian war dance. Neither got far in these occupations.

"Welcome, fellow blockheads," declared the phrenological head.

Las Bombas choked in midsentence. Theo's war whoop died on his lips. The voice had come from the wooden head.

"Come on, don't be shy," it continued. "Have a taste of that mess. Look what it did for me. I rubbed some on my hair. Now I save a fortune in barbering."

The onlookers burst into laughter, taking these remarks as part of the show.

"I'll thank you not to interrupt," said the count, hastily collecting his wits and trying to behave as if he had expected this to happen. "Please hold your tongue, sir. Or madam. Whichever you are."

The phrenological head answered with a loud, wet, and rasping noise, adding, "At your age, can't you tell the difference?"

The impudence of the head and the discomfort of Las Bombas sent the crowd into new gales of laughter. Some of the onlookers began tossing coins onto the table. This encouraged the head to inquire if there were moths in the count's wig, to comment on the size of his paunch, and the uselessness of his lazy assistants. The audience guffawed, more coins sailed through the air. When it was clear that the onlookers had emptied their pockets, the phrenological head announced it had nothing more to say. Las Bombas had sold not one bottle of elixir, but the profits were as great as if he had fobbed off his entire stock.

Once the audience had drifted away, the count seized the phrenological head, turned it upside down, shook it, and rapped it with his knuckles.

"Speak up! What's the trick?"

Meantime, one of the urchins crept from under the coach and stood watching them. It took Theo a moment to realize this collection of skin and bones was a girl. She wore a pair of ragged breeches tied with a rope about her bony hips, and dirty shirt with more holes than cloth. She was drab as a street sparrow, with a beaky nose in a narrow face. Her eyes were blue, but pale as if the color had been starved out of them.

Theo had never seen such a pitiful waif. The count, however, was less deeply touched.

"Off with you," Las Bombas ordered. "We are conducting a scientific investigation."

"Give her something. You can see she's hungry." Without waiting for the count's approval, Theo picked a coin from the table. The waif snatched it and held out a filthy palm.

"Let's have my share. You wouldn't have peddled a drop of that muck without me, not to that crowd."

"What are you saying?" demanded the count. "That you did all that nonsense?"

"Cough it up," declared the phrenological head. "Pay out fair and square or I'll never speak another word."

Las Bombas gaped. "Do that again."

"You heard me the first time."

The voice came from inside the coach. Startled, Theo turned to look. Las Bombas had not taken his eyes from the girl's lips. He studied her closely with genuine admiration.

"In all my travels, I've only met three people better at that trick. Who taught you?"

"Nobody. I learned it myself, when I was in the Queen's Home for Repentant Girls. The charity mistress wouldn't let us talk to each other. So I used to send her into fits. She never knew who to blame. She must have been glad when I escaped."

"And you've been living on your own, in the streets?" put in Theo, dismayed.

"Hanno was my friend for a while. He was a burglar — the best. He said I could be as good as he was. He was teaching me the trade," the girl added proudly. "Then he got hanged."

The dwarf had finished collecting the stray coins. The girl looked him up and down. "Hallo there, Thumbling. Give us a pull on your pipe."

The dwarf grinned and handed it over. She squatted down, stretched out her legs and, to Theo's further distress, puffed away happily. The urchin luxuriously scratched her washboard of ribs through the holes in her shirt.

"Now," she said, "where's the rest of my money?"

Las Bombas did not answer immediately. His eyes seemed fixed on some distant vision. He smiled with a look of pure greed and innocent joy.

"My dear lady," he said at last, "whatever your name is —"

"Mickle is what they call me."

"Mickle, then. I take it you have no permanent attachments. I urge you to join me and my colleagues. The possibilities are vast. The sums could be enormous."

"Sums?" said Mickle. "Does that mean money?"

"All you could desire. Eventually, that is."

"Done!" cried Mickle, spitting in her palm and seizing the count's hand. Theo could not keep silent.

"Wait a minute," he said to Las Bombas. "You can't just pick her up like a stray cat. She ought to be someplace where she can be looked after properly. It's not fair to the girl —"

"He was talking to me, not you," broke in Mickle. "You stay out of it with your 'It's not fair to the girl, she ought to be looked after properly.'"

The girl had spoken these last words in Theo's own voice. Though lighter in tone, the accents were identical. Theo did not find it flattering.

Las Bombas clapped his hands. "Marvelous! Still another gift! We'll find good use for it."

Theo said no more, knowing it would be labor lost. He was, moreover, unwilling to open his mouth and have his words tossed back into it. He smarted at the girl's mimicry. He went to the ditch and set about washing off the paint.

When Theo returned, Las Bombas announced they would travel no further that day. Musket hurried into Born to buy provisions. Mickle flung herself on the food, gobbled it as if it could be snatched away at any moment, wiped her hands on her breeches, and contentedly sucked her teeth. At nightfall, Las Bombas opened one of the coach seats, turning it into a cot, and bedded down on it. Musket curled up on the box while Theo stretched out under the coach. Mickle sprawled on the turf beside Friska.

The moon was still high when Theo woke to a thin, trembling sound, like a small animal in pain. He listened a moment. It came from the direction of Friska and the girl. He crawled out and walked cautiously toward them. The mare switched her tail and snuffled gently. Mickle lay on her side, one arm beneath her head, the other outflung. She was motionless, but sobbing as if her heart would break.

Alarmed, Theo knelt. "What's the matter?"

The girl did not answer. Tears flooded her cheeks. He waited silently a while, then went back to the coach. The girl had never stirred. Through all her weeping, she had been fast asleep.

Chapter Eight

y the time Theo opened his eyes, Las Bombas was already up and stirring, dressed in an embroidered caftan and red fez.

"There you are, awake at last," said the count while Theo climbed stiffly to his feet. "Great plans are in store. We'll talk them over at breakfast. I'll pack away Dr. Absalom's Elixir. I suggest you go and rouse our young lady. She'll be in your charge. Your first responsibility, on the earliest occasion, will be to make certain she takes a bath. She's a natural genius, but she smells like a fox."

Mickle still sprawled on the turf. Twice during the night, Theo had gone anxiously to her side. Except for that one strange spell of weeping, she had slept peacefully as she slept now, a half-smile on her wan face. Reluctant to wake her, for some moments he looked down at the girl, feeling like an eavesdropper on a secret part of her life. At last, he took her by the shoulders and gently shook her.

"Come along. It's morning."

"Go away," mumbled the girl. "I get up at noon."

Theo continued urging, but what finally brought Mickle to her feet was the aroma of eggs which Musket was frying in a saucepan. While she attacked her breakfast, the count polished the lens of a lantern, then set it down beside several large round looking glasses.

"The tools to fame and fortune," said the count. "Oh, we'll do The Phrenological Head, I have some further thoughts on that. But what I have in mind is far more spectacular: The Undine. That's a mermaid, my dear, half human, half fish. A fabulous creature of the sea, charming, alluring. Picture it. A dimly lit chamber — we'll use the lantern for that. The Undine seeming to float in midair — I've worked out a clever arrangement of those mirrors. The beautiful sea-child speaks. She knows all. She reveals the mysteries of the future. At a good fee, of course. For a costume, she only needs a fishtail. Any seamstress can stitch it up."

The count beamed. "There's my plan. Simple, elegant, and cheap. What do you say to that?"

Mickle shrugged. "It's easier than housebreaking."

"If you ask me," said Theo, "I think it's nonsense."

"My dear boy!" Las Bombas gave him a wounded glance. "How can you say —"

"Look at her," Theo went on. "Who'll pay to see a scrawny little street bird decked out as a mermaid?" This was his honest, but less than complete, opinion. For some reason, the idea of Mickle being gawked at gave him a peculiar twinge.

Las Bombas drew himself up in injured pride. "No doubt you have a better suggestion."

"Yes, well — in fact, I do," Theo declared. Having made this claim, he wondered how to justify it. He paused, hastily seeking an idea, then went on. "Didn't you tell me something about summoning spirits?"

"They proved reluctant," the count admitted. "In other words, I couldn't pull it off."

"Now you can. Put those arms and legs together with the phrenological head. Dress the girl in a black robe and hood, at a table with one candle in front of her. The spirit appears out of thin air — Musket and I can pull it up and down on strings — and seems to talk. You know she's good at that."

The count said nothing for a long moment. His face shone, his moustache quivered, and he whispered in a voice filled with awe. "The Oracle Priestess. I can see her now. Marvelous!"

"We have paints and brushes," added Theo. "I can make a signboard announcing it."

Las Bombas turned a smile of admiration on Theo. "My boy, I'm proud of you. You have the mind of a first-rate mountebank."

The count, on the spot, produced a square of pasteboard from his store of oddments and ordered Theo to begin work immediately.

Collecting his drawing materials, Theo sat on the ground a little distance away and began to sketch the letters, sorry Anton had ever taught him the skill. He had only intended to keep Las Bombas from making a spectacle of the girl; instead, he had put the count onto a scheme equally disreputable. The count's compliment had unsettled him further. He wondered if indeed he had the heart of a mountebank. He already knew he could have been a murderer.

Mickle had been circling him, venturing closer until she was able to peer over his shoulder. "What's it say there?"

Having put himself into his predicament entirely by his own efforts, Theo was out of sorts with everyone else, especially the girl. "It's plain enough, isn't it?"

Mickle shook her head. "I don't know letters."

"You can't write?" Theo put down his brush. "You can't even read?"

"I wanted to. Nobody would teach me. Hanno said it was a waste of time for a burglar. In the home, they mostly gave us repentance and oatmeal. So I never learned."

"Didn't your parents teach you?"

"They couldn't."

"Couldn't read or write, either?"

"I don't know. They were dead. I don't even remember them. I used to live with my grandfather until he died, too. Now I'll never learn."

"Yes, you will." Theo forgot he was supposed to be vexed. "It's easy. I can show you, for a start. Right now. Do you want to?"

Mickle nodded. Theo put aside the poster and picked up a sheet of paper. Mickle crouched beside him, eyes wide.

"We'll begin with block letters." Theo plied his brush. "Look here. This is the first: *A*."

"I've heard of that. So that's what it looks like?"

"Remember now: *A* stands for *apple*."

"What?" cried Mickle. "I know apples. That isn't one."

"It's only for the sound," said Theo. "All right. Make it *A* for — for *arrowhead*."

"That's better. Yes, I can see that."

"Then comes *B*. It's a *boat*, with wind in the sails. Now, for *C* —"

"How long do they go on?" protested Mickle. "Just tell me the best ones."

"You'll have to know them all, twenty-six of them."

The girl whistled. "That many? I don't have to use them all at once, do I?"

"Of course not. But when you go to write a word, you have to do it letter by letter."

"That's a slow business. I know something faster." Mickle made small, quick gestures with her fingers. "That's how my grandfather and I used to talk. He was deaf and dumb, you see. I worked it out better after I ran off. When they caught me and put me in the home, I showed the other girls how to do it. The charity mistress didn't know we were talking. She thought we were only fidgeting. Then, with Hanno, we made up all kinds of signals. Just lifting your knuckle — like this — it meant 'Look out, someone's coming.' In the burglar trade, it helps if you can talk without making noise."

"Will you teach me?"

"Why? Are you going in for burgling?"

"I like to learn things, that's all. Come on, I'll make a bargain with you. Teach me your language and I'll teach you numbers as well as letters."

"All right," said Mickle. "But no skimping. Show me all twenty-six. And all the numbers, too."

The paint had begun to cake. Promising to go on with the lesson as soon as he finished, Theo turned back to his work. Mickle stayed beside him, watching closely.

After a time, he turned to her and asked quietly, "Are you all right now?"

The girl frowned. "What do you mean?"

"You were crying last night."

"Was not! I never cried in all my life. Not when my granddad died, not when the mistress strapped me, not even when Hanno —"

"I heard you," said Theo. "I saw you. You must have been having a bad dream."

The girl drew back and jumped to her feet. She did not answer, only darted to the coach. Theo called after her. She paid no attention. Las Bombas was urging him to finish quickly so they could be on their way. Theo's hand trembled and he blotted a letter.

Chapter Nine

abbarus was happy. Going about his duties, he paced the corridors of the Juliana with his head bowed, the corners of his mouth turned down. Following His Majesty's collapse, the chief minister had suffered some uneasy moments. If the prospect of Cabbarus for a son had been enough to bring on a seizure, Augustine, recuperating, might have dismissed him outright. On the contrary, the king needed him more than ever, and refused to see any other councillor. And so Cabbarus was happy. As a principle, he tried only to show feelings admirably grave. Pankratz alone understood that his master's morose frown and air of aggressive gloom indicated that Cabbarus was in the best of spirits.

The desired state of affairs had come about very simply. Dr. Torrens had refused to bleed the king, to purge him, blister him with poultices, or dose him with potions. To the dismay of the chief minister, Augustine regained some of his health.

As Torrens admitted, it was health only of the body. The king spent his new energy pursuing his old obsession. Cabbarus had no intention of turning him from it. Instead of warning him against disappointment, Cabbarus provided Augustine with still more occultists and spiritualists, each with a different method of summoning the departed. They shared one thing in common: failure. Each disappointment took its toll of Augustine's health, undoing the best efforts of the court physician.

Dr. Torrens was furious. He entreated the king to give up a ruinous, futile quest. Cabbarus, naturally, sided with the king. By serving his monarch's desires, which was no less than his sacred duty, Cabbarus set His Majesty and the court physician at loggerheads: a situation that grew more bitter each day.

The storm broke sooner than Cabbarus hoped. It followed an audience granted to the latest necromancer, a hairless little man in tinted spectacles: a fraud who actually believed in his nonexistent gift and was sincerely dismayed when he could raise no spirits at all. He left the king on the brink of new collapse.

Dr. Torrens had word of it within the hour. He burst into the royal apartments unsummoned, unannounced. The king, pale and shaking, slumped in his chair. Cabbarus sprang to defend the patient against his doctor.

"You have no business here," declared Cabbarus, holding off the angry Torrens. "His Majesty is suffering."

Torrens addressed himself bluntly to Augustine. "Sire, I have warned you against the consequences of dealing with these charlatans. As your physician, I insist —"

"You shall insist upon nothing," broke in Cabbarus. "The tender emotions of a bereaved father, indeed of a royal father, do not fall within your competence."

"Grief is not only the privilege of kings," said Torrens, disregarding the chief minister. "We all have a right to it. But enough is enough. Your Majesty has made progress. I will not see my work destroyed by quackery."

"If your work can be destroyed so easily," said Cabbarus, "then your methods, Doctor, are ineffective to begin with. His Majesty has been disappointed, for one simple reason. The inducements have not been sufficient to attract those of highest ability. We have agreed — is that not correct, Your Highness? — to offer a more substantial sum. The individual who enables His Majesty to communicate with the late princess will receive the highest reward."

"Call it bait," replied Torrens. "Every knave in the kingdom will try for it. The greater the sum, the greater the knave. As you, Chief Minister, appreciate better than anyone. Sire, have you agreed to this?"

King Augustine's lips moved, but the words were too faint to be heard.

"His Majesty says he fully agrees," declared Cabbarus. "He desires to speak with you no further."

Dr. Torrens was not famous in the Juliana for sparing anyone the rough side of his tongue, but he said with unusual gentleness, "Majesty, none of us knows what lies beyond the tomb. I can only tell you this: Death is not unfamiliar to me. I have seen more of it than I wish. Disease, accident — the forms are different, the end is the same. What befalls us afterward is a mystery. Death is a fact. Forgive me, Sire, if I wound you, but the princess is dead. Unless you accept that simple fact, you will be prey to every false hope."

Augustine's face twisted in anguish. "No! She will return!"

"Majesty, I must forbid any further exertion in these useless —"

"You will forbid nothing!" cried Cabbarus. "Do you dare stand between a father and his daughter?"

"Yes!" flung back Torrens. "Yes! By heaven, Cabbarus, I shall do all in my power to end this folly."

"Your Highness, do you hear the fellow?" Cabbarus recoiled in shock and indignation. "The truth at last! He admits it. He works against you. A loyal subject would seek only to reunite you and the princess, however briefly. What, then, are we to think of one who desires the opposite?"

Cabbarus stretched out an accusing finger at the court physician. "You have gone too far. You are dismissed from His Majesty's service. Banished from the kingdom. Return at your peril, under pain of death. Be grateful your punishment is so light."

"These are your words, not the king's. You have done your best to make a puppet of him, and have done all too well." The court physician was a vigorous man with the arms and shoulders of a peasant. He pushed Cabbarus aside and dropped to one knee before Augustine.

"I beg you, Sire, listen to me. You risk your life and sanity for no purpose. This villain puts words in your mouth. Speak for yourself."

Augustine's lips trembled, but the words were clear. "We banish you. Set foot again in our kingdom and your life is forfeit. Such is our Royal Will."

Torrens drew back as if the king had struck him.

Cabbarus folded his arms. "I would say, Dr. Torrens, you have been answered."

There was, as the chief minister had long observed, a noose to fit every neck. The court physician had found his with very little guidance. It had been easier than Cabbarus expected.

In his apartments, Dr. Torrens finished packing a few surgical instruments and personal belongings he would carry with him. He turned at the sound of his door opening. It was Queen Caroline.

If the court physician was surprised to see her in his quarters, he was more concerned to see her so distraught. It was not the queen's custom to give way to visible emotion, but all her will could not keep her hands from trembling. Dr. Torrens bowed and gave a wry smile of apology for the disordered chamber.

"As you gather, Madam, I have been obliged to deal with the inconveniences of a hasty departure. The chief minister has already prepared a warrant for my execution. He has the satisfaction of seeing me exiled. I prefer not to give him the pleasure of seeing me hanged."

"I feared you had left the palace," Queen Caroline said. "This is despicable. Even a common criminal is granted more time to set his affairs in order."

Torrens laughed. "To Cabbarus I am a most uncommon criminal. I spoke the truth to His Majesty. In any case, I would not have gone without taking leave of you and explaining my side of it. Cabbarus will no doubt spread his own version."

"He has done so, and of course I did not believe it. I went immediately to the king. He refused to see me. I was unable to help you. Thus His Majesty loses his strongest friend."

"Not altogether."

"How not? Most of the ministers do as Cabbarus orders, the rest hold their tongues. When you go, the king's one strength goes with you. Cabbarus has played his hand cleverly."

"A scoundrel is no more clever than an honest man; he only works harder at it. He has not won all the stakes."

The queen gave him a questioning look.

Dr. Torrens went on. "My baggage will soon be taken to the port. I have ordered inquiries made of vessels ready to sail; the more remote their destination, the better."

"Must you go so far? There are closer kingdoms where you would be safe."

"I spoke of my baggage, not myself. I do not intend leaving Westmark. I shall try to send you word as often as I can. It may not always be possible. If you hear nothing from me, assume the best. Or the worst. In either case, do not lose heart. You and His Majesty have yet another strength. I will seek it out and do all I can to nourish it. In time, it may prove the strongest. I speak, Madam, of the people of Westmark."

"Our subjects? But how, then —"

"I said 'people,' Madam. They are your subjects through affection and loyalty. They are people in their own right. I believe most understand that Cabbarus, not the monarchy, is to blame for the injustices, the punishments, indeed the whole sorry state of the kingdom. I hope to find those who will rally to your side against him."

"You expect much from commoners," said the queen.

"I do," said Torrens. He smiled. "Being one of them myself."

It was close to midnight when Dr. Torrens finished his preparations and the hired wagon arrived to carry his baggage to the port. He traveled ahead in an open coach with all lamps lit, loudly declaring that he wished to be driven to the waterfront. He kept only the small bag with him. He had resigned himself to sacrificing his other belongings.

At the quayside, he entered a seafarer's inn where his inquiries had been received. There he met the master of an outward-bound merchantman and struck a bargain with him to be taken on as a passenger. He paid openly in gold and requested the captain to have his luggage immediately stowed on board. He asked about the tides, the hour the vessel would sail, and the length of the voyage. He demanded assurance that his cabin would be comfortable. He did not say he had no intention of occupying it.

This business concluded within earshot of all the company, Dr. Torrens settled himself at a table and called for a bottle of wine. He drank hardly a glass before telling his host that he would return momentarily and to keep an eye on the bottle, which he would attend to when he came back.

He left the inn and strode briskly along the docks. By now he had singled out the spy he knew Cabbarus would send: a seaman in canvas slops and a grimy jacket. The man was dressed as roughly as any common sailor; he was, however, the only one in the room without dirt or tar under his fingernails.

The doctor's plan was not to avoid the eyes of the chief minister's agent but, on the contrary, to make sure the man saw him. The fellow, of course, would keep him under scrutiny until Torrens was aboard. Just before setting foot on the gangplank, Torrens would make a show of having forgotten his bottle at the inn. He would turn, go back, then suddenly lose himself in one of the alleyways. With luck, he would have a few moments head start before his observer realized he had vanished. Torrens calculated in advance the most suitable unlit alley.

The sailor was following too closely. The man was incompetent if he thought to go unnoticed. It was all Torrens could do to pretend not to see him. The man was at his heels. Torrens halted, reckoning no other course but to confront him. The man held a knife. Torrens, too late, realized he had done what he had never done in his medical practice. He had overlooked the obvious. He expected a spy. He had not counted on an assassin.

Chapter Ten

They reached Felden by midafternoon. Las Bombas judged the town would suit them perfectly.

"It's big enough," he said as they halted in the market square, "to have gentry with money in their pockets, and small enough so they won't be too critical. An excellent place for the Oracle Priestess to learn the business. Then, on to greater fame and fortune."

Las Bombas had pinned a number of royal honors and medals to his uniform, unidentifiable but unmistakably noble. Thus decked out, he strode into the largest lodging house and demanded the best suite of furnished apartments. The landlord, too dazzled and flattered to dare bring up the question of advance payment, hurried to show the count the most elegant he could offer. The rooms, on the second floor, had been occupied by a dancing master. The main salon, spacious and high-ceilinged, attracted Las Bombas immediately. He hired the apartments then and there.

Seeing Friska comfortably stabled, the count and Musket went off to survey the town and post the signboard where it would best catch the public eye. Theo, having unpacked the count's gear, was left to his own devices. He had never set foot in such luxurious quarters; nor, he was sure, had Mickle. But the girl only glanced at the ornaments, remarking that Hanno would have found little worth stealing.

As if that settled the matter, she lost interest in exploring and flung herself onto the sofa, her legs outstretched, feet on an end table. Before entering Felden, Theo had persuaded her to make at least a token effort at washing at a streamside. Las Bombas had given her the Trebizonian costume, which suited her scarcely better than it had suited Theo.

The girl had barely spoken to him since leaving Born. Why he found this both painful and aggravating, he did not know. To pass the time, he rummaged in the count's oddments and found clean paper and a charcoal stick. He went to the casement, thinking to sketch the marketplace for his own amusement. His attention wandered. His eyes returned continually to Mickle. He began what he expected to be a quick portrait of her. Though he had learned to draw as easily as he lettered, the closer he studied Mickle the more difficult she became. He tore up the paper and started again.

Mickle spoiled his new attempt by jumping up. Whatever had caused her to ignore him, her curiosity got the better of her.

"Is that supposed to be me?" She peered over his shoulder and made a face.

"Supposed to be. But it isn't." Theo felt he was blushing, but there was nothing he could do about it. "I can't make you pretty —"

Mickle tossed her head. "Didn't ask you to."

"No, I mean it's more than that. One minute, you look like a scared little bird, and the next as if you could stand up to Cabbarus himself. You say you didn't cry when your friend got hanged, but you cry in your sleep and don't remember it. Sometimes you look as though butter wouldn't melt in your mouth; then you swear like a dragoon, smoke like a chimney — The count called you a genius, and you can't read or write. I can't catch all that on paper. I don't know what you are."

"That's all right." Mickle grinned at last. "I don't know what you are, either. The count's a rascal, that's plain as a pikestaff. Thumbling's a good fellow. But I don't see how you came to take up with them."

Theo hesitated. He felt a sudden urge to tell the girl what had happened to him and an equal unwillingness to admit anything at all. Before he could decide which to follow, the provisioner's errand boy hauled in a huge basket of food; in another moment, the wine merchant entered with an armload of bottles; and finally Las Bombas himself leading a brigade of tailors, barbers, dressmakers, and carpenters.

Before he understood what was happening, Theo had bolts of cloth draped over his shoulders, and he was being measured, chalked, pinned, and fitted for waistcoats, jackets, and breeches. Mickle had vanished in clouds of lace

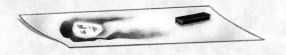

and billows of satin. Of Musket he saw nothing; only the dwarf's bellowing rose above the din, ordering the carpenters about their work.

"How did you manage all this?" the astonished Theo asked Las Bombas, who was in the hands of two barbers trying to shave and powder him. "How did you pay?"

"By a miracle, my boy." The count beamed. "The miracle of credit. The more we manage to owe these fellows, the better they'll look after us."

By nightfall, when the carpenters had left after nailing up a platform and wooden frame at the end of the salon, the landlord and his wife arrived to serve an enormous supper. Las Bombas interrupted each course to drink a toast to their good fortune, present and future. Theo, overstuffed and exhausted, was glad at last to find his way to the luxury of his own bed in his own chamber. Mickle stayed at the table, making certain nothing remained on the plates.

Too tired even to enjoy the feather pillows and mattress, Theo sank into them like a stone. He had been asleep, he did not know how long, when a scream ripped apart his slumber.

He sat up, head spinning. His body answered before he could gather his wits. By the time he realized the sound had come from Mickle's room, he was on his feet and plunging through the connecting door.

A candle guttered on the night table. Mickle crouched amid a heap of bedclothes. Her face was dead white, streaked with sweat, her eyes wide and staring, empty of everything but terror. He was not sure she even recognized him. He ran to her.

She threw her arms around him. He rocked her back and forth like a child, smoothing her tangled hair. Her cheeks and forehead were icy.

"Nothing, it's nothing," he said. "You had another bad dream. It's gone."

"I was drowning. Water over my head. I kept sinking. I couldn't breathe."

Theo was only now aware that Las Bombas and Musket had been standing behind him. The count, nightcap askew, ordered the dwarf to fetch a glass of wine, then peered anxiously at the girl.

"You'll be fine in a moment. A nightmare, eh? Too much supper, I shouldn't wonder." He sat down beside her and laughed good-naturedly, though giving Theo a quick glance of concern. "Drowning, you say? In that case, you're perfectly safe. No one, to my knowledge, has ever drowned in bed."

Mickle sipped the wine Musket brought. She snuffled and wiped her nose on the back of her hand. Some color had come back to her cheeks. She smiled at last. After a few more moments, she was making impudent remarks about the count's nightcap, joking with Musket, and mimicking Theo.

Even so, when Las Bombas and Musket went back to their chambers, Theo sensed she was still frightened and stayed, waiting until she fell asleep. He sat watchful the rest of the night. Mickle did not stir.

Next morning, she was quiet and polite, which worried Theo all the more. Musket was busy stringing together the false arms and legs. Las Bombas had gone to hire more chairs for the salon. To distract her and put her in better spirits, Theo started her portrait again.

This time, he had her sit by the casement and ordered her not to move. He worked rapidly at first, with somewhat better result. Then he found himself looking at her so intently that his charcoal stayed poised above the paper as if he had forgotten what he was doing.

Mickle began fidgeting. She complained of a stiff neck and refused to pose longer. She brightened when he offered to go on with her lessons. They sat heads together in a sunny corner while Theo quickly went over the whole alphabet. He planned to go back and teach her a few letters at a time. But when he started his review, Mickle rattled off all twenty-six in nearly perfect order.

"That's all there is to it?"

"I told you it was easy." Theo did not add that he never expected her to do so well so fast. He would gladly have taken credit to himself as school-master. He knew it was not the case. It was not his doing. The girl astonished him. Las Bombas, he thought, had been right. She was a genius. "Next, you'll start making words."

Mickle had lost interest. She looked out the window, turned back, restless.

Finally, she said to him, after much hesitation, "Do you think — about last night, does it mean someday I'm going to drown? The girls in the home used to say that dreams told what was going to happen to you."

"That's nonsense. You had a bad dream, that's all. It's gone, it won't come back."

"It — it's never gone," Mickle burst out. "I've always had it. Not the same every time. Sometimes there's a well and I'm trying to get a drink. Or there's a ditch full of water, but the sides are so high I can't climb out. But it always ends the same: I'm drowning and there's nobody to help.

"Last night, there was a voice, someone saying terrible things. I can't remember what they were. And somebody was laughing. It's the first I ever dreamed that. It was the worst of all."

Theo frowned. "That's what you always dream about?"

"No." The girl had taken his hand, gripping it tightly. "There's another dream I have. It doesn't frighten me. It only makes me want to cry. I dream about my mother and father. It's a nice dream at first. We're happy, laughing, playing hide-and-seek the way we used to do. Then it's my turn to hide and they can't find me. They're calling for me but when I answer they can't hear me. They're very sad and so am I. Because I know I'll never see them again."

She was trembling. After a moment, she pulled away and without another word went to her room.

Theo stood, about to follow. Musket was bellowing for him to come and lend a hand. Something in the girl's account puzzled him. He was sure, outside Born, Mickle had told him her parents were long dead, that she had never known them.

Chapter Eleven

he phrenological head was now a working ghost. Swathed in white gauze and attached to the false arms and legs, it appeared a startling spectral figure. Theo and Musket had rigged pulleys from the ceiling, and fixed thin black cords to the mannequin. From their hiding place behind a black screen, they could hoist the figure and make it seem to float across the salon. Las Bombas, meanwhile, instructed Mickle in her role as Oracle Priestess. Before the end of the week, the count was satisfied with all preparations and, that night, flung open his doors to the public.

Theo privately doubted there would be any audience. No one, he believed, would be taken in by such hoaxing. Squinting through a peephole in the screen, he could not believe his eyes. The room was too dim for him to be certain of the number, but most of the chairs were filled. Mickle, robed in black, sat in the light of a single candle, as Theo had suggested. At her signal, he and Musket tugged away at the cords. The ghost obediently rose into the air. The audience gasped; there were a few screams of delicious terror. Someone in the back of the salon paid Theo's handiwork the compliment of fainting dead away.

Las Bombas urged the company to consult the spirit on any matter of concern. Theo braced himself for disaster as questions showered on the Oracle from all sides. One gentleman demanded to know where his late uncle had hidden his will, as he expected to inherit all the estate. A lady anxiously sought spiritual advice on what colors would be coming into fashion. He expected Mickle to burst out laughing, but the girl kept a straight face. Sitting motionless, eyes closed, she gave every sign of being lost in the deepest trance; with a trick of her voice, she made the phrenological head seem to speak in eerie, sepulchral tones. The answers, however, were so vague that the questioners could take any meaning they chose.

Instead of indignant outcries at being cheated, the audience clamored for more. Las Bombas finally had to declare that the Oracle Priestess was too fatigued; the ghost was dismissed to rejoin its fellow shades. Advising the spectators to come back another day, Las Bombas hustled them out as quickly as possible and locked the doors behind them.

"Magnificent!" cried the count as Theo and Musket came from their hiding place. He threw his arms around Mickle. "Dear girl, you were superb!"

Las Bombas delved into his bulging pockets and tossed handfuls of coins into the air. "Look at this! So much that I lost count of it!"

"No matter how you add it up," muttered Theo, "it still comes to a fraud."

"Indeed it does, my boy," Las Bombas happily answered. "The best I've struck on. Credit where it's due, I have you to thank. You thought of it, you put me onto it. A brilliant notion, and it's all yours."

Theo said nothing in reply. He was ashamed of himself, appalled that his scheme had worked so well. He also had to admit that he was not entirely displeased.

Mickle seemed to have no qualms whatever. During the days following, she was in the best of spirits. The nightmare had not come back, nor had the other dream. Since the Oracle Priestess had no duties until evening, the rest of the time was her own. Mornings she spent with Theo going over the alphabet.

She knew her letters perfectly and had begun writing them as quickly as she had learned to say them.

Mickle kept her part of the bargain. Afternoons were her turn to play schoolmistress and teach her sign language to Theo. He did not learn as quickly as his former pupil.

"No, no, you've got it all wrong again," Mickle told him. "Move your thumb up, not sideways. Here, watch my fingers."

Little by little, he caught the knack. He practiced with her at every opportunity, adding improvements. Now that Mickle could spell, he devised a finger motion for each letter. Thus, when Mickle's gestures did not exactly suit the circumstances, she spelled out words of explanation. Within little more than a week, they could signal anything they pleased, so quickly that no outsider could guess they were using a silent code. Though Las Bombas and Musket could not fail to notice the two young people passed most of their time in each other's company, they did not comment.

For the rest, Theo expected, even hoped, the novelty of The Oracle Priestess would wear off. The Feldeners, instead, crowded the salon each night in growing numbers. Las Bombas crowed over the receipts. Theo's conscience smarted like a skinned knee.

He finally asked the count when they would move on.

Las Bombas blinked at him. "What an idea! We've barely skimmed the cream. In fact, I'm thinking of doubling the admission price."

"I'm thinking we should stop altogether," blurted Theo. "I've gone along this far, which I shouldn't have done. There must be something better than cheating people."

"Who's cheating anyone?" protested the count. "Harmless amusement! Do you think for a moment they believe one bit of it? Are they complaining? Set your mind at rest, my boy. Now, here's a thought for you. Suppose we put up refreshment tables in the hall. That would be a new attraction."

Next night, Theo was almost willing to admit the count was right. The Oracle Priestess had become fashionable among the Felden gentry, probably through lack of better diversion. The audience, more and more, came to see and be seen; to be amused by the antics of the phrenological head; to admire the wistful charms of the Priestess. There was much gossip and laughter; no one, as far as Theo could gather, truly believed in the girl's ghostly pronouncements. Las Bombas might as well have opened a comedy theater.

However, among the spectators who used the occasion to put on all their finery, Theo glimpsed a man and woman dressed in deep mourning. Their garb alone would have set them apart. From the woman's raw hands, the man's weathered face and heavy shoulders, Theo guessed the couple to be smallholders or tenant farmers. The two sat ill at ease amid the town dwellers.

Only toward the end of the evening did the woman venture to stand. She made an awkward curtsy to Mickle and to the phrenological head, causing a few titters among the audience. She glanced around uncomfortably and looked ready to sit down again without a word.

"Come, madam," said Las Bombas, "the Priestess grows fatigued. If you wish to consult the spirit, come out with it."

"Sir" — the woman hesitated, reddening — "our girl's dead a week now. It was the fever, you see. We can't have her back, I know that. All I want to ask, can you tell us: Wherever she is, is she happy there?"

The phrenological head assured its questioner that the girl was happier than she had ever been in all her life. The woman stammered her gratitude for setting their hearts at rest.

Las Bombas then asked for more questions. None came. The audience had turned restless and embarrassed; some stood up to leave, as if the woman's grief had cast a shadow over their entertainment. The count finally declared the séance ended.

"How can you do it?" Theo demanded, as soon as the last of the spectators had gone. "They were heartbroken, those two. It wasn't just foolishness for them. They took it seriously. We told them a pack of lies."

"My boy, they were quite satisfied," answered Las Bombas. "What do you want?"

"No more of it," said Theo, "that's what I want. Call it harmless amusement if you like. You're taking advantage of people who don't know any better. It's dishonest, it's contemptible." He rounded on Mickle. "You understand what I mean, don't you? You see what we're doing."

"I'm doing what you wanted," the girl retorted. "It was your idea in the first place, wasn't it?"

"No, you don't understand, either," burst out Theo. "Can't you even see what's right or wrong? Or don't you care? I shouldn't have expected any better from you."

Mickle gasped as if he had slapped her in the face. Instead of answering, she pulled the hood over her head and ran to her chamber.

Theo could have bitten his tongue as soon as he had spoken the words. He started after her. Las Bombas held him back.

"Let be. You've hurt the child's feelings already, and you'll make matters worse, the state you're in. Patch it up in the morning."

"Let's leave here," said Theo. "There must be something else we can do."

"Change The Oracle Priestess? When it's working so marvelously? Ridiculous! Out of the question! Have a good sleep. You'll feel better tomorrow."

Without replying, Theo went to his room and flung himself on the bed. Tormented at wounding Mickle, he only hoped he could make it up to her. That still did not satisfy his conscience. Las Bombas had no intention of changing his ways. He was fond of the count, as fond as he had ever been of Anton. But the man was a born rogue, and Theo was well on the road to becoming one himself. Anton would not have been proud of him. The answer was clear. He had gone far enough, perhaps too far. To save whatever shreds of honesty were left him, he would have to quit Las Bombas, the sooner the better. Now, he told himself, this very night. If he waited, he feared he would not have strength to do it.

No sooner had he made up his mind to that than he realized he could not leave Mickle. The idea was unbearable to him. Much as he had hurt the girl, he believed he could finally make her understand. She would come with him, if he tried his best to persuade her.

He stood and went quickly to her room. He raised his hand to tap on the door, but the motion froze in midair. To his dismay, he realized he had forgotten one thing. He was a wanted criminal, a fugitive who could be arrested at any moment. He did not dare ask her to stay with him. Even if she wanted to, he could not let her. She would be as much at risk as himself. She would be safe with Las Bombas, mountebank though he was.

He let his hand fall to his side. He stood, uncertain, at the door. Finally he turned away. The portrait, unfinished, lay on a table. He was about to pick it up. He shook his head. It would pain him less if he had no reminder of her.

He carried nothing with him as he went quietly down the stairs. He could not trust himself to say farewell. He strode across the market square. The town slept. Though nearly summer, the night was cool.

There was no question in Theo's mind. He had done the right and honorable thing. For the first time since taking up with Las Bombas, his conscience was at ease.

And he felt miserable.

Part Three
Florian's Children

Chapter Twelve

he lodging house at the end of Strawmarket Street stood as one of the marvels of Freyborg: the marvel being that it stood at all. The spider webs in every corner appeared to be its strongest support. The narrow staircase lurched up three flights and stayed in place out of habit. Mold flowered from cracks in the walls. The roof shed its tiles like autumn leaves. The lodgings, nevertheless, had two things to recommend them: cheap rent and a landlord who never asked questions.

The topmost room was a little bigger than a baker's oven. In summer, the stifling tenant could take comfort knowing that he would, in due season, freeze. This cubbyhole was often vacant. For the past two months, however, it had been occupied by a public letter writer calling himself De Roth.

His new name had been Theo's choice. His new occupation and living quarters he owed to Florian.

On the night he had left Felden, he struck out across country, heading generally south. He trudged without a halt until daybreak. Even then he did not stop until some hours later when his legs gave out. He had made up his mind not to think of Mickle, the count, Musket, or anything connected with them. In consequence, he thought of nothing else. Mickle's absence crept over him like a toothache: at first ignored, then denied, then taking command altogether.

He kept on a straight path for the next few days. He slept in barns or hayricks, if one happened to be in his way. Otherwise, he crawled under bushes or flung himself down in open fields. He neither asked for nor refused hospitality from the farm folk. Sometimes he mucked out stables or chopped logs for a sack of food. Convinced that he had acted honorably, he was proud of his strength of will. He also caught a cold.

He limped into Freyborg around midday, bursting with lofty sentiments and a stopped-up nose. Perhaps he had intended going there from the first. In the days before Cabbarus, when Anton worked for the university scholars, the ancient town had come to be a sparkling, almost magical, fountainhead of learning for Theo. He found it gray, the streets narrow, the famous university tower smaller than he had imagined. He was too hungry to think of being disappointed.

There was a tavern on the near side of the square, facing a statue of Augustine the Great. He went inside, hoping to trade work for a meal. In the busy room, he saw no one who might be the host. The waiters ignored him. He squeezed onto the end of a bench and leaned his head against the wall.

His tablemates, half a dozen young men and women, were talking and laughing. What drew Theo's attention was the bowl of soup in front of his neighbor, a massive-browed, bullnecked youth whose hair had already begun thinning. Theo's nose was not too blocked to keep out the aroma, and he lost himself in it.

"Stock," said the young man directly across from Theo, "this gentleman appears to be memorizing your soup."

Theo started, realizing his head had come forward little by little as if the bowl were a magnet. He stammered an apology, which only brought him under scrutiny of all the party.

"What has now to be determined," the speaker went on, as attentive silence fell over the table, "is the reason for such fascination. Is it the essential nature of the soup, hidden from all of us? Stock's table manners, hidden from none of us? Or still another cause?"

Though only a few years older than Theo, the speaker seemed to have crossed some invisible line giving him an authority beyond the number of his birthdays. His hair was light brown and he wore it long and loose. Pockmarks sprayed his cheeks and the bridge of his finely drawn nose. He was studying Theo with apparently idle amusement; but his gray eyes took in everything at once, observing, calculating, and summing up the result.

Theo sensed he was being laughed at or soon would be. Had he looked in a mirror these past days he would have seen good reason for it. His hair was matted, his clothes wrinkled and muddy, his face dirty and wind-raw.

"He's hungry, Florian," put in one of the young women, fair-haired and broad-faced, with the swollen hands of a laundress.

"Obviously. But to what degree? Is he hungry enough to risk Master Jellinek's concoction? This remains to be seen, theory proved in practice. Pass him your bowl, Stock. Go on, don't be a pig about it."

Chuckling and grumbling at the same time, Stock did as he was asked. Florian raised a finger and two waiters arrived instantly. One set a goblet in front of Theo, the other poured wine into it.

Florian lifted his own glass. "To the health of one who is ever in our thoughts: our chief minister."

Theo reddened. He was too tired to be polite. He pushed away the glass. "Drink to him yourself. I won't."

"My children!" cried Florian. "Do you hear? This youngster, clearly perishing from hunger, stands nevertheless on his principles. He sets us an example. Put to the same test, would we do as well?" He turned to Theo. "Spoken bravely but carelessly. You haven't the mind of a lawyer, which is a great blessing for you. Otherwise, you would have observed the health was not specified as 'good.' You jumped to a conclusion. In this case, a wrong one. Would you care to reconsider?

"Seize the opportunity," Florian continued. "Don't think we banquet like this every day. We are celebrating the anniversary of Rina's birth." He nodded at the laundress, who rose and made a mocking curtsy. "With us, it is feast or famine, more often the latter."

Theo ventured to ask if they were students. Hoots and whistles followed his question.

"We forgive your unintended offense," Florian said. "No one with a thirst for knowledge goes to the university now. Half the faculty has resigned, the other half gives courses in advanced ignorance. The Royal Grant is no longer very royal nor much granted. Public intelligence, in the view of Cabbarus, is a public nuisance, like a stray cat. If unfed, it will go away. But allow me to present my children, my fledgling eagles waiting impatiently to spread their wings.

"Our worthy Stock, though he may look like a prize bull, is by inclination a poet; by temperament, a dreamer. This one, Justin" — he pointed to a thin, pale youth, close to Theo's age, with hair so yellow it shone almost white, and with long-lashed eyes of astonishing violet — "Justin has the face of an angel; whereas, in fact, he is a bloodthirsty sort of devil. The result, possibly, of seeing his father hanged. Our two goddesses, the golden Rina and the russet Zara, guide and inspire us."

Florian stood, laid a hand on his bosom, and struck an exaggerated oratorical pose. "As for me, I pursued the study of law until I learned there is only one: the decree of Nature herself that men are brothers; and the only criminals, those who break her statute. Students? Yes. But our classroom is the world."

When his companions, playing audience, finished cheering and pounding the table, Florian went on more quietly.

"And you, youngster? What brings you here? Your trade appears to be professional scarecrow. You may find little call for your services."

Theo's fever was singing lightly in his ears. The food and drink had turned him a little giddy. Florian, on top of that, seemed to have the odd power of drawing him out. Though he kept enough caution to say nothing of Dorning, Theo hardly stopped talking long enough to catch his breath. He gladly unburdened himself, having spoken no more than a dozen words in a dozen days. He detailed his journey with Las Bombas and tried to explain that he had left Mickle for her own good. He finally realized he had been babbling and let his account trail off.

"He loved her," sighed Rina. "It was noble of him. It was beautiful."

"It was stupid," said Zara.

Florian raised a hand. "Children, we are not called upon to render a verdict, only to ponder what should be done."

He spoke apart with the auburn-haired Zara for a moment, and turned back to Theo. "The russet divinity will see you housed for the time being, Master — would you care to tell us your name?"

"It's" — Theo paused, remembering the order for his arrest, and hoping to cover his tracks as best he could — "it's — De Roth."

"Go along with her, then, Master De Roth." Florian grinned. "Here, we feed our stray cats."

Zara led him to Strawmarket Street. The girl said little, as did Theo, still rankling at her comment. When he told her he had no money for rent, Zara shrugged. He could, she advised, settle it with the landlord some other time. Florian, meanwhile, would vouch for him.

"What does Florian do?" Theo asked. "What's his work?"

"His work?" Zara gave him a hard smile. "He works at being Florian."

ext day, having slept the clock around, Theo found his way back to the tavern. He wanted to thank Florian and take leave of him. He saw none of the company in the public room. Jellinek, a stout little man, surprisingly good-natured for a landlord, recognized Theo. He motioned with his thumb toward a cubicle beside the kitchen. Because of the commotion behind the door, Theo's knock went unheard or ignored. He let himself in, though uneasy at intruding on what sounded like a furious oration.

It was Stock and, as Theo would learn, only his way of holding forth on any subject. The burly poet stalked back and forth, arms waving. Florian, Justin, and several others unknown to Theo sat around a plank table.

"A battle, I say, is a poem," Stock was declaiming. "A sonnet of death, men for verses, blood for punctuation. Attack and counterattack, rhyme against rhyme, cavalry against foot —"

"How do you reckon artillery, then?" broke in one of the listeners, called, as Theo later found out, Luther. "The exclamation marks? Clever notion. It only has one flaw. It has nothing to do with real fighting. Take my advice, keep to scribbling."

Glimpsing Theo, Florian beckoned. "Stock has given up being a field marshal of poetry in favor of being a poetic field marshal. And what are you up to?"

"I'll have to move on. I'll try to send you money for my lodging."

"Going, are you? Where?"

"It doesn't matter. Wherever I can find some sort of work."

"These aren't the best days to go wandering around the country," said Florian.

"I need to make a living, one way or another."

Florian thought for a while. "Do you write a clear hand? There's room for a public letter writer here in Freyborg. The previous incumbent is no longer with us, and Stock finds the profession demeaning to his genius."

"Yes, I could do that," Theo began eagerly. He stopped short. The day before, he had said nothing of what had happened in Dorning. He was still reluctant to do so. If Florian knew the truth about him, he might well withdraw his offer. Harboring a fugitive was as much a crime as being one. He took a breath and hurried on. "You may not want me to stay. There's something I have to tell you."

"Go at it, then." Seeing his discomfort, Florian motioned for the others to leave.

"What you ought to know," said Theo, once they were alone, "is — I'm in some trouble."

"We all are. Go on."

After his painful hesitation, Theo poured out the whole account. His surprise, when he finished, was Florian's lack of surprise.

"Youngster, I'm sorry," said Florian. "A brutal business, but I've heard far worse."

"If I stay here, it could put you in trouble. And your friends, too."

"Don't worry, we can manage it," said Florian. "In fact, you couldn't be in a safer place. So, it's settled."

"One more thing."

"Oh? You seem to have quite a lot on your mind."

"My name. It isn't De Roth."

Florian laughed. "We have something in common. My name isn't Florian."

From then on, a bench and table were reserved for Theo in Jellinek's tavern, with pen, ink, and paper supplied by the host until he earned enough to buy his own. It had all been arranged so quickly, as if Florian needed only to snap his fingers. With Florian, he came to know, this was how things happened.

In the following days, as he became a familiar sight in his corner, he drew a small but steady stream of customers.

Some were able to write slowly and painfully, others not at all. None could draft a letter setting out what they had in mind to say. The task of Theo was to sort their ideas and try to put them on paper.

An old woman needed an appeal to the Royal Prosecutor on behalf of her son, in prison for a crime he did not commit. A kitchen maid expecting a child wished to write her sweetheart, who had gone off to Marianstat, and lie to him that all went well with her. There were letters swearing undying love; letters begging for it; furious letters threatening lawsuits; timid letters asking more time to pay a debt. To the public letter writer, as much a piece of furniture as the bench he sat on, none hesitated to pour out every sorrow, shame, fear, and hope. Most of the letters went unanswered.

Nights, Theo often lay awake tossing and sweating on his pallet in the loft, chewing over his clients' misfortunes as if he had to absorb them before he could rest. Sometimes, on the contrary, he could not go to sleep fast enough to escape them. He was overwhelmed, appalled. Finally, he grew modest. Until then, he had believed he suffered a very high quality of misery. It took him a little time to accept the humbling idea that most of his customers were in worse case than himself.

Mornings, he went to Jellinek's tavern. Florian was sometimes there, sometimes not. He had the habit of disappearing for several days on end. When he reappeared, something in his bearing warned Theo against asking him where he had been.

Stock and the others were used to these absences and did not comment on them. Theo, again, sensed that he should not raise questions. Otherwise, he got on well with them and enjoyed their company.

The golden divinity and the russet divinity, he soon realized, were clearly in love with Florian: the former, dreamily and happily; the latter, bitterly and almost against her will. Stock, who usually turned furious at the least criticism of his poetry, listened closely to Florian's opinions. For the most part, Florian kept a wry good humor. Sometimes, however, his remarks could sting. The others were able to shrug them off, but on one occasion when Florian made a mildly sarcastic remark to Justin, the latter nearly burst into tears.

"You should have answered back," Theo later told him. "You shouldn't have let him hurt your feelings."

Justin turned his eyes on Theo. "If he asked me to, I'd die for him."

To be called "my child" by Florian was a title of honor. It had not been granted to Theo. Nevertheless, he yearned for it. Despite Florian's help and interest, Theo was aware of a certain lack of acceptance. Perhaps he had not yet earned it, perhaps he did not deserve it. In the lives of Florian and his children, some part was held back from him, and he was puzzled by it.

What also puzzled Theo was how Florian stayed out of prison, for the man spoke his mind whenever and wherever he chose. The townsfolk worshiped him, and Theo first believed the officers feared a riot if they laid hands on him. Theo was wrong, as he learned one afternoon when two constables strode into the tavern and began badgering Jellinek for information about a runaway apprentice.

Theo broke into a sweat, sure it was himself they were asking about. Jellinek, sweating as much as Theo, kept wiping his hands and face with his apron. Florian finally got up from his usual seat.

He sauntered over to the constables. Smiling, he quietly suggested they leave. He did not raise hand or voice. The smile never left his face, but his gray eyes had turned bright and hard as ice. The officers blustered a few moments, then declared the matter unimportant and hurried out. Theo understood. It was not the townsfolk they feared. It was Florian.

Florian's assurance of safety had not been idle boasting, and Theo was grateful. His spirits had begun mending a little. At times, however, he turned restless, feeling his days were without sense or point.

"I'm glad for the work," he told Florian one morning in the tavern, "but none of it does much good. I write their letters, but nothing comes of it. I'm not making anything better for them. What's the use?"

"The use," answered Florian, "is that they need you. There's always a chance something may work out. You give them a grain of hope, at least. Be satisfied you can do anything at all.

"As a matter of fact," he went on, "I might have something else for you. I warn you, it won't be easy."

"What is it?"

"We'll talk about it when the time comes."

Theo, excited, pressed him for some hint, but Florian left, saying no more. The old woman whose son was in prison had been waiting patiently. Theo had written her same letter to the Royal Prosecutor so often that he knew it word for word. He had, until then, considered that the best service he could do would be to tell her to go away, that it was a lost cause. He beckoned to her.

"Come along, mother," he said. "Let's try again."

Chapter Fourteen

There's a dead one." The boy held up his lantern and leaned over the side of the rowboat. "Pull hard, Sparrow."

The girl did as her brother asked. The craft bobbed alongside the stone steps leading from the embankment to the dock. The boy, Weasel, was small and as thin as his namesake. Sparrow, a few years older and the stronger, took charge of the rowing on their nightly ventures into the port.

The man lay on his belly, half in, half out of the water. His legs swung gently in the tide.

Sparrow shipped her oars. "Drowned, is he?"

Weasel threw a line around the iron stanchion and hopped out of the boat. He squatted by the body but could not turn it. Sparrow came to help. They saw the knife hilt.

"A brawl." Weasel nodded his head in solemn professional judgment. He tugged until the weapon came free of the breast. "It's a good blade."

He put the knife in his belt. Sparrow had been deftly going through the pockets. She had no fear of the dead. On the other hand, she was terrified of spiders.

The jacket and canvas slops yielded nothing. She made a face and shrugged her shoulders. The lantern light showed a bulky form a few steps higher. Sparrow got to her feet. The boy, too, noticed the figure and clambered after his sister.

"I knew it was a brawl," Weasel declared with satisfaction.

 This man was white-haired and blunt-featured. One sleeve, bloodsoaked, had been slashed up the arm. The girl rummaged in the pockets. This time she whistled. She had discovered a purse of coins, and something else: The man was alive. Weasel crouched beside her, greatly interested. They had never found a live one.

"What shall we do with him, Sparrow?"

The girl chewed her lower lip. She was a sharp-faced creature, more vixen than bird. The man was looking at her, muttering something she could not make out.

She bent closer, listening, then glanced at Weasel. "I don't know what he's saying, but I don't think he wants to stay here."

"I shouldn't wonder," said Weasel.

Like her brother, Sparrow wore a garment of sacking. Her one vanity was the kerchief about her head. She undid it and awkwardly bound up the man's arm. Her patient groaned and made a feeble gesture.

"What's he after?" Until then, Weasel had given all his attention to the unusual find. Now, at the edge of the circle of light, he glimpsed a leather case. He scuttled over and picked it up. "This?"

Weasel snapped open the catch and peered inside. "Knives and things. They'll be worth something."

Sparrow had finished her work and had come to her decision. "We'll keep him."

"What will Keller say?"

"He'll be glad. It's company for him, isn't it?"

The two set about hauling the man down the steps and aboard the boat. He was conscious enough to make some small effort to help. Otherwise, his salvagers would have had to leave their prize where they found it. Weasel cast off the line. Sparrow labored to get the craft under way before the tide turned against her.

The River Vespera flowed through Marianstat. Near the port, narrow spits of land reached out from the banks: The Fingers. Part marsh, part scrub lining a maze of inlets, The Fingers formed a hand grasping whatever floated by. Human bodies, as well as animal carcasses, sometimes came to bob among the reeds. They were picked over for anything useful and sent on their voyage again by the scavengers who lived and made a living there.

These river and shore dwellers avoided each other. They had their favorite backwaters which they defended jealously, tending and harvesting them like frugal farmers, selling their crop for a pittance in Marianstat. When the harvest was lean, those lucky enough to have a boat explored other waters. The docks usually offered gleanings of some value.

It was toward The Fingers that Sparrow plied her oars, eager to examine her passenger at greater length and leisure. It was nearly full daylight by the time she beached the rowboat. The man, eyes closed, slumped in the stern. The scavengers could not move him.

"Keller!" Sparrow shouted. "Come help."

From a crude hut amid the bushes a little distance from shore, a lanky figure cautiously put out his head, then strode toward the youngsters.

"Hurry," ordered Sparrow. "We brought company for you. He may be dead."

"Marvelous," the man tartly replied. He was youngish, with rumpled chestnut hair and a pale face. "Exactly what I need."

Weasel was pulling him by his coatsleeve. Keller glanced at the man in the stern, then hurried closer, paying no heed to the water sloshing about his knees.

"Come on," said Sparrow. "Give us a hand."

"Water rats," said Keller, with a bemused laugh, "You've caught yourselves a Royal Physician."

Dr. Torrens, opening his eyes, could be certain only of two things: He was alive and his arm hurt. His recollections, otherwise, were dim and confused. He had been hauled off by a pair of goblins. Or he might have dreamed it. Lying on a dirt floor, a stranger bending over him, he had no idea where he was. A ragged girl and boy were staring at him.

"We've been waiting two days for you to wake up," the stranger said. "I can tell you, there were moments when I had my doubts. This is Sparrow and her brother, Weasel. They would have me believe you put a knife in a sailor's ribs. They find that intriguing. They are much impressed by you, Dr. Torrens."

"You know me?" The physician, astonished, managed to sit up.

"By sight and by reputation. You are one of the few who do not employ the services of leeches. Very sensible, since we already have a large one disguised as a chief minister. Ah — forgive me for imposing my opinion on someone too weak to disagree with it."

Torrens grimaced. "I would hardly do so. You recognize me, but I cannot say the same for you."

"You might know me better if I presented myself as Old Kasperl."

In spite of his discomfort, Dr. Torrens laughed in surprise at hearing the name. It was the title of a comic journal circulated throughout Marianstat. "You? Is that possible?"

"Since I pen the words to put in his mouth and, in fact, created him, I suppose I may claim his identity. The Bear's, too."

"Your journal has given me pleasure," said Torrens. "Those talks between Old Kasperl and his bear show a nice wit. But — Old Kasperl? With his peasant jacket, his tankard, his gray whiskers? I would expect his author to be a much older man."

"The times we live in age us rapidly," said Keller. "Even so, I take it as a compliment. I make nonsense of the world to help others make sense of it."

"A remark worthy of Old Kasperl," said Torrens.

"Actually, the Bear is the smarter. He usually sets Old Kasperl straight, as you may have noticed. The chief minister, I am happy to say, finds their humor cuts a little close to the bone. They were — embodied, that is, in their creator — quite recently invited to a hanging: their own. A tribute to their ability to nettle Cabbarus, but an honor I was grateful to forgo. A whole crew of us scriveners awaited the writing of our last pages in the Carolia Fortress. A few succeeded in escaping. I joined them, not wishing Old Kasperl to make his final public appearance on the gallows. Once out, we all separated. I made my way here. These water rats have been most hospitable. They admire lawbreakers.

"But I weary you, Doctor. Tell me how I may set you on your path, since you are clearly not here by choice. Trust my discretion about the dead sailor."

"I killed him," Torrens answered flatly. "I have not forgiven myself for that. My occupation is to save life, not take it. But he would have taken mine. Unfortunately for him, I know the vulnerabilities of the human body better than he did. He was not a sailor, by the way. Cabbarus had sent him. For you see, Master Keller, I too am under sentence of death."

"Bravo!" cried Keller. "You'll be a hero in the eyes of our generous water rats. In mine, too, for that matter."

Dr. Torrens was grateful he had fallen into the hands of a journalist and two urchins rather than those of another physician. Instead of dosing and cauterizing him, in their ignorance they merely let him rest, fed him as best they could, and kept his wound clean. As a result, he recovered quickly. Keller, following the doctor's instructions, made a sling from a linen garment he found in a pile of rags.

"Sparrow and Weasel will not object to our making free with their rubbish collection," said Keller, adjusting the sling. "Some of it no doubt was here when they arrived: like an ancestral heritage. Good stewards, they have added to it."

"This is not their home, then?"

"It is now. If I understand Sparrow, they found it empty and simply moved in. They have no parents, except in the biological sense. They may stay, they may move on. They are here now, which is all that matters to them."

"It is monstrous to think of them growing up in this — sewer, for it is hardly better than one."

"On the contrary," said Keller, "they are among the lucky. Marianstat swarms with waifs and strays, as you surely know. Sometimes I think they must live in the cracks of the sidewalks. For them, what you call a sewer would be a holiday in the country. We, too, should be glad of it as long as we are obliged to stop here."

"In my case, it cannot be much longer," said Torrens. During his recovery, the court physician and the journalist had come to have confidence in each other. Though gloomier by temperament than Torrens expected from the creator of Old Kasperl, the writer could be comical and scathing in his remarks about Cabbarus. When their two hosts were off on their daily rounds, Torrens revealed his hope of rallying opposition to the chief minister.

"Master Cabbarus hardly lacks admirers," said Keller. "That is, they would admire him most if he were at the end of a rope. They are scattered throughout the kingdom. Which sums up the difficulty. They are scattered."

"Are there no leaders among them? None who can help me?"

"A colleague wrote to me earlier this year," said Keller. "He lives in Belvitsa, some leagues up-country. He mentioned rumors of one individual, something of a firebrand."

"Can you put me in touch with your colleague?"

"I should like to put myself in touch with him. Old Kasperl and the Bear will have to go to ground, as far as possible from Marianstat. The Fingers are delightful in their own peculiar way, but not as a permanent address."

"The roads, of course, will be watched."

"Closely. Except for one. An excellent highway, it may get us clear of the city. From that point, it will be up to us. I say 'us' because I suggest we travel together."

"Agreed," said Torrens. "But this highway?"

"At our door. The Vespera. Since we cannot walk it, we shall have to sail it. Since we have to sail it, we require a boat. As for the boat —"

"Take the children's?" Torrens frowned. "It's their only means of livelihood."

"Although by trade a journalist," said Keller, "I nevertheless decline to rob children. Our water rats might row us beyond the city and put us ashore well upriver. Money, I think, might induce them."

"No doubt," said Torrens, "but my purse is gone."

"Sparrow has it. I saw her with it. Let me convince her to part with it. I shall appeal to her better nature, to her sense of honor, of which she must have some remaining trace."

When Sparrow and Weasel came back, Keller sat them down in front of him. "Water rats, I shall ask you a question. Are you thieves?"

"No," piped up Weasel, "but I'd like to be."

"I'm no thief either," said Sparrow. "I never had the luck."

"Even so," Keller went on, "I believe you have a purse of money belonging to this gentleman. In effect, you stole it from him."

"Did not!" cried Sparrow. "It's my pickings. I found it."

"Yes, you found it. In his pocket," said Keller. "Now, pay attention to my reasoning. Had you taken it from a dead man, that would be one thing. Since he was very much alive, that's something else. That is stealing."

"I shan't give it back."

"You shall keep it," Keller agreed, "but under different conditions. This gentleman and I have urgent business upriver. Were you to row us a certain distance, the purse would be quite honorably and honestly yours — to pay our passage and to compensate you for your hospitality. You may not understand the finer points of my logic, but —"

"We'll take you," said Sparrow. "Why didn't you just come straight out and ask?"

"So much for logic." Keller sighed. "So much for honor."

Chapter Fifteen

ome nights after his hint of new work for Theo, Florian led him to a wine merchant's warehouse near the market square. The merchant himself unbolted the door and motioned them down a flight of steps. In the cellar, behind a wall of vats, a space had been cleared to provide a large, low-ceilinged room. On a trestle table were candles and wooden boxes. Stock was pacing back and forth while Zara and Justin rummaged through the boxes. Rina had just set down a wooden plank.

"My children," declared Florian, "greet your architect and artificer." He bowed to Theo. "Youngster, you are no longer an apprentice, but master."

Theo had no idea what Florian was talking about. His eyes fell on a pile of lumber and odd bits of ironware. It was a press — the fragments, rather, of several presses.

"Cabbarus makes it his business to close print shops," Florian said. "We make it our business to open them. At least one, so far. When the king's officers tear down a press, we salvage a few pieces, like little birds picking up crumbs."

"But — how? How did you manage to bring all this here?"

"That doesn't matter," said Florian. "The question is: Can you put it together?"

"I don't know." Theo was staggered at the work needed. "Each press is a little different. It's not just cobbling one piece to another. I don't know. But, yes, I'll try."

"Do it," said Florian. "If you want anything, you'll have it."

"Like the phoenix!" cried Stock. "Like the legendary bird that rises from its own ashes, this press will rise from its own rubbish heap."

"Leave off," said Zara. "If you mean to work, stay. If not, go to Jellinek's."

The bulky poet seized a sheet of paper from the table. "I shall set to work immediately. I have some verses in mind. They shall be the first offsprings of our mechanical phoenix. The original laid only a single egg, but we can hatch thousands."

"Your verses can wait," said Florian. He glanced at Theo. "When our young friend first came here, he told me something in private. If he agrees, I think now it should be made public. The killing of an innocent man by Royal Officers should not be kept a secret."

Theo, still puzzled, nodded and Florian went on. "I suggest you write an account of your master; why they destroyed his press and, indeed, destroyed him. Set it all down, exactly as it happened. Print it. We'll get it into as many hands as we can. The people of Westmark will have another example of how Cabbarus goes about his business."

Theo agreed willingly. From then on, he worked at three occupations. Days, he sat in the tavern and drafted letters for his customers. Evenings, he labored over the press in the warehouse. Afterwards, far into the night, he tried to write his account.

It was not as easy as he had supposed. Anton had been as much a father as a master to him. He found himself thinking more of his own upbringing than what had happened that night in Dorning. He tried to see Anton through the eyes of a stranger: a provincial tradesman who had seen little of the world beyond his shop, whose life was in the books he printed. He remembered Anton reproaching him for wishing to have Cabbarus by the throat. Yet, the man had fought furiously to defend his press. Trying to define Anton, he tried to define himself. None of it, however, was useful to his pamphlet, and he began all over again.

The press, meanwhile, took shape little by little. He had chosen Zara for his devil. She was sharp-tongued but quick-witted and, by trade a dressmaker, clever with her hands. Rina and Justin sorted the hodgepodge of type: a tedious job but, since it was for Florian, neither complained. Stock did the heavy work, grumbling that he was a poet, not a packmule.

When the press at last was ready — Stock had insisted on naming it The Westmark Phoenix — Florian treated them to a supper at Jellinek's: a double celebration, since Theo had finished his pamphlet and Florian had praised it.

While Stock declaimed verses and Justin nodded over the remnants of the feast, Florian left the table at a signal from Jellinek. Returning shortly, he drew Theo aside and led him to the cubicle next to the kitchen.

Luther was waiting. Of all Florian's friends, he was least seen and least known to Theo. A graying, leathery man older than the others, he could have been a wheelwright, stonemason, or artisan of some sort. His clothes were damp and travel-stained.

"Luther has come up from the south," said Florian, "by way of Nierkeeping. You may be interested in what he can tell about some friends of yours."

"I've never been to Nierkeeping," said Theo. "I have no friends there."

"I think you do," said Florian. "Your former colleague. Whatever he's calling himself at the moment, Luther's description matches what you told me."

"There was a girl with him," cried Theo. "Mickle —"

"And still is," said Luther. "A half-size fellow, too. They're both in the town lockup."

"Why?" Theo's heart sank as quickly as it had leaped. "What have they done?"

"I don't know," said Luther. "They're better off than the other one. He's in the middle of the market square. Locked in a cage."

"What for?" Theo seized Luther's arm. "What are they doing to him?"

"From what I gather, punishing him for some kind of mischief. He's been caged up for a couple of days. They aren't even feeding him."

"I have to go there. Zara can manage the press."

"When we first met," said Florian, "I recall you seemed delighted to be rid of the fellow."

"He wasn't in trouble then. Mickle's there, too. And Musket. I have to get them out."

"You can't," said Luther. "Nierkeeping's full of troops, for one thing. For another, the town's in an ugly mood. You wouldn't last a minute."

"I can't stay here and do nothing. There must be some way. I'm going. I'll take my chances."

"I won't let you do that," said Florian.

"Won't let me?" cried Theo. "No one's going to stop me. Not even you."

Theo was astonished at his own words. No one spoke that way to Florian. Nevertheless, he stood his ground and looked him squarely in the face.

Florian half smiled. "You're more a hothead than I supposed. No, I won't let you. That's to say I won't let you go alone."

"You'll help me, then?"

Florian's gray eyes had a light in them. "As I think of it, a visit to Nierkeeping might suit all of us very well. We could profit from a breath of country air." He glanced at Luther.

"It could be profitable, as I was telling you," replied the artisan. "Large risk, but large gain."

"We'll do it," said Florian. He turned to Theo. "But I'm afraid we can't leave immediately."

"When? How soon?"

Florian grinned. "Within the hour. Would that stretch your patience beyond bearing?"

"I'm in your debt," said Theo. "I'll make it up to you. I give you my word."

"Accepted and valued," said Florian. "Go and tell the others."

Chapter Sixteen

heo huddled under the straw in the back of the wagon. The moon was down, the sky beginning to pale. Justin, beside him, was curled up and sleeping soundly. In front, Florian held the reins lightly, allowing the horse to make its own pace. Zara, dressed as a peasant woman, drowsed with her head on his shoulder. She had insisted on going with them, so Rina, under protest, had stayed in Freyborg: to keep an eye on the press and await any urgent word from Florian. Stock and Luther had ridden ahead on fresh mounts. Theo marveled that Florian had set all in train so quickly. It was, he understood, part of the business of being Florian. He was grateful.

He had tried to thank Florian, who shrugged it aside as if the journey were, in fact, only a jaunt through the countryside. For a while, so it appeared. The wagon rattled along dirt roads with flat, stubble fields on either side. Morning, when it came, was bright and crisp. There was an air of holiday, with Florian in the best of spirits.

They reached a paved road and, later, a fingerpost pointing toward Nierkeeping. Instead of following it, Florian turned off and drove into the woodlands covering the swelling hills.

When Theo ventured to ask why, Florian only replied, "Leave that to me. For the moment, all you need to do is enjoy the view. It's one of the most beautiful parts of the country. The nobility have their summer estates and hunting lodges hereabout. And a few rustic cottages, with all the comforts the rustics themselves never see. It amuses the nobles to play at being peasants. I wonder if they'd be equally amused if the peasants took it into their heads to play at being nobles."

Soon after, Florian pulled up the wagon in the yard of a cluster of buildings screened by woods. The main house was of timber, with a high-pitched roof. Several horses occupied the stables; two more stood tethered near a stone-sided well.

Stock was sitting on a barrel by the door. He jumped off and hurried to the wagon. Justin and Zara climbed down and went directly inside, seeming to be familiar with the place.

"You have visitors," Stock announced to Florian. Theo followed them into a long room with white plaster walls and a huge fireplace. Luther was there, along with half a dozen men Theo had never seen before. Some wore hunter's garb, with game bags over their shoulders; others, the rough jackets of farm laborers. Fowling pieces and muskets were stacked in a corner.

Two men sat at a plank table, the remains of a meal in front of them: the younger, ill-shaven and glum-looking; his companion, white-haired and with one arm in a sling. Both were grimy, their clothes torn and burr-clotted.

The company warmly greeted Florian, who waved a hand and turned his attention to the men at the table. The younger stood up.

"My name is Keller. We have certain acquaintances in common. Thanks to them, we were put on our way here. Though I have to tell you, sir, you are devilish hard to find."

"I'm glad of that," said Florian. "For my own sake, if not yours. I would have preferred meeting Old Kasperl in easier circumstances."

"You know of me, so far from Marianstat?" Keller's glum expression turned into a delighted smile. "I take that as high praise.

"My traveling companion," Keller went on, "looks like one of his own patients. How that came about he shall tell you himself: Dr. Torrens, formerly court physician, presently an exile — as long as he manages to stay alive. As for the unlikely association of a scrivener with a physician, you may wish to know —"

"I should rather know why a courtier is here at all."

"I can answer that very simply," Dr. Torrens said. "I take it for granted that you despise Chief Minister Cabbarus as much as I do. You know, certainly, that Augustine is now hardly able to rule and may never be. What you do not know, since you are not close to the inner workings of the court, is that Cabbarus schemes to make himself Augustine's adoptive heir. For these six years, the chief minister has been king in all but name. Now he seeks the title as well as the power."

Instead of sharing the doctor's outrage, Florian made a small gesture.

"King Augustine or King Cabbarus? To me, Doctor, kings are one and the same."

"You cannot believe that!" cried Torrens. "Do you see no difference between a monarch and a tyrant? The chief minister has been a disaster for the country. As king, he will be still worse. At court, the only one who dares oppose him is Queen Caroline. Her life may be in danger as a result. Cabbarus will let no one stand long in his way. He has banished me, he has tried to have me murdered. But I will not leave the kingdom. I seek honest men to join me and support the queen's cause, to bring force to bear —"

"Let us understand each other," Florian broke in. "You are correct on two counts. We are honest men here. Our opinion of Cabbarus matches yours. As for supporting your cause, I see no reason. We intend, Doctor, to support our own."

"Whatever that may be," said Torrens, "it is less urgent than putting an end to the influence of Cabbarus. The villain must be brought down, without delay, whatever the cost. There is no other way to preserve legitimate monarchy."

"Preserve it?" returned Florian. "Preserve a power fixed by an accident of birth? Unearned, unmerited, only abused? You have been sadly misled, Doctor, if you come to me for that. Legitimate monarchy? The only legitimate rulers are the people of Westmark."

"That, sir, is a dream. I do not share it with you. There are abuses; I do not deny it. They must be corrected. But not through destruction. If I have a patient with a broken leg, I mend the leg. I do not bleed him to death. I do what is possible and practical."

"So do I," said Florian. "You urge me to join you. Let me ask: How many troops do you command? How many weapons?"

"None," said Torrens. "And you?" He gestured toward the stack of firearms. "If that is your arsenal, it does not impress me."

"We hope to improve it within the next twenty-four hours. Our resources are modest, but only a beginning. Now, Doctor, if you will excuse me, we have plans to make."

As much as Florian had spoken bitterly and angrily against the chief minister, Theo had never until now heard him oppose the whole monarchy. The idea stunned and excited him. The sheer daring of it was only what he might have expected from Florian. He suddenly understood his willingness to make the journey to Nierkeeping. The man's boldness dazzled him. It also horrified him.

"You're going to attack the town!" cried Theo. "You said you'd help my friends."

"So I will," Florian said. "Did you imagine we'd simply stroll into Nierkeeping and ask politely to have them set loose?"

"No. But not this way. There's going to be bloodshed."

"That's certain. Some of ours. Some of theirs. As little as possible, but no avoiding it. Yes, youngster, it may end with killing. We'd be a band of innocent idiots if we didn't expect it. You want your friends. My people want guns. We'll do whatever we must. Will you?"

Theo did not reply. Florian looked at him and said quietly, "It's very simple. Are you going with us or not? You need our help, but we need yours if my plan has any chance of working."

Theo turned away. He had tried to kill the Royal Inspector in the heat of anger, unthinking. What Florian asked of him was something calculated, accepted in advance. Yet he could not bring himself to abandon Mickle, or even Las Bombas and Musket. He tried to guess what Anton would have done. He could not. He had no answer, nor could any answer have satisfied him; and that, more than anything, tore at him. Finally, without speaking, he nodded his head.

"You'll get through it," said Florian. "The first time is the worst."

Stock, meanwhile, had brought a wooden chest to the table and had begun taking pistols from it. Florian handed one to Theo, who drew back a little.

"It won't bite you," said Florian.

"I don't want it."

"Take it, even so. You may not want it, but you may need it. Do you know how to use one?"

Theo shook his head.

"Go along with Justin, then. He'll show you."

Chapter Seventeen

t was still dark when they left the farm: Theo and Justin, Stock and Zara in the wagon; Florian and the rest of the company on horseback. A short distance from town, Zara halted in the shadow of a gravel embankment. Florian embraced each one, and they parted there — Florian to lead his men into Nierkeeping from another quarter, Theo and the others to go the rest of the way on foot.

Justin strode out eagerly, urging them to speed their pace until Zara told him to be quiet. Stock yawned and grumbled at being abroad in the dregs of the night.

Once within the town limits, no one spoke. Theo clenched his jaws to keep his teeth from chattering. The chill of the hours at the thin edge of daybreak had seeped into his bones. The pistol butt drove into his belly at every step. Following Luther's directions, they passed through a winding lane and soon reached the square. In the middle of it stood a narrow cage hardly taller than the shape inside.

Theo broke from the others and ran across the square. The cage reeked like an animal's pen. The man inside groaned. It was Las Bombas, hardly recognizable. His lips were swollen and split, a stubble of beard covered his cheeks. Theo grappled the bars. The count hunched up his shoulders and turned his face away.

"Let me be."

"It's all right," whispered Theo. "We're going to get you out."

The count shifted his position and raised his head. His voice was raw and rasping. "Who's that? My dear boy, is it you?" He put his hands through the bars and passed his fingers over Theo's face. "Merciful heaven, so it is!"

Stock and Justin had come up behind Theo. Zara followed. She crouched and peered into the cage, then wrinkled her face.

"Is this what we've come to rescue?"

"Shut up, Zara," Theo flung back. "You know Florian's plan. He wants a diversion. He'll have one. But this man's my friend, even so."

The count was pleading for water. Theo pulled the flask from his belt and passed it through the bars. Las Bombas seized it and downed the contents in one gulp. "Thank you, my boy. You've saved my life. It's gone badly with us since you left. But now that you're back again —"

"Not to stay. I'm working in Freyborg. I heard you were in trouble."

"Don't leave us again. We need you. Mickle's lost spirit, she won't do The Oracle Priestess. Nothing's worked right, not even this: The Escaping Prisoner. Nothing simpler. A sheet over the cage, an instant later I'm out, lock untouched, no key in sight. Marvelous effect. It would have gone splendidly if some blockhead hadn't made me open my mouth. They found the picklock I'd hidden there.

"Stupid yokels! Claimed I was cheating them. They said I promised to escape and they'd leave me here until I did. Mickle tried to open the lock, but they caught her at it and threw her in jail, with Musket for good measure."

"We'll see to them now and come back for you," Theo said. "What became of Friska and the coach?"

"In the blacksmith's stable, near the barracks."

Theo glanced at Stock, who nodded agreement and set off immediately across the square.

Zara stood up. "Are the two of you ready?"

Theo hurried after Justin, with Zara at his heels. The jail, as Luther had told them, was at the back of the town hall. They found it easily. At the door of the guardroom, Theo halted and gripped Justin by the scruff of the neck.

"Don't act up yet," he whispered. "Wait until we're inside and see how many we have to deal with. Then start shouting your head off."

Zara stayed back. Theo tightened his grasp on Justin and hauled him through the door. One constable drowsed at a table. At a glance from Theo, Justin began struggling and protesting furiously. The startled officer jumped to his feet and seized the pistol in front of him.

"Thief!" Theo hung on to his pretended captive. "I caught him trying to pick my pocket."

"Who the devil are you?" The constable eyed him suspiciously. He waved his pistol. "You're not from around here, neither of you."

"I'm staying at the inn," Theo said hastily. "I've just come from — from Freyborg. I'd no sooner set foot in town than this fellow tries to rob me. I'll see him behind bars. Lock him up, officer. I'll swear charges against him."

"No business of mine. He's not one of our thieves." The constable frowned. "As for you, let's see your travel permit."

At this instant, Zara burst into the guardroom, weeping and wringing her hands. "Sir, that's my brother. He meant no harm. I beg you, don't take him away."

The officer hesitated, uncertain whether to deal first with the distraught young woman or the thief and his captor. Adding to the man's confusion, Justin broke loose and Theo made a show of trying to recapture him. The constable spun around, groping for one, then the other.

Zara chose this moment to dart behind the table. She picked up the chair and brought it down on the constable's head. The constable dropped to his knees. Theo leaped on him and locked his hands around the man's throat. "Keys! Where?"

The constable motioned with his head. A ring of keys hung on the wall beside a rack of muskets. Justin had begun ripping away the man's shirt.

"Who's with you?" demanded Theo.

"Alone," gasped the officer. "Night watch. Nobody else."

Theo tore off the man's neck stock and crammed it into the constable's mouth. He beckoned Zara to finish trussing up the officer with the strips of shirt. He snatched the ring and raced down a short flight of steps. Iron-studded doors lined the corridor. Theo fumbled with the keys and found one to unlock the first cell. Musket was inside.

"Go to the marketplace!" cried Theo. "Stay with the count."

The dwarf asked no questions. He took to his heels and dashed up the steps. Theo snapped open the lock on the next cell. Mickle stared at him. Her face was dirty and haggard. Straw from the cell floor clung to her hair.

He held out his arms, but Mickle gave him a haughty glance and drew away.

"Come out! Hurry!" Theo shouted. "What's wrong with you?"

"Don't touch me," Mickle flung back. "You went off without a word! Not a word to me! You can go to the devil, for all I care."

Seizing the girl by the shoulders, Theo pulled her from the cell and sent her stumbling up the stairs ahead of him. Outside, he clamped a hand around her arm and half dragged her, still in icy silence, toward the square.

A shot rang from the direction of the barracks. He glimpsed Justin and Zara beside the cage, along with Musket. More shots rattled through the still air and the clatter of hooves. He glanced back. Friska was galloping into the marketplace, the coach jolting behind her. Stock, upright on the box, was roaring at the top of his voice. By now, Theo judged, the Nierkeeping garrison must be awake and tumbling out of the barracks.

This was the moment Florian and his company had counted on to break into the arsenal holding the garrison's store of weapons. Theo had given Florian his diversion. Now he could turn his efforts to setting Las Bombas free and rely on the others to help him. Whatever else happened, Florian had ordered them to get clear of the town and rejoin him at the farm.

Mickle twisted away and ran to the cage. Swearing furiously, she struggled with the lock. Meantime, Stock had pulled up Friska. He jumped down and went toward Zara. The dressmaker, like Justin, carried two muskets, seized from the rack in the guardroom. She tossed one to the poet.

"To the wagon!" shouted Stock. "If the lock won't open, we'll drag him out, cage and all."

Mickle's face was streaked with grime and sweat. "I can't do it without tools. Hanno knew how, but I don't. Damn him for getting himself hanged!"

Stock rummaged in his pockets and brought out a penknife. He threw it to the girl. Mickle set to work again. The blade snapped in two. She spat and flung it away.

Soldiers from the garrison had begun pouring into the marketplace. Mickle jumped to her feet and ran to Zara. She tore at the dressmaker's shawl.

"This should do it." She seized Zara's brooch and slid the point of the pin into the lock. She turned it deftly, one way then another. The cage opened. Mickle crowed in triumph.

Theo and Musket sprang to haul out the count, who was barely able to crawl from his narrow prison. Las Bombas threw his arms around Mickle. "Bless you for a housebreaker!"

"Go, the rest of you," Theo ordered Zara. "Get out of here. We'll catch up with you."

Las Bombas had slipped to the cobbles. Even with the help of Mickle and the dwarf, Theo could scarcely put the count on his feet and heave him into the coach.

Stock and Zara had already started off, with Justin following. After a few paces, Justin suddenly halted and turned back.

He had unslung one of his muskets. His eyes shone with a terrible joy. Before Theo could stop him, Justin flung himself to the cobbles and began firing at the soldiers.

"You fool!" shouted Theo. "Get in the coach!"

That same instant, Theo caught sight of horses milling through the rear ranks of the troops. He thought, first, that cavalry had joined the fray. Then he saw they were riderless and unsaddled. Florian had not only stormed the arsenal. His company had broken into the stables to send the animals galloping in panic among the soldiers.

The ranks broke and scattered at the threat of being trampled. One officer, bawling for his men to advance, beat at them with the flat of his saber until he managed to lead some of them clear of the stampede.

The officer ran toward the coach. Justin fired again. He missed his mark. The man was on top of him in a moment. Justin scrambled to his feet. He tried to fend off the saber stroke with his musket. The force of the blow knocked the weapon from his hands. By the time Theo reached him, the officer had brought up his blade again. Had Theo not pulled Justin aside, the saber would have struck him in the throat. Instead, it laid open the lad's forehead and cheek. The man braced to make another attack.

"Kill him!" Justin turned his bloody face to Theo, violet eyes blazing. "Kill him!"

Theo swung up his arm and leveled the pistol. He hesitated an instant. Justin was screaming for him to shoot. Theo cried out as the explosion echoed through his head. A look of bewilderment froze on the officer's face. He staggered and fell. Theo stared at the weapon in his hand. His finger had not moved on the trigger.

He glanced up to see Florian. He was on horseback, a smoking musket across the saddlebow. His long hair hung matted, smears of gunpowder blackened his cheeks. His gray eyes fixed squarely on Theo. He half smiled, as if observing a child fumbling to tie a shoe.

Florian motioned with his head toward Justin. "See to him."

He wheeled his horse back across the square. The rest of his company had galloped into the marketplace in the wake of the riderless mounts, driving them toward the outskirts of the town. The soldiers, regrouping, sent volleys of musketry after the raiders, who sharply returned their fire. Florian's men pressed their retreat, leaving half a dozen of the garrison sprawled on the cobblestones.

Theo flung away his pistol. Mickle was beside him. Between them, they dragged Justin into the coach. Friska plunged forward.

Part Four

The Garden of Cabbarus

Chapter Eighteen

ut of respect for his position, the chief minister allowed himself certain small luxuries. One of these was a private garden that yielded, in all seasons, blossoms of information. Cabbarus fertilized it with generous applications of money. The harvest was always more plentiful and usually more accurate than the labored, vegetablelike reports of provincial constables and police spies. Cabbarus earnestly believed his rank entitled him to this higher quality of produce. Since he cultivated his garden personally, he saw no reason to share it.

As in the most carefully tended gardens, the occasional weed sprang up or plant withered. Cabbarus had his disappointments. The individual he counted on to deal with Torrens had not thrived. This in itself did not trouble the chief minister. As a precaution, the man would have been pruned, in any case. What nettled Cabbarus was that he had no inkling of the doctor's fate.

Torrens and his opponent might have killed each other. Cabbarus found that unlikely. The court physician might have fallen from the embankment and been borne away on the tide. But no corpse had surfaced. The chief minister's informants could report only that Torrens had vanished. Cabbarus was not pleased to accept this. No one truly vanished except by the chief minister's order.

Nevertheless, until he learned otherwise, Cabbarus counted Torrens as dead — if not in fact, for all practical purposes. The king required his urgent attention. Augustine was presenting difficulties.

First, the king had no recollection of banishing Torrens and called for the court physician to attend him.

"He grievously offended Your Majesty," said Cabbarus. "Your Majesty had no choice but to dismiss him."

"No matter. I desire him back again."

Cabbarus assured his monarch it was impossible. For some days, however, Augustine continued to demand the presence of the physician. Finally, he let the matter drop. But he refused the services of any other doctor, even those whom Cabbarus highly recommended. The king's health improved alarmingly.

His mind, too, grew somewhat clearer. Cabbarus blamed this on the occultists, necromancers, and spiritualists; rather, on the lack of them. What had been a constant procession dwindled to a handful.

"The reward is still not adequate," Augustine declared. "I direct you to double the sum."

"As Your Majesty commands." Cabbarus bowed his head. Since he was sure the reward would go unclaimed, he had no objection to doubling, or even trebling it. "It shall be so proclaimed."

"You shall add one thing further to the proclamation. As we offer a reward for success, we judge it fitting, as well, to impose a penalty for failure."

"I do not entirely understand, Sire. A penalty? Of what nature?"

"These men have claimed spiritual powers, but they have disappointed me beyond bearing. Nevertheless, they have been enriched by their failures. Now it is my command: If they accomplish nothing, they are to be paid nothing."

"As Your Majesty so aptly expresses it, this is only fitting. They shall not be paid."

"That is not the penalty."

"What then, Sire?"

"If they fail," said the king, "they shall be put to death."

"Majesty," exclaimed Cabbarus, "a penalty of such severity —"

"A severe punishment for severe disappointment," said Augustine. "Proclaim it, Chief Minister. I command you to do so."

The king held to that point in spite of the chief minister's protests. Cabbarus, for all his influence, could not move him to revoke it. Cabbarus devoutly believed in punishment, but in this case he saw the consequences immediately. There were rogues aplenty who would venture anything for gain. There was an even greater number of fools. Finding a combination of the two was another matter. No rogue would be foolish enough to risk his neck attempting the impossible. The penalty for failure ended all visitations.

Worse, the court physician had been right. Without the daily arrival of charlatans to feed his obsession, Augustine recovered some of his former calm.

Cabbarus fumed inwardly. The proclamation showed that Augustine was regaining some of his wits. For the good of the kingdom, Cabbarus wished its ruler would suffer a relapse. But wishes, Cabbarus knew, seldom came true without enterprise on the part of the wisher. Throughout his private garden, he planted word that he required a fresh supply of necromancers. The seeds did not sprout.

For several weeks, the chief minister showed every sign of cheerfulness. In the same way that he cloaked his pleasure in frowns, he wreathed his fury in smiles. His good humor astonished the courtiers. As usual, only Pankratz appreciated how matters really stood. A smiling Cabbarus was a dangerous Cabbarus.

Pankratz, therefore, dealt very gingerly with his master. Cabbarus, in private, made little attempt to hide his feelings. Not long before, over some inconsequential failing, Cabbarus had struck his councillor full in the face. Pankratz merely rubbed his jowls and bowed his way out of the minister's chambers. The Minister's Mastiff accepted that dogs were made to be occasionally beaten. He respected his master all the more for it, and passed along the chief minister's bad temper, in kind, to his own underlings.

Nevertheless, Pankratz held himself at arm's length one evening when he announced that a certain individual desired a private audience.

Cabbarus, in his apartments, had just finished supper and it was not sitting happily with him. In any case, he disliked conducting business directly with his creatures. It made him feel that he had put his fingers into something disagreeable: a task better entrusted to Councillor Pankratz. Cabbarus shook his head.

"I do not wish to see him. Let him discuss the matter with you."

"Excellency, he insists." Pankratz half bowed and spread his hands in a gesture both deferential and defensive. "It has to do with — what Your Excellency has been inquiring about."

The chief minister's eyes flickered an instant with excitement. He kept his face impassive. "I doubt that he offers much of value. However, as he insists, you may send him to me." He motioned with his head. "Below."

Cabbarus put on his robe and made his way without haste to one of the cellars of the Old Juliana. It had once been a torture chamber. None of the instruments remained. They had been dismantled during the reign of Augustine the Great — a wastefulness Cabbarus would never have allowed had he been in office at the time. Iron rings and staples, however, had been left in the walls. In one corner, a wooden trapdoor covered an opening somewhat larger than the girth of a man. It was the mouth of a deep well, roughly faced with stones and mortar.

Although the bottom of this well was too heavily shadowed to be seen, a torrent of water could be heard. The shaft tapped into an underground stream whose course had never been fully traced. Presumably it flowed to join the Vespera. It once had served as a means of disposing of prisoners or portions of them. The flagstones around the trap sloped inward, making it easier to wash down the chamber floor and send the sweepings into the shaft.

The present Augustine had commanded the well to be bricked over and sealed at the same time he had ordered the Juliana Bells to be silenced. The latter order had been carried out, but not the former. Cabbarus had taken it on himself to ignore it. The chief minister found it pointless to destroy such a useful feature merely because of the king's hindsight.

Awaiting his guest, the chief minister stood by the trapdoor, studying it thoughtfully. When Cabbarus granted a rare personal audience, he always chose this chamber. There was no mistaking what it had been, and it impressed his visitors with the seriousness of their endeavors.

He glanced up as Councillor Pankratz ushered in the man, then went to sit behind a heavy oaken table. Pankratz discreetly vanished. Cabbarus did not invite his guest to be seated, and eyed him silently for several moments.

The man was short and stout. Perspiration filmed his plump cheeks. Cabbarus noted the fur-trimmed cloak and the gold chain around his visitor's neck.

"You have, I see, bettered your station in life," said Cabbarus. "I believe you formerly went about as a tinker."

"That is correct, sir," the man replied. "It served its purpose. Alderman, though, carries more weight and substance. It conveys, you might say, the aroma of prosperity. It suits well enough at the moment."

"Your choice of profession is up to you. Get on with your business. You say you have found a ghost-raiser."

"Ah, well, sir, perhaps I have and perhaps I haven't."

"I urge you," said Cabbarus, "to decide which, and to do so quickly."

"Well, sir, you see it's a curious thing. A few months ago I was in Kessel, and I came upon a knave calling himself, if memory serves, Bloomsa. He took me for a greater fool than himself. He had the impudence to swindle me. Try to, that is."

"And you, naturally, ended by swindling him."

"As you say, sir, naturally." The man allowed himself a wink. "But that only begins the tale. I thought no more of him until a while after. I happened to be passing through a town called Felden. The local gossip was all about a fellow who had made quite a splash there. Some sort of flummery: spirit apparitions, a wench playing at being an oracle, and all such great nonsense.

"He was doing well for himself until something happened, I don't know what. The wench, for some reason, turned skittish. In any case, the novelty wore off. But the fellow had run up a fortune in bills. His creditors started coming down on him. They'd have thrown him in jail. He saved them the trouble by leaving town one night — in something of a hurry. From what the Feldeners told me of him, I thought: Aha, here's Master Bloomsa up to another of his tricks.

"The constables were still searching his lodgings. He and his crew had gone off so quickly, the constables thought they might find some valuables left behind. Out of curiosity, I did a little poking about, too.

"It's a matter of nose, sir," continued the self-styled alderman, tapping his own. "My nose told me there might be something of interest, though I didn't know what. I trust my nose, sir, and always follow it. This time, I feared it disappointed me. There was nothing worth mention. Except one thing. I took it along. Again, I didn't know why. The nose advised me, very likely."

The chief minister's patience had worn threadbare. He was about to tell the man to take his nose and himself to the devil. Then his visitor drew a rumpled sheet of paper from his cloak and spread it on the table.

"The Feldeners tell me it's a good enough likeness."

It was the portrait of a young girl. Only by effort was the chief minister able to compose himself.

"And so, sir," the man was going on, "when I later heard you were looking for ghost-raisers, I wondered if our Master Bloomsa might be of some use after all, especially with the wench."

Cabbarus barely heard him. He was engrossed in the portrait. Once more, his confidence had been justified. Opportunity always arose when it was needed. He suddenly understood how simple it was. He need no longer be concerned with forcing the queen's approval, or even being named adoptive heir. The answer lay within reach. Cabbarus nearly did something he had seldom done in all his life. He nearly laughed. Instead, he scowled with joy.

"Where are they now?"

The visitor shrugged. "There's the difficulty, sir. I didn't follow them, you see. Had I known you'd be wanting someone in that line of work, I'd have kept a finger on them. Now it may take some doing, as the trail is cold. And so I came to ask your instructions, sir. If you think it worth the time and toil — and the money."

"Find them," said Cabbarus. "I want them."

Chapter Nineteen

usket, clearly experienced in avoiding pursuit, did not trouble to ask their destination. He drove Friska at top speed and sent the coach careening through the outskirts of the town, deep into the countryside, up and down lanes hardly suitable for an oxcart. Justin, sprawled across the seat, was bleeding heavily. Mickle had torn a strip from her dress and, despite the jolting vehicle, tried to stanch the wound.

Theo helped her, his hands moving mechanically. The girl barely spoke to him. His joy at finding her was gone. Half his thoughts were in Nierkeeping. He still saw the bodies in the square, and himself ready to fire the pistol. Justin, too, could have been killed. His bloody face was a silent reproach. Theo raged at himself. He should have pulled the trigger. He wanted to beg forgiveness. Unconscious, Justin could not have heard him.

Musket, judging they had outdistanced any troopers who might have followed, reined up Friska and ran to ask Theo where he wanted to go. The dwarf had saved them and, at the same time, lost them. Theo climbed out and tried to regain his bearings in the unfamiliar countryside.

Las Bombas took the opportunity to stretch his cramped legs. His uniform was wrinkled and befouled, his cheeks sunken. He had perked up enough, however, to brush the grit from his moustache.

"You were right, my boy. Honesty is the best policy. That cage was a blessing in disguise. Public humiliation, private starvation! I vowed to mend my ways if ever I got free. My ordeal reduced me in body, but fortified me in spirit."

Since Theo carried no food and there was none in the coach, Las Bombas had further occasion to fortify his spirit. He climbed back into the coach, resigned to the benefits of continued hunger. Justin had turned restless. Las Bombas held him in his arms and soothed him with a gentleness Theo had never suspected.

Their only choice, Theo decided, was to circle back and, in spite of risk, find the Nierkeeping road. He jumped onto the box beside Musket and tried to guide him. Partly by luck, partly by the dwarf's own sense of direction, they finally came upon it. Theo recognized the fingerpost where Florian had turned. They followed the road into the hills. Even then, they would have missed the farm if some of Florian's men, stationed as guards, had not shown them the rest of the way.

It was late afternoon when they rolled into the farmyard. Florian was in the doorway. Though obviously relieved to see them, he exchanged only the briefest greetings. He himself carried Justin into the house. Stock, Zara, and the others were sorting the captured weapons.

The court physician had been standing by the fireplace. He went immediately to examine Justin's wound and called for clean bandages and a basin of water.

"More bloodshed." Torrens glanced up at Florian. "I have seen enough of it this day."

"So have I," said Florian. "You forget, I was at Nierkeeping, too. And let me remind you: You were not much impressed, yesterday, by our modest store of arms. Perhaps now you have changed your opinion. In any case, I lost three of my best men. Do your work, Doctor. I don't want to lose a fourth."

Florian turned away. Seeing Mickle, he smiled and bowed gracefully. "So this must be the young lady in question?"

666

"I didn't know there was any question about me," said Mickle.

"This is Florian," said Theo. "Without him, you'd still be in jail."

"And with him," replied Mickle, "we nearly got shot. He's dangerous."

Florian laughed. "I sincerely hope I am. But only to my enemies. You're quite safe. I suggest you go along with Zara and see if she can find something better for you to wear."

"We are in your debt, sir," put in Las Bombas. "I must say your line of work entails certain, ah, hazards. I should be glad to provide you with special remedies of my own preparation, at wholesale rates."

When Florian declined the offer, Las Bombas turned his attention to the larder.

Theo took Florian's arm. "There's something I have to know — about what happened this morning."

"We couldn't have done without you," said Florian. "We needed that fracas of yours to draw off the garrison. You have your friends back; we have guns and horses. We paid a price. Does that still trouble you? Believe me, it could have been worse."

"It's not only that. It's Justin. You saved his life."

"Luckily. What of it?"

"I should have. I was there beside him. I should have been the one to do it."

Florian shook his head. "Justin won't worry over who takes the credit."

"If anything," replied Theo, "he'll be proud it was you. But the man was right in front of me. I had the pistol."

"And you held back," said Florian. "I saw you. Beware, youngster. Next time, don't hesitate. It may cost your life."

"But you," said Theo. "You didn't hesitate. You shot him without having to think."

"Some things are best not thought about."

"I have to," said Theo. "I have to understand. You know what happened in Dorning. I swore then I'd never try to take another man's life. Killing is wrong. I believed that. I still do. But now I wonder. Do I believe it because I want to be a decent man? Or — because I'm a coward?"

"In which case, you're no different from the rest of us." Florian gave a wry smile. "We're all afraid. And afraid of being afraid. You'll get used to it."

"I don't want to get used to it," cried Theo. "If I'd really known what it would be like —"

"You wouldn't have gone to Nierkeeping? Would you rather see your friends still in jail? Starving in a cage? And even if you'd shot that officer, what then? Half his trade is killing; the other half, being killed."

"The first day I met you," said Theo, "at Rina's birthday party, you said there was only one law, that all men are brothers."

Florian nodded. "Yes. And sometimes brothers kill each other. For the sake of justice. For the sake of a higher cause."

"Who decides what's right? Me? You? Dr. Torrens? He's against you. He holds with the monarchy. But he seems a good and honorable man."

"He is," answered Florian. "Curious that being a commoner he should take that side. Perhaps he knows less of it than I do. I can tell you of peasants flogged half to death, forced to weed a noble's garden while their own crops rot in the ground, having their cottages pulled down to make room for a deer park. I know the aristocracy better than Torrens ever can. I was born into it.

"Yes," Florian went on, smiling at Theo's astonishment. "You might recognize my family's name if I mentioned it, which, by the way, I have no intention of doing. This farm is theirs. They've forgotten they even own it, among so many others. They would be highly displeased if they knew the purpose it served.

"As for Torrens thinking merely to correct abuses — he is almost as innocent as you are. Abuse is in the very grain of the monarchy's power. And I can tell you one thing more. Men give up many things willingly: their fortunes, their loves, their dreams. Power, never. It must be taken. And you, youngster, will have to choose your side. Though I assure you the monarchy will be as unsparing with its enemies as I am, at least there is justice in my cause."

"Even if the cause is good," said Theo, "what does it do to the people who stand against it? And the people who follow it?"

"Next time you see Jellinek," said Florian, "ask him if he's ever found a way to make an omelet without breaking eggs."

"Yes," Theo said. "Yes, but men aren't eggs."

Chapter Twenty

Dr. Torrens was calling Florian, who left Theo unanswered and went anxiously to the court physician.

"The lad is in no danger now," said Torrens, rolling down his sleeves. He had taken off the sling and crammed it into his pocket. "Though I fear he will be badly scarred."

"We may all be," said Florian. He strode to the table and called the rest to join him.

"My children," he said to Stock and Zara, "we'd best take leave of each other for a while. Our worthy opponents in Nierkeeping had too close a look at me. After today's business, I can't even risk staying in Freyborg. You two should be safe enough there. For me, the wiser course is to disappear. Better to be wanted than found. Give my greetings to Jellinek. Tell him I shall miss those concoctions he fancifully calls stew. You shall have word from me later. Take some of the muskets. We shall find a good hiding place for the remainder. Justin will stay with me. Luther, too."

He turned to the court physician. "And you, Doctor? We have our differences. I suggest, for the time being, we bury them — if you will forgive my using the term with a physician. We are both marked men. If caught, we shall be equally dead. We can agree on that much."

Torrens nodded. "Who knows, you may change your views, or I, mine. I judge either unlikely. Indeed, sir, the day may come when we find each other very bad companions. Until then, I shall go with you."

"Since I've brought Dr. Torrens this far," put in Keller, "I think the time has come for the Bear to go into hibernation; and for Old Kasperl to make his way with the doctor and yourself."

"Old Kasperl would keep us amused," said Florian. "But if he is silenced, then Cabbarus might as well have hanged you. You would do greater service if you kept on with your journal."

"Gladly," said Keller. "But without the means, it is impossible. For one thing, I would have to stay hidden."

"Old Kasperl and the Bear can find a safe lair in Freyborg," said Florian. "Trust my children for that."

"Even so, a journalist is nothing without a press. Nothing, sometimes, with one. But it is essential to the trade."

"You shall have a press in Freyborg," replied Florian. "Whether you may also have a printer" — he glanced at Theo — "I leave it up to this young man. He may want to talk over the matter with his friends. Do it quickly, youngster. We must all be gone before daybreak."

"Meantime," said Las Bombas, wiping his plate clean with a slice of bread, "I should welcome an opportunity for professional discourse with a colleague."

"Do you refer to me, sir?" Torrens raised an eyebrow. "I was not aware that we were colleagues in any way at all."

"We are both men of science," the count replied. "That is, in our respective endeavors. My present endeavor is for my coachman and me to leave the country at the earliest possible moment. I feel things are pressing in upon us a little too closely for comfort. Trebizonia, a realm long familiar to me during my attendance on the prince, will surely welcome my services."

Mickle and Zara had come into the room. Zara had given the girl an old woolen skirt, a man's jacket, and a shawl. Zara went to Florian's side. Mickle strode out of the farmhouse. Leaving Las Bombas to expound his scientific discoveries to the court physician, Theo followed her.

Dusk was gathering quickly. The trees had not yet dropped all their leaves and the ragged branches laid heavy shadows across the yard. He heard Musket working in the stables and Friska whinnying among the tethered horses.

Mickle stood near the well. She had pulled the shawl closer around her shoulders. He called to her. The girl turned and looked coolly at him. She had grown even thinner. The oversized garments seemed to hold a bundle of sticks.

"Florian wants me to go back to Freyborg," Theo began. "That's where I've been living, since —"

"Since you ran off without so much as a fare-thee-well," said Mickle. "You had me thinking you liked me. Next thing I knew, you were gone."

"I didn't want to leave."

"Then why did you?"

"I thought it was best. There's a lot you don't know about me."

"I doubt it," Mickle said. "The count told me why you took up with him. Zara told me the rest."

"Well, then you see why I couldn't ask you to come with me. I'm a criminal; the police are looking for me. I could be arrested any time. By now, I suppose, I would have been. If Florian hadn't helped me."

"The police are looking for everybody I know," Mickle said. "That's not much of a reason."

"For me it is. Suppose they'd caught me? They'd have arrested you, too."

"It's happened before. I'm used to it."

"I'm not. I'm not used to anything that's happened to me. I'm not used to hoaxing gullible people, or pretending to be a High Brazilian savage —"

"You were very good at it." Mickle grinned for the first time since their meeting.

"That's the trouble, don't you see? When I ran into the count, I thought it would be a chance to see the rest of the world. That's really what I wanted. Not swindling people with elixirs made from ditch water, or claiming to raise ghosts. Least of all, trying to kill someone. But I've done all that. Even getting you out of jail, I lied like a thief. Worse, it didn't bother me at all. What kind of person does that make me?"

"No different from anyone else," Mickle said. "Did you think you were?"

"I don't know. I don't know what I am anymore."

"Tell me when you find out," said Mickle. "As you're so itchy to go traveling, I suppose you'll run off again."

"That can wait. I have work to do in Freyborg now."

"That's fine for you," said Mickle. "You needn't wonder what becomes of me."

"I thought — I took it for granted you'd stay with the count and Musket."

"You could ask, at least."

"Will you come to Freyborg with me?"

Theo heard his own voice, not from his lips but seeming to come from the bottom of the well. Taken aback for an instant, he realized it was Mickle. The girl was laughing.

"I'm not the phrenological head," protested Theo, laughing himself. "You needn't put words in my mouth."

"You weren't putting them there yourself."

"All right," said Theo. "Will you come with me? What else happens, I don't care. Florian wants to bring down the monarchy, Torrens wants to patch it up, the count's off to humbug the Trebizonians. All I want is — I don't want us to be apart any more."

He thought she was still laughing at him when he put his arms around her. He was surprised to discover, then, what he had not been able to see in the dark. The girl's cheeks were wet.

"It's bad enough crying when I'm asleep," said Mickle. "Why should I do it when I'm awake?"

Chapter Twenty-one

t first light, Florian and his party said their farewells. Justin, bandaged and pale but looking very proud, had been given one of the cavalry mounts. Florian sat astride a bay mare with a blanket for a saddle.

"Do well, youngster," he said to Theo. "I count on you for that."

Theo watched them ride from the farmyard. Florian had still not given him the honor of calling him his child. Theo was uncertain whether to be sorry or glad.

Zara, Stock, and Keller left soon after. Theo and Mickle would have gone in the cart with them, but Las Bombas, for the sake of old times, insisted on driving them to Freyborg in the coach. While Musket hitched up Friska, Theo stayed at Mickle's side. The two had not ceased talking since breakfast, using Mickle's private sign language, so none of the company realized they were in fact chattering like a pair of magpies.

Theo had put aside his own anxieties. He was happy, with no room in his mind for them. He was impatient for Mickle to see the Strawmarket cubbyhole, Jellinek's tavern, the press, as if these were treasures he had been storing up for her.

Las Bombas had changed his ruined uniform for the robes of Dr. Absalom. He had slept well, eaten still better, and had trimmed his moustache into something close to jauntiness.

"I urge you both to reconsider," he told Theo and Mickle as they climbed into the coach. "A fascinating country, Trebizonia. I promise you, my boy, no oracles, no undines, not even Dr. Absalom's Elixir. I intend to follow the path of virtue. It will not be overcrowded."

Seeing his persuasive powers had no effect, Las Bombas sighed and settled into a corner of the coach. The day promised to be sharp and bright.

Musket set off at a walking pace, looking for a road that would carry them north and, as well, give Nierkeeping the widest berth.

The Demon Coachman's instincts for the lay of the land proved sound. Before noon, he struck a good highway several leagues above Nierkeeping. By luck, there was a posthouse at the crossroads. Friska needed fodder and water. Las Bombas required something more substantial. Musket reined up, but the count now realized he was suffering from the return of an old ailment.

"I haven't a penny to my name. Honesty tends to reduce one's cash in hand. But wait — this may answer: my lodestone from Kazanastan, from the Mountain of the Moon. It's worth a king's ransom. If I can remember where I put it, I'd be willing to part with it for a modest sum."

He rummaged in a box under the seat and at last brought out the black, egg-sized pebble which Theo recognized from their first meeting. The count's good resolutions were still too new and unexercised to withstand his appetite. He would hear none of Theo's objections, and strode into the public room. Mickle and Theo followed reluctantly, with Musket behind them.

The uncrowded room gave the count a meager choice of customers. At a table, some travelers were playing a game of dominoes. One of them, with several stacks of coins in front of him, was clearly winning handsomely over his opponents. Las Bombas, about to approach, suddenly halted. He stared at the winning player, a pudgy man with a gold chain around his neck.

"See that rascal?" Las Bombas gripped Theo's arm. "That villain sitting there as bold as brass?"

It took Theo a moment to recall the inn at Kessel and the false alderman. Las Bombas muttered, "He robbed me then. He'll pay for it now, with interest. There's justice in the world, after all. Forgiveness is a virtue, but I'll forgive him some other time. Wretch! He's likely rigged those dominoes in some fashion, to fleece innocent wayfarers. They'll be grateful to me for warning them."

"Let him be," whispered Theo. "We don't dare stir up trouble. Get out. We'll find another inn."

Las Bombas had already started for the table. Robes flapping, he shook his fist in the air.

"Gentlemen, I denounce this creature for what he is: a cheat and a fraud! He swindled me out of a fortune and is doing the same to you. Alderman, is he? Thimblerigger! Stand up, Skeit, and deny it if you dare!"

The count's outburst brought players and onlookers to their feet. The losers shouted agreement with Las Bombas. The others, seeing a prosperous gentleman defamed by a gross figure in a shabby robe, defended the alderman. The landlord hurried to the table, waving his arms and ordering all of them to settle their differences outside.

Skeit, during this, kept his seat and his composure. He was staring at Las Bombas with a look of joy. Far from cringing at the count's accusation, he beamed.

"My dear sir! My dear — Bloomsa, I believe? This is the happiest of meetings. Indeed, sir, I had been hoping our paths might cross. I have, in fact, been at some pains to make sure they did. I would have found you sooner or later. Now you save me further effort. This is a moment you will come to regard with a pleasure as great as my own. You, my good Mynheer, stand to gain a fortune."

At this word, Las Bombas pricked up his ears. He hesitated, then glared at the self-styled alderman.

"You cannot turn me from my duty. Fortune, you say? No, you'll not wiggle away by trying to corrupt me. On the other hand, as a just and reasonable man, I must in all fairness let you state your case. I shall allow you to do so in private."

The commotion had brought the rest of the company to the group of quarreling travelers. An army captain shouldered his way to Las Bombas and peered at him.

"Sir, do we not know each other?"

"Eh?" Las Bombas gave him a hasty glance. "Not in any degree. Be so good as to leave us. This gentleman and I have a matter to discuss."

"But I recognize you, sir," the officer insisted. "You are General Sambalo. This is your servant — but I recollect he was Trebizonian. And yourself, no longer in uniform —"

"At my tailors'," replied the count in a stifled voice. Assuming a military bearing, he eyed the captain. "I was merely testing your memory. An officer must always keep his wits about him. I commend you, sir. Your commander shall have a glowing report from me."

"Begging the General's pardon," replied the officer, "this is most irregular. I heard you accuse this individual. I presume, sir, you will press charges against him. I shall see to it on your behalf."

"Not necessary. I shall deal with him myself."

"Begging the General's pardon again, there is another question. A mere formality. Since you are in plain clothes, I am required to ask for your papers."

"Excellent," said the count. "Very dutiful. They are in my uniform."

"Sir, my orders oblige me. There has been a serious incident at Nierkeeping. Without proper identification, even if it were the field marshal himself, I would be required to place him under arrest. I cannot go against regulations. You, sir, must appreciate that more than anyone."

"I'll see you court-martialed!" cried Las Bombas. "Arrest, indeed! I'll have you drummed out of your regiment."

"The captain is in error," said Skeit. "He will not arrest anyone."

"This is not your business," returned the officer. "Hold your tongue or you'll be under lock and key."

The officer, in the unhappy position of being at odds with a superior, was delighted at the chance to berate a civilian.

Skeit, however, drew a paper from his jacket. "Read this. Do you recognize the signature and seal?"

The officer stared at the document and brought up his hand in a stiff salute.

Skeit nodded. "You understand I have full authority. This man and his party are indeed under arrest. Not by your command. By mine. They shall be in my custody."

"As you order, sir. The girl, too?"

"All of them," replied Skeit. "And, most assuredly, the girl."

Chapter Twenty-two

Captain," said Skeit, "report to your commander immediately. Tell him that I require an armed escort for myself and these four."

The domino-players, unwilling to be caught up in a serious matter over their heads, drew away. The false alderman took a pistol from under his cloak.

"This is outrageous!" cried Las Bombas. "The man's a fraud. Authority? That scrap of paper's a forgery. I warn you, captain, I have connections at the highest levels."

The count's protest went unheeded by the officer, who turned on his heel and strode from the inn to carry out Skeit's orders. Had he alone been arrested, Theo would have been less surprised. He had lived in fear of it for months. Skeit had barely glanced at him. The man's eyes, instead, were on Mickle.

The girl appeared unconcerned. She drew her shawl closer around her. Then she made a startled movement and stared, half smiling, past Skeit's head.

"Don't move," a voice commanded. "Stand as you are or you're a dead man. Throw down the pistol."

For that instant, Theo was sure Mickle's ruse had saved them. Skeit stiffened, his face was furious, but he let the gun drop from his hand. Musket scurried to pick up the weapon. Skeit had turned to confront his captor. Seeing no one behind him, without pausing to wonder how he had been tricked, the pudgy man moved with astonishing speed. A booted foot shot out to stamp on the dwarf's reaching hand. Musket roared in pain. Skeit drove a heel into the dwarf's ribs, then snatched up the weapon. Losing all caution, Theo flung himself on the man and shouted for Mickle to run.

The landlord, during this, had seized a blunderbuss from the chimney corner. He aimed the heavy firearm at the girl.

"Stand away," Skeit cried to him. "This is my business."

Theo had fallen back. Skeit held the muzzle of the gun to Theo's head.

"Listen to me, all of you," he muttered through clenched teeth. "I don't want you damaged, but I'll have you one way or another. As for this one," he added, indicating Theo, "he had a hand in getting you out of Nierkeeping. I know that and it's not your concern how I know it. He's mixed up with that band of rebels, and I can turn him over to the military here and now. They'll put him against a wall and shoot him. Or you can all come nicely and quietly, and that other matter stays a friendly little secret among us. That's a fair bargain, wouldn't you say?"

Las Bombas nodded glumly. Skeit lowered his pistol and beamed as if he had concluded a difficult but profitable transaction. "We understand each other, then. It will be all in your best interest. And in mine."

"What do you want from us?" Theo demanded.

"I? Nothing whatever. But other people have something in mind." Skeit winked. "What that may be, you'll have to ask them."

"I should have listened to you, my boy." Las Bombas drew a heavy sigh. "I should have let the little snake cheat them all blind. I rue the day I turned honest."

After assuring the landlord and the frightened onlookers that he would personally undertake to burn their brains if they gossiped about the incident, Skeit calmly ordered the trembling host to put up some hampers of provisions.

That they were captives was, to Theo, all too clear. Not clear at all was the nature of their captivity. When the officer returned with a cavalry escort, Skeit went to great pains over the comfort of his prisoners. He demanded quilts and blankets for them in case the weather turned colder. He did not shackle them, as Theo had expected, but advised them pleasantly that they should consider themselves his guests.

They were allowed, in fact obliged, to ride in the coach. Musket, forbidden to drive, at first stayed with them while Skeit took the reins. Friska turned so skittish under an unfamiliar hand that the dwarf had to climb back onto the box. Theo hoped the Demon Coachman would seize a chance to break free of the escort, but the vehicle was too closely hemmed in by the cavalrymen trotting alongside.

Skeit occasionally sat next to the dwarf, directing him when and where to halt: sometimes at the inn of a small town, or at a posthouse along the road. More often, he stayed inside the coach, where his presence made impossible any serious talk among his prisoners.

Theo and Mickle avoided being overheard by using the girl's sign language. While their captor drowsed or looked through the window, Mickle's hands made slight, unnoticeable motions.

Her quick fingers told Theo, "I can try to take his pistol."

"Too dangerous," he signaled back.

"What then?"

"I don't know. Wait. Be careful. Our chance may come." Theo's look of despair needed no signal.

Skeit, for his part, was in high good humor. Sure of his prisoners, he brightened with every passing mile. He grew expansive and talkative, as if he were sharing a pleasant journey in the friendliest company.

"Be still, you little snake," muttered Las Bombas. "I can't bear the sight of you, let alone your gabble."

Skeit gave him a wounded glance. "My dear sir, you'll be grateful to me. You don't know it yet, but I'm putting you in the way of making a fortune."

Las Bombas snorted in disbelief. The pudgy man winked at him. "Indeed so. Take my word for it. You'll come out of this a very rich man."

Skeit cheerfully added, "Or a very dead one."

If it suited him, Skeit did not hesitate to commandeer and pay for the use of an entire inn. On the strength of the document he carried, he ordered the guests to find lodgings elsewhere. He then chose the largest room and herded his charges into it. Relays of troopers mounted constant guard at the door and within the room itself.

As much as Theo racked his brain and Mickle recalled every trick she knew of housebreaking, they struck on no plan. Escape, Theo had to admit, was impossible. One thing tormented him more than that. Mickle's nightmares had come back.

The guards, forbidden to speak with their prisoners, kept stolid, silent watch as the girl tossed violently in her sleep, wept, and cried out. When Theo made a move to go to her side, a trooper leveled a musket at him.

The stages of their journey grew more exhausting. Skeit seemed to become impatient. One morning, he roused them well before dawn and ordered the escort to press on with all speed. In the coach, he kept the curtains tightly drawn. Theo had ceased to care whether it was day or night. Only when the coach halted and Skeit, snapping his fingers, urged his prisoners to climb out, did Theo realize it was sundown. They were in a courtyard between two high buildings. Mickle, half-asleep, shivered beside him. Las Bombas blinked.

"Not possible," he whispered. "The little worm's brought us to Marianstat, to the Juliana. There's the bell tower. I've seen it enough — from the outside, that is. No mistake, that's where we are. But — inside?"

Skeit, that moment, was approached by a stocky, bandy-legged man in court dress.

"Delivered, sir," declared Skeit, "as requested."

"Those?" said the courtier, with a look of distaste. He handed over a purse, which Skeit immediately tucked away under his cloak. "Now get out.

Don't show your face around here. Your work is done. Even so, you should have had them cleaned before the chief minister sees them."

Theo felt Mickle's hand tighten in his own. Before he could digest what he heard, a detachment of palace guards fell in around them. They were marched into the older, fortresslike building, and through a corridor. The bandy-legged courtier, who had gone ahead, beckoned them to enter a sparsely furnished chamber. Behind a table sat a black-robed man studying a sheaf of papers. He continued his work for several moments, then glanced up.

"I am given to understand you have come from our northern provinces. I trust the journey was not fatiguing."

Cabbarus smiled.

Chapter Twenty-three

heo expected a monster. He saw only a gaunt, thin-lipped man he could have taken for a town clerk or notary. Yet, suddenly, he had a taste of tarnished metal in his mouth. The man reeked of power, it hung in the air around him. Theo felt light-headed. He was choking with what he thought was hatred, then realized how much of it was terror. Still smiling, Cabbarus glanced at each of the captives. His eyes came at last to fix on the girl. He made a small motion with his head. Mickle's cheeks had gone gray. A thready sound rose in her throat. The girl had begun shuddering violently. Afraid she might fall, Theo held her arm.

"Does the young woman require assistance?" asked Cabbarus. "I should have provided refreshment. Forgive my oversight, but I have been at my desk all this day. Councillor Pankratz will see to any of your needs."

Las Bombas was the first to find his voice. "There has been, sir, a deplorable misunderstanding, some judicial error. Our lives have been threatened, we have been brought here as prisoners, for no discernible reason."

"The reason," said Cabbarus, "is very simple. I ordered it. The individual I employed may have been overzealous in his duties, but you are not prisoners."

Las Bombas heaved a sigh of relief. Cabbarus raised his hand and went on.

"Not necessarily prisoners. That remains to be seen. For some days, I have been studying a number of reports. I find that serious charges have been laid against this young man. Assault, attempted murder, armed rebellion — an extensive list."

Cabbarus leafed through his papers. "As for you — not long ago a band of rebels attacked the Nierkeeping garrison. I am led to conclude you were present."

"In a cage!" protested Las Bombas. "And my colleagues were —"

"Freed by the selfsame rebels. By the strict letter of the law, you were, therefore, at the scene of a brutal crime, where nearly a dozen soldiers were killed. You did nothing to prevent it. You offered no assistance to the authorities, you came forward with no information. A tribunal must look severely on your conduct. It would, in fact, have no choice but to sentence you to the extreme penalty.

"I am prepared to order all charges dropped. You and your associates will be released and generously compensated. Depending on how well you are able to serve me. A service which is also a duty."

"I have no duty toward you," broke in Theo. "I've done what I'm charged with. Yes, even attempted murder. But you've done more than attempt it."

"Be quiet, for heaven's sake," whispered the count. "If we have any chance at all, don't ruin it."

Cabbarus was unruffled by Theo's outburst. He appeared, instead, grieved by it. "I am quite aware of those among the king's subjects who accuse me of severity. They do not understand that justice must be severe for the sake of a higher cause. When the very foundation of the realm is at stake, stern, selfless devotion to duty is the noblest virtue. The welfare of the kingdom is my only interest."

The chief minister turned to Las Bombas. "Let me speak with utter honesty. It is no secret that King Augustine is gravely ill. He has not ceased to mourn his daughter, to such a point that he is no longer capable of ruling.

"However, I am given to believe that you are a man of certain talents. I ask you to put them at the service of your monarch."

"My dear sir," cried Las Bombas, "I consider it an honor. Had I known this was what you wanted, I would have presented myself willingly. Now, sir, only tell me what is required. Do you wish me to treat His Majesty with Dr. Absalom's Elixir? It has worked wonders for man and beast and will do no less for a king. Also, I have in my possession a remarkable stone from Kazanastan. Or, if you prefer, a vat of magnetized water."

"Trash," said Cabbarus.

"I beg your pardon?"

"Trash," Cabbarus repeated. "You are a common fraud, a despicable cheat and swindler."

"Yes, and a better man than you," cried Theo, before Musket, reddening, could come to his master's defense. "You talk about virtue and duty. You've turned them into lies."

"My boy, I beg you! Hold your tongue," the count pleaded. "Let him call me what he will. If he wants something I can provide and we can save our necks with it, let's hear what he has to say."

Mickle, Theo abruptly realized, was no longer at his side. Cabbarus, ignoring Theo's words, looked past him toward a corner of the chamber. "Fetch the girl."

The chief minister's voice had an edge of alarm. "Keep her away from there."

The girl was staring down at a wooden trapdoor set in the stone flooring. She did not turn when Theo reached her. She stood frozen, her eyes glazed. Musket had followed Theo and between them they drew her back from the sloping edge.

"It stinks of blood," she murmured. "He's killed people here. I know it."

Mickle's brow was burning to his touch. Theo turned to Cabbarus. "The girl is sick. She must have a doctor. Take her out of this place."

"I doubt that her complaint is serious," replied Cabbarus. "She will recover. In fact, she must."

"Whatever you require of me," put in Las Bombas, "she has no part in it. I urge you to release her. My cures and treatments — she has nothing to do with any of that."

"She has everything to do with it," said Cabbarus. "The king wishes to communicate with the spirit of his daughter. And so he will. There have been reports from a town called Felden. You are known to have summoned ghosts and apparitions with the girl's assistance."

"Do you believe that?" cried Las Bombas, turning pale. "My dear sir, you must understand — and I ask you to keep this a matter of confidence between us — these apparitions, spirit-raisings and all such are, shall we say —"

"False," said Cabbarus. "No more than a mountebank's trickery."

"Exactly!" returned the count, with a certain tone of pride. "Mere illusions, theatrical entertainments. For a moment, I thought you took them as genuine. If His Majesty wishes to reach the spirit of the late princess, the girl can't help him. She can't summon a ghost of any sort, let alone Princess Augusta."

"She will not summon the spirit of the princess," said Cabbarus. "She herself will be the spirit of Augusta. The resemblance between them is striking. She is the age the princess would now have been."

"Impossible!" protested Las Bombas. "She's a street girl. There's no way she can make the king believe she's his daughter."

"How convincing her performance will be," said Cabbarus, "is entirely up to her. For her sake, and yours, I hope it will be persuasive. His Majesty has proclaimed a sentence of death for any who fail him. This is the king's command, not mine. I can do nothing to change it.

"His Majesty knows of your presence. He will grant you a special audience tonight. You will not disappoint him."

"There's no time," said Las Bombas, beginning to sweat. "There are special arrangements to be made. It can't be done."

"You shall have whatever you need," said Cabbarus. "The girl will have only one task. As princess, she will convey a message to her father."

"Message? She can't know what to say to the king."

"She will say what I instruct her to say," replied Cabbarus. "The message is simple, but she must give it precisely. Young woman, I advise you to listen carefully.

"You are to tell His Majesty that your unhappy shade will never rest unless he does what you entreat him. For the sake of his love for you, for his own peace of mind, and for the good of the kingdom, he will give up his throne."

"What?" cried Las Bombas. "Ask the king to abdicate? Leave the throne because — because a ghost wants him to? He'll never do it."

"He will do as his daughter prays him to," said Cabbarus. "As he has always done. In her life, he refused her nothing. He will not refuse her now.

Indeed, more than ever, he will grant whatever she desires. I know His Majesty's mind and can assure you of that.

"But there is one thing more. The princess will not only plead for the king to abdicate. She will also urge His Majesty to name a successor. She will tell him that he is to resign his throne in favor of his chief minister."

"You're mad!" cried Theo. "You dare make yourself king!"

"Not I," said Cabbarus. "Princess Augusta shall do it for me. I had once contemplated His Majesty naming me adoptive heir. This is much simpler and saves tiresome waiting. It is only a formality. I rule in fact. I intend to do so in name, as well: Cabbarus the First."

The chief minister stood. "I go to advise His Majesty that I have spoken with you and am convinced your powers are genuine. Meanwhile, you shall make certain the girl understands what she must do. When I return, you shall specify the preparations you desire. If you need a further spur to your efforts, I can tell you that His Majesty offers quite a substantial reward for success. If avoiding death is not sufficient incentive, I am certain that money will be."

Cabbarus strode from the chamber. Las Bombas clapped his hands to his head.

"We're cooked! We'll never pull it off. Oh, my boy, I wish you'd never thought of The Oracle Priestess in the first place. Mickle's a wonder, I know that. But — as Princess Augusta? She'll never manage."

"Do you want her to?" Theo demanded. "King Augustine or King Cabbarus? Florian said there was no difference. I think he was wrong. I don't know whether he's right about the monarchy, or whether Dr. Torrens is. All I know is that I won't have any part in setting that murderer on the throne."

"The idea of King Cabbarus is distressing, I admit," said the count. "Being dead, even more so. We've got to try it. No, by heaven, we'll do better than try. We'll give him a princess that Augustine can't help but believe. Once the money's in hand, let Cabbarus rule as he pleases. For us, out of the country and on to Trebizonia! Mickle, my dear, listen to me —"

"Don't be a fool," cried Theo. "Do you think any of us will get out of this no matter what we do? Do you think Cabbarus will let us live a moment longer than he has to? Knowing what we know? That he set himself up as king on the word of a sham princess? That the whole business was nothing but a trick? He won't dare keep us alive."

The count choked off his words. His face fell. "I hadn't looked at it that way. I'm afraid you have a rather strong point."

Musket, during this, had been examining the trapdoor. Shaking his head in discouragement, he came to rejoin them.

"I thought we could try climbing down that drain or whatever it is. But there's water at the bottom. How deep or where it goes I don't know, and I'm not sure we'd last long enough to find out. Even so, we might risk it."

"Before plunging into some bottomless pit," said Las Bombas, "I'd rather explore another possibility. Let Cabbarus think we'll go along with his scheme. Once we're before the king, we confess the whole business. Throw ourselves on his mercy. Let him know his own chief minister forced us into it."

"Will Augustine believe it?" said Theo. "It's our word against Cabbarus."

Las Bombas nodded ruefully. "I'm afraid you're right. I don't see us winning that argument. It's the end of us, no matter what. We have everything to lose and absolutely nothing to gain. At this point, the only question is our choice of demise: wet or dry?"

Chapter Twenty-four

n Freyborg, what seemed years ago, Justin had said he would give up his life if Florian asked him. The idea had seemed heroic and admirable to Theo at the time. Now he was furious. Dying for Florian was one thing; dying for the benefit of the chief minister made him feel soiled. He thought, for a moment, of simply throwing himself at the throat of Cabbarus and satisfying at least some of his rage before the guards killed him. That would be no help to Mickle, or Musket, or Las Bombas, who was bemoaning deprivation of life and fortune both in the same day.

"Chance it, that's what I say," declared Musket. "Feet first down the shaft, take a breath, and hope for the best."

"All very well for you," said Las Bombas, who had gone to see the trapdoor himself. "I'm not the size for it. I'd end up like a cork in a bottle."

Mickle crouched in a corner, arms clasped around her shoulders. She stared at the open drain as if unable to turn away.

"Not there," she whispered. Her voice was thin, a frightened child's.

Theo went to kneel beside her. He glanced at the count. "She's not fit to try anything. I'm not sure she's even able to walk."

Las Bombas glumly nodded. "I feel much the same. Poor girl, if anyone could outface Cabbarus I'd have thought she'd be the one. She's been scared out of her wits from the moment she set foot in here. I don't blame her." The count brightened for a moment. "That might be a blessing in disguise. What if she took sick, eh? Performance canceled due to serious indisposition."

"You won't get away with it," said Musket. "That fish-eyed scoundrel doesn't look the sort to hear excuses. She can't be sick forever. He'll wait. The girl's the one he wants; and suppose in the meantime he decides he doesn't need the rest of us? If we're going to try our luck, it's now or never."

"There's one thing we can do," said Theo, after a time. He hurried on as the idea took better shape in his mind. "Go along with Cabbarus."

"What?" cried Las Bombas. "After all you said against it?"

"Hear the rest," said Theo. "If the king doesn't believe she's his daughter, we're lost from the start. But — suppose Mickle can really make him think she's Princess Augusta? It's doubtful, but she just might be able to do it. If the king listens to her and believes what she says, we may have a chance."

"I don't see that," said the count. "How's it going to help us?"

"Cabbarus wants her to tell the king to give up his throne. What if she does the opposite?"

"Eh? Opposite of what?"

"She tells him to keep it. She tells him never to abdicate, no matter what his chief minister advises. She warns him against Cabbarus, begs the king to dismiss him —"

"And Cabbarus denounces us as frauds."

"Let him," said Theo. "Even if he does, he'll still have a lot to account for."

"It comes to the same," said Las Bombas. "The king may believe us, or he may not. It doesn't answer the question uppermost in my mind: What becomes of us later? Master Cabbarus, I suspect, has a long arm. And the state Mickle's in — Even so, anything's better than jumping into drain pipes."

"Will you try it?" Theo turned to Mickle. On her face was a look of terror he had never seen before. She finally nodded. He smiled at her and would have taken her hand, but she drew away from him.

He had expected Cabbarus. Instead, it was Pankratz who came to order Las Bombas to make his preparations. Theo was unwilling to leave Mickle alone. The count assured him he and Musket could do all that was needed.

Mickle still crouched motionless. Once, she cried out as if in a waking nightmare. The rest of the time, she kept silent. He wondered if she understood or remembered anything of what she must do. He began to despair of his plan. He had thought of no other when the door was unlocked and Las Bombas hurried in.

The count helped Mickle put on a white robe, meantime whispering to Theo, "Musket's waiting. We have it all ready. The draperies, the lights — marvelous, the best I've ever done. It could work. Mickle might well save all our skins."

They were escorted from the chamber, across the courtyard, and entered what Las Bombas told Theo was the New Juliana. Cabbarus awaited them in a large audience hall.

"His Majesty never leaves his apartments," said Cabbarus. "On this occasion, he has consented to do so. I have promised him an event of utmost importance. Queen Caroline will attend, as well, along with His Majesty's high councillors and ministers. It is essential for all to hear for themselves what the princess will instruct her father."

"It's better than what we had in Felden," said Las Bombas, leading Theo and Mickle behind the curtains screening a low platform. "One thing I'll say for Cabbarus, he gave me all I wanted. He found some excellent tripods and braziers. I've worked it out so they'll give off quite impressive smoke. I could have had fireworks and rockets, but they seemed a touch excessive."

Las Bombas helped Mickle to a tall chair, where she sat with her head bowed. From the murmur of voices beyond the curtains, Theo guessed the courtiers were arriving. The count went to the front of the platform. Mickle's breathing had turned shallow. She did not answer when Theo spoke to her and gave no sign she heard him.

Las Bombas ducked around the curtains. "The king and queen are here. Cabbarus wants us to begin."

"We can't. Not now. Mickle's taken a turn for the worse. Tell Cabbarus there's been a delay. Tell him — tell him anything."

"Too late," groaned the count. Musket had lit the tripods. Clouds of smoke billowed upward. Mickle raised her head. The girl seemed to be forcing herself past the limits of her strength.

Theo pulled on the cords that opened the curtains. In the hall, the candles had been snuffed out. He saw only a crowd of shadows, two dim figures on a dais at the far end of the room, and the dark shape of Cabbarus beside them.

The count had arranged lanterns on either side of Mickle, and their glow fell on her face. The courtiers drew in their breath at their first sight of the girl. Her eyes were lowered, her features a pale mask. Her lips parted slightly but did not move. She spoke in a tone that seemed to come from a great distance.

"Help me. Please help me. I'm going to fall."

The terror and pleading that underlay the words were so real that Theo started forward.

"Please," Mickle went on, "give me your hand."

"What's she doing?" Las Bombas whispered frantically to Theo. "She's not supposed to go at it like that. She's ruining the whole business. If we ever had a chance, it's gone!"

Mickle had risen from her chair. "Hurry. I can't hold on any longer."

A cry of anguish rang through the chamber, not from the king, but from Queen Caroline.

"That is my child! My child is calling!"

Chapter Twenty-five

heo's head whirled. He had staked all on Mickle's acting her part well; but to mimic a voice she had never heard, the voice of a child long dead, was impossible.

Mickle's tone changed and deepened. It was a new voice, cruel and mocking.

"You seem, Princess, to have put yourself in a fine fix. Let that be a lesson not to pry into places that don't concern you."

The child's voice spoke again. "I was playing hide-and-seek. It was only a game. Please, I'm getting tired."

Mickle had begun making her way like a sleepwalker to the middle of the hall. Theo and Las Bombas were too dumbstruck to prevent her. She spoke once more.

"You take a different air with me now, Princess. I was never one of your favorites. How quickly you change your manner, with your life in my hands. Do you beg me to help you? I am not sure I wish to oblige."

The courtiers gasped. They had realized the same thing Theo had in the same instant. The voice was a girl's imitating a man; but in tone and cadence, unmistakable: the voice of Cabbarus.

Before Mickle could go on, the chief minister burst out, "What is this monstrous trickery? Majesty, they have deceived me with their promises. They are frauds —"

"Be silent!" cried Augustine. "The spirit of my child at last speaks to me. She tells me truly how she came to her death!"

A dry laugh rose from Mickle's lips. "Many before you, little Princess, made their last journey down this well. Would you find it amusing to join them?"

For all its terror, the child's voice took on a tone of command. "Lift me out. My father shall know how you treated me. He won't like to hear how you stood up there and made fun of me. Some of the ministers want him to send you away. I heard them talking about it. My father hasn't made up his mind. But he will, once he finds out you wouldn't help me."

"He will only know if you live to tell him."

Mickle's eyes were wide, staring upward as she cried out, "My hands are slipping! Cabbarus, don't! You're hurting my fingers!"

Someone was calling for lights. Theo sprang from behind the curtains. Mickle screamed and dropped to the floor. King Augustine was on his feet.

"My daughter did not die by mishap! It was you, Cabbarus! You told me you came too late to save her life. A lie! You were there with her in the Old Juliana. You let her fall to her death. Her spirit accuses you!"

Queen Caroline had reached Mickle. She flung herself beside the unconscious girl. "No spirit! This is my child!"

"Murderer!" cried Augustine. He took a step toward Cabbarus. "Murderer! Seize him!"

Cabbarus leaped away. The guards were as stunned as the courtiers. He forced his way through the ranks of attendants and fled the chamber. Leaving Mickle and the queen, Theo bolted after him. Cabbarus had gained the corridor and was making for the courtyard.

Theo at his heels, Cabbarus halted, uncertain which way to turn. A company of soldiers had come into sight from one of the arcades. Finding this path of escape blocked, Cabbarus darted through the gate of the Old Juliana. He broke his stride to turn and strike at Theo, who fell to one knee and clutched at the man's robe.

Cabbarus tore free. Guards from the audience chamber were in the courtyard, the alarm raised throughout the palace. Theo grappled with Cabbarus, who threw him aside and clambered up a flight of stone steps.

Theo stumbled after him. The steps narrowed and twisted. It was the belfry of the old fortress. A square gallery with a low railing surrounded the massive bells. Stone arches, open to sky and wind, gave him a dizzying glimpse of the courtyard below.

Cabbarus halted and spun around. Theo heard the growling of an enraged animal. To his horror, he realized it came from his own throat.

He flung himself on the chief minister. Cabbarus fought to break loose. His fingers locked around Theo's neck. Theo pitched backward. Still in the grip of Cabbarus, he lurched against the railing and hurtled over it. He fell, clutching at air for an instant. His hand caught one of the bell ropes.

Cabbarus, toppling with him, loosened his grasp. The man screamed and would have plummeted to the bottom of the tower if Theo had not snatched his arm and held on to it with all his strength.

The jolt nearly wrenched Theo's own arm from its socket. He cried out in pain. The man's weight was dragging at him. Another moment, he feared, and both would fall to their death. He needed only to open his hand to rid himself of his burden.

Cabbarus was staring up at him, eyes bursting with hatred. Theo's own fury choked him. That instant, he wanted nothing so much as to fling the man away. Half sobbing, he clamped his legs around the rope and tightened his grip on Cabbarus.

The guards were racing up the steps into the belfry, with Musket scuttling ahead of them. The dwarf's mouth was open, shouting. Theo heard none of his words. Above him, the bell had stirred into life, its voice resounding in the others that hung beside it. The clangor exploded in his ears. He was being hoisted up and pulled back over the railing, still gripping Cabbarus. Theo's hand had frozen on the man's arm. Someone was prying his fingers loose.

The face of Las Bombas loomed in front of him. Deafened, dazed, he wondered why Mickle had not come. Then he remembered there was no such person. There was only one who had called herself by that name.

Chapter Twenty-six

They keep telling me I'm Princess Augusta," said Mickle. "I know that. What I can't decide is whether I'm a princess who used to be a street girl, or a street girl who used to be a princess."

Mickle sat cross-legged amid a pile of cushions on her bed in the Royal Chambers. She wriggled her shoulders as if her silken gown made her itch. She grinned at Theo, who waited for her to continue her story. He had not been allowed to see her for two days, while physicians, maids, nurses, and her parents constantly hurried in and out. Finally, Mickle had declared herself perfectly well and demanded Theo, Las Bombas, and Musket.

Queen Caroline sat in a chair by the casement, keeping an anxious eye on her daughter, although the girl had clearly regained health and spirit.

"I remember everything," said Mickle. "That's what makes it feel so odd. Because I can't understand why there were so many years when I'd forgotten everything."

"You didn't forget," said Theo. "It was there, somewhere in your mind. It was in your nightmares."

"They're gone now," said Mickle. "I haven't had any more. Yes, I must have been dreaming about what Cabbarus did to me, but there wasn't any way I could know that. When I saw the trapdoor again, it all started coming back."

"You were living through it again," said Theo. "It was worse than a nightmare because you couldn't wake up from it."

"You gave an impressive performance," put in Las Bombas. "I thought at the time: amazing how you could pretend to be Princess Augusta."

"She wasn't pretending," said Theo. "She was telling us how Cabbarus tried to kill her."

"I suppose it was my own fault," said Mickle. "I was always getting into one scrape or another. I even climbed the bell tower. That day, I wanted to see what was under the trapdoor. I thought it would be a good place for hide-and-seek. Nobody would ever look for me there. But I slipped and couldn't pull myself back. That's when Cabbarus came in and saw me.

"He kicked my hands until I let go. I remember falling down, down into the water. Then there was the river taking me away —"

Queen Caroline came to smooth her daughter's hair. "Do not think of it any longer. We believed you dead. You are alive and with us again. No more need be said."

"Oh, it wasn't too bad after that," Mickle answered. "I was lucky. I floated into the marshes. The Fingers, they're called. The old man who fished me out really saved my life. There's no way I can thank him now. I grew up thinking he was my grandfather. By then, I'd lost my memory of whatever happened before. I couldn't have told him who I was. I didn't know. It was as if I'd always been there. Poor man, he couldn't have heard me, or spoken to me anyway. Even after he taught me his sign language, he never told me how he found me. I suppose he wanted me to stay. And I did, until he died. Then I went off on my own.

"I'll tell you one thing," she added to Queen Caroline. "That Home for Repentant Girls: Something has to be done about it, starting with that oatmeal they serve."

"You shall see to it yourself, my dear," said the queen. "It shall be one of your Royal Duties."

"Oh. Those." Mickle made a face. "I'd rather not think about them."

"Be glad you are able to perform any duties at all," said the queen. "In the audience chamber, we feared you might never wake. You fainted and nothing could bring you back until the bells rang."

"Yes, the bells! How I loved them! Well, Cabbarus tried to kill me — and he turned out to be the one who woke me up. That's fair enough."

"Actually, it was our young friend here," put in Las Bombas. "He was hanging on to the bell rope and Cabbarus at the same time."

"A moment more and the two of them would have ended up with broken necks at the bottom of the tower," added Musket. The dwarf, through methods of his own, had come into possession of a new hat, which he brandished at Theo.

"I kept telling you to let him drop. You didn't hear me. That may be just as well, for some of the names I called you, least of which was 'idiot.'"

"I never hated anyone before," said Theo. "But I hated Cabbarus. Why should I have been the one to save his life?"

"Even so, his life will not be long."

King Augustine had come unannounced into the chamber and had been listening silently. Though he moved with the gait of an invalid still unsure of his legs, his face had regained a little of its color. Although one weight had been lifted from him, he seemed to bear another.

"I blame only myself for raising him to chief minister. It was true, as Princess Augusta told it: I had thought of dismissing him as superintendent of the Royal Household. My senses left me when I believed my child was dead; but I neither excuse nor forgive myself on that account. I will set right all that can be set right. What Cabbarus did in my name can never be forgiven.

"He awaits execution in the Carolia Fortress," the king went on. "He will be put to death justly, as he put to death so many others unjustly. That is the only price he can pay, though it is far too little."

"Majesty, I ask one favor," Theo said. "I didn't save his life to have him lose it. I want no one's death on my conscience, not even his."

"You plead for him?" cried Augustine. "He is a monster!"

"Then let him live with his monstrousness. Banish him —" Theo stopped. "I'm not the one to ask that. Mickle — Princess Augusta — suffered most at his hands. The judgment is hers."

"Well," said Mickle, "I saw what they did to my friend Hanno. I say, no more of it. Yes, send Cabbarus into exile. He's lost his power, and for him that's worse than hanging."

"As you wish," said King Augustine. "He shall know who kept him from the scaffold, and be grateful — if he is capable of gratitude."

"I don't want his gratitude," said Theo. "Majesty, he must not be told I spoke for him."

"So be it," said Augustine. "Councillor Pankratz, too, will be exiled with his master."

"I suggest a desert island," said Las Bombas. "They can take turns ruling each other. But, Your Majesty, since the matter of granting favors has arisen: I recall the former chief minister mentioning something about a reward."

"You're asking for money?" Theo rounded on Las Bombas. "You want to be paid for something you'd have done anyway? You ought to be ashamed!"

"I am," replied the count. "On the other hand, I'm even more ashamed of being penniless."

"A reward was offered," said King Augustine. "You claim it rightly and shall be given it. But the princess grows tired. You have our permission to withdraw."

Royal permission being a royal command, Theo, against his own wishes, found himself ushered from the chamber with no further chance to talk with Mickle. Or Princess Augusta. How much of her was the one, how much the other, he was afraid to guess.

"I can't believe you'll take that reward," Theo told the count as they went to their apartments. "You're a worse rogue than I thought, if that's possible."

"My boy, what do you expect from me?" protested Las Bombas. "I'm only flesh and blood — more so than most."

Theo laughed and shook his head. "I can't argue that. I'm not the one to blame you, either. I was trying to be better than I am. I'm not as virtuous as I thought I was — or wanted to be. I wonder if anyone is, even Florian. I suppose we should be glad if we're able to do any good at all."

Las Bombas shrugged. "I never had that kind of problem."

Las Bombas, despite Theo's reproaches, insisted on claiming his due. Next day, unable to persuade Theo to come with him, the count set off with a light heart and heavy purse. Alone, at loose ends, Theo paced his chambers. To his surprise, he found himself looking back with a measure of longing for the days of The Phrenological Head, even The Oracle Priestess: when Mickle still was Mickle.

He saw little of her during the following week, the princess being hedged about with courtiers paying their respects. The only event to raise his spirits was the arrival of Dr. Torrens.

News of all that had led to the downfall of Cabbarus had spread throughout the kingdom. The court physician had set out for Marianstat as soon as word reached him. Torrens brought the king and queen a curious gift.

"The river — that is to say, two young water rats — took me where it had taken the princess, indeed to the hut itself. At first, I did not realize it. Then I found this."

Torrens handed Queen Caroline the stained piece of linen he had worn as a sling. It was a child's garment embroidered with the Royal Crest, faded and torn but still visible. "I took it as proof the princess was dead. Instead, it was a token that she still lived."

King Augustine, over the doctor's protest, named Torrens chief minister. Augustine then ordered him to announce pardon to all whom Cabbarus had unjustly sentenced, as well as those who had attacked the Nierkeeping garrison. The doctor, describing Florian to the king, doubted this would satisfy him.

"We spent many days together," said Torrens. "We did not agree, nor did I expect us to. As a man, I respect him more than I imagined I would. As chief minister, I am troubled by him. He has not rejoined his friends in Freyborg. Where he is, I do not know. But he has not changed his views of the monarchy. I suspect we shall hear again of Master Florian."

Later, he spoke apart with Theo.

"Their Majesties are concerned for your future and so am I. Certain matters must be discussed, of importance to you and to the kingdom."

"And Princess Augusta?"

"Naturally. We shall speak of this another time. Meanwhile, I have something Florian wished me to give you. It amused him that you, of all people, were the one to bring down Cabbarus. I think he was a little envious, too. He had counted on doing that himself. He would, no doubt, have gone about it differently. The fact remains: Cabbarus is gone."

"Was I a fool?" asked Theo. "Should I have let him drop? I didn't want his death on my conscience, but I don't want his life on my conscience, either."

"I do not know what I would have done in the same circumstances," replied Torrens. "How easy it is to think well of ourselves. Until the moment is upon us, we can never be certain."

Torrens handed Theo a folded scrap of paper.

"From Florian. He asks you to remember some things you said to him at the farm. It would appear you gave him much to think about."

Afterwards, in his chambers, Theo smiled over the hastily written lines:

My Child,
You did well. Perhaps you even did right.

It was unsigned.

Chapter Twenty-seven

orrens finally did what Mickle had not managed to do. As physician as well as chief minister, he ended the endless visitations by the courtiers. Instead, he prescribed fresh air. Theo was permitted to walk with her in the Juliana gardens, leaving her ladies-in-waiting behind them to cluck over such a breach of etiquette. For a while, the two were silent, content simply to be in each other's company.

"There's quite a difference between all this and the way I lived in Freyborg," Theo said at last. "Jellinek's tavern, the wine merchant's cellar. Stock and the others. I miss them. I even miss my cubbyhole on Strawmarket Street. But I realize I'd have been a fool to bring a princess there."

"I didn't know I was a princess, so it wouldn't have mattered."

"But you are a princess, and it matters now. There's no way around it."

"I'm still Mickle, aren't I? One part of me."

"The king and queen don't think so. I have an idea they wish you'd forget that part."

"Not likely!" Mickle suddenly imitated the voice of a street peddler and laughed at the startled look on Theo's face. "They've been talking to you, haven't they? Yes, well, they've been talking to me, too. They mainly come back to the same thing: I'll be queen of Westmark some day."

"And so you will."

"Not if Florian has his way. Not if I have mine, either. There must be a royal cousin somewhere who's foolish enough to like this kind of work. Anyhow, I told them I didn't care about it, I wouldn't let them separate us. So that settles it." When Theo did not answer immediately, her face fell. "Doesn't it? Unless — What did they say to you?"

"Only that I had to make my own choice."

A flurry of excitement from the court ladies interrupted him.

Theo turned to see Las Bombas hurrying up the path, and called out to him. "You, back again? I thought you'd be well away by now, money and all."

"No," said Las Bombas. "That's why I'm here."

"You changed your mind about keeping it!" exclaimed Theo. "I never imagined you would. Bravo, then!"

"I admit having such a large sum made me feel uncomfortable. I'm more used to pursuing a fortune than having one handed to me."

"So you had to return it." Theo clapped Las Bombas on the shoulder. "You do have some sort of conscience after all."

"Yes, and it's been a torment to me." The count sighed. "I can't forgive myself."

"Of course you can," said Theo. "You'll feel better as soon as you turn back the reward."

"You misunderstand," said Las Bombas. "I can't forgive myself — for losing it.

"Bilked out of it," he went on ruefully. "Gulled out of it, as if I'd been an innocent babe. That's what's unforgivable. I fell in with a gentleman — Gentleman? A barefaced scoundrel! He showed me a letter from a nobleman who'd been clapped into a Trebizonian prison. If we'd pay his ransom and get him out, he'd show us where he'd discovered an enormous buried treasure. We'd go shares — ah, no need to parade the details of my shame before the world. The money's gone. Oh, let me come across that wretch again!

"So I've only stopped to bid you farewell once more, Princess. And you, my boy. Musket's impatient to be off. You two, I daresay, are busy making your own plans."

"I have none," said Theo. "But Dr. Torrens has one for me. I don't know. I was telling Mickle — the princess — I'll have to decide. Dr. Torrens wants me to travel around Westmark."

"You'll do it in fine style," said Las Bombas. "Rather better than we did."

"No. Just the opposite. He wants me to be on my own and see for myself what the kingdom's like. He thinks I can find out what the people want and what's to be done about it. But I don't know if I can. I don't even know whether Florian's right, or the monarchy."

"Permit me to say," put in Las Bombas, "no offense, you understand, but a princess who smokes a pipe, swears like a trooper, and scratches wherever she itches might be a blessing for the entire kingdom. Even Florian might approve."

"What if —" Theo took Mickle's hand. "What if you and I went together? You'd know more than I would. I've hardly been away from Dorning."

The girl's eyes were dancing, but she shook her head. "I'll stay here. For now, at any rate. My parents broke their hearts over me once. I won't have them break again. I didn't like it when you walked off last time. I won't mind so much now. It's not the same thing. Do what Dr. Torrens asks. You want to. I know it. I can tell by looking at you."

"I don't want to leave you."

"You won't," said Mickle. "Call it being slightly apart for a while."

The ladies-in-waiting had come to insist on taking the princess indoors. Mickle stuck out her tongue at them, but finally let them escort her to the New Juliana. She turned back once and Theo read the quick motion of her hands.

"Find what you want. I will find you."

Responding to *Westmark*

Thinking and Discussing

Though the kingdom of Westmark is an imaginary setting, the author creates a sense of time and place to make the story more believable. What clues help establish the time and place?

How does the reader learn about the kind of person Theo is? Which experiences help him mature, and how do they affect him? When does Theo himself recognize the change that has taken place?

What details about Mickle are revealed in the climax of the story? How does this turning point lead to the outcome for each character? What clues did the author give earlier in the book that might have led the reader to predict this scene?

Choosing a Creative Response

Recommending Changes in Westmark Theo will tour Westmark to report on the state of the kingdom and recommend changes to be made. What recommendations do you think he might make? Write a series of newspaper headlines describing laws that come about as a result.

Creating Your Own Activity Plan and complete your own activity in response to *Westmark*.

Exploring Language

Many expressions used in conversation by the inhabitants of Westmark are outdated by today's standards. Make a list of some of these words and phrases and translate each one into modern-day language. For example, "to write a clear hand" could be translated as "to have neat handwriting." Use the context to help you decipher the meaning of unfamiliar terms.

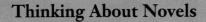

Thinking About Novels

Plotting the Plot Working with a group, discuss what you would include if you were to make a story web showing the plot and subplots in *Westmark*. The main plot line should map Theo's travels and adventures. The subplot lines should trace events surrounding minor characters, such as the attack on Dr. Torrens. As you complete the web, consider these questions:

- Does the author relate the story in sequential order? How can you use the web to explain how the story unfolds?

- Which incidents foreshadow events that occur later in the novel? How does this build suspense?

- Which incidents make future events possible or even probable?

Designing a Poster Posters often persuade people to visit faraway, exotic lands. Design an intriguing poster that might convince readers to travel to Westmark through the pages of Lloyd Alexander's novel. Bring one of the characters described in the story to life, or portray one of the settings.

Panel Discussion   Do you like fantasy novels like *Westmark*? Realistic novels? Science fiction? Romances or mysteries? With a group, organize a panel discussion to talk about the many types of novels you and your classmates enjoy reading. Then think about what distinguishes one novel from another. What do the novels have in common? Have any of the novels been made into movies or television programs? How do the programs compare with the originals?

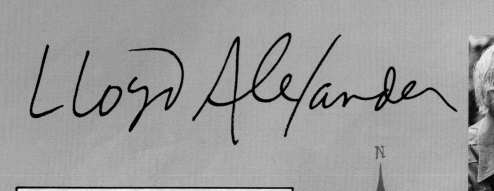

Author Lloyd Alexander was born in Philadelphia, Pennsylvania, in 1924. He enjoyed reading at an early age; a great treat was to be allowed to buy books from a store in West Philadelphia. Unable to afford a college education, Alexander worked briefly as a bank messenger, then joined the U.S. Army to fight in World War II.

The High King, the fifth book of the Prydain Chronicles, received the Newbery Medal in 1969, and *The Marvelous Misadventures of Sebastian* won the National Book Award in 1971. Says Alexander of his writing, "I start work at the crack of dawn, but if things go badly at the typewriter, I may sneak back to bed. Janine, my wife, claims I'm snoozing. I claim I'm thinking horizontally." Alexander continues to live in Pennsylvania, where he enjoys playing the violin in an informal chamber music group, printmaking, and animals, especially cats.

As part of a military intelligence unit, Alexander was sent to England, and later to Wales, which he found to be a land of enchantment. Imagining the days of King Arthur and his Round Table, Alexander says, "My sense of Wales was of a land far more ancient than England. . . . The companions of Arthur might have galloped from the mountains with no surprise to me."

It took seven years before any of his books were accepted for publication, and it was another four years before he wrote his first book for children. His first fantasy, *Time Cat*, was published in 1963. Then came *The Book of Three*, the first of the Prydain Chronicles series in which the history and mythology of Wales were to have such a strong influence. Other books by Alexander followed, including *The Cat Who Wished to Be a Man*, the Westmark trilogy, *The First Two Lives of Lukas-Kasha*, and the adventures of Vesper Holly.

After Wales, Alexander was sent to Paris as a translator-interpreter. He married a French woman, earned a degree at the University of Paris, and returned to Pennsylvania, where he settled down to become a part-time writer.

More from the Imagination

The Dark Is Rising by Susan Cooper
(Macmillan, 1973)

Eleven-year-old Will Stanton is the last of the Old Ones and must search for the six Signs of the Light, which will help defeat the Dark. Other books in this series are *Over Sea, Over Stone* (1966), *Greenwitch* (1974), *The Grey King* (1975), and *Silver on the Tree* (1977).

Nightpool by Shirley Rousseau Murphy (Harper, 1985)

The Dragonbards trilogy begins with this tale of sixteen-year-old Tebriel, who is injured by Dark invaders and healed by the talking otters in the colony of Nightpool. Teb aids a singing dragon in fighting the forces of evil.

The Black Cauldron by Lloyd Alexander (Holt, 1965)

Taran knows that as long as the Black Cauldron remains in the wrong hands, the kingdom of Prydain cannot be safe.

The Hobbit by J.R.R. Tolkien (Houghton, 1938)

This is a fantasy about Bilbo Baggins, the hobbit, who lives in the land of dragons, dwarfs, elves, and goblins. The tale of his adventures with the dwarfs who try to recover the treasure stolen by the dragon Smaug is a classic.

The Westmark Trilogy by Lloyd Alexander
(Dutton; Dell, 1982, 1983, 1985)

This award-winning series, originally published by Dutton, portrays the imaginary kingdom of Westmark. The trilogy begins with the book you have just read, continues in *The Kestrel* (1982), and concludes in *The Beggar Queen* (1984).

Glossary

Some of the words in this book may have pronunciations or meanings you do not know. This glossary can help you by telling you how to pronounce those words and by telling you the meanings with which those words are used in this book.

You can find out the correct pronunciation of any glossary word by using the special spelling after the word and the pronunciation key that runs across the bottom of the glossary pages.

The full pronunciation key opposite shows how to pronounce each consonant and vowel in a special spelling. The pronunciation key at the bottom of the glossary pages is a shortened form of the full key.

FULL PRONUNCIATION KEY

Consonant Sounds

b	**b**i**b**	k	**c**at, **k**i**ck**, pi**que**	th	pa**th**, **th**in
ch	**ch**ur**ch**	l	**l**id, need**le**	*th*	ba**the**, **th**is
d	**d**ee**d**	m	a**m**, **m**an, **m**u**m**	v	ca**ve**, **v**al**ve**,
f	**f**ast, **f**i**fe**, o**ff**,	n	**n**o, sudde**n**		**v**ine
	phase, rou**gh**	ng	thi**ng**	w	**w**ith
g	**g**a**g**	p	**p**o**p**	y	**y**es
h	**h**at	r	**r**oa**r**	z	**r**o**se**, **s**i**ze**,
hw	**wh**ich	s	mi**ss**, **s**au**ce**, **s**ee		**x**ylophone,
j	**j**u**dge**	sh	di**sh**, **sh**ip		**z**ebra
		t	**t**igh**t**	zh	gara**ge**,
					plea**s**ure, vi**s**ion

Vowel Sounds

ă	p**a**t	î	d**ear**, d**eer**,	ou	c**ow**, **ou**t
ā	**ai**d, th**ey**, p**ay**		f**ier**ce, m**ere**	ŭ	c**u**t, r**ou**gh
â	**air**, c**are**, w**ear**	ŏ	p**o**t, h**o**rrible	û	f**ir**m, h**ear**d,
ä	f**a**ther	ō	g**o**, r**ow**, t**oe**		t**er**m, t**ur**n,
ĕ	p**e**t, pl**ea**sure	ô	**a**lter, c**augh**t,		w**or**d
ē	b**e**, b**ee**, **ea**sy,		f**or**, p**aw**	yo͞o	ab**u**se, **u**se
	s**ei**ze	oi	b**oy**, n**oi**se, **oi**l	ə	**a**bout, sil**e**nt,
ĭ	p**i**t	o͝o	b**oo**k		penc**i**l, lem**o**n,
ī	b**y**, g**uy**, p**ie**	o͞o	b**oo**t		circ**u**s
				ər	butt**er**

STRESS MARKS

Primary Stress ′	*Secondary Stress* ′
bi•ol•o•gy [bī **ŏl**′ə jē]	bi•o•log•i•cal [bī′ə **lŏj**′ĭ kəl]

Pronunciation key © 1986 by Houghton Mifflin Company. Adapted and
reprinted by permission from *The Houghton Mifflin Student Dictionary.*

Abject *is from the Latin word* abjectus, *meaning "cast away," from* ab-, *"away from," and* jacere, *"to throw."*

A

ab·ject (ăb′jĕkt′) *or* (ăb jĕkt′) *adj.* **1.** Lacking all self-respect or resolve. **2.** Deeply hopeless and miserable.

a·bout-face (ə bout′fās′) *or* (ə bout′fās′) *n.* A change of attitude or standpoint to the opposite of an original one: *The candidate did an **about-face** in regard to that issue.*

ab·solved (ăb zŏlvd′) *or* (-sŏlvd′) *adj.* Released, as from a promise or an obliga-tion: *Because things have changed, he is **absolved** of his earlier promise.*

a·buse (ə byo͞os′) *n.* A corrupt practice or custom: *The new governor has prevented gov-ernmental **abuse**.*

a·dorn (ə dôrn′) *v.* **a·dorned, a·dorn·ing.** To decorate with something beautiful or or-namental: *The committee **adorned** the table with flow-ers for the banquet.*

af·firm·a·tive (ə fûr′mə tĭv) *n.* A positive answer or re-sponse.

af·ford (ə fôrd′) *or* (ə fōrd′) *v.* **af·ford·ed, af·ford·ing.** To give or furnish; provide.

af·ter·im·age (ăf′tər ĭm′ĭj) *or* (äf′-) *n.* An image that con-tinues to be seen when the original picture or object is no longer there.

ag·gres·sion (ə grĕsh′ən) *n.* Hostile action or behavior.

a·ghast (ə găst′) *or* (ə gäst′) *adj.* Shocked or horrified, as by something terrible.

a·gil·i·ty (ə jĭl′ĭ tē) *n.* The quality or condition of being able to move quickly and easily.

al·che·my (ăl′kə mē) *n.* An early system of beliefs and practices, somewhat akin to modern chemistry, that had among its aims the changing of common metals into gold and the preparation of a po-tion that gives eternal youth.

a·li·en (ā′lē ən) *or* (āl′yən) *adj.* Foreign; unfamiliar; strange.

a·lign·ment (ə līn′mənt) *n.* Arrangement or position in a straight line.

al·le·vi·ate (ə lē′vē āt′) *v.* **al·le·vi·at·ed, al·le·vi·at·ing.** To make more bearable; relieve; lessen: *Aspirin can **alleviate** the pain of a headache.*

al·ly (ăl′ī′) *or* (ə lī′) *n.* A per-son who is joined or united to another for a specific purpose; a friend.

a·miss (ə mĭs′) *adj.* Wrong; faulty; improper: *Something seems to be **amiss**.*

an·es·the·tize (ə nĕs′thĭ tīz′) *v.* **an·es·the·tized, an·es·the·tiz·ing.** To put

The practice of **alchemy** *has often been associated with magic. The word has its origin in ancient Egypt. The Late Greek word* khem(e)ia *meant "art of transmutation (to change from one form to another) practiced by the Egyptians," from Greek* Khemia, *meaning "Black Land." The Late Greek word moved into Arabic in the form of* al-kīmiyā, *which meant "art of transmutation."*

ă pat / ā pay / â care / ä father / ĕ pet / ē be / ĭ pit / ī pie / î fierce / ŏ pot / ō go / ô paw, for /

into a condition in which some or all of the senses stop operating, either completely or in part.

an•guish (ăng′gwĭsh) *n.* A pain of the body or mind that causes one agony; torment; torture.

an•i•mos•i•ty (ăn′ə mŏs′ĭ tē) *n.* Long-held hatred or hostility.

an•o•nym•i•ty (ăn′ə nĭm′ĭ tē) *n.* The condition of not being well-known.

ap•pa•ri•tion (ăp′ə rĭsh′ən) *n.* A ghost; specter.

ap•pre•hen•sion (ăp′rĭ hĕn′shən) *n.* Fear or dread of what may happen; anxiety about the future.

ap•pren•tice (ə prĕn′tĭs) *n.* A person who works for another without pay in return for instruction in a craft or trade.

apt•ly (ăpt′lē) *adv.* In a suitable or appropriate manner: *He is **aptly** trained for the job of supervisor.*

a•que•ous hu•mor (ā′kwē əs hyōō′mər) *or* (ăk′wē-) *n.* A clear fluid that fills the space between the cornea and lens of the eye.

ar•is•toc•ra•cy (ăr′ĭ stŏk′rə sē) *n.* A social class based on inherited wealth, status, and sometimes titles.

ar•ti•san (är′tĭ zən) *n.* One manually skilled in making a certain product; a craftsman.

as•sent (ə sĕnt′) *n.* Agreement, as to a proposal, especially in a formal or impersonal manner: *The prime minister desired the king's **assent**.*

as•sert (ə sûrt′) *v.* **as•sert•ed, as•sert•ing.** To insist upon recognition of: *She went to court to **assert** her claim to the money.*

at•trib•ute (ə trĭb′yōōt) *v.* **at•trib•ut•ed, at•trib•ut•ing.** To regard or consider as belonging to or resulting from someone or something: *He **attributed** his lack of energy to the fact that he hadn't slept the night before.*

au•ra (ôr′ə) *n.* A distinctive air or quality that characterizes a person or thing: *The stranger had an **aura** of mystery about him.*

au•thor•i•ty (ə thôr′ĭ tē) *or* (ə thŏr′-) *n., pl.* **au•thor•i•ties.** An accepted source of expert information, as a book or person: *Those two professors are well-known **authorities** on American history.*

a•vert (ə vûrt′) *v.* **a•vert•ed, a•vert•ing.** To keep from happening; prevent: *The police **averted** any further violence.*

Apprentice *and* "apprehend" *have the same origin. Both are from the Latin* apprehendere, *"to take hold of" (ad-, "toward," + prehendere, "to grasp"). In Old French,* apprehendere *became* aprendre *and came to mean "to learn." From* aprendre *the word* aprentis, *"one who learns," was formed. This was borrowed into English as* **apprentice.**

oi oil / ŏŏ book / ōō boot / ou out / ŭ cut / û fur / *th* the / th thin / hw which / zh vision / ə ago, item, pencil, atom, circus

707

Barbarism *comes from the Greek word* barbaros, *which meant "babble-speaking," i.e., "foreign, non-Greek." The ancient Greeks were not interested in foreign languages and regarded foreign peoples as inferior. In fact, however, most of the peoples with whom they came into contact, such as the Persians, the Celts, and the Romans, spoke languages related to Greek. The languages spoken by these people and the Greek language all belong to the Indo-European family of languages, but the Greeks did not know this.*

bioluminescence

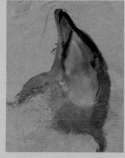
blowhole

awe (ô) *n.* A feeling of wonder, fear, and respect inspired by something mighty or majestic: *We gazed in* **awe** *at the mountains ahead.*

B

badg•er (băj′ər) *v.* **badg•ered, badg•er•ing.** To trouble with many questions or protests; pester: *The angry audience began* **badgering** *the speaker.*

ban (băn) *v.* **banned, ban•ning.** To prohibit by law, decree, etc.; forbid: *The state legislature* **banned** *billboards on all highways.*

bank (băngk) *v.* **banked, bank•ing.** To pile ashes or fuel onto (a fire) to make it burn slowly.

bar•ba•rism (bär′bə rĭz′əm) *n.* A brutal or cruel condition, act, or custom reminding one of uncivilized society: *Mob violence brings about sickening* **barbarism.**

bar•rage (bə räzh′) *n.* A concentrated firing of guns or missiles, often as a screen or protection for military troops.

bear (bâr) *v.* **bore** (bôr) *or* (bōr), **borne** (bôrn) *or* (bōrn), **bear•ing.** To carry.

be•nign (bĭ nīn′) *adj.* Kind; gentle: *His face was fatherly and* **benign.**

be•rate (bĭ rāt′) *v.* **be•rat•ed, be•rat•ing.** To scold severely; upbraid.

be•reaved (bĭ rēvd′) *adj.* Being deprived of a loved person by death: *The* **bereaved** *family left for the funeral.*

ber•serk (bər sûrk′) *or* (-zûrk′) *adj.* In or into a crazed or violent frenzy: *He went* **berserk** *and started screaming at everyone in sight.*

be•speak (bĭ spēk′) *v.* **be•spoke** (bĭ spōk′), **be•spok•en** (bĭ spō′kən) *or* **be•spoke, be•speak•ing.** To be or give a sign of; indicate: *The haggard look on her face* **bespoke** *years of suffering.*

bi•o•lu•mi•nes•cence (bī′ō lōō′mə nĕs′əns) *n.* The giving off of light by living organisms such as fireflies or certain fish or fungi.

blood•let•ter (blŭd′lĕt′ər) *n.* A doctor; refers to doctors of the fifteenth, sixteenth, and seventeenth centuries who took blood from patients in the belief that the practice would cure their illnesses.

blow•hole (blō′hōl′) *n.* A nostril at the top of the head of a whale, dolphin, or related animal.

blus•ter (blŭs′tər) *v.* **blus•tered, blus•ter•ing.** To utter noisy boasts or threats.

boat•swain (bō′sən) *n.* A warrant officer or petty officer

ă pat / ā pay / â care / ä father / ĕ pet / ē be / ĭ pit / ī pie / î fierce / ŏ pot / ō go / ô paw, for /

in charge of a ship's deck crew, rigging, and anchors.

bog•gy (bô′gē) *or* (bŏg′ē) *adj.* Like a marsh or swamp; full of soft, water-soaked ground.

borne (bôrn) *or* (bōrn) *v.* Carried. A past participle of **bear.** [See the entry for **bear.**]

boy•cott (boi′kŏt′) *n.* An organized group refusal to use a product or service or to buy from or deal with a business, nation, etc., as a means of protest or pressure.

bran•dish (brăn′dĭsh) *v.* **bran•dished, bran•dish•ing.** To wave or exhibit in a dramatic or threatening way: *The cave man was **brandishing** a club.*

bra•zen (brā′zən) *v.* **bra•zened, bra•zen•ing.** To face or undergo with bold self-assurance: *Danger was upon him, but he **brazened** it out.*

bul•bous (bŭl′bəs) *adj.* Bulb-shaped: *He has a round, **bulbous** nose.*

bur•ly (bûr′lē) *adj.* Heavy and strong; muscular.

butte (byo͞ot) *n.* A hill that rises sharply from the surrounding area and has a flat top.

ca•dence (kād′ns) *n.* The general rise and fall of the voice in speaking.

caf•tan (kăf′tən) *or* (kăf tän′) *n.* A coatlike robe having long sleeves and sometimes tied with a sash, worn in the Near East.

can•tank•er•ous (kăn tăng′kər əs) *adj.* Ill-tempered and quarrelsome; disagreeable; contrary.

ca•per (kā′pər) *v.* **ca•pered, ca•per•ing.** To jump about playfully: *The lambs **capered** about the meadow.*

cas•cade (kăs kād′) *v.* **cas•cad•ed, cas•cad•ing.** To fall in or like a small waterfall: *The cards **cascaded** to the floor.*

cask (kăsk) *or* (käsk) *n.* A barrel of any size for holding liquids.

cas•u•al•ty (kăzh′o͞o əl tē) *n.* A person who is killed, wounded, captured, or missing during a military action.

cat•e•gor•i•cal (kăt′ə gôr′ĭ kəl) *or* (-gōr′-) *adj.* Without exception or qualification; absolute: *He gave a **categorical** rejection of the job offer.*

char•la•tan (shär′lə tən) *n.* A person who deceives others by

caftan

Boycott *is a coined word from the name of Charles C. Boycott, the Earl of Erne, a landowner in County Mayo, Ireland, who in the 1800's refused to lower the rents on his land.*

Oliver Goldsmith, a British playwright, developed **cantankerous** *from the Middle English word* conteck *or* contak, *meaning "quarrelsome."*

oi **oil** / o͝o **book** / o͞o **boot** / ou **out** / ŭ **cut** / û **fur** / *th* **the** / th **thin** / hw **which** / zh **vision** / ə **ago, item, pencil, atom, circus**

Charlatan *developed from the name of the town of Cerreto, Italy, which is known for its fakes and quacks.*

falsely claiming to have expert knowledge or skill in a special subject or field of activity.

cloak (klōk) *v.* **cloaked, cloak·ing.** To cover up; hide.

cob·ble (kŏb′əl) *v.* **cob·bled, cob·bling.** To put together roughly; to make parts fit together: *He tried cobbling a chair out of leftover pieces of wood.*

co·in·cide (kō′ĭn sīd′) *v.* **co·in·cid·ed, co·in·cid·ing.** To correspond exactly; be identical.

co·in·ci·dence (kō ĭn′sĭ dəns) *n.* A combination of events or circumstances that, though accidental, is so remarkable that it seems to have been planned or arranged.

com·mand (kə mănd′) *or* (-mänd′) *v.* **com·mand·ed, com·mand·ing.** To dominate by position; overlook: *The hill commands the approach to the city.*

com·mend (kə mĕnd′) *v.* **com·mend·ed, com·mend·ing.** To speak highly of; praise: *The mayor will commend the firefighter for saving the children.*

com·mon·er (kŏm′ə nər) *n.* A person without noble rank or title.

com·pen·sate (kŏm′pən sāt′) *v.* **com·pen·sat·ed, com·pen·sat·ing.** To make

payments or amends to or for; repay: *You will be compensated for the work you have done.*

com·pen·sa·tion (kŏm′pən sā′shən) *n.* Something given as payment or amends, as for work, loss, or injury: *The money was compensation for the lost jewels.*

com·pe·tence (kŏm′pĭ tns) *n.* Ability to do what is required; skill: *Mathematics is his area of competence.*

com·pla·cent·ly (kəm plā′sənt lē) *adv.* In a contented or self-satisfied manner.

com·ple·men·ta·ry col·or (kŏm′plə mĕn′tə rē kŭl′ər) *n.* One of a pair of contrasting colors that form gray (paint) or white (light) when mixed in the proper proportions.

com·ply (kəm plī′) *v.* **com·plied, com·ply·ing.** To act in accordance with a request, rule, order, etc.: *If you comply with the requirements, you will be able to join the class.*

com·pose (kəm pōz′) *v.* **com·posed, com·pos·ing.** To make calm, controlled, or orderly: *Stop giggling and try to compose yourself.*

con·cede (kən sēd′) *v.* **con·ced·ed, con·ced·ing.** To give; yield; grant.

ă pat / ā pay / â care / ä father / ĕ pet / ē be / ĭ pit / ī pie / î fierce / ŏ pot / ō go / ô paw, for /

con•ceive (kən sēv′) *v.*
con•ceived, con•ceiv•ing.
To imagine: *We could not*
conceive *that such a beautiful*
place really existed.

con•coc•tion (kən kŏk′shən)
n. Something made by mixing or combining ingredients:
We mixed a ***concoction*** *of ba-*
nanas, honey, and milk.

con•de•scend (kŏn′dĭ sĕnd′)
v. **con•de•scend•ed,**
con•de•scend•ing. To agree
to do something one regards as
being beneath one's social rank
or dignity.

cone (kōn) *n.* Any of the
structures in the retina of the
eye that are sensitive to light
and that perceive differences
between colors.

con•fla•gra•tion
(kŏn′flə grā′shən) *n.* A large
fire.

con•front (kən frŭnt′) *v.*
con•front•ed, con•front•ing.
To meet or face boldly or de-
fiantly: *He felt it was time to*
confront *the bully.*

con•fron•ta•tion
(kŏn′frən tā′shən) *n.* A direct encounter; a clash, as of
rivals, opponents, or opposite
political points of view.

con•nive (kə nīv′) *v.*
con•nived, con•niv•ing. To
cooperate secretly or under-
handedly: *The two robbers*
connived *to steal all the*
jewelry.

con•serve (kən sûrv′) *v.*
con•served, con•serv•ing.
To use (a supply) carefully,
without waste: *We need to*
conserve *gas during an en-*
ergy shortage.

con•sis•ten•cy (kən sĭs′tən sē)
n. The degree of firmness,
stiffness, or thickness: *Mix*
water and clay to the
consistency *of thick cream.*

con•sole (kən sōl′) *v.*
con•soled, con•sol•ing. To
comfort in time of disappointment or sorrow.

con•sume (kən sōōm′) *v.*
con•sumed, con•sum•ing.
To overwhelm or take over:
Anger will ***consume*** *you if*
you don't escape its source.

con•sumed (kən sōōmd′) *adj.*
Overwhelmed or engrossed:
She was ***consumed*** *by the*
urge to scream.

con•sump•tion
(kən sŭmp′shən) *n.* The act
of eating or drinking.

con•tem•plate (kŏn′təm plāt′)
v. **con•tem•plat•ed,**
con•tem•plat•ing. 1. To look
at, often quietly and solemnly:
We quietly ***contemplated*** *the*
sunset. **2.** To expect: *They*
contemplated *various kinds of*
trouble.

con•tempt•i•ble
(kən tĕmp′tə bəl) *adj.* Deserving to be regarded as inferior or undesirable: *It was a*

Confront *comes*
from the Old French
word confronter,
which in turn came
from Medieval Latin
confrontare, *mean-*
ing "to have a com-
mon border."

Connive *comes from*
the French conniver,
from Latin connivere,
meaning "to close the
eyes" or "be indulgent."

---

oi **oil** / o͞o **book** / o͞o **boot** / ou **out** / ŭ **cut** / û **fur** / *th* **the** / th **thin** / hw **which** /
zh **vision** / ə **ago, item, pencil, atom, circus**

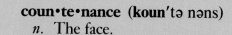

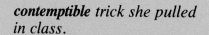

The two meanings of **conviction** are so different that they might well be thought of as separate words, but the etymology of the word shows that it is a single unit. Latin convincere basically meant "to defeat," but it had two special applications: (a) "to defeat someone in argument, persuade," and (b) "to prove someone guilty of a crime." Convincere was borrowed into English as "convince," taking on only sense (a); and its abstract noun convictio was borrowed as **conviction**, taking on both senses.

contemptible trick she pulled in class.

con•tra•dict (kŏn′trə dĭkt′) *v.* **con•tra•dict•ed, con•tra•dict•ing.** To declare to be untruthful or untrue.

con•trast (kŏn′trăst′) *n.* The placement of colors, shapes, or lines in opposition to one another in order to affect what a viewer sees: *The contrast of blue and white stripes makes the shirt look brighter than this one.*

con•vey (kən vā′) *v.* **con•veyed, con•vey•ing. 1.** To take or carry from one place to another: *A helicopter conveyed us to the city.* **2.** To make known; communicate: *Words convey meaning.*

con•vic•tion (kən vĭk′shən) *n.* A strong opinion or belief; the condition of being sure: *He waited for the announcement to be made with the conviction that he had won.*

con•viv•i•al (kən vĭv′ē əl) *adj.* Jolly; sociable.

coop•er (kōō′pər) *n.* A person who makes or repairs barrels.

cor•ne•a (kôr′nē ə) *n.* A tough, transparent membrane that forms the forward portion of the outer coat of the eyeball. It covers the iris and lens.

coun•sel (koun′səl) *n.* Opinion.

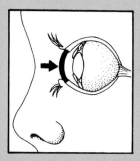

cornea

coun•te•nance (koun′tə nəns) *n.* The face.

crack•er•jack (krăk′ər jăk′) *n.* *Slang.* Something or someone of excellent quality or ability.

cred•i•tor (krĕd′ĭ tər) *n.* A person or firm to whom money is owed: *Banks are creditors for people who have borrowed money from them.*

cringe (krĭnj) *v.* **cringed, cring•ing.** To shrink back, as in fear; cower: *He could not keep from cringing when the bully came near.*

crit•i•cism (krĭt′ĭ sĭz′əm) *n.* A review or report giving an opinion or opinions of the worth of something.

cul•prit (kŭl′prĭt) *n.* A person guilty or believed to be guilty of a crime or offense.

cum•brous•ly (kŭm′brəs lē) *adv.* In a clumsy and awkward manner.

D

da•is (dā′ĭs) *or* (dās) *n.* A raised platform for a throne, a speaker, or a group of honored guests.

de•bris, also **dé•bris** (də brē′) *or* (dā′brē′) *n.* The scattered remains of something broken, destroyed, or discarded; fragments; rubble.

ă pat / ā pay / â care / ä father / ĕ pet / ē be / ĭ pit / ī pie / î fierce / ŏ pot / ō go / ô paw, for /

de·cline (dǐ klīn′) *v.*
de·clined, de·clin·ing. To
refuse to accept or do: *I must
decline your job offer.*

de·cree (dǐ krē′) *n.* An authoritative order; a law; edict:
*The king's decree called for a
day of celebration.*

de·crep·it (dǐ krĕp′ĭt) *adj.* In
poor condition because of old
age or long use; worn-out;
broken-down.

def·er·en·tial (dĕf′ə rĕn′shəl)
adj. Marked by courteous respect: *She shook hands with
the President in a deferential
manner.*

de·mean·ing (dǐ mēn′ĭng) *adj.*
Low in dignity or stature: *She
found the task of sweeping
demeaning.*

de·mise (dǐ mīz′) *n.* The
death of a person: *Nathan
Hale faced his demise with
bravery.*

de·nounce (dǐ nouns′) *v.*
de·nounced, de·nounc·ing.
To accuse formally; inform
against: *I denounce this person for the crimes she has
committed.*

de·plor·a·ble (dǐ plôr′ə bəl)
or (-plōr′-) *adj.* Worthy of
strong disapproval or re-
proach: *The child had
deplorable behavior.*

de·sign·ing (dǐ zī′nǐng) *adj.*
Scheming or conniving: *A
designing person plans and
schemes.*

de·sist (dǐ zǐst′) *or* (-sǐst′) *v.*
de·sist·ed, de·sist·ing. To
cease doing something: *Please
desist from speaking out of
turn.*

des·pi·ca·ble (dĕs′pǐ kə bəl)
or (dǐ spǐk′ə-) *adj.* Deserving
contempt or disdain; vile: *You
committed a despicable act.*

de·spon·dence (dǐ spǒn′dəns)
n. Hopelessness; low spirits.

des·ti·ny (dĕs′tə nē) *n.* The
fortune, fate, or lot of a particular person or thing, considered as something determined
or appointed in advance: *His
destiny was a life spent at
sea.*

de·tach (dǐ tăch′) *v.*
de·tached, de·tach·ing. To
send on a special mission; as-
sign.

de·ter (dǐ tûr′) *v.* **de·terred,
de·ter·ring.** To prevent or
discourage, as by fear: *Despite
the storm, she was not
deterred from making her
flight home.*

dev·il (dĕv′əl) *n.* A student
who works, usually without
pay, for a printer in order to
learn the craft of printing.

de·void (dǐ void′) *adj.*
—**devoid of.** Completely lacking; without.

de·volve (dǐ vǒlv′) *v.*
de·volved, de·volv·ing. To
pass or be passed on to a successor or substitute: *During*

Deferential *devel-
oped from the Latin
word* deferre, *mean-
ing "to bend away."*

oi **oil** / o͞o **book** / o͞o **boot** / ou **out** / ŭ **cut** / û **fur** / *th* **the** / th **thin** / hw **which** /
zh **vision** / ə **ago, item, pencil, atom, circus**

Dexterity *comes from the Old French* dexterite, *which descended from the Latin* dexteritās, *from* dexter, *meaning "skillful."*

Disperse *comes from the Middle English* dispersen *and from the Old French* disperser. *These forms came from the Latin* dispergere, *meaning "to scatter on all sides."*

the President's illness his duties **devolved** upon the Vice President.

dex•ter•i•ty (dĕk stĕr′ĭ tē) *n.* Skill in the use of the hands or body: *A diamond cutter must have great **dexterity**.*

di•a•bol•i•cal (dī′ə bŏl′ĭ kəl) *adj.* Of or like the devil; extremely wicked: *a **diabolical** murder.*

di•lem•ma (dĭ lĕm′ə) *n.* A situation that requires a person to choose between courses of action that are equally difficult or unpleasant: *He faced the **dilemma** of giving in or losing his job.*

dil•i•gence (dĭl′ə jəns) *n.* Long, steady effort in one's job or studies: *Her **diligence** was rewarded with good grades.*

di•plo•ma•cy (dĭ plō′mə sē) *n.* Skill in dealing with others; tact: *She used **diplomacy** to settle the neighbors' dispute.*

dis•con•so•late (dĭs kŏn′sə lĭt) *adj.* Very sad; gloomy; dismal.

dis•count (dĭs′kount′) *or* (dĭs kount′) *v.* **dis•count•ed, dis•count•ing.** To disregard or doubt (something) as being an exaggeration; ignore: *His invention was **discounted** for not being practical.*

dis•course (dĭs′kôrs′) *or* (-kōrs′) *n.* A formal discussion, either spoken or written, of a subject.

dis•cre•tion (dĭ skrĕsh′ən) *n.* The exercise of caution or good judgment in speech or behavior; prudence: *Her **discretion** in telling the story spared hurt feelings.*

dis•gorge (dĭs gôrj′) *v.* **dis•gorged, dis•gorg•ing.** To pour forth or throw up.

dis•heart•ened (dĭs här′tnd) *adj.* Having lost courage, spirit, or hope: *After the loss, the team was **disheartened**.*

dis•or•der (dĭs ôr′dər) *n.* A public disturbance; violation of the peace: *Police were posted to prevent **disorder** in the streets.*

dis•perse (dĭ spûrs′) *v.* **dis•persed, dis•pers•ing.** To move or distribute in different directions; break up; scatter: *She convinced the angry group to **disperse**. The fog **dispersed** in the wind.*

dis•rep•u•ta•ble (dĭs rĕp′yə tə bəl) *adj.* Not honorable or proper: *We were punished for carrying out his **disreputable** idea.*

dis•taste (dĭs tāst′) *n.* A dislike or aversion: *From his look of **distaste**, we found out how he feels about music.*

dis•tinc•tion (dĭ stĭngk′shən) *n.* The condition or fact of

ă pat / ā pay / â care / ä father / ĕ pet / ē be / ĭ pit / ī pie / î fierce / ŏ pot / ō go / ô paw, for /

being distinct; a difference; unlikeness: *a **distinction** between capital letters and small ones.*

dis•traught (dǐ **strôt′**) *adj.* Anxious or agitated; worried: *She was **distraught** because he was so late arriving home.*

di•ver•sion (dǐ **vûr′**zhən) *or* (-shən) *or* (dī-) *n.* **1.** Something that relaxes or entertains; recreation: *Today many people enjoy the **diversion** of sports.* **2.** The act or an example of drawing the attention to a different course, direction, etc.

di•vin•i•ty (dǐ **vǐn′**ǐ tē) *n.* A god or goddess: *She is as beautiful as any **divinity** of ancient Greece or Rome.*

do•main (dō **mān′**) *n.* A territory or range of rule or control; realm: *the queen's **domain**.*

dom•i•nance (**dǒm′**ə nəns) *n.* The condition or fact of having the most influence or control.

dom•i•nate (**dǒm′**ə nāt′) *v.* **dom•i•nat•ed, dom•i•nat•ing.** To control, govern, or rule by superior power or strength: *No country can **dominate** the world.*

dot•ing (**dōt′**ǐng) *adj.* Lavishing excessive fondness or affection: *His **doting** parents had spoiled him completely.*

dow•ry (**dou′**rē) *n.* Money or property brought by a bride to her husband.

dra•goon (drə **gōōn′**) *or* (drǎ-) *n.* A heavily armed soldier.

drudg•er•y (**drǔj′**ə rē) *n.* Hard, tiresome, or menial work: *She enjoyed housework, while others considered it **drudgery**.*

E

ef•fi•gy (**ěf′**ǐ jē) *n.* A crude image or dummy fashioned in the likeness of a hated or despised person.

e•lix•ir (ǐ **lǐk′**sər) *n.* A mixture often sold as a medicine.

em•bar•go (ěm **bär′**gō) *n.* A suspension by a government of foreign trade: *the U.S. **embargo** on Cuban exports.*

e•merge (ǐ **mûrj′**) *v.* **e•merged, e•merg•ing.** To come into view; appear: *The butterfly **emerged** from the cocoon.*

en•deav•or (ěn **děv′**ər) *n.* A major effort or attempt: *You are to be congratulated for your **endeavor**.*

en•dow (ěn **dou′**) *v.* **en•dowed, en•dow•ing.** To provide or invest with certain talents, qualities, rights, etc.: *Nature has **endowed** her with both beauty and charm.*

Dragoon *developed from the French word* dragon, *which was used to name the mythical animal and a rifle, the latter being "something that breathes fire," like a dragon.*

Emerge *comes from the Latin word* ēmergere, *"to unsink, to rise to the surface, to come out":* ē- *"out,"* + mergere, *"to sink."*

oi **oil** / ōō **book** / ōō **boot** / ou **out** / ǔ **cut** / û **fur** / *th* **the** / th **thin** / hw **which** / zh **vision** / ə **ago, item, pencil, atom, circus**

715

en•dow•ment (ĕn dou′mənt) *n.* A natural gift or quality, such as beauty or talent.

en•gross (ĕn grōs′) *v.* **en•grossed, en•gross•ing.** To occupy the complete attention of; absorb wholly: *The play engrossed me for the first act.*

en•grossed (ĕn grōsd′) *adj.* Having one's attention completely occupied; absorbed wholly: *Engrossed in a new book, he read for hours.*

en•snared (ĕn snârd′) *adj.* Caught in or as if in a trap.

en•tail (ĕn tāl′) *v.* **en•tailed, en•tail•ing.** To have as a result; involve: *Your paper entails research and an outline.*

en•ter•prise (ĕn′tər prīz′) *n.* Systematic work: *Enterprise helped her realize her dream of owning a restaurant.*

en•treat (ĕn trēt′) *v.* **en•treat•ed, en•treat•ing.** To ask earnestly; beg; implore: *He entreated the business owner for a job.*

et•i•quette (ĕt′ĭ kĭt) *or* (-kĕt′) *n.* Rules of correct behavior among people: *Knowing the proper etiquette is important when attending a formal dinner.*

ex•as•per•a•tion (ĭg zăs′pə rā′shən) *n.* Extreme irritation: *Mom threw up her hands in exasperation at all their questions.*

ex•e•cute (ĕk′sĭ kyo͞ot′) *v.* **ex•e•cut•ed, ex•e•cut•ing.** To put into effect: *We will execute the voters' wishes.*

ex•ile (ĕg′zīl′) *or* (ĕk′sīl′) *n.* Someone who is or has been banished from his or her country, either by force or voluntarily.

ex•ude (ĭg zo͞od′) *or* (ĭk so͞od′) *v.* **ex•ud•ed, ex•ud•ing.** To give or come forth, by or as if by oozing: *His brow exuded sweat.*

ex•ult•ant•ly (ĭg zŭl′tnt lē) *adv.* With great joy; jubilantly: *The winner smiled exultantly.*

ex•ul•ta•tion (ĕg′zŭl tā′shən) *or* (ĕk′sŭl-) *n.* Great joy; jubilation: *He wanted to shout with sheer exultation.*

fac•tion (făk′shən) *n.* A group of persons forming a united, usually discontented and troublesome, minority within a larger group: *The club's membership includes three factions.*

fal•low (făl′ō) *adj.* Plowed and tilled but left unseeded during a growing season.

Execute *is from Medieval Latin* execūtāre, *"to follow out"* (ex-, *"out,"* + secūt-, *"follow"). Its basic meaning was "to follow a thing through, to carry out a task or order."*

Fallow *comes from the Middle English* falow *or* falwe, *which came from the Old English* fealh, *meaning "arable land."*

ă pat / ā pay / â care / ä father / ĕ pet / ē be / ĭ pit / ī pie / î fierce / ŏ pot / ō go / ô paw, for /

fa·mil·i·ar·i·ty (fə mĭl′ē ăr′ĭ tē) *n.* Friendship or informality; forwardness: *The army discourages familiarity between officers and enlisted men.*

far·sight·ed (fär′sī′tĭd) *adj.* Having a defect of vision in which parallel rays of light are brought to a focus behind the retina of the eye, making it easier to see distant objects than those that are nearby.

fez (fĕz) *n.* A high felt cap, usually red with a black tassel, worn chiefly in eastern Mediterranean countries.

fiend (fēnd) *n.* An evil spirit; demon.

fire·brand (fīr′brănd′) *n.* A person who stirs up trouble.

fis·sion·a·ble (fĭsh′ə nə bəl) *adj.* Capable of undergoing nuclear fission, a reaction in which an atomic nucleus splits into fragments whose mass does not quite equal the mass of the original nucleus, the remaining mass being transformed into energy.

fleece (flēs) *v.* **fleeced, fleec·ing.** To defraud of money or property: *He tried to fleece the people at our club.*

flub (flŭb) *v.* **flubbed, flub·bing.** *Informal.* To botch, fumble, or ruin: *Did she flub her opportunity to win?*

fluke (flo͞ok) *n.* One of the two flattened, finlike divisions of a whale's or dolphin's tail.

flum·mer·y (flŭm′ə rē) *n.* Nonsense.

foal (fōl) *v.* **foaled, foal·ing.** To give birth to (a colt).

fob (fŏb) *v.* **fobbed, fob·bing. —fob off.** To put off or palm off by being tricky or dishonest: *He fobbed off the reporter with a false lead.*

fo·cus (fō′kəs) *v.* **fo·cused** *or* **fo·cussed, fo·cus·ing** *or* **fo·cus·sing.** To bring or come together in a single point.

fore·bod·ing (fôr bō′dĭng) *n.* An uneasy feeling that something bad is going to happen. —*adj.* Giving a hint or warning of (something bad to come): *They knew they would find trouble in the foreboding alley.*

forge (fôrj) *or* (fōrj) *n.* A furnace or hearth where metal is heated so that it can be worked more easily.

for·go (fôr gō′) *v.* **for·went, for·gone** *or* **for·go·ing.** To give up: *If you decide not to clean your room, you will have to forgo your allowance, too.*

for·lorn (fôr lôrn′) *adj.* Wretched or pitiful in appearance, condition, or effect: *the forlorn sound of the crying child.*

fez

---

oi **oil** / o͝o **book** / o͞o **boot** / ou **out** / ŭ **cut** / û **fur** / *th* **the** / th **thin** / hw **which** / zh **vision** / ə **ago, item, pencil, atom, circus**

The word **fortitude** appeared in both Middle English and Old French. It comes from the Latin word fortitūdō, from fortis, for "strong."

Fracas probably developed by blending the Latin words frangere, "to break," with quassāre, "to shatter."

garland

for·ti·tude (fôr′tĭ tōōd′) *or* (-tyōōd′) *n.* Strength to deal with pain or adversity.

foun·tain·head (foun′tən hĕd′) *n.* A primary source or origin: *She found that book a* **fountainhead** *of knowledge about horses.*

fra·cas (frā′kəs) *n.* A disorderly uproar: *The party turned into a* **fracas.**

fray (frā) *n.* A fight; brawl; battle. —*v.* **frayed, fray·ing.** To make or become ragged, worn, or raveled at the edge so that loose threads show: *His old coat had* **frayed.**

fre·quen·cy (frē′kwən sē) *n.,* *pl.* **fre·quen·cies.** The number of complete cycles of a wave that occur within a period of time.

fru·gal (frōō′gəl) *adj.* Thrifty; not wasteful, because of lack of money: *Frugal people use their money wisely.*

fru·gal·i·ty (frōō găl′ĭ tē) *n.* The act of being thrifty, not wasteful: *Since we are not rich, we must practice* **frugality** *in our everyday lives.*

fu·gi·tive (fyōō′jĭ tĭv) *n.* A person who flees; a runaway; refugee.

fume (fyōōm) *v.* **fumed, fum·ing.** To feel or show anger or agitation; seethe: *The boy fretted and* **fumed.**

fu·tile (fyōōt′l) *or* (fyōō′tĭl′) *adj.* Having no useful result; useless; vain.

gait (gāt) *n.* A way of walking or running: *He plodded along with a slow* **gait.**

gal·lows (găl′ōz) *n.* A framework with a suspended noose, used for execution by hanging.

game·cock (gām′kŏk′) *n.* A rooster trained for fighting.

garb (gärb) *n.* Clothing or way of dressing: *For Halloween he wore a sailor's* **garb.**

gar·land (gär′lənd) *n.* A wreath or chain of flowers, leaves, etc., worn as a crown or used for ornament.

gaunt (gônt) *adj.* Thin and bony; haggard: *The hungry woman's face was pale and* **gaunt.**

gaunt·let (gônt′lĭt) *or* (gänt′-) *n.* An old form of punishment in which a person was forced to run between two lines of men who struck him or her with clubs, sticks, or other weapons.

gen·try (jĕn′trē) *n.* Well-bred people of good family and high social standing.

ă pat / ā pay / â care / ä father / ĕ pet / ē be / ĭ pit / ī pie / î fierce / ŏ pot / ō go / ô paw, for /

gin•ger•ly (jĭn′jər lē) *adv.* Cautiously; carefully: *She tiptoed **gingerly** around the sleeping snake.*

glean•ings (glē′nĭngz) *pl. n.* Items left behind or dropped and which are gathered bit by bit: *The farmer lets them pick up and sell the **gleanings**.*

glow•er (glou′ər) *v.* **glow•ered, glow•er•ing.** To look or stare angrily or in a threatening manner: *She was **glowering** at the mischievous students.*

grim•ace (grĭm′əs) *or* (grĭ mās′) *n.* A facial contortion expressing pain, disgust, etc.

grov•el•ing (grŭv′əl ĭng) *or* (grŏv′-) *adj.* Humble; cringing.

gul•li•ble (gŭl′ə bəl) *adj.* Easily fooled: *He sold fake medicine to the **gullible** people.*

hag•gard (hăg′ərd) *adj.* Appearing worn and exhausted because of suffering, worry, etc.: *Her face was drawn and **haggard**.*

hail (hāl) *v.* **hailed, hail•ing.** To designate by tribute: *They **hailed** the old man as their leader.*

har•assed (hăr′əsd) *or* (hə răsd′) *adj.* Bothered or tormented with repeated attacks.

heft (hĕft) *v.* **heft•ed, heft•ing.** To estimate or test the weight of by lifting.

hind•sight (hīnd′sīt′) *n.* A looking back to past events with full understanding or knowledge that was lacking when they occurred: *Coach used **hindsight** and changed all our plays.*

hoax•ing (hōks′ĭng) *n.* A trick or action intended to deceive others, often in the form of a practical joke, false report, etc., that fools the public.

hodge•podge (hŏj′pŏj′) *n.* A confused or haphazard mixture; a jumble.

hum•bug (hŭm′bŭg′) *v.* **hum•bugged, hum•bug•ging.** To deceive or trick.

hy•poth•e•size (hī pŏth′ĭ sīz′) *v.* **hy•poth•e•sized, hy•poth•e•siz•ing.** To put forth a theory or explanation for which there is no direct supporting evidence: *The class **hypothesized** about the nature of the mineral.*

i•dyl•lic (ī dĭl′ĭk) *adj.* Full of quiet beauty and peacefulness.

Groveling *comes from the Middle English word* gruflinge, *meaning* "in prostrate position," *from the phrase* on grufe, *"on the face." The phrase comes from the Old Norse* a grufu: a, *"on,"* + grufa, *"proneness."*

Haggard *developed from the Old French word* hagard, *meaning "wild hawk."*

oi **oil** / o͞o **book** / o͞o **boot** / ou **out** / ŭ **cut** / û **fur** / *th* **the** / th **thin** / hw **which** / zh **vision** / ə **ago, item, pencil, atom, circus** il•lu•sion (ĭ lōō′zhən) *n.* An appearance or impression that has no real basis; false perception.

im•pas•sive (ĭm păs′ĭv) *adj.* Feeling or showing no emotion; calm: *Her face was impassive.*

im•pede (ĭm pēd′) *v.* im•ped•ed, im•ped•ing. To obstruct or slow down; block.

im•pen•e•tra•ble (ĭm pĕn′ĭ trə bəl) *adj.* Not capable of being entered or penetrated: *The boat stalled in the impenetrable swamp.*

im•pu•dence (ĭm′pyə dəns) *n.* Boldness; rudeness; disrespectful action: *The children's impudence showed in their remarks to the old man.*

im•pu•dent (ĭm′pyə dənt) *adj.* Bold and disrespectful; impertinent; rude.

im•pul•sive (ĭm pŭl′sĭv) *adj.* Caused by a sudden urge or whim; uncalculated: *Her impulsive outbursts often got her into trouble.*

in•an•i•mate (ĭn ăn′ə mĭt) *adj.* Not living: *A rock is an inanimate object.*

in•au•di•ble (ĭn ô′də bəl) *adj.* Incapable of being heard: *A dog whistle is inaudible to human ears.*

in•cen•tive (ĭn sĕn′tĭv) *n.* Something provoking an action or effort: *A scholarship is an incentive for making good grades.*

in•ces•sant•ly (ĭn sĕs′ənt lē) *adv.* Without interruption; constantly.

in•cline (ĭn klīn′) *v.* in•clined, in•clin•ing. To depart or cause to depart from a true horizontal or vertical direction; to lean, slant, or slope.

in•con•stant (ĭn kŏn′stənt) *adj.* Not constant or steady; changeable or fickle.

in•cred•u•lous•ly (ĭn krĕj′ə ləs lē) *adv.* With disbelief or astonishment: *He stared incredulously at his wrecked car.*

in•cum•bent (ĭn kŭm′bənt) *n.* A person currently holding an office.

in•de•struc•ti•ble (ĭn′dĭ strŭk′tə bəl) *adj.* Not capable of being destroyed.

in•dif•fer•ent (ĭn dĭf′ər ənt) *or* (-dĭf′rənt) *adj.* Having or showing no interest; not caring one way or the other.

in•dig•nant•ly (ĭn dĭg′nənt lē) *adv.* With anger aroused by something unjust, mean, etc.: *She indignantly denied the rumors about her.*

in•dis•tin•guish•a•ble (ĭn′dĭ stĭng′gwĭ shə bəl) *adj.* Without distinctive qualities; hard to tell apart from others.

Impudent *is a Middle English word that came from the Latin* impudēns: in-, "*not,*" + pudens, *from* pudere, "*to be ashamed.*"

Incline *comes from the Middle English* inclinen *or* enclinen, *and the Old French* encliner. *The Latin ancestor of the word is* inclīnāre, *meaning* "*to bend or lean toward.*"

ă pat / ā pay / â care / ä father / ĕ pet / ē be / ĭ pit / ī pie / î fierce / ŏ pot / ō go / ô paw, for /

in·duce (ĭn dōos′) *or* (-dyōos′) *v.* **in·duced, in·duc·ing.**
1. To cause or stimulate the occurrence of: *The smell of baked turkey induced thoughts of Thanksgiving.*
2. To persuade; influence: *She left because nothing could induce her to stay.*

in·dul·gent (ĭn dŭl′jənt) *adj.* Showing, marked by, or given to pampering; leniency: *The child was spoiled by the indulgent parent.*

in·dul·gent·ly (ĭn dŭl′jənt lē) *adv.* With a willingness to yield or be forgiving; leniently: *The teacher indulgently allowed the class one more day to finish their reports.*

in·es·cap·a·ble (ĭn′ĭ skā′pə bəl) *adj.* Not capable of being avoided, denied, or overlooked: *Death is inescapable.*

in·flam·ma·to·ry (ĭn flăm′ə tôr′ē) *or* (-tōr′ē) *adj.* Tending to arouse strong emotion.

in·flu·en·tial (ĭn′flōo ĕn′shəl) *adj.* Having or exercising considerable power to produce effects or changes: *As the newspaper grew, it became more influential.*

in·fuse (ĭn fyōoz′) *v.* **in·fused, in·fus·ing.** To impart or instill: *The best painters infuse their work with the bright colors of nature.*

in·got (ĭng′gət) *n.* A mass of metal shaped in the form of a bar or block.

ink-daub·er (ĭngk′dôb′ər) *n.* A printer's tool used to place ink on type before a page is printed.

ink·ling (ĭngk′lĭng) *n.* A slight indication; a hint; a vague idea: *This was our first inkling that something was wrong.*

in·stinc·tive·ly (ĭn stĭngk′tĭv lē) *adv.* With or by an inner influence, feeling, or drive that is not learned: *Birds instinctively build nests.*

in·ter·cede (ĭn′tər sēd′) *v.* **in·ter·ced·ed, in·ter·ced·ing.** To mediate in a dispute: *Congress can intercede in certain labor disputes.*

in·ter·fer·ence (ĭn′tər fîr′əns) *n.* A physical effect in which two or more waves alternately reinforce and cancel each other at different points in space or time.

in·ter·fer·ence fring·es (ĭn′tər fîr′əns frĭnj′əz) *n.* Bands, lines, or gaps produced by the meeting and overlapping of two or more waves (as light or sound).

in·ter·lock·ing (ĭn′tər lŏk′ĭng) *adj.* United firmly or joined closely; overlapping.

Induce *comes from the Middle English word* inducen, *from the Latin* indūcere, *meaning "to lead in."*

Ingot *comes from a combination of* in-, *"in," and the Old English* goten, *past participle of* geotan, *"to pour or cast in metal."*

ink-dauber

oi **oil** / ŏŏ **book** / ōō **boot** / ou **out** / ŭ **cut** / û **fur** / *th* **the** / th **thin** / hw **which** / zh **vision** / ə **ago, item, pencil, atom, circus**

721

Intrepidity *and its root word, "intrepid," come from the Latin word* intrepidus: in-, *"not,"* + trepidus, *"agitated or alarmed."*

in•tol•er•ant (ĭn tŏl′ər ənt) *adj.* Not tolerant of; prejudiced against: *Their teacher is **intolerant** of bad behavior.*

in•tre•pid•i•ty (ĭn trə pĭd′ĭ tē) *n.* Courage; boldness; fearlessness.

in•tri•guing (ĭn trēg′ĭng) *adj.* Curious; fascinating: *They watched an **intriguing** mystery.*

in•vin•ci•bil•i•ty (ĭn vĭn′sə bĭl′ĭ tē) *n.* The state of being or feeling too strong, powerful, or great to be defeated or overcome.

jos•tle (jŏs′əl) *v.* **jos•tled, jos•tling.** To push or bump by running into suddenly: *The teams **jostled** each other as they poured onto the field.*

knack (năk) *n.* A special skill or talent: *He has the **knack** of getting along with people.*

knave (nāv) *n.* A dishonest, crafty man.

knoll (nōl) *n.* A small, rounded hill; a hillock.

In Middle English, **libel** *meant the formal written claim of a plaintiff. The word comes from the Latin* libellus, *"a little book."*

lan•cet (lăn′sĭt) *or* (län′-) *n.* A surgical knife with a short, broad, double-edged blade that tapers to a point.

lar•der (lär′dər) *n.* A room, cupboard, etc., where food is stored; a supply of food.

leech (lēch) *n.* A worm that lives in water and sucks blood from other animals, including human beings. Used by doctors in the past to suck blood from patients in the belief that it would cure their illnesses.

le•git•i•mate (lə jĭt′ə mĭt) *adj.* Being or acting in accordance with the law; lawful: *Queen Elizabeth is a **legitimate** monarch.*

lens (lĕnz) *n.* A piece of glass or other transparent material that has been precisely shaped so as to cause parallel light rays that pass through it to concentrate to a focus or to spread out as if coming from a focus.

li•bel (lī′bəl) *v.* **li•beled** *or* **li•belled, li•bel•ing** *or* **li•bel•ling.** To commit the act or crime of making a statement that unjustly damages a person's reputation or exposes him or her to ridicule.

ă pat / ā pay / â care / ä father / ĕ pet / ē be / ĭ pit / ī pie / î fierce / ŏ pot / ō go / ô paw, for /

li•cen•tious•ness
(lī sĕn′shəs nəs) *n.* A state or quality of unrestrained immorality or defiance of all rules of conduct.

lit•er•al (lĭt′ər əl) *adj.* Reflecting exactly what is meant by a word or group of words: *He knew the literal meaning of the phrase but not what it was meant to suggest.*

log•ger•head (lô′gər hĕd′) *or* (lŏg′ər-) *Idiom.* **at loggerheads.** In disagreement or in a dispute with; at odds: *The two countries were at loggerheads.*

lull (lŭl) *n.* A temporary lessening of activity, noise, etc.: *There was a lull in the storm.*

M

maim (mām) *v.* **maimed, maim•ing.** To disable, usually by depriving of the use of a limb; cripple.

mal•ice (măl′ĭs) *n.* The desire to harm others or to see others suffer; ill will; spite.

man•i•fes•ta•tion
(măn′ə fĕ stā′shən) *n.* Something that makes itself apparent or reveals itself, as in a supernatural occurrence: *She insisted the ghostly mist was some sort of manifestation.*

mas•tiff (măs′tĭf) *n.* A large dog with a short, brownish coat and short, square jaws.

mat•ter (măt′ər) *n.* The stuff of which the physical bodies of the universe are made.

mea•ger (mē′gər) *adj.* Lacking in quantity; few: *He kept only a meager store of food for the winter.*

med•i•tate (mĕd′ĭ tāt′) *v.* **med•i•tat•ed, med•i•tat•ing.** To think deeply and quietly; reflect.

mel•an•chol•y (mĕl′ən kŏl′ē) *n.* Low spirits; sadness: *The old man's melancholy was worse on holidays.* —*adj.* Sad; gloomy: *That melancholy time makes me cry.*

mer•chant•man
(mûr′chənt mən) *n.* A ship used in commerce.

me•thod•i•cal (mə thŏd′ĭ kəl) *adj.* Orderly and systematic in one's habits or thinking: *The director was methodical in laying out the stage plan.*

mi•li•tia (mĭ lĭsh′ə) *n.* A body of citizens who receive military training outside the regular armed forces and who are on call for military service in times of emergency.

mil•ling ground (mĭl′ĭng ground′) *n.* A place where people move about and mingle informally.

mim•ic•ry (mĭm′ĭk rē) *n.* The practice or art of copying or imitating closely, as in speech, expression, or gesture.

Loggerhead was formed by combining logger, *"a block of wood," and* head.

Mastiff may have developed from the Latin word mānsuĕutus, *which translates as "accustomed to the hand," and means "tame."*

mastiff

Melancholy is found in Middle English as malencolie *or* melancholye, *and in Old French as* melancolie. *The word comes from the Greek* melankholia, *meaning "sadness" (literally "an excess of black bile").*

---

oi **oil** / o͝o **book** / o͞o **boot** / ou **out** / ŭ **cut** / û **fur** / *th* **the** / th **thin** / hw **which** /
zh **vi**s**ion** / ə **ago**, **item**, **pencil**, **atom**, **circus**

min•ute•man (mĭn′ĭt măn′) *n.*, *pl.*-**men** (-mĕn′). In the Revolutionary War, a member of the American militia or any armed civilian pledged to be ready to fight on a minute's notice.

mi•rage (mĭ **räzh′**) *n.* An optical illusion in which nonexistent bodies of water and upside-down reflections of distant objects are seen. It is caused by distortions that occur as light passes between layers of air that are at different temperatures.

mired (mīrd) *adj.* Muddy.

mode (mōd) *n.* A way, manner, or style of doing: *Deaf people use sign language as their **mode** of communication.*

mol•ten (mōl′tən) *adj.* Made liquid by heat; melted.

mo•rose (mə **rōs′**) *or* (mô-) *adj.* Ill-humored; sullen; gloomy.

mor•ti•fied (môr′tə fīd′) *adj.* Embarrassed; ashamed: *The actor was **mortified** at making his entrance onstage too soon.*

moun•te•bank (moun′tə băngk′) *n.* Any swindler.

mun•dane (mŭn dān′) *or* (mŭn′dān′) *adj.* Ordinary; commonplace: *He hated his **mundane** duties at the shop.*

Nimble *comes from the Middle English* nemel *or* nym(b)yl, *meaning "agile," and from Old English* næmel, *meaning "quick-witted; quick to seize or understand."*

murk (mûrk) *n.* Darkness; gloom.

murk•y (mûr′kē) *adj.* Cloudy and dark with sediment: *Pools of **murky** water dotted the swampy shore.*

nec•ro•man•cer (nĕk′rə măn′sər) *n.* A person who professes to be able to call up the spirits of the dead and communicate with them in order to predict the future.

net•tle (nĕt′l) *v.* **net•tled, net•tling.** To annoy; irritate.

nim•ble (nĭm′bəl) *adj.* Moving or able to move quickly, lightly, and easily; agile.

noi•some (noi′səm) *adj.* Harmful or injurious: *The old basement was filled with a **noisome** odor.*

null and void (nŭl ănd void) *adj.* *Idiom.* Having no legal force or effect; not binding.

o•blige (ə **blīj′**) *v.* **o•bliged, o•blig•ing.** To require; to compel.

ob•nox•ious (əb **nŏk′**shəs) *adj.* Extremely unpleasant or offensive.

ă pat / ā pay / â care / ä father / ĕ pet / ē be / ĭ pit / ī pie / î fierce / ŏ pot / ō go / ô paw, for /

ob•scure (əb skyōor′) *v.*
ob•scured, ob•scur•ing. To
make less clear; cause to be
difficult to sense or understand: *Static **obscured** the music on the radio.*

ob•ses•sion (əb sĕsh′ən) *n.*
An idea, thought, or emotion
that occupies the mind continually: *Collecting rocks became an **obsession**.*

ob•struc•tion (əb strŭk′shən)
n. Something that makes im-
passable or gets in the way:
*The **obstruction** was a huge
tree that had fallen across
the road.*

oc•cult•ist (ə kŭl′tĭst) *or*
(ŏk′ŭl-) *n.* A person who
believes in or studies magic,
astrology, or the supernatural.

o•paque (ō pāk′) *adj.* Not capable of letting light pass
through.

op•pressed (ə prĕst′) *adj.* Per-
secuted or subjected to harsh
treatment. —*n.* People who
are subjected to persecution or
harsh treatment.

op•tic nerve (ŏp′tĭk nŭrv′) *n.*
Either of the two nerves that
connect the retinas of the eyes
to the brain.

or•a•cle (ôr′ə kəl) *or* (ŏr′-) *n.*
Any person considered to be a
source of wise advice or pre-
dictions of the future.

or•a•tor•i•cal (ôr′ə tôr′ĭ kəl)
or (ŏr′ə tŏr′-) *adj.* Of or appropriate to the art of public
speaking: *Her **oratorical** skills
are superb.*

out•face (out fās′) *v.*
out•faced, out•fac•ing. To
win a confrontation or success-
fully deal with a situation
boldly or bravely; defy; stare
down: *He can **outface** an angry dog.*

out•rage (out′rāj′) *n.* An extremely vicious or wicked act.

out•ra•geous•ly (out rā′jəs lē)
adv. In a manner that exceeds
all bounds of what is right or
proper; shockingly: *He was
punished for playing an
outrageously cruel prank.*

o•ver•mas•ter (ō′vər măs′tər)
v. **o•ver•mas•tered,
o•ver•mas•ter•ing.** To get
the better of; subdue; overpower: *Her desire to make
the trip **overmastered** her fear
of flying.*

o•ver•sight (ō′vər sīt′) *n.* An
omission or mistake that is
not made on purpose; an unintentional error: *It was an
oversight that your name
was left off the list.*

par•fleche (pär′flĕsh′) *n.* A
bag or other container made

Opaque *comes
partly from the
Middle English word*
opake *and partly
from the Old French
word* opaque. *Both
of these words devel-
oped from the Latin*
opācus, *meaning
"dark."*

Latin ōrāre, *"to
speak," had two dis-
tinct meanings:
(1) "to speak in pub-
lic, to address a
crowd," and (2) "to
pray." In sense (1) it
formed* oratio,
"speech," orator,
"speaker," and (ars)
oratoria, *"(the art
of) public speaking";
from these we have
"oration," "oratory,"
"orator," and*
oratorical.

oi **oil** / ŏŏ **book** / ōō **boot** / ou **out** / ŭ **cut** / û **fur** / *th* **the** / th **thin** / hw **which** /
zh **vision** / ə **ago, item, pencil, atom, circus**

*The word **passive** is found in Middle English and developed from the Latin* passīvus, *meaning "capable of suffering."*

from a raw hide that has been soaked in lye and dried.

pas•sive (**păs′ĭv**) *adj.* Acted upon or forced to act by an outside influence or agency: *Each representative is a **passive** servant of the people.*

pem•mi•can (**pĕm′ĭ kən**) *n.* A food made by North American Indians from a paste of lean meat mixed with fat and berries.

per•pet•u•al (**pər pĕch′ōō əl**) *adj.* Lasting forever or for an indefinitely long time: *They made a vow of **perpetual** friendship.*

per•se•ver•ing (**pûr′sə vîr′ĭng**) *adj.* Holding or persisting without giving way; steadfast: *With her **persevering** work, the job was completed in half the usual time.*

per•turb (**pər tûrb′**) *v.* **per•turbed, per•turb•ing.** To make uneasy or anxious; disturb; upset.

pes•ti•lence (**pĕs′tə ləns**) *n.* A deadly epidemic disease, especially bubonic plague.

pe•ti•tion (**pə tĭsh′ən**) *v.* **pe•ti•tioned, pe•ti•tion•ing.** To make a formal request: *His lawyer **petitioned** the court for a retrial.*

phe•nom•e•non (**fĭ nŏm′ə nŏn**) *n., pl.* **phe•nom•e•na** (**fĭ nŏm′ə nə**) *or* **phe•nom•e•nons.** Any occurrence or fact that can be perceived by the senses: *Floods are natural **phenomena**.*

phi•los•o•pher (**fĭ lŏs′ə fər**) *n.* A person who develops or expands a formal set of ideas based upon the study by logical reasoning of the basic truths and laws governing the universe, nature, life, morals, etc.

pho•ton (**fō′tŏn′**) *n.* A stable particle of light or other electromagnetic energy that travels at the speed of light and has a mass of zero.

phren•o•log•i•cal (**frĕn′ə lŏj′ĭ kəl**) *or* (**frē′nə-**) *adj.* Having to do with the method of attempting to determine intelligence and character by studying the shape of the head.

pi•geon (**pĭj′ĭn**) *n.* A person who can be tricked and swindled.

pig•ment (**pĭg′mənt**) *n.* A substance or material used to give color to something.

pit•tance (**pĭt′ns**) *n.* A small amount of money.

plum•met (**plŭm′ĭt**) *v.* **plum•met•ed, plum•met•ing.** To drop straight down; plunge.

pock•mark (**pŏk′märk′**) *n.* A pitlike scar left on the skin as a result of smallpox, acne, or a similar disease.

Petition *developed from the Middle English* peticioun *and the Old French* petition. *Its Latin root is* petītiō, *meaning "attack; solicitation," from* petere, *meaning "to seek or demand."*

ă pat / ā pay / â care / ä father / ĕ pet / ē be / ĭ pit / ī pie / î fierce / ŏ pot / ō go / ô paw, for /

pon•der (pŏn′dər) *v.*
pon•dered, pon•der•ing. To
think or consider carefully and
at length: *She will have to
ponder the decision.*

post mor•tem (pōst **môr′**təm)
adj. Occurring or done after
death: *A **post mortem** investigation revealed murder.*

press (prĕs) *n.* Pressure, haste,
urgency: *The **press** of business weighs heavily on him.*

pri•ma•ry col•ors (prī′mər´ē
kŭl′ərz) *or* (-mə rē) *pl. n.*
1. The three colors of light,
red, green, and blue, from
which light of any color can
be made by mixing. **2.** The
three colors of pigment, pur-
plish red, greenish blue, and
yellow, from which pigment
of any color can be made by
mixing.

prin•ci•ple (prĭn′sə pəl) *n.* A
rule or moral standard of behavior.

prism (prĭz′əm) *n.* A geomet-
ric solid, usually with triangular bases and rectangular sides,
made of a transparent material
and used to refract light or
break it up into a spectrum.

pro•nounce•ment
(prə **nouns′**mənt) *n.* An
authoritative statement or
judgment: *The scientist made
several **pronouncements**
about the rocket launch.*

pro•phet•ic (prə **fĕt′**ĭk) *adj.*
Having or showing the ability

to predict the future: *Her
warning proved to be
prophetic.*

pro•spec•tive (prə **spĕk′**tĭv)
adj. Expected to be or occur;
forthcoming; future; possible:
*We finally met our son's
prospective bride.*

prox•im•i•ty (prŏk sĭm′ĭ tē) *n.*
The quality or fact of being
near; closeness: *We stayed in
proximity to the fire during the
bitter cold.*

quack•er•y (kwăk′ə rē) *n.*
The practice or claims of a
person who pretends to have
knowledge, especially medical
knowledge, that he or she does
not have.

qualm (kwäm) *or* (kwôm) *n.*
A pang of conscience: *He had
no **qualms** about telling lies.*

quar•ter (kwôr′tər) *n.* An un-
specified person or group of
persons: *Help arrived from
unexpected **quarters**.*

ra•di•ant en•er•gy (rā′dē ənt
ĕn′ər jē) *n.* Heat and light
formed by atomic reactions on
the surface of the sun.

ran•kle (răng′kəl) *v.*
ran•kled, ran•kling. To fill

---

*Post mortem is lit-
erally Latin for "after
death." Most words
that exist in Modern
English in their lit-
eral Latin forms are
used in the medical or
legal professions.*
*Post mortem is
usually used in the le-
gal sense of an
investigation or ex-
amination after
death.*

---

*Rankle is from the
Old French word
rancler, meaning "to
fester." The word
originated in Late
Latin as dracunculus,
meaning "something
curled or twisting
like a serpent."
The original word
was draco, which
was Latin for
"dragon or serpent."*

---

oi **oil** / o͞o **book** / o͞o **boot** / ou **out** / ŭ **cut** / û **fur** / *th* **the** / th **thin** / hw **which** /
zh **vision** / ə **ago**, **item**, **pencil**, **atom**, **circus**

someone with nagging resentment; annoy: *His lack of sympathy was **rankling** the others.*

ra•tion•al (răsh′ə nəl) *adj.* Consistent with or based on reason; logical: *I made the only **rational** decision.*

rav•age (răv′ĭj) *v.* **rav•aged, rav•ag•ing.** To bring heavy destruction upon; devastate: *The coast was **ravaged** by a hurricane.*

real im•age (rē′əl ĭm′ĭj) *or* (rēl-) *n.* A picture of an object that can be viewed on a screen.

re•cede (rĭ sēd′) *v.* **re•ced•ed, re•ced•ing.** To become farther away: *Her memory of that night **receded** over the next few months.*

reek (rēk) *v.* **reeked, reek•ing.** To give off a strong or unpleasant odor: *The open garbage can **reeked**.*

ref•er•ence, (rĕf′ ər əns) *or* (rĕf′rəns) *n.* An allusion or mention: *He only made one **reference** to his trip to Europe.*

re•flect (rĭ flĕkt′) *v.* **re•flect•ed, re•flect•ing.** To send or turn back, as radiation, particles, etc., that strike a surface: *Light was **reflected** from the shiny glass.*

Reluctant *comes from the Latin word* reluctāns, *meaning "struggling against." That word is the present participle of* reluctārī, *meaning "to struggle against, resist, be reluctant":* re-, *"against, back,"* + luctari, *"to struggle."*

re•fract (rĭ frăkt′) *v.* **re•fract•ed, re•fract•ing.** To cause the path of (light or other radiation) to bend or deflect.

re•gard (rĭ gärd′) *v.* **re•gard•ed, re•gard•ing.** To look at; observe: *The farmer stood **regarding** the trespassers with a fixed stare.*

reg•i•men (rĕj′ə mən) *or* (-mĕn′) *n.* A system or method of treatment or cure: *He must add diet and exercise to the other **regimens**.*

reg•is•ter (rĕj′ĭ stər) *v.* **reg•is•tered, reg•is•ter•ing.** To be indicated, as on a scale or device: *The temperature will **register** 100 degrees on a thermometer.*

re•lent•less•ness (rĭ lĕnt′lĭs nĭs) *n.* A steady and persistent manner; something unstoppable: *The wind blew with fierce **relentlessness**.*

re•luc•tant (rĭ lŭk′tənt) *adj.* Unwilling: *They were **reluctant** to leave the party.*

re•morse•ful (rĭ môrs′fəl) *adj.* Having or showing bitter regret or guilt for having done something harmful or unjust: *The child was **remorseful** for having told a lie.*

rend (rĕnd) *v.* **rent** (rĕnt) *or* **rend•ed, rend•ing.** To tear, pull, or wrench apart violently: *He **rent** his jeans on a nail.*

ă pat / ā pay / â care / ä father / ĕ pet / ē be / ĭ pit / ī pie / î fierce / ŏ pot / ō go / ô paw, for /

ren•der (rĕn′dər) *v.*
ren•dered, ren•der•ing. To
pronounce; hand down: *The
judge will render a verdict.*

ren•dez•vous (rän′dā vōō′) *or*
(-də-) *v.* **ren•dez•voused,
ren•dez•vous•ing.** To meet
together or cause to meet together at a certain time and
place: *The choir will
rendezvous at the auditorium
today.*

rent (rĕnt) *v.* A past tense and
past participle of **rend.**

re•peal (rĭ pēl′) *v.* **re•pealed,
re•peal•ing.** To withdraw or
annul officially; revoke: *Congress repealed the new tax
law.*

re•pose (rĭ pōz′) *v.* **re•posed,
re•pos•ing.** To place (faith,
trust, etc.): *Their hopes were
reposed in her.*

re•proach (rĭ prōch′) *v.*
re•proached, re•proach•ing.
To rebuke severely or sternly;
blame: *The teacher is
reproaching the ones who
cheated.*

re•pub•lic (rĭ pŭb′lĭk) *n.* A
country governed by the
elected representatives of the
people.

res•o•lute•ly (rĕz′ə lōōt′lē)
adv. With a strong will and
determination: *Our team continued resolutely in the game.*

res•o•lu•tion (rĕz′ə lōō′shən)
n. **1.** A solution or answer:
This resolution will end the
controversy. **2.** A formal
statement or expression of
opinion proposed or adopted
by an assembly, legislature, or
other organization: *The senate
passed a new resolution.*

re•spec•tive•ly (rĭ spĕk′tĭv lē)
adv. Each in the order named:
*Albany and Atlanta are,
respectively, the capitals of
New York and Georgia.*

re•strain (rĭ strān′) *v.*
re•strained, re•strain•ing.
To check; suppress; hold back:
*He restrained his appetite to
stay on his diet.*

re•straint (rĭ strānt′) *n.* The
act of checking; suppressing;
holding back: *Restraint kept
him from crying.*

re•tal•i•ate (rĭ tăl′ē āt′) *v.*
**re•tal•i•at•ed,
re•tal•i•at•ing.** To reply to or
pay back an unfriendly act
with a similar one: *We will
retaliate against an enemy
attack.*

ret•i•na (rĕt′n ə) *or* (rĕt′nə) *n.*
A delicate, light-sensitive
membrane that lines the inside
of the eyeball and is connected
to the brain by the optic
nerve.

re•tire (rĭ tīr′) *v.* **re•tired,
re•tir•ing.** To withdraw; go
away; disappear: *The judge
retired to her study.*

re•voke (rĭ vōk′) *v.* **re•voked,
re•vok•ing.** To make void, as
by reversing or withdrawing;

Rendezvous *is from
French* rendezvous, *a noun formed from
the phrase* rendez
vous, *meaning "pre-
sent yourselves." This
was originally a com-
mand to soldiers, and
the English word,
which was first bor-
rowed in the sixteenth
century, remains in
technical military
use.*

Republic *is from
Latin* rēspublica, *a
compound noun
meaning "public
affairs, the state":*
res-, *"affairs, busi-
ness,"* + publica,
*"public." The Roman
idea of the state is ef-
fectively summed up
by the word*
rēspublica; *the
Romans regarded
government as being
"the public concern, the
business of the whole
community." The
Romans were never
truly democratic like
some of the Greeks, but
they strongly believed
that it was everyone's
duty to serve "the
common good, the
commonwealth."*

oi **oil** / ōō **book** / ōō **boot** / ou **out** / ŭ **cut** / û **fur** / th **the** / th **thin** / hw **which** /
zh **vision** / ə **ago**, **item**, **pencil**, **atom**, **circus**

cancel: *The principal will* **revoke** *permission for the party.*

rev•o•lu•tion•ar•y (rĕv′ə loo′shə nĕr′ē) *adj.* Characterized by radical change: *He lectured on a* **revolutionary** *new teaching idea.*

rig (rĭg) *v.* **rigged, rig•ging.** To manipulate dishonestly: *The game was* **rigged** *and will have to be replayed.*

rit•u•al•is•tic (rĭch′oo ə lĭs′tĭk) *adj.* In accordance with a procedure faithfully and regularly followed.

rod (rŏd) *n.* Any of the elongated cells in the retina of the eye that are sensitive to dim light and incapable of distinguishing colors.

rogue (rōg) *n.* A person who tricks or cheats others; a scoundrel; rascal.

rout (rout) *v.* **rout•ed, rout•ing.** To defeat overwhelmingly; crush: *We will* **rout** *the opposing team.*

rue (roo) *v.* **rued, ru•ing.** To feel shame, sorrow, or regret: *She will* **rue** *her mistake.*

ruse (rooz) *n.* An action meant to confuse or mislead an opponent; a deception: *The quarterback's* **ruse** *helped the running back score a touchdown.*

S

sac•ri•le•gious (săk′rə lĭj′əs) *or* (-lē′jəs) *adj.* Disrespectful toward something sacred.

sad•dler (săd′lər) *n.* A person who makes saddles for horses or other animals.

saun•ter (sôn′tər) *v.* **saun•tered, saun•ter•ing.** To walk at a leisurely pace; stroll.

scaf•fold (skăf′əld) *or* (-ōld′) *n.* A platform for the execution of condemned prisoners.

scath•ing (skā′*th*ĭng) *adj.* Extremely severe or harsh: *Their teacher gave them a* **scathing** *reprimand.*

scav•en•ger (skăv′ĭn jər) *n.* Someone who searches through rubbish or discarded material for food, useful objects, etc.

scriv•en•er (skrĭv′ə nər) *or* (skrĭv′nər) *n.* A scribe; a writer.

scru•ple (skroo′pəl) *v.* **scru•pled, scru•pling.** To hesitate as a result of conscience or principles: *She did not* **scruple** *at stealing money for food.*

scru•ti•ny (skroot′n ē) *n.* A close, careful look or study: *The class quieted under the* **scrutiny** *of the principal.*

Sacrilegious *developed from the Latin words* sacer, *meaning "sacred," and* legere, *meaning "to steal, gather, or pluck."*

Scruple *developed from the Old French* scruple, *and from the Latin word* scrupus, *which means "a rough stone."*

ă pat / ā pay / â care / ä father / ĕ pet / ē be / ĭ pit / ī pie / î fierce / ŏ pot / ō go / ô paw, for /

sé·ance (sā′äns′) *n.* A meeting at which persons attempt to communicate with the dead.

se·duc·tive (sĭ dŭk′tĭv) *adj.* Tempting; alluring: *He couldn't resist the seductive aroma of baking bread.*

self-styled (sĕlf′stīld′) *adj.* As characterized or described by oneself: *He is a self-styled artist.*

se·pul·chral (sə pŭl′krəl) *adj.* Suggestive of tombs or burial rites; funereal; mournful: *Her sepulchral moan raised the hair on my head.*

ser·rat·ed (sĕr′ā tĭd) *adj.* Edged with notched, toothlike projections: *The knife blade was serrated.*

sev·er·ance (sĕv′ə rəns) *or* (sĕv′rəns) *n.* The act of cutting or breaking from the whole: *Their revolt was a severance of the union.*

shade (shād) *n.* A spirit; a ghost.

sham (shăm) *adj.* Pretended; not genuine. —*v.* **shammed, sham·ming.** To pretend to have or feel; feign; pretend: *He is shamming illness to stay out of school.*

shim·my (shĭm′ē) *v.* **shim·mied, shim·my·ing.** To shake, vibrate, or wobble.

shrewd (shrood) *adj.* Clever and practical: *She is a shrewd business person.*

shroud (shroud) *v.* **shroud·ed, shroud·ing.** To conceal; screen; hide: *The sun was shrouded by clouds.*

si·mul·ta·ne·ous·ly (sī′məl tā′nē əs lē) *or* (sĭm′əl-) *adv.* Happening or done at the same time.

sin·is·ter (sĭn′ĭ stər) *adj.* Suggesting an evil force or motive: *A sinister man was seen lurking in the shadows.*

sin·u·ous (sĭn′yoo əs) *adj.* Having many curves or turns; twisting or writhing: *Imitating a snake, the dancer performed a sinuous dance.*

skir·mish (skûr′mĭsh) *n.* A minor encounter between small bodies of troops.

skirt (skûrt) *v.* **skirt·ed, skirt·ing.** To pass around rather than across or through: *We skirted the marshes.*

skit·tish (skĭt′ĭsh) *adj.* Frivolous in action or character; capricious or fickle: *The skittish young girl could not make up her mind.*

smite (smīt) *v.* **smote** (smōt), **smit·ten** (smĭt′n) *or* **smit·ing.** To inflict a heavy blow on.

sni·per (snī′pər) *n.* A person who shoots at others from a hiding place.

sol·i·tude (sŏl′ĭ tood′) *or* (-tyood′) *n.* The state of being alone or remote from others: *She enjoyed the*

Serrated *developed from the Latin word* serratus, *"saw-shaped," from* serra, *meaning "saw."*

Sinister *is a Latin word that means "left or on the left side." In ancient Roman fortunetelling, the left side of something was not good or favorable.*

---

oi **oil** / oo book / oo boot / ou **out** / ŭ **cut** / û **fur** / *th* **the** / th **thin** / hw **which** / zh **vision** / ə **ago, item, pencil, atom, circus**

Squat *came from the Middle English word* squatten, *"to crush or flatten," and from the Old French* esquatir. *These words probably developed from the Latin word* cogere, *meaning "to drive or press together."*

solitude of her vacation home.

sou'west·er (sou **wĕs′**tər) *n.* A waterproof hat, often of oil-skin or canvas, with a broad brim in back to protect the neck.

sparse·ly (spärs′lē) *adv.* Not crowded; mostly empty: *The region was sparsely settled.*

spec·tral (spĕk′trəl) *adj.* Of or resembling a spirit or ghost: *The mist blew in spectral forms.*

spec·trum (spĕk′trəm) *n.* **1.** The bands of color seen when white light, especially light from the sun, is broken up by refraction, as in a rainbow or by a prism. **2.** A broad range of related qualities, ideas, or activities: *We investigated a wide spectrum of careers.*

spec·u·la·tion (spĕk′yə lā′shən) *n.* The act of thinking deeply about a given subject or idea; consideration; contemplation.

spec·u·la·tive·ly (spĕk′yə lā tĭv lē) *or* (-lə-) *adv.* In a meditative, deeply thoughtful, or inquisitive way: *The students were talking together speculatively.*

spiel (spēl) *n.* A talk designed to persuade.

spir·i·tu·al·ist (spĭr′ĭ chōo ə lĭst′) *n.* A person who claims to be able to

steppe

communicate with the dead.

spite (spīt) *n.* Malice or ill will causing a person to desire to hurt or humiliate another.

squat (skwŏt) *adj.* Short and thick; low and broad: *The tea kettle had a squat shape.*

stake (stāk) *n.* Often **stakes.** The amount of money or the prize awarded to the winner of a bet, gambling game, etc.: *The stakes of the tennis match are high.*

stanch (stônch) *or* (stănch) *or* (stänch) *v.* **stanched, stanch·ing.** To stop or check the flow of blood from a wound: *The doctor used pressure and a cloth to stanch the flow of blood.*

stan·chion (stăn′chən) *or* (-shən) *n.* A vertical pole, post, or support.

stat·ute (stăch′ōot) *n.* A law or order.

steppe (stĕp) *n.* A vast, somewhat dry plain, covered with grass and having few trees, as found in southeastern Europe and Siberia.

sti·fled (stī′fəld) *adj.* Being held back; suppressed: *She turned red with stifled laughter.*

stock (stŏk) *n.* Cloth worn around the neck, such as a tie, scarf, or cravat.

stom·ach (stŭm′ək) *v.* **stom·ached, stom·ach·ing.**

ă pat / ā pay / â care / ä father / ĕ pet / ē be / ĭ pit / ī pie / î fierce / ŏ pot / ō go / ô paw, for /

To bear, tolerate, or endure: *She had to **stomach** undeserved criticism.*

sub•dued (səb dōōd′) *or* (-dyōōd′) *adj.* Quiet; under control; toned down: *The restaurant's **subdued** music made him sleepy.*

sub•ject (sŭb′jĭkt) *adj.* Liable to incur or receive; exposed. —*n.* Someone who owes allegiance to a government or ruler: *The British people are Queen Elizabeth's **subjects**.*

sub•stance (sŭb′stəns) *n.* **1.** That which has mass and occupies space; matter: *We learned about the **substance** known as carbon.* **2.** Wealth; quality; importance: *A millionaire is a person of **substance**.*

sub•tle (sŭt′l) *adj.* Not immediately obvious; devious: *The mystery had a **subtle** solution.*

sub•tly (sŭt′lē) *adv.* In a manner so as to be difficult to detect; not obviously.

suc•ces•sor (sək sĕs′ər) *n.* A person who replaces another in an office or position: *Her **successor** was a much younger woman.*

suf•fer (sŭf′ər) *v.* **suf•fered, suf•fer•ing.** To permit; allow.

sump•tu•ous (sŭmp′chōō əs) *adj.* Of a size or splendor suggesting great expense; lavish: *Jewels decorated the **sumptuous** temple.*

sup•press (sə prĕs′) *v.* **sup•pressed, sup•pres•sing.** To put an end to forcibly; subdue: *Police had to **suppress** the riot.*

swathe (swŏth) *or* (swôth) *v.* **swathed, swath•ing.** To wrap or bind with a strip or strips of cloth: *Her right hand was **swathed** in bandages.*

swin•dle (swĭn′dl) *v.* **swin•dled, swin•dling.** To cheat or defraud (a person) of money or property: *He **swindled** the couple out of their life savings.*

tails (tālz) *n.* A swallow-tailed coat worn as a part of men's most formal evening clothes.

tap•es•try (tăp′ĭ strē) *n.* A rich, heavy cloth woven with designs and scenes in many colors, usually hung on walls for decoration and sometimes used to cover furniture.

ten•ta•cle (tĕn′tə kəl) *n.* One of the narrow, flexible, unjointed parts extending from the body of certain animals, such as an octopus, and used for grasping, moving, etc.

the•o•ry (thē′ə rē) *or* (thîr′ē) *n., pl.* **the•o•ries.** A statement or set of statements designed to explain a phenomenon or class of phenomena, generally consisting of

Substance[1] *is from Latin* substantia, *a scientific term for basic matter, "that which underlies things, the underlying stuff of which all objects are made":* sub-, *"under,"* + stant-, *"standing, existing."* **Substance**[2] *developed from the Latin word* substare, *which means "to stand up or be present."*

Tentacle *developed from the New Latin word* tentaculum, *which came from the Latin word* temptare, *meaning "to feel or to touch."*

tentacle

oi **oil** / ōō **book** / ōō **boot** / ou **out** / ŭ **cut** / û **fur** / *th* **the** / th **thin** / hw **which** / zh **vision** / ə **ago, item, pencil, atom, circus**

Transparent *is found in Middle English, from the Medieval Latin word* transparens, *"to be seen through."*

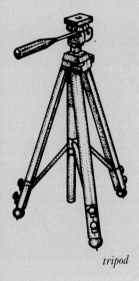

tripod

Try *developed from the Middle English* trien, *and from the Old French word* trier, *meaning "to sift out or sort."*

Ultimatum *developed from the Medieval Latin word* ultimatus, *meaning "last or ultimate." Thus, an* **ultimatum** *is a last chance to meet certain terms or demands.*

conclusions drawn from known facts and various assumptions by mathematical or logical reasoning: *We discussed Isaac Newton's* **theories** *about gravity.*

thim·ble·rig·ger (thĭm′bəl rĭg′ər) *n.* A person who cheats and swindles others through gambling or games of chance.

thwart·ed (thwôrt′əd) *adj.* Frustrated, blocked, or prevented from doing something: *She was* **thwarted** *in her efforts to make the team.*

tin·ker (tĭng′kər) *n.* A traveling mender of metal household utensils.

tract (trăkt) *n.* A propaganda pamphlet.

trans·lu·cent (trăns loo′sənt) *or* **(trănz-)** *adj.* Transmitting light, but scattering it enough so that images become blurred or are destroyed: *Silhouettes could be seen through the* **translucent** *glass.*

trans·mog·ri·fi·ca·tion (trăns mŏg′rə fĭ kā′shən) *n.* The ability to change shape or form: *Werewolves use* **transmogrification**.

trans·mu·ta·tion (trăns′myoo tā′shən) *or* **(trănz′-)** *n.* The transformation of base metals into gold or silver.

trans·par·ent (trăns pâr′ənt) *or* **(-păr′-)** *adj.* Capable of transmitting light so that objects and images are clearly visible.

trea·tise (trē′tĭs) *n.* A formal, systematic account in writing of some subject: *We had to read all of the professors'* **treatises** *on mathematics.*

tre·ble (trĕb′əl) *adj.* Increased by three times; triple: *She has* **treble** *the amount I have.*

tri·bu·nal (trī byoo′nəl) *or* **(trĭ-)** *n.* A seat or court of justice: *I am waiting for the verdict of the* **tribunal**.

tri·pod (trī′pŏd′) *n.* A stand or holder with three legs.

trump (trŭmp) *n.* Something that can be used to help win, like the card that outranks all other cards in a card game: *A fast finish is a runner's* **trump**.

truss (trŭs) *v.* **trussed, truss·ing.** To tie up securely; bind: *We saw the guards* **trussing** *up the criminals.*

try (trī) *v.* **tried, try·ing.** To examine or hear (a case) in a court of law; to put on trial.

ty·rant (tī′rənt) *n.* A ruler who exercises power in a harsh, cruel manner.

ul·ti·ma·tum (ŭl′tə mā′təm) *or* **(-mä′-)** *n.* A statement of terms that expresses or implies the threat of serious penalties

ă pat / ā pay / â care / ä father / ĕ pet / ē be / ĭ pit / ī pie / î fierce / ŏ pot / ō go / ô paw, for /

if the terms are not accepted; a final demand or offer.

un·al·ien·a·ble (ŭn āl′yə nə bəl) *adj.* Not capable of being given up, taken away, or transferred to another person.

un·bid·den (ŭn bĭd′n) *adj.* Not asked or invited: *No one knew the **unbidden** guest.*

un·der·ling (ŭn′dər lĭng) *n.* A person in a subordinate position: *The manager praised his **underlings**.*

un·der·tow (ŭn′dər tō′) *n.* A current beneath the surface of a body of water running in a direction opposite to that of the current at the surface: *Two swimmers were carried out to sea by the **undertow**.*

un·nerv·ing (ŭn nûrv′ĭng) *adj.* Frightening or startling: *She found the roller coaster ride **unnerving**.*

up·heav·al (ŭp hē′vəl) *n.* A sudden and violent disturbance: *The storm's **upheaval** overturned our boat.*

up·start (ŭp′stärt′) *n.* A person of humble origin who has suddenly risen to wealth or high position, especially one who becomes snobbish or arrogant because of success.

ur·chin (ûr′chĭn) *n.* A small child, especially a mischievous or needy child.

vac·u·um (văk′yoo əm) *or* (-yoom) *n.* A space that is empty of matter: *There is absolutely nothing inside a **vacuum**.*

val·id (văl′ĭd) *adj.* Well-grounded; sound; supportable: *She made a **valid** objection.*

var·i·e·gat·ed (vâr′ē ĭ gā′tĭd) *adj.* Having streaks, marks, or patches of different colors: *Many butterflies have **variegated** wings.*

venge·ance (vĕn′jəns) *n.* The act of causing harm to another person in retribution for a wrong or injury: *A victim of a practical joke may seek **vengeance**.*

vexed (vĕksd) *adj.* Irritated; annoyed; bothered.

vic·tro·la (vĭk trō′lə) *n.* A device that reproduces sound from a disk, especially one that operates by a spring that is wound by hand cranking.

vig·il (vĭj′əl) *n.* A period of alert watchfulness during normal sleeping hours: *The night-duty security guard's **vigil** was rewarded when he caught a thief.*

vig·i·lant (vĭj′ə lənt) *adj.* Alert and watchful: *A police officer must be **vigilant** at all times.*

vir·tu·al im·age (vûr′choo əl ĭm′ĭj) *n.* An image, such as

> **Urchin** *is a Middle English variant of* (h)irchon, *from the Norman French word* herichon. *These words developed from the Latin word for* hedgehog, hericius.

> **Vacuum** *developed from the Latin word* vacare, *meaning* "empty."

victrola

oi **oil** / oo **book** / oo **boot** / ou **out** / ŭ **cut** / û **fur** / *th* **the** / th **thin** / hw **which** / zh **vision** / ə **ago, item, pencil, atom, circus**

735

vixen

one seen in a mirror, from which rays of reflected or refracted light appear to come and which cause the image to appear reversed.

vir•tue (vûr'chōō) *n.* Moral excellence and righteousness; goodness.

vis•u•al noise (vĭzh'ōō əl noiz') *n.* Something that causes the brain to misunderstand what the eye has seen; an optical illusion.

vit•re•ous hu•mor (vĭt'rē əs hyōō'mər) *n.* A thick, clear liquid that fills the eyeball.

vix•en (vĭk'sən) *n.* A female fox.

voile (voil) *n.* A sheer fabric of cotton, rayon, wool, or silk used in making lightweight curtains, dresses, etc.

vol•ley (vŏl'ē) *n.* The discharge of a number of missiles, such as bullets or cannonballs, all at the same time: *The guards fired a volley to warn the intruders.*

vul•ner•a•bil•i•ties (vŭl'nər ə bĭl'ə tēz) *pl. n.* Unprotected parts; areas in which one can be injured.

> **Voile** *is a French word that developed from the Latin word* velum, *which can mean "veil or cloth."*

wave•length (wāv'lĕngkth') *or* (-lĕngth') *n.* The distance between two points of identical phase in successive cycles of a wave.

wench (wĕnch) *n.* A young woman or girl.

wheel•wright (hwēl'rīt') *or* (wēl'-) *n.* A person who makes or repairs wheels.

winch (wĭnch) *v.* **winched, winch•ing.** To lift; raise up.

wise•a•cre (wīz'ā'kər) *n.* A person that pretends to be clever; a smart aleck.

wiz•ened (wĭz'ənd) *adj.* Shriveled; withered: *The elderly woman's wizened face softened as she smiled.*

wreathe (rē*th*) *v.* **wreathed, wreath•ing.** To encircle; decorate; surround.

writ of as•sis•tance (rĭt ôv ə sĭs'təns) *n.* A written legal order allowing customs officials to search private establishments for smuggled goods without first having to obtain a search warrant.

wry (rī) *adj.* Dryly humorous, often with a touch of irony.

W

wan (wŏn) *adj.* Unnaturally pale, as from an illness.

Y

yo•kel (yō'kəl) *n.* A simple country fellow.

ă pat / ā pay / â care / ä father / ĕ pet / ē be / ĭ pit / ī pie / î fierce / ŏ pot / ō go / ô paw, for / oi oil / ŏŏ book / ōō boot / ou out / ŭ cut / û fur / *th* the / th thin / hw which / zh vision / ə ago, item, pencil, atom, circus

action The series of events that make up a **plot.**

alliteration The repetition of a consonant sound, usually the first sound in a group of words, as in "trumpeted two times."

allusion A brief mention of a person or thing with which the reader is presumed to be familiar.

anecdote A short account that gives details of an interesting event.

antagonist The character who opposes the main character, or **protagonist,** in a story, play, or poem.

archaic language Words and expressions that once were part of the language, but are no longer in use.

author's purpose What the author means to say or accomplish in his or her work.

autobiography A person's account of his or her own life.

ballad A fairly short poem that tells a story. Ballads typically consist of **stanzas** and a **refrain.** They were originally meant to be sung.

biography The factual account of a person's life, written by someone else.

blank verse A form of poetry that does not rhyme and has five beats per line.

chapter One of the main sections of a book, usually labeled with a number or title.

characterization The process of making a character seem real and lifelike. An author uses description of the character's physical features, personality traits, actions, thoughts, speech, and feelings to achieve characterization.

characters The people or animals in a story. The main character handles the problem or **conflict** in the story. Minor characters help advance the **plot** and reveal information about the main character's personality.

character traits Qualities that make one character different from another. Such qualities — bravery, intelligence, stinginess, and so on — are as various in literature as they are in real life.

climax The point in a play or story where the **conflict** reaches its highest intensity and must be resolved. The climax is the most exciting moment in a story and holds the most interest for the reader. (See also **turning point.**)

comedy Writing that is designed to amuse. Comedy uses such devices as sarcasm,

exaggeration, satire, and **wit.** Comedies typically have happy endings.

conclusion In dramatic structure, the part of a story or play that gives the final results; the ending.

conflict The problem in a story faced by the main character. The character may face one (or more) of the following four kinds of conflict: a struggle against nature, a struggle against another character, a struggle against society, or a struggle against himself or herself.

connotation The feelings, emotions, and ideas associated with a word, as opposed to its dictionary definition. (See also **denotation.**)

context The words and ideas that surround a particular word. A reader can often figure out the meaning of a new word from its context.

denotation The exact meaning of a word as it might appear in a dictionary. (See also **connotation.**)

description Writing that provides details of time, place, character, and setting. An author uses description to create images of the "world" in which the story takes place.

descriptive language Language that is rich in sensory details. It evokes sights, smells, sounds, and textures.

dialect The way of speaking used by the people of a particular region or group. A writer achieves a dialect by using words that are spelled differently to show local or regional pronunciations, and by using words and sentence structures that are part of local or regional sayings and manners of speaking.

dialogue The words spoken by characters to one another in a story or play.

diction **1.** The choice and arrangement of words in a story or play. **2.** The quality of speech or singing judged by clearness and distinctness of pronunciation.

drama A serious play designed to be acted on a stage.

dramatize **1.** To turn a story into a play or screenplay. **2.** To relate an incident in a very dramatic way.

epic A long poem or literary work, usually written in a formal style, about heroes and their adventures. Ancient epics, such as Homer's *Iliad* and *Odyssey*, are often written versions of the oral legends of a nation or culture.

essay   A brief piece of prose writing about a specific topic. An essay usually expresses the opinions of its author.

exaggeration   Deliberate overstatement used for emphasis, effect, or **humor.**

expository writing   Informational writing that enlightens or explains. Most **nonfiction prose** is expository.

fable   A short story, often with animal characters who speak and act like humans, that teaches a lesson about human nature.

falling action   In dramatic structure, the part of a story or play that tells what happens after the **climax.**

fantasy   Fiction that tells about events that are impossible in the real world because they do not obey known scientific laws. **Science fiction** and fairy tales are types of fantasy writing.

fiction   Stories created from the imagination of the author. **Novels, short stories,** and **fables** are all forms of fiction.

fictionalized biography   An account of a person's life that is based on facts but includes some imagined elements.

figurative language   Writing that uses figures of speech such as metaphors, similes, and personification. (See also **metaphor, simile,** and **personification.**)

figures of speech   Various imaginative uses of language that create special effects or meanings. (See also **metaphor, simile,** and **personification.**)

first person   The **point of view** from which one of the characters tells the story using the pronoun *I*. This character may experience the events of the story personally or may simply be a witness to them. (See also **narrator** and **third person.**)

flashback   A writing technique that interrupts the present action to explain something that happened earlier.

folklore   Traditions, beliefs, legends, customs, and stories handed down by a particular people from generation to generation by word of mouth. Folklore includes folk **ballads,** folk **dramas,** folk **heroes,** and **folktales.**

folktale   A traditional story of a particular place or people, handed down from generation to generation and eventually written down.

foreshadowing   A writing technique involving clues that a writer gives early in a selection to hint at future events.

formal language   Careful, precise language, more frequently used in writing than in everyday speech. (See also **informal language.**)

free verse   Poetry that does not follow a regular pattern of rhythm or line, and has either irregular rhyme or no rhyme.

genre   A category or type of literary work. Works can be grouped into genres by form, technique, or type of subject. Thus, the adventure story, the **folktale,** and the **novel** are all examples of literary genres.

haiku   A **lyric** poem of three lines and usually seventeen syllables. Traditionally, a haiku expresses a person's feelings inspired by nature.

hero/heroine   **1.** The central character in a work of fiction, poetry, or drama. **2.** A strong and courageous man or woman who performs brave deeds or who risks his or her life for a good cause. In mythology, heroes and heroines were descended from gods.

historical fiction   A story based partly on historical events and people and partly on the author's imagination.

humor   **1.** A type of writing intended to make people laugh. **2.** The quality of being funny.

idiom   A use of words, such as a **figure of speech** or a common saying, that is unique to one language and cannot be translated literally into another.

image   A mental picture of something not present or real.

imagery   Word pictures; mental images. In writing or speech, the use of **figurative language,** vivid **description,** or **sensory words** to produce **images.**

informal language   Casual language used mainly in conversation. (See also **formal language.**)

interpretation   The art of understanding what a work of literature means. Complex works can be interpreted in several different ways.

introduction   In dramatic structure, the part of a story or play that creates the mood, presents some of the characters, and supplies background information.

irony   The use of words or situations to contrast what is expected with what is actually meant or occurs. In *verbal irony,* the speaker says the opposite of what he or she means. In *dramatic irony,* the audience knows more about events than the characters do, which makes for **suspense** as the characters act out the story.

jargon   Special or technical language used by people in a particular job or by people with a particular hobby or interest.

legend   An imaginative story that is often connected with a national hero or a historical event and may be based on truth.

literature   Imaginative writing that possesses recognized artistic value.

lyric poetry   Poetry that expresses personal feelings and thoughts.

memoir   A form of **autobiography,** usually written by someone famous or by someone who has witnessed an important event. A memoir focuses on other people and events, rather than on the writer, as in autobiography.

metaphor   An implied comparison between very different things, used to add vividness to writing. In a metaphor, the two things compared are said to be the same, as in "Her mind is a computer." (See also **simile.**)

monologue   A long speech delivered by one character in a play, story, or poem.

mood   The effect of a story, poem, or play on the feelings of a reader or an audience; the emotional **tone** of a piece of writing.

moral   A lesson taught by a story or **fable.**

motivation   The combination of plot events and personality traits that determines a character's actions.

motive   A reason, a need, or an emotion that causes a character to act in a certain way.

mystery novel   Fiction that deals with a puzzling event, often a crime. (See also **novel.**)

myth   A story handed down from the past that gives an imaginary explanation of how certain things in nature, such as the moon, the sun, and the stars, came to be.

narration   The act or example of narrating, or telling a story.

narrative   In an account of an event, the description of characters, scenes, or events that is not dialogue.

narrative poetry   A type of poetry, sometimes rather long, that tells a story.

narrator   The character who tells the story or, in a play, who explains the events to the audience by addressing them directly. (See also **point of view, first person, third person.**)

nonfiction Writing that is about the real world rather than an imagined one.

novel A long fictional **narrative,** usually showing how a **character** develops as a result of events or actions, and organized around a **plot** or **theme.**

onomatopoeia The use of a word that imitates the sound it describes. *Buzz, splash,* and *honk* are all onomatopoetic words. In poetry, onomatopoeia may be more subtle, as the sound of the verses may help create a particular mood.

oral tradition A tradition in which songs and tales are passed by word of mouth from one generation to another.

outcome The final result; how something ends.

personification A **figure of speech** in which human traits are given to something that is not human.

plot The action or series of events in a story. The plot is traditionally divided into sections. The **introduction** creates the mood, presents some of the characters, and supplies background information. The **rising action** establishes and develops the **conflict.** At the **climax,** or turning point, the conflict is resolved through a key event or through the actions of the main character. In the **falling action,** the reader learns what happens as a result of the climax. The **conclusion** gives the final results.

point of view The position from which a story is told. A story may be told from the point of view of one of its characters, or from the position of an observer who is outside the action. (See also **first person, third person,** and **narrator.**)

prose Ordinary speech or writing as distinguished from verse or poetry.

protagonist The main character in a story. (See also **antagonist.**)

proverb A sentence or phrase that expresses a truth about life. "The early bird catches the worm" is a proverb.

realism Fiction that tells about true-to-life people, places, or events that could actually exist or happen.

refrain A phrase or verse repeated several times, usually at regular intervals throughout a song or poem.

repetition A writing technique in which a word or phrase is repeated for emphasis.

rhyme The repetition of the same or similar sounds of syllables, often at the ends of lines of verse.

rhyme scheme The pattern in which rhymes occur in a poem.

rhythm In poetry, a regular pattern of accented and unaccented syllables.

rising action In dramatic structure, the part of a story or play that establishes and develops the **conflict.**

romance novels **Novels** about extraordinary events in extraordinary settings. Romance novels are more concerned with action — love, adventure, combat — than with characters.

satire The use of **humor** or **irony** to expose hypocrisy or foolishness.

scene A section of a novel or play that focuses on the actions of one or several characters in one place and time.

science fiction Imaginative writing that has some basis in scientific fact and usually takes place in a time other than the present. Science fiction writing is sometimes used by an author as a vehicle for making a statement about society.

sensory words Words that appeal to one or more of the five senses (hearing, sight, smell, touch, and taste).

setting The time and place in which events in a story or play occur.

short story A brief fictional **narrative** in prose. It has unity in **theme, tone, plot,** and **character.** Often a short story reveals a character's true nature through a series of events.

simile A comparison of two unlike things, using *like* or *as*. "He was as brave as a lion" is a simile. (See also **metaphor.**)

slang Words and phrases that occur most often in **informal language.** Slang is often humorous, vivid, and extremely casual. Slang tends to be in a state of constant change, words and phrases experiencing popularity for a time, only to be replaced by new terms.

stage directions Instructions in the script of a play that tell the characters their movements on the stage. They also describe the use of props and sound effects.

stanza In poetry, a group of lines united by a pattern of rhyme and rhythm.

subplot An additional, but secondary **plot,** that makes the action in a work of fiction more complex and more interesting.

suspense Uncertainty, on the part of the reader or the audience, about what will happen in a story or play. Authors deliberately create suspense to hold the reader's or audience's interest.

symbolism   The use of an object, character, or incident to represent something else.

symbols   Objects, characters, or incidents that represent something else.

synopsis   A summary of a story's events.

theme   The underlying idea or message in a story. The theme may be directly or indirectly stated.

third person   The **point of view** in which the author acts as an unidentified **narrator** to tell the story about the characters. (See also **first person**.)

tone   The attitude toward the subject and the reader in a work of literature. The tone of a work may be formal or informal, for example, or light-hearted or serious. (See also **mood**.)

tragedy   A serious play that ends with a great misfortune that could not have been prevented. In a classic tragedy, the main character, a worthy, noble person, meets his or her fate with courage and dignity.

turning point   An important moment in the **plot**, when events that have led to the moment of greatest intensity in the story come to a peak, and the main conflict must be resolved. (See also **climax**.)

universal themes   Themes that occur in the stories of every culture, in every time. The conflict between good and evil is a traditional theme. Universal themes are particularly apparent in traditional tales.

verse   **1.** A part of a poem, such as a line or a **stanza**. **2.** Rhythmic, and usually rhymed, poetry.

wit   The ability to describe events that are amusing or odd, or to point out similarities in things that seem to be very different. Wit is a type of humor that depends mainly on the clever use of words.

Acknowledgments

For each of the selections listed below, grateful acknowledgment is made for permission to excerpt and/or reprint original or copyrighted material, as follows:

Major Selections

"The All-American Slurp," by Lensey Namioka, from *Visions: Nineteen Short Stories by Outstanding Writers for Young Adults*, edited by Donald R. Gallo. "The All-American Slurp" copyright © 1987 by Lensey Namioka. Reprinted by permission of Lensey Namioka. All rights reserved.

Excerpt from *The Big Sea*, by Langston Hughes. Copyright © 1940 by Langston Hughes. Copyright renewed 1968 by Arna Bontemps and George Houston Bass. Reprinted by permission of Farrar, Straus and Giroux, Inc., and Serpent's Tail.

"The Boy with Yellow Eyes," by Gloria Gonzalez from *Visions: Nineteen Short Stories by Outstanding Writers for Young Adults*, edited by Donald R. Gallo. "The Boy with Yellow Eyes" copyright © 1987 by Gloria Gonzalez. Reprinted by permission of Dell Books, a division of Bantam, Doubleday, Dell Publishing Group, Inc.

"But Who Can Replace a Man?" by Brian W. Aldiss. Copyright © 1958 by Royal Publications, Inc. Reprinted by permission of the author and the author's agents, Scott Meredith Literary Agency, Inc., 845 Third Avenue, New York, New York 10022. From *Infinity*.

"Colors and Waves," from *How Did We Find Out About Microwaves?* by Isaac Asimov. Text copyright © 1989 by Isaac Asimov. Reprinted by permission of Walker Publishing Company, Inc.

"Crispus Attucks," adapted from pages 33–40 of "Two Famous Patriots," in *Black Heroes of the American Revolution*, by Burke Davis. Copyright © 1976 by Burke Davis. Reprinted by permission of Harcourt Brace Jovanovich, Inc.

"Dark They Were, and Golden-eyed," by Ray Bradbury. Originally published in *Thrilling Wonder Stories* as "The Naming of Names." Copyright © 1949, renewed 1977 by Ray Bradbury. Reprinted by permission of Don Congdon Associates, Inc.

"Dolphin's Way," by Gordon R. Dickson. Copyright © 1991 by Gordon R. Dickson. Reprinted by permission of the author and the author's agent, the Pimlico Agency, Inc.

Excerpt from *The Empire Strikes Back Notebook*, edited by Diana Attias and Lindsay Smith. Copyright © Lucasfilm, Ltd. (LFL) 1980. TM: a trademark of Lucasfilm, Ltd. Reprinted by permission of Ballantine Books, a division of Random House, Inc.

"The Eye and How It Works," from *Optics: Light for a New Age*, by Jeff Hecht. Copyright © 1987 by Jeffrey Hecht. Reprinted by permission of Charles Scribner's Sons, an imprint of Macmillan Publishing Company.

"The Fifer of Boxborough," by Elizabeth West and Katherine S. Talmadge, from *Cobblestone*, September 1983: "Patriotic Tales of the American Revolution." Copyright © 1983 by Cobblestone Publishing, Inc., Peterborough, New Hampshire 03458. Reprinted by permission of the publisher.

"The Fuller Brush Man," by Gloria D. Miklowitz, from *Visions: Nineteen Short Stories by Outstanding Writers for Young Adults*, edited by Donald R. Gallo. "The Fuller Brush Man" copyright © 1987 by Gloria D. Miklowitz. Reprinted by permission of Delacorte Press, a division of Bantam, Doubleday, Dell Publishing Group, Inc.

Excerpt from *I Know Why the Caged Bird Sings*, by Maya Angelou. Copyright © 1969 by Maya Angelou. Reprinted by permission of Random House, Inc.

"In the Middle of the Night," from *What the Neighbours Did and Other Stories*, by Philippa Pearce (Kestrel Books, 1972). Copyright © 1972 by Philippa Pearce. Reprinted by permission of Penguin Books Ltd.

"Kintu and the Law of Love," from *Myths and Folk Tales Around the World*, edited by Robert R. Potter, Ed.D. and H. Alan Robinson. Copyright © 1963 by Globe Book Company, Inc. Reprinted by permission of Globe Book Company, Inc.

Excerpts from *Letters of a Loyalist Lady*, by Anne Hulton. Copyright © 1927 by The President and Fellows of Harvard College; © 1955 by Kenneth B. Murdock. Reprinted by permission of Harvard University Press.

Excerpt from *The Magic of Color*, by Hilda Simon. Copyright © 1981 by Hilda Simon. Reprinted by permission of Lothrop, Lee & Shepard Books (a division of William Morrow & Co.).

"Maria Morevna," from *The Maid of the North: Feminist Folk Tales from Around the World*, by Ethel Johnston Phelps. Copyright © 1981 by Ethel Johnston Phelps. Reprinted by permission of Henry Holt and Company, Inc.

"More Than Meets the Eye: Illusions that Baffle Your Brain," text by Russell Ginns, from *3-2-1 Contact* magazine. Copyright © 1989 Children's Television Workshop. Used courtesy of *3-2-1 Contact* magazine.

"On Shark's Tooth Beach," from *Throwing Shadows*, by E. L. Konigsburg. Copyright © 1979 by E. L. Konigsburg. Reprinted with the permission of Atheneum Publishers, an imprint of Macmillan Publishing Company, and Lescher & Lescher, Ltd. for the author.

Excerpt from *Ordinary Jack* by Helen Cresswell. Text copyright © 1977 by Helen Cresswell. Reprinted with permission of Macmillan Publishing Company, Helen Cresswell, and Faber & Faber.

"Pandora . . . The Fateful Casket," from *The Firebringer and Other Great Stories*, by Louis Untermeyer. Copyright © 1968 by Louis Untermeyer. Reprinted by permission of the publisher, M. Evans and Company, Inc., New York.

Excerpt from Paul Revere's letter to Dr. Jeremy Belknap, edited by Charles Deane, adapted from *Proceedings of the Massachusetts Historical Society*, XVI (1879), pages 370–376. Reprinted courtesy of the Massachusetts Historical Society.

"The Piano," by Aníbal Monteiro Machado, from *Modern Brazilian Short Stories*, translated by William Grossman. Copyright © 1967 by the Regents of The University of California. Reprinted by permission of The University of California Press.

Excerpts from *Platero and I*, by Juan Ramón Jiménez, translated by Eloise Roach. Copyright © 1957 by Juan Ramón Jiménez. Reprinted by permission of the University of Texas Press.

"Shots Heard Round the World" and "Writings that Changed History," (originally titled "Times That Tried Men's Souls") from *The War for Independence*, by Albert Marrin. Copyright © 1988 by Albert Marrin. Reprinted with permission of Atheneum Publishers, an imprint of Macmillan Publishing Company, and Toni Mendez Inc.

Excerpts from *The Story of Prince Rama*, retold by Brian Thompson (pages 5, 34, 35, 36, 38, 40, 50, 52, 54, 56, 58, 60, and 62). Copyright © 1980 by Brian Thompson. Illustration from page 35 copyright © 1980 by Jeroo Roy. (First published by Kestrel Books, 1980.) Reprinted by permission of Penguin Books Ltd.

"Victory Unintentional," by Isaac Asimov, from *The Days After Tomorrow*, edited by Hans Stefan Santesson. "Victory Unintentional" copyright 1942 by Fictioneers, Inc., renewed © 1970 by Isaac Asimov. Reprinted by permission of Isaac Asimov.

Westmark, by Lloyd Alexander. Copyright © 1981 by Lloyd Alexander. Reprinted by permission of the publisher, Dutton Children's Books, a division of Penguin Books USA Inc., and Brandt & Brandt Literary Agents, Inc.

Poetry

"Alexander Throckmorton," from *Spoon River Anthology*, by Edgar Lee Masters. Copyright 1914, 1915, 1916 by Edgar Lee Masters, renewed 1942, 1944 by Edgar Lee Masters. Published by the Macmillan Company. Reprinted by permission of Ellen C. Masters.

"And the days are not full enough . . . ," from *Personae*, by Ezra Pound. Copyright 1926 by Ezra Pound. Reprinted by permission of New Directions Publishing Corporation and Faber and Faber Ltd.

"Apple," by Nan Fry, from *Plainsong* magazine, Vol. IV, No. 1, Spring 1982. Copyright © 1982 by Plainsong, Inc. Reprinted by permission of Plainsong, Inc.

"Autobiographia Literaria," from *The Collected Poems of Frank O'Hara*, by Frank O'Hara. Copyright © 1958, 1967, 1971 by Maureen Granville-Smith, Administratrix of the Estate of Frank O'Hara. Reprinted by permission of Alfred A. Knopf, Inc.

"The Bagel," from *Rescue the Dead*, by David Ignatow. Copyright © 1966 by David Ignatow. Reprinted by permission of Wesleyan University Press.

"Big Wind," from *The Collected Poems of Theodore Roethke* by Theodore Roethke. Copyright 1947 by The United Chapters of Phi Beta Kappa. Reprinted by permission of Doubleday, a division of Bantam, Doubleday, Dell Publishing Group, Inc., and Faber and Faber Ltd.

"Blue Cornucopia," from *Robert Francis: Collected Poems, 1936–1976*, by Robert Francis (Amherst: University of Massachusetts Press, 1976). Copyright © 1965, 1974 by Robert Francis. Reprinted by permission of the University of Massachusetts Press.

"Boy at the Window," from *Things of This World*, by Richard Wilbur. Originally published under the title "Exodus" in *The New Yorker* magazine. Copyright © 1952, renewed 1980 by Richard Wilbur. Reprinted by permission of Harcourt Brace Jovanovich, Inc.

"Bubbles," from *Wind Song*, by Carl Sandburg. Copyright © 1960 by Carl Sandburg and renewed 1988 by Margaret Sandburg, Janet Sandburg, and Helga Sandburg Crile. Reprinted by permission of Harcourt Brace Jovanovich, Inc.

"Counting-out Rhyme," from *Collected Poems*, by Edna St. Vincent Millay. Copyright © 1928, 1955 by Edna St. Vincent Millay and Norma Millay Ellis. Published by Harper and Row. Reprinted by permission.

"Fire and Ice," from *The Poetry of Robert Frost*, by Robert Frost, edited by Edward Connery Lathem. Copyright 1916, 1923 by Holt, Rinehart and Winston and renewed 1944, 1951 by Robert Frost. Reprinted by permission of Henry Holt and Company, Inc., and Jonathan Cape Ltd. on behalf of the Estate of Robert Frost.

"Lament," from *Collected Poems*, by Edna St. Vincent Millay. Copyright 1921, 1948 by Edna St. Vincent Millay. Published by Harper and Row. Reprinted by permission.

"May—T'aatsoh," from *Alice Yazzie's Year*, by Ramona Maher. Copyright © 1977 by Ramona Maher. Reprinted by permission of Ramona Maher.

"Miss Blues'es Child," from *Selected Poems of Langston Hughes*, by Langston Hughes. Copyright © 1959 by Langston Hughes. Reprinted by permission of Alfred A. Knopf, Inc.

"Mother to Son," from *Selected Poems of Langston Hughes*, by Langston Hughes. Copyright 1926 by Alfred A. Knopf, Inc., and renewed 1954 by Langston Hughes. Reprinted by permission of Alfred A. Knopf, Inc.

"Museum Vase," from *Robert Francis: Collected Poems, 1936–1976*, by Robert Francis (Amherst: University of Massachusetts Press, 1976). Copyright © 1965, 1974 by Robert Francis. Reprinted by permission of the University of Massachusetts Press.

"Not Forever on Earth," from *In the Trail of the Wind*, edited by John Bierhorst. Copyright © 1971 by John Bierhorst. Reprinted by permission of Farrar, Straus and Giroux, Inc.

"Old Deep Sing-Song," from *Wind Song*, by Carl Sandburg. Copyright © 1958 by Carl Sandburg and renewed 1986 by Margaret Sandburg, Janet Sandburg, and Helga Sandburg Crile. Reprinted by permission of Harcourt Brace Jovanovich, Inc.

"Silver," from *The Complete Poems of Walter de la Mare*, by Walter de la Mare. Copyright © 1969 by the Literary Trustees of Walter de la Mare. Reprinted by permission of The Literary Trustees of Walter de la Mare and The Society of Authors as their representative.

"Two Girls . . .," from *By the Waters of Manhattan*, by Charles Reznikoff. Copyright © 1959 by Charles Reznikoff. Reprinted by permission of New Directions Publishing Corporation.

"The Weary Blues," from *The Dream Keeper and Other Poems*, by Langston Hughes. Copyright 1926 by Alfred A. Knopf, Inc. and renewed 1954 by Langston Hughes. Reprinted by permission of Alfred A. Knopf, Inc., and Harold Ober Associates, Inc.

"Zimmer's Street," from *The Zimmer Poems*, by Paul Zimmer. Copyright © 1976 by Paul Zimmer. Reprinted by permission of Paul Zimmer.

Quotations from Authors/Illustrators

From *Life in the West* by Brian W. Aldiss. Copyright © 1980 by Brian W. Aldiss. Reprinted by permission of A. P. Watt Ltd. and Robin Straus Agency, Inc., as agent for Brian W. Aldiss.

From "Meet Your Author" by Lloyd Alexander in *Cricket* magazine. December, 1976. Copyright © 1976 by Open Court Publishing Company. Reprinted by permission of *Cricket* magazine.

Quotation by Lloyd Alexander from his Newbery Award acceptance speech. Copyright © 1969 by the *Horn Book Magazine*. Reprinted by permission of the *Horn Book Magazine*.

Quotation by Maya Angelou from "Talks with Two Singular Women" by Carolyn Seebohm. Originally appeared in *House and Garden* magazine, November, 1981. Copyright © 1981 by Carolyn Seebohm. Reprinted by permission of Carolyn Seebohm.

Isaac Asimov quotation from *People Weekly* article by Brad Darrach, November 22, 1976. Copyright © 1976 by PEOPLE Weekly. Reprinted by permission of *People Weekly*.

Quotation from Isaac Asimov from *Contemporary Authors New Revision Series*, Vol. 19. Copyright © 1987 by Gale Research Inc. Reprinted by permission of the publisher.

Quotations from Ray Bradbury, reprinted by permission of the author.

From the introduction to *Tom Tiddler's Ground* by Walter de la Mare. Copyright © 1961 by Walter de la Mare. Reprinted by permission of the Literary Trustees of Walter de la Mare and the Society of Authors as their representative.

Quotation from David Ignatow from *Contemporary Authors*, Vols. 9–12. Copyright © 1974 by Gale Research Inc. Reprinted by permission of the publisher.

Quotation by Juan Ramón Jiménez from the prologue to *Libros de Prosa* by Juan Ramón Jiménez by Donald Fogelquist. Copyright © 1976 by Aguilar S. A. de Ediciones and G. K. Hall & Co. Reprinted by permission.

Quotation from Aníbal Monteiro Machado from "The Piano" from *Modern Brazilian Short Stories*, translated by William Grossman. Copyright © 1974 by the Regents of the University of California. Reprinted by permission of the University of California Press.

Quotation by Philippa Pearce from *Books for Keeps*, No. 23, November, 1983. Copyright © 1983 by the School Bookshop Association.

Quotation by Hilda Simon from *Illustrators of Children's Books, 1957–1966*, edited by Lee Kingman. Copyright © 1968 by the *Horn Book*. Reprinted by permission of the *Horn Book*.

Credits

Program Design   Carbone Smolan Associates

Cover Design   Carbone Smolan Associates

Design   **13–19** Sheaff Design;   **111–189** Appleton Design;   **191–253** Pronk & Associates;   **257–359** Carbone Smolan Associates;   **361–399** Martine Bruel;   **401–499** Ligature, Inc.;   **501–581** WGBH

Introduction   (left to right) 1st row: Andrew Myer; James L. Ballard; Andrew Shachat;   2nd row: Robert Appleton; Sotheby Parke Bernet Publications; Ron Chan;   3rd row: Frank Siteman; Sonder/Gamma Liaison; Jacqui Morgan;   4th row: Deborah Blackwell; Robert Appleton; Frank Siteman

Table of Contents   **4** Fred Lynch;   **5** Scott Van Sicklin;   **6** David Edmunds;   **7** Alan Okamoto;   **9** The Shelburne Museum, Shelburne, Vermont;   **10** Andrew Meyer, (type and borders) Jeff Hodgkinson;   **11** Kim Nelson

Illustration   **16–17** Jeroo Roy;   **20–21** The British Library;   **24–25** Sotheby Parke Bernet Publications;   **26–27** Director of the India Office Library and Records;   **32–33** The British Library;   **38–47** Paul Schulenburg;   **48–52** David Frampton;   **68–79** Fred Lynch;   **111–189** (xerography and collage) Robert Appleton;   **190–193** Jun Park;   **195** Steve Van Gelder;   **200–203** Kimberly Britt;   **205** Jun Park;   **209** Mark Summers;   **210** Marcel Durocher;   **212** Mark Summers;   **214–215** Jun Park;   **218–222** David Edmunds;   **224–227** Steve Van Gelder;   **231** Walt Gunthardt;   **232–233** Steve Van Gelder;   **232–234** Jeff Hecht;   **238–239** Joe Lepiano;   **242–245** Precision Graphics;   **246–247** Thach Bui;   **257–258** Alex Schomburg;   **259, 306–327** Sharmen Liao;   **260–285** Ron Chan;   **286–287** Greg Nemic;   **290–303** Alan Okamoto;   **304–305** Carl W. Rohrig;   **328–353** Jacqui Morgan;   **405** Mapping Specialists;   **414** Brian Battles;   **416** Ligature, Inc.;   **422–425, 427** Johanna Bandle;   **501** Andrew Myer;   **501–503, 580–581** (type and borders) Jeff Hodgkinson;   **502, 504–515** Kevin Hawkes;   **516–531** Andrew Shachat;   **532–533** Elwood Smith;   **503, 534–549** Cat Bowman Smith;   **551** Roz Chast;   **552–575** Deborah Blackwell;   **577** Elivia Savadier;

583–584, 610, 633, 659, 697, 698–703 Kim Nelson;   **591, 598, 600, 607, 621, 625, 636, 639, 642, 656, 666, 673, 690, 694** Linda Phinney;   **712** Robin Brickman;   **718, 734–736** Robert Frank/Melissa Turk, The Artist Network

Photography   **13** type: Digital Art/Westlight;   **34–35** (puppets) Courtesy of The Children's Museum, Boston. Photo by Sam Gray.   **54–67** (objects) Courtesy of the Plains Indian Collection, The Children's Museum, Boston. Photos by Sam Gray.   **81** T. O'Neill/Sygma; (background) Digital Art/Westlight;   **82–83** Digital Art/Westlight;   **84–85** TM & © Lucasfilm 1980. All Rights Reserved;   **86–88** Digital Art/Westlight;   **89** TM & © Lucasfilm 1980. All Rights Reserved;   **90–97** Digital Art/Westlight;   **94** TM & © Lucasfilm 1980. All Rights Reserved;   **96** Courtesy of Lucasfilm 1980. All Rights Reserved;   **98–99** TM & © Lucasfilm 1980. All Rights Reserved;   **99–100** Digital Art/Westlight;   **101** Courtesy of Lucasfilm. All Rights Reserved;   **102–103** Digital Art/Westlight;   **106** T. O'Neill/Sygma (bottom);   **106** Wide World Photos (center);   **107** Courtesy of Richard Phelps (top);   **107** AP/Wide World Photos (bottom);   **107** Courtesy of Robert R. Potter (center);   **107** Courtesy of Brian Thompson (center);   **110–111** Frank Marchese;   **112–113** Frank Marchese;   **114** Scott Van Sicklin;   **115** Mary Ellen Mark/Library   **118** daisy: Scott Van Sicklin; girl: Frank Marchese;   **123** Scott Van Sicklin;   **126** Scott Van Sicklin;   **126** UPI/Bettman Newsphotos (bottom);   **131** Scott Van Sicklin;   **133** Scott Van Sicklin;   **134–135** Todd Eller;   **136** Scott Van Sicklin;   **139** Scott Van Sicklin;   **142–143** Scott Van Sicklin;   **143** UPI/Bettmann Newsphotos;   **144** Scott Van Sicklin;   **148** portrait: Frank Marchese; glasses: Scott Van Sicklin;   **155–156** Scott Van Sicklin;   **160** Scott Van Sicklin;   **163–164** Scott Van Sicklin;   **171** Frank Marchese;   **177** Frank Marchese;   **183** Scott Van Sicklin;   **185** Scott Van Sicklin;   **186** AP/Wide World Photos (top);   **186** UPI/Bettmann Newsphotos (bottom);   **186** Gloria Gonzalez (center);   **187** UPI/Bettmann Newsphotos (top);   **187** Courtesy of Dell Publishing Company (bottom);   **187** Courtesy of Atheneum, imprint of Macmillan Publishing Company (center);   **188** Frank Marchese;   **189** Frank Marchese;   **195** Harald Sund/ The Image Bank;   **203** Visuals Unlimited;   **206–207** Spencer Grant/Photo Researchers, Inc.;   **207**

Sander/Gamma-Liaison; **217** Don King/The Image Bank; **228** J. Carmichael, Jr./The Image Bank; **237** J & L Weber/Peter Arnold, Inc.; **241** ©1938 M. C. Escher/Cordon Art - Baarn - Holland©; **252** AP/Wide World Photos (top); **252** Courtesy of Russell Ginns (bottom); **253** Courtesy of Macmillan Publishing Company (top); **253** Courtesy of Hilda Simon (bottom); **257–258** Alex Schomberg; **259** TSW-CLICK/Chicago Ltd.; **288–289** Jeffrey Milstein/Paperhouse Productions; **289** Peter Menzel; **306** J. Barry O'Rourke/The Stock Market; **314** J. Barry O'Rourke/The Stock Market; **316–317** Nasa; **325** J. Barry O'Rourke/The Stock Market; **354–355** Alex Schomberg; **356** Jerry Bauer (top); **356** John Olson/ Gamma Liaison (center top); **356** ©1986 by David W. Wixon (bottom); **356** B. Herman/Globe Photos (center bottom); **358–359** K. Iwasaki/The Stock Market; **361** John G. Zimmerman; **363** © Henri Cartier-Bresson/Magnum; **365** © Elliott Erwitt/Magnum; **366** Courtesy, Laurence Miller Gallery, NY; **369** International Museum of Photography at George Eastman House: Bequest of Edward Steichen by Direction of Joanna T. Steichen; **370** Association des Amis de Jacque Henri Lartigue-France, Courtesy of the Center for Creative Photography, University of Arizona, (center); **374** Photograph by the Trustees of the Ansel Adams Publishing Rights Trust. All Rights Reserved; **376** Reproduction courtesy of the Art Museum, Princeton University, The Minor White Archive, Copyright ©1982 by the Trustees of Princeton University; **379** Horace Bristol/Time Inc.; **380** UPI/ Bettmann Newsphotos; **382** Pete Turner; **384** Library of Congress; **387** Gilles Peress/Magnum (center); **388** Reproduction courtesy of the Art Museum, Princeton University, The Minor White Archive, Copyright © 1982 by the Trustees of PrincetonUniversity; **390** Burt Glinn/ Magnum; **393** Nina Leen, LIFE Time Inc.; **395** © Wayne Miller/Magnum (center); **399** © Henri Cartier-Bresson/ Magnum (center); **401** Library of Congress, Hand-colored by Karla Cinquanta; Library of Congress; **407** Massachusetts Historical Society; **408** Library of Congress; **409** Daughters of the American Revolution, Boston Tea Party Chapter; **411** The Granger Collection; **413** Photograph courtesy of The Concord Museum, Concord, MA; **415** The Granger Collection; **417** Minute Man National Historical Park, Concord, MA, © Rob Huntley for Chromographics,

Inc.; **418** Steve Dunwell; **419** Frederick A. Szarka; **421** Library of Congress; **425** Massachusetts Historical Society; **428–429** American Antiquarian Society; **430–431** The Parson Capen House, Topsfield, MA, © Rob Huntley for Chromographics, Inc.1989; **431** National Archives of the United States, Photographer: Jonathan Wallen (top right); **432** Essex Institute, Salem (top); **432** American Antiquarian Society (bottom); **433** Library of Congress; **434** Peabody Museum of Salem, Photo by Mark Sexton (left); **434** Peabody Museum of Archaeology, Harvard University (right); **435** Peabody Museum of Archaeology, Harvard University; **436** American Antiquarian Society (left); **436** Massachusetts Historical Society (right); **437** American Antiquarian Society; **438** The John Carter Brown Library, Brown University; **439** Library of Congress; **440** The John Carter Brown Library, Brown University (top); **440** Lexington Historical Society, © Rob Huntley for Chromographics, Inc. 1990; **441** I.N. Phelps Stokes Collection, Miriam Ira D.Wallach Division of Art, Prints and Photographs, The New York Public Library, Astor, Lenox and Tilden Foundations; **442** Museum of Fine Arts, Boston, Deposited by the City of Boston; **443** American Antiquarian Society (top); **443** Lexington Historical Society, © Rob Huntley for Chromographics, Inc. 1990 (bottom); **444** Courtesy Museum of Fine Arts, Boston, Gift by Subscription and Francis Bartlett Fund; **445** Cary Memorial Library, Lexington (left); **445** Minute Man National Historical Park, Concord, MA, © Rob Huntley for Chromographics, Inc. 1990 (right); **446** Minute Man National Historical Park, Concord, MA, © Rob Huntley for Chromographics, Inc. 1990; **447** Minute Man National Historical Park, Concord, MA, © Rob Huntley for Chromographics, Inc. 1990 (top); **447** The Concord Museum, Concord, MA, © Rob Huntley for Chromographics, Inc. 1990; **448** Lexington Historical Society, © Rob Huntley for Chromographics, Inc. 1990; **449** The Concord Museum, Concord, MA, © Rob Huntley for Chromographics, Inc. 1990; **450** Bedford Public Library, Bedford, MA; **450–451** Frederick A. Szarka; **452–453** Lexington Historical Society, © Rob Huntley for Chromographics, Inc. 1990; **454** Lexington Historical Society, © Rob Huntley for Chromographics, Inc. 1990; **455** The Massachusetts Historical Society; **456** Steve Dunwell; **457** Courtesy of CBS Inc., © James

Dee, 1990; **458** The Bostonian Society (top); **458–459** The Massachusetts Historical Society; **460** The Concord Museum, Concord, MA, © Rob Huntley for Chromographics, Inc. 1990; **461** Museum of Fine Arts, Boston, Pauline Revere Thayer Collection (left); **461** Museum of Fine Arts, Boston Gift of Joseph W., William B., and Edward H. R. Revere (right); **462** Nichipor Collection, © Rob Huntley for Chromographics, Inc. 1990; **462–463** Anne S. K. Brown Military Collection, Brown University, Providence, RI; **463** Nichipor Collection, © Rob Huntley for Chromographics, Inc. 1990 (top); **464–465** Lexington Historical Society; **465** The Concord Museum, Concord, MA, © Rob Huntley for Chromographics, Inc. 1990 (bottom); **466** The Nichipor Collection, © Rob Huntley for Chromographics, Inc. 1990; **467** Veronica M. Stanley, © 1990; **468** Massachusetts Historical Society (left); **468** Minute Man National Historical Park, Concord, MA, © Rob Huntley for Chromographics, Inc. 1990; **468–469** Anne S. K. Brown Military Collection, Brown University, Providence, R.I.; **469** Minute Man National Historical Park, Concord, MA, © Rob Huntley for Chromographics, Inc., 1990; **470** Minute Man National Historical Park, Concord, MA, © Rob Huntley for Chromographics, Inc. 1990 (top, bottom); **470** Courtesy of National Archives of the United States, Photographer: Jonathan Wallen (middle); **471** Courtesy of Historical Commission of Boxborough (top); **471** "Commemorative of Calvin and Luther Blanchard" by Alfred Sereno Hudson, 1899 (bottom); **472** North Wind Picture Archives (top); **472** Lexington Historical Society, © Rob Huntley for Chromographics, Inc. 1990 (bottom); **473** Minute Man National Historical Park, Concord, MA, © Rob Huntley for Chromographics, Inc. 1990; **474** Guildford Courthouse National Military Park (left); **474** American Antiquarian Society (center); **475** Minute Man National Historical Park, Concord, MA, © Rob Huntley for Chromographics, Inc. 1990 (top); **475** Anne S. K. Brown Military Collection, Brown University, Providence, R.I.; **476–477** The Parson Capen House, Topsfield, MA, © Rob Huntley for Chromographics, Inc.1990; **478–479** American Antiquarian Society; **480** Independence National Historical Park; **481** National Archives (top); **481** The Smithsonian Institution, Washington, D.C. (bottom); **482–483** © David Binder, Stock Boston 1989; **483** Massachusetts Historical Society; **484** Alan D. Carey/Visual Resources for Ornithology; **484–485** National Archives of the United States, Photographer: Jonathan Wallen; **486–487** Courtesy of National Archives of the United States, Photographer: Jonathan Wallen (bottom); **487** The Shelburne Museum, Shelburne, Vermont; **488–489** Yale University Art Gallery; **489** North Wind Picture Archives (bottom); **490** The Bostonian Society; **491** American Antiquarian Society; **492** Independence National Historic Park Collection; **493** Philadelphia Museum of Art, Gift of John T. Morris; **494** Courtesy of the Trustees of the Boston Public Library (top); **494** The New York Historical Society (bottom); **495** Massachusetts Historical Society; **496** The Bostonian Society (left); **496** The Museum of Fine Arts, Boston, Gift of Joseph W., William B., and Edward H. R. Revere (right); **496–497** The Hancock-Clarke House, © Rob Huntley for Chromographics, Inc. 1990; **497** Courtesy of Elizabeth West (top left); **497** Courtesy of Katherine S. Talmadge (top right); **497** Wide World Photos (bottom left); **497** Courtesy of Toni Mendez, Inc. (bottom right); **498–499** © Steve Dunwell, 1990; **578** Courtesy of Atheneum, imprint of Macmillan Publishing Company; **579** Rulan C. Pian (top left); **579** Harper & Row (bottom right); **700** A. Limont; **708** Kenneth Lucas at Steinhart Aquarium/Biological Photo Service (top); **708** Brian Parker/Tom Stack and Associates (bottom); **709** Martin Rogers/Stock Boston; **717** Owen Franken/Stock Boston; **718** © The Stock Market/Bo Zaunders; **721** Greg Mancuso/Jeroboam, Inc.; **723** Animals Animals/© Susan L. Jones; **732** Superstock; **733** Gary Milburn/Tom Stack and Associates; **Assignment Photographers** Sam Gray **13**, **14–15**, **34–35**, **36–37**, **53–67**, **104–105**, **108–109**; Rob Huntley/Chromographics **402**; Kenji Kerins **254–255**.

751